W9-ADD-853

One Hundred Years of
Huckleberry Finn

PS
1305
.O54
1985

ONE HUNDRED YEARS

OF *HUCKLEBERRY FINN*

THE BOY, HIS BOOK, AND

AMERICAN CULTURE

PS
2384
C54

Centennial Essays Edited by

Robert Sattelmeyer and J. Donald Crowley

Salem College
Gramley Library
Winston-Salem, NC 27108

UNIVERSITY OF MISSOURI PRESS

Columbia, 1985

Copyright © 1985 by
The Curators of the University of Missouri
University of Missouri Press, Columbia, Missouri 65211
Printed and bound in the United States of America

All rights reserved

Library of Congress Cataloging in Publication Data

Main entry under title:

One hundred years of Huckleberry Finn:
The boy, his book, and American culture

    Bibliography: p.
    Includes index.
    1. Twain, Mark, 1835–1910. Adventures of Huckleberry
Finn—Addresses, essays, lectures. I. Sattelmeyer,
Robert. II. Crowley, J. Donald (Joseph Donald)
PS1305.A7   1985   813'.4   84–19574
ISBN 0–8262–0457–0

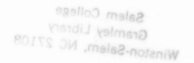
Salem College
Gramley Library
Winston-Salem, NC 27108

Acknowledgments

We are grateful to William H. Loos, Curator of the Rare Book Room of the Buffalo and Erie County Library, for making available to us copies of the unsigned Swedish and Japanese illustrations included in this volume; to Allison R. Ensor for copies of the illustrations by Rockwell, McKay, Burra, Falter, and Lhotak as well as those by unsigned Bulgarian and Russian artists; and to R. S. Brownlee, Director, and James W. Goodrich, Associate Director of The State Historical Society of Missouri, for making available copies of the Kemble frontispiece illustration and the bust of Mark Twain from the 1885 first American edition.

We would also like to thank Julie Apple, Paul Taylor, and Tom Quirk, of the University of Missouri–Columbia Department of English, for their generous assistance in the preparation of this volume.

R.S.
J.D.C.
Columbia, Mo.
October 1984

Contents

III

Contexts and Conventions, *147*

IV

Extensions and Transformations, *243*

V

A Document of American Culture, *309*

x / Contents

Preface

Faced on the one hand with Mark Twain's threats of prosecution, banishment, and execution in his "NOTICE" to readers of the first edition of *Adventures of Huckleberry Finn* and, on the other, with the prodigious length of the bibliographical checklist that closes this volume (a survey of the criticism, after all, only since the 1968 *Modern Fiction Studies* bibliography), wary editors and other registered voters alike, no doubt, will ask: Do we really need, in 1985, another couple dozen essays on that novel? Hasn't more than enough ink already and long since been spilt? The appearance of a comet might suffice perhaps, but another collection? Editorial feet question whither and whether to proceed at all—but only for a moment.

Necessity overwhelms trepidation. The occasion—first, the centennial of the book's publication in this country, but also, as if an advertising agency had planned the whole affair, the one-hundred-fiftieth of the author's birth and the seventy-fifth of his death—turns out to be obligatory, something like Emerson's idea of "Fate." The occasion, that is, stirs some sort of imperative Moral Sense into the temptation to try to give an account of how things stand between us—the boy, the book, the author, their readers—from a long century's perspective. Time still once more, then, for Huck's readers to "resk the truth" if they can about the one book, as Ernest Hemingway some years ago had it, "All modern American literature comes from."

It is an occasion that forces the fresh realization of the extent to which Twain, having written the book, wrote us. It is an occasion that, in an age of exhaustion, brings us back to sources of fascination at once Paleface and Redskin, to such intersections of, say, popular and elite that our Interstate Highway culture so rarely provides us. The occasion is a reminder of the way in which critics, going again to Huck's book, are not altogether unlike the swarms of families who, making their summer pilgrimages to Hannibal or taking snapshots of themselves in front of Twain's birthplace, ground themselves more surely in the substance and the illusions of their own being. Indeed, the reader standing before *Huckleberry Finn*, if the history of the criticism is any indication, seems more often than not transfixed, caught up in an intense exercise of self-examination: he becomes a John Updike, say, returning to the home of his parents and staring, awe-struck, at that old photograph of himself as a boy.

When such rare monuments as *Huckleberry Finn* are in question, the task of the American poet as defined by William Carlos Williams—"how to begin to begin again"—becomes the task of the critic. That task is how to recover the book itself for ourselves from all those unfolding versions that have necessarily ripened into cliché. Few books, after all, have so fulfilled Emerson's crusty, demanding injunction that their sole purpose is but to inspire. And if *Huckleberry Finn* has also attracted to itself those "restorers of readings, the emendators, the bibliomaniacs of all degrees" whom Emerson debunked as Man Not Thinking, we can now, from our privileged inheritance, understand far better than he just how much of the inspiration has depended upon the slow progress of the scholar as bookworm. The fact is that *Huckleberry Finn* has many mansions, many Huck Finns. Twain himself had several, and Clemens, apparently, had at least one or two others. Even Hollywood has not been able to make do with just a couple. Between the bourbons and the back-scratchers marketed under the Twain logo there are Huck Finns filling the interstellar spaces, probably more of them, and in much less time, than there are Robinson Crusoes, that other fictional creation who keeps moving around in the world as if he were a real person. *Huckleberry Finn*'s strange, surprising adventures include two complete rewritings: John Seelye's *The True Adventures of Huckleberry Finn* (1970) and *The Further Adventures of Huckleberry Finn* (1983) by Greg Matthews, an Australian writer camped out in Kansas. T. S. Eliot, W. H. Auden, as well as Hemingway—and Fitzgerald, Faulkner, Ralph Ellison, Saul Bellow, Wright Morris, and Walker Percy—are but a few of our most distinguished writers who have written about their own Huck Finns. There is the Huck who belongs to Norman Rockwell and therefore to a great many other Americans, there is the Illustrated Classics comic-book Huck, the current cable-television serialized Huck, there is the Huck after whom restaurants have been named, the Huck of various abridged and illustrated editions on the children's shelf of family libraries. Seen as eminently safe and palatable in many quarters, the boy and his book have been declared sinister and subversive in others. From the beginning: the Huck seen upon publication by the Public Library board in Concord, Massachusetts (according to a squib in the *Boston Transcript*, 17 March 1885), prompted members to ban his book as "the veriest trash." And in recent years: there is the Huck of various public school board members scattered around the territory, some of them, curiously, at a place called Mark Twain High School, who also ban the book or remove it from required-reading lists. Somewhere between these two extremes is the Huck of all those Americans, young and old alike, who have never read the book or the comic book, never seen the movies or the Benton lithograph, never put together the cardboard picture puzzles or bolted a Huckburger—but still think that, naturally, they know Huck.

"In the long run," said Walt Whitman, in 1891, of *Leaves of Grass*, "the world will do as it pleases with the book." One wishes for the right Twainian deadpan-manner adverb that would express the greater fullness of truth that comment has for *Adventures of Huckleberry Finn*. Clearly, the world has read and misread the book, appropriated and misappropriated, revised and revisioned it, in purely literary and impurely extraliterary ways, for better and for worse, in sickness and in health, in sometimes gaudy displays of clarity and confusion for now these hundred years. What Whitman hoped for regarding *Leaves of Grass*—that the world would not view it "distinctively *as literature* . . . as a literary performance"—Twain seems to have triumphantly wrought and won. *Adventures of Huckleberry Finn*, one hundred years later, assumes the proportions of being Samuel Clemens/Mark

Twain/Huck Finn's Gift Outright, purchased, as it were, by each of them at no small cost. And like our native land in the Frost poem of that title, Clemens/Twain/Huck made the book ours. Possessing the book, critical/creative readers gradually, "vaguely realizing westward" and possessed by the book, have at their best learned the art of the necessity of reappraisal and thus, in Wright Morris's terms, of repossessing the book.

To make the book ours again, freshly, still one more time, then, is the attempt of this collection of critical essays. To mark time—no more, but no less.

Written independently and arranged with no conscious design of dialectic, the essays illustrate the enormous range and variety of problem and interest, of interpretation and analysis, that still, after so many years, attach to so many dimensions of the book and its life. They constitute a series of necessarily partial portraits about central aspects of the numerous worlds of the book—the making and meanings and living out of it. Taken together, the essays add up to something more than the sum of their parts. They suggest, for one thing, how inexhaustible a source of the need for fresh commentary *Adventures of Huckleberry Finn* has been, is, will no doubt be. Taken together, they make the point that when such books as *Huckleberry Finn* exist, such books as this one will have their reason for being. Commemorative in intent, the essays are not uncritically celebrative. Celebration comes, though, as it should, in retrospect and in effect: in the rediscovery of the book's powers to help create its creative readers and to make them, like Huck's songbirds of Chapter 19, be "just going it!"

The editors have not consulted any of Tom Sawyer's authorities in arranging the essays collected here. John Gerber's, a survey of the development of the criticism on the novel and of some of the current popular uses American culture has made of the book, we employ as our introduction. The other essays are arranged under general topic headings that begin with the private life behind the book—"The Imagination and Its Amanuensis: Huck, Twain, and Clemens"—and end with a group of essays focusing on the current stature of the book as nothing less than "A Document of American Culture." The second section, "The Conscious Craft of Telling the Truth, Mainly," contains essays devoted primarily to elucidating several dimensions of Twain's controlled artistry; the third, "Contexts and Conventions," treats some of the ways in which Twain's novel embodies and transmutes numerous traditional literary conventions, stereotypical social attitudes of the day, and the author's own earlier works; "Extensions and Transformations," the fourth section, is put together in a picaresque mode and has a necessarily half-horse, half-alligator character, containing as it does four essays that trace some of the book's "translated" lives—in college classrooms, in the different styles of the book's illustrators, in the current Japanese children's Saturday-morning television serialization, in the life of the humor beyond the book. The essays are diverse and, no doubt, here and there the placement of one or two of them might strike some readers as bordering on the arbitrary. In general, however, the arrangement moves in gradual stages from a consideration of the pressures in the making of the book—from the past and the unconscious—to the public power and presence of the book today. If readers insist on seeing this rationale as so much flapdoodle, it is nonetheless the conviction of the editors that a little such flapdoodle is, after all, neither totally irrelevant to this book's subject nor completely unbefitting of the occasion.

Robert Sattelmeyer
J. Donald Crowley

Note on the Text

All citations to *Adventures of Huckleberry Finn* are taken here from the reproduction of the first American edition of 1885 included in *The Art of Huckleberry Finn: Text, Sources, Criticism*, edited by Walter Blair and Hamlin Hill (San Francisco: Chandler Publishing Co., 1962). The present editors have silently corrected typographical errors allowed to stand in that facsimile.

Abbreviations used in Footnotes and Bibliography

AAus	*Americana-Austriaca*
ABC	*American Book Collector*
AL	*American Literature*
ALR	*American Literary Realism*
AmerS	*American Studies*
AN&Q	*American Notes & Queries*
AQ	*American Quarterly*
ArAA	*Arbeiten aus Anglistik und Amerikanistik*
ArQ	*Arizona Quarterly*
AS	*American Speech*
ASch	*The American Scholar*
BNYPL	*Bulletin of the New York Public Library*
BP	*Banasthali Patrika*
BSUF	*Ball State University Forum*
CE	*College English*
CEA	*CEA Critic*
CentR	*The Centennial Review*
CimR	*Cimarron Review*
CollL	*College Literature*
CR	*The Critical Review*
CRevAS	*Canadian Review of American Studies*
CritI	*Critical Inquiry*
DQ	*Denver Quarterly*
EA	*Etudes Anglaises*
EAA	*Estudos Anglo-Americanos*
EJ	*English Journal*
ELN	*English Language Notes*
ELWIU	*Essays in Literature*
EngR	*English Record*
ES	*English Studies*
ESELL	*Essays & Studies in English Language and Literature*
ESRS	*Emporia State Research Studies*
Expl	*Explicator*
GaR	*The Georgia Review*
HR	*Hispanic Review*
IEY	*Iowa English Bulletin: Yearbook*
JAmS	*Journal of American Studies*
JAPA	*Journal of the American Psychoanalytic Association*
JJQ	*James Joyce Quarterly*
JNT	*Journal of Narrative Technique*
KanQ	*Kansas Quarterly*
L&P	*Literature & Psychology*
MASJ	*Midcontinent American Studies Journal*
MFS	*Modern Fiction Studies*

MissQ	Mississippi Quarterly
MLQ	Modern Language Quarterly
MLS	Modern Language Studies
MMisc	Midwestern Miscellany
ModA	Modern Age
MP	Modern Philology
MQ	Midwest Quarterly
MQR	Michigan Quarterly Review
MR	Massachusetts Review
MSpr	Moderna Sprak
MTJ	Mark Twain Journal
MTQ	Mark Twain Quarterly
NALF	Negro American Literature Forum
NAR	North American Review
NCF	Nineteenth Century Fiction
NDQ	North Dakota Quarterly
PoT	Poetics Today
PR	Partisan Review
RS	Research Studies
SAR	South Atlantic Review
SAF	Studies in American Fiction
SAQ	South Atlantic Quarterly
SCL	Studies in Canadian Literature
SLJ	Southern Literary Journal
SNNTS	Studies in the Novel
SoQ	The Southern Quarterly
SoR	The Southern Review
SR	Sewanee Review
StAH	Studies in American Humor
TAIUS	Texas A & I University Studies
TSE	Tulane Studies in English
TSER	T. S. Eliot Review
TSLL	Texas Studies in Literature & Language
UMSE	University of Mississippi Studies in English
VQR	Virginia Quarterly Review
WAL	Western American Literature
WIRS	Western Illinois Regional Studies
WN	A Wake Newslitter
YES	Yearbook of English Studies
YR	The Yale Review

One Hundred Years of
Huckleberry Finn

JOHN C. GERBER

Introduction: The Continuing Adventures of *Huckleberry Finn*

In his preface to *Mark Twain and Huck Finn*, published in 1960, Walter Blair wrote that *Huckleberry Finn* was "unique in being held in the highest esteem by critics and at the same time prodigiously popular in the United States and throughout the world."[1] A quarter of a century later the same statement can be made, and with even more confidence. Revised and rerevised by editors and publishers, argued over by critics, and even occasionally banned by school boards and libraries, the book still retains its appeal for millions of readers. Scores of scholars, moreover, continue to argue over it and thousands of teachers to discuss it in class. The trip down the Mississippi River on a raft has become legendary, and like Rip Van Winkle the main characters have become firmly fixed in the public consciousness. Not a bad record for a book that came into the world by fits and starts and that at one point was thought by its author to be possibly not worth finishing.

In what follows I attempt to assemble evidence that demonstrates both the general popularity of the book and its particular ability to attract, charm, and confound the scholars and critics. Chiefly this evidence is American. Judging from the fact, however, that from 1884 to 1976 there were 696 foreign editions representing 53 languages and 47 countries it seems safe to assume that *Huckleberry Finn* has consistently been one of our most popular books abroad as well as at home.[2]

I

A swatch of figures may be the quickest and most useful means of suggesting the dimensions of *Huckleberry Finn*'s domestic popularity. Through 1976 the book appeared in 145 American editions.[3] Since 1976 there have been least eight more editions, and others are on the way. According to *Books in Print*, there are thirty-five editions currently available, of which seven are intended for grade-school students, nine for high-school students, and the others for college students and the general market. One is a facsimile edition, one is in large print, two come with cassettes and tapes, and several have study aids. Five have introductions by such respected scholars as Alfred Kazin (Bantam), Leo Marx (Bobbs), Claude Simpson (Prentice-

1. *Mark Twain and Huck Finn* (Berkeley: University of California Press, 1960), p. v.
2. Robert M. Rodney, *Mark Twain International* (Westport, Conn.: Greenwood Press, 1982), p. 264.
3. Ibid.

Hall), Henry Nash Smith (Houghton-Mifflin), and Lionel Trilling (Holt, Rinehart and Winston). Walter Blair has been preparing the historical introduction and explanatory notes, and Robert Hirst and his aides the text, for the authoritative Iowa-California edition. Gale publishers have brought out an elegant two-volume facsimile edition of the extant manuscript. The story has also become available on cassettes, and versions of it have appeared in motion pictures, teleplays, three *Encyclopedia Britannica* films with Clifton Fadiman as commentator, and *Illustrated Classics* (a comic book). Hal Holbrook includes selections from it in his lectures and records, and the whole book or excerpts from it appear in many anthologies. *Across the River* is a new musical adaptation of the book, and at least two more are to follow. Furthermore, as Michael Hovland at the University of Iowa informs me, Charles Wakefield Cadman made the narrative the subject for an overture in the 1940s, Hall Overton and Judith Stampfler used it as the basis of an opera in the early 1970s, and Kurt Weill at the time of his death was working with Maxwell Anderson on a musical to be called *Raft on the River*. This centennial year, 1985, will see the most extraordinary outpouring of commentary and dramatic adaptions that we have yet experienced as universities hold celebratory conferences and presses pour out articles and books hailing the work as one of the few American novels that can properly be called a classic.

Accurate sales figures are difficult to obtain because many publishers consider them classified information. Only eight of twenty-four provided useful replies to written queries about current sales. Fortunately, these eight represent the spectrum of the houses that publish the book. Taken together, Norton, Houghton-Mifflin, Bobbs Merril, and Macmillan sell approximately 30,000 copies annually, a figure that represents a modest drop from sales in previous years. The sales of Longman's Simplified Educational Edition have stabilized at about 9,000, and those of Penguin at about 50,000 (35,000 of the American Library edition and 15,000 of the Puffin Children's Edition). Through increased marketing emphasis, Bantam has upped its sales to 100,000 a year, and for a special book-fair edition Andor sold 100,000 in two years. Though by no means exhaustive, these figures are indicative: *Huckleberry Finn* remains a best-seller, in some instances the best-seller among American literary classics. All-time worldwide sales probably exceed 20 million in number.[4]

A side glance at the market for first editions shows that the first issue of the first American edition of *Huckleberry Finn* is also a best-seller. Many booksellers attest that among American books first editions of the works of Mark Twain are the most eagerly sought.[5] Three sell for especially high

4. For this information I am indebted to Edwin Barber of W. W. Norton and Co.; Charles E. Hayward of Macmillan Publishing Co.; Longman, New York; Paul F. O'Donnell, Jr., of Andor Publishing, Inc.; Kathy Rosenthal of Bantam Books; Mary Stephenson of Bobbs-Merrill Educational Publishing; and Stephanie Wallace of Penguin Books.

5. I attempt to support this statement in "Collecting the Works of Mark Twain," *Mythologizing Mark Twain* (Tuscaloosa: University of Alabama Press, 1984).

prices: *The Jumping Frog of Calaveras County and Other Tales*, Twain's first book, now quite rare; *The Adventures of Tom Sawyer*, scarce in part because of the handling it received from youngsters; and *Adventures of Huckleberry Finn*, especially treasured for its scarcity, for its reputation as a masterpiece, and for the continuing brouhaha over the identity of the first edition. On this last, one argument has it that a few copies of the book had been bound and distributed before some joker altered the illustration on page 283 and turned Uncle Silas, of all people, into an exhibitionist. If this contention is correct, then these copies represent the first issue. The opposing argument is that no copies left the bindery before the defacement was discovered and a new page tipped in showing Uncle Silas once more properly buttoned up. If this contention is correct, the copies with page 283 as a tip-in represent the first issue.[6] Although a prospectus containing the mutilated illustration has been found, no bound volume containing it has surfaced. With the identity of the first issue somewhat in doubt, booksellers play it both ways, advertising as a first issue both a copy with the page tipped in and a copy in which Uncle Silas's famous fly seems ever so slightly more curved than it does on the tipped-in page. Faced with this momentous dilemma the avid collector tries to hedge his bets and buy any copy with a claim to being a first. Thus the price continues to go up. Van Allan Bradley's 1982–1983 *Handbook of Values* reports that normally a first issue of *Huckleberry Finn* in fine condition sells for $1,500 to $2,500; the *American Book Prices Current* for 1982, however, lists one copy at $3,000, and *Book Auction Records* for 1981–1982 lists one for $3,800.

In the schools *Huckleberry Finn* is still widely taught, though perhaps not so widely as it once was. In recent years English teachers have had to contend with organized groups that want the book banned from the curriculum because it contains the word *nigger* and because they believe it portrays blacks unfavorably. Although formal protests against the book in such states as Texas, New York, Virginia, and Iowa have been set aside, no one knows how many teachers have quietly taken *Huckleberry Finn* off their reading lists, either because they agree with the protestors or because they want to avoid possible trouble. For whatever reasons, the *Senior High School Library Catalogue*, the bible for librarians on readings for adolescents, no longer lists *Huckleberry Finn*, though it formerly awarded the book two stars. Nevertheless the book does get read in the schools, probably as often as any American "classic." As early as the fifth grade some teachers read parts of it aloud to their classes or assign a simplified version for the students to read. Interestingly, a sizable fraction of fifth graders, until told otherwise, believe Huck was a real person or a folk hero like Paul Bunyan. By the end of the ninth grade the great majority have at least been introduced to the book in class and recognize it as an exciting adventure story— and as a companion volume to *Tom Sawyer*, with which they frequently confuse it. But it would be a mistake to believe that many fourteen year olds

---

6. A detailed treatment of this subject is in Blair, *Mark Twain and Huck Finn*, pp. 385–87.

have read it in its entirety. At the senior high-school level it most frequently appears in the eleventh-grade course in American literature. Since this course is most commonly taught from an anthology, most students read only the excerpt in the anthology unless the teacher sends them to the school library for the book itself. Among these sixteen and seventeen year olds, moreover, there is a problem of motivation. Because the book, understandably, is read only as an adventure story in grade school and because it is so frequently shelved in the libraries with children's books, high-school juniors tend to look upon it as babyish and resist reading it. Except in the honors sections, therefore, high-school teachers have difficulty developing class discussions that penetrate beyond the most obvious psychological and sociological questions. But again we must say that *Huckleberry Finn* somehow does get read, at least among college-bound students.[7] Librarians in both high-school and town or city libraries report a modest but steady demand for the book, a demand that would be much greater if it were not so easy for students to buy their own paperback copies. Over the years my own experience with college freshmen and sophomores has been that about half profess to have read *Huckleberry Finn* before coming to college. Once in college, undergraduates encounter it as required reading in such courses as Introduction to Literature, Reading Fiction, American Literature Survey, American Novel, Nineteenth-Century American Literature, and the Rise of Realism. Occasional English majors complain of an overdose: *Huckleberry Finn* as required reading in three of their courses.

Those out of school speak of *Huckleberry Finn* enthusiastically but remember it imperfectly. Six graduate students at the State University of New York at Albany interviewed some four hundred adults selected at random on the street, in homes, in a high-school faculty lounge, in an electrical plant, and in Macy's store in Colonie (Albany), New York.[8] A third of those interviewed professed to have read the book, and fewer than a dozen said they had never heard of it. Those who had not read the book but knew about it said they had picked up their information from such sources as relatives and friends, grade-school and high-school teachers, newspaper and magazine articles and advertisements, motion pictures and television programs, Hal Holbrook's lectures and records, children's card games, and an exhibit at Walt Disney World in Florida. The third who had read it talked about it readily and nostalgically as an adventure story, as escape reading, and as a reminder of their own youth and America's past. Many mentioned the humor and a few the social criticism. More than a few confessed to having it confused with *Tom Sawyer*. Some of their specific impressions were fascinating. Here is a potpourri of representative comments:

7. G. Robert Carlsen, author of *Books and the Teen Age Reader*, and Robert F. Hogan, executive associate for research and development of the National Council of Teachers of English, have been most helpful in supplying information about the use of *Huckleberry Finn* in the schools.

8. These students were Maria Baranchuk, Tim Dayton, Phylis Dryden, Norman Freckman, Gregory McGarvey, and Raymond Werking, Jr. They, of course, are not responsible for my handling of the material they assembled.

—A social studies teacher: Huck's adventures represent a microcosm of what happened to the people who crossed the plains before the closing of the frontier in 1888.

—A bus driver: Wasn't Huck an orphan of sorts? They all felt sorry for him. Who the heck took him over?

—A reading specialist: The book is difficult to teach because the kids do not find it interesting. The slower pace is not what our kids identify with. In high school it is presented as a period piece.

—A housewife: I always get Tom Sawyer and Huck Finn mixed up. They were rowdy little boys, but they could get adventure and excitement out of life without harming people—which is more than you can say today for the kids who are taking drugs.

—An engineer: It's the best picture we have of the pre–Civil War South.

—A town councilman: The book makes me think of carefree childhood days when every day was an adventure. Huck is happy and carefree without a problem in the world.

—An eighth-grade English teacher: The book gives a picture of the entire Mississippi valley, and judges slavery, feuding, and many other weaknesses of human nature.

—A young businesswoman: The life-style is definitely one of escapism. It makes me think of summertime and gives me that lazy-day feeling one gets when sitting underneath a tree chewing on a piece of grass.

—Her mother: Tom and Huck bring back Norman Rockwell paintings; they are so carefree.

—Her grandmother: The book always reminds me of going huckleberrying.

—A sixty-five-year-old surgeon: I've read *Huckleberry Finn* every year for the last twenty-three years, read it for the humor, and I'm damned if I'm going to listen to the theories of the so-called experts.

Possibly the surest proof of *Huckleberry Finn*'s current popularity is that journalists and advertisers use Huck's name and references to the book without explanation. In a recent issue of the *New York Times* a sportswriter called a tight end in the NFL a Huck Finn, clearly assuming that all his readers would know what he meant. Not long afterward in the same paper an editorial began with a reference to Huck's remark about "stretchers," as though every reader of the *Times* would know what Huck said. Furthermore, just as advertisers trade on Mark Twain's name to push everything from Mississippi River cruises to cigars and bourbon, so they use Huck's name to help sell their wares. There are, for example, Huckleberry Finn furniture stores (so called because the original store was built beside a Tom Sawyer Motel that has—you guessed it—a Huckleberry Finn cocktail lounge), Huckleberry Finn pontoon kits, Huckleberry Finn fruits, and Huckleberry Scrim. None of these is a Missouri product. The closer one gets to Hannibal, of course, the more frequently one sees the name used commercially. Although Tom Sawyer has helped to make Huck Finn famous, tie-ins with events and phrases in *Huckleberry Finn* show that newspaper writers and advertisers bank primarily on a general knowledge and respect for the Huck Finn of that book. Add this evidence to the evidence of editions, sales, use in schools and colleges, library circulations, and the testimony of the general public, and the conclusion is overwhelming: *Huckleberry Finn* continues to be read by tens of thousands and to be remembered affectionately, though not very accurately, by millions.

II

The history of the scholarship on *Adventures of Huckleberry Finn* is an adventure story in itself. Except for *Moby-Dick* and possibly *The Scarlet Letter*, no other work in American literature has received so much attention from both literary historians and literary critics. It has been the subject of three books and of over six hundred articles—and of eight collections of the best of these articles. In addition, it has been discussed, sometimes extensively, in hundreds of works on broader topics. Obviously the narrative has had an extraordinary appeal for scholars as well as for the public at large. In this section I try to suggest the extent and diversity of the scholarship on the book since its publication. For convenience, I am dividing the hundred years into approximate thirds: 1885 to 1919, 1920 to 1949, and 1950 to the present. General assessments dominate the first third, historical studies the second, and critical analyses and interpretations the third.

Some fifty articles on *Huckleberry Finn* appeared before 1920, many of them reviews published in the late 1880s. This figure does not include scores of short notices and brief discussions of the book appearing in works on broader topics. Writers of the period tended to address themselves to questions concerning the overall worth of the book and often came up with absurdly contradictory judgments. Consider a few examples of the questions raised and the contrary opinions voiced: Is *Huckleberry Finn* a work of art? (Yes, it is a literary masterpiece; no, it is trash.) Is the narrative true to life? (Yes, it is highly realistic; no, it is no more truthful than a dime novel.) Is the humor of high quality? (Yes, it is the finest that has appeared in America; no, it is coarse, flat, dated, and grotesque.) Can a humorist really produce a work of high literary merit? (Yes, if as in the case of Mark Twain the humorist is a profound observer of life and a craftsman of great literary skill; no, a clown is always a clown.) We forget today how bothersome this last question was and how much attention it received. Even as fine a critic as Brander Matthews admitted that Mark Twain's humor held down his literary reputation. H. L. Mencken, however, would have no truck with such an idea. In the *Smart Set* in 1913 he wheeled up his heavy artillery:

> No, there is not the slightest disharmony between sense and nonsense, humor and respectability, despite the almost universal tendency to assume that there is. But, why, then, that widespread error? What actual fact of life lies behind it, giving it a specious appearance of reasonableness? None other, I am convinced, than the fact that the average man is far too stupid to make a joke.[9]

What one notices especially about this early criticism is that with few exceptions it speaks to the general effect and effectiveness of the book rather than to the specifics of its genealogy and design. But the result was important. By

9. *The Smart Set* 39 (February 1913): 151.

1920 such critics as William Archer, Barrett Wendell, Andrew Lang, Fred Lewis Pattee, and Matthews and Mencken had firmly established the judgment that *Huckleberry Finn* was Mark Twain's masterpiece—and quite possibly one of the masterpieces of the English language.

From 1920 to 1949 the scholarly output on *Huckleberry Finn* was half again as great as it had been in the preceding period: some eighty essays and, again, sizable segments in many books and essays on broader subjects. For comic relief there were ten articles on the defacement of the illustration on page 283. Since this was a period when literary history was still in the saddle, it is not surprising to find ample attention to influences (folklore, Western humor, Mark Twain's Missouri upbringing), specific sources (for Huck, for the Grangerford piano, for the Duke and his tooth powder), and literary comparisons (with *Don Quixote, Tom Sawyer, Penrod,* the Alger books). In his *Mark Twain, the Man and His Work* (1935) Edward Wagenknecht dealt with the biographical background of the book, and DeLancey Ferguson in his *Mark Twain, Man and Legend* (1943) devoted a chapter to its sources and composition. Some innocent asked why Jim could not have gotten free simply by crossing the Mississippi to the Illinois shore and was promptly squelched by several who knew that residents of southern Illinois would have immediately turned him in for the reward money. Leslie Fiedler infuriated Huck Finn lovers with his "Come Back to the Raft Ag'in, Huck Honey!" though the title was not a quotation from the book and the article not primarily about *Huckleberry Finn*.

The main controversy of the period, however, was the one touched off by Van Wyck Brooks's argument in 1920 that Mark Twain by moving to the East arrested his development. He pulled *Huckleberry Finn* into the dispute by agreeing with Arnold Bennett that though episodically magnificent, the novel is "of quite inferior quality" as a complete work of art.[10] Bernard DeVoto, as is well known, disagreed:

> With him [Huck Finn] goes a fullness made and shaped wholly of America. It is only because the world he passes through is real and only because it is American that his journey escapes into universals and is immortal. His book is American life formed into great fiction.[11]

In attenuated form, the argument started by Brooks still goes on, but Brooks himself tried to lift *Huckleberry Finn* out of it when he wrote to Sherwood Anderson that Anderson

> showed me clearly where my study had fallen short. I had failed to write the most important chapter, in which I should have praised "Huckleberry Finn." I was too much concerned with the psychological problem, and the psychologist inhibited the poet in me.[12]

At the very end of the 1940s in "The Greatness of *Huckleberry Finn*,"[13] Lionel Trilling anticipated the flood of New Criticism in the following years by dis-

10. *The Ordeal of Mark Twain* (New York: E. P. Dutton & Co., 1920), p. 151.
11. *Mark Twain's America* (Boston: Little Brown, 1932), p. 321.
12. Foreword to "Letters to Van Wyck Brooks," *Story* 19 (September–October 1941): 43.
13. Introduction to Rinehart Edition (1948). Reprinted, somewhat revised, in *The Liberal Imagination* (New York: Viking Press, 1950), pp. 104–17.

cussing the book's language and structure ("in form and style *Huckleberry Finn* is an almost perfect work"), its symbolism (the river as god, Huck as its servant), and its psychological tensions (Huck vis-à-vis Jim). Though he was not the first to reflect upon them, Trilling's guarded defense of the last ten chapters ignited an argument that *still* continues. Obviously his was an essay whose time had come.

Since 1950 commentary on *Huckleberry Finn* has exploded: three books on it exclusively (one in India), over five hundred articles including more than a dozen introductory essays to new editions, at least eight collections of previously printed essays plus this collection of new essays, a score or more of books in which *Huckleberry Finn* receives a chapter, and literally hundreds of works in which it gets attention. The literary historians have dealt exhaustively, it would seem, with sources as well as with the book's composition, publication, reception, and sales. Most notably, Walter Blair produced a 436-page book, *Mark Twain and Huck Finn* (1960), in which he defined the forces that gave the book its substance and form. Ever since, this study has been the benchmark for all serious work on where Mark Twain got the materials for *Huckleberry Finn* and what he did with them. Other historians (I name only a few) have extended our understanding in dealing with such relevant topics as the Southwestern vernacular (James M. Cox), folklore and superstition (Daniel G. Hoffman), the occult (Howard Kerr), confidence men (Susan Kuhlmann), Southwestern humor (Kenneth Lynn), Mark Twain and the South (Arthur G. Pettit), Mark Twain's burlesque patterns (Franklin R. Rogers), the writings of the literary comedians (David E. Sloane), Mark Twain's struggle with the assumptions and language of the dominant culture (Henry Nash Smith), and earlier Romantic fiction (William Spengemann).

One of the funnier disagreements of the scholars resulted from their penchant for classifying. True to the Germanic tradition, they asked what genre or subgenre *Huckleberry Finn* belongs in. Here are some of the answers.[14] Taking their cue from the title, a few avowed simply that it is an adventure story. More ardent classifiers, however, have seen it variously as an allegory, a romance, an epic, a Protestant-American epic, not an epic, a boybook, a picaresque novel, a historical novel, a Gothic novel, a realistic novel, a revolutionary novel, a comic novel, a great World Novel, and not a novel at all because it is too loosely structured. Dipping into minor categories, still others think of it as local color, a pastoral, a tall tale, gentle satire, bitter satire, social commentary, a comic portraiture, a myth, a dreambook, and a dithyramb. As if this were not enough, we are also assured that it is a Socratic dialogue, an elemental tragedy, a Shakespearian tragedy, an Odyssey, and an anti-Odyssey.

Turning from the historical scholars to the critics, we are more than ever

14. The words and phrases in the lists that follow come directly from the original sources or from excerpts in Thomas A. Tenney's valuable *Mark Twain: A Reference Guide* (Boston: G. K. Hall, 1977) and follow-up articles appearing once a year in *ALR*. I have not used quotation marks and footnotes because they would be so numerous as to make reading hazardous. Besides, most would be references to only single words or short phrases.

engulfed. The interpretations of *Huckleberry Finn* written since 1950 have been so extensive and so diverse in subject matter and methodology that no brief account can possibly do them justice. I propose here simply to record sample opinions about three of the most commonly treated aspects of the work: its structure, its main character, and its major themes. Such a procedure will level out the studies, coordinating a penetrating analysis with a trivial one, but it will, I hope, suggest the extraordinary variety of opinion the book invites. *Huckleberry Finn* is like the doubloon Ahab nailed to the mast; all who view it interpret it in the light of their own predispositions and their own knowledge (which in the case of *Huckleberry Finn* includes their awareness of earlier interpretations).

Take, for example, the discussions of the book's structure. Impelled by the popularity of the New Criticism, about a third of the work in the last three decades has consisted of analyses of the narrative's form, the relation of the parts to one another and to the whole. On the one hand there are those critics like T. S. Eliot who find it both unified and coherent with a closeness of grain and a firmness of texture. They unearth a myriad of parts that result in a happy whole: for example, Huck as narrator, the frame with Tom as the focal center at the beginning and at the end, the river, the journey, the flight, Huck's increasing awareness of the selfhood of Jim, the humor, the satire, the language, the basic form of the story in the shape of a circle, the basic form of the story in the shape of a horseshoe. Alternations, say other interpreters, add interest and variety to the structure, alternations between river and shore, light and dark, the romantic and the realistic, the material and the ideal, appearance and reality. For a sociologist the key to the design is the games people play. And for a structuralist such as George C. Carrington a whole book is necessary for an explanation of the novel's dramatic unity.

Critics being critics, however, there are equally passionate arguments to the effect that the narrative is disunified and therefore incoherent and not a creditable work of art. Especially, we are told, expectations are unfulfilled: the Sunday school picnic comes to nothing, Pap disappears, the flight from the sheriff is forgotten, too much depends on coincidence, and we have to turn to *Tom Sawyer Abroad* to discover what happens to Tom, Huck, and Jim. A few contend the book would be more coherent had the "raft passage" not been deleted. One writer says the story is too blandly predictable, and another that the beginning is improvised, the middle uncertain, and the end anticlimactic. In a much anthologized essay, William Van O'Connor argued that *Huckleberry Finn* is not the great American novel.[15] But a year later he admitted rather plaintively that he had discovered that "criticizing Twain is apparently as irreverent and sacrilegious as criticizing Mother's Day."[16]

Particularly, the New Critical types have fastened on the last ten chapters—and still do. Those who dislike the ending charge that in it Mark Twain changes the mode from satire to burlesque, the prevailing tone from

15. *CE* 17 (October 1955): 6–10.
16. *CE* 18 (November 1956): 108.

seriousness to farce, the characters from flesh and blood to pasteboard. The action depends upon outrageous coincidence, and Tom's antics are anti-climactic, silly, unfunny, and ruinous to the story as a whole. As he (Tom) takes over, Huck becomes uninteresting and weak and Jim a minstrel-show darky. Mark Twain is up to his old tricks, burlesquing what he has just treated seriously and movingly. The section is much too long, even unneces-sary because the story reaches its climax when Huck makes his decision not to return Jim to Miss Watson. As one critic poetically puts it, the last chap-ters are simply flotsam and jetsam.

Increasingly, though, the defense of the ending has grown in strength and ingenuity, witness such arguments as these: Since the book is a frame story, the reentry of Tom is inevitable and amply prepared for throughout. More importantly, it puts Huck back in proper perspective. Without Tom as con-trast, Huck might end up seeming more imaginative and competent than he really is. In the last chapters we see that he has matured—but only to a point; we perceive with special clarity his horse sense, his compassion, and his ability to come to terms with his environment. But we also perceive that though he has come to realize the selfhood of Jim he cannot extend this real-ization to all blacks. Thus the ending permits Huck to fade into the world from which he has emerged; he does not merit tragedy, and a happy ending would be silly. The last chapters thus keep the story from becoming mawkish and provide a final note of poignancy as we realize that Huck in lighting out is just one step ahead of the others; inevitably he will have to light out again. In the conclusion of the narrative, too, we see most clearly Jim's ability to adapt to whatever role the whites demand of him. Far from being the min-strel darky, he shows himself to be an extraordinarily shrewd human being who knows how to adapt in order to survive. And the depths of his compas-sion finally become manifest as he is willing to risk his freedom so that Tom can receive medical help. Importantly, too, the last chapters reveal the true extent of Tom's aggressiveness and cruelty. Finally, there are those who be-lieve the last chapters cap the satire of the book, for in them we see how slavery corrupts even decent people. They present a travesty on how the na-tion freed the slaves, and a parable on the theme of the damned human race. The fact that Jim has been free all along ends the work with an ironic bang instead of a whimper. Besides, the conclusion carries out the principle of rhythmic repetition that gives the book its basic coherence. But there are always killjoys. One or two critics have had the temerity to call the whole argument over the last chapters silly.

If the structure of the work has fascinated critics in the last three or four decades, Huck has entranced them. They have not been able to reach too deeply into their verbal bags for ways of describing him. Disregarding Mark Twain's injunction to avoid the adjective, they have called Huck accepting, accommodating, compassionate, decent, dirty, good-natured, helpful, hon-est, humorless, imaginative, innocent, lonely, passive, pathetic, practical, pragmatic, poker-faced, mature, naive, bad, good, heroic, and unheroic. He is called a real boy, an unspoiled boy, a town boy, a river boy, a ragamuffin, a river rat, a picaresque saint, a liar, an imagist poet, a fugitive, a figure from folklore, an existential hero, the first absurd hero, a keen observer, and a literary sport. Metaphorically, he is a Prometheus, a frontier Thoreau, a Mississippi Moses, a Tocquevillian hero, and the devil's disciple who has become God's own child. We learn that he is both a fugitive and a joiner who longs for freedom and for acceptance by the community, an innocent as well as one who feels innately guilty. He is much like his father; indeed he has his father's strength. But he is searching for a mother substitute. He matures, but there is little that he really learns. He is hurt by experience, fears loneliness, and finds no code adequate for the demands of his moral nature. He is torn by the Leckian conflict between his heart and his conscience. His moral triumph (and agony) is when he decides not to return Jim to Miss Watson, but he learns little from the episode and never thinks of it again. He is nonjudgmental but exists to furnish us with a means of judging the world. He is the contemplative side of Mark Twain, the lonely spirit. He is also a shield behind which Mark Twain can let go. Despite all this and more, we learn from other critics that Huck is not a coherently developed character, his moral growth is overrated, and he lacks many of the basic interests and drives of a normal adolescent. In *The True Adventures of Huckleberry Finn* (1970) John Seelye attempts to show what Huck would have done had Mark Twain been really interested in depicting a true-to-life boy.

Arguments over the theme of the book have kept critics spinning and twirling. Here are a few of the nominations for major theme: alienation, conscience, death, disguise, faith in human goodness, fear, freedom, mock freedom, initiation, justice, liberation, loneliness, lying, morality, suffering, superstition, theft, setting a free man free, and, of course, the damned human race. Some see the theme in oppositions: accommodation versus transcendence, black magic versus white, fantasy versus reality, appearance versus reality, imagination versus reality, imagination versus common sense, freedom versus slavery, the individual versus society, power versus love, Miss Watson's Providence versus the Widow Douglas's Providence, wish versus belief, and—two favorites—head versus heart, and a sound heart versus a deformed conscience. One statistically minded critic in developing the head–heart dichotomy finds that the characters cry seventy-one times. Those critics of a moral and psychological bent explore Huck's inner conflicts; those more interested in social issues present the book as an attack on the conventions and institutions of Mississippi valley culture, which they variously describe as slave, Southern, genteel, and Victorian. These critics vigorously deny that the book is racist and argue that when properly read it is one of the most powerful attacks on racial prejudice ever published. Philosophically minded critics allude to a strain of determinism; one suggests that the book exhibits the beginnings of Mark Twain's descent into epistomological uncertainty.

After all these commentaries on *Huckleberry Finn*, one would think that everything that can be said about the book has been said. Yet a few of the most recent studies are among the most perceptive. In his essay about Mark Twain scholarship for 1982, Louis Budd lists articles that deal with Huck as a confidence man, Huck's rejection of society because of the false identifica-

Salem College
Gramley Library
Winston-Salem, NC 27108

tions it places upon him, Huck's attempt to escape society because he real-izes that both the aristocrats and the poor in the South suffer from the fact that they live in a slave culture. Other articles suggest that Huck's psychic wavering grows into a wish for oblivion, that Twain elevates the common in backwoods Southern life by avoiding mention of sexuality, that there are three strong linguistic relationships in the book: Huck as narrator versus Huck as character, Huck versus Tom, and Huck versus the other charac-ters.[17] Other useful essays have followed in the past year, all of them capped, it seems to me, by Alfred Kazin's section on *Huckleberry Finn* in *An Ameri-can Procession*. Kazin finds the book an exploration of the human bottom, the world of the totally powerless and unsettled. In confronting forces bigger than himself—he knows who runs things—Huck has only his wits. By these, however, he manages to keep going until there is no place for him to go except back to Tom Sawyer's fun and games. "The sense of necessity that only bottom dogs know is what gives such unmediated, unintellectualized beauty to the style. Mark Twain, fully for the first time, knew how to let life carry out its own rhythm."[18]

Although the output of articles on *Huckleberry Finn* has slackened to about ten a year in a normal year, that number will be at least tripled in 1984. There is no strong indication that the *Huckleberry Finn* industry is preparing to bank its fires. Nor that the famous raft in the foreseeable future will sink from public consciousness. This extraordinary narrative still at-tracts both young and old, the general reader and the literary specialist. Mark Twain would be pleased to know that on its hundredth birthday his "so noble" a book and "so beautiful" a book is still alive and well and doing just fine.

17. *American Literary Scholarship: An Annual/1982* (Durham: Duke University Press, 1984), pp. 104–6.
18. *An American Procession* (New York: Alfred A. Knopf, 1984), p. 209.

Salem College
Gramley Library
Winston-Salem, NC 27108

I

The Imagination and Its Amanuensis: Huck, Twain, and Clemens

T HE essays in this section extend, often in surprising ways, the truism that Samuel Clemens, his literary persona and alter ego, Mark Twain, and his most remarkable fictional creation, Huck Finn, are bound together by intricate psychological threads that hint at the mysterious depths of the author's psyche and imagination. From relatively early in Twain's career there was a profound public consciousness of highly demarcated "sides" to the man—the wild humorist of the Pacific slope domesticated in genteel Victorian respectability at Nook Farm, for example—and the course of criticism subsequently has been to find and explore with increasing sophistication more such dichotomies and elements of a divided self. Like the intricacies of the Mark Twain/Samuel Clemens locus, however, Stephen Gilman's essay is difficult to classify without violating its complexity and integrity: by turns contextual, allusive, analytical, and personal, it manages to place *Huck Finn* provocatively against the tradition of the European novel, from the primitive picaresque to the nearly contemporary and highly conscious artistic experimentation of Flaubert. At the same time it celebrates what one inchoately feels in the presence of the novel, the delicate mediation of Mark Twain's literary skill in projecting through Huck's voice the primal sensibility of his creator.

Louis J. Budd's exploration of this same Twain/Clemens dichotomy employs a more conventionally scholarly and Jamesian "density of specification" to place the achievement of *Huckleberry Finn* in the context of the genesis of "Mark Twain," whom he views not so much as a pseudonym or a persona as "a nimble troupe of personae" out of which the diverse elements of the novel emerged. His speculations are based—all the more intriguingly—on the now nearly forgotten bust of himself that Twain had commissioned from his protégé Karl Gerhardt to serve as the frontispiece for *Huckleberry Finn*—a visual benchmark that we are pleased to reproduce in the present volume. Tom Quirk explores the obverse and rather startling attempt by Twain shortly after the writing of *Huckleberry Finn* to reinterpret a crucial episode in his own life as a replication of the most significant act of his young hero. He shows how, in "The Private History of a Campaign That Failed," Twain reimagined his Civil War experiences, so as to justify his lighting out, like Huck, for the Territory in the face of socially induced horrors. There were powerful stimuli for Twain the reconstructed southerner,

Republican, the friend and publisher of General Grant to account for his stint as a member of a Confederate militia during the war, of course, but it is nevertheless startling to realize that he portrayed himself—in contravention of the known facts—as fleeing in the pattern of his recently created protagonist the absurdities and cruelties of border civilization.

Clearly Huck, although he was Twain's first important first-person narrator not explicitly based on the autobiographical "Mark Twain" persona, was a character who projected vibrantly certain deep fears and longings of the author. Jay Martin's "The Genie in the Bottle: Huckleberry Finn in Mark Twain's Life" offers a thoroughgoing and arresting psychoanalytic interpretation of the novel. Now a practicing analyst as well as a gifted critic, Martin renders a portrait of Twain's unconscious life that accounts both for his persistent feelings of loss, guilt, despair, and insignificance and for his momentary masked disclosure and transcendence of these feelings in *Huckleberry Finn*. It is a portrait and an interpretation that will be controversial, but the essay has a rare virtue for exercises in this vein in that it leads to no diminution of the novel as a work of art but only to increased admiration for and wonder at its achievement.

1 STEPHEN GILMAN

Adventures of Huckleberry Finn: Experience of Samuel Clemens

Novel reading is an activity best engaged in by avid novel readers—amateur, professional, or both—with the result that each individual novel reaches its plenitudes of meaning in the context of other novels.[1] *Huck Finn* is not an American *Don Quixote*, but those who have not read and loved and assimilated that father of novels will not excavate all of the river's richness. Or as Stendhal would say: will not play its full symphony in their "souls." However, this rapport is not the subject of the present essay. Instead, as a student of more than one Romance literature, I should like to comment on the theme of *Huck Finn* and its peculiar stylistic point of view in the light of other areas of my reading, specifically Spanish picaresque novels and those of Twain's great contemporaries: Flaubert and Galdós. Perhaps in so doing, I may be able to shed light on certain aspects of the novel—our novel—that critics who bring with them only the English tradition may not have noticed. Or may think not worth noticing.

The *Lazarillo de Tormes* and the *Guzmán de Alfarache* (primordial picaresque novels, neither of which there is any reason to believe Mark Twain had read)[2] have one thing in common with *Huck Finn*. All are written in the first person by fictional egos engaged in remembering and assessing—"accounting for" as Claudio Guillén puts it[3]—their lives. In so doing, all three challenge the lives and values of their expected and unexpected readers. However, there is a crucial difference between Huck and those remote forebears. Both Spanish seventeenth-century authors took great pains to invent more or less credible grown-up personae ostensibly capable of writing about themselves and indeed anxious to do so—personae who for different reasons enjoy looking back across time with mature irony at their youthful illusions, mistakes, fears, and miseries. However, in the case of Huck it is impossible to imagine him as grown up and capable of putting on paper what we are reading. He himself tells us that he has only been to school for three or four months and that he can "spell, and read, and write just a little" (p. [34]). And at the end, as we know, he literally deserts "sivilization." Only on that occasion (and when he acknowledges his incapacity to reproduce ei-

1. This article is for Augusto Centeno, Roy Harvey Pearce, Kurt H. Wolff, and Claudio Guillén, without whom . . . .
2. Not mentioned in Alan Gribben's exhaustive *Mark Twain's Library: A Reconstruction* (Boston: G. K. Hall, 1980).
3. "La disposición temporal del *Lazarillo de Tormes*," HR 25 (1957): 270.

ther fake or real English accents) does he mention the act of writing at all: "there ain't nothing more to write about, and I am rotten glad of it, because if I'd a knowed what a trouble it was to make a book I wouldn't a tackled it and ain't agoing to no more" (p. 366).

The comparison is not intended to be disparaging. Rather it points directly at the central marvel of the book, the irresistibly enticing mystery at its heart that engages us from the moment Huck leaves Tom and until they are rejoined: who—or what—is Huckleberry Finn? There have been many answers to this riddle—felon, saint, mythological creature, unwitting homosexual, and, most profound of all, a "touchstone" for estimating the perils and possible salvation of being American.[4] Which is to say, corruptible or already corrupted "innocents" from Europe "abroad" in a New World. But in the end, the question itself matters more than the answers. Such is the lesson of reading *Huck Finn* in a picaresque context; in so doing we realize that in spite of apparent past tenses,[5] his adventures are radically present and that he, like Christ for his disciples after the Crucifixion, remains with us after we finish reading, not so much as a character than as a "presence." The mystery has been made more mysterious.

Only on one occasion are we allowed dimly to perceive a span of time separating the "I" of the writer from an earlier self, and it is so surprising and so moving that in quoting it I sense a commotion in my own life. Speaking of Mary Jane Wilks, Huck remembers:

> You may say what you want to, but in my opinion she had more sand in her than any girl I ever see; in my opinion she was just full of sand. It sounds like flattery, but it ain't no flattery. And when it comes to beauty—and goodness too—she lays over them all. I hain't ever seen her since that time that I see her go out of that door; no, I hain't ever seen her since, but I reckon I've thought of her a many and a many a million times, and of her saying she would pray for me. (P. 245)

If only for a narrative instant Huck shares the human condition. No longer a presence, loss has submitted him to the irreversibility and inevitability of time and personal history.

The passage just cited is the exception that confirms the rule. With instinctive wisdom and unerring insight Samuel Clemens built his book in a different way: as a salvation of time rather than a picaresque loss. But it does help us to comprehend his recurrent and sly insistence on Huck's pathetic efforts to pretend to be *"real."* One thinks, for example, of the miniature autobiographies of his lies in so many of which he creates and destroys the family he never had. Or of his self-presentation to the reader and the people he meets as a "boy." When he explains his desire to risk boarding the *Sir Walter Scott*, he tells us, "I felt just the way any other boy would a felt" (p. 96). And in so saying, he betrays a tacit concern that he may not be one.

4. Roy Harvey Pearce, "Huck Finn in His History," *EA* 24(1971): 294.

5. Käte Hamburger in her *Die Logik der Dichtung* (Stuttgart: E. Klett, 1957), excludes narration in the first person ("Ich-Erzählung") from the general tendency of narrative past tenses to become present during the process of reading. This may be partially true of certain picaresque novels, but certainly not of *Huck Finn*. It is marvelous to observe how blithely and systematically Mark Twain exploits the "illogic" of his "Dichtung."

Tom Sawyer, Huck's Amadís of Gaul because he is the archetype of boyhood (in the sense that he plays being grown-up), would never have said such a thing. Nor would he have identified himself to the besieged Grangerfords as "only a boy." Here is a statement that is immediately belied by the conversation that ensues the next morning with young Buck, a genuine boy who tells riddles, brags about wild and domestic pets, and is impatient to grow so that he, too, can shoot the neighbors. He is thus diametrically opposed to Huck, who cannot understand the riddles, does not want pets (during the flood on Jackson's Island, "We could a had pets enough if we'd wanted them"), and is appalled by the feud (p. 76). No, Huck is not a boy; he is—as "old lady" Grangerford describes him without realizing the meaning of her words and as Samuel Clemens created him with far more awareness—a "little stranger." This is to say, a "stranger" as "mysterious" in his own way as the one so described.

Hence, Huck's inability to play and to comprehend the nature of playing, an inability that refers not just to the much-criticized framing chapters that imitate the pattern but not the profundity of *Don Quixote* (Tom's gang at the beginning and the rescue of Jim at the end), but also to the circus, to the charades of the Duke and the King, to the bellicose frontier rhetoric of Bob the Corpsemaker and the Child of Calamity, to the crude practical jokes of the inhabitants of Bricksville, to Pap's pretense of reform, to the assassination so accurately imitated by the "lanky man, with long hair and a big white fur stove-pipe hat" (p. 188), to Pokeville rituals of repentance, and in general to the behavior of men immersed in history and society. On occasion, Huck does try to play, but his efforts in general show his incompetence—for example, when he pretends to be a girl for the benefit of Mrs. Judith Loftis, when his imitations of Tom's practical joke on Jim turn out so pathetically, and on those occasions when conscience tries in vain to compel him to fulfill his proper cultural role, that is, to play being someone else.

What Huck cannot be and cannot do are thus made evident by his vain attempts to surpass limitations. Yet this apparent impotence is, as we know, the condition of his special kind of heroism. Not picaresque antiheroism but the real thing, for Huck is armed not with shield and lance but with the clear vision and invincible language of the perfect reporter. As is well known, the making of the novel is intertwined with the writing of Mark Twain's first-person memoirs of *Life on the Mississippi*, "old times" relived on the occasion of his 1882 visit to the river that inspired him to return to the abandoned manuscript of *Huckleberry Finn*. The point is that the Mark-persona who remembers his travails with the river and with Horace Bixby is Tom Sawyer as a young man, alternately credulously humble and cockily riding for a fall. In short, given to believing and telling "stretchers." Only Huck can tell us the truth of the river, *both* the inner underwater truth of its perilous and fickle inevitability and the outer truth of its intense marvel and beauty.[6] He *is* Samuel Clemens, not a surrogate or a persona, but Clemens's naked sensibility stripped of the flattened restrictive self-image of reminis-

---

6. In *Life on the Mississippi*, Mark Twain remembers that his training as a pilot destroyed his sense of the river's beauty, but in the creation of Huck it was miraculously restored.

cence and autobiography. Pastness remembered foreshortens in its dream-like quest for lost perfection (as in *The Adventures of Tom Sawyer*) or in its rueful self-irony (as in the two Mississippi memoirs), but Huck's irrefutable presence seeks and finds and preserves lost time.

Both the truth of the river and the truth of the narrative consist in sheer indivisible temporality. Not comically and rhythmically juxtaposed, as in the stop-and-go hoofbeat gait and narrative "Vorgang" of Jacques "le fataliste" or the varying locomotion of Parson Adams, the world's first jogger, but an immense single flow of consciousness and water translated into words, sentences, and paragraphs. In *Tom Sawyer* the river is a background, part of an "endless summer" far away and long ago, and the climactic adventure occurs appropriately in the timeless isolation of the cave. In *Huck Finn*, on the contrary, time is present truth, and, as such, it is literally smelled, heard, seen, tasted, and felt. Here the river is crucial. Before embarkation, Huck's experience of time is rudimentary and lyrical, readily recognizable by anyone who has ever been afraid of the dark: a lonesome, seemingly endless night punctuated by the sounds of rustling leaves, a hooting owl, a howling dog, the whispering wind, a restless ghost, and finally relieved by the mechanical reassurance of the chimes of the town clock. Imprisoned domestically and still potentially a boy, Huck has not yet escaped downriver.

But on the very first night of his liberation ("I fool Pap and get away") Huck has a far more private and arresting encounter with time. He is lying on the bottom of the stolen canoe:

> I was pretty tired, and the first thing I knowed, I was asleep. When I woke up I didn't know where I was, for a minute. I set up and looked around, a little scared. Then I remembered. The river looked miles and miles across. The moon was so bright I could a counted the drift logs that went a slipping along, black and still, hundreds of yards out from shore. Everything was dead quiet, and it looked late, and *smelt* late. You know what I mean—I don't know the words to put it in. (P. 58)

The result—or the cause—of this "Proustian" conjunction of time and space are the chapters we love the best: the endlessly flowing aorta of the novel.

Time is not "smelt" but heard and overheard directly on the following page:

> And how far a body can hear on the water such nights! I heard people talking at the ferry landing. I heard what they said, too, every word of it. One man said it was getting towards the long days and the short nights, now. 'T other one said *this* warn't one of the short ones, he reckoned—and then they laughed. . . . The first fellow . . . said that warn't nothing to some things he had said in his time. I heard one man say it was nearly three o'clock, and he hoped daylight wouldn't wait more than about a week longer. After that, the talk got further and further away, and I couldn't make out the words any more, but I could hear the mumble; and now and then a laugh, too, but it seemed a long ways off. (P. 59)

A stupid joke about sidereal time, another about psychological time (Is dawn a week away?), and then the direct audible evanescence as the canoe drifts away downstream into distant space. The whole passage is so apparently simple that it conceals the complexity of its orchestration.[7]

We actually taste time in the same chapter:

> And so for three days and nights. No difference—just the same thing. But the next day I went exploring around down through the island. . . . I wanted to know all about it; but mainly I wanted to put in the time. I found plenty strawberries, ripe and prime; the green summer-grapes, and green razberries; and the green blackberries was just beginning to show. They would all come handy by-and-by, I judged. (Pp. 64–65)

Again we experience an overlapping plurality of time: the empty mind-time of Huck, which he tries to fill or "put in" (the same idiom had just been used to explain his counting driftwood and stars), and the seasonal fruition of time now and in the future. In the next few paragraphs we go on to *see* time and to *feel* it in all its immediacy: Jim's campfire is discovered "still smoking." Then on the following morning: "A little ripply, cool breeze begun to blow, and that was as good as saying the night was about done" (p. 66). For all the five senses, then, valley, river, and island space and every kind of time blend into an integrated, self-evident experience that the "Mark Twain" of *Life on the Mississippi* could never have provided.

Nevertheless, without Mark Twain's training as a pilot this creative identification of space and time as a fluvial phenomenon would not have been possible. If the quotation that follows seems overextended, it perhaps may be pardoned as appropriate recognition of the debt every American reader owes to Horace Bixby:

> I went to work now to learn the shape of the river, and of all the eluding and ungraspable objects that ever I tried to get mind or hands on, that was the chief. I would fasten my eyes upon a sharp, wooded point that projected far into the river some miles ahead of me and go to laboriously photographing its shape upon my brain, and just as I was beginning to succeed to my satisfaction, we would draw up toward it and the exasperating thing would begin to melt away and fold back into the bank! If there had been a conspicuous dead tree standing upon the very point of the cape, I would find that tree inconspicuously merged into the general forest and occupying the middle of a straight shore, when I got abreast of it! No prominent hill would stick to its shape long enough for me to make up my mind what its form really was, but it was as dissolving and changeful as if it had been a mountain of butter in the hottest corner of the tropics. Nothing ever had the same shape when I was coming down-stream that it had borne when I went up. I mentioned these little difficulties to Mr. Bixby. He said:
>
> "That's the very main virtue of the thing. If the shapes didn't change every

7. The sight and sound of time merge in the sharply etched description at the beginning of Chapter 19: "Next you'd see a raft sliding by, away off yonder, and maybe a galoot on it chopping, because they're most always doing it on a raft; you'd see the ax flash, and come down—you don't hear nothing; you see that ax go up again, and by the time it's above the man's head, then you hear the *k'chunk!*—it had took all that time to come over the water" (p. 158). Note also the combined feeling and glimpse of time in Chapter 15: "I was floating along, of course, four or five miles an hour; but you don't ever think of that. No, you *feel* like you are laying dead still on the water; and if a little glimpse of a snag slips by, you don't think to yourself how fast *you're* going, but you catch your breath and think, my! how that snag's tearing along" (p. 117).

three seconds they wouldn't be of any use. Take this place where we are now, for instance. As long as that hill over yonder is only one hill, I can boom right along the way I'm going, but the moment it splits at the top and forms a V, I know I've got to scratch to starboard in a hurry or I'll bang this boat's brains out against a rock, and then the moment one of the prongs of the V swings behind the other, I've got to waltz to larboard again or I'll have a misunderstanding with a snag that would snatch the keelson out of this steamboat as neatly as if it were a sliver in your hand. If that hill didn't change its shape on bad nights there would be an awful steamboat graveyard around here inside of a year."

The narrator surely exaggerates as he remembers, but nevertheless his peculiarly intense training in observing space in terms of time and time in terms of space, grafted onto his reproduction of that naked sensibility which is Huck's "presence," is what made *Huck Finn* possible. Many critics, including Twain himself, have emphasized his vivid experience of the river as a special, equally intense, and profoundly American way of life that enabled what might be called the "population" of the novel: "met 'em on the river." This is, of course, true; but for my present purposes I am less interested in experience as a gathering in, a form of unofficial education, or what the Germans call "Erfahrung" (recollection of the journey) than as an "Erlebnis": what is smelt, heard, tasted, seen, and felt now. As well as exactly how it is smelt, heard, tasted, seen, and felt. No wonder Hemingway was entranced with this particular novel. Thus it is that Clemens-Huck, like their great nineteenth-century fellow connoisseurs of time and space—Stendhal, Flaubert, Proust—perceive all they observe. When it comes to judging people Huck is a naif in the eighteenth-century tradition, meaning that his instincts are infallible and his comprehension is erratic, whereas his author, we know, was just the opposite.[8] But it is the precise intersection of river "nowness" and "hereness" that was instilled in "Mark Twain" by Horace Bixby and conferred on Huck that commands our unconditional assent.

At this point, we are ready to consider the title, *Adventures of Huckleberry Finn*. In view of what has just been said, is it not misleading, and would not something resembling Dickens's *The Personal History and Experiences of David Copperfield the Younger* have been more suitable? I think not because, in spite of all that has been said so far, the river chapters do constitute an immense adventure of the sort defined by Georg Simmel as essentially hermetic. An adventure, he says in the brilliant essay published in English translation by Kurt Wolff, occurs outside "the usual continuity of this life":

> It is like an island in life which determines its beginning and end according to its own formative powers and not—like the part of a continent—according to those of adjacent territories. This factor of decisive boundedness, which lifts an adventure out of the regular course of a human destiny, is not mechanical but organic: just as the organism determines its spatial shape not simply by adjusting to obstacles confining it from right and left but by the propelling force of a life forming from inside out, so does an adventure not end because something

---

8. From his business dealings we may conclude that Samuel Clemens, while consciously suspicious and disabused with human nature, was instinctively gullible.

else begins; instead its temporal form, its radical being ended, is the precise expression of its inner sense.[9]

This seems to me to help clarify the anguishing novelistic problem that confronted the author. The novel could not end where the adventure ended (with the decision to "*go* to hell" [p. 272]); his readers, like those of Dickens's *Great Expectations*, would have been up in arms. And so, remembering the post–*Tom Sawyer* beginning, he framed the "organic" adventure with a "mechanical" imitation. The not so hermetic walls of the play-prison replace the confines of the authentic raft.

If questioned, I surmise that Simmel would have assented enthusiastically to the notion that rafts are even more adventurous than "islands." The immense adventure of the river (perhaps the longest and most vivid adventure that as readers we are privileged to share) as a result of this particular means of locomotion—the isolating current—is subdivided into a multiplicity of episodic adventures. Once Huck and Jim are back on the raft and out of sight each chapter is sealed and closed—"soaked up." Yet, just as in the case of *Don Quixote*, there is also an unceasing and crucial transition of adventure to experience, from hermeticism to temporal continuity. In almost every sentence we witness the fecundating penetration of the "thresholds" of adventure by time—experience in time. The special intensity of the river voyage is derived from this confrontation, which is also a coexistence. On the one hand, each adventure is by definition discrete, and, on the other, it is shot through with a relentless and continually entrancing flow of experienced time. The novelist does not say here, as he did in *Tom Sawyer*, "Verweile doch; du bist so schön," but rather "Hör nicht auf."

When the larger adventure comes to an end and Huck decides, like Galdós's Fortunata,[10] to abandon imposed conscience ("sivilization") for good, the sum of his experienced time coalesces into a final reminiscence: "And got to thinking over our trip down the river; and I see Jim before me, all the *time*, in the day, and in the night*time*, some*times* moonlight, some*times* storms, and we a floating along, talking, and singing, and laughing" (p. 271; italics added). For Huck this is what Percy Lubbock called with moderate desperation the "right form" of the novelistic whole: memory of the past as the passing of time. Which in turn implies that sentence by sentence it is the latter that makes the book as irrefutable as it is. Stylistically, the maitrise with which Samuel Clemens accomplishes this—by which he infiltrates adventure with experience—results, as we have seen, in a flow of prose that is surprisingly complex in spite of its apparent simplicity.

There are at least four distinct narrative modes that exhibit the same temporal concern: decelerated individual scenes such as the thunderstorm over Jackson's Island; passages of transition during which days and nights "swim

9. *Georg Simmel, 1858–1918*, ed. Kurt H. Wolff (Columbus: Ohio State University Press, 1959), pp. 244–45.

10. See my *Galdós and the Art of the European Novel, 1867–1887* (Princeton: Princeton University Press, 1981), chap. 11, for a detailed thematic comparison of the two novels. In their castigation of "conscience" they coincide remarkably.

by"; descriptions of local color such as that of Bricksville or the campmeeting; and finally actual happenings in the "present." The first two are obvious: the present participles of the storm—the branches "tossing their arms," "the tree-tops a-plunging," the thunder "rumbling, grumbling, tumbling down the sky" (pp. 75–76). Then on the next pages: "The river went on raising and raising for ten or twelve days" followed by the plural "Daytimes," "We went winding," "you could see," and then "One night" and "Another night" and "every day" (pp. 76–[79]). The most memorable of these is, of course, the passage at the beginning of Chapter 19 ("Here is the way we put in the time"), which communicates the sound ("bull-frogs a-cluttering"), the sight ("you could see little dark spots drifting along, ever so far away—trading scows, and such things"), and the feel and the smell ("then the nice breeze springs up, and comes fanning you from over there, so cool and fresh, and sweet to smell, on account of the woods and the flowers; but sometimes not that way, because they've left dead fish laying around, gars, and such, and they do get pretty rank") (pp. [157]–58).

The use of the present tense, present participles, temporal adverbs, "coulds" and "woulds," and the present perfect is supplemented by the use of repeated plurals, particularly in the local-color description:

> There was as much as a thousand people there, from twenty mile around. The woods was full of teams and wagons, hitched everywheres, feeding out of the wagon troughs and stomping to keep off the flies. There was sheds made out of poles and roofed over with branches, where they had lemonade and gingerbread to sell, and piles of watermelons and green corn and such-like truck.
>
> The preaching was going on under the same kinds of sheds, only they was bigger and held crowds of people. The benches was made out of outside slabs of logs, with holes bored in the round side to drive sticks into for legs. They didn't have no backs. The preachers had high platforms to stand on, at one end of the sheds. The women had on sun-bonnets; and some had linsey-woolsey frocks, some gingham ones, and a few of the young ones had on calico. (P. 172)

The very multiplicity of the typical converts this particular campmeeting from a snapshot or single image into a re-creation of a thousand campmeetings, an endless temporal procession of the same superstitious celebration. Time is extended forward and backward in such a way as to embrace what Unamuno would have called the "intra-history" of the Old South.

Finally, let us examine the incident at the funeral in which Clemens provides us with a new version of the interrupted sermon in *Tom Sawyer*. There the action had been primarily sequential:

> The dog spied the beetle; the drooping tail lifted and wagged. He surveyed the prize; walked around it; smelt at it from a safe distance; walked around it again; grew bolder, and took a closer smell; then lifted his lip and made a gingerly snatch at it, just missing it, made another and another, began to enjoy the diversion; subsided to his stomach with the beetle between his paws.

In contrast, when another dog interrupts the funeral sermon, the undertaker, "the softest, glidingest, stealthiest man" Huck "ever saw," makes

> a sign to the preacher as much as to say, "Don't you worry—just depend on me." Then he stooped down and begun to glide along the wall, just his shoul-

ders showing over the people's heads. So he glided along, and the pow-wow and racket getting more and more outrageous all the time; and at last, when he had gone around two sides of the room, he disappears down cellar. Then, in about two seconds we heard a whack, and the dog he finished up with a most amazing howl or two. . . . In a minute or two here comes this undertaker's back and shoulders gliding along the wall again; and so he glided and glided, around three sides of the room. (Pp. 232–33)

Here the specific action—the whack and the howl—is encased in the open-ended time of the gliding—just as the King's confession of piracy is encased in the open-ended time of custom. In *Tom Sawyer*, on the other hand, the time of the witnessing ("the whole church was red-faced and suffocating with suppressed laughter") is encased in the sequence of actions.

At this point, we are ready to imagine Flaubert translating *Huck Finn*. There can be no doubt at all in the minds of faithful "flaubertians" that in all four of the narrative modes just exemplified he would have put his verbs in the imperfect tense. By which I mean not the traditional "passé imparfait" of the grammarians (a past tense of duration as contrasted to the "passé défini") but rather that experiential imperfect of time-going-by which (according to Albert Thibaudet) he had dredged out of spoken language.[11] This superb novelistic instrument, which is unhappily lacking in English, appears at the very beginning of *L'Education sentimentale* with the departure of a steamboat, an event not without interest for the author of *Huck Finn* or for Horace Bixby, past master of a tenseless metier:

> Le 15 septembre 1840, vers six heures du matin, *la Ville de Montéreau*, près de partir, fum*ait* àgros devant le quai Saint-Bernard.
> Des gens arriv*aient* hors d'haleine; des barriques, des cables, des corbeilles de linge gên*aient* la circulation; les matelots ne répond*aient* a personne; on se heurt*ait*; les colis mont*aient* a personne; on se heurt*ait*; les colis mont*aient* entre les deux tambours, et le tapage s'absorb*ait* dans le bruissement de la vapeur, qui, s'échappant par les plaques de tôle, envelopp*ait* tout une nuée blanchâtre, tandis que la cloche, a l'avant, tint*ait* sans discontinuer.

In spite of the temporal precision of the first sentence—year, day, and hour—we are then immediately invited to share the experience of being there at the moment, or as my teacher Américo Castro used to say: the novel does not just tell us what happened but "how it feels to exist within the happening." Flaubert in the above passage uses the same means employed by Mark Twain to create Huck's present and presence (plurals and present participles), but the achievement was made immensely easier by his marvelous rediscovery of the lost potentialities of the imperfect.[12] So that in rereading

11. *Gustave Flaubert* (Paris: Plou, 1922). For further references to the extensive bibliography on the grammatical redefinition of the imperfect tense, see my "The Imperfect tense and the *Poema del Cid*," *CL* 8 (1956): 31–37. More recent observations and bibliography may be found in Stephen Ullman, *Style in the French Novel* (Cambridge: Cambridge University Press, 1957), and Dorrit Cohn, *Transparent Minds* (Princeton: Princeton University Press, 1978).

12. In a translation that I have examined there is a tendency to equate the present and the imperfect. Chapter 19 begins as follows: "Deux ou trois jours s'écoulèrent; je devrais dire glissèrent, tant il furent calmes et reposants. Le Fleuve était énorme dans ces parages, atteignant parfois, jusqu'à trois kilomètres de large. Nous naviguions la nuit comme d'habitude. Au petit

him after rereading *Huck Finn* we come to appreciate with renewed admiration all the techniques, shades, contrivances, and modulations of style by means of which Mark Twain used English to convert adventure into experience.[13]

In conclusion we may remark that this rapprochement of two such apparently dissimilar novelists as Clemens and Flaubert not only helps us to marvel at the stylistic miracle of *Huckleberry Finn* but also may serve to illuminate its thematic engagement with history. As readers of *L'Education sentimentale* will remember, the "experiential" (or sentimental) climax of that novel is the carriage ride of Frédéric and Rosanette through the forest of Fontainebleau. The unfolding perspectives of "large verdures," the sylvan silence, the tender Romantic rapture of the lovers are all communicated in prose as moving and temporally decelerated as the best of the river descriptions. However, the punctuation of this sustained idyll by rumors of a "bataille épouvantable" taking place in Paris (the time is 1848) and by the distant beat of regimental drums reminds us that these two are merely playing at love (if the companion had been Mme. Arnoux, the novel could not and would not have been written) and that the stern truth of history is waiting in the wings.

The crucial point is that in the American novel the situation is antithetical. The two who love, love as truly as they perceive (and in so saying no genuflection to Leslie Fiedler is intended), and their authentic "life-time" or "river-time" is presented intentionally in contrast to the corrupt, cruel, or at best foolish "play-time" of those who live onshore. I refer here not just to Tom, the two theatrical confidence men, the fools they fool, the dog torturers of Bricksville, but also, and above all, to Pap and the two colonels, each of whom at his own level of dignity or indignity enables us to comprehend the incipient atrocity built into that portion of American history. *Huckleberry Finn* is more than just a critique of the penchant for Sir Walter Scott among Southern gentlemen and ladies. In this "play-time" of feud, of murder, of lynching, of tarring and feathering, and of ignorant racial prejudice, Samuel Clemens comprehends and leads us to comprehend how the Civil War was possible. The rushing mobs that on at least four occasions surge ignorantly through the latter portion of the novel,[14] are they not precursors of the Blue and the Gray? *Huckleberry Finn* thematically is more

---

jour nos attachions le radeau soigneusement camouflé au moyen de branches de cotonniers, posions nos ligne, puis piquions une tête dans le fleuve pour nous refraîchir. Apr'cela nous restions assis dans cinquante centimètres d'eau, sur le sable des bords, à regarder le jour se lever. A cette heur-là, il n'y a pas un bruit sur la terre ou dans le ciel. Tout est parfaitement calme."

13. Among the expressions and techniques not mentioned specifically in my text or the quotations are the following: "used to," "warn't often," "as a general thing," "whenever," "mornings," "went on and on," "now and then," "generly," "by and by," the emphatic "did" ("the wind *did* scream along"), the description of weather itself as a form of time as in the Romance languages, and the use of the second person that brings the reader's present into the act of reading. A full inventory surely would be much more lengthy.

14. I refer, of course, to the disinterment, to the lynch mob, to charging the stage, and to the rush to confess in Pokeville. One might also think of the chase after the rescue of Jim.

than a book of sheer adventures and experience; in its devious anti-Scottian fashion it is also North America's most profound historical novel.

Here Clemens is much closer to the Galdós of the *Episodios nacionales*[15] than he is to the author of *Salammbo*—about which he remarked that it might be "great art" but he would not reread it unless he were "on salary."[16] Both the American and the Spaniard were appalled at their compatriots' penchant for civil war; both attempted to explain it novelistically; both were avid readers of history;[17] both presented the Middle Ages as blackly humorous; and both expressed their revulsion from what they perceived to be the fatuous and fatal cult of historicism that had infected their shared century. In the case of Galdós, this led to a magnum opus, *Fortunata y Jacinta*, in which, as we remarked, an illiterate heroine, equally a presence and hence equally unconcerned with "dead people," literally coincides with Huck in her rebellion against socially and historically imposed "conscience"[18] and in her consequent willingness "to go to Hell." In the case of Samuel Clemens, it resulted not only in *A Connecticut Yankee* and *The Gilded Age* but also in the marvelous invention of the King and the Duke, as shabby and exploitative a pair (as both Huck and Jim come to realize) as their genuine counterparts in the past. Why should English royalty not have been replaced by "a family of cats"? It is a question that Galdós might well have asked concerning Fernando VII and Isabel II, whose behavior he had castigated in the *Episodios*. The thematic coincidence is all the more remarkable for being a coincidence. For both novelists, worship of history was at once ridiculous and fraudulent, whether that read about in books or that imposed capriciously and atrociously by the game-playing "Bosses" of their own times.

15. A series of historical novels extending from Trafalgar to the Bourbon restoration. Galdós tells us indirectly that he learned how to use the novel as a means of historical comprehension—not archaeological reconstruction—from Balzac.

16. He had also read *Madame Bovary* in translation while on shipboard, according to Gribben. But in spite of his friend Howells's enthusiasm, there is no evidence that he ever opened any novel by Galdós.

17. So concludes Gribben with an admirable collection of evidence. For Galdós the same affirmation can be made not only from his novels but also from the inventory of his library published by H. Chonon Berkowitz, *La biblioteca de Bemito Pérez Galdós* (Las Palmas, 1951).

18. My colleague Zeph Stewart in a paper unfortunately not yet published gets to the heart of the matter: Saint Paul's "con-scientia" is consciousness *shared* with some external and morally imperative entity: God, society, or most compelling of all, god-society.

2 LOUIS J. BUDD

"A Nobler Roman Aspect" of
Adventures of Huckleberry Finn

$\mathbf{B}$Y now it takes a Tom Sawyer to dream of finding the master-clue to *Adventures of Huckleberry Finn* that has been overlooked by all the capable scholars and critics who have ransacked the apparently simple text, and not even Poe's Auguste Dupin would dare to sneer that it was in plain sight all along. But an important clue to appreciating *Huckleberry Finn* stands right there up front for anyone who looks at a very early printing. I mean the full-page photograph or, more precisely, the heliotype of a bust of Mark Twain. Only descriptive bibliographers and collectors have looked hard because they find it useful for trying to establish the earliest states of the first edition. That fact is revealing in itself. Because of technical problems, the plate had to be remade about a hundred times for the first printing of thirty thousand.[1] Perhaps because of that, the heliotype was soon dropped.

It was expensive also because of the timing: it held up publication or at the least incurred charges for rush service. On 19 August 1884, from his summer hideout in Elmira, New York, Twain wrote to Charles L. Webster, the nephew running a newly founded publishing firm for him in New York City: "Gerhardt is completing a most excellent bust of me." There was an accident, however, and not until 31 August could Twain inform William Dean Howells that the "finishing touches" would come the next day. Indeed on 9 September he described the bust as "just finished," adding that the sculptor "has just gone" to Philadelphia for the casting into bronze. Then, as early as 20 September, Twain was fuming that the "heliotype Co." in Boston had not sent "that bottle of ink for the autographs."[2] It still had not arrived four days later. These details gain significance from the timetable of publication. Twain had mailed the revised manuscript on 12 April 1884 and had finished with the proofs—galley and page—before the end of August. But long before one of his books issued, he was impatiently counting on the

---

1. Jacob Blanck, *Bibliography of American Literature* (New Haven: Yale University Press, 1957), describes three distinct states but praises Merle Johnson whose *A Bibliography of Mark Twain* (New York: Harper, 1935) discusses the "literally dozens of states" in "almost as many colors" and gives the "last-minute addition" of the heliotype as a main cause for the exceptional tangle of minor textual points. For convenience I later use *frontispiece* more loosely than experts might like.

2. Samuel C. Webster, *Mark Twain, Business Man* (Boston: Little, Brown, 1946), pp. 273–77; this volume is the source for any further letters from Twain to Charles L. Webster. See also Henry Nash Smith and William M. Gibson, eds., *Mark Twain–Howells Letters* (Cambridge: Harvard University Press, 1960), 2:500–502.

The heliotype bust of Mark Twain.

royalties. Also, his letter to Webster on 20 September had called for an unbound copy, probably to use in getting ready for his barnstorming tour with
George Washington Cable.

In fact, unbound copies were available by 19 September. Why did Twain
take on the problems of inserting that helioptype so late? It surely was not
meant to add comedy. Twain, who had been doggedly trying to educate his
tastes and had learned deeper respect for fine art than seems likely from *The
Innocents Abroad*, assured Howells that the bust was "about as good a one
as nearly anybody could make." Serious in expression, it was sternly imposing from the front, and he must have worried that some apprentice Mark
Twain might make sparkling fun of it. It came from the hands of his protégé,
Karl Gerhardt, fresh back from Paris after more than three years of study
paid for by Twain, who ordered his nephew to make sure that the sculptor's
name showed on the bust (as it does in only some of the plates). Twain
hoped to launch Gerhardt, probably not to recover an investment but to
prove an ability to recognize a gifted artist in the rough. Obviously Twain
would also enjoy getting credit for generosity, all the more because the envious were starting to gossip about his success at raking in dollars. His
"P.S." primed Howells with: "If you run across anybody who wants a bust,
be sure & recommend Gerhardt on my say-so."

Another obvious motive was royalties from *Huckleberry Finn*. The short
ad for "agents" would dangle a "Fine Heliotype of the Author" as a wedge
for their door-to-door battle. As early as 1869 an alert operator in Cleveland
had sold photographs of Twain after his lecture. During the 1870s he had to
notice that his face evidently helped various lines of business—cigars, "White
& Fancy Goods, Sewing Machines, & C," and the services of "Plumbers,
Steam and Gas Fitters." A haggler over words could argue that the first separate biography of Twain was packed in Duke's Cigarettes soon after 1886.
Of course it put his portrait on the cover, which measures 1½ by 3 inches.
Partly to tap such demand, *A Tramp Abroad* (1880) carried a solemn engraving of Twain in coat and tie. Suggestively for my argument to come, it
balanced (or was balanced by) a spurious "Titian's Moses," featuring a
bawling infant holding a dish with a live frog on it.

The plausible motives fall short of explaining why the heliotype, even
with the side view it used, clashes so sharply with the tone of *Huckleberry
Finn*. Pseudo-classical in the style that the early nineteenth century had established for our statesmen, it lacks only the folds of a toga gathered at one
of the bare shoulders. The *Boston Literary World*, more impressed than
quizzical, decided that it "gives the humorist a nobler Roman aspect than
that which he wears in real life."[3] The *New York Critic*, a weekly devoted to

3. *Literary World* 16 (7 February 1885): 49. For Warner see *Critic* 2 (18 October 1884):
185; reprinted from *Hartford* (Conn.) *Courant*, 9 October, p. 1. For front photographs of the
bust see *Harper's Monthly* 71 (October 1885): 721 and *Harper's Weekly* 31 (2 April 1887):
248; the side view used can be seen in Hamlin Hill and Walter Blair, eds., *The Art of Huckleberry
Finn* (San Francisco: Chandler, 1962 [1st ed.] or 1969 [2d ed.]). Twainians have wondered over
a stripped-to-the-waist photograph, reproduced in Milton Meltzer, *Mark Twain Himself* (New
York: Crowell, 1960), p. 182. Perhaps it was posed for the use of Gerhardt, who wanted

aesthetic and intellectual affairs, cautiously quoted from a long description by Charles Dudley Warner—Twain's neighbor in Hartford, to be sure, but a genteel prophet honored nationally. He especially admired the bust's "broad masses, full of strength and character—no pettiness, here. . . . It is simple in all its lines, but massive and solid in treatment, and it has a noble dignity and repose." While professing tentativeness, Warner grew positive that it was "more worthy of study than anything of the sort that has appeared here in a long time." The creator of Huck Finn had seemingly modeled for a near-masterpiece himself.

Twain, we know, carefully supervised the illustrations in his books. For *Huckleberry Finn* he came up with a young artist whom he treated like a draftsman or a tailor. Incongruously with the yet unmade bust he picked E. W. Kemble through his centerspread in *Life*, a new comic weekly. Kemble's cartoon had seized on the latest technology to imagine "the applying of electrical protectors to door-knobs, door-mats, &c & electrical hurriers to messengers, waiters &c." He would draw the now familiar frontispiece of Huck holding a dead rabbit and a rifle. But for the second frontispiece Twain did not choose Kemble or the *Life* artist who had him (22 March 1883) studying a skull while an owl and black cat glare from a weird set of props.[4] By 1884 at least twenty other cartoonists, including Twain's famous friend Thomas Nast, had run him through a gamut of exaggeration, but none of them got an offer. Avoiding a humorously stylized portrait of himself was a significant decision at some level of consciousness.

He likewise ignored the models for another engraving like the one in *A Tramp Abroad*. Fascinated by the newfangled camera, he had already posed for it many times. We have to suspect self-ridicule beneath his insistence that it's human nature to center on your own face in a group picture. Furthermore, anybody whose photograph has never appeared more publicly than in a college yearbook may underestimate the trauma when it gets national visibility. In 1887 Twain raged: "leave out that woodcut of me [from *The Library of American Literature* published by his firm]. The more I think of the gratuitous affront of wood where [a] steel [engraving] is lavished upon the unread & the forgotten, the more my bile rises. Don't leave it out, simply—put it in the fire."[5] Some sympathy is due here. How many of his would-be betters had already sat for at least two portraits by established artists?

Besides those oil portraits Twain might have used the one taken recently by Napoleon Sarony, since 1870 or so "the photographer of the country"

photographs of his subject; see the anecdote in *Mark Twain–Howells Letters*, 2:498. The *Hartford Courant* reported (28 November 1884, p. 2) that the bust "has been more recently shown in New York" and "will be taken to the New Orleans exposition." It now rests in the entrance hall of Twain's restored Hartford house.

4. For Twain's comment on Kemble's *Life* cartoon, see *Mark Twain, Business Man*, p. 246. Meltzer reproduces many cartoons of Twain, and I have been locating others.

5. *Mark Twain, Business Man*, pp. 388–89; see also Robert Pack Browning et al., eds., *Mark Twain's Notebooks and Journals: Vol. III (1883–1891)* (Berkeley: University of California Press, 1979), p. 348.

according to the *New York Times* obituary. "His pictures are as well known in the shops of Paris as they are in Broadway and in the theatres of the United States."[6] As for his head-and-shoulders photograph of Twain, the subject sighed in 1905 that it had "spread about the world" and "turns up every week in some newspaper some where or other." But at first it pleased him so much that soon he went back to Sarony with Cable and then, ten years later, alone. In March 1885 he instructed Webster: "Don't forget that I want a dozen of my photos from Sarony's." Eventually he joked at length that it made him look like a gorilla. It did give him a fierce stare and would have suited almost as well what I think he was after. However, the bronze bust had more "tone" in the ironic sense in which he often used that word.

Given the kaleidoscope of Twain's career, my argument should stick close to 1884. Still, it is relevant that alertness toward his visual image never sagged. In 1905 he drolled for a prearranged, syndicated interview:

> Many people think I am a happy man, but I am not; it is because my portraits do me justice. I have a highly organized and sensitive constitution and an educated taste in esthetics, and I cannot abide a portrait which is too particular. I am as I was made—this is a disaster which I cannot help and am in no way responsible for; but is there any fair reason why the artist should notice that? I do him no harm, yet he always exercises this wanton and malicious frankness upon my portraits.
>
> I should like to be drawn once, before I reach 70 again, as I should look if I had been made right instead of carelessly.[7]

Revealing by omission, very few photographs of a smiling Twain survive despite such typical clowning. When asked why his face froze even for snapshots, he explained he did not want to go down to posterity with a foolish grin. The caricatures of Twain as a madcap entertainer must have left him edgy and rueful. However welcome the publicity, he must have brooded about upgrading it. The persons illustrated in his books whom a reader could take for Mark Twain rise in sedateness from *The Innocents Abroad* through *Life on the Mississippi* and of course beyond. So we should ponder that heliotype inserted at the cost of money and vexation to an impatient man. He proposed it to Webster with: "I suppose it would help sell the book." The next day he added, "I thought maybe it would advantage the book." Curiously tentative words from somebody poor in false modesty and increasingly rich in confidence as a promoter.

---

6. 10 November 1896, p. 5. Dating of the first Sarony photograph (reproduced often, as in Meltzer, *Mark Twain Himself*, p. 182) is still unsure; it could have been made as early as 1883. Interestingly, the 1895 photograph was highly similar in pose and clothing, including the overcoat. Twain went back to the firm in 1900. Around 1886–1887 Twain went also to the studio of Benjamin J. Falk, the "prominent New York Photographic artist and innovator"—*Notebooks and Journals*, 3:275. The comment in 1905 comes from a longer passage in a letter to Samuel H. Row, printed in Marlen E. Pew, "Samuel L. Clemens Interviews the Famous Humorist, Mark Twain," *Seattle* (Wash.) *Star*, 30 November 1905, p. 8.

7. From the interview just cited.

II

To present all sides of Twain's mind properly would outdo Emmeline Grangerford's spidery drawing. So I may slight his aesthetic impulses by concentrating on his awareness of his public image. Still, the heliotype represents deep anxieties about the novel ready to appear, not just about its sales and those of previous books and any to come but also about his future as a personality conducting a range of enterprises—from authorship to lecturing to hard-sell merchandising. Those anxieties had intensified since 1876, when he decided to start Huck's "Autobiography" yet worked at it only sporadically before the summer of 1883. Comedy that often depended on irreverence ran to the heart of Twain's genius; but practical self-interest, his share of the submissive instinct, and his sense for communicable reality hobbled him. My approach to that bust expands into the still-open questions: Why did he soar to the heights of *Huckleberry Finn* just once; why did its acclaimed solution of a lowly vernacular hero, boyish yet wise, evade him before 1876 and after 1884? Posterity, I add, should put such questions humbly, not accusingly.

Many of Twain's devotees cannot help dismissing his nonliterary activity as a quirky distraction, especially when he was winding up *Huckleberry Finn*. They cannot understand how he could put tense effort into a board game for teaching historical facts, finally patented as Mark Twain's Memory Builder in August 1885. Likewise numb to his considering his books a commodity, they pay little attention to a private letter of 13 December 1876 that, angry over royalty problems, declares: "If I can make a living out of plays, I shall never write another book. For the present I have placed the three books in mind, in the waste basket."[8] They need to size up the first edition of *Huckleberry Finn* as a physical object designed to catch the eye and sell through a big drive instead of word-of-mouth praise from readers. Twain the publisher, hoping for trailed glory from *The Adventures of Tom Sawyer*, first proposed marketing the old and new novels as a pair; to bring them closer in size, he easily agreed to cut the raftsmen's passage borrowed earlier for *Life on the Mississippi*. Comparing the original *Huckleberry Finn* with its format in the collected editions that began in 1899 leads into the changing faces of Twain's career. The respective readers had significantly different experiences, particularly because of the illustrations.

Both for better and worse, Twain thought of himself as publishing under a brand name, tied first to the Jumping Frog story and then to *The Innocents Abroad*, which, he bragged, kept selling right along like the Bible. As early as 1873 he fought literary pirates by contending in court that Mark Twain was a trademark, not a pseudonym, and he pushed another such case in 1883. An interview in 1891 had him discussing the "trademark" the public stamps on authors where we would say it "types" them. Testifying later in

8. Hamlin Hill, ed., *Mark Twain's Letters to His Publishers, 1867–1894* (Berkeley: University of California Press, 1967), pp. 106–7.

behalf of Rudyard Kipling, he "expressed the view that trade marks ought to be respected, and there is no difference between counterfeiting a label on a book, a box of blacking, or a bottle of whiskey."[9] It was logical to incorporate under his pen name in 1908, creating a legal grayland still with us. That made a triumphant answer to the warning—or threat—from genteelist critics that comic writers better count on a brief run. Some of those critics had even ranked him well down among the pack of funny-men. In 1882 a fellow humorist—long forgotten—who spent a day knocking around St. Louis with Twain commented that he was "too sensible a man not to realize that humor, of all things, is the most ephemeral, and that which will convulse the world today, will appear flat and insipid tomorrow."[10] The prospects for immortality aside, writing a comic novel was a short-term gamble of much effort. In fact, *Huckleberry Finn* took daring risks under a trademark worth protecting.

Like an impresario (or a smart rock-music star) Twain worried about the next step when his vogue started to fade. As the dollars rolled in during the 1870s from several fronts, such as Mark Twain's Self-Pasting Scrapbook, newspaper stories noted his fine head for business. He was gaining status as a self-made tycoon, not just as a self-taught writer or a self-promoting personality. That fellow humorist thought Twain's abilities "might be profitably employed in directing the practical every-day affairs of life." Reporters who dogged the river trip were impressed by his traveling secretary. He had begun to look like a one-man syndicate. To that interviewer in 1891 he would sigh that the dictaphone had not proved useful so far to a "literary or business man." Ironically, he must have decided that a businessman operates on firmer ground than an author, especially a humorist with a fickle public. By 1889 Twain believed that *A Connecticut Yankee in King Arthur's Court* was his "swan song," that he would not have to write for money anymore. Huck, in his first paragraph, calls his creator "Mr. Mark Twain." Mr. Twain had already come to feel entitled to let himself go at his own best gait.

Huck would have goggled at both Mr. Twain's luxurious home and the family's expensive travels. Their style of life took a lot more cash than rafting. In spite of the surefire coups ahead like the mechanical typesetter, Twain's books and lecturing still covered most of the bills and investments. Some of the final touches on *Huckleberry Finn* may reflect the fact that he was mounting a tour with Cable, which carried its own conflicts of imagemaking. As the tour's financial backer, Twain went in for brash advertising and colorful interviews; as the costar he fretted that Cable showed greater dignity with audiences. Eventually Cable produced an anecdote that seems to mark a crisis in 1885. But the problem, which festered long ago, had the clarity of a syndrome by the time *Huckleberry Finn* was projected. A persona—really a nimble troupe of personae—had grown famous as Mark Twain. With the public watching always more intently, that persona

9. Raymond Blathwayt, "Mark Twain on Humor . . . ," *New York World*, 31 May 1891, p. 26; *New York Times*, 27 March 1901, p. 6.

10. John Henton Carter (Commodore Rollingpin), "A Day with Mark Twain," reprinted in my *Critical Essays on Mark Twain, 1867–1910* (Boston: G. K. Hall, 1982), pp. 61–64.

had to narrow his erratic swings and move up from buffo capers while increasing his appeal, had to—we now see—keep adjusting a synthesis of his strengths and improved opportunities. Privately, as Justin Kaplan suggests, Twain hobnobbed with the gentry but understood that his pass listed the trade of entertainer as the reason for admission. Would they keep inviting him to banquets if he no longer gave a hilarious speech? In the marrow of his character did he want to join their clubs if that required taming his humor into polite banter? He knew he could not suppress its wild side if he tried, yet he realized that some of them would find Huck too gamey.

Though a few biographers make him close to paranoiac, his tactical problems were treacherous. He had to feel wary that Huck's attitudes might irritate not just the gentry but also the lions of respectability. The reaction from the directors of the Concord (Massachusetts) Public Library proves that some of the danger was real. They had allies not only in New England but also across the country, not merely in Sunday schools but also throughout a society hoping for enough discipline to give capitalism a smooth roadbed. The biography packed with Duke's Cigarettes held up at praising Huck as "this young scapegrace of a hero" whose courage and manliness are the "better side of ruffianism, which is the result of American independence of character." [11] Later, Twain himself was no more positive than to describe him as a boy of "sound heart & a deformed conscience." That left plenty of distance between a river-rat and an upper-middle-class ornament of Hartford. Huck has worn well because his creator tempered his own dissenting instincts and comic impetus with shrewd calculation of the risks he was running.

Just as some biographers cannot forgive Twain for showing any caution, others cannot mediate between the outside or psychic pressures and his backbone of glorious autonomy. [12] As yet, after all, nobody has come close to matching *Huckleberry Finn*. But while composing it Twain struggled through a series of cruxes for his public image. As he started he was agonizing over how to support Rutherford B. Hayes for president without stirring up the comic paragraphers. His speech at the Whittier dinner soon gave him a vivid lesson in the handicaps of his persona and the bad bounces of his

---

11. Among other places, no doubt, this booklet can be found at the Manuscripts Department of the Duke University Library and the Meine Collection at the University of Illinois (Urbana). Its opinion of Huck Finn was a close paraphrase from the review by Thomas Sergeant Perry in *Century* 30 (May 1885): 171. From the shelter of Twain's Oxford degree, the sedate critic Hamilton Mabie could defend *Tom Sawyer* only obliquely: "there was a grave question in the minds of some people whether such a stage of society was a proper subject for literary presentation; whether it was not too rudimentary for art"—*Outlook* 87 (23 November 1907): 652.

12. Of course Twain encouraged the overreading of his character. Henry Nash Smith has done most to move beyond the Brooks-DeVoto debate by exploring Twain's changing attitudes toward his writing. Though rightly acclaimed, Justin Kaplan finds too much inner melodrama in Twain's career. A fresh wave of biographical analysis is proceeding more dispassionately; for example, see Leland Krauth, "The Proper Pilot: A New Look at 'Old Times on the Mississippi,'" *WIRS* 2 (1979): 52–69. More specifically, Krauth argues that in shaping the cub-pilot essays for an *Atlantic Monthly* audience Twain took care to imply the solidity and seriousness of his own character in 1875.

reputation.[13] However, his triumph with impudent humor at the Grant banquet in 1879 left him giddy as he was completing *A Tramp Abroad* (1880), which vacillated on how to present Mark Twain. Then *The Prince and the Pauper* (1881) puzzled his hardcore readers, who were only partly reassured by *Life on the Mississippi* (1883). Meanwhile, his three daughters now flanked him in hotel lobbies and depots, observed and observing. Thirteen-year-old Susy, around as Gerhardt shaped that bust, started a biography of her father in the spring of 1885 because the press kept underrating him. Of course her devotion imposed a handicap, too. Above all, *Huckleberry Finn* was a bold move, but it pulled against solid forces. We have to follow both strands without stumbling into confusion, without forgetting that humor feeds on psychic release.

Howells had given Twain a prestigious boost through an essay in *Century* magazine for September 1882. That reinforced his confidence but perhaps worried him about reaching a status he could not afford to honor or might disgrace impulsively. In April 1884 a poll for literary "Immortals" still alive left him tied at fourteenth with Warner and no doubt torn among smugness, jealousy, surprise, and uncertainty about how he ought to feel. While sitting for Gerhardt and checking the page proofs of his masterpiece, he dashed off an impious sketch for the much despised *New York Sun*.[14] Yet he sent it both free and unsigned; his tactics had wavered again. Once published, *Huckleberry Finn* influenced the shifting images, too. As it slowly gained ground with respectable critics, he paraded his downhome side more publicly. Nevertheless, as late as the 1890s his own praise usually showed less enthusiasm than an interviewer's leading questions. For the right audience he could volunteer some other book as his best, particularly *Personal Recollections of Joan of Arc*.

Why didn't he sign the sketch for the *New York Sun*? Why did he insert the heliotype? Because, realizing that his novel was fundamentally serious, he wanted to post a warning for the public? If so, what about that almost silly "Notice" to readers also added very late? Or did the bust say: Don't confuse me totally with the ragged, naive, barely literate narrator? Many reviewers assumed that *Huckleberry Finn* was aimed at the juvenile audience.[15] That cooking of the witch-pie (chap. 37) is kid stuff, and much of the Evasion anticipates the Our Gang cliché of children outwitting the adults. Too conscious of position and fame to merge into a poor-white "scape-

13. Critics have yet to analyze exactly how the persona of the narrating miner failed to work. Anybody who sees the sketch as hidden aggression ought to ponder "The Nature of Deference and Demeanor" in Erving Goffman, *Interaction Ritual: Essays in Face-to-Face Behavior* (Chicago: Aldine, 1967).

14. I make the case for ascription in "Who Wants To Go To Hell? An Unsigned Mark Twain Sketch?" *StAH*, n.s. 1 (1982): 6–16. On reading my essay, Robert H. Hirst, general editor of the Mark Twain Project, Bancroft Library, University of California, Berkeley, sent me a copy of the galleys for "Hunting for H———" that evidently were mailed to Twain by W. M. Laffan of the *Sun*.

15. See Victor Fischer's beautifully thorough "Huck Finn Reviewed: The Reception of *Huckleberry Finn* in the United States, 1885–1897," *ALR* 16 (1983): 1–57.

grace," Twain would never again pitch Huck's voice above the firmly boyish level. His next vernacular heroes have at least the maturity of Hank Morgan and Captain Stormfield, waiting long in the wings. But they fascinate posterity much less than Huck. The man behind him had also aged. While not drooping emotionally before his bankruptcy anyway, he had built the new dimensions of his image that left less room for surrender to comic élan.

III

My basic argument risks the charge of being too elitist to appreciate a natural, uncombed democrat, especially after it contends that Huck's origins guarantee neither nobility nor wisdom. Most of the other plebeian characters Huck records verge on the contemptible. Only a chucklehead will deny that the vernacular style liberated some of Twain's best instincts or, more precisely, widened his comic range, so much so that he uneasily took longer with *Huckleberry Finn* than with any other book. But Huck's virtues get overstated except for his empathy with Jim. (An underdog boy could not afford to oppose racism itself.) Perhaps the kindest criticism is that Huck, softening his ties to the humorists of the Old Southwest, sneaks in dollops of Victorian sentimentality.[16] But his much acclaimed kindness can shut off. Always referring to Joanna Wilks as the "hare-lip" (changed meticulously from "hair-lip" in the holograph manuscript) he bursts out once, "Why, Hare-l—why, Joanna" (p. 223). Ridicule of the inherited face and body, which flickers throughout, is cruel, even in the case of Miss Watson, that "tolerable slim old maid, with goggles on" (p. 19). Huck is sometimes more ignorant (including the colloquial sense) than innocent. We grin at his folklore that ranges from horseshoes to cosmology, but we know that we know better. Anyone who takes him as a rounded figure has to pity his reasoning: "Jim said bees wouldn't sting idiots; but I didn't believe that, because I had tried them lots of times myself, and they wouldn't sting me" (p. 71).

Far from belittling Huck, however, I mean to argue that Twain used him with brilliant flexibility as a satirist and a yokel on the same page, as a trumpet of conscience and, if not as a ruffian, as something of a rapscallion. An indulgent tone colors the "stretchers" by Huck, whom the *New York Sun* called "this uncommonly able descendant of Ananias" but whom a bluenose might see as apprenticed to the King and Duke at deceit that glories in its own brass. Twain's lead-in for the excerpts published in the *Century* chuckled: "Readers who have met Huck Finn before . . . will not be surprised that whenever Huck is caught in a close place and is obliged to explain, the truth gets well crippled before he gets through." Is Huck less flesh and blood than a wheel of masks? The habitual liar was an ancient type passed along from the Southwestern school to the literary comedians. In

16. See Leland Krauth, "Mark Twain: The Victorian of Southwestern Humor," *AL* 54 (1982): 368–84.

other scenes, as David E. E. Sloane has pointed out, Huck plays the straight man for many of their routines, including outrageous puns and spellings.[17]

But Sloane also demonstrates that the ablest literary comedians recognized the effects of urbanized industrialism. In boyhood, before falling into history, Twain's spirit had already proved unusually sensitive to the pressures from what Emerson calls the not-Me; while honed intellects feel "free and easy and comfortable" with *Candide*, the everyday mind finds more specific, familiar coordinates in *Huckleberry Finn*. Next, Twain's humiliations in the West had taught him the power of economic and social class and of the reigning mores, however artificial. Political questions, as distinct from campaign rhetoric, had engaged him since his apprenticeship to journalism in Hannibal, and the modernist goal of Reconstruction troubled him as possibly another lost cause. Psychically he bent with the opposite, emotional pull toward primitivity, toward escape from the rush of Progress. On his personal calendar, meantime, he needed to assure himself that his fiftieth birthday in November 1885 would find him soaring above mental arthritis. Therefore, as soon as we concentrate on Huck as a strolling clown we feel that we are missing both intended and involuntary probing into profundities, that in laughing at his corny jokes we ignore the Swiftean angers of a man who both promised and regretted that "There is no laughter in heaven."

Always too demanding of human potentiality, Twain was increasingly nauseated by the machine politics that led to the Blaine-Cleveland election of 1884. But his European trip of 1878–1879 had refired his delight in the American freedom of movement and self-assertion that underlies *Huckleberry Finn*. His equations were complicated, unstable. Before getting to Huck's first paragraph, we can frustrate ourselves by trying to harmonize the ornate binding, the two frontispieces, the warning "Notice" countersigned by the "Chief of Ordnance," the niggling "Explanatory" about dialects, and the sometimes arch tone of the table of contents and of the captions listed for the illustrations. Yet for the reader the novel is magnificently "there" in the Jamesian sense. We should avoid dulling its concreteness under any scheme of abstractions. Most critics will force a logical resolution or build a theory on its failure to offer one. Unsatisfied with its power to imply differing views of experience, they now overdo its dark episodes, ignoring how much of the humor is lighthearted, even featherbrained. Expounding Twain's profundity is safest; Buck Grangerford learns that explaining a joke can leave you looking like a muggins. Highly verbal academic critics search for finer grist than the idea that *Huckleberry Finn* is not solely yet organically comic, that its serious thrust and flare-ups of rage give the humor weight without dominating it.

---

17. *Mark Twain as a Literary Comedian* (Baton Rouge: Louisiana State University Press, 1979), esp. chap. 8. I grant the complexities in distinguishing between Huck as a character and the voice forced on him as narrator; they are admirably expounded by Alan Trachtenberg, "The Form of Freedom in *Adventures of Huckleberry Finn*," *SoR*, n.s. 6 (1970): 954–71.

IV

Few of them are now misled by the heliotype. But they can partly blame Twain by accepting my second major clue—a negative one—for appreciating *Huckleberry Finn*: Its author would never supply a minimally nourishing discussion of humor. Our overuse of "How To Tell a Story" shows how slim the pickings are. It deals only with oral or platform technique; furthermore, it satisfied the wish of the editor of *The Youth's Companion* that the subject "should, of course, be treated in a way suitable for boys and girls."[18] Twain fumbled elsewhere with the old distinction between comedy and wit, and if the modish subject of international differences was forced on him he juggled it feebly. When the organizer of a banquet tried in 1885 to wheedle a speech on "Humor," he labored to come through before refusing adamantly. After that he was quick to plead incompetence. Another interviewer who wanted a British-American comparison got instead: "That is a question I am particularly and specially unqualified to answer. I might go out into the road there, and with a brickbat I would knock down three or four men in an hour who would know more than I about humor and its merits and varieties."[19] During his world tour, mindful of needing a good press, and during his return with his Oxford degree, mindful of the reasons cited at the ceremony, he declined with more grace. But the installment of his autobiography published in May 1907 had a crisp footnote:

> Humor is a subject which has never had much interest for me. That is why I have never examined it, nor written about it nor used it as a topic for a speech. A hundred times it has been offered to me as a topic in these past forty years, but in no case has it attracted me.

I suggest two reasons for this reaction by so qualified a spirit. First, Twain was anxiously aware that the workings of laughter, in both its creator and its respondent, are subliminal. Navigating masterfully by the flow of response from an audience, he was often surprised at what went over best. But he stood baffled before himself from boyhood, phrasing instinctively the perceptions that, as he came to count on, amused most people. A late scrap of manuscript asked: "Can the mind that *lacks* the infirmity of humor afflict itself with it by study & teaching?"[20] The answer was "Obviously not,"

18. Letter from William H. Rideing, 23 January 1894—in the files of the Mark Twain Project.

19. Blathwayt, "Mark Twain on Humor." For his most forthcoming responses, see my "Mark Twain Talks Mostly about Humor and Humorists," *StAH* 1 (1974): 4–22.

20. DV127, no. 3, and an AMS scrap in #4 of Box 37 in Mark Twain Project. Previously unpublished materials by Mark Twain are © 1981 by Edward J. Willi and Manufacturers Hanover Trust Company as trustees of the Mark Twain Foundation and are published with the permission of the University of California Press and Robert H. Hirst, general editor of the Mark Twain Project. For a revised version, see p. 182 in Paul Baender, ed., *"What Is Man" and Other Philosophical Writings*, vol. 19 in *The Works of Mark Twain* (Berkeley: University of California Press, 1973). Robert A. Wiggins's chapter "Humor and Realism" in his *Mark Twain: Jackleg Novelist* (Seattle: University of Washington Press, 1964) concludes that Twain was "limited in his understanding" of humor.

while "infirmity" and "afflict" carried more than mock humility. For a deterministic thesis *What Is Man?* instanced the flash of wit that surprises the speaker, too. This narrowing to a turn or phrase of idea had already simplified the problem; an earlier manuscript version made humor itself the automatic product of one's "machine." Nevertheless, the second, much more important reason for Twain's refusal to spin theories about humor was his perception that none he could invent or borrow covered him fully, that they were neat and—foolishly often—unitary.[21] His most vibrant performances, above all *Huckleberry Finn*, mocked such guidelines.

Ironically, though humor rebels against ratiocination, we yearn to systematize it. Without an owner's manual it can seem too mysterious. I suspect that the most rarefied readings of *Huckleberry Finn* are encouraged either by guilt over taking sheer delight in Huck's tactile and pungent world, guilt that pays the tariff or duty for subconscious release, or else by uneasiness at the power to compel laughter, uneasiness that regains courage through structured ideas. Most explications omit details that upset their tight diagram.[22] An eminent critic who labels Huck "always passive" thereby ignores the tricks he plays on Jim or the ingenuity of his finding Jim after the King and Duke sell him. The other, heavily populated extreme makes Huck a born nonconformist though he several times shows the tact of a barefoot chargé d'affaires and bumbles along as Adolphus the "valley." A recent critic praises him as "singularly free from the desire to be either entertainer or entertained," but did anybody enjoy that circus more? He even found the Royal Nonesuch "awful funny." Often described as taciturn, he rattles on for Mary Jane Wilks while distracting us with a seldom-noticed bit of clowning about telling the truth for the first time in his life. My rebuttals do not lead toward uncovering a yet deeper, ultimate layer. I have already proposed that *Huckleberry Finn* outreaches any conceptual scheme for it.

My proposition would oblige a theorist to codify the farce, burlesque, comedy, humor, wit, satire, and parody in *Huckleberry Finn*. It's simpler to deny that any species from a sound taxonomy is missing. Twain races up and down the scale: from physical clowning (Huck's brains oozing from under his hat) to educated wordplay (such as fake etymology), from visual gags (Jim as Sick Arab) to mordant ridicule (of Christian burial), from libidinal exuberance to topical barbs (at the "violent" South), from warm escapist fantasy to the grim pleasure of confronting human paltriness, from deflation of pretense (in the Grangerford parlor) to a gratifying smugness (about the Grangerford parlor), from timeless motifs (the biter bit, the con

---

21. The theories continue to multiply. An excellent, up-to-date survey that accepts their differences is Peter Farb's "Speaking Seriously about Humor," *MR* 22 (1981): 760–76. James M. Cox, in chap. 7 of *Mark Twain: The Fate of Humor* (Princeton: Princeton University Press, 1966), argues shrewdly that *Huckleberry Finn* turns serious themes into the "central good humor pervading the book." Smith and Gibson, *Mark Twain–Howells Letters*, 2:462, speculate that Twain soon was "eager" to make up for his "comic self-indulgence."

22. Harold H. Kolb, Jr., "Mark Twain, Huck Finn, and Jacob Blivens: Gilt-Edged, Tree Calf Morality in the *Adventures of Huckleberry Finn*," *VQR* 55 (1979): 653–69, states the broader point in terms of the major readings that conflict with each other.

men stripped of their gold in the Wilks episode) to a guffawing at Victorian ladyhood, from tickling of sectional prejudice to stroking of chauvinist feathers, from whimsy to boot-stamping chuckles over the drowning of Stephen Dowling Botts, from deriding schoolbook language to flattering a higher literacy (in the year that also saw the founding of the Modern Language Association), from mock inferiority to mock superiority, from the groping folk wisdom of Jim to literary parody, and—with an unintended humor of contrast—from the pseudo-classical heliotype to the near-cartoon tone of the illustrations. I eagerly grant that anybody can expand the list.

Whatever the list's rationale it must include contradictory qualities. One favorable reviewer found *Huckleberry Finn* a "popular work in a broad vein of low comedy by a popular writer";[23] but the Concord Library had already banned it as dangerously irreverent. Many scenes evoke smiling nostalgia, and Norman Rockwell would inevitably illustrate an edition; but citifying Americans also felt the Hobbesian glow of superiority toward clodhoppers, while Northerners snorted at the tacky, benighted South. Though egalitarianism backs some sharp ridicule, plebeian dignity is crippled by faith in a magic hairball, and the King chortles that the "damn fools" hold a majority anywhere. Just as cynical, the Duke, "uncommon bright" and better educated than the average person Huck meets, cools our faith in the effects of upward mobility. Together, the con men leave us grinning, yet edgy about mocking the Bible, sobriety, the received cultural tradition, and the work ethic; besides, they are satiric targets themselves.[24] Gripped by the sardonic realism in *Huckleberry Finn*, we waver at surrendering to the comedy that unmistakably takes over with the Evasion sequence.

Herman Wouk marvels at the "insanely comic parody," the last fling of a "jerky, uneven, patchwork tale, as jerry-built as a pioneer's hut on the prairie, or a real estate development on Long Island."[25] Actually, the Evasion itself spans the poles of Twain's humor. Hypnotized by his own imagination (and revising very little of the holograph version) he piled improbabilities on each other as if his fairy-tale success had blurred the barrier between daydreams and stubborn fact. The Evasion suggests a world of absurd contingency (seen more darkly in the climax of the Wilks episode) or of Bergsonian flux sweeping over petrified attitudes like those of Silas Phelps or of a Quixotic floating above the literal-minded drudges. Closer to Twain's origins it echoes the joviality of Southwestern humor in which physical torture of simpletons was regarded not as sadism but, like yarnspinning, as competi-

23. *Sacramento* (Calif.) *Record-Union*, 26 March 1885, p. 2—from Victor Fischer's typescript.

24. Harold Kaplan, *Democratic Humanism and American Literature* (Chicago: University of Chicago Press, 1972), sums up, for *Huckleberry Finn*, the "paradoxical and difficult task of the moral critic in a democracy" (p. 252).

25. "America's Voice Is Mark Twain's," *San Francisco Chronicle*, 5 August 1956, "This World" section, p. 20; this essay was syndicated by the Associated Press. I am willing to accept Twain's insistence that he "should never be able to acquire the novel-writer's art"—Blathwayt, "Mark Twain on Humor." Nor would calling *Huckleberry Finn* a romance encompass its dedication to humor beyond any other consideration.

tive variation on a cliché. However, Tom's fun collides with flesh-and-bone pain in the cry, "What kine er time is *Jim* havin'?" (p. 330). We are challenged to enjoy both Tom's inventiveness and its collapse—triggered when his "britches catched fast on a splinter on the top rail" of a fence. Those of us who hug the reality principle can feel gratified—and grateful—that it had again pulled Twain back from comic anarchy.

Ransacking its ancient mode, *Huckleberry Finn* builds a castle as individualistically turreted and boldly cantilevered as seems possible without toppling over or losing touch with common day. Practically everybody finds several kinds of humor to respond to and ignores or else forgives the rest if, for instance, so mature as to dislike masked aggression. Twain's own tensions had released into a complexity of laughter based in as well as on human nature but also in the imperatives of his society, contemporary and historical. A few critics close *Huckleberry Finn* angry at man-unkind or hopeless about communication; instead they should be heartened to learn that humor has so many ways and means and can get away with such wild risks. Giving the book its true unity, Twain's daring earned that bust of himself. Whatever tragedy, classical or bourgeois, touched his private life, in *Huckleberry Finn* he reigns, nobler than a Roman, as the American god of the comic gift.

3 TOM QUIRK

Life Imitating Art: *Huckleberry Finn* and Twain's Autobiographical Writings

> Cyril: What do you mean by saying life, "poor, probable, uninterest-
> ing human life," will try to reproduce the marvels of art? I can quite
> understand your objection to art being treated as a mirror. You think it
> would reduce genius to the position of a cracked looking glass. But you
> don't mean to say that you seriously believe that life imitates art, that
> life is in fact the mirror, and art the reality?
> Vivian: Certainly, I do.
>
> Oscar Wilde, *Decay of Lying* (1889)

On 1 March 1883, Mark Twain wrote William Dean Howells and reported on a lecture he had attended the previous evening given by "an idiot by the name of Stoddard." Twain found the stereopticon pictures John L. Stoddard showed full of interest but the lecturer's comments about them "chuckleheaded" and wished Stoddard had kept "still" or had "died in the first act."[1] Nevertheless, Twain evidently approved of the lecturer's description of "how retired tradesmen and farmers in Holland load a lazy scow with the family and the household effects and then loaf along the waterways of the Low Country all summer long, paying no visits, receiving none, and just lazying a heavenly life out in their own unpestered society, and doing their literary work, if they have any, wholly uninterrupted." Twain obviously envied this lazy and unpestered existence and felt Howells would as well: "If you had hired such a boat and sent for us we should have a couple of satisfactory books ready for the press now with no marks of interruption, vexatious weariness, and other hellishness visible upon them anywhere." The editors of the Twain/Howells correspondence comment on this portion of the letter: "The effect upon Mark Twain of Stoddard's slides depicting a lazy existence aboard a Dutch scow suggests that he may have taken up the MS of *Huckleberry Finn* again, after driving himself hard to complete *Life on the Mississippi*." However, Twain's "recollection" of this portion of Stoddard's lecture appears to have been imaginative invention, not timely reaction.

If Stoddard's published collection of his illustrated talks contains "the identical discourses" he had delivered on tours for some eighteen years, as the subtitle to the collected lectures indicates, then he made no mention of

---

1. Henry Nash Smith and William M. Gibson, eds., *Mark Twain–Howells Letters* (Cambridge: Harvard University Press, 1960), 1:426–29. Hereafter cited as *MTHL*.

retired farmers lazily floating on a canal in a scow. The only printed passage that resembles Twain's recollection is this:

> Many of the barges in Amsterdam form the abodes of people who have no other homes. Among a certain class of Hollanders, when a young man has saved or borrowed money enough he buys a huge, broad-shouldered boat; and like the Patriarch Noah, leads into it not only his family, but also all the animals of which he is possessed, including poultry, hogs, even cows. Thenceforth he is independent; and as the master of a floating house, stable, farmyard, and express cart, all in one, and never absent from his family, he transports loads of merchandise from town to town, and even sells a few superfluous eggs, or a little milk.[2]

It is possible, of course, that Twain was recollecting an impromptu remark, not properly a part of the written lecture, but if Stoddard made such a remark, it went against the whole tenor of his talk, for he consistently portrayed the Dutch as an industrious, persevering, ingenious people whose only occasion for relaxation was during the winter months when they might skate or glide down the frozen canals and visit friends and relatives. More likely, however, Twain summoned this image, quite unconsciously, from his own fiction—from the not yet completed *Huckleberry Finn.*

In itself, this discrepancy between fact and fiction is relatively insignificant. But it does provoke certain interesting, if unanswerable questions: Did Twain really believe he had heard Stoddard describe retired farmers loafing along the waterways? Certainly he had no reason to lie or to fictionalize the account of his experience in a private, informal letter to a trusted friend. Had Twain drawn the inference from this image that he would have desired and profited by such an existence while completing *Life on the Mississippi,* free from interruptions and other vexations? Or was the process all the other way round? Had those actual feelings of "hellishness" prompted the familiar image of escape and drift he had created several years before, in the first phase of composing *Huckleberry Finn?* In short, was the report on the Stoddard lecture an instance of factual description or of life imitating art? Either alternative is possible, for Twain possessed a projective as well as an assimilative imagination. It is equally possible that Twain did not recognize that he was inventing rather than reporting on an event, for, as Justin Kaplan has observed, the creative unconscious lay closer to the surface in Twain than in most writers.[3] In fact, Twain described himself as the "amanuensis" of his own art, a servant to the mysterious operations of his own creative imagination. In either case, it is clear that Mark Twain was identifying with the fictional hero of *Huckleberry Finn* and preferring that outcast's imagined situation to his own. It was this sort of identification that sometimes supplied the imaginative and emotional coherence that Twain's reports on his own experiences lacked.

Ever since the publication of Walter Blair's "When Was *Huckleberry Finn*

2. *John L. Stoddard's Lectures,* 10 vols. (Boston: Balch Bros. Co., 1898), 7: 193–94.
3. *Mr. Clemens and Mark Twain: A Biography* (New York: Simon & Schuster, 1966), p. 253.

Written?" we have been able to examine the influences upon the composition of that novel, and Blair himself did so exhaustively in *Mark Twain and Huck Finn* (1960). Often we may observe in the works written during the years when the manuscript of *Huck Finn* was "pigeonholed" tentative rehearsals for a return to that book, anticipations of episodes and themes, unconscious percolations that, once the author's "tank" filled, would be dramatized in his novel. However, we know as well that Twain's imagination also worked in "reverse" (as Blair put it), that the fiction of *Huckleberry Finn* also spilled over into his purportedly autobiographical writing. But that reverse operation has not been sufficiently charted, and, as Kaplan justly remarked, Twain's reshaping of his own biography possesses its own kind of truth.[4] To look at familiar evidence in this way is not to add substantially to what we already know but to regard it in a new light, and it allows us to measure, however vaguely, the degree and nature of the author's involvement with his creation, to implicate Twain in his book, by identifying not how much of his life was put into it, but how much of the book was put into his life, or rather the autobiographical representation of his life. For Twain, Huck Finn seems to have represented not the boy he had been but the boy he wished he had been. And, though the basis of his identification with Huck surely began in simple envy of Huck's free and unpestered situation, that basis changed during the seven-year gestation of the novel. Huck became the hero of his own life in a way that Twain personally admired and, in the end, fictitiously attributed to his own history. Although the author finished *Huckleberry Finn* in the autumn of 1883, the book was not finished with him until he published "The Private History of a Campaign That Failed" in December 1885.

II

The first autobiographical piece Twain published after he set aside the manuscript of *Huck Finn* in late August 1876, liking it only "tolerably well," was a four-installment series of sketches for the *Atlantic* about his trip to Bermuda with Joe Twichell in May 1877. "Some Rambling Notes of an Idle Excursion" is flat and uninspired, though it begins promisingly enough as a trip of "pure recreation" and provides the occasion to be absolutely "free and idle."[5] But Twain forfeited whatever narrative opportunity an aimless excursion with a companion offered in preference for the anecdotal, and the relation between himself and the "Reverend" is never adequately developed. Perhaps because Twain placed his narrative persona under no particular obligation, no dramatic conflict occurred to him. In any event, his subsequent efforts to write a book about his travels in Germany, Switzerland, and northern Italy the next year seem to have begun in the same way, for much of the anecdotal material in *A Tramp Abroad* was written before he discovered

4. Ibid., "Preface," n.p.
5. *The Writings of Mark Twain* (New York: Gabriel Wells, 1923), 19:242. Hereafter cited as *Writings*.

a narrative plan for the book.[6] It was not until August 1878, after Twichell joined him in Europe, that he hit upon the "joke" that provided a narrative foundation to unify his already completed burlesques, tales, and legends. He would appear as an authentic pedestrian, in proper costume, but, as he told Howells, "mount the first conveyance that offers, making but slight explanation or excuse, and endeavoring to seem unconscious that this is not legitimate pedestrianizing."[7]

By casting Twichell as an agent named Harris whom he could assign to do his traveling for him, Twain provided his narrative persona with a mischievousness that complemented his apparent naiveté. In effect, he was Tom Sawyer again and might delegate his felt responsibilities to another. But there was a Huck Finn quality in this narrative persona as well, for he steadily resisted the obligation to become enlightened and civilized by the European experience. Thus, Twain found narrative justification for his already written burlesques of Wagnerian opera and his own attempts to learn German and permitted himself to lampoon Turner and Titian and to display his seemingly guileless pride in his own crude drawings, which he juxtaposed to those of professional illustrators. These masks must have proved an antidote to the "smileless state of solemn admiration" Twain felt shortly after he arrived in Germany,[8] but they also permitted him a creative latitude his own proper voice was incapable of. "A man can't write successful satire except he be in a calm judicial good-humor," he wrote Howells, "whereas I *hate* travel, & I *hate* hotels, & I *hate* the opera, & I *hate* the Old Masters—in truth I don't ever seem to be in a good enough humor with ANYthing to satirize it; no, I want to stand up before it & *curse* it, and foam at the mouth."[9]

Incapacitated by his own indignation, at times Twain found he could convey his own contempt by simply displaying an undiluted sense of admiration and stupefaction. He did this when he wrote the chapters on student duels in Germany. The description of the "knightly graces" of this bloody sport is handled in much the same way he handled the feud chapters of *Huck Finn* when he wrote them in 1879–1880; he reports on the duels matter-of-factly and ironically calls into question not the custom itself but his own feelings of repulsion as somehow being an untutored reaction to venerable European tradition. And, as Huck does in describing the killing of Buck Grangerford in Chapter 18 of the novel, he refuses to go into "details" about the most brutal exchanges. There is anticipation of the novel, too, in Chapter 24, in which his misplaced sympathy for a meanly dressed and evidently embarrassed parishioner, whom he eventually discovers is the Empress of Germany, resembles Huck's sympathetic response to the supposed drunken bareback rider in the circus.

These instances foreshadow Twain's treatment of certain episodes in *Huck*

6. Hamlin Hill discusses the composition of *A Tramp Abroad* in *Mark Twain and Elisha Bliss* (Columbia: University of Missouri Press, 1964), pp. 132–48.
7. 30 January 1879, *MTHL*, 1:248–50.
8. 4 May 1878, *MTHL*, 1:227–28.
9. 30 January 1879, *MTHL*, 1:248–50.

Finn, but he was recollecting what he had already written when he imaginatively "chartered" a raft for a journey down the river Neckar. This invented account of a raft trip occupies only five chapters of *A Tramp Abroad*, and much of that space is given over to local legends and other interpolated matter. Indeed, from a practical point of view, this raft is simply a "conveyance" and fitted neatly into the planned "joke" of the book. But there may have been more than literary convenience involved in transporting Huck's raft to Germany; it was as well a private evocation of the idyllic mood he had already created in his novel and an identification of himself with the easy circumstances of Huck Finn.

His confessed "hate" for Europe and homesickness for America may have contributed something to his motives for creating this episode, and a lazy drift on a river probably served as symbolic compensation for his personal feelings of anger and vexation. Certainly, Twain recommended such a voyage to his reader, and no doubt the image provided a salve to his immediate situation:

> The motion of a raft is the needful motion; it is gentle, and gliding, and smooth, and noiseless; it calms down all feverish activities, it soothes to sleep all nervous hurry and impatience; under its restful influence all the troubles and vexations and sorrows that harass the mind vanish away, and existence becomes a dream, a charm, a deep and tranquil ecstasy.[10]

Indeed, in these chapters Twain consistently draws upon the contrast between the soothing ease on the river and human sorrow and vexation on shore.

On land there is drudgery (represented by the women he observes working in the fields, or those he remembers who work in town), the busy activity of progress (symbolized by the massive and destructive construction work on a railroad that levels mountains and tunnels through bluffs), and sleepless nights (experienced by young "Z" at the Naturalist Tavern). And there is the felt constraint of propriety, which makes the narrator confused and uncomfortable (epitomized by the perplexing custom of bowing or the rules of dress for admittance to a ball or the baffling and contradictory regulations governing admission into the student corps, all described in Chapter 17). On the raft, however, Twain is content; he observes naked children happily swimming and describes peaceful landscapes. Even Harris and Twain doff their outer clothing, dangle their legs in the water, and occasionally go for a swim. However well the fiction of a raft voyage fitted into his plans, this is the only "conveyance" that suggested these contrasts to him. But in the end, this idyllic voyage and the raft itself are disposed of in the same way Twain disposed of Huck and Jim's raft at the end of the first phase of composition of the novel—by a smash-up. The raft hit the center pier of a bridge and "went all to smash and scatteration" (p. 164), but for five chapters it had served as an adequate carrier for such anecdotal freight as he

---

10. *Writings*, 9:107; citations hereafter included parenthetically in the text. In the summer of 1891, Twain actually did float down a European river; he bought a flat-bottomed boat and made a ten-day trip down the Rhone, apparently as a remedy for certain feelings of financial desperation. See Kaplan, *Mr. Clemens*, pp. 368–69.

cared to bring to it, and the journey evoked an emotional tranquility that contrasted sharply with his own feelings of vexation.

In a later chapter of *A Tramp Abroad*, Twain described the delights of idle traveling and easy companionship, this time in reference to casual walking. "Walking is good to time the movement of the tongue by," he wrote:

> And what a motley variety of subjects a couple of people will casually rake over in the course of a day's tramp! There being no constraint, a change of subject is always in order, and so a body is not likely to keep pegging at a single topic until it grows tiresome. We discussed everything we knew, during the first fifteen or twenty minutes, that morning, and then branched out into the glad, free, boundless realm of the things we were not certain about. (Pp. 202–3)

It was precisely this relaxed, associative, speculative mode of creation that Twain did not permit himself when he wrote *Life on the Mississippi* two years later. Evidently, he felt intensely the "constraints" of "pegging at a single topic."

A recent genetic study of this book by Horst H. Kruse modifies the familiar view of *Life on the Mississippi* and, implicitly, of its relation to the composition of *Huckleberry Finn*. The significant relation of *Life on the Mississippi* to *Huckleberry Finn*, unlike that of *A Tramp Abroad*, ought not be sought simply in the recovery of episodes from the completed portion of the novel, nor in the invocation of the dream of drift. To be sure, there are borrowings from the novel: in the clear echoes of *Huck Finn* in Chapter 38 ("The House Beautiful"), in the discussion of Southern feuding in Chapter 26, and in the direct importation of a segment of the manuscript in Chapter 3. However, Kruse has shown that these borrowings do not constitute evidence that the subject of the river impulsively drew Twain back to the pigeonholed manuscript, nor is there evidence that these appropriations were filched from the novel because of flagging invention or the pressure of a contract deadline.[11] Rather, the use of them was calculated well in advance and, except for the directly quoted raft passage of the *Huck Finn* manuscript, they were modified to suit the immediate purpose of the book at hand.

While it may be true, as Kaplan suggests, that the relation of *Life on the Mississippi* to *Huckleberry Finn* was in a sense "symbiotic" and that for Twain the books possessed a certain "overlapping" interest; and while, as William Gibson has contended, following Blair, *Life on the Mississippi* "may be regarded as a rich mine for episodes and characters in *Adventures of Huckleberry Finn*,"[12] these were, nevertheless, distinctly different books, in character and in conception. It is that very difference that has the most suggestive interest for us here. In fact, Kruse has argued persuasively that *Life on the Mississippi* (except for the earlier "Old Times on the Missis-

11. See Horst H. Kruse, *Mark Twain and "Life on the Mississippi"* (Amherst: University of Massachusetts Press, 1981), esp. chap. 4, "A Summer's Work," pp. 43–91.

12. See Kaplan, *Mr. Clemens*, p. 289; and William M. Gibson, *The Art of Mark Twain* (New York: Oxford University Press, 1976), p. 65.

sippi" portion) was an altogether different sort of book from the earlier autobiographical works, indeed of a different genre.

From the beginning, Twain strove to write a definitive account of life on the river, a "standard" work as Twain himself had described it, and his return trip to the Mississippi was something of a "field trip" to insure accuracy and objectivity. As a result, he did not speak in the voice of an innocent or a tenderfoot; he adopted an authoritative persona and painstakingly and purposefully supplemented his recent experience on the river by reading and research. He was committed, in short, to pegging away at a single topic, and the genesis of the book shows that the author continually exercised a rational control upon his treatment of the material that checked his customary and persistent inclination to make for the glad, free realm of speculation and irrelevant anecdote and curtailed his impulse toward random invective and social criticism.[13]

Twain's ambitions for *Life on the Mississippi* were high ones and his commitment to his original purpose and its completion transcended the simple, nagging obligation of a contract deadline. Nevertheless, he seems to have questioned the value of the authentic and documentary account of river life, even as he was writing it. When an Arkansas traveler brags about the size of his state's mosquitoes, the traveler's friend deflates these exaggerations: "Wait—you are getting that too strong; cut it down, cut it down—you get a leetle too much costumery onto your statements: always dress a fact in tights, never in an ulster. . . . what these gentlemen want for a book is the frozen truth."[14] Rightly or wrongly, Twain was committed for the most part to dressing his "standard" work in tights, and the net effect of this commitment is often an austere, even antiseptic journalism. *Life on the Mississippi* is occasionally fastidious and frequently filled with statistical information— gross revenues of river towns, population increases, and the like—and it gives several pages over to quoting accounts of other Mississippi travelers. But in writing *Life on the Mississippi*, Twain apparently recognized that direct observation and dedication to the "frozen truth" were more often desiccating than vitalizing.

Twain found that a surfeit of experience, however extraordinary, disables the imagination, and he said as much in Chapter 35. After enumerating the known facts related to "Vicksburg During the Trouble," he asks, "Could you, who did not experience it, come nearer to reproducing it to the imagination of another non-participant than could a Vicksburger who *did* experience it?" (p. 298). Though it seems impossible, the novel rather than the repeated experience, argues Twain, better outfits the "tongue or pen" for rendering the experience, for it takes a "deathless grip upon his imagination and memory." The first voyage out, the experience "bristles with striking novelties," but by the tenth "the thing has lost color, snap, surprise; and has become commonplace" (p. 299).

---

13. See Kruse, *Mark Twain*, esp. pp. 5–19.
14. *Writings*, 12 : 294–95; citations hereafter included parenthetically in the text.

Surely these statements have particular application to his own return to the river after so many years, for he had written "Old Times on the Mississippi" from memory and must have recognized how much more feeling he had put into that than he was able to get into part 2 of *Life on the Mississippi*. He perceived as well that, in contrast to the "grown-up" mask he had adopted for his standard work, with a young and innocent persona all experience may be portrayed as novel, full of color. In Chapter 54 ("Past and Present"), Twain walks the streets of Hannibal and spots the house of a boyhood friend: "It carried me back more than a generation in a moment, and landed me in the midst of a time when the happenings of life were not the natural and logical results of great general laws, but of special orders, and were freighted with very precise and distinct purposes—partly punitive in intent, partly admonitory; and usually local in application" (p. 434). Even as he was advancing his theme of progress in *Life on the Mississippi*, he opposed to the universal and statistical the particularizing atmosphere of the youthful imagination that invigorates experience and perception; he was contrasting the world of fact with the world of feeling.

Nor, though devoted to speaking authoritatively about the Mississippi, did he seem to find factual matter the adequate substitute for such feeling. "Emotions are among the toughest thing in the world to manufacture out of whole cloth," he wrote; "it is easier to manufacture seven facts than one emotion" (p. 226). This statement is even more revealing when one recognizes that Twain's efforts to collect factual material for his book were by no means always easy and were sometimes frustrating.[15] Life on the river had changed, but so had Mark Twain, and he eventually discovered that his strongest feelings for the Mississippi were wedded to his memory of it and could not be automatically regained by renewed observation. A standard work might possess authority, but it lacked life, and he endorsed the atmospheric vitality of fiction over "frozen truth" when he praised Cable's *The Grandissimes*: "In him the South has found a masterly delineator of its interior life and its history. In truth, I find by experience, that the untrained eye and vacant mind can inspect it and learn of it and judge of it more clearly and profitably in his books than by personal contact with it" (p. 355). He might have said the same about "Old Times on the Mississippi" or *Huckleberry Finn* itself.

The "difficulties" Twain complained of in writing *Life on the Mississippi*, as Kruse has shown, were not principally related to anxieties over his contractual obligations to finish the book, as had been supposed.[16] One suspects they rather derived from his own, self-imposed constraints to write a standard work, the result of constantly trying to hold in check his impulses to indulge in the peripheral, the anecdotal, the atmospheric, to harness his own strong feelings and maintain an authoritative, dispassionate persona.

Not the least of those feelings was that of moral indignation. Howells had

15. See Kruse, *Mark Twain*, pp. 48–53, 58–60.
16. Kruse, *Mark Twain*, questions this supposition throughout; see esp. chaps. 3–4.

published the first lengthy appreciation of Twain in the *Century Magazine* for September 1882. Twain's humor, he wrote, was "at its best the foamy break of the strong tide of earnestness in him," and he had praised the humorist's "indignant sense of right and wrong," his "ardent hate of meanness and injustice."[17] Twain had seen the essay in manuscript as early as June 1882 and had thanked Howells for his evaluation: "I hope the public will be willing to see me with your eyes."[18] And his work in progress provided the occasion to verify Howells's perception of him, for he indulged in some strident social commentary, even though it went against the purpose of a standard work. Twain's recognition of this deviation from his plan (partly pointed out to him by his publisher and partly detected by himself) caused him to temper his moral indignation. Deferring to Osgood's judgment on the point, he deleted two chapters devoted exclusively to strong social criticism; he muzzled his ardent Republicanism and intense anti-Southern feeling, partly to insure, one supposes, that the book might have a market value in the South; he even toned down his familiar, virulent attack on Sir Walter Scott in Chapter 46.

In short, Twain seems to have been champing at the bit throughout the composition of *Life on the Mississippi*. No doubt Twain's serious ambitions for his river book and his persistent commitment to an objective detachment contributed to the success of *Life on the Mississippi*, but it was an unfamiliar and stiff collar for him to wear. And it is perhaps significant that when he returned to *Huck Finn* in that last furious burst of composition, he began with Colonel Sherburn's verbal attack on the mob,[19] for in that episode Twain was indulging in his own indignant sense of right and wrong again, and with a vengeance. Though he resumed the mask of Huck shortly after creating that episode, for the moment he would speak through Sherburn, and with the force of personal conviction. In any event, when he returned to the novel, he was no longer under the obligation to peg away at a single subject; he was able to speak for himself, even if he spoke, for the most part, through Huck.

He took up the manuscript of the novel again in the summer or spring of 1883, and wrote with an energy and ease that even he found remarkable; he would "sail right in and sail right on, the whole day long, without thought of running short of stuff or words." The experience was in dramatic contrast to the difficulties he had encountered in writing *Life on the Mississippi*. He had willingly assumed the role of an adult in writing his river book and had attempted to speak rationally and temperately throughout, but Huck's was clearly a more comfortable and artistically satisfying mask for him. "I expect to complete it [*Huckleberry Finn*] in a month or six weeks or two months more," he wrote Howells. "And *I* shall *like* it, whether anybody else

17. *Century Magazine* 24:5 (September 1882):783.
18. 16 June 1882, MTHL, 1:405.
19. Walter Blair in *Mark Twain and Huck Finn* (Berkeley: University of California Press, 1960), contends that when Twain threw himself into the novel again in the summer of 1883, he probably began with Chapter 22; see p. 300 and n. 2, p. 411.

does or not." [20] He should have liked it, having put so much of himself into it.

III

In September 1884, Twain wrote Howells about the upcoming presidential election: "I only urge you not to soil yourself by voting for Blaine," he advised. "It is not necessary to vote for Cleveland. The only necessary thing to do, as I understand it, is that a man shall keep *himself* clean (by withholding his vote for an improper man) even though the party and the country go to destruction in consequence." [21] He reaffirmed this notion of ethical independence in *A Connecticut Yankee* a few years later when he wrote that a man ought to preserve the single "atom" of self that is worth preserving and let the rest land in "Sheol." Yet when he insisted to Howells that "a man's first duty is to his own honor," Twain was not so much indulging in self-righteousness as he was emulating the moral nature of Huck Finn, who had preserved his own "sound heart" in the face of circumstance and against the claims of his own "deformed conscience" and had promised to "light out for the Territory" to avoid the contaminating effects of "sivilisation." The following year, when he came to write "The Private History of a Campaign That Failed," Twain would once again and even more strongly identify himself with Huckleberry Finn.

"The Private History" was printed in *Century Magazine*'s "Battles and Leaders of the Civil War" series in December 1885 and was the first extended piece Twain published after the completion of *Huckleberry Finn*. The author's absorbing interest in his new publishing company, his lecture tour with Cable, and his commercial and personal involvement with Ulysses S. Grant, whose memoirs he had contracted to publish, provided ample preoccupation to divert him from the now painful business of writing. In view of the fact that these ventures occupied much of his time and taxed his creative energy, his interest in writing his own "war paper" must have been a strong one, and the motives for it may have been several.

In part the piece served in a practical way as advertisement for the Grant *Memoirs*. But, as John Gerber has suggested, Twain's "Campaign" may also have been an effort to justify his own role in the war and was probably prompted by his renewed acquaintance with those familiar with and perhaps disdainful of his military record when he traveled to Hannibal in 1882 and again in 1885. [22] Justin Kaplan believes the story is a symbolic working out of Twain's own complicated relationship with Grant, his feelings for whom sometimes bordered on idolatry. [23] In either case, this "private history" is an attempt at self-vindication on ethical grounds and is more fiction than fact. In a sense, it resembles Melville's "inside narrative" of *Billy Budd*

20. 20 July 1883, *MTHL*, 1:435–36.

21. 17 September 1884, *MTHL*, 2:508–9.

22. John Gerber, "Mark Twain's 'Private Campaign,'" *Civil War History* 1:37 (March 1955):37–60.

23. Kaplan, *Mr. Clemens*, pp. 316–25.

(composed, incidentally, at around the same time), constructed, as it were, from the other side of the cloth. Melville created a fiction that had private reference to and qualified, even if it did not ultimately justify, the recorded conduct of his cousin Guert Gansevoort in the *Somers* mutiny case. Twain, on the other hand, created a "private history," publicly presented as fact, which he must have felt vindicated him of his own questionable conduct during the war and, at the same time, justified his association with the nation's most eminent war hero. Whatever his motives, however strong his pangs of conscience, this invented autobiography, reminiscent of the many "autobiographies" Huck spontaneously manufactures in the novel, represented a symbolic cleansing of the contaminated self. For the first time Twain identified not simply with Huck's free and easy circumstance but with his moral nature as well.

Gerber, who has provided the most thorough analysis of the discrepancies between recorded fact and narrative detail in this memoir, has also identified the multiple parallels between the story and *Huckleberry Finn*. So extensive are the echoes of the novel, in fact, that Gerber suggested, "In the 'Private History,' Huck becomes Twain." [24] Still, since the fictional details of Huck's life at times displace the autobiographical details of Twain's, one may, without really contradicting Gerber, accept as equally true the converse formulation that Twain became Huck, that, consciously or unconsciously, he enlisted his little outcast to give shape and substance to his own ambiguous experience. In short, this report on an important phase of the author's history was another instance of life imitating art.

The pattern of action of the "Private History," Gerber observes, "is precisely the pattern which recurs repeatedly in *Huckleberry Finn.* . . . Huck gets into a series of scrapes of increasing complexity and annoyance until finally when matters reach a climax and he can't stand it any longer, he 'lights out.'" [25] From the first sentence, the "Private History" recalls the novel, for Twain strikes an immediately familiar note, though his story is told from the point of view of an outsider, a deserter: "You have heard from a great many people who did something in the war; is it not fair and right that you listen a little moment to one who started out to do something, but didn't?" [26] Though he undertakes to speak for the thousands of like-minded young men who deserted in the early days of the war, Twain assumes a Huck-like pose when he admits that perhaps these men, himself included, ought not be allowed much space "among better people," people who "did something" in the war. Nevertheless, he maintains that even the soldiers who skedaddled ought to be given a chance to explain *why* they didn't do anything. Thus, Twain begins his "war paper" as an effort at self-justification, speaking from the vantage point of a social pariah.

Twain's company, the Marion Rangers, reminds us of Tom Sawyer's band of robbers. Indeed, Gerber notes that the volunteers all talk like Tom, and

24. Gerber, "Mark Twain's 'Campaign,'" p. 42.
25. Ibid.
26. *Writings*, 15:255; citations hereafter included parenthetically in the text.

their leader, Tom Lyman, is constantly urging in Sawyeresque fashion the heedless crew to conform to military custom. One young soldier especially recalls Tom Sawyer's romantic pretensions. He is described as "young, ignorant, good natured, well-meaning, trivial, full of romance, and given to reading chivalric novels and singing forlorn love-ditties" (p. 257). His "nickel-plated aristocratic instincts" are burlesqued in the opening pages, but Twain describes his own reactions to them in a way that reminds us of what Huck's or Tom's might have been: he thought Peterson Dunlap's giving his own familiar name a French accent "the bravest thing that can be imagined" (p. 257).

On the whole, the young soldiers have little inclination to obey orders, post lookouts, and the like, preferring to indulge in such innocent pastimes as fishing, swimming, smoking, and playing games. These soldiers are more like boys out on a lark than men engaged in the serious business of war. Much like Tom's gang, they react to danger by hiding out and, safe from real conflict, are free to quarrel over the rights and privileges of rank. On one occasion, they lose their guns and a keg of powder scurrying up and down hills in a retreat to the Mason farmhouse. In fact, as Henry Nash Smith has pointed out, this farm itself is reminiscent of the Phelps plantation, though both probably had their emotional origin in the author's .memory of the Quarles farm where he often spent his summers as a boy.[27] In any event, like Huck when he arrives at the Phelpses, these soldiers are greeted by several barking dogs, and each one "took a soldier by the slack of the trousers and began to back away with him" (p. 268); this skirmish, Twain claims, was "perhaps the most terrifying spectacle of the Civil War" (p. 268). The repeated burlesque of their ready impulse to retreat and their undisciplined antics stamps them as a "curious breed of soldiers"; and the upbraiding they receive from the "grown up" Mr. Mason makes them feel "shabbier than the dogs had done" (p. 269).

Despite their wounded dignity and bruised feet, war for them is more a welcome escape from responsibility and routine than a call to duty. "For a time," wrote Twain, "life was idly delicious, it was perfect, there was nothing to mar it" (p. 266). Their "holiday" (p. 258) is periodically interrupted by retreats, but, however discomfiting these may have actually been, Twain's description of his several flights from the enemy in this memoir possesses nothing of that "hard baked" familiarity with feelings of "death-on-a-pale-horse-with-hell-following-after" that he confessed to in a letter to an unidentified correspondent in 1890.[28] Rather, as the multiple parallels between this history and *Huckleberry Finn* indicate, Twain, once again, was recovering from his novel the mood of an easy and free existence.

However, the essential relation between *Huck Finn* and this autobiographical piece is somewhat different from that between the novel and either *A Tramp Abroad* or *Life on the Mississippi* because here Twain seems not to have simply envied Huck's easy circumstance but to have identified with his

27. *Mark Twain: The Development of a Writer* (New York: Atheneum, 1967), pp. 130–31.
28. Reprinted in *The Portable Mark Twain*, ed. Bernard DeVoto (New York: Viking Press, 1946), pp. 773–75.

natural sympathies as well. This difference signals a shift in the basis of Twain's identification with his created character. For it was not nostalgia that drew him toward his subject and prompted his importation of Huck into his autobiography. If anything, Twain was dredging up bad memories, not fond ones. Under the circumstances, his published account of this episode in his life invited public scorn. But Twain saved his war paper from becoming pure burlesque and, to a degree, justified his behavior during the war when he provided his own adventures with a significant dramatic climax, almost surely a fabrication,[29] and described his moral revulsion in a way that linked him to his fictional character.

The nervousness created by rumors of enemy troops in the area causes the undisciplined soldiers to fire precipitately at a man who happens to ride past their encampment in Mr. Mason's barn one night, and the Rangers watch the man gasp out his dying breath: "The thought shot through me that I was a murderer, that I had killed a man—a man who had never done me any harm. That was the coldest sensation that ever went through my marrow" (p. 277). Even as the narrator regards the dying man with "pitying interest," his conscience begins to gnaw at him: "my imagination persuaded me that the dying man gave me a reproachful look out of his shadowy eyes, and it seemed to me that I would rather he had stabbed me than done that" (pp. 277–78). The thought of this dying man "preys" upon him every night. This senseless killing, he decides, was "an epitome of war" (p. 278). His campaign was "spoiled," and he resolved to "retire from this vocation of sham soldiership while I could save some remnant of my self-respect" (p. 279). His desertion, we are to understand, is not the shirking of duty but the attempt to keep himself "clean" and is prompted by the introduction of the sort of dramatic incident that Melville in *Billy Budd* called a "moral emergency."

It is not so much that this invented shooting resembles any particular episode in *Huckleberry Finn* (though the dying man's outspread arms, bloody front, and gasping breaths recall the Boggs killing, and Twain's reaction to it resembles Huck's reaction to Buck Grangerford's death). The significance instead lies in the dramatization of a certain revulsion of feeling that Huck had had throughout the novel, especially in the latter half. Nor, for that matter, was it necessary for Twain to resort to this strategy to exonerate his conduct during the war. As Gerber has pointed out, Twain made explicit certain common and understandable reasons why a young man in Missouri might have deserted the army during the early days of the war. Like many new recruits at the time, Twain had mixed loyalties, which, coupled with his own lack of training and discipline, created in him an ambivalence, if not a genuine moral confusion. Twain was not the only soldier to desert under similar conditions. But these constituted complicating and extenuating circumstances which, though they might *excuse* his behavior, could not *sanctify* it. What was missing was a demonstration of innate and superior moral impulses, what Thomas Jefferson had called a "generous spasm of the heart."

29. See Gerber, "Mark Twain's 'Campaign,'" p. 42, on this point.

Walter Blair has observed, "For all his talk about believing man 'merely a machine automatically functioning,' Mark had not been completely converted by his own eloquence." [30] In opposition to his announced cynicism, he had attributed to Huck a "sound heart," and in the "Private History" had appropriated it as his own.

The bouts Twain has with his conscience (what he calls in the "Private History" the "diseased imagination") are of the same sort Huck has in the novel. His overwrought and, to a degree, unwarranted display of guilt, as Smith notes, reminds us of Huck's feelings of blame when he sees the tarred and feathered Duke and Dauphin: "it don't make no difference whether you do right or wrong, a person's conscience ain't got no sense, and just goes for him *anyway*. If I had a yaller dog that didn't know no more than a person's conscience does, I would pison him. It takes up more room than all the rest of a person's insides, and yet ain't no good, nohow" (p. 292). While he pretends to recognize the legitimacy of this killing as the unfortunate but natural consequence of a nation at war, his sympathies run in the opposite direction: "He was killed in war; killed in fair and legitimate war; killed in battle, as you may say; and yet he was as sincerely mourned by the opposing force as if he had been their brother" (p. 278). His resolution to quit soldiering is attended by some feelings of guilt, to be sure, but it is the kind of compromised guilt Huck has about his "sinfulness" in helping Jim escape: "It seemed to me that I was not rightly equipped for this awful business; that war was intended for men, and I for a child's nurse" (p. 279). He would take up the wicked business of desertion, for he was not "brung up" to the bloody business of war. However, one may judge from his characterization of those who stayed in the army that the proper "equipment" for war is a callous, desperate, even sinister quality that though "manly" by society's reckoning, was at odds with his own natural, if childlike, sympathies.

In essence, Twain invested his own life with the ethical superiority he had supplied his little outcast. There is no evidence that Twain later remembered this fictionalized killing as a real occurrence, as he apparently remembered coming within a "few hours" and a "few miles" of meeting Grant on the battlefield, though he and Grant had together determined their close call was nearer twenty-five miles and two weeks. [31] But the net effect of this alteration of autobiographical detail was that he rewrote his own life in terms of his fiction, identified his own character with Huck's. It is a matter of record that Twain himself "lit out for the territory" only a week or two after he quit the Marion Rangers, though his trip was probably more a search for opportunity than a blameless escape from the contaminating circumstance of public responsibility and "sivilization." Several years after he wrote the "Private History," Twain insisted to Kipling that a "joggle to circumstance"

30. See Blair, *Mark Twain and Huck Finn*, p. 343.

31. As Kaplan points out (*Mr. Clemens*, pp. 312–22), Twain was fascinated by the possibility that he and Grant had come close to facing each other on the battlefield. Shortly after Grant had established that they had missed each other by a few weeks, Twain recorded in his notebook that their possible meeting was separated by "a day or two," and his published memoir brought them even closer together.

would alter the fundamental nature of Tom Sawyer, make of him either an "angel or a rip" as his creator saw fit.[32] It was just such a "joggle" to the details of his own life that must have made Twain, in his own mind at least, a fit companion to share with Grant the national prominence and esteem that both enjoyed so many years after the war and that verified Howells's assessment of him as a moral spokesman for the times, a view Twain hoped the public would share. Whatever the nature of Twain's private feelings concerning his war record, his published account of it provided him with a sound heart that triumphed over his deformed conscience. Though "The Private History" ends in burlesque, Twain had turned to the fiction of *Huckleberry Finn* to give his memoir its emotional center and its shape. But, then, he had been there before.

32. Reported in DeLancey Ferguson, *Mark Twain, Man and Legend* (New York: Charter Books, 1963), pp. 241–42.

4 JAY MARTIN

The Genie in the Bottle:
Huckleberry Finn in Mark Twain's Life

Adventures of Huckleberry Finn was written during a dark time in Mark Twain's life; the intensity of his suffering and the anguish of his emotional confusion during this period made desirable, and perhaps necessary, that Twain should attempt to resolve his griefs in literary acts of creative restitution.[1] Almost from the beginning of his career, his writing had constituted a kind of mourning process for him, in which the pleasures of recollection, tale-telling, and humor compensated him for loss. If Twain could not personally clap his hands with gladness over his losses and consequent griefs, he could at least tell stories that made light of the dark tatters in his mortal dress. For a time—the first ten years of his career—his astonishing, increasing success itself helped to push his earlier losses undercover. But after the publication of *The Adventures of Tom Sawyer* (1876) his present grievances piled so rapidly upon previous griefs that they surfaced visibly, undeniably.

During the years when *Huckleberry Finn* was composed, there existed such an even balance between Twain's accumulations of sorrows and his increasing skill and mastery of his own style of literary creation that in this book, as in no other, the divisions in his being were transformed naturally—though not at all easily—into the complexity of his work. Fresh new griefs freshened older ones at this, the height of his powers, making *Huckleberry Finn* Twain's great effort at achieving personal and artistic unity, identity, consolidation—a holding together of himself and his book, even as he also was experiencing himself and his works as falling apart. His efforts to unify or centralize his life and art proved, in the outcome, unsuccessful: after *Huckleberry Finn* Twain's life and art alike evinced more and more fragmentation. No wonder. Even during the years when he composed *Huckleberry Finn*, his personal life, like his book, clearly exhibited deconstructive processes; nonetheless, the emotional *effort* to achieve unity, so evident in both, was central and powerfully centralizing during 1876 to 1884.

Twain had always had trouble with the dark. From his earliest infancy, he had slept fitfully; he walked in his sleep and was often found "in the middle of the night . . . fretting with cold in some dark corner." No wonder he

1. The theory of creative restitution for loss in the mourning process is in George H. Pollock, "Mourning and Adaptation," *International Journal of Psycho-Analysis* 42 (1961): 341–61.

could remark that by his old age he had lost enough sleep to supply a "worn-out army." He had had troubles enough to justify almost any degree of insomnia. Like unwelcome visitors, these came early and never left. The years when he wrote *Huckleberry Finn* crystallized a period of self-doubt and social distraction from which Twain never really recovered. During this time Twain experienced the decline of his popularity as an author; the disruption by the Beechers of the previously calm life of his Nook Farm community; a final break with Bret Harte; fatal trouble with his publisher, Bliss; temporary alienation from the New England worthies through his Whittier birthday dinner speech; "business responsibilities and annoyances; . . . the persecution of kindly letters from well-meaning strangers"; disenchantment with travel abroad, especially with the French and English; struggle with seven books in addition to *Huckleberry Finn*, while feeling that his creative powers were exhausted; financial troubles, ruinously expensive involvements with the Paige typesetter and other patents; a disappointing return to the Mississippi River, Hannibal, and boyhood scenes; and the beginnings of chronic ill health for the four female members of his family. All of this was, for him, deeply disillusioning. He tried to combat this disillusional process in his personal life through the distractions of superficial illusions of many sorts—masquerades, empty play, domestic games, social frippery, and so on; he often gave in to these temptations. But the only process of reillusioning that really worked for him was the restitutive process of literary creation.

Even literature did not sufficiently reillusion him; it sufficed only while he was engaged in writing. And, though he did write voluminously, he could not compose continuously. Sorrows settled into the interstices between compositions; creative capacity came and went, but depression was permanent. Increasingly life lost its meaning for Twain; more and more he saw experience as delusion, an affair of masks; what is more, he saw that this was especially true of himself. There were obvious reasons for him to think of himself as an impostor, to be confused about his true identity, to be overwhelmed by his contradictoriness. An unrefined Southerner who aspired to the gentility of Nook Farm and the acceptance of Republicans, a "backwoods humorist" who wished to be taken seriously as a writer, a popular writer who doubted the taste of the public, and a success who saw himself becoming a failure, Twain camouflaged his true being to preserve his sense of safety, to protect himself against unwanted but expected criticism, hurt, or rejection. But he increasingly felt the cost at which this protection was purchased. In hiding himself from others, he began to experience an instability of identity or self-image along with personal confusion, inexplicable fits of temper, imaginative paralysis, social alienation, depression, and self-doubt.

But there were still deeper reasons for his uneasy feeling that he was an impostor. He knew his inner impulses at least well enough to know that he was wearing a mask in society and in all social relations. He didn't know exactly what his deepest self was, but he felt it would be a mistake to expose it, and so in public he displayed an expurgated, censured self that departed widely from the authentic self of which he had occasional glimpses. This made literary composition, though it was his chief defense against depression, highly problematical since authorship threatened to expose the very self he felt he must hide. In his correspondence, his public appearances, his life-style, even in his family relations, Twain was busy constructing the concept of himself that he wished others to have. He ended by concealing himself from himself. At times, he doubted that he had a self at all. He believed (rather, in his grief, he wished) that he himself was an empty dream; for that would make his griefs illusions too.

Sometimes, though, he did try to locate and define the core of his being. He had hidden it so well that in his anguish he thought it had been in his adolescence or even preadolescence when he was "really himself"; he felt it was this time that he wished to revive and recapture. When this image of his "true" self took hold of him, he tried—in correspondence, in household games, in fantasies, and in literature—to construct a literary and personal version of a perfect childhood, a paradise he had lost, even though he knew, when he could afford to remember, how desperately unhappy his childhood had been. He told many young admirers that he wished to be a boy again, a cub pilot, in "eternal summer." Sometimes he thought, alternatively, that he wished to become his "savage" self—though when he really *had* known savagery on the frontier in Missouri and Nevada, he had been appalled by it.

Driven sometimes by more extreme fantasies, he half-seriously imagined that the Garden of Eden still existed somewhere and that he could become an Adam. What did it matter that his wishes conflicted with experience— that, for instance, he knew the Hawaiian islands to have been irredeemably despoiled?—he could still tell Charles Warren Stoddard that he wished to see his Connecticut house burn down and his possessions be consumed, so that he could "pack up the cubs and fly to the isles of the blest, and shut ourselves up in the healing solitudes of the crater of Haleakala and get a good rest . . . and eat poi and dirt and give thanks . . . and never house-keep any more." These dreams were mournful, deeply mournful, expressions of weariness and depression. They did not so much describe his inner self as they indicated his wish just to escape self altogether—to achieve oblivion in any manner available: by repression if possible, by imposture if allowed, or by drunkenness and billiards when no other routes remained.

He could be neither cub pilot nor Sandwich Islander, boy nor savage, of course. Far from being able to regain a lost self, mostly he felt that his self had been irredeemably lost. He felt as if he had died—only his body went on. Many times he said that his mind was filled with corpses, and consciously he yearned for death. Death, he wrote in 1909, "was man's best friend." He often spoke of the time in 1866 when "I put the pistol to my head but wasn't man enough to pull the trigger," and he remarked just the year before his death, "Many times I have been sorry I did not succeed but I was never ashamed of having tried. Suicide is the only really sane thing the young or the old ever do in this life."

Twain's external impostures, his inner inability to scrutinize his deepest motives, and his dream of surcease from mental pain in death are all related to the global omnipotence of his guilt. Guilt pervaded his being. Hamlin Hill refers to "the guilt which . . . stalked [Twain] throughout his career"[2] as a self-evident condition. Twain's superego was sensitive and hyperactive. Between legitimate guilt, which he usually embraced (though sometimes warding it off angrily), and unwarranted guilt, which he also accepted eagerly, was a large shifting pool of uneasy, uncertain, troubled self-accusations. From his first writings to his final works; in accounts by others concerning Twain from early to late in his life; and in his letters and recorded conversations for four decades, Twain's expressions of his guilt, moral responsibility, and sense of personal depravity, along with the resulting self-castigations, are constant, suffusing almost every area of his life.

Twain's guilt and its consequences for *Huckleberry Finn* are the subjects I will investigate in this essay. Guilt was the genie in the bottle for Twain: all he or his experiences had to do was rub the lamp a certain way and in his life, as well as his writing, guilt would assume monstrous proportions, strange shapes, astonishing aspects—and incredible power. I am going to trace out the presence of two sources of guilt and one mode of defense against guilt, in Twain's life, and then consider the way that these affected *Huckleberry Finn*. I hope to be suggestive since I cannot be conclusive in tracing out in Samuel Langhorne Clemens's life and Mark Twain's writing (1) the guilt associated with his relations to his father and his younger brother Henry and (2) the way in which Twain defended against these by a special sort of derangement of his body-ego that resulted in a defensive distortion of perception.

II

I will first take up Sam Clemens's relation to his father. John Marshall Clemens was always cold and distant; he behaved in a remote manner toward everyone, even his wife. And so Jane had to seek the intimacy she desired not from her husband but from her children—especially, it seems, from Sam and Henry. Certainly they would have wanted to receive the affection she gave them and to give it back, but such a transaction would have grated against the icy domestic tone established by the father and made the children uneasy. This, in any event, was its effect upon Sam. Kenneth Lynn has characterized John Marshall Clemens as a "strange, austere, loveless man."[3] Certainly his household was reserved and formal. Each night Sam shook hands with his father before he retired to listen to Uncle Ned's or Uncle Dan'l's ghost tales. Uncle Dan'l, Sam must have pretended as a boy, was the sort of father he wished to have—a slave, not a master; an affectionate caretaker, not an austere taskmaster; a father who would give him love unmodified by rivalry for mother's love. But Uncle Dan'l wasn't his father: John Marshall, named after the lawyer and judge, was—and *he* laid down the law. Mark could not remember more than one time when a kiss was exchanged between members of the Clemens family. "My father and I,"

2. *Mark Twain: God's Fool* (New York: Harper & Row, 1973), p. 256.
3. *Mark Twain and Southwestern Humor* (Boston: Little, Brown, 1959), p. 210.

Twain wrote, "were always on the most distant terms when I was a boy—a sort of armed neutrality, so to speak." Twain's guilty feelings and troubled conscience were to a large extent the deformed products of his relation to his father; the accusations and rejection implied in his father's coldness toward him helped to create a conscience that in later life ever accused him of wrongdoing or inadequacy, even in times of success, but certainly in periods, like 1876–1884, of difficulty.

Twain's deepest symbol for his relation to his father derived from the young Sam's identification of his own helplessness with the slave's and of his tyrannical father with the slavemaster who was scornful of the slave and everyone associated with the black. His father had owned slaves; as a local magistrate, Twain knew, John Marshall Clemens had even sentenced abolitionists to jail. Twain had a vivid memory of seeing a dozen male and female blacks chained together on the Hannibal wharf—"the saddest faces I have ever seen," he recalled. He watched his father tie up, then whip, their slave girl Jennie; and later he saw her sold South. To oppose his father, then, was to identify with the black—to imagine that Uncle Dan'l or Uncle Ned and Jennie were his real parents and that, like Tom and Valet in *The Tragedy of Pudd'nhead Wilson*, he too was divided; his selves were interchangeable, but his real self was a black child disguised as a white man. He supported two black students at Yale, as if these were his own secret children.

Yet, in identifying himself with the slave, Sam would also, as a Southerner, have been aware of the frequent slave rebellions in the South; of the career of Toussaint L'Ouverture; of course, the Civil War and the Reconstruction period, with its Negro Governments, were recent facts. Thus, by identifying with the black man in relation to his father, he was secretly asserting his rebelliousness and his wishes to seize control. Twain saw blackness as covert, rebellious power. It was no accident that in December 1894, at the most desperate moment of his public life—barely a few hours after he learned that the Paige typesetter was a failure and he was ruined financially—Twain went into his bedroom and then reappeared: "blacked up as Uncle Remus, . . . it drove my troubles out of my mind." The real, hidden self appeared when the public mask was devastated.

The consequences of these identifications and the conflicts behind them are obvious in *Huckleberry Finn* in the allegory of Huck and Pap. Huck escapes Pap by committing symbolic suicide and murder. He feigns his own death by killing a wild pig and sprinkling the blood—itself a ritual act— around the cabin. "But this act," as Lynn has observed, "has a double meaning, which emerges only when we recall Pap Finn's notorious habit of lying drunk amongst the hogs in the tanyard, as well as the drunkard's . . . identification of himself with his sleeping companions: 'There's the hand that was the hand of a hog.' Huck's slaughter of the pig not only symbolizes the desire to end his own miserable life, but to slay his father."[4] In the novel the theme of the murderous relation between father and son is repeated sev-

4. Ibid., p. 211.

eral times—in the rejected (as perhaps too revealing) story of Dick Albright's murder of his child, who pursues him even in his coffin; in the mutilation of Hamlet's soliloquy following his talk with his father's ghost; and in the reiterated situation that each time Huck is forced to tell about himself, he tells the same tale—of the death of his father. The same distressing feelings and the guilt arising over them burned in Twain's conscience.

The fable of the son's relation to the father set forth in *Huckleberry Finn* is clarified by Freud's *Totem and Taboo* and Theodor Reik's 1915 lecture "The Puberty Rites of Savages."[5] Working from Darwin's hypothesis that the earliest state of society was one ruled by a jealous father who kept all the females for himself and drove away his sons as they grow up, Freud argued that totemism, already present in the earliest observable state of society, was the result of the son's guilt over the killing of the father: "the brothers who had been driven out came together, killed and devoured their father and so made an end to the patriarchal horde. United, they had the courage to do and succeeded in doing what would have been impossible for them individually. . . . The violent primal father had doubtless been the feared and envied model of each one of the company of brothers; and in the act of devouring him they accomplished their identification with him, and each one of them acquired a portion of his strength."[6] Once the father had been disposed of, according to the conclusions of J. J. Atkinson in *Primal Law* (1903), the horde would disintegrate in a bitter struggle between the victorious sons. Still, in ancient society, Freud argued, such overt hostility would last only briefly. Renewed social control would be exerted, Freud suggested, by the ambivalent father complexes of the sons who at once hated the father who had driven them out and exiled them from both mother and sexual gratification, and also admired him and identified with him. Their affection would make its appearance as remorse for his murder; and, following the impulses of the psychic mechanism of "deferred obedience," sons would forbid the killing of the totem, a substitute for the father, as well as the incestuous possession of the mother, the fruit of their victory. To the taboos thus formed against murder and incest are traceable the origin of the superego and the foundation of social organizations and moral restraints, and thus the beginnings of civilization. Reik has remarked on the continuance of these ambivalent impulses into puberty rites. The adult members of the tribe show both affection and hostility toward the young men who are initiated into the totemic system. At the very same time that they may subject the initiates to tortures, and often circumcision—the vengeful "bite" of the totemic ancestor-monster and a clear reminder of the prohibition against incest—the adults also manifest concern for the novices' safety and

5. Freud, *Totem and Taboo* (1913), *The Standard Edition of the Complete Psychological Works of Sigmund Freud*, trans. James Strachey (London: The Hogarth Press, 1958), 13:1–161; Reik, "Die Pubertätsriten der Wilden," *Imago* 6 (1915–1916): 125–44, 189–222, translated in *Ritual: Psycho-Analytic Studies* (New York: International Universities Press, 1958), pp. 91–166.
6. Freud, *Totem and Taboo*, pp. 141–42.

pretend to assist them in their fight against the monster. This is a memory, Reik suggests, of the fear of retaliation and consists of the displacement of hostility from the father to the totem-ancestor.

These totemic systems and their origin vividly illuminate the work buried in *Huckleberry Finn*. In their light, the fable of the first sixteen chapters is clear. Twain's notes for these chapters show, as Franklin Rogers has proved, that he regarded their primary theme as the death and disappearance of Pap. (Indeed, during the gestation of the book, Twain was absorbed in murder plots and detective stories.) Huck, an adolescent nearing the age of puberty, and moderately contented in the matriarchal family of Miss Watson and the Widow Douglas, is forced from it by Pap, who robs him of everything he has for putting "on airs over his own father and let[ting] on to be better'n what *he* is" (p. 40); later, Pap threatens to kill Huck. Though weak, Huck cunningly and symbolically triumphs over his father through a hoax to regain his freedom, or life. Then, exiled in nature, where the monstrous powers of ghosts and demons of the totem monster prevail, he is aided by Jim, a slave who does not threaten, only cares, for him. In testing Jim's strength as one would a hostile father, Huck virtually kills him, and he shows his superiority by tricking and humiliating him. Meanwhile, Pap is killed and Jim sees Pap's dead body. The father is split into two; the hostile, threatening father is killed, while the affectionate, protecting father is tested and accepted. One reason that Twain dropped the book at this point was that his ambivalent attitudes toward his own father had been objectified in this narrative; he had found a way of recalling both sides of his father-complex—his nightly dismissal by his real father and the care with which Uncle Dan'l had put him to bed. He had been able to imagine losing the bad father and getting the loving father he desired. Yet this resolution was not satisfactory for long. Emotionally for Twain the story was over. But Twain was also a professional novelist who needed to write a novel of considerably greater length. Besides, Twain's emotional needs were omnivorous, and he could not long accept this solution of his imagination. So he sent Huck, Jim, and the raft into the chaotic deeps at the end of Chapter 16.

Now he was faced with two problems: finding a way to extend his narrative and simultaneously giving new expression to his ambivalent, guilty attitudes toward his father. He was obsessed by both needs, but they were often in conflict, and Chapters 17 and 18 consist of his attempt to satisfy both. These two chapters are devoted to Huck's life with the Grangerfords; the colonel becomes a new father-substitute. Now, when an outsider, Harney Shepherdson, steals a female, Miss Sophia, from the primal horde, fighting breaks out, the father is killed, and society falls into chaos. Virtually all the male members, as Atkinson supposed would happen in primitive society, are killed; and Huck, who bears the guilt only of his desire to kill his own father, declares: "I reckoned I was to blame, somehow" (p. 154). Huck wasn't to blame, but he couldn't shake off his guilty feelings, and besides Twain displaced onto Huck a good dose of the considerable guilt that this narrative engendered in him.

Immediately after the deaths of the father and most of the males, however, the affectionate father Jim reappears, saying: "'Good lan' is dat you, honey?' . . . and Jim grabbed me and hugged me" (p. 155). Again, Twain ceased work on the book; again, in effect, it was ended on the emotional level. He had to struggle to continue the book as a novel. The next time he picked it up, in June 1880, he set it going through the appearance of two hostile fathers—the King and the Duke. These subdue Huck and Jim through power and cruelty. Only when Huck escapes the King and Duke can he regain Jim; but by that time another father, Silas Phelps, is on the scene, and Huck must go through the whole effort again. Now, just as he had "killed" his hostile father symbolically through a Tom Sawyer—like hoax in the beginning, at the end he regains his affectionate father through another hoax in which Tom Sawyer aids him. Huck has tested the affections of Jim, his totemic second father, first in the masculine Sacred Forest of Jackson Island, then in the feminine coils of the river monster, and at last in civilized society. Jim has passed the test of the good totem in all three. At the end, as throughout, the totemic prohibition against women is maintained. But, symbolically, Huck has a mother, too, in Jim. Aunt Sally, Huck says, had "mothered me so good I felt mean, and like I couldn't look her in the face," and Huck resolves he will "never do nothing to grieve her any more" (pp. 353, 354). But Jim is ultimately disguised in Aunt Sally's gown and in this motherly appearance is stolen from the threatening father, Silas, by the boys. At the very end, Jim, who has become mother and father, reveals that Pap is dead, that fatherly affection kills authoritarian regulation. So Huck can give up his protective social mask—his disguise as Tom Sawyer—and be "resurrected" with his true name, to tell his tale.

Jim is free, but the slave system remains as a sign of the regulative father; Huck will not again challenge it. He attempts to evade father's rules by fleeing into the Territory. He will go there, he says, "ahead of the rest"—an only child again, without a father, without a brother: alone. The fable has progressed from the father-son hostility of primal law toward the beginnings of civil and psychic benevolence, and it projects a virgin territory where these might be perfected. This psychic, inner drama of the book takes place, psychosexually speaking, in an entirely pregenital arena—yearning for mother, fears of father, identification with father, rivalry with a brother. It tells us something of Sam Clemens's fixations, Mark Twain's fantasies, and Huck Finn's fears.

Twain's guilt concerning his father would have been intensified by his father's death, which occurred when Sam was twelve years old and just entering puberty. At this time, following the relative quietude of sexual drives during the latency period, the sexual wishes that had earlier been attached to a mother (and, to a degree, to a father), ordinarily shift to adolescent girls, or young women, and to masculine career goals. When the father dies at this time, as Sam's did, there occurs a strong regressive pull back toward the original love of mother, bringing not only new unconscious guilt for the old wish to supplant father but also a deflection of sexual development backward. The result for the early adolescent boy has been separately described by Phyllis Greenacre and Lionel Finkelstein as the feeling of imposture: just as the ego is making new sexual and career choices, it is thrust backward; the adolescent forced by a father's death into a father's position (without his sexual role) feels like an imposter—father, yet not father.[7] Twain's feelings of imposture, the sense of isolation that tormented him, and the depression and sense of loss that were a constant source of anguish, are certainly related importantly to his father's death during Sam's early adolescence.

Death and sickness and loneliness and depression are Huck's constant companions. Though he claims—too offhandedly and too insistently—"I don't take no stock in dead people" (p. 18), his omnipresent, underlying tone of mourning surfaces at the smallest provocation:

> Then I set down in a chair by the window and tried to think of something cheerful, but it warn't no use. I felt so lonesome I most wished I was dead. The stars were shining, and the leaves rustled in the woods ever so mournful; and I heard an owl, away off, who-whooing about somebody that was dead, and a whippowill and a dog crying about somebody that was going to die. . . . Then . . . I heard that kind of a sound that a ghost makes . . . [and] I got so down-hearted and scared, I did wish I had some company. (P. 20)

At various times, Huck feels like an orphan; and over and over again he tells how such feelings came about—through successive deaths: "Then I told her my father and mother were dead" (p. 89); "and then there warn't nobody but just me and pap left, and he was just trimmed down to nothing, on account of his troubles; so when he died" (p. 136); "they all died off but me and pa and my brother" (p. [167]). This sense of loss Huck often transforms, of course, into empathy for others; but we should not forget that both his tale-telling capacity and his empathy are reactions against the depression that lies beneath them. Huck is no less obsessed with death and loss than Emmeline Grangerford; she has but one defense against grief, and when her poetry fails she is overwhelmed. More resourceful, yet much more needy, Huck has a considerable repertoire of defenses.

To a considerable degree, Huck's imagination of disaster and loss revolves around his wish for his father's death and his subsequent fear that should his wish be realized he will be all alone. Usually, in Huck's autobiographical romances his father is the only other member of Huck's family left alive; that is to say, the death of father, in Huck's imagination, is tantamount to real loneliness. This is a projection onto Huck of Twain's continuing feelings about Sam Clemens's loss of his father. The mechanism of projective identification that Twain employed in this instance is a familiar defense by which unwanted or unacceptable feelings are projected onto another person. It serves two purposes: first, the feelings are thereby displaced; second, it is possible to see what someone else—or, in literature, some character—might do with these feelings. How does Huck handle Sam's old sense of loss and guilt? Ultimately, he refuses to accept guilt or, indeed, any unrealistic responsibility for

---

7. See Greenacre, "The Relation of the Imposter to the Artist," in *Psychoanalytic Study of the Child* (New York: International Universities Press, 1958), 13:521–40; and Finkelstein, "The Imposter: Aspects of His Development," *Psychoanalytic Quarterly* 43 (1974): 85–114.

loss; for instance, he remarks about the drowning of a gang of cutthroats whom he had tried to save: "I reckoned if they could stand it, I could" (p. 107). As a character, Huck gave Twain the instructions that Sam needed to deal with his childhood and adolescent guilt.

III

But Sam's guilt was not confined to his father's death; nor could it be resolved simply by the creation of a literary character. On top of his primary guilt was piled guilt arising from his ambivalent relation to his brother Henry, who was three years younger than Sam. Henry was the subject of one of Twain's earliest memories:

> I used to remember my brother Henry walking into a fire outdoors when he was a week old. It was remarkable in me to remember a thing like that and it was still more remarkable that I should cling to the delusion for thirty years that I *did* remember it—for of course it never happened; he would not have been able to walk at that age.

Twain goes on to say that, though many people believe impressions "deposited in a child's memory" disappear very early, he himself is convinced otherwise. He thus brands his "memory" an illusion even as he makes claims for the authenticity of early memory traces. He seems to be saying, in an altogether inexplicable manner, that Henry couldn't walk at his age, but Sam could have remembered it at his. Twain breaks off his account in mid-sentence, perhaps wary of the paradoxical character of his claims. Then he seems to shift subjects and delivers his famous quip: "when I was younger I could remember anything, whether it happened or not; but my faculties are decaying now, and soon I shall be so I cannot remember any but the things that didn't happen." Of course, he *is* still reflecting on his memory of Henry: it didn't happen, yet it did; he couldn't remember it, yet he could; Henry couldn't walk into a fire, but without a doubt he did so. One *can* remember what happened, but also what "didn't happen"—that is, what one invented, what one wished to happen.

Psychoanalysts and literary psychologists have frequently asserted correctly that dreams and screen memories can be fully interpreted only through an associative process that might slowly disclose the unconscious and its connections. It is equally true, however, that dreams and screen memories possess manifest verbal content that can be adequately analyzed and understood at the level of conscious symbolization. Twain's memory of Henry's walking into a fire when the infant was a week old is a screen memory that scarcely expresses an event, but it certainly condenses a wish: it quite clearly expresses the burning anger and jealousy of the three-year-old Sam at the arrival of this unwanted intruder and especially the recognition, following some period of time, that the usurper of mother's attention was not going to go away and allow Mrs. Clemens to return to her proper business of taking care of Sam. Then, murderous feelings arose that gave expression to Sam's seething anger through the fire metaphor. Undoubtedly, Jane Clemens had earlier taught the young Sam that the fire was dangerous: logs burned up and disappeared in it. So, clearly, the boy identified his dangerous anger with the conflagration and wished that Henry would walk into it, just as he had, by his birth, walked into Sam's narcissistic, all-consuming wrath. Sam's evident wish was that, thereby, he could be rid of two unwanted things—his murderous anger, projected onto the fire, and the infant Henry. The event didn't happen, but the wish was real and was remembered as if it had happened, so fervently was its fulfillment desired.

But immediately apparent in the screen memory is the guilt that the young Sam probably experienced in connection with his rage at the newcomer's receiving attention from everyone in the house. Sam's guilty feelings would have almost certainly remained unconscious at age three. Yet guilt would be almost inevitable when everyone in the household would have prepared Sam for the birth of a sibling by telling him how happy he would be to have a little brother, how welcome the little darling would be; instead, secretly, he "realized" he wanted the interloper to go back into the stove where he had been "cooking" all these months. Without any sense of certainty at this point, then, we can hypothesize guilt, and perhaps see its presence in yet one more aspect of the fantasy's choice of fire to express Sam's anger and the infant's punishment. In a fundamentalist religious household, one meaning of fire was perfectly clear: bad boys went to hell, where they were burned up by fires. The corpus of Twain's work is strewn with images, too numerous to count, in which anger, bitterness, aggression, and hellfire are associated. Twain's famous description of his inner being in his sermonlike "text" for his autobiography says very clearly what his inner world was like: "The mass of [a man] is hidden—it and its volcanic fires that toss and boil, and never rest, night or day. These are his life." If Sam felt hellish guilt over his anger at the infant, an inner accusation that he was a bad boy, he warded it off by assigning blame to Henry, therefore requiring punishment of him. Henry was the bad boy because he disrupted the household, and he should be thrown into the fires of hell for his transgression of disturbing the peace—Sam's peace.

We can get a direct look at Twain's feelings of guilt in another episode involving a fire. In his *Autobiography* he begins a section with a tale in which he was exposed to shame and humiliation by being seen naked by two young girls. Then he proceeds from shame to guilt. He tells the story of how he gave matches to a drunken tramp. Later, in jail, the tramp started a fire and, when the door could not be opened, burned to death before young Sam's eyes:

> A boy's life is not all comedy [that is, shame]; much of the tragic [that is, guilt] enters into it. The drunken tramp who was burned up in the village jail lay upon my conscience a hundred nights afterward and filled them with hideous dreams—dreams in which I saw his appealing face as I had seen it in pathetic reality, pressed against the window bars, with the red hell glowing behind him—a face which seemed to say to me, "If you had not given me the matches, this would not have happened; you are responsible for my death." I was *not* responsible for it, for I had meant him no harm, but only good, when I let him have the matches; but no matter, mine was a trained Presbyterian conscience

and knew but the one duty—to hunt and harry its slave upon all pretexts and on all occasions, particularly when there was no sense nor reason in it. The tramp—who was to blame—suffered ten minutes; I, who was not to blame, suffered three months.

In this section of the *Autobiography*, Twain goes on to give accounts of several other "tragedies" that, he says, proved to him that he would be condemned to hell. He does not so much as mention Henry in connection with the tramp's death, and so seems to give me no warrant for connecting his angry, jealous "memory" that Henry would burn up in a fire with his guilt over "causing" the tramp's death.

Yet the fact that Henry *is* intimately associated with Sam's guilt over the tramp's death becomes clear in *Life on the Mississippi*.[8] There, Twain tells the story of the tramp and writes movingly about his own boyish paranoid projections: *everyone* in the town, he thought, *must* know that he was the culprit who had provided the matches through whose agency the tramp incinerated himself. Sam's dreams were haunted by grisly pictures and fears— created by guilt, maintained by suppression, and intensified by a horror of exposure and a fear of punishment. He felt that everyone knew about his culpability even as he desperately tried to conceal the part he had played in the death.

> All this time I was blessedly forgetting one thing—the fact that I was an inveterate talker in my sleep. But one night I awoke and found my bed-mate—my younger brother [Henry]—sitting up in bed and contemplating me by the light of the moon. I said:
> "What is the matter?"
> "You talk so much I can't sleep."
>
> * * *
>
> "What did I say? Quick—out with it—what did I say?"

Sam's fears so overwhelm him that he nearly exposes the very guilt he wishes to hide. It would be a relief to be caught and accused, however. So he keeps interrogating Henry with hypothetical situations. Suppose a drunken man asked you to loan him a pistol and you forgot to tell him to be careful, it was loaded, and he shot and killed himself with it . . . would that be murder? "'Well,' Henry says, 'probably murder, but I don't quite know.'" Sam is insistent. Regarding the man burned up in the calaboose, Sam says,

> "The man wanted some matches to light his pipe. A boy got him some. The man set fire to the calaboose with those very matches, and burnt himself up."
> "Is that so?"
> "Yes, it is. Now, is that boy a murderer, do you think?"
> "Let me see. The man was drunk?"
> "Yes, he was drunk."
> "Very drunk?"

8. Though reaching rather different conclusions from either, I have benefited in what follows from both Coleman O. Parsons, "The Devil and Samuel Clemens," *VQR* 23 (1947): 582–606; and Forrest G. Robinson, "Why I Killed My Brother: An Essay on Mark Twain," *L&P* 30 (1980): 168–81.

"And the boy knew it."

"Yes, he knew it."

There was a long pause. Then came this very heavy verdict:

"If the man was drunk, and the boy knew it, the boy murdered that man. This is certain."

Are Twain's memories of his instrumentality in the death of the town drunk and of his guilt-ridden talk with Henry memories of things that happened, or screen-"memories" of what "didn't happen" except in the symbolmaking faculty of fantasy? Was there a tramp at all? Did Sam "really" give the tramp matches by which he was consumed in a fire? If he did, was his guilt really over that, where guilt was highly oblique? Or was it the continuing expression of his guilt over wishing Henry (and before him, his father) incinerated? Did Henry really spy out Sam's guilty secrets? It *is* Henry, in any event, who in Twain's account announces Sam's guilt for murder, Henry who represents Sam's guilty conscience. But it was Sam's wish for Henry's death (and behind that, his father's death) for which he really felt guilt. Whatever the elements of truth or invention in these tales concerning real fires, symbolic fires, and the hellfires of guilt, we must read the stories together as accounts of Twain's rage at Henry's birth and his continued jealousy of the younger rival who had displaced him in his mother's affections and continued to be the favored son.

In 1858 Sam and Henry traveled together by steamboat to St. Louis. A cub pilot, Sam was ordered to stay two days there in order to catch another boat, while Henry, a passenger, continued the journey to New Orleans. The night before Henry was to leave, the two brothers discussed steamboat catastrophes, and "we decided that if a disaster ever fell within our experience we would at least stick to the boat, and give such minor service as chance might throw in the way." Following Henry's departure, Sam had a dream of Henry as a corpse, lying in a metallic coffin, dressed in a suit of Sam's clothes. A bouquet of white roses, with a red rose at the center, lay on his chest. The manifest content of the dream is clear enough: the wish for Henry's death is at the center. He has walked into the fire again—he is inside something that is most like a Franklin stove; the flame-red rose burns at his heart. At the same time, the fact that he wears Sam's clothes shows for whom the punishment of hellfire is really meant—the guilty Sam.

Very possibly, Twain would never have "remembered" any of the "events" whose "history" I have been recounting—the infant's walking into the fire, the tramp's fate, the "accusation" by Henry, the dream of Henry's death— except for the fact that Sam's murderous wish was actually fulfilled in the most dramatic way possible: Henry died as a result of an explosion and fire aboard the steamboat on which he traveled alone. Twain's account of the episode is ambiguous; but it seems likely, too, that Henry's injuries were sustained when, abiding by their last night's agreement, Henry returned to the boat to render "minor service" to the injured. Twain wrote in *Life on the Mississippi* that "Henry remembered this [conversation] afterward, when the disaster came, and acted accordingly." Most likely Henry died— as many other passengers did—from inhaling scalding steam from the burst boilers. He had finally walked into the fire, as his older brother had long ago wished him to do. No wonder that when Sam described the event to his sister-in-law, Mollie Stotts Clemens, his sense of guilt overpowered him. He himself is "poor" and "wretched," a "lost and ruined sinner," who wishes for God to pour "just wrath upon my wicked head"; he is lower than the "vilest beggar." He wishes that he might change places with Henry and prays that God would blast him "but have mercy, mercy, mercy upon that unoffending boy."[9]

Twain reported Henry's death to their mother, including a full account of his anticipatory dream—though years later, he believed he had not told her of the dream since it would have been, he felt, the last thing he would have wanted her to know. Clearly, he recognized the wish contained in his dream. He didn't want Jane to know about his dream; but he himself secretly treasured it, calling it "that wonderful dream," and so he told her of it.

What is the story, the "inside narrative," told about Twain's unconscious in his variations upon the theme of fire?—Henry's fire, the tramp's fire, the steamboat's fire, and Sam's inner hellfire? I would interpret this sequence—in a very schematic, summarizing way—as follows: Sam's guilty wish to do away with his unwanted father was intensified by the birth of an unwanted sibling; the wish was unexpectedly fulfilled in the case of the tramp, and this temporarily revived the guilt connected with his original wishes concerning father and Henry. After all, the earliest wishes persisted in his unconscious and were the source of recurring guilt-ridden dreams about Henry's death. Then, by chance, following one such dream, the wish was fulfilled, a fact that led both to omnipotent feelings of power and triumph (that is, what he wishes will come true), and grandiose guilt feelings. These together made him both want to repress his wishes and to confess them. Sam Clemens in 1858 was stuck between guilty repression and triumphant proclamation. He was left with Henry's corpse on his hands—or at least on his mind.[10]

So much for Sam. Six years after the steamboat incident Clemens decisively shuffled off the identity he had derived from steamboating and assumed a new name and a new identity based on authorship. Mark Twain was not free of Sam Clemens's history and inner torments, but he had acquired a new instrument—literary composition—through which to deal with the conflicts of his earlier, other life. If Sam Clemens was left with a corpse, Mark Twain could turn that dead weight into the body of a book. The "mood of writing," Twain often said, "attacked [him] when some mentally dead people brought their corpses with them for a long visit." By the end of 1875 Twain's mind was frightened with corpses, especially (but not only) Henry's. Twain was haunted by his own dead past, his youth; and by his present, which to him increasingly seemed dead, ghostly, sterile. Sam's

9. Quoted from Robinson, "Why I Killed," p. 169.

10. Twain, characteristically, developed more than one reason to make himself feel responsible for Henry's death. Paine states that Clemens actually felt more responsible for Henry's death because of an overdose of morphine, which Sam allowed to be given to Henry in treatment, than because he had told Henry to help passengers should an explosion occur. See Albert Bigelow Paine, *Mark Twain: A Biography* (New York: Harper & Brothers, 1912), pp. 142–44.

relation to his father was, as we have seen, represented in many of the elements of plot and symbol in *Huckleberry Finn*. The same is equally true of his conflicts concerning Henry. Henry's death was certainly on Twain's mind as he prepared to begin *Huckleberry Finn*. From January to August 1875, his series of articles "Old Times on the Mississippi" ran in the *Atlantic Monthly*. Eventually, these became chapters 4–17 in *Life on the Mississippi*—the chapters beginning with "The Boys' Ambition" and ending with "Cut-offs and Stephen." In these he came right up to the account—as it eventually appeared—of Henry's death, but he stopped his series abruptly just before he was to tell that tale. It was still waiting to be told when he started his new novel, and he soon put two "brothers"—Huck and Jim— on a raft in the Mississippi, heading toward a catastrophic collision with a steamboat. Stories of Huck's adventures with other "brothers" follow one after the other.

Huckleberry Finn involves Huck not only in a series of parent-son situations but also in an equally potent succession of brotherly arrangements. Throughout his career, Twain took up the theme of the varied relations between two brothers—twins, doubles, intimate friends, older brother and younger, dandy and squatter, sophisticate and innocent, the powerful and the weak, Negro and white. From book to book, of course, he considered their relations in a variety of ways, but one basic plot feature that emerged early held on and became a fundamental feature of Twain's stories. He starts with two brothers, one apparently more powerful than the other. Then he reverses their positions. As a result, the weaker, younger, more innocent "brother" wins or gains a superior position.[11] Finally, he returns to the original relation. Just as Sam had proclaimed his triumph concerning Henry's death by confessing his wishes, even as he condemned himself for them; so, in his literary work, he restored the "brothers" to their "proper" positions. In brief, the action of the novel shows the superior brother losing his position, changing places with the weaker, then, at last, regaining his original position. The psychological purpose of this pattern of power relations, considered from Twain's point of view, is clear. He identified with the older brother; he suffered punishment by losing his power; then, having expiated his guilt, he reassumed his position of power. This pattern of doubling, reversal, and release from guilt was not only a literary device but also a deeply personal response operating automatically in Twain's books and Twain's psyche.

Twain famously described the theme of *Huckleberry Finn* as the conflict between "A sound heart & a deformed conscience." The terms are of fundamental importance. In Huck's story, conscience suffers defeat. Twain was himself engaged in the same struggle to defeat his conscience and reveal his "sound heart." Huckleberry Finn is, as Twain doubtless wished himself to be, an only child, without parents, without brothers. He is free from a guilt-

11. This subject has been brilliantly pursued in all its varieties by Robert Regan in *Unpromising Heroes: Mark Twain and His Characters* (Berkeley: University of California Press, 1966).

ridden conscience and the influences of a Christian civilization in general. Yet, he gets subjected to various authorities, "fathers," or rule-givers, from the judge and Miss Watson and the Widow Douglas, to his own father, the Grangerfords, the King and the Duke, and finally Uncle Silas and Aunt Sally. He manages to escape from all of these and resume his own ways. At the same time, he gets associated with several "brothers"—with Tom Sawyer and the gang (they become "blood brothers"), with Jim, with Buck, and finally again with Tom Sawyer masquerading as Sid. Huck's doubling and reversal of roles, allied with an attack upon parental superegos from which he escapes, gave Twain a chance, at least temporarily, to extricate himself through Huck from the guilty tangle that Sam Clemens had gotten him into.

In the very narrative form of the book itself Twain creates his own younger-older, weak-powerful, "unsivilized"-civilized, tale-telling twins: Huckleberry Finn and Mr. Mark Twain. The same pattern is evident here. As a professional novelist, Mr. Mark Twain is the older, stronger brother in the telling of tales. He has told *The Adventures of Tom Sawyer*. But the new novel begins as Huck seizes the story from him and in the process vindicates Mr. Twain from wrongdoing by assuring us that he had mainly told the truth. Still, Huck is bent on conveying a different level of truth. There is a considerable distance between the boy's tale and a conventional narrative by a professional novelist. The sort of narrative Huck tells opposes all accepted conventional narrative rules of novels. On the surface, it is full of defects— false starts, contradictions, mixed genres, and plot confusions. But Huck's tale turns out to be superior. Underneath, it has the "sound heart" of a true tale. Twain revealed his own sound artistic heart precisely by using his weaker novelistic brother, Huck, to destroy the surface order, the literary conscience and aesthetic appeal of the novel-narrative, and finally by going behind Huck's vernacular language to tell the truth—which he knew but could not speak—of his own heart.

The book ends with what Huck calls The Evasion—but it begins in evasion as well. The opening words of this book are as simultaneously revealing and concealing as those of *Moby-Dick*. "You don't know about me," Huck challenges the reader; and then he goes on, as Twain's shadow, to challenge the author, who had in a previous book "mainly . . . told the truth" about him. Twain attempted to collaborate with Huck in self-disclosure by submerging the literary forms of the novel and by making, behind them, a work that explores primitive man and so encourages the flow of unconscious impulses that mock both the formularizations of the superego and the "wisdom" of the ego. As experienced by Huck, these opened Twain's book to the expression of the violent, the anarchic, and the nightmarish. Twain accepted the nineteenth-century romantic notion that the common ground of all men is primitive man, and he assumed that by exposing the primitive in himself he could reveal the real core and sound heart of his nature. The Polish critic Konstanty A. Jelenski describes this as a postmodern aesthetic: "In order to open (or to attempt to open) the creative processes . . . [the artist] has to do away with consciousness and produce within himself an emptiness that will allow him to plunge headlong into the power of instinct."[12] Sharing this assumption and investigating himself, trying to get at the rock-bottom character of his self, Twain killed conscience in order to put the primitive (and thus, he supposed, his own authentic being) in the center of his book. In this manner he wrote a work in which he wished to reveal the underlying psychic reasons for his own and man's enslavement, especially to guilt, and the conditions for liberation.

In order to surrender his book to the primitive and the unconscious, Twain had to write a work in which all levels of experience would be marked by terror. No wonder that an early review of *Huckleberry Finn* in *Life* magazine was titled "Mark Twain's Blood-Curdling Humor"; the reviewer complained that he found no humor whatsoever in the book—only one bloody episode after another. Whence comes this primitive terror? Twain wrote in the prefatory note to *Tom Sawyer*: "the odd superstitions touched upon were all prevalent among children and slaves in the West at the period of this story." He began his new novel in this context; later, in 1882, when he visited the Mississippi valley, his memories of its "dreams and superstitions" were revivified. Ghostlore, demonology, witchcraft, divination, lucky and unlucky signs, magic, portents and omens, covenants, riddles, spells, and numerous superstitions fill *Huckleberry Finn*.

In these Twain was not only revealing the power that superstitious fears had over him; more important, he exposed the importance for his psyche of the *way* he learned his ghostlore. That tales of the supernatural in the book congregate around Jim seems to be because Jim's prototype, Uncle Dan'l, was a black servant in the Clemens household who told bedtime stories to the young Sam; the adult Mark could still recall in 1900 "the creepy joy which quivered through me when the time for the ghost story was reached." As I remarked earlier, in connection with Sam's affective relation to John Marshall Clemens, Uncle Dan'l was everything that Sam's father was not— but there was no chance that Twain could consciously entertain the fantasy that he could have a slave for a father. In Dan'l's powerlessness, he was more easily imagined as a big younger brother who would *give* to Sam, not (as Henry did) *take* anything from him. Twain had not been able to "save" Henry from disaster and death, but he wrote a story in which Huck saved Jim (while almost killing him) several times. Temporarily, Twain thus found himself able to deal with his deepest sorrows and anxieties, arising from his uneasy relations with his father and younger brother. What is more, he was able to treat them with an extraordinary humorous exaltation.

IV

The first words of *Huckleberry Finn* reverberate at the novel's end: "You don't know about me, without you have read a book." Once the reader has read the book, he knows something of Huck and, if he has read carefully, of Mark Twain as well. In 1868, even before he had published his first book, he had written to a friend: "I don't care anything about being humorous, or

---

12. Personal communication.

poetical, or eloquent, or anything of that kind—the end and aim of my ambition is to be authentic—to be considered authentic." He had been *considered* authentic from the first; but not until *Huckleberry Finn* was he *really*
authentic in beginning to expose his true self.

What he revealed was not simply the tormenting ambivalence of his attitudes toward his father and brother and the continuing pressure these put
on him through his conscience; he showed, as well, the beginnings of his
freedom from conscience in his ability to dissect his attitudes and, at last
in the Evasion, even, as it appears, to burlesque himself. So far as he was
able to reveal his self in public, he could make a beginning at knowing himself in private. Psychotherapists like Sidney Jourard have argued that self-
knowledge is a collaborative product. It is an "empirical fact," Jourard
wrote, "that no man can come to know himself except as an outcome of
disclosing himself to another person."[13] *Huckleberry Finn* was Twain's best
attempt at making himself transparent, at least, to himself and, if they could
understand him, to his audience.

But I am far from wanting to claim that in *Huckleberry Finn* or elsewhere
Twain entirely gave up his defenses and stepped from behind his disguises.
He could certainly blame his culture for his inability to do so and for the
highly covert character of his confessions. What nineteenth-century American could openly confess the revelation that Twain indirectly made: that he
wished to be his own double, but black, and to have a black father or
brother? "Lincoln's proclamation," he once hopefully remarked, "not only
set the black slaves free, but set the white man free also." But Twain was still
chained. What nineteenth-century American could clearly admit that he
would rejoice in the news of his father's demise? What prominent citizen and
member of genteel society—such as Twain wished to be—could acknowledge that he wanted to do away with his brother as well as his father, yet feel
no twinge of guilt about either? Certainly cultural mores were partly responsible for Twain's concealments.

But Twain's personal defenses were far more restrictive than society's
mores. Often he submitted his writings to others, such as Howells or his
own wife, encouraging them to represent cultivated society for him and to
censor his work; and he could usually cajole criticism from them, as he had
from Henry. But when they finished, he censored himself still more severely;
he refused to allow manuscripts to be published; or he assumed additional
pseudonyms so as to dissociate himself from his work. In this essay I have
been examining the way in which many ordinary defenses against guilt, depression, and anxiety were transformed in *Huckleberry Finn*. Projection,
projective identification, displacement, reversal, splitting, doubling, sub-
limation, repression, denial, and regression are some of the mechanisms
whose operation is sporadic and temporary in Twain and have surprising
consequences for his literary work. But one fairly unusual defense is exhibited rather continuously in both Twain's life and work. Indeed, this de-

13. *The Transparent Self* (New York: Van Nostrand Reinhold Co., 1964), p. 5. (I have omitted
the italics in the original.)

fense is so characteristic of Twain—in Wilhelm Reich's phrase, a part of his "character armor"—that it seems more an aspect of his identity than a defense of self.

The defense I refer to is a basic distortion of body-ego that made Twain see himself (and his projections of himself) as smaller than these were; while others (or his projections of them) were seen as larger than they were. Associated with seeing himself as smaller was his imagination of himself as younger, weaker, more exposed, and more victimized than he was; in an opposite manner, he imagined others as larger, older, stronger, more protected, and more masterful than he. Among the analysts who have studied these processes of distortion, Paul Kramer, William G. Niederland, and V. D. Volkan agree on calling it the "little man" phenomenon, while Woodbury speaks more generally of "altered body-ego experiences," and would consider the microscopia-macroscopia sequence which is most evident in Twain not only a defense but also a derangement of the ego at the level of the primary body image.[14] I use *little man* and *microscopia* in what follows rather interchangeably. At the period of the composition of *Huckleberry Finn*, the distortion remains, I think, at the level of defense; by around 1905, as we shall see, it increased in intensity and entered the sphere of the perversions.

Twain said in 1900 that to his childish perception the world was "peopled with . . . mysterious dwarfs and giants and goblins," such as he heard about in the tales of the Negro slaves. Certainly, his was no special, unique experience. The Egyptians believed that every man has a *ka*, an exact counterpart of himself in features, gait, and dress—only miniature in size. Egyptian funerary monuments representing the divine judgment of a king show the ruler accompanied by a little king, exactly duplicating him, standing in back of him. "Little" doubles appear in many different forms in folklore and mythology—the dwarf with magical powers, such as Rumpelstiltskin; creatures who are tiny but powerful, such as fairies, elves, and leprechauns, or the genie who is condensed into a bottle but can become gigantic. In more formal literature, the experiences of Swift's Gulliver or Carroll's Alice exhibit the continuing belief that little creatures, to whom we have some relation, exist—around us, within us. In stories about giants, or those concerning incredible shrinking men (or women), we see ourselves as small; often such a perception is accompanied by feelings of terror.

But just as often, especially when the self is seen as shrinking, the process is accompanied by relief: to be small means to be inconspicuous, easily hidden, too insignificant for retaliation, too tiny to be an easy target. That there is also a psychological defensive aspect to the perception of otherwise large and powerful fears or objects as small is clear, as Sandor Ferenczi pointed out in his article on "Gulliver's Fantasies."[15]

14. See Kramer, "On Discovering One's Identity: A Case Report," *Psychoanalytic Study of the Child* (New York: International Universities Press, 1955), 10:47–74; Niederland, "Clinical Observations on the 'Little Man' Phenomenon," *Psychoanalytic Study of the Child* (New York: International Universities Press, 1956), 11:381–95; V. D. Volkan, *Primitive Internalized Object Relations* (New York: International Universities Press, 1976), esp. pp. 9–12; and Michael A. Woodbury, "Altered Body-Ego Experiences," *JAPA* 14 (1966): 273–303.

15. *International Journal of Psycho-Analysis* 9 (1928): 283–300.

Microscopia and related phenomena are frequently met in clinical practice. One of my patients pictures a part of himself as a tiny monster living in a dark slimy cavity inside his body; the monster eagerly gobbles up whatever comes near his hiding place and winks at my patient in a friendly, collaborative way. This young man is deeply distressed by his rageful feelings and wants desperately to deny his anger by splitting it off as a little monster within him. Woodbury treated a patient who gave an explanation of another feature of this process in simple phenomenological terms; his perceptions of size were related to his investments of affective energy in object- or self-representation; for instance, he said, "a girl in the streets becomes very big and everything [else] very small if I feel horny." [16] When one of Volkan's patients "looked into a mirror she saw herself as no more than an inch or two in height. . . . When in reality she was sitting on a chair, looking in the mirror, she could see the chair reflected truly but her own person as diminutive": [17] hers was a distortion not of perception (she saw the chair accurately), but of inner feelings about her value and need to protect herself. Such hallucinations as those reported to Woodbury and Volkan represent inner reality, as Herbert Silberer put it, "autosymbolically," [18] finding adequate symbols for internal feelings in body-"reality." Clearly, like Volkan's patient, Twain did not have a disease of perception; his microscopia was psychological, not physiological. But he did regard himself as small—in the colloquial phrase that applies to his perspective on himself, he "saw" himself as tiny, a child, weak, easily hidden. This is why, when he wanted to be noticed, he felt he had to call dramatic attention to himself, by wearing white suits in the winter, for instance, or his scarlet Oxford academic robes at his daughter's wedding. But mostly he wanted to hide behind a mask rather than use masks to bring attention toward himself.

What benefits did the young Sam derive from seeing himself or part of himself as tiny? Three are immediately apparent, and all relate to his feelings of rivalry and are defenses against loss or defeat. In the first place, by being small and insignificant he could avoid both his father's angry regulative attention and his older siblings' jealousy, as well as claim continued attention from his mother. He was no threat to them, but he needed her. In the second place, after Henry's birth, when the little baby got the attention Sam wanted, littleness must have seemed all the more desirable: Sam imagined that *he* was the little one, while Henry grew so rapidly that by the end of a week he could walk into a fire. Third, by being tiny he could try to evade his guilt feelings; what guilt could a baby be accused of? Or else he could separate off a tiny part of his ego and say that this tiny creature, not he—a part of him but not him—was guilty.

Only a few months before beginning *Huckleberry Finn*, Twain wrote a sketch that gave very vivid representation to this last possibility. Titled "The Facts Concerning the Recent Carnival of Crime in Connecticut," the sketch

16. "Altered Experiences," p. 278.
17. *Primitive Object Relations*, p. 21.
18. "Bericht über eine Methode, gewisse symbolische Halluzinations-Erscheinungen hervorzurufen und zu beobachten," *Jb. Psychoan. Psychopath. Forsch.* 1 (1909): 513–25.

portrayed a terrible figure who pursued him without remorse or surcease—a repulsive, deformed dwarf. This little man, Twain says, "with exquisite cruelty . . . recalled to my mind . . . wrongs and unkindnesses I have inflicted and humiliations I had put upon friends." The narrator murders the dwarf, his conscience, enjoys his life, and concludes, "Nothing . . . could persuade me to have a conscience again." Niederland has reported a case involving the "little man" phenomenon that closely resembles Twain's "Carnival of Crime":

> In a dream the patient saw an ugly and deformed little man in a dirty cellar. In his associations the patient referred to the dwarf Alberich who presided over the golden hoard in the saga of the Nibelungs, and to other dwarfs in mythology and literature such as Rumpelstiltskin in [the] Grimms' fairy tales, and Victor Hugo's hunchback of Notre Dame. At last the patient indicated in his associations recognition of the fact that "the little man" was himself, and he gradually identified more and more with "the dwarf" whenever he mentioned any kind of shady deal in which he had been engaged.[19]

Niederland says that this patient eventually learned to distinguish between his ego, his central self, and the "dwarf" aspect of his self that had been split off from his ego proper. For his part, Twain used literature as a vehicle by which to make and consolidate these distinctions. He wanted to keep his guilt from childhood separate from his wish for innocence.

But even though he constructed innumerable stories in which the good wins by decisively rejecting the bad, Twain could not keep his feelings of guilt from welling up and contaminating his wishes for innocence. Often the dark dwarf won out—bad destroyed good. One of the earliest versions in Twain's writing involving distinguishing one child aspect of himself from another—the good and bad little selves, the "angel" self and the "dwarf" self—occurs in the pair of sketches written around 1865: "The Story of the Bad Little Boy" and "The Story of the Good Little Boy." In these sketches two boys, Jim Blake and Jacob Blivens, share one basic identity—expressed in the initials *J. B.*—but are otherwise completely opposite. Everything is reversed: evil succeeds while morality suffers defeat:

> Somehow nothing ever went right with this good little boy; nothing ever turned out with him the way it turned out with the good little boys in the books. They always had a good time, and the bad boys had the broken legs; but in his case there was a screw loose somewhere, and it all happened just the other way. When he found Jim Blake stealing apples, and went under the tree to read to him about the bad little boy who fell out of a neighbor's apple tree and broke his arm, Jim fell out of the tree, too, but he fell on *him* and broke *his* arm, and Jim wasn't hurt at all. Jacob couldn't understand that. There wasn't anything in the books like it.
>
> And once, when some bad boys pushed a blind man over in the mud, and Jacob ran to help him up and receive his blessing, the blind man did not give him any blessing at all, but whacked him over the head with the stick and said he would like to catch him shoving him again, and then pretending to help him up. This was not in accordance with any of the books. Jacob looked them all over to see.

19. Quoted from Volkan, *Primitive Object Relations*, p. 11.

> One thing that Jacob wanted to do was to find a lame dog that hadn't any place to stay, and was hungry and persecuted, and bring him home and pet him and have that dog's imperishable gratitude. And at last he found one and was happy; and he brought him home and fed him, but when he was going to pet him the dog flew at him.

Clearly, in 1865, Twain saw his self as radically split between two "little men," a good one that had little power and a bad one that committed numerous transgressions, yet went unpunished. His "good" self deserved the rewards it wished for; but the "bad" self would not be condemned.

I do not need to give a chronicle of Twain's varied representations of the "little men" or continuing child selves splitting his identity, as they appeared in one book after another. I have already mentioned some of the variants of his tendency to split himself into two, then reverse the split-off parts—making the good self a failure and the bad a success; the "educated" man a buffoon and the uncultivated boy a wise man; the black slave a father-figure and the father a pig; the prince a pauper and the pauper a prince. It is certainly the case that during the second half of the nineteenth century nearly every major writer of fiction in America dealt importantly with children. Even Henry James, who seems in so many ways to be the opposite of Twain, wrote about children frequently—in novels (for instance, *What Maisie Knew*), stories (such as "The Turn of the Screw"), and autobiography (*A Small Boy and Others*). But no other writers in Twain's period—even those like Thomas Bailey Aldrich and Charles Dudley Warner who were famous for children's stories—restricted themselves as thoroughly as Twain did to representing childhood life. Even his adults he portrayed simply as big children: witness Hank Morgan and King Arthur in *A Connecticut Yankee*, the passengers in *Innocents Abroad*, and Satan in *No. 44, The Mysterious Stranger*. In *Roughing It*, Twain represents himself as a presexual tiny child, even though the events of the book took place when he was twenty-six years old; a Mormon says to Orion of Sam: "Ah—your child, I presume? boy, or girl?" In a way that no other major novelist has ever done—indeed, in a way that would seem intolerably restrictive—Twain virtually confined his work to the representation of children or childlike behavior.

Huckleberry Finn is clearly, to my mind, the character in whom, more than any of his others, Twain found himself able to combine his little boy and little man selves into one complex being. With Huck, he broke out of the restrictions that representing only child life imposed on him. Huck is a child, of course, but he is a complex one; whereas adults in Twain's work are ordinarily represented as children, Huck is a child drawn with the complexity of an adult. Huck is, at last, neither the good boy who acts through convention nor the bad boy who defies it, but the human boy on his way to adulthood who balances good and bad in a series of moral decisions concerning human freedom. He is willing to "go to hell" in order to do right, knowing what Twain found it difficult to know on his own—that good and bad are always mixed in real boys, real worlds, and real books. A wild boy who inherits money at the end of *Tom Sawyer*, Huck participates in both innocence and civilization; he thrives, or at least survives, under all sorts of tutelage—that of the Christian sisters, of the romantic Tom, of a criminal father, of the escaped slave, of the "aristocratic" Grangerfords, of the King and the Duke, of the Wilks girls, and at the Phelps plantation—because he has and can acknowledge in himself elements of all the responses and feelings signified by each of these. Huck has little of the rigidity that is so marked in most of Twain's characters and in Twain himself. The basic psychological pleasure given by Huck is that he can become whatever he needs to be; thus he can get—almost—whatever he wishes. With considerable ease he goes through the developmental stages that we all follow—by learning to survive without living in mother's house; by abandoning his abandoning parents, then learning to accept both a more tolerant second father and also a more distant but more generous mother; by seeing that he can triumph over his brothers (Tom, Jim, "Sid") and still retain their friendship; and at last by feeling confident in striking out for an unknown territory in his first gesture of tentative independence. Huck can grow up because he can experience, accept, and gather together all his varied "little boy" selves and learn to fuse them into one self, thereby seeing himself big, the same size as other objects, inhabiting the same object-world.

In *Tom Sawyer*, Tom's "little" brother Sid (who very much resembles Henry) is a perfect representative of the superego; he is prim, proper, morally correct, and wholly insufferable. The last we see of Sid is when Tom boots him out of the novel for his mean-spiritedness. He is like Twain's malicious "dwarf," and Tom unhesitatingly gets rid of him. More than any other episode, this expulsion from *Tom Sawyer* of the superego representation, the "Sid"-side of Twain's personality, helped to prepare the ground for his composition of *Huckleberry Finn*.

In Huck and the Sid aspect of Tom, Twain represented two sides of his own being. But in *Huckleberry Finn* he was able to create in Huck a good-bad little boy, without completely calling the good boy bad. He seemed able to accept both sides of the child "little men" inside himself. Early in the novel, Huck and Tom discuss one "little man" phenomenon, and each argues for the side appropriate to his nature, one stressing fears—and the other, hope:

> Tom Sawyer said I was a numskull.
> "Why," says he, "a magician could call up a lot of genies, and they would hash you up like nothing before you could say Jack Robinson. They are as tall as a tree and as big around as a church."
> "Well," I says, "s'pose we got some genies to help *us*—can't we lick the other crowd then?"
> "How you going to get them?"
> "I don't know. How do *they* get them?"
> "Why they rub an old tin lamp or an iron ring, and then the genies come tearing in, with the thunder and lightning a-ripping around and the smoke a-rolling, and everything they're told to do they up and do it. They don't think nothing of pulling a shot tower up by the roots, and belting a Sunday-school superintendent over the head with it—or any other man."
> "Who makes them tear around so?"
> "Why, whoever rubs the lamp or the ring. They belong to whoever rubs the lamp or the ring, and they've got to do whatever he says. If he tells them to build

a palace forty miles long, out of di'monds, and fill it full of chewing gum, or whatever you want, and fetch an emperor's daughter from China for you to marry, they've got to do it—and they've got to do it before sun-up next morning, too. And more—they've got to waltz that palace around over the country wherever you want it, you understand."

"Well," says I, "I think they are a pack of flatheads for not keeping the palace themselves 'stead of fooling them away like that. And what's more—if I was one of them I would see a man in Jericho before I would drop my business and come to him for the rubbing of an old tin lamp."

"How you talk, Huck Finn. Why, you'd *have* to come when he rubbed it, whether you wanted to or not."

"What, and I as high as a tree and as big as a church? All right, then; I *would* come; but I lay I'd make that man climb the highest tree there was in the country."

"Shucks, it ain't no use to talk to you, Huck Finn. You don't seem to know anything somehow—perfect sap-head."

I thought all this over for two or three days, and then I reckoned I would see if there was anything in it. I got an old tin lamp and an iron ring and went out in the woods and rubbed and rubbed till I sweat like an Injun, calculating to build a palace and sell it; but it warn't no use, none of the genies come. (Pp. 32–33)

Since his youth, Twain had tried to keep the genies in the bottle. He knew from experience—centrally with his father and younger brother—how quickly a hidden impulse could become a raging giant; he knew, too, how a tiny, "dwarf" guilt could grow suddenly into a monster, threatening to destroy him. He wished to keep the genie in the bottle, under control, small, without aggression. Every now and then, the genie popped out of the bottle and Twain vented his fear and anger and disappointments on anyone near, and then he visited his self-accusations upon himself.

In *Huckleberry Finn* he let his genies out; by seeing himself microscopically, through the eyes of a small boy who was growing up, he became the genie—he accepted for the moment what he had bottled up—and he made a book from the process. His imaginative achievement did not endure for him. After the book was completed Twain was soon following his old pattern again, using characters to represent and test his own divisions; these divisions, rather than any possible complex personal unity, preoccupied him. He couldn't hold his little selves together to the extent that Huck could. He barely got the mischievous, disappointed, bitter genies back in the bottle in *A Connecticut Yankee*, and he never quite let them out in a richly realized book again.

By 1905, in *Three Thousand Years Among the Microbes*, he represented himself as microscopic, lost among the innumerable microscopic fragments of his split-up self. He had become so tiny he had to pass through a microscope to find his random pieces. Interestingly, the tramp figure, with whom so much guilt was connected, makes his final appearance in this tale: through an error in his experiment, a scientist enters the bloodstream of the tramp, living in the microbe world inside the body of the giant. A terrible, monstrous genie had taken hold of Twain's sensibility and laid waste to his art. When Twain's artistic capacities became paralyzed, no aesthetic means remained for him to get the genie back into the bottle, and he had never had any means other than art for doing so. Inevitably, he fell into despair and his protective microscopia took possession of his behavior.

Mark Twain told himself on his seventieth birthday in 1905 that his life had ended in fragmentation and depression. "Old Age, white headed, the temple empty, the idols broken . . . nothing left but You, a remnant, a tradition, belated fag-end of a foolish dream, a dream so ingeniously dreamed that it seemed real all the time; nothing left but You, centre of a snowy desolation, perched on the ice-summit, gazing out over the stages of that long *trek* and asking Yourself, 'would you do it again if you had the chance?'" For years Twain's dreams had been filled with these images of his own desolation, of himself in pieces, stranded in a great white waste, locked in place by blank snow and ice, beached on an endless shore under a merciless sun, tormented by a great white glare. He tried to make stories of these dreams; but such works as *The Enchanted Sea Wilderness, Three Thousand Years Among the Microbes,* and *Which Was the Dream?* remained incomplete, as chaotic and uncompletable as bad dreams.

In Twain's personal activities during his last decade the persistence of microscopia was pervasive, and not just in his work. It was especially evident in the enormous amounts of energy and attention he devoted to creating and augmenting his collection of what he called "Angel Fish" for his "Aquarium." His "Angel Fish" were young, preadolescent, presexual girls whom he induced to gather around him; from them, as Hamlin Hill says, "he demanded unquestioning devotion and frequent companionship," and he "lavished affection" on them in return. He gave each an angel-fish pin. "Don't get any older," he wrote to one in 1906; "I can't have it." When this same girl became sixteen, he demanded that she regress to fourteen for his sake. By 1908, he was obsessed with adding new Angel Fish to his Aquarium. Isabel Lyon remarked that "his first interest when he goes to a new place is to find little girls." Two years before his death nearly half of his correspondence was devoted to a dozen angel fish. He had always liked to be called "Youth." His wife, Olivia, called him that. Now, he lived entirely in a microscopic world, imagining himself reflected in his young companions as not only young but also tiny, presexual, weak, girlish.

In Bermuda, just before the onset of Twain's final illness, there is a report that "something very terrible . . . happened. . . . something unprintable," involving Twain's behavior with Helen Allen, the fifteen-year-old daughter of the American consul in Bermuda.[20] However the Allens might have interpreted Twain's actions, it is clear that he would not have regarded her sexually, but as an extension of himself—what Heinz Kohut calls a selfobject[21]—a part of himself, a beautiful little fragment of the self that, like microbes, darted about in the by now completely unstable, fluid aquarium of his self. If he treated her familiarly it would have been because he regarded her as a microscopic part of his tiny being.

20. Hill, *God's Fool,* quoted pp. 127, 128, 195, 261.
21. See *The Restoration of the Self* (New York: International Universities Press, 1977).

Twain, then, ended his literary career and personal life in a floodtide of fragments, "fag-ends" of possible identities. But once, during the years 1876 to 1884, when he created and contemplated Huckleberry Finn, he seemed to be able to fuse his fragments into one magnificent, varied, whole being. He could not maintain that identity for himself in life, but by the grandeur of his momentary powers and the permanency of art he preserved it for us in literature.[22]

22. Those readers interested in pursuing the psychological study of Mark Twain and *Huckleberry Finn* should consult especially Jose Barchilon and Joel S. Kovel, "Huckleberry Finn: A Psychoanalytic Study," *JAPA* 14 (October 1966): 775–814; and three articles by Robert Sears, "Episodic Analysis of Novels," *Journal of Psychology* 85 (1973): 267–76; "Episodic and Content Analysis of Mark Twain's Novels: A Longitudinal Study of Separation Anxiety," in Joseph Strelka, *Literary Criticism and Psychology* (University Park: Pennsylvania State University Press, 1976); and "Content Analysis of Mark Twain's Novels and Letters as a Biographical Method," *Poetics* 7 (1978): 155–75.

II

The Conscious Craft of
Telling the Truth, Mainly

I T was in 1876 that Twain began writing what he called then
"Huck Finn's Autobiography," four hundred manuscript pages he said he
liked "only tolerably well" and even, he claimed, thought of burning. Not
until the winter of 1879–1880 and then again in the following summer, according to Walter Blair, did he manage to put together the book's next five
chapters, 17 through 21, only to find himself at still another dead end. Some
of the most pressing reasons for these fits and starts of composition are
made clear in Jay Martin's essay preceding this section and tracing the dark,
demonic id-driven pressures that Twain's creative unconscious was bringing
to the book. From 1880 to the summer of 1883, a period when he was writing other works with accustomed ease, Twain apparently could not, did not
attempt other efforts on this novel. But when he did pick it up again, in the
seventh year of the process, he had what he called "booming working-days"
and piled up "manuscript in a really astonishing way." The high drama of
Twain's long and arduous composition of *Huckleberry Finn* is one of several
issues in his career that have made for lively debate about the nature of his
genius and the reliability of his claims that his books rather wrote themselves. What part, critics have asked, is played by instinct, spontaneity, and
inspiration? Where lie the elements of conscious craft and of a deliberately
imposed and sustained style gradually discovering and revealing its subject
matter?

"Art is the path of the creator to his work," Emerson wrote, and the
thought is apt enough to serve as an epigraph for the four essays grouped
here. Charting in fact various paths by which Twain at last made his way to
Huckleberry Finn, each of these essays attempts to define those transactions
between the writer and his materials that mark the points where they master
or threaten to master him and those others where he exerts the authority of
an often highly deliberate and conscious control. Jeffrey Steinbrink, focusing
on the 1876 manuscript, analyzes the ways in which Twain's initial conflicting desires and intentions—to make Huck's book a continuation of *Tom
Sawyer*, to make it a very different kind of book altogether—led to complications roughly the equivalent of taking one's first horse ride up on the
back of a genuine Mexican plug. The efforts Twain made to stay in that
saddle, Steinbrink shows, are evident still, especially in the book's early
chapters, in which Twain is hard at work "testing ideas, proposing and experimenting with lines of action, revising aspects of characterization, and

abandoning blind leads *in the text itself.*" They were efforts that turned out to be ineffectual, and Twain was thrown, at least temporarily, when his darkening materials ran right out from under him at the end of Chapter 16.

Whatever those difficulties that came in 1876 to seem unmanageable, Twain's achievement in having captured the basic cadences of Huck's idiom is evidenced that early. Nonetheless, as Victor Doyno demonstrates in his essay on the word and phrase changes Twain made both within the manuscript and between the manuscript and the first edition, Huck's voice did not arrive in the world as either fully consistent or always capable of "throw-[ing] in an amount of style that was suitable." Twain's brilliant strategy of removing himself from Huck's storytelling created problems requiring a talent for controlled revision. The alterations Doyno selects illustrate that Twain, too, had his appreciation for what Hawthorne had called "the very gem of a word" even when he was creating an unwashed vernacular.

A literary-critical crux if ever there was one, the Evasion episode at the Phelps farm, Twain's conclusion of the novel, is a topic that has been bully-ragged as if it too had to sit up straight at table with Miss Watson. Mr. Eliot and Mr. Trilling and Mr. Marx, in having had their say some years ago, managed only to open up a subject that is more than a crux. In the words of Jim Baker's enterprising blue jay atop that abandoned mining cabin: "It looks like a hole, it's located like a hole—blamed if I don't believe it *is* a hole!" And so, in a world where "Animals talk to each other, of course," it's a mistake to think that critics won't do as much. The debate thus goes on here, in two essays that contend, on grounds radically different, that Twain is completely in control of his narrative and that, far from wrenching and ruining the rich vitality of Huck's vision, he created a conclusion that has an inexorable logic. Fritz Oehlschlaeger's argument is that Twain's burlesque embodies his bitter and savage irony and registers the uncompromising view he takes of the grim choice Huck is left with: society, safety, and not being himself on the one hand, freedom and perhaps death on the other. Whereas Oehlschlaeger assumes the referential reality of the novel, Millicent Bell, in her formalist/post-structuralist reading, finds the ending consistent, controlled, and steadily prepared for by the novel's earlier incidents because it is absorbed totally into the "textuality"—the tyrannically game-playing literary imagination—of Tom Sawyer's make-up. The Twain whom Bell evokes is an author who has clearly mastered the storytelling and in doing so has taken revenge on the possibilities of authenticity residing in storytelling itself. Huck's fate, in this controversial interpretation, might well be seen as something worse than death.

5   JEFFREY STEINBRINK

Who Wrote *Huckleberry Finn?*
Mark Twain's Control of the Early Manuscript

ALTHOUGH we celebrate the centennial of *Huckleberry Finn* in 1985, it was actually one hundred-nine years earlier, in the summer of 1876, that Mark Twain began the novel at Quarry Farm in Elmira. He wrote William Dean Howells in August that he was underway in "another boys' book—more to be at work than anything else"—and that after 400 pages he liked it "only tolerably well."[1] Shortly thereafter he set Huck aside—for about three years, as it turned out[2]—and with considerably more enthusiasm launched into *1601* for Joe Twichell, "A Canvasser's Tale" for Howells's *Atlantic*, and the play *Ah Sin* with Bret Harte. He subsequently gave his attention to projects that led to *A Tramp Abroad, The Prince and the Pauper,* and *Life on the Mississippi* and to literary burlesques and other short pieces that Bernard DeVoto has characterized as "mostly painful reading now."[3] So it is that you undertake the writing of a masterpiece—if you are Mark Twain.

That he liked the beginning of *Huckleberry Finn* only tolerably well and that he lavished affection and praise on such lesser books as *The Prince and the Pauper* and *Joan of Arc* are often cited as indications of Clemens's imperfect appreciation or even comprehension of his own work. Such testimony reinforces the impression that his was an undisciplined, unselfconscious genius and lends plausibility to his claim that he allowed his books to "write themselves." Were we to take him at his word in this, we would have reason to regard *Huck Finn* as among the most remarkable instances of automatic writing on record, a kind of speaking in American tongues—allowing for a certain amount of garbling, perhaps, toward the end of the recitation. While no one seems willing to go quite this far, it has become a critical commonplace that Mark Twain "builded" better than he knew, that his finest writing arose all but spontaneously from a reverie whose focus was his boyhood in the antebellum Mississippi valley.[4]

---

1. Henry Nash Smith and William M. Gibson, eds., *Mark Twain–Howells Letters* (Cambridge: Harvard University Press, 1960), 1 : 144. Subsequent references to this text (abbreviated *MTHL*) appear parenthetically in the essay.

2. Walter Blair, "When Was *Huckleberry Finn* Written?" *AL* 30 (March 1958): 1–25.

3. *Mark Twain at Work* (Cambridge: Harvard University Press, 1942), p. 56.

4. DeVoto puts the familiar case succinctly: "[Mark Twain] wrote on impulse, and when impulse was in circuit with the deeper levels of his phantasy things went well, but when the circuit was broken he could only improvise. Improvisation was responsible for the worst and commonest blemishes in his books. . . . He caught fire easily and when an 'idea' inflamed him,

How much control, and what kind of control, did Mark Twain exercise over his best work? The beginning of *Huckleberry Finn*, that part of the book written in 1876, offers evidence that can sharpen our understanding of the interplay between inspiration and deliberation that shaped the novel.[5] Clemens's correspondence at the time reveals something of his intention regarding *Huck* as well as his impression, after 400 manuscript pages, of what he had in fact accomplished. More immediately, these early chapters of the book *show* Mark Twain at work on an "inspired" story—testing ideas, proposing and experimenting with lines of action, revising aspects of characterization, and abandoning blind leads *in the text itself*. This is not simply to say that Clemens made up *Huck* as he went along, but that he left a record of that making-up in the book, especially at its outset, when he himself was trying to bring the story to life and sustain its vitality.[6] To uncover this record, the ambition of this essay, is to catch Mark Twain in the process of creation, to glimpse the pattern of choice that allows a book to "write itself."

Huckleberry Finn was born out of two related but in some ways contradictory impulses, Clemens's intention to produce a sequel to *Tom Sawyer* and his desire to write what might be called its supplement. This second impulse is most clearly revealed in a letter he wrote Howells on 5 July 1875, having just completed the *Tom Sawyer* manuscript. "I . . . didn't take the chap beyond boyhood," he says.

> I believe it would be fatal to do it in any shape but autobiographically—like Gil Blas. I perhaps made a mistake in not writing it in the first person. . . .
> By & by I shall take a boy of twelve & run him on through life (in the first person) but not Tom Sawyer—he would not be a good character for it. (*MTHL*, 1:91–92)

Here is the germ of *Huck*, couched in terms that suggest it would be the book *Tom Sawyer* was not, the realization of possibilities that were left unexplored or undeveloped in the earlier work. Seen in this light, *Huck* was clearly to be something *other* than *Tom* rather than its continuation; it was

---

he attacked it with verve and enthusiasm, trusting to luck, providence, or his demon to make it good" (ibid., p. 52). For an extended general consideration of the relationship among inspiration, planning, and revision in Clemens's work, see Sidney J. Krause, "Twain's Method and Theory of Composition," *MP* 56 (February 1959): 167–77.

5. Recent studies of the portion of *Huckleberry Finn* written in 1876 have focused exclusively on its first chapter. See Robert J. Lowenherz, "The Beginnings of *Huckleberry Finn*," *AS* 38 (October 1963): 196–201; James R. Bennett, "The Adventures of Huck Finn in Chapter One," *IEY* 12 (1967): 68–72; and Eugene McNamara, "*Adventures of Huckleberry Finn*: Chapter One as Microcosm," *MTJ* 18 (Summer 1977): 17–18.

6. I think it is legitimate to assume that the first sixteen chapters of *Huckleberry Finn*, as we have them today, are essentially similar to the manuscript Mark Twain completed in 1876, allowing for the addition of the *Walter Scott* episode and the deletion of the "Raft Passage." My assumption is based upon what we know about Clemens's manner in conducting other revisions at about this time, upon a simple comparison of the bulk of the manuscript and that of these early chapters, and upon the notes he made in reviewing the manuscript when he later returned to it. Even if Clemens did substantially revise, however, the record of his experiments and choices—the matter I treat here—evidently survived such revision.

the book that Mark Twain's simultaneous recognition of Tom's richness and misdirection had prepared him to write.

There is nothing contradictory, of course, in a sequel's realizing possibilities that were only latent in its predecessor, but *Huck* was to be generically unlike *Tom* by virtue of its remarkable first-person narrator. Moreover, it was to be a book in which boys were "run" into manhood. With these rather confusing ambitions in mind, Clemens began *Huckleberry Finn*, apparently in July 1876, while he was correcting proof for *Tom Sawyer* and otherwise preparing for that novel's long-delayed publication. His immersion in *Tom Sawyer* is obvious at the outset of Huck's book, whose narrative line begins with a synopsis of *Tom* and whose action appears to commence on the very night of the day upon which *Tom* concludes (with Tom's promising to hold his robber-gang's initiation ceremony "to-night, maybe"[7]). Huck has the last word in Tom's book, pledging to "stick with the widder till I rot" (*TS*, p. 236), and Walter Blair has even proposed that Huck's book begins with the reworking of a chapter excised from *Tom Sawyer*.[8] DeVoto has reinforced our sense of the interrelation of the two books by pointing out "the original impetus that launched" *Huckleberry Finn* in Chapter 25 of *Tom Sawyer*,[9] where Huck says of the money the boys hope to find, "O, that ain't any use. Pap would come back to thish-yer town some day and get his claws on it if I didn't hurry up, and I tell you he'd clean it out pretty quick" (*TS*, p. 177). Then, too, the title page of Huck's book reminds us that he is "Tom Sawyer's comrade." For all the differences between *Tom* and *Huck*, Clemens himself tended quite often to think of them in tandem, at one point remarking to Howells, "Although I mean to publish Huck in a volume by itself, I think I will also jam it & Sawyer into a volume *together* at the same time, since Huck is in some sense a continuation of the former story" (*MTHL*, 1:445−46; letter dated 15 October 1883).

Given the intimate connection between the two books, it seems fair to suppose that Clemens's convictions about the former might have helped to shape his intentions for the latter. If, as he said, he considered *Huck* "another boys' book," what did he believe about the boys' book that so immediately preceded it? Ironically, one of his strongest beliefs upon finishing the manuscript of *Tom Sawyer* was, "It is *not* a boy's book at all." He wrote Howells, "It will be read by adults. It is only written for adults" (*MTHL*, 1:91; letter dated 5 July 1875). Just what brought him to this conclusion is not entirely clear, although his disdain for contemporary juvenile fiction no doubt colored his judgment. As early as 15 March 1871 he wrote his

---

7. *The Adventures of Tom Sawyer; Tom Sawyer Abroad; Tom Sawyer, Detective* (Berkeley: University of California Press, 1980), p. 235. Subsequent references to *The Adventures of Tom Sawyer* (abbreviated *TS*) are to this edition and appear parenthetically in the essay.

8. *Mark Twain and Huck Finn* (Berkeley: University of California Press, 1960), p. 99. "*Tom Sawyer* was much on its author's mind that summer," Blair observes, speaking of Clemens's beginning *Huckleberry Finn* in 1876. "Chapter proofs followed him to the Farm. In August he acknowledged receipt of copies of the British edition and mentioned at least partially dramatizing the book."

9. *Mark Twain at Work*, p. 47.

brother Orion, "My opinion of a children's article is wholly worthless, for I never saw one that I thought was worth the ink it was written with. . . . I have no love for children's literature."[10] However fervidly he held this attitude while writing *Tom Sawyer*, he did not hold it long thereafter. At Clemens's request, Howells read the manuscript of the book in November 1875 and wrote him upon finishing it that it was "altogether the best boy's story I ever read. It will be an immense success, but I think you ought to treat it explicitly *as* a boy's story. Grown-ups will enjoy it just as much if you do; and if you should put it forth as a study of boy character from the grown-up point of view, you'd give the wrong key to it" (*MTHL*, 1 : 110–11; letter dated 21 November 1875). A bit earlier, on 15 October, Clemens had written Howells that in regard to literary matters, "Yours is the recognized critical Court of Last Resort in this country; from its decision there is no appeal" (*MTHL*, 1 : 107). Now he acted on that belief, acquiescing immediately to Howells's judgment of *Tom Sawyer*. "Mrs. Clemens decides with you," he wrote Howells, "that the book should issue as a book for boys, pure & simple—& so do I. It is surely the correct idea" (*MTHL*, 1 : 112; letter dated 23 November 1875).

This radical, almost instantaneous reversal in Clemens's conception of *Tom Sawyer* is startling if not altogether unaccountable. He had been and was to remain impatient of labels and critical abstractions, after all, and was much more likely to be struck by Howells's liking of the book than by his categorization of it. Moreover, *Tom Sawyer* surely contained much that was atypical in children's literature of the time—violence, drunkenness, brutality, and murder; a cast of vernacular characters in a vernacular setting; and satire, particularly satire directed at excesses of piety and propriety. In many respects it is a tribute to Howells's iconoclasm that his definition of juvenile fiction was broad enough to hold such elements. Still, Clemens's capitulation raises questions about his grip on his material and his apprehension of the audience for which he wrote. Having allegedly had "only adults" in mind as he produced (or at least as he completed) *Tom Sawyer*, he was nevertheless persuaded, evidently without a struggle and in the space of less than two days, that *Tom*'s best and most appropriate audience was made up of children. When he made final revisions in the manuscript in January 1876, he agreed with virtually all of the minor prunings and softenings that Howells had suggested "since the book is to be for boys & girls,"[11] and he even initiated the best-known substitution himself—Huck's "they combed me all to thunder" for "they combed me all to hell"—because, he assured Howells, "the book is now professedly & confessedly a boy's & girl's book" (*MTHL*, 1 : 122; letter dated 18 January 1876). Having discovered that he

10. *Mark Twain's Collected Letters, Vol. 3*, ed. Michael B. Frank (Berkeley, Los Angeles, London: University of California Press, forthcoming).

11. Howells's suggestions and Clemens's subsequent revisions of the *Tom Sawyer* manuscript are treated in DeVoto, *Mark Twain at Work*, pp. 12–14, and in Blair, *Mark Twain and Huck Finn*, pp. 78–82. For a consideration of Clemens's strategic choices in telling Tom's story, a discussion in many ways complementary to the one presented here, see Hamlin Hill, "The Composition and Structure of *Tom Sawyer*," *AL* 32 (January 1961): 379–92.

had written a book for children, Mark Twain was determined to do his best to erase any fingerprints he might have left when he thought he was writing for adults.

While this discovery appears to have affected the character of *Tom Sawyer* in only minor ways, coming as it did after the fact of the manuscript's composition, it would have—it must have—been clearly in Clemens's mind as he began *Huckleberry Finn* in July 1876. On 24 June, apropos of *Tom Sawyer*'s status as a book for boys and girls, he had written his fellow members of the Board of Directors of Elisha Bliss's American Publishing Company that *Tom* was "a new line of writing for me"; [12] and on 22 July, by which time *Huck* was no doubt well underway, he again acknowledged his anxiety over having turned to the production of children's books. "I am solicitous about Tom Sawyer," he told Bliss, "because this is an experiment." [13] As the immediate follow-up to this experiment, *Huck* was the first of Mark Twain's major works intended from the outset as juvenile fiction. Having written one boys' book without trying, he was self-consciously trying, in the summer of 1876, to write another.

So we come to an initial benchmark against which to measure Mark Twain's control over his material in *Huckleberry Finn*: To what extent is the novel, or at least that portion of it written in 1876, adequately described as a boys' book? Did the term have any real critical significance for Clemens, and, assuming it did, how is its influence evident in the text? The first of these questions has provoked a chorus of answers, but the predominant voices of popular and scholarly opinion seem in one way or another to echo T. S. Eliot's observation that while "*Huckleberry Finn* is, no doubt, a book which boys enjoy, . . . [it] does not fall into the category of juvenile fiction." [14] The pertinent question for the purposes of this inquiry, however, is not how—or by whom—*Huck* is to be read, but how it was written. Do the novel's first sixteen chapters bear witness to Clemens's expressed intention to write a boys' book?

There can, of course, be no final answer to a question whose crucial term—*boys' book*—is so patently subjective. To complicate the question further, the possibility exists that Clemens put his intention to write for children entirely out of his mind in 1876, reckoning that if he accidentally produced a child's book in writing *Tom Sawyer*, there was no need to do so deliberately in the case of *Huck Finn*; this would be to say that, at least in respect to creating juvenile fiction, he sought to exercise no control at all. But such reasoning, if it can be called reasoning, seems specious even by Clemens's volatile critical standards. He had before him an operational definition of a "boys' book" in *Tom Sawyer*, whose galleys were still wet from the presses. That he revised *Tom* with an eye toward its young readers, tem-

12. Typescript in Mark Twain Papers.

13. *Mark Twain's Letters to His Publishers, 1867–1894*, ed. Hamlin Hill (Berkeley: University of California Press, 1967), p. 101.

14. T. S. Eliot, "Introduction," *The Adventures of Huckleberry Finn* (New York: Cresset Press, 1950), p. vii.

pering its language and taming its satire, implies that writing for a juvenile audience meant *something* special to him and that this "something" largely took the form of a mild protectiveness regarding the sensibilities of boys and girls. This is not to say that *Tom Sawyer* became a conventional children's book as a consequence of Mark Twain's revisions, but that these revisions reflect his willingness—even his anxiety—to bring his work at least superficially into line with some of the genre's prevailing conventions.

To what extent, then, do the first sixteen chapters of *Huckleberry Finn* seem to conform to this admittedly elusive and implicit set of standards for boys' books? Given Mark Twain's stunning innovation in point of view, perhaps the most surprising observation one might make about *Huck* is that its language, however colloquial, is never merely coarse. Huck's narrative voice is remarkably free of the kinds of indelicacies that Clemens had pruned in revising *Tom Sawyer* (substituting "water" for "foul slop," for instance, and "drenched" for "reeking"). Further, such critics as Blair, Kenneth S. Lynn, and Albert E. Stone have maintained that the book does not truly darken until *after* Chapter 16, and/or that its serious social commentary begins only at that point.[15] Such observations give rise to speculation that, by the time he returned to the manuscript in 1879–1880, Clemens may no longer have regarded *Huck* as a book for children and that he accordingly allowed himself greater freedom as an ironist and social critic at that time than he had in 1876. These are useful and provocative generalizations, but like most generalizations about Clemens's work they admit to exceptions, and the major exception here is Pap Finn.

To say that Pap is a "dark" presence in the 1876 portion of *Huckleberry Finn* is something of an understatement: He bullies the widow, threatens Judge Thatcher, defiles St. Petersburg, and kidnaps and abuses his son, all with a drunken fanaticism that operates just beyond the fringe of comedy. Still, *Tom Sawyer* serves to remind us, as it may have served to reassure Clemens, that such a figure is not necessarily off-limits in a boys' book. Injun Joe, after all, had been a pretty hard lot. But Pap is different from Injun Joe in the intensity of his impotent fury and in the single-mindedness with which he comes to direct that fury and its concomitant violence at Huck. Huck's first-person narration shortens our distance from this violence, this extraordinary *parental* violence, and even if we don't directly take Pap's beatings, we feel them in Huck's line, "I was all over welts" (p. 47). Ultimately, toward the end of Chapter 6, we experience the full force—and terror—of this violence as Pap tries to kill Huck in the cabin in which he has imprisoned him.

The episode begins with Pap's determining that "he had enough whiskey . . . for two drunks and one delirium tremens" and then dropping into what Huck calls a "blind drunk," from which he awakens "looking wild and skip-

---

15. See, for example, Blair, *Mark Twain and Huck Finn*, p. 152; Kenneth S. Lynn, *Mark Twain and Southwestern Humor* (Boston: Little, Brown, 1959), pp. 198–245; and Albert E. Stone, *The Innocent Eye: Childhood in Mark Twain's Imagination* (New Haven: Yale University Press, 1961), pp. 144–45.

ping around every which way and yelling about snakes. He said they was crawling up his legs. . . . I never see a man look so wild in the eyes" (p. 51). The wildness mounts in Pap, father becoming monster, as he "crawls" and "wallows" around the cabin until Huck's full horror is realized:

> By-and-by he rolled out and jumped up on his feet looking wild, and he see me and went for me. He chased me round and round the place, with a clasp-knife, calling me the Angel of Death and saying he would kill me and then I couldn't come for him no more. I begged, and told him I was only Huck, but he laughed *such* a screechy laugh, and roared and cussed, and kept on chasing me up. . . . I thought I was gone.

Pap exhausts himself in the chase, Huck tells us, "and said he would rest a minute and then kill me." But even at that, Mark Twain has saved a final detail, one last bit of action to drive the horror home:

> By-and-by I got the old split-bottom chair and clumb up, as easy as I could, not to make any noise, and got down the gun. I slipped the ramrod down it to make sure it was loaded, and then I laid it across the turnip barrel, pointing towards pap, and set down behind it to wait for him to stir. (P. 52)

Surely this is among the most powerful images in the 1876 portion of *Huckleberry Finn*—the boy, with the chilling deliberation to which his fear has brought him, preparing to shoot his father to save his own life. Animal brutality has been met by animal cunning and the drive for self-preservation. In the end the two animals are saved from one another by the onset of the same animal necessity, sleep.

However one were to define the term, it is hard to imagine that Clemens regarded such material as the stuff of which a "boys' book" is rightly made. It is conceivable that the same sensibility that balked at including *hell* and *reeking* in one such book would deliberately admit the very graphic possibility of parricide in another, but not likely; even Clemens's sensibility, for all its whimsy and lack of discipline, was not so divided.[16] It seems to me, rather, that this episode in the early *Huck* manuscript demonstrates how little effect his intentions had in a piece of "inspired" writing. Even, as in this case, where those intentions had been sharpened by his earlier experience in revising *Tom Sawyer*, the prerogatives of the narrative itself took precedence over resolutions and formulations arrived at before the fact. This is at least part of what Clemens meant when he said that his books wrote themselves: His preconceptions about a work were easily displaced by the possibilities and demands fashioned by his autocratic imagination. Howells had recognized the point in the *Tom Sawyer* manuscript, about a third of the way through, where this imagination was fully engaged, and he thereafter virtually stopped making suggestions for revisions. "When you fairly swing

16. That Clemens's conception of his boys' books would have disallowed the inclusion of such an episode is further suggested by Stone's contention that the juvenile fiction he wrote "modeled itself on local products" of his Nook Farm neighbors. These genteel products, turned out by such neighbors as Harriet Beecher Stowe and Charles Dudley Warner, typically "exploited . . . experiences of childhood and domestic life and [were] written to interest all members of a family" (*The Innocent Eye*, p. 5).

off," he wrote Clemens, "you had better be let alone" (*MTHL*, 1:111; letter dated 21 November 1875). Clemens himself came to something of the same conclusion, and in his desire to "let alone" the creative impulses that shaped some of his best work he figuratively endowed that work with its own energy and volition. "As long as a book would write itself," he said, "I was a faithful and interested amanuensis and my industry did not flag, but the minute that the book tried to shift to *my* head the labor of contriving its situations, inventing its adventures and conducting its conversations, I put it away and dropped it out of my mind."[17] A book can write itself only when invention is free to override intention. This account of the creative process implicitly acknowledges Mark Twain's willingness to relinquish conscious control of a manuscript and offers a rationale for his forfeiture of—or at least his impatience with—such burdensome responsibilities as planning and managing a narrative.

It is, of course, Mark Twain himself who has done more than anyone to promote his image as an automatic writer. While he was at work on *Tom Sawyer*, for example, he wrote to thank Howells for some suggestions regarding the story but then added, "Since there is no plot to the thing, it is likely to follow its own drift, & so is as likely to drift into manhood as anywhere—I won't interpose" (*MTHL*, 1:87–88; letter dated 21 June 1875). Similarly, in an 1879 interview he described his latest project, *A Tramp Abroad*, as a "gossipy volume": "It talks about anything and everything, and always drops a subject the moment my interest in it begins to slacken. It is as discursive as a conversation; it has no more restraints or limitations than a fireside talk has."[18] Then, too, there are the familiar accounts of the ease with which he sometimes wrote. "I haven't piled up MS so in years," he told Howells as he neared the end of *Huckleberry Finn*. "Why, it's like old times, to step straight into the study, damp from the breakfast table, & sail right in & sail right on, the whole day long, without thought of running short of stuff or words" (*MTHL*, 1:435; letter dated 20 July 1883). Later he added, "I've written eight or nine hundred MS pages in such a brief space of time that I mustn't name the number of days; *I* shouldn't believe it myself" (*MTHL*, 1:438; letter dated 22 August 1883). The beginning of *Huck* seems to have come almost as easily as its conclusion, its 400 manuscript pages occupying Clemens for just about a month.

These accounts further the notoriety of Mark Twain's unconscious genius and leave the impression that he was somehow better off *not* to try to control his gifts but to trust to the providence of his untrammeled imagination to summon and shape his material. He is the great writer above all great

17. Bernard DeVoto, ed., *Mark Twain in Eruption: Hitherto Unpublished Pages about Men and Events* (New York and London: Harper, 1940), p. 196.

18. "Mark Twain Interviewed," *New York World*, 11 May 1879, p. 1, clipping in Mark Twain Papers. About a year later Clemens wrote in the same vein in advising his brother Orion to worry less about planning his own work: "Keep in mind what I told you—when you recollect something which belonged in an earlier chapter, do not go back, but jam it in *where you are*. Discursiveness does not hurt an autobiography in the least" (holograph in Mark Twain Papers; letter dated 6 May 1880).

writers whose work, in its diversity and unevenness, its soaring successes and stunning failures, makes such a thesis plausible. The evidence of such texts as the early *Huck Finn* manuscript, however, allows us to refine our understanding of Mark Twain's creative faculty. At least as revealingly as anything else in his canon, it demonstrates that while it was the function of Clemens's imagination to provide him with a galaxy of possibilities, openings, and alternatives, it was his judgment, every bit the active partner, that determined which constellations to follow in plotting the course of his narrative.

"*Huckleberry Finn*," said Eliot, "is not the kind of story in which the author knows, from the beginning, what is going to happen." [19] The portion of *Huck* written in 1876 suggests the degree to which Eliot's remark accurately characterizes Mark Twain's fictional method, especially when he was caught in the throes of inspiration. That "method" might best be described by Huck's words in the first chapter: "All I wanted was to go somewheres; all I wanted was a change, I warn't particular" (p. 19). For Mark Twain, "going somewheres" meant keeping a narrative line moving, in this case a line that Huck immediately inherited from *Tom Sawyer* and that his own book at first seeks merely to continue. At the end of Chapter 1, just at midnight, Huck is happy to discover "sure enough there was Tom Sawyer waiting for me" (p. 21). Tom waits for us, too; the adventures begun in his book are bound to continue.

For a short while they do, Chapter 2 treating Tom's tricking Jim and conducting the robber-gang's initiation ceremony. This boys'-book stuff gives way at the beginning of Chapter 3 to Huck's comic meditation on the efficacy of prayer, the anecdotal nature of all three episodes reinforcing the impression that Clemens "warn't particular" at this point about the course of his story as long as it went "somewheres." But beginning with the third paragraph of Chapter 3 two things signal that Clemens was making conscious choices to affect that course. First, Huck reminds us of Pap's existence and so prepares the way for the important plot action that Pap will initiate. In doing so he makes it clear that he "didn't want to see [Pap] no more" and that he "warn't comfortable" because he feared that rumors of Pap's death were unfounded, his candid hope that his father is dead amounting to the first significant trespass of the bounds of conventional juvenile fiction in the book (p. 30). Second, Huck becomes disillusioned with the robber-gang, and Mark Twain summarily dismisses Tom Sawyer from the story. "I judged that all that stuff was only just one of Tom Sawyer's lies," Huck says of Tom's play-world. "I reckoned he believed in the A-rabs and the elephants, but as for me I think different. It had all the marks of a Sunday school" (p. 33). Because the writer concurs in this judgment, and especially because he has

19. Eliot, "Introduction," p. viii. Henry Nash Smith has amplified Eliot's comment and anticipated a portion of my argument in remarking of *Huckleberry Finn* that Mark Twain "did not see clearly where he was going when he began to write, and we can observe him in the act of making discoveries both in meaning and in method as he goes along." *Mark Twain: The Development of a Writer* (Cambridge: Harvard University Press, 1962), p. 114.

come to appreciate the ways in which his narrator "thinks different," Chapter 3 becomes a watershed in the early portion of *Huckleberry Finn*, establishing the real line of demarcation between Tom's book and Huck's and describing a sharp turning away from the lighter Matter of Hannibal to the darker themes of tyranny, escape, and tenuous freedom that the latter will pursue. Mark Twain is not simply warming up in these first three chapters; he is testing his materials, his ideas, and his characters and making vital choices as the story unfolds, determining who is to prevail—or at least to survive—and under what circumstances. Tom Sawyer simply fails to make the cut.

Jim, on the other hand, remarkably succeeds. Every indication in the story's early going is that Mark Twain conceived of Jim as a two-dimensional comic character whose simplicity made him a likely object of Tom's pranks and whose innocent chicanery and sense of self-importance (at having been flown around the world by witches) made him fair game for the writer's mildly derisive humor. This early vision of Jim comes clearly into focus in Chapter 4, when Huck, having seen Pap's tracks in the new snow, consults Jim and his hair-ball about the future. Jim responds to Huck's anxiety no more nobly than the King or the Duke would have, telling him that sometimes the hair-ball "wouldn't talk without money." When Huck offers "an old slick counterfeit quarter" Jim accepts it, saying that if he places it between the halves of a new Irish potato overnight, "it wouldn't feel greasy no more, and . . . anybody in town would take it in a minute, let alone a hairball." But Huck does not have to wait overnight for this counterfeit to be accomplished; Jim simply places the greasy brass quarter under the hair-ball and tells Huck his fortune. Jim has merely been thinking out loud about how *he* can eventually make use of the coin. His innocent duplicity is transparent—and funny—to the reader but not, of course, to Huck, and it prepares the way for Jim's mumbo-jumbo fortune-telling ("You gwyne to have considable trouble in yo' life, en considable joy"). One can only wonder whether Mark Twain had *any* inkling of the role that either Jim or the river would play in the book when he had Jim end the performance by warning Huck, "You wants to keep 'way fum de water as much as you kin" (pp. 36– 38). The effect of the episode as a whole is to define Jim as an engaging minor character whose usefulness and range are largely exhausted in the comic interlude that immediately precedes Pap's eruption into the story.

As soon as he arrives on the scene at the end of Chapter 4, Pap dominates the action of the novel. His power diminishes but never wholly abates until the book's last page, when Jim tells Huck that Pap was the murdered man in the house of death. Until that moment Huck's flight has been at least in part from his father. Significantly, Pap seems to have been the one character/plot device that Mark Twain had firmly in mind when he began *Huckleberry Finn*, Huck's prediction of his return toward the end of *Tom Sawyer* suggesting that Pap would likely be of some importance in *Tom's* sequel. Pap's advent offers possibilities for coherent action in the narrative, something that its early chapters lack, but the action that he actually precipitates raises logical problems that show Mark Twain at his managerial worst. To account for the widow's inability to wrest custody of Huck from Pap, even with the help of the influential Judge Thatcher, he invents a "new judge that had just come" and in a single short paragraph dismisses the widow's just and sensible claims (p. 42). In the process of doing so, Mark Twain spots a chance for burlesque and so has the new judge undertake Pap's reformation. In the wake of the resulting disaster the new judge "felt kind of sore" and "reckoned a body might reform the ole man with a shot-gun, maybe," but he apparently remains adamant in his determination that Pap is a better guardian for Huck than the widow or Judge Thatcher (p. 44).

A similarly loopy logic underlies, even if it does not entirely undermine, the principal action of the 1876 manuscript, Pap's abduction of Huck in Chapter 6. Pap has "[gone] for Judge Thatcher in the courts to make him give up that money" and apparently believes he has a good chance of win-ning. We know this because even *after* Pap kidnaps Huck, "his lawyer said he reckoned he would win his lawsuit and get the money" (pp. [45]–47). We know, too, that this is all Pap is after; the burden of Huck's upbringing is a responsibility he has long since learned to ignore. Yet in a kind of snit at the widow's condescension he catches Huck, carries him away, and imprisons him in the hut on the Illinois shore, thereby diminishing the legal ground he has to stand on in suing for Huck's money. In fairness to Clemens it ought to be acknowledged that this is an instance of Pap's illogic, not the writer's, but it is a substantial such instance, nevertheless, as well as one of enormous consequence in the story. It is compounded by our suspicion that even Pap would eventually have come to recognize that to confine Huck was also to confine himself, and that to do so was in no way likely to bring him closer to the $6,000 that brought him back to St. Petersburg in the first place. Finally, although the widow and the Judge are conjecturally in a position to strike a deal with Pap—exchanging the money for Huck—they do not, leaving us, by default, to construe their motives.

My purpose here is not to indict Mark Twain for inelegant manipulations of plot nor to catalog the creaking coincidences—the strategic arrival and disappearance of canoes, for instance—upon which Huck's book sometimes depends. For the most part we gladly overlook these problems, our pleasure more than keeping pace with Clemens's determination that the narrative move forward at almost any cost; *Huckleberry Finn* is a remarkably well-told story even if it is indifferently plotted. But I do mean to bring attention to the process of choice that guided that forward movement. Up until the point in the novel where Pap kidnaps Huck, in Chapter 6, those choices are as often as not arbitrary, unconvincingly motivated, and plot-ridden, Clem-ens's anxiety to get some action underway betraying itself in the narrative like the brass in Huck's counterfeit quarter. Some of that action centers around Tom Sawyer, a character Mark Twain knew but had come to dis-dain; more of it is driven by Pap, a character—actually a caricature or a grotesque—whom he saw, ultimately, from without. Only when these vital choices are generated by Huck himself, as they are in most of the balance of the 1876 manuscript, could the story easily and experimentally evolve.

By "experimentally" I mean by virtue of a process of trial and error whose record remains in the text. Once Huck has been abducted in Chapter 6, his story ceases in any substantial way to be a sequel to *Tom Sawyer*. The important characters of the earlier book have fallen away as Huck himself has grown more compelling. St. Petersburg has receded into the distance, its place taken by a more primal, universal, natural environment. Huck functions well in this environment, as does Mark Twain, the two of them together relying on their wits and their instincts to make the tough decisions upon which the vitality of both the boy and the book depend. Once Huck is in control of these vital choices, beginning with his determination to escape from Pap in Chapter 6, Mark Twain unselfconsciously "thinks out loud," through Huck, about the course the narrative is to take, provisionally pursuing an idea or a line of action until a better one presents itself. The developing affinity between the writer and his narrator allows the book to "write itself" in this sense: The myriad plans of escape that dominate the rest of the 1876 manuscript arise simultaneously from the schemings of a thirteen- or fourteen-year-old boy on how best to avoid pursuit and capture and from those of a forty-year-old author with an interest in providing his story with direction, complexity, and resonance. The text itself becomes the proving ground for these schemes, as well as a record of their varying utility.

Huck's escape from the hut on the Illinois shore begins not with a scheme but with an impulse born of desperation. "I was scared," Huck says of Pap's increasingly violent beatings. "I made up my mind I would fix up some way to leave there" (p. 47). Driven and determined, he shortly formulates a plan that will save him from both Pap's brutality and the widow's civility:

> I thought it all over, and I reckoned I would walk off with the gun and some lines, and take to the woods when I run away. I guessed I wouldn't stay in one place, but just tramp right across the country, mostly night times, and hunt and fish to keep alive, and so get so far away that the old man nor the widow couldn't ever find me any more. (P. 48)

As do all of Huck's subsequent plans, this one suggests a line of action that the book might follow. In this case he would become the solitary backwoods runaway, trusting to the wilderness and to darkness to obscure the trail of his flight and necessarily avoiding settlements as he ran. Mark Twain may well have had reservations about the narrative possibilities suggested by such a plan, if he ever considered it seriously, since it carried Huck away from the complexities that "civilization" had earlier put so promisingly in his way. At any rate he dismisses the plan, or at least postpones the opportunity to set it in motion, simply by having Huck fall asleep before Pap drops into a stupor that would allow him to act (p. 51).

Shortly thereafter, at the beginning of Chapter 7, Clemens providentially supplies Huck with a drift-canoe, just the piece of luck to give rise to a revision of Huck's plan:

> I struck another idea; I judged I'd hide her good, and then, stead of taking to the woods when I run off, I'd go down the river about fifty mile and camp in one place for good, and not have such a rough time tramping on foot. (P. 54)

This is clearly an improvement on the scheme from Huck's point of view, but it seems unlikely to have been so from Mark Twain's: after the fifty-mile drift downriver Huck would become the static loner whose chief concerns were food, shelter, and avoiding detection. This is the plan, though, that Clemens allows Huck to perfect and begin to put into practice. Moreover, in doing so Huck determines to figure a way to circumvent the only part of the initial plan with any real narrative promise:

> I got to thinking that if I could fix up some way to keep pap and the widow from trying to follow me, it would be a certainer thing than trusting to luck to get far enough off before they missed me. (P. 55)

Sure enough, Pap's timely comment about a prowler helps Huck complete the scheme: "what he had been saying to me give me the very idea I wanted. I says to myself, I can fix it now so nobody won't think of following me" (p. 55).

At this point Huck has the final, ingenious escape plan fully in mind. We know this because Mark Twain immediately gives him the chance to put it into practice—by causing the river to provide Pap with the fragment of a log raft that he conveniently goes off to sell—and he does so unhesitatingly. It is a remarkably complex and deceptive piece of ingenuity, the kind of thing, Huck himself believes, that is worthy of Tom Sawyer. What had begun as an impulse to flee had become a means of escape, provision, and anonymous freedom.

Mark Twain can be seen from time to time stage-managing the process that carries Huck to this plan—providing necessary props, incentives, and opportunities. Although Huck seems satisfied with each of his schemes as it comes to mind, he quickly jettisons a good idea when a better one comes along. The process of arriving at the final escape plan seems to have unfolded easily for Huck and for his creator; certainly it transpires quickly in the text. But one has to wonder what Mark Twain had in mind at this point. Each of Huck's improvements in the plan seems to diminish the literary possibilities inherent in his escape. The more admirable and satisfying the plan becomes, the safer (and so less interesting) will be Huck's situation when the plan succeeds. In fact, the end result of his elaborate and ingenious "murder" scheme is that Huck is free at its conclusion simply to float away from Pap and the widow and the threats they pose; he realizes that after a bit of fuss "they . . . won't bother no more about me" (p. 58). It could be argued that in his eagerness to provide Huck's story with a Tom Sawyer–like "effect" Mark Twain jeopardized his narrative by denying it the tension that derives from pursuit.

He remedies this problem, however, almost as soon as it arises by means of two unlooked-for twists—one in character, the other in plot. The first involves Huck's deciding not to "go down the river about fifty mile" as he had earlier planned but to stay close by St. Petersburg:

> All right; I can stop anywhere I want to. Jackson's Island is good enough for me; I know that island pretty well, and nobody ever comes there. And then I can

> paddle over to town, nights, and slink around and pick up things I want. Jackson's Island's the place. (P. 58)

I have described this as a twist, or change, in characterization; perhaps it could more accurately be called a clarification. Despite his uneasiness with "civilization" and the torments it poses, Huck wants to remain in proximity to "his" town, observing it and slinking unseen through it as he did much of the time he lived there. There are practical advantages to living near the town as well, but Huck here implies that keeping St. Petersburg at just the proper distance might be an anodyne for his curious lonesomeness. The decision to settle on Jackson's Island is the last wrinkle in Huck's escape plan. It represents an enormous improvement in the story line, if only because it revives the possibility of exploiting Huck's tenuous relationship to his community and allows for a series of "adventures" as he shuttles between the island and the town.

The second twist, a twist in plot, is of course Huck's discovery of Jim on the island. It is impossible to say when Mark Twain hit upon the idea of reintroducing Jim and giving him the chance for a larger role in the book, but bringing him to the island at this point was just the right piece of business to open wide new prospects for the narrative. Such an instance of strategic imaginative power calls to mind Howells's admiring exclamation to Clemens, "What a fancy you *have* got!" (*MTHL*, 1:224; letter dated 16 March 1878). Still, to bring Huck and Jim together, Mark Twain has to build one more idiosyncrasy into Huck's nature: He makes him so stubborn and curious as to take unaccountable and foolhardy chances. When Huck stumbles upon the smoking ashes of a campfire in Chapter 8, he responds exactly as we might expect: "I got all my traps into my canoe again so as to have them out of sight, and I put out the fire and scattered the ashes around to look like an old last year's camp, and then clumb a tree" (p. 65). Apparently it never occurs to him simply to leave the island; yet flight has been and continues hereafter to be his instinctive response to danger. But not this time: "By-and-by I says to myself, I can't live this way; I'm agoing to find out who it is that's here on the island with me; I'll find it out or bust" (p. 66). This brashness allows Huck and Jim to meet, and once again our pleasure in the outcome of a narrative inconsistency or manipulation overcomes the skepticism it generates. Although character and plot relate more harmoniously in this portion of the book than they did earlier, Clemens remains willing to take liberties with the former for the sake of the latter. Each of these manipulations demonstrates how unlike a "faithful amanuensis" he could be when an attractive line of action suggested itself.

Jim's reappearance in the novel is clearly among the major milestones of the 1876 manuscript, yet even at this point Mark Twain seems not to have conceived of the status Jim would eventually achieve in the book. Jim is still primarily a comic character whose first lines upon being reintroduced are straight from the minstrel-hall repertoire: "Doan' hurt me—don't! I haint ever done no harm to a ghos'. I awluz liked dead people" (p. 67). No sooner has Mark Twain brought Jim back onstage, moreover, than he has Huck engage him in a comic dialogue about his speculations in "stock." Jim is kindly, gullible, and superstitious; he initially seems even more naive or opaque than Huck and somewhat less resourceful: Both of them were familiar with the ways in which the townspeople would attempt to recover Huck's drowned body from the river, and both watched the booming ferryboat pass by the island, but only Huck was sharp enough to turn his knowledge to a profit by anticipating the floating loaves laden with quicksilver. That Jim "grows" in the course of the novel is due fundamentally to Mark Twain's stressing—or indeed creating—richer aspects of his endowment as the story progresses. In Chapters 8 and 9, however, the greatest problems Jim poses have to do with the logic, or the illogic, of his remaining on Jackson's Island.

Like Huck's, Jim's escape plan has undergone a series of modifications by the time he reaches the island, but the immediate goal of the plan has evidently remained unchanged: to reach the Illinois shore. Modern commentators have remarked that this is not a particularly sound idea, given that the laws of Illinois permitted and even encouraged the capture of fugitive slaves, but the fact remains that it *is* Jim's plan. His luck has brought him only as far as the island, where he has lived for at least three days and nights only on "strawbries en sich truck" (p. 67). When Huck arrives, the provisions improve and the two set up housekeeping, evidently planning on an indefinite stay. This is, after all, just what Huck said he wanted; he has the town at a comfortable distance, a full larder, and the unexpected blessing of companionship. "Jim, this is nice," he says toward the middle of Chapter 9. "I wouldn't want to be nowhere else but here" (p. 76). But what about Jim? Huck tells us, "The river went on raising and raising for ten or twelve days," during which time, apparently, Jim is content to remain on the island, even though Huck's canoe makes the Illinois shore easily accessible (p. 76). Mark Twain needs Jim on the island but has no very satisfactory rationale for keeping him there. In the absence of any convincing motivation on Jim's part, he simply avoids the issue and offers two significant diversions later in the chapter, again by means of the obliging river. It first produces "a little section of lumber raft— . . . twelve foot wide and about fifteen or sixteen foot long"—and sometime thereafter the floating frame house in which Jim discovers a murdered man (p. 76). Whether Clemens knew at the outset the full use he would make of these properties is, again, debatable. Although he discreetly waits almost two entire chapters to put the raft into play, its arrival in Chapter 9 has many of the earmarks of such coincidences as the appearance of the canoe and the *other* raft fragment—the one that propitiously drew Pap away so that Huck could escape—that have previously served to advance his plot. It seems likely, in other words, that he knew what would become of the raft when he introduced it.

I have less confidence in making a similar statement about the house of death. Perhaps it made its way into the book simply as an "adventure," something to punctuate the pleasant but rather dull time the two fugitives spend on the island, as well as an early opportunity for Jim to behave protectively toward Huck. Or is that what he does? Did Mark Twain "know" when he wrote the scene that Pap was the dead man? If he did, then of course Jim would have known, too, and, so knowing, must have chosen not to tell Huck. Why? If he had learned anything at all about Huck in the twelve days they had spent together on the island, it ought to have been that few things would give him greater peace of mind than a firsthand report of Pap's death; Huck himself had told *us* earlier that hearing a rumor that Pap had died made him "comfortable." It seems to me that Jim's more likely motivation in not identifying Pap for Huck, if indeed he knew the dead man to be Pap, was selfish: With Pap safely out of the picture, Jim may well have believed that Huck would return to St. Petersburg. *We* may doubt that Huck would do so, understanding his antipathy to being "sivilized," but to what extent would Jim have been in a position to comprehend such an attitude? If Huck *were* to return to the town, Jim had good reason to fear that Huck might inform on him; and even if he did not suspect this treachery on Huck's part, he would at the very least be losing a useful companion and ally in Huck's departure.

This dark reading of Jim's character is to a degree inconsistent with what we come eventually to believe of him. We might expect the "better" Jim whom we know from the rest of the story to understand Huck's feelings toward Pap and to waste no time in sharing the "comfortable" news of Pap's death, whatever the personal consequences. Perhaps the only reading that makes sense and consistently preserves Jim's "better" character is that the murdered man is *not* Pap Finn when Jim finds him, that Mark Twain had not yet made that "discovery" when he wrote the chapter. In that case, Jim is simply and admirably protecting Huck from the sight of a corpse, a corpse as anonymous to the two of them as it was at the time to their creator. Mark Twain seems to have identified the corpse as Pap by the time Huck talks with Mrs. Judith Loftus in Chapter 11; there Mrs. Loftus speaks of Pap's disappearing with "a couple of mighty hard looking strangers" and having been missing since (p. 86). He certainly made the identification by the time he prepared review and working notes for the continuation of the novel, probably before the summer of 1880. One of the notes, clearly a reference to the house of death, reads, "the dead man is Huck's father." [20] But when he first conceived and wrote the episode, it is entirely possible—even likely—that Mark Twain was thinking simply of the dramatic and comic possibilities it provided, and only as the story further evolved did he see the advantage of identifying the murdered man as Pap.

Such conjectures about the gradual revelation of plot and character to Clemens himself as he worked his way through a narrative are in keeping with his own disclosures about his largely spontaneous and unpremeditated fictional "method," especially in the 1870s. By the time he had finished nine chapters of *Huck Finn* in 1876, *that* story had evolved to the point where Huck and Jim were enjoying a placid idyll on Jackson's Island. Huck's comment at the end of Chapter 9, as they return from the floating house, epito-

20. The notes are reproduced by DeVoto in *Mark Twain at Work*, p. 71. DeVoto's dating of the notes has been corrected by Blair, although Blair is noncommittal about dating the notes in Group B–2, where this reference to Pap occurs. "When Was *Huckleberry Finn* Written?" pp. 10–20.

mizes the feelings of ease and security that their stay on the island has engendered: "We got home all safe" (p. 78). However appealing this sense of well-being may have been to Clemens, and however much he may have felt his outcasts deserved to enjoy it, he realized that it could not be allowed to continue for long in a book of "adventures." So in Chapters 10 and 11 he sends Huck, eager for "a stirring up," off to meet Mrs. Loftus and to learn that the island sanctuary is about to be invaded. By the time Huck returns to the island, now no longer "home," he has formulated *another* plan of escape. Mark Twain has found a way to drive his fugitives back onto the water and in so doing to bring the island-idyll to an end.

Before long, though, a river-idyll threatens to take its place. The raft drifts easily along at three or four miles an hour, and Huck and Jim are once again at ease. "We catched fish, and talked," Huck says, "and we took a swim now and then to keep off sleepiness . . . , and nothing ever happened to us at all, that night, nor the next, nor the next" (pp. 94–95). This is exactly the problem, perhaps the unexpected problem, that Huck and Jim's rafting posed for Mark Twain. The opening pages of Chapter 12 show how unsatisfactory life on a raft might be from the point of view of a writer concerned with the vitality of his story. They contain a catalog of miscellaneous and trivial activity that betrays the lack of focus and absence of significant incident inherent in a "drifting" narrative. Nothing suggests that Mark Twain solved this problem in 1876, and it was probably this failure more than anything else that led him to pigeonhole the manuscript after having written what are now its first sixteen chapters. His ingenuity and the gradually unfolding story it produced kept his characters in motion to this point, but, beyond escaping one kind of pursuit or another, it had given them nothing to do. His provisional responses to this difficulty—sending Huck ashore nightly to buy or borrow supplies and allowing him to hitch a ride with storytelling raftsmen—could relieve but not resolve the issue. These episodes may be interesting, but they are ultimately inessential to the novel, as Clemens's excision of the "Raft Passage" for the purpose of expanding *Life on the Mississippi* convincingly demonstrates. He could likewise simply insert the *Walter Scott* episode at this point in the story (Chapters 12, 13, and 14), probably in 1883, without appreciably distressing the narrative.[21]

These merely anecdotal episodes give way to Huck and Jim's further development of their plans as they approach Cairo at the beginning of Chapter 15: "We would sell the raft and get on a steamboat and go way up the Ohio amongst the free States, and then be out of trouble" (p. [115]). The exigencies of the situation no doubt drove Clemens, like Huck, to this sensible proposal, but he seems from the outset to have had little enthusiasm for it and in fact spent the remainder of the 1876 manuscript trying to avoid or at least to forestall the solution it offered to Jim's dilemma. Critics have observed that Clemens's unfamiliarity with the Ohio made him reluctant to consign Huck and Jim to its waters, even as the lure of the lower Mississippi, intimately familiar and rich in associations, grew more powerful as the raft con-

21. The dating is from DeVoto, *Mark Twain at Work*, pp. 62–63.

tinued its southward drift. At this point, characteristically, he resorted to a kind of holding action, an interlude that postponed his having to face the difficulties that geography and common sense had conspired to create. By separating Huck and Jim in the fog, reuniting them, and treating in detail Huck's trickery and the lesson it affords him, Mark Twain diverts our attention from his problems with plot and in the process gives his characters a chance to grow.

It is among the ironies of the textual history of *Huckleberry Finn* that the last two chapters written in 1876 (Chapters 15 and 16), those that apparently brought Mark Twain's frustration with the book to the point where he chose to discontinue it, are those that more than any of their predecessors demonstrate new depths in his main characters. They include both Huck's implicit recognition of Jim's humanity in "humbling himself" to apologize for the cruel joke with which the fog sequence ends as well as his decision to protect Jim from the slave-hunters after his conscience has driven him from the raft with duty on his mind and treachery in his heart. While Mark Twain was no doubt *interested* in the development of his characters, Chapters 15 and 16 suggest that he delineated some of this development in rather a left-handed way, while his primary energies were directed at fretting over the course of his recalcitrant plot. Even as we take satisfaction in the stature that Huck and Jim achieve in these chapters, we ought to recognize that Clemens's own satisfaction was apparently insufficient to allay his anxiety over the management of events in the story. A skeptical reader in fact suspects that, like the gorgeous Raft Passage that was lifted from Chapter 16, he regarded these revelations of character either as essentially extraneous to the narrative or as being at the service of plot.

Consider, for example, Huck's determination to betray Jim in Chapter 16. To this point Huck has given no sign of uneasiness about helping Jim escape. In Chapter 8 he says, "People would call me a low down Ablitionist and despise me for keeping mum—but that don't make no difference. I ain't ago-ing to tell" (p. 69). Every indication is that he has remained faithful to this pledge, and in fact most recently he and Jim have planned together to sell the raft at Cairo and travel up the Ohio to freedom. In the second paragraph of Chapter 16 the two discuss the possibility that they might already have missed Cairo. Huck says, "That disturbed Jim—and me too" (p. [122]). Although this can be taken to suggest that Huck is undergoing a change of heart, the text makes it more likely that the cause of Huck's uneasiness is identical to Jim's—the fear that they are being carried ever further into the slave states and thus ever further from Jim's best chance to be free. The Raft Passage, an interlude of several thousand words, immediately followed this paragraph in the 1876 manuscript. When the narrative continues Huck is suddenly "all over trembly and feverish" at the thought of Jim's impending freedom: "I begun to get it through my head that he *was* most free—and who was to blame for it? Why, *me.* . . . It hadn't ever come home to me before, what this thing was that I was doing. But now it did" (p. 123). What accounts for this turnabout? It is possible, as Huck himself suggests, that the enormity of his villainy in helping Jim escape comes home to him only as the proximity of Cairo brings Jim's freedom within reach. It is just barely conceivable, as he further suggests, that he is moved by remorse at the thought of helping to deprive "poor Miss Watson" of her property (p. 123). It seems to me at least as likely as either of these explanations, however, that Clemens was anxious for a "stirring up" in his plot and that he was happy for the chance to create another diversionary episode while the raft drifted further downriver. At any rate, if this unlooked-for turnabout in Huck's regard for Jim is an instance of simple manipulation on Mark Twain's part, it is at least a plausible instance, and it opens the way for Huck's encounter with the slave-hunters, one of the richest and most dramatic episodes in the book. It demonstrates Clemens's willingness, once again, to take certain liberties with his characters—in this case with the sudden reversal in Huck's attitude toward Jim's escape—for the sake of a narrative possibility. This is the first time, though, that the possibility thus realized assumes the moral cast of social criticism. The cowardice and duplicity of the slave-hunters—their anxiety that smallpox not contaminate their community, their willingness that it contaminate another, and their guilty handout—are of a piece with the shorebound hypocrisy with which much of the rest of Huck's book will deal. Yet it was almost precisely at this point in Chapter 16 that Mark Twain abandoned the manuscript in 1876.[22]

If Clemens's "tank ran dry" after his first month's work on *Huckleberry Finn*, it was not because his characters were unpromising or his narrative lacked significance; especially in the later 1876 chapters the former had assumed new complexity and the latter had turned more resolutely in the direction of social criticism. His habit of narrative trial and error, of advancing a line of action until it suggested or intersected with another, had, together with his marvelous "fancy," carried the story remarkably forward. But in the course of Chapter 16 problems of the kind that this method of composition creates simply accumulated to the point of bringing the narrative to a standstill. One page toward the end of the chapter shows Mark Twain typically scrambling, through Huck, to come up with a plan that will allow him to follow his impulses (down the Mississippi) without violating the integrity of his story. Trouble begins to mount as Huck and Jim "suspicion" that they have passed Cairo in the fog. When their fears are confirmed, they resolve to make their way back upriver as best they can. "There warn't no way," Huck says, "but to wait for dark, and start back in the canoe and take the chances" (p. 129). This plan promises well in that it allows Huck and Jim to have more Mississippi "adventures" before reaching Cairo. Perhaps it was to extend this possibility that Mark Twain risked another blatant manipulation:

22. Given Clemens's unpremeditative and happenstantial manner in advancing his narrative, it is just possible that his primary purpose in including the slave-hunter episode was simply to provide Huck and Jim with the money they would need if they were to take deck passage on a steamboat up the Ohio, as Jim subsequently suggests. DeVoto has emphatically made a similar case regarding the *Walter Scott* episode, claiming that it "exists solely to furnish Huck with books of history so that he can prepare the coming of the vagabonds [the King and the Duke]" (*Mark Twain at Work*, p. 90). That such conjectures can be made without maligning our sense of Clemens's managerial gifts is perhaps the most telling observation of this kind concerning his control of a manuscript.

"when we went back to the raft about dark the canoe was gone!" (p. 129). Huck, at least, can blame this piece of bad luck on the threadbare snakeskin that began its work in Chapter 10; the reader realizes that the lost canoe is the same one that came along so conveniently when Huck was plotting to escape from Pap. Parts of Huck's story may have written themselves, but Mark Twain himself has to be held accountable for purveying that canoe.

With the disappearance of the canoe Huck and Jim devise yet *another* plan, the last in the series of such plans that have formed the skeleton upon which the 1876 manuscript depends for its structure: "there warn't no way but just to go along down with the raft till we got a chance to buy a canoe to go back in" (p. 129). While this scheme has the advantage of lengthening even further the time Huck and Jim will be likely to spend on the Mississippi, one can sense Clemens's growing managerial desperation in Huck's "there warn't no way . . . there warn't no way." Others have speculated before me that that desperation led to Mark Twain's violent destruction of the raft on what is now the last page of the chapter in a kind of frenzy of anger, frustration, and resignation.[23] He may well have realized at this point that while he could contrive to keep Huck and Jim marginally alive, he had arrived at no satisfactory way to allow them spontaneously to thrive on the river below Cairo. The process of experimentation, improvisation, and choice that had served adequately—and sometimes brilliantly—to this point seemed finally to have let him down. He may well have believed that he had followed one of the blind leads he had so carefully or so fortunately avoided to this point in the novel.

The text of that portion of *Huckleberry Finn* written in 1876 offers a record of the choices Mark Twain made and of the ingenuity he invested in carrying Huck and Jim through the myriad plans by means of which the course of their story was plotted. When he later continued the book he sometimes worked from notes in which he would propose incidents or lines of action for the narrative to follow. Some of them we recognize in the finished text; some of them leave us feeling grateful *not* to recognize them: "Farmer has bought an elephant at auction. Gives him to Tom Huck & Jim & they go about the country on him & make no end of trouble."[24] No comparable notes pertaining to the writing of the 1876 manuscript have survived. Such notes would at any rate be in a sense extraneous, since the manuscript itself contains an inventory of the raw material from which it was constructed. In watching Clemens work through this material, allowing his characters to propose and pursue options as he goes, we come closer to understanding the nature of the tension between spontaneity and discipline upon which he characteristically depended in the best of his "inspired" fic-

23. "At this point," remarks Blair, for example, "I suspect that the cannon-cracker Clemens' temper exploded and blew the book from the writing table to a pigeonhole." The fire of that temper, Blair believes, is reflected in the violence of the accident that befalls Huck and Jim: "This is as ferocious a steamboat as ever split a raft into splinters—a dragon-like monster breathing fire through red-hot teeth" (*Mark Twain and Huck Finn*, pp. 149, 151).

24. DeVoto, *Mark Twain at Work*, p. 77.

tion, and we gain an appreciation, perhaps more accurate than his own, of what it meant to him to allow a book to "write itself."

By the time Clemens stopped writing *Huck* in 1876, the story had taken greater control of him than he had of it. When he wrote Howells that he was only "tolerably" satisfied with this second "boys'" book," he was masking—primarily from himself—some basic truths about the novel to that point. For Huck had ceased to be a boy—that is, a typical or representative boy like Tom Sawyer—even as his story had grown out of the juvenile trappings with which it began. Driven by Mark Twain's imagination and endowed by Huck's voice with a guileless authority, the evolving narrative tapped more and more deeply the unconscious sources of Clemens's art while his energy and attention were focused primarily on problems relating to plot. There was a kind of liberation for him in this imperfectly understood mix of deliberation and inspiration: As he fumed and fretted over the course of his narrative line, his "fancy" spun out nuances of character, complexities of motivation, and revelations of kindness, nobility, and hypocrisy. Mark Twain worked *hard* on the early *Huck Finn* manuscript, even if he worked quickly, and he allowed the record of some of that work to remain in the text, particularly where it involved the choices that guided his plot. What cannot be recorded or discovered is the process by which that fancy, that imagination, produced the book's lasting richness. Concerning that last mystery we must remain, like Mark Twain himself, simply in the dark.

6 VICTOR DOYNO

Adventures of Huckleberry Finn:
The Growth from Manuscript to Novel

In the Rare Book offices of the Buffalo and Erie County Library, behind two doors of a double safe, the partial manuscript of *Adventures of Huckleberry Finn* rests, compact and well preserved. Over six hundred and eighty-seven pages (circa 21.3 by 13.5 centimeters each), usually with sixteen to eighteen lines per page, survive. The sheets reveal numerous legible cancellations, interlinear insertions, and, occasionally, large block insertions on the reverse sides. Some sheets appear to be early drafts, and some must be copy sheets, presumably transcriptions of Twain's complicated revisions of earlier, simpler versions. Renumbered sheets and inserted sheets indicate reorderings and expansions. Significant changes within the manuscript and between the manuscript and the first edition make this material a complex, fascinating record of Twain's creative process and so allow us to observe closely his artistic practices.

Subsequent generations of scholars and critics have been grateful to James Fraser Gluck for securing this national treasure from Mark Twain, and the manuscript has of course been studied to explore several mysteries.[1] Did Olivia Clemens bowdlerize the artistic achievement of her creative husband? No evidence exists in the manuscript to convict her of censorship. Walter Blair has examined the manuscript in his determination of the dates of composition. DeLancey Ferguson and Sidney Krause, among others, pointed out that Twain revised with artistic rather than "popular" considerations uppermost in mind. The publication of the facsimile edition, edited by Louis J. Budd, now offers the fascinating material to any inquiring mind.

1. For example, DeLancey Ferguson wrote "Huck Finn Aborning," *Colophon*, n.s. 3 (1938): 171–80, and then *Mark Twain, Man and Legend* (Indianapolis: Bobbs-Merrill, 1943). Although Ferguson was concerned with the possibility of censorship by Olivia Clemens, he must be credited with realizing the importance of the manuscript for aesthetic study. Bernard DeVoto, in *Mark Twain at Work* (Cambridge: Harvard University Press, 1942) concludes that the evidence reveals Twain was self-censoring, especially about sexuality. Walter Blair's convincing article, "When Was *Huckleberry Finn* Written?" *AL* 30 (March 1958): 1–25, draws upon the manuscript, and in *Mark Twain and Huck Finn* (Berkeley: University of California Press, 1962), he discusses the craftsmanship of the revisions. Sidney J. Krause has used the manuscript to survey "Twain's Method and Theory of Composition," *MP* 56 (February 1959): 167–77. Krause finds Twain "a far more scrupulous craftsman than he is generally given credit for being" and presents to the scholarly world two pages of citations comparing the manuscript and printed text in tabular form.

I am grateful to the late Miss Jane G. Van Arsdale and Mr. William H. Loos, Curators of the Rare Book Room of the Buffalo and Erie County Public Library.

Can any further insight be gained by continued exploration? For the past dozen years, I have studied the manuscript, almost microscopically, with a view toward understanding the genetic process and can now share some examples of how Twain's artful revisions create dynamic, interactive meanings in the novel.

Because Sam Clemens promoted the public persona of Mark Twain as a careless, naive native genius, too casual to do anything so difficult as worry a sentence into shape, the scholar-critic who insists on Twain's deliberate artistry still has an uphill battle. Let a small example serve as an introduction to this problem. One of Huck's comments about Tom Sawyer is surprisingly emblematic of Twain's actual compositional practice. The first manuscript version reads:

> In them circumstances he could always throw in an amount of style that was suitable.[2]

"Throw in" creates an impression of casual imprecision, and "an amount of style" phrases style as a measurable quantity. But Twain crossed out "he could always throw" and substituted above the line an insertion that makes the second version read:

> In them circumstances it warn't no trouble to him to throw in an amount of style that was suitable. (P. 286)

Huck's double negative, grammatically asserting a positive, helps to characterize his idiom. There is only a slight difference between the versions; the constancy of "always throw" becomes "it warn't no trouble to throw" (making the action less difficult, less burdensome). But, of course, the increased casualness is itself the product of revision; thus the tone of bravado conceals the trouble; *ars celare artem*. The manuscript permits us to examine precisely how much trouble Twain took to throw in an amount of style and how each change dynamically affected the completed work of art.

Let us observe first how Twain modulated his narrator's voice. The main surviving portion of the manuscript begins in the Sherburn episode (Chapter 22) where Huck is describing the mob's attempt to avenge the shooting of Boggs by lynching Colonel Sherburn. The townspeople have arrived at Sherburn's house and torn down his fence as he appears:

> Sherburn never said a word—just stood there, looking down. It seemed to me that the stillness was as awful, now, as the racket was before; and somehow it was more creepy and uncomfortable. Sherburn run his eye slow along the crowd; and wherever his eye struck, the people tried a little to outgaze him, but couldn't;

2. MS p. 500; I present first the earliest surviving version, then describe the growth into the finished text. In the following transcriptions, contractions are silently expanded. Illegible cancellations are represented by [XXX]. Cancellations are presented in square brackets, and insertions are heavily underlined. Thus a word that was immediately corrected in the initial writing would be shown as "The man [said] stopped and muttered," but if the passage was later revised it would be noted as "The man [said] stopped and muttered." The second notation represents cancellation and insertion, above the line, with a caret. MS p. _____ indicates the location in the manuscript; the quotations from the first American edition are noted simply by page number.

> they dropped their eyes and looked [sickish and] sneaky. Then pretty soon Sherburn sort of laughed; not the kind of laugh you hear at the circus, but the kind that's fitten for a funeral—the kind that makes you feel crawly. (MS pp. 162–63)

This is Huck's voice, but with a touch of his author's more sophisticated accent; the syntax is far too measured and balanced, the diction too formal and abstract. By the time we reach the climactic vernacular coinage, "crawly," we have the sense of a word that is truly Huck's but nonetheless fails to objectify the pervasive emotions of the crowd. Twain revised the passage at least twice. He canceled "sickish and," preferring to portray the townspeople as furtive but not ill. (A fair number of changes of this type drop acceptable but unemphatic phrases.)

A more important revision affecting Huck's voice happened when Twain was revising the novel for print. He compressed the one sentence with measured literary balance: "It seemed to me that the stillness was as awful, now, as the racket was before; and somehow it was more creepy and uncomfortable." The revised, shorter form does not declare a concern with Huck's point of view; instead it characterizes the scene with a sense of palpable reality: "The stillness was awful creepy and uncomfortable."

A similar modification of Huck's skill in rendering complex psychological states as vivid sense impressions occurred at this paragraph's conclusion. Twain had originally written, "Not the kind of laugh you hear at the circus, but the kind of laugh that's fitten for a funeral, the kind that makes you feel crawly." But perhaps the author thought the negative comparison would appear as an obvious foreshadowing of the immediately following circus episode with the trick rider and the ringmaster. The purely conceptual funeral-circus polarity was canceled when the grim laughter was re-created as "not the pleasant kind, but the kind that makes you feel like when you are eating bread that's got sand in it" (p. 190). Twain enabled Huck to speak in the concrete, tactile, ordinary words that express both his verbal ability and his physical experience. The unrealized feeling "crawly" is now dramatized in a vivid image of physical discomfort. The result of revisions such as these is a tone of voice and set of words for Huck that live precisely because any apparent literary polish has been concealed.

Many who love the novel and think of it as a nonliterary book will be surprised to find out how central a role literary topics played in the earliest surviving version. But, of course, these thematic concerns caused difficulties with Huck's voice, because such matters were beyond his experience. In early drafts literary diction and topics push through Huck's voice and burden it with inappropriately bookish language. For example, at one point, Huck originally related, "The king was saying—in the middle of a sentence." But clearly Huck would be unlikely to say "sentence" in this context, as Twain realized when he revised to "in the middle of something he'd started in on—" (p. 217). A similar, angrier authorial voice breaks through Huck's original explanation to Jim about the King's morality while Huck is conflating the Scheherazade demand for stories with Henry VIII's beheading his wives:

[F e t c h] 'Ring up fair Rosamun.'" Fair Rosamun answers the bell. Next morning, 'Chop off her head'—and next thing you see is the Chief of police with it in [a blanket] a rag. [Ole] And he made every one of them tell him a tale every night; and he kept that up till he had hogged a thousand and one tales that way, and then he got out a copyright, and published them all in a book, and called it Domesday Book—which was a good name, and stated the case. Of course most any publisher would do that, but you wouldn't think a king would. (MS pp. 199–200)

Apparently Clemens's/Twain's own attitude toward some publishers seethes through the boy's voice. But Twain deleted both the bloody description and the "copyright" and "publisher" segments in a deliberate and artistic effort to cancel this appearance of the adult Hartford author behind Huck's voice. Contemporary critics should be aware simultaneously of the extent to which Twain had literary concerns and of the effort he exerted to expunge them from Huck's voice, thereby not only preserving the consistency of his narrative mask but also creating Huck's character by way of his original voice.

The appeal of the novel resides largely in the consistency of this severely restricted point of view and voice: the struggle of that creation arises from the conflict of the adult's knowledge and evaluation with the boy's voice and perception. The creation of the imaginative fusion—almost seamless in the finished novel—can be observed in the manuscript. Huck's remarks about the other characters are, of course, self-characterizations because phrased in his language; they are also descriptions, so that Twain's problem was how to indicate precisely the character of other characters in language that would be appropriate to Huck. Twain lavished much attention in this regard upon Huck's comments about the King, the aging con man. For example, when the King and Duke begin to deceive the Wilks family by posing as distant relatives, they approach a townsperson to inquire where Peter Wilks lives. The local man replies:

> "I'm sorry, sir, but the best we can do is to tell you where he *did* live, yesterday evening."
> The derned old cretur fell up against him; and put his chin on his shoulder, and cried down. (MS p. 233)

The novelist modified, momentarily, the awkward and ineffective up-down physical gestures of the King. First Twain wrote in "kerflummoxed," a word he tried repeatedly to apply to this character, but then decided to make the action more flamboyant by inserting "went all to smash." And he added a splendid ironic simile that captures the King's duplicity: "Sudden as winking, the derned old cretur went all to smash." The simile combines unexpected speed and deception, for the wink also conveys collusion. Moreover, the revised version is open to at least two interpretations; the King may have planned a performance of this sort, or perhaps the simile implies instead his instinctive, unplanned, spur-of-the-moment genius for con games.

By the time the passage reached print, Twain had again touched up the description, inserting "ornery" for "derned." This minor change makes the segment slightly more polite, because the slang for "damned" is dropped.

But the major aesthetic effect is part of a pattern of Twain's revising words that assert to words that dramatize. In this instance, the simple explicit condemnation of "derned" was transformed when Twain substituted a word that justified the attitude.

Once their deception is underway, the King and Duke must not talk in public because of the Duke's pretense about being a deaf semimute. Only in private can the rascals plot their moves. Twain originally has the King explain his plan to the Duke, saying, "after we disappear" (MS p. 290). But when revising, reseeing—and perhaps even refeeling—the novel for print, Twain created a more tactile and perhaps a more ominous turn of phrase, "after we've slid" (p. 228). The elusive deception thus carries relevant connotations of both moral sliminess and the precariousness of the King and the Duke's position.

In his public speech, the King must adopt a different verbal style, one appropriate to his pose as the bereaved English brother, the Reverend Harvey Wilks. The King assumes a higher level of diction—which Twain has him control only imperfectly—and a sanctimonious, condescending tone. He ingratiates himself with the townspeople by making the correct invitations:

> "—they being partickler friends of <u>the</u> diseased. That's why they're invited here this evenin'; but to-morrow we want *all* to come—everybody; for he respected everybody; he liked everybody, and so it's fitten that his funeral orgies should be public." (MS pp. 256–57)

Many readers have not perceived how cleverly Twain constructed this paragraph, giving the speaker two outrageous malapropisms that characterize him as careless and ignorant. Most readers catch the mistake of "orgies," but the earlier error of "diseased" for "deceased" is seldom observed. Because readers perceive at least one error, but probably do not realize the full extent, their situation resembles Dr. Robinson's, and the similarity of perception may predispose readers to sympathize with the honest doctor in the verbal confrontation.

The King repeats "orgies" and receives a corrective note from the Duke, but nonetheless blathers on pretentiously:

> "I use the word orgies, not because it's the common term, because it ain't—obsequies is the common term—but because it's the right term." (MS p. 258)

This passage Twain revised in an enormously subtle way; the modified manuscript version reads: "obsequies bein' the common term—but because orgies is the right term." The insertion of "bein'" subordinates the correct word, makes it more parenthetical, more under the breath, as if less time and emphasis are needed. In addition, the shift to the more declarative, emphatic "orgies is the right term" boldly asserts the malapropism.

The King's voice seems to be in command of the situation as he explains:

> Obsequies ain't used in England no more, now—it's gone out. We say orgies, now, in England. Orgies is better, because it means the thing you are after, more exact. It's a word that's made up out of the Greek *orgo*, outside, open, abroad; and the Hebrew *jeesum*, to plant, cover up; hence *inter*. So, as you see, funeral orgies is an open or public funeral. (MS pp. 258–59)

Twain's meticulous care for the exact sound led him to revise for the printed version, changing "out of" to "out'n" and, with equal attention to detail, turning the "open or public funeral" to "open er public funeral." Tiny changes of this sort certainly improve the dialect, but more importantly such fine tuning of the voice gives greater emphasis to the humorous incongruity between the King's pedantic derivations and his nonstandard usage. His pretentious and ignorant arrogance appears in his voice; he is a master of wordy mispronunciation.

A dramatic conflict arises as the King's ignorance alerts Dr. Robinson to the fraud. The surface conflict involves the two characters, but a deeper contrast exists in how Twain—typically—revised the doctor's speech to emphasize his difference from the King. After Dr. Robinson laughs at the King's imitation of an English accent, he turns to the girls and says:

> "I was your father's friend, and I'm your friend; and I warn you *as* a friend, and an honest one, that wants to protect you and keep you out of harm and trouble, to turn your backs on that scoundrel, and have nothing to do with him, the ignorant hog, with his putrid and idiotic Greek and Hebrew as he calls it. He is the thinnest of thin imposters." (MS p. 262)

Because the doctor is an educated person, he can use unusual words—such as "putrid"—accurately. But Twain revised to make the doctor's language more ordinary, less aristocratic in vocabulary and structure. His contempt is moderated slightly, in the printed version, by the removal of "the ignorant hog" and "putrid." The easy, predictable, intensive "thinnest of thin imposters" Twain simplified to "the thinnest kind of an imposter." Such changes create a characterization of a more approachable, less livid doctor.

In the manuscript, Dr. Robinson first has a vocabulary that is polysyllabic and elevated. He states that the rascal

> "has come here with a lot of empty names and facts which he has picked up somewhere, and you weakly take them for *proofs*, and are assisted in deceiving yourselves by these thoughtless unreasoning friends here, who ought to know better." (MS pp. 262–63)

But his diction becomes more ordinary as "assisted in deceiving yourselves" changes to "helped to fool yourselves." Twain also modified the doctor's characterization of the townspeople by revising "thoughtless unreasoning friends" to "foolish friends." The doctor, in obvious contrast to the King, appears unpretentious and blunt. Moreover, Twain refocused the doctor's judgmental ire by suppressing "weakly." The resulting "you take them for *proofs*" recognizes his fellow townspeople's desire for evidence, and the resulting printed passage characterizes the doctor as a forceful, intelligent, but ordinary person who confronts his neighbors forthrightly.

Originally, the doctor's impassioned pleas had been melodramatic in tone:

> "Mary Jane Wilks, you know me for your friend, and your honest and unselfish friend. Now listen to me: cast this paltry villain out—I beg you, I beseech you to do it. Will you?" (MS p. 263)

But Twain had already had the doctor describe himself as "honest" in his earlier speech, and this self-characterization was dropped. The clichéd phrase—"cast this paltry villain out"—sounds so melodramatic that a standard gesture, a pose, and a tableau spring immediately to mind; the printed "turn this pitiful rascal out" seems more contemptuous. "I beseech you" was dropped, but the printed form of the request gains a lifelike emphasis of tone with "beg" in italics. With revisions of this sort, the doctor's voice becomes more genuine, less pedantic, clichéd, or melodramatic, and the contrast between the pretentious King and the correct, blunt, honest country doctor can be heard more clearly in the finished text. Twain's attention to voice, tone, characterization, and dialogue contributes to the sense of realism and guides the reader's precise allocation of sympathy among the characters.

The development of a more significant character, such as Mary Jane Wilks, apparently required additional novelistic skills. Interacting changes in description or imagery usually also affect the tonality of a passage. When Huck explains the fraud to Mary Jane, his tone is fairly serious in the first version:

> and she set there, mighty impatient and excited and beautiful, but looking kinder happy. So I went to studying it out. I says to myself, [so] I reckon [that] a body that tells the truth [,] when he is in a tight place, is taking considerable many risks; though I ain't had no experience, and can't say for certain. (MS p. 329)

A minor change lightened the tone; Twain added the nonstandard verb "ups," which conveys irregular or surprising action as a young boy would express it: "a body that ups and tells the truth." But a more significant change in imagery reinforces the change to a lighter tone. Creating an additional description of Mary Jane, Twain inserted a simile picturing her as "eased-up like a person that's had a tooth pulled out." The brilliant addition conveys exactly relief from pain and anxiety. Moreover, the ordinariness of the description makes Mary Jane more familiar, hence a less threatening person to whom to tell the truth. The informality of the revised version fits Huck's voice. By the time the passage reached print, it read:

> and she set there, very impatient and excited, and handsome, but looking kind of happy and eased-up, like a person that's had a tooth pulled out. (P. 240)

The change from the manuscript's "beautiful" to "handsome" is in accord with other changes, deemphasizing Mary Jane's physical attractiveness, that keep Huck's point of view appropriate to that of a prepubescent youth. "Handsome" conveys an implication of admiration for a pal. These revisions present an example of the kaleidoscopic interrelationship of speaking voice, characterization, and description. In context they also lighten the tone of the full passage sufficiently to make Huck's moral-philosophical questioning seem spontaneous rather than cunning or conniving.

Similar modifications about sexuality, as well as a change about religion, happen in Huck's emotional farewell scene with Mary Jane, when she offers to pray for him. The first manuscript version reads:

> Pray for me—good land! I reckoned if she'd knowed me she'd tackle a job that was nearer her size. But I bet you she done it, just the same—she was just that kind. She had the grit to pray for Judas Iscarott if she took the notion—

there warn't no back-down *to* her, if *I* know a girl by the rake of her stern; and I think I do. You may say what you please, but in my opinion that girl had more sand in her than any girl I ever see; in my opinion she was just *full* of sand. And when it comes to beauty—*and* goodness—she lay over them all. I hain't ever seen her since that time I see her go out at that door, turn at the stairs and kinder throw a kiss back at me; no, I hain't ever seen her since; but I reckon I've thought of her a many and a many a million times, and of her saying she would pray for me; and if ever I'd a thought it would do any good for me to pray for *her*, I'm dum'd if I wouldn't a done it or bust. (MS pp. 351–52)

Mary Jane's femme fatale gesture, throwing a kiss from the stair, is excised in the manuscript. Had Twain allowed it to stand, the novel would have had an explicit suggestion of a topic it studiously avoids. Part of Huck's innocence is his presexual condition; however appropriate the gesture may have been for the slightly older Mary Jane, it would have complicated Huck's characterization. Either he must ignore it or respond to it, and either choice would have changed the novel. Instead, Twain wrote in an insertion above the cancellation so the section reads, "I hain't ever seen her since that time that I seen her go out at that door, like light and comfort a-going out of a body's life." This simile pays explicit attention only to the emotional impact of separation.

Similar considerations about sexuality—and about tone and characterization—clearly influenced Twain's later revisions for print. Huck's voice first used a slang phrase, and then, perhaps, the author's mind shifted to the girl's figure. The result was a complex tone more appropriate to an experienced Mississippi riverboat pilot than to Huck's presexual naturalness: "there warn't no back-down to her, if I know a girl by the rake of her stern; and I think I do." But Huck's innocent voice is restored in the final version, as he simply praises, "There warn't no back-down to her, I judge" (p. 245).

His innocence is also preserved by a suppression of some intricate satire on religion. The passage opens with Mary Jane's offer to pray for Huck, and he concludes, in the manuscript version, by saying, "if ever I'd a thought it would do any good for me to pray for *her*, I'm dum'd if I wouldn't a done it or bust." The dialect statement, "I'm damned if I wouldn't have prayed for her," carries a witty involution that was lost when Twain shifted the word choice for print to "blamed." Once more Huck seems younger, and the adult author's potential for satiric sharpness is concealed.

The wake and funeral of Peter Wilks provide several opportunities for humor, satire, and social criticism, but much rewriting involved toning down what might have been regarded as too strong or too cruel a satire. One such instance arises after the King and Duke, posing as the relatives, have cried over the coffin:

every woman, nearly, went up to the girls, without saying a word, and kissed them, solemn, on the forehead, and then put their hand on their head, and looked up towards the throne, with the tears running down, and [then let go] then busted out and went off sobbing and swabbing, and give the next [heifer] <u>woman</u> a show. I never see anything so disgusting. (MS pp. 240–41)

The satire on religion is diffused—even to the point of disappearance—by the revision of the manuscript's "throne," a reference to the seat of God, to the printed text's general "sky." The revised text keeps the satire on the woman striking a melodramatic pose, in the manner of Emmeline Grangerford, but omits the religious component in the mockery. Similarly, Twain's original comparison of the women to heifers pictures them as large, dumb, and easily led, and the cancellation of "heifer" and substitution of "woman" was clearly less offensive. The target of the satire remains ostensibly the King and Duke, and only by extension and implication the manipulated townspeople.

The funeral itself could, of course, be a dismal part of the novel, but Twain managed to brighten the ceremony in a remarkable way. After the people have filed past the coffin, while the family is sobbing, Huck observes: "There warn't no other sound but the scraping of feet on the floor, and blowing noses." Then Twain inserted, on the back of MS p. 302: "because people always blows them more at a funeral than they do at other places except church" (p. 232). The scene is lightened by Huck's quasi-philosophical comment; the range of human activity is momentarily summoned and compared. There is a deft jab at church behavior, but Huck's innocent observation seems objective, and whatever emotion the scene deserves is placed in a cultural context.

Huck's narration of the rest of the ceremony is subtly comic: "They had borrowed a melodeum; and when everything was ready, a young woman set down and pumped up its sufferings, and everybody [joined] jined in and sung" (MS p. 304). Twain inserted, after "a melodeum," "a sick one," a qualification clarifying the idea of the instrument as having "sufferings." However, "sufferings" may have been uncomfortably close to the understandable emotions of the Wilks girls, and the printed version relates that "a young woman set down and worked it, and it was pretty skreeky and colicky, and everybody joined in and sung" (p. 232). The idea of sickness is thus redefined in nonemotional but audible fashion. "Skreeky" is a brilliantly created portmanteau word conveying, one assumes, a discordant combination of "scream" and "shriek," while "colicky" suggests minor sickness in a rasping, irregular cough.

Twain's humor was also frequently spontaneous, subtle, and on occasion intricate. The quickness of his verbal wit is aptly demonstrated by a minor revision in his original composition. After the funeral, the real brothers arrive and the townspeople must then determine which pair of brothers is genuine. The doctor says:

> Come along, Hines; come along, the rest of you. We'll take these fellows to the tavern and [confront] affront 'em with the t'other couple. (MS p. 379)

This is an amusing modification; "confront" would be perfectly satisfactory, but "affront" is an apt malapropism, implying insult. Twain had the quickness to seize an ordinary word and spin it in midsentence, converting conventional serviceable language into humor.[3] The doctor's word choice reveals his

3. A similar, midword change occurs when the King is looking for another town to swindle:

Well, early one morning we hid the raft in a good safe place, about two mile below a little bit of a shabby village, named Pikeville, and the king he went ashore, and told us all to stay hid

human imperfections, and the following confrontation will, accordingly, be more interesting.

During the trial scene, Twain originally planned to use the word "kerflummox"; the genuine brother tries to trap the king by asking what Peter Wilks had tattooed on his chest:

> I'm blamed if the king didn't have to brace up mighty quick, or he'd a kerflummuxed, it took him so sudden—and mind you it was a thing that was calculated to make most *anybody* kerflummux, to get fetched such a stunner as that without any notice. (MS pp. 391–92)

However, in print, the unusual "or he'd a kerflummuxed" is canceled and replaced by a different word joined to a simile drawn from the locale: "or he'd a squshed down like a bluff bank that the river has cut under" (p. 256). The coinage—"sqush" for collapse into liquid—reinforces the striking image of a large, impressive facade sinking.

Twain apparently kept an attentive eye on creative transformations of his settings. When Huck is exploring the Phelps farm, an important location—the area where Jim will be imprisoned—was first described as "three little log nigger-cabins in a row beyond the smoke-house; one little hut by itself, down against the back fence" (MS p. 463). Later, probably after Twain had imagined some details of Jim's imprisonment, he added to the manuscript so that the single cabin is portrayed as "one little hut <u>all</u> by itself, <u>away</u> down against the back fence." With admirable verbal economy, with the magic of words the cabin and the fence are moved and Jim's prison made more isolated; hence the tricks and descriptions become more possible and plausible. One could even speculate that the boys attempting to reach Jim would be able to conceal their approach behind the distant fence.

Deliberately, I've reserved two examples of Twain's re-creative artistry, those involving Jim, for the concluding portion of this survey. Quite late in the novel, after Tom and Huck have engineered Jim's escape, Huck and Jim are talking. Huck's voice was obviously continuously present to Twain, but because Jim had been silent for many pages, Twain did not, at first, "hear" Jim:

> "*Now*, old Jim, you're a free man *again*, and I bet you you won't ever be a slave [any] <u>no</u>more."
>
> "En a mighty good job it was, too, Huck. It was planned beautiful, en it was *done* beautiful; en [day] dey ain't *nobody* kin git up a plan dat's mo' mixed up [XXXX] den what dat one wuz." (MS p. 707)

The fascinating revision develops when Twain's aural imagination works on Jim's voice. The change of "day" to "dey" was done in the original flow of the composition, and thereafter no dialect changes are needed because

---

whilst he went up to town and smelt around to see if anybody had [hear] got any wind of the Burning Shame there yet. (MS p. 428)

Shortly before completing the word *heard*, Twain self-critically changed his word choice to be consistent with the emphasis on sense of smell. His artistic imagination, then, was rapid enough to censor mixed sense imagery in midword. But then the significance of the olfactory imagery decreased when, in print, the phallic romp became retitled "The Royal Nonesuch."

Twain was listening to Jim in his mind. But once the voice was "heard" accurately, Twain had to revise, rehearing, to change the earlier "was" to "wuz" or "'uz," capturing precisely Jim's speech.

At an earlier point in the novel, when Jim discusses his daughter's deafness, Twain made the highly unusual change of modifying Jim's speech toward standard. And he inserted a reinforcing phrase in standard English as well. Although the idea might seem surprising, I ask the open-minded critic to read Jim's speech, keeping in mind the conclusion of Shakespeare's *King Lear*, when Lear speaks of Cordelia's death with the overwhelming line of five words, "Never, never, never, never, never." Jim relates that he had punished the child for disobedience and that she did not hear the door slam:

> "—en my lan', de chile [nuvver] <u>never</u> move'! My breff mos' hop outer me; en I feel so—so—I doan know *how* I feel. [XX] I crope out, all a-tremblin', en crope aroun' en open de do' easy en slow, en poke my head in behine de chile, sof' en still, en all of a sudden I says *pow*! jus' as loud as I could yell. <u>She never move'</u>! O, Huck, I bust out a-cryin', en grab her up in my arms en say, 'O de po' little thing! de Lord God Amighty fogive po' ole Jim, kaze he never gwyne to fogive his-seff as long as he live!' O, she was plumb deef en dumb, Huck, plumb deef and dumb—en I'd ben a treat'n her so!" (MS pp. 209–10)

Could the moving passage include an allusion in situation and word choice to *Lear*? There is relevant contextual evidence to support this view. Twain was working at the time on a parodic play in which a bookseller wanders about in the middle of *Hamlet*. Earlier in *Huck* the King had used a garbled soliloquy, and after the Grangerford-Shepherdson elopement and massacre the King and Duke practice *Romeo and Juliet* and *Richard III*. And there is evidence from the manuscript itself—just two paragraphs after Jim's speech—in a passage where the King and the Duke dress Jim up. At first Twain has them costume Jim as King Richard, but that is heavily canceled, and instead Jim assumes the hitherto unmentioned clothing of "King Leer."

The significance of this revision goes far beyond implying that the admirable slave has Shakespearean feelings, as indicated by his speech about his daughter. Once the notion of *King Lear* was echoing in Twain's mind, he had, in his next episode, the King and Duke attempt to rob the inheritance of three orphan daughters. Twain's inverse duplication of *King Lear* has its trial scene, its stormy scene, its revelation of a body. Moreover, when Huck flees and returns to the raft, he jumps into Jim's arms, but is frightened because he has forgotten that Jim is dressed as Lear. It must be emphasized that nonbookish Huck has no idea in the Wilks episode that he may be wandering around in a parodic version of *King Lear*.

Indeed, Twain could "always throw in an amount" of art that is suitable, and far more often than not his efforts at revision and re-creation create a more consistent voice and a more compelling novel. Genetic criticism of this sort remains attentive to the words of the text and the words that were excluded. Exploring the actions of these dynamic, interactive revisions, we can more fully appreciate not only the genius but also the craft of Twain's creative process.

7   FRITZ OEHLSCHLAEGER

"Gwyne to Git Hung": The Conclusion of *Huckleberry Finn*

T HE ending of *Huckleberry Finn* has long posed a problem to readers of the novel. After Huck's climactic decision to "go to hell" in order to free Jim from prison at the Phelps plantation, it is difficult to accept his easy submission to Tom Sawyer in the "Evasion" sequence. The accompanying shift in tone from one of high seriousness to one of low burlesque is so abrupt as to be almost chilling. Clemens has simply made the issues too serious for us to accept a return to the boyhood world of the novel's opening. We are asked to forget Huck's process of moral education, his growing awareness of Jim's value as a human being. Similarly, we are asked to forget Jim's nobility, revealed to us repeatedly in the escape down the river. Instead Jim becomes again the stereotyped, minstrel-show "nigger" of the novel's first section, a figure to be manipulated, tricked, and ridiculed by the boys. Perhaps even less acceptable is Clemens's apparent decision to allow Miss Watson a partial redemption through her death-bed freeing of Jim. At the end Jim is free and considers himself rich, and Huck is left to pursue further adventures in the Territory. Everything is just "old pie," as Huck would say, except that something in us longs for quite a different outcome, one that would allow Jim to retain his heroic stature and force Huck to live up to the decision that accompanies his tearing up of the letter to Miss Watson.

Perhaps the kind of conclusion we should prefer is that proposed by Leo Marx in what is undoubtedly the best-known criticism of the novel's ending.[1] Marx argues that a successful ending would leave "Jim's fate as much in

1. "Mr. Eliot, Mr. Trilling, and *Huckleberry Finn*," *ASch* 22 (1953): 423–40. Marx's essay responds to arguments by Lionel Trilling and T. S. Eliot that the ending possesses a certain "formal aptness" (Trilling's phrase). Trilling's essay appeared originally as the introduction to an edition of *Huckleberry Finn* (New York: Holt, Rinehart & Winston, 1948); Eliot's was also an introduction to the novel (New York: Cresset Press, 1950). All three essays have been widely reprinted. Another significant discussion of the novel's ending is James M. Cox, *Mark Twain: The Fate of Humor* (Princeton: Princeton University Press, 1966), pp. 172–84. Cox disputes Marx's reading of the novel's central action as a quest for freedom. Instead he sees the journey as "primarily a negation, a flight *from* tyranny, not a flight toward freedom." Cox then argues for the ending's consistency by suggesting that Huck actually "negates himself" when he decides to "go to hell," for this is to renounce the pleasure in freedom from conscience that he has consistently sought. "To commit oneself to the idea, the *morality* of freeing Jim, is to become Tom Sawyer," and thus Huck is prepared for the role he assumes in the final chapters. A less strained argument for the novel's unity is Richard P. Adams, "The Unity and Coherence of *Huckleberry Finn*," *TSE* 6 (1956): 87–103. Adams praises the novel's ending as a final expression of "contempt for adult society" and maintains that Huck does not merely capitulate to Tom. Instead he "has arrived at maturity and self-sufficiency, and he is poised at the end in a

doubt as Huck's. Such an ending would have allowed us to assume that the principals were defeated but alive, and the quest unsuccessful but not abandoned." For Marx, the novel's ending represents a "glaring lapse of moral imagination" caused by Clemens's inability to "acknowledge the truth his novel contained." That truth made a "partial defeat . . . inevitable," but instead the novel's final chapter creates a mood of "unclouded success." Clemens had effectively drawn the contrast between the corrupt society along the river's shore and the microcosmic community of the raft, but he "could not, or would not, accept the tragic fact that the one he had rejected was an image of solid reality and the other an ecstatic dream." The unconvincing moral regeneration of Miss Watson, a preeminent representative of the shore and all its values, signifies Clemens's ambition to reconcile these conflicting orders. Fortunately, Marx concludes, Clemens does break through to the truth of his novel's symbols in Huck's final sentences: "But I reckon I got to light out for the Territory ahead of the rest, because Aunt Sally she's going to adopt me and sivilize me and I can't stand it. I been there before" (p. 366). The statement is a "confession of defeat," one that means the abandonment of the raft as an ideal of human freedom. But even this final tragic moment remains unconvincing for Marx because its tone differs so radically from the concluding chapter's prevailing mood of success.

I have outlined Marx's views at length because I wish to respond to them specifically. I should say first that I generally agree with Marx's delineation of the weaknesses of the Evasion sequence as a whole: the trivializing of Huck and Jim, the implausibility of Huck's "awestruck submission" to Tom's romantic fantasies, the shift from a serious tone to one of burlesque. I do wish, however, to offer a quite different reading of the final chapter, one that sees it as savagely ironic and morally courageous. In my view, Clemens's final chapter does face the meanings implicit in the novel: the quest fails, both for Jim

---

delicate balance, ready at any moment to 'light out for the territory.'" For a structuralist assertion of the ending's logic, see George C. Carrington, Jr., *The Dramatic Unity of "Huckleberry Finn"* (Columbus: Ohio State University Press, 1976), pp. 153–87. For Carrington, the novel's central concern is with Twainian man's response to the pressure of situations through drama-making. The ending, then, has an "outrageous logic" of its own, for it is a "final devastating demonstration of the principles developed earlier in the novel: the power of situation, the need for reciprocal activity, the need for dramatic organizing of situations." Other important studies that bear directly on the novel's ending include Martha Banta, "Rebirth or Revenge: The Endings of Huckleberry Finn and The American," MFS 15 (1969): 191–207; Millicent Bell, "*Huckleberry Finn*: Journey without End," VQR 58 (1982): 253–67; Thomas A. Gullason, "The 'Fatal' Ending of *Huckleberry Finn*," AL 29 (1957): 86–91; Chadwick Hansen, "The Character of Jim and the Ending of *Huckleberry Finn*," MR 5 (1963): 45–66; Laurence B. Holland, "A 'Raft of Trouble': Word and Deed in *Huckleberry Finn*," Glyph 5 (1979): 69–87; Cecil L. Moffitt, "The Historical Ending of *Adventures of Huckleberry Finn*: How Nigger Jim Was Set Free," ALR 13 (1980): 280–83; Roy Harvey Pearce, "'The End. Yours Truly, Huck Finn': Postscript," MLQ 24 (1963): 253–56; and Neil Schmitz, "The Paradox of Liberation in *Huckleberry Finn*," TSLL 13 (1971): 125–36. Pearce's article is particularly significant as the first to point out the implications of Huck's saying he will light out "ahead of the rest." With those four words Clemens commits himself finally to "a conception of a Huck Finn whose fate it must always be to seek a freedom beyond the limits of any civilization." One last work of relevance is John Seelye's "true" account of Huck's adventures, in which Huck is left despairing at the end after Jim is drowned while escaping pursuers. See *The True Adventures of Huckleberry Finn* (Evanston: Northwestern University Press, 1970), pp. 326–39.

and for Huck, and there is no attempt to reconcile the social orders of raft and and shore.[2] Instead, the corrupt social order of the shore triumphs entirely, and and freedom once again receives definition not from Jim and Huck but from those who will never be free and could not stand it if they were.

The shore's final triumph is even ironically evident in Miss Watson's freeing of Jim, that act which seems so implausible and unanticipated by events in the narrative. As Marx notes, Clemens makes "little attempt to account for" this "change of heart," a fact that is itself significant. Clemens's interest is not in explaining Miss Watson's change of heart or in suggesting that it signifies her moral regeneration; instead he uses it to reaffirm the terrible and absolute dependence of Jim upon her. Miss Watson's freeing of Jim effectively defeats his quest for freedom, and it is the worst kind of defeat imaginable. Her act simply declares Jim's quest irrelevant. Jim is free not because he is a natural creature, not because he is a human being, not because he is a man of immense nobility and moral worth, and not because he has striven with determination and courage and in great peril for his freedom. Instead he is "set free" by the same code that has sanctioned and enforced his slavery. Being set free by Miss Watson is the one act from which he will never be free, for in that very act of giving freedom she affirms her right to own him. Isaac Mc-Caslin of *Go Down, Moses* comes to understand this paradox well as he turns through the pages of his family's ledger books and encounters the history of Thucydus, a slave of Carothers McCaslin whom Carothers had set free at the time of his death. Thucydus refused to accept freedom on these terms, however, preferring instead to "stay and work it out." As Isaac looks through the many pages of the ledgers recording Thucydus's slow accumulation of the wages needed to buy himself, he understands the black man's motivation for refusing manumission. Indeed Thucydus's sacrifice becomes so real to Isaac that he can "actually see the black man, the slave whom his white owner had forever manumitted by the very act from which the black man could never be free so long as memory lasted."[3] Like Thucydus himself, Isaac recognizes the brutal irony that the slave's lack of freedom is never more apparent than in his receipt of freedom from his master's arbitrary hand.

I am convinced, too, that Clemens must have fully understood the terrible irony in Miss Watson's freeing Jim, for he plays on a similar irony in an earlier episode, the one in which Huck first ponders betraying Jim. Part of what moves Huck to his near betrayal is Jim's disturbing talk of stealing his children out of slavery:

> Thinks I, this is what comes of my not thinking. Here was this nigger which I had as good as helped to run away, coming right out flat-footed and saying he would steal his children—children that belonged to a man I didn't even know; a man that hadn't ever done me no harm. (P. 124)

2. In my use of the terms *shore*, *raft*, and *river*, my general debt to the work of Walter Blair and Henry Nash Smith will be apparent. See Walter Blair, *Mark Twain and Huck Finn* (Berkeley: University of California Press, 1960), and Henry Nash Smith, *Mark Twain: The Development of a Writer* (Cambridge: Harvard University Press, 1962).

3. William Faulkner, *Go Down, Moses* (New York: Random House, 1942), p. 266.

The irony here turns on a distinction between natural rights and legal rights that we as readers perceive but Huck does not. By natural right, Jim's children obviously belong to him, but Huck acknowledges only the purely legal right of the slaveowner. Huck's conscience is grinding him at this point, and he speaks squarely from it, condemning Jim's desire to steal his children without seeing the perversion of nature by law that makes such action necessary. Actually there is a double irony present here, for Jim's children do belong, in the natural and not simply the legal sense, to a man Huck does not really know in any deep way at this point in the novel, a man who also has never done Huck any harm, only good—Jim himself.

The same ironic playing on the difference between legal and natural right is introduced again by Clemens near the end of the novel when Tom Sawyer finally yields up the cruel news of Miss Watson's having freed Jim. After his capture, Jim is returned to the cabin, a fact that outrages Tom's delicate sense of right: "They hain't no *right* to shut him up! *Shove!*—and don't you lose a minute. Turn him loose! he ain't no slave; he's as free as any cretur that walks this earth!" (p. 360). The irony lies in Tom's seeming to attribute Jim's freedom to natural right, to his being a "cretur" endowed with freedom by his creator. Natural freedom is of course the true longing of the novel, the goal of the raft's quest, but it is hardly a freedom that Tom Sawyer understands. For Tom, this boy devoted to the authorities, to the "regular" way of doing things, and even to suing those who might use the mark of his gang without permission, Jim's freedom is purely a matter of law, a legal fiction. Tom's comment also invites us to ask what it means to be as free as the other creatures who walk the earth in *Huck Finn*. Is Tom free? Or the Grangerfords, the Shepherdsons, the Wilkses, or any of the other shore dwellers whom we see imprisoned by their own stupidities, their untested or outworn values, and their commitment to vicious institutions? Presumably these are the people whom Jim will return to live among, as a free man among free men. Such people can be said to be free, but only as a matter of legal fiction.

Clemens uses the difference between natural and legal freedom ironically again at the very beginning of the novel's last chapter. Huck has of course been puzzled throughout the Evasion by Tom's willingness to help set Jim free. Huck simply does not expect such meanness from a boy of Tom's upbringing. When Huck learns that Jim is legally free, Tom's behavior begins to make sense to him. Still in a quandary about Tom's ultimate intentions, however, Huck asks him "what it was he'd planned to do if the evasion worked all right and he managed to set a nigger free that was already free before?" (p. [364]). The question is a final chilling reminder of the limitations of Huck's perceptions, his own inability to free a legally free man—himself— from his conscience. Huck is perplexed by the absurdity of freeing a "nigger" who is already legally free, but he does not—indeed cannot—see the fundamental absurdity that Clemens has prepared his readers to see. Huck should be asking Tom what gives him the right to set free a man whose freedom is already a matter of God-given natural right. But Huck cannot ask this question, for he accepts the code of slavery, that legal fiction which calls Tom Sawyer free and Jim a slave, even though Tom Sawyer will never be free while Jim is at least capable of freedom, as he demonstrates on the raft. The bitter tone of this first paragraph of "Chapter the Last" is reinforced as well by part of Tom's response to Huck's question. Tom reveals that he planned to "have adventures plumb to the mouth of the river, and then tell him about his being free" (p. [364]). The idea that Tom could tell Jim anything significant about freedom, conceived in a larger than legal sense, must strike us as repulsive as well as patently absurd.

Tom is really Jim's fifth liberator. The first is Jim himself; the second, the river; the third, Huck, or at least that part of Huck which would risk hell to help his friend; the fourth, Miss Watson; and the last, Tom Sawyer. Jim, the river, and Huck all ultimately fail; Miss Watson and Tom succeed. What could be a more bitter ending to the quest, or a more honest acknowledgment on Clemens's part of the overwhelming power of the shore? What could more effectively suggest the ultimate degradation of Jim by the slave society than his being told by Tom Sawyer that he is free? The complete triumph of the shore over the raft is reinforced by Tom's desire to run Jim "down the river, on the raft, and have adventures plumb to the mouth of the river" (p. [364]). To have "adventures," as Tom uses the word, is to impose the mentality of the shore, with all its respect for authorities and "regular" behavior, upon what has seemed at least briefly to be the novel's sole haven of freedom, the raft; it would be a still crueler imposition than that earlier one of the Duke and the King on the raft. In a terribly poignant line, Huck expresses a profound hope to Jim after his marvelously confused recapitulation of the history of kings: "Sometimes I wish we could hear of a country that's out of kings" (p. 201). At least for a short time in the novel, the raft is that country, as America might have been, but it is no longer so when the Duke and King arrive and establish their microcosmic aristocracy. And it would be no longer so with Tom Sawyer aboard, quoting his authorities all the way down to the mouth of the river.

Other details of the last chapter also undercut the apparent "mood of success" surrounding Jim's freeing and the family reunion. It is impossible, for instance, to see Tom's giving Jim forty dollars as anything but an act of monstrous insensitivity. Tom gives Jim the money "for being prisoner for us so patient" (p. 365): that is, for being a "good nigger," for enacting the role the slave code demands of him. Jim is rewarded for conforming to the institutionalized fiction of himself as the patient, docile, and long-suffering slave. But certainly we are meant to see the irony of Jim's being rewarded for this conformity, for this "lowering of himself," to adapt Huck's phrase, rather than for the qualities of devotion and nobility that he reveals on the raft. Lest we miss this irony, Clemens takes us back for a moment to Jackson's Island, to a time when freedom and wealth were conceived as natural rights rather than legal fictions. Upon receiving the forty dollars, Jim "busted out, and says":

> *Dah*, now, Huck, what I tell you?—what I tell you up dah on Jackson islan'? I *tole* you I got a hairy breas', en what's de sign un it; en I *tole* you I ben rich wunst, en gwineter to be rich *agin*; en it's come true; an heah she *is*! (P. 365)

But Jim has been rich in a quite different sense on Jackson's Island. There, after explaining the hairy breast sign to Huck, Jim realizes, "I's rich now, come to look at it. I owns mysef, en I's wuth eight hund'd dollars. I wisht I had de money, I wouldn' want no mo'" (p. 73). Jim here is beginning to equate wealth with freedom itself, not the freedom allowed him by society at the end of the novel but that God-given or natural freedom that is his true inheritance and that he gains only by escaping to the middle of the river, first on Jackson's Island and then on the raft. By alluding to this earlier passage in "Chapter the Last," Clemens invites us to compare the wealth Jim receives from Tom Sawyer to his wealth on Jackson's Island. Once again the irony is unmistakable: society rewards for all the wrong reasons. It rewards Jim not for his heroic assertion of freedom, for taking possession of himself, but instead for conforming to the slave code's abstraction of the "good nigger."

Clemens's allusion to the earlier "hairy breast" passage adds another dimension to the final chapter as well. Family is of major importance in that final chapter: Clemens gives us the "cozy family reunion" to which Marx objects and reveals the death of Pap Finn, thereby cutting Huck loose from all family ties. Moreover, as I have previously suggested, the very first sentences of "Chapter the Last" allude to the distinction between natural and legal freedom brought home to us by Huck's earlier dismay at Jim's plan to buy his wife and children or to steal them if need be. Within this context, the cozy reunion of the Phelps clan forces us to remember another family who will not be reunited, Jim's. And by alluding to the Jackson's Island passage, Clemens reinforces this sad reminder. Jim would consider himself rich and "wouldn' want no mo'" if he had eight hundred dollars. Why? If the answer is not immediately apparent on Jackson's Island, it certainly is when Jim speaks of his wish to buy his wife and children: eight hundred dollars would go far toward doing that. At the end of the novel, however, society, in the person of Tom Sawyer, awards Jim only forty dollars. Thus even in the midst of Jim's rejoicing about his wealth, we perceive the discrepancy between society's recompense and Jim's hope, as it has been defined throughout the novel: the hope to buy his family. The irony is deepened if we remember too that the eight hundred dollars is associated by Jim with owning himself, as he does truly own himself, in a more than monetary way, on Jackson's Island and the raft. In short, if the free life of Huck and Jim on the river were a model for all society, Jim would naturally possess what the corrupt society of the shore values at a paltry eight hundred dollars and what his merely legal possession of himself fails to bring him: unity with his family. Jim is not to be united with his family, and the pattern of allusions embedded in "Chapter the Last" underscores the savage and unavoidable irony that family reunions are for white people, not for blacks.

Neither do blacks adopt whites. "Chapter the Last" reveals Pap Finn's death and leaves Huck in need of a family. In a world organized around the values of the raft, Jim would clearly be the obvious candidate to adopt him, for, as Kenneth Lynn has argued, he has served as a father figure to Huck throughout the journey.[4] Jim protects and consoles Huck, provides him

---

4. See "You Can't Go Home Again," in *Adventures of Huckleberry Finn*, ed. Sculley Bradley et al. (New York: W. W. Norton & Co., 1977), p. 403. Reprinted from *Mark Twain and Southwestern Humor* (Boston: Little, Brown & Co., 1959).

moral instruction by his example, and lavishes upon him the love that society prevents him from giving to his own children. Yet the last chapter of the novel presents quite a different parent for Huck, Aunt Sally, who plans to "adopt" and "sivilize" him—in short, to inculcate all the corrupt values associated throughout the novel with the shore. Once again the moral honesty of Clemens's last chapter is apparent, and the triumph of society over the raft is complete. Aunt Sally is a potential parent to Huck because her adoption has the sanction of law. Jim, on the other hand, has no recognized claim as Huck's father, despite his paternal caring for Huck on the raft. Clemens drives the irony home by reminding us of Jim's fatherly protectiveness. It is Jim who tells Huck of Pap's death, and only after continuing his attempt to protect Huck from the gruesome truth about the old man's demise:

> "He ain't a comin' back no mo', Huck."
> I says:
> "Why, Jim?"
> "Nemmine why, Huck—but he ain't comin' back no mo'."
> But I kept at him; so at last he says:
> "Doan you 'member de house dat was float'n down de river, en dey wuz a man in dah, kivered up, en I went in en unkivered him and didn' let you come in? Well, den, you k'n git yo' money when you wants it; kase dat wuz him." (Pp. 265–66)

It is supremely appropriate that Jim recalls his first moment of fatherly concern for Huck, the moment in which he first realizes Huck's need for a father. Clemens juxtaposes this moment of deep parental caring, possible during the free life of the raft, with the legal fiction of parenthood represented by Aunt Sally's proposed adoption of Huck. The juxtaposition of Jim's parenthood with Aunt Sally's also makes us realize that they are markedly different in kind: the purpose of Aunt Sally's adopting Huck is to "sivilize" him, to make him a useful member of a corrupt society. The effect of Jim's parental care, on the other hand, has been to help Huck toward freedom.

Certainly the real bitterness of Clemens's last chapter is suggested, too, by the forty dollars Tom gives Jim. Using that amount, Clemens invites us to compare the morality of Tom's act to the kind of morality evident in two previous incidents in which the sum of forty dollars appears prominently.[5] The first of these occurs in Chapter 16 when Huck, paddling ashore to betray Jim, experiences a change of heart and then protects Jim by lying to the two slave-hunters in the skiff. Huck's lie, that the sick man aboard his raft is his pap, both deceives the slave-hunters and reveals a profounder truth of which Huck himself remains unaware. What follows is a savage satire based loosely perhaps on the parable of the Good Samaritan: our two shore dwellers discharge their responsibility to their brother sufferer by giving Huck two

---

5. For more on Clemens's use of the forty dollars, see Victor A. Doyno, "Over Twain's Shoulder: The Composition and Structure of *Huckleberry Finn*," *MFS* 14 (1968): 3–9. Doyno argues that "these financial dealings reveal one important way in which the novel is structured. Twain created in *Huckleberry Finn* three parallel sequential patterns of action," each involving "first the meeting of Huck with someone who thinks him dead, the formation or renewal of a partnership to free the slave which ends in failure, and finally, the exchange of forty dollars" (pp. 3–4).

twenty-dollar gold pieces and suggesting that he take his pap ashore at a town twenty miles downriver. The same sum appears again when the King betrays Jim and causes his incarceration at the Phelps plantation. The King's are "forty dirty dollars" (p. 269), Huck realizes, because, like the slave-hunters' gold pieces, they have been obtained by trading in human life. That sum, so repeated, should prepare us for Clemens's harsh rebuke of Tom Sawyer's actions in the final chapter, after Tom's Evasion not only subjects Jim to misery and prolonged imprisonment but also exposes him to death. Then, for the pleasures attached to risking Jim's life, Tom casually pays him forty dollars, his thoughtless estimation of Jim's worth. The inclusion of this telling detail in the final chapter suggests once more that the chapter represents no "faint hearted" failure of Clemens's to face "the truth his novel contained," as Marx avers. Throughout that final chapter Clemens's unrelenting irony exposes the viciousness of society along the Mississippi shore. That viciousness is never more apparent than in Tom's paying Jim off for what he calls "lost time."

Still another detail with sinister suggestions is, indeed, Tom's infatuation with time, with his watch. Huck begins his parting paragraph: "Tom's most well, now, and got his bullet around his neck on a watch-guard for a watch, and is always seeing what time it is" (p. 366). Certainly clock time is man's most fundamental imposition of artificial order upon the eternal flow of nature. That Clemens understood time in this fashion is clearly apparent from *The Mysterious Stranger*, in which Theodor Fischer marvels at "the mastery Satan had over time and distance. For him they did not exist. He called them human inventions, and said they were artificialities."[6] Tom's obsession with the watch is a potent reminder of his status as representative of the artificialities of the shore. We should recall, too, that early in the novel Tom's love of watches is associated with his fantasies of murder and dirty dollars. When he explains to his gang the difference between ordinary burglars and highwaymen, Tom emphasizes that highwaymen "stop stages and carriages on the road, with masks on, and kill the people and take their watches and money" (p. 27).

We should also recall the prominent place given to a timepiece by those other eminent devotees of abstraction and style, and of murder in the name of both, the Grangerfords. The Grangerfords are inordinately proud of their clock, so much so that they value it even above money; when she was all shined up, "They wouldn't took any money for her," as Huck says. The clock rests in an honored place "on the middle of the mantel-piece" and has a "picture of a town painted on the bottom half of the glass front." The picture of the town is especially significant for, as Huck innocently reveals, the Grangerford place is nothing but a "house out in the country" trying to be "the same as houses in a town." On each side of the clock is a "big outlandish parrot" which, like the Grangerfords, is "painted up gaudy" but actually "made out of something like chalk" (pp. 136–37). The clock, then, is inti-

6. In *Selected Shorter Writings of Mark Twain*, ed. Walter Blair (Boston: Houghton Mifflin Co., 1962), p. 372.

mately associated with the lies of the Grangerfords, the lies they live, pray, and die. Their lives, and that of Tom Sawyer, are ordered not by the continuous and eternal flow of nature that governs Huck and Jim's life on the raft but by artificial social institutions and values that themselves depend upon the central fiction of time conceived as a mechanical system of measurement represented by the workings of the clock. By noting Tom's obsession with his watch in "Chapter the Last," and by associating watch and bullet, Clemens reaffirms the link between the Grangerfords and Tom, who resembles them also in living according to abstract notions of style and honor. It is perfectly appropriate as well that Clemens reminds us of the Grangerfords in this final chapter with its undercurrent of ironies about the family as natural bond and as legal fiction. The Grangerfords represent a perversion of family, for they are held together, and buried together, more by the abstract fiction of their honor than by love and care.

Tom's obsession with his watch marks him further as mechanical man and allows us to establish his place in American literature. His brethren are those people in *Walden* who believe so completely in the fidelity to the schedule of the Fitchburg railroad that they set their clocks, and their lives, "railroad fashion," even as Henry Thoreau is discovering the eternal sequences of nature in his microcosm at the pond.[7] Tom's spiritual heir is another man who is always seeing what time it is, Jason Compson, Faulkner's symbol of mechanical man perversely alienated from nature.

Tom's brethren and heirs are also those who will constitute the inevitable advance of civilization into the Territory where Huck decides finally to flee. After disclaiming any intention to make another book, Huck closes this one with what T. S. Eliot has called "the only possible concluding sentence"[8]: "But I reckon I got to light out for the Territory ahead of the rest, because Aunt Sally she's going to adopt me and sivilize me and I can't stand it. I been there before" (p. 366). Roy Harvey Pearce has noted Huck's "curious prescience" in recognizing that "he will be only one step ahead of the rest: boomers, dukes and dauphins, Aunt Sallies, Colonel Sherburns, and Wilkses—civilizers all."[9] And if Huck is to be pursued into the territory, and history confirms that he has been, what should we expect for him? The novel suggests one possible answer to that question, an answer that confirms the bitter and unremitting moral honesty of its conclusion.

"Chapter the Last" reminds us of the importance of superstition and folklore to Jim and Huck. After Jim recalls his prediction of future wealth, he reminds Huck of the value of signs: "*Dah*, now! doan' talk to *me*—signs is *signs*, mine I tell you; en I knowed jis' 's well 'at I 'uz gwineter be rich agin as I's a stannin' heah dis minute!" (p. 365). Certainly Jim's words should prompt us to ask whether Huck's ultimate fate can be foreseen from any of the novel's signs. Jim has made just such a prediction for Huck at the end of his

---

7. See the "Sounds" chapter of *Walden*, ed. J. Lyndon Shanley (Princeton: Princeton University Press, 1971), esp. p. 117.

8. "An Introduction to *Huckleberry Finn*," in *Huckleberry Finn*, ed. Bradley et al., p. 335.

9. "The End. Yours Truly, Huck Finn," p. 256.

divination from the hairball in Chapter 4: "You wants to keep 'way fum de water as much as you kin, en don't run no resk, 'kase it's down in de bills dat you's gwyne to git hung" (p. 38). Daniel G. Hoffman has dismissed this as a "counterfeit prophecy," [10] but I would suggest that it is remarkably consonant with the meanings implicit in the novel. In evaluating the prophecy, we should first remember Jim's situation at the time he makes it. While Jim is a slave at Miss Watson's, "de water" can mean for him escape, with all its attendant dangers, or, what is more likely (and made more explicit in *Pudd'n-head Wilson*), sale down the river to worse treatment, brutality, and probable death. In either case, the river is a potent symbol of danger and death. Indeed, in receipt of Tom's forty dollars at the end, Jim has, for all his and Huck's travails on that river, been in fact "sold." Obviously the dangers of "de water" are not the same for Huck as for Jim, but the prophecy can be read as a revelation of Jim's sense that the power of organized society is overwhelming. What Jim gives Huck is sound practical advice: to be safe, stick to the shore and "don't run no resk." Clemens may even intend a brilliant pun on Jim's use of "gwyne" in his warning to Huck that he is "gwyne to git hung." "Gwyne" of course signifies future action, but it may also suggest movement. "Going" takes one to hanging; safety lies in stasis. If we recall this prophecy when we come to the very end of the novel, as I think we are intended to, Clemens's pun on "gwyne" works as a powerful antithesis to Huck's last statement: "I been there before." As Hoffman has commented, Huck's "*'there'* means the stasis of being a part of society." [11] Huck prefers "gwyne" to "there," going to stasis, the flux of nature to the ordered repetition of social life. In that preference lies his fate.

If we remember Jim's hairball prophecy when we are pondering Huck's fate at the end of the novel, we should see that it poses with remarkable aptness the choices available to him. He can become a Tom Sawyer or "git hung." Tom Sawyer is one who "don't run no resk," who sets free "niggers" free. Tom may unwittingly risk his life as part of his games, but he will not risk violating what is far more important to him, the code of his society. In this he is but a grace note removed from the Grangerfords, who risk their lives repeatedly and really but who would never risk their sacred honor. Huck, on the other hand, has run great and true risks and experienced the freedom of life on the raft, on the water. His lighting out for the Territory is a continued search for this freedom. But when "the rest" arrive, Huck will face a choice; he can stop running risks, stop being a free man, or "git hung." Jim's divination from the hairball may suggest Huck's choice, for Jim says it is "down in de bills" that Huck is "gwyne to git hung." The novel's ending, then, forces us into the difficult and painful hope that Huck will choose "de water" and freedom rather than safety and society, even though the choice may mean his death. In the last chapter Clemens faces the meanings implicit in his novel without flinching. What Leo Marx calls the final "illusion of success" is precisely that: an illusion whose almost saccharine

---

10. *Form and Fable in American Fiction* (New York: Oxford University Press, 1961), p. 334.
11. Ibid., p. 342.

quality itself ironically underscores the bitter logic of the book's conclusion. Clemens's judgment of society is as uncompromising as society's triumph is complete. There is no room for a free man in a corrupt society. The compelling and perhaps tragic quality of the ending lies in its offering no middle ground: Huck can either survive by giving up what is best in him or "git hung" by the "sivilization" he cannot ultimately elude.

8 MILLICENT BELL

Huckleberry Finn and the Sleights of the Imagination

LIKE the second half of *Don Quixote*, *Huckleberry Finn* begins with a reference by the hero to his previous existence as a literary character: "You don't know about me, without you have read a book by the name of 'The Adventures of Tom Sawyer,' but that ain't no matter. That book was made by Mr. Mark Twain, and he told the truth, mainly. There was things which he stretched, but mainly he told the truth" (p. [17]). It is sometimes thought that this opening is a remnant, merely, of Twain's intention to write a sequel to his earlier success made up out of discarded portions of it, parts he might have eliminated as the book grew into an independent and very different act of the imagination.[1] But the literary self-consciousness introduced by Huck's awareness of his status as fiction is perhaps quite significant. Borges remarks that it disquiets us to know that Don Quixote is a reader of the *Quixote* because "if the characters in a story can be readers or spectators, then we, their readers or spectators, can be fictitious."[2] Making allowance for Borges's particular readiness to see fictionality in existence, we still can take note of the way in which fiction and "life" are mixed as the result of the promotion of character to reader. And as the author, the maker of fictions, becomes the author of what is also "real," we are also reminded of reality's fictionality.

Huckleberry Finn seems to eliminate the author by the superior authority of its hero's first-person narrative. Yet it admits, indeed incorporates into that pretended reality, a profounder awareness than its predecessor of the role of the imagination in all human gestures. The three opening chapters are, in fact, highly relevant to this awareness, as are the last ten chapters, so often considered a regrettable superfluity that Twain would have done better to eliminate.[3] John C. Gerber has properly identified *Huckleberry Finn* as a

1. Compare *Adventures of Huckleberry Finn*, ed. Sculley Bradley et al. (New York: W. W. Norton & Co., 1977), n. 1, p. 7.
2. *Other Inquisitions: 1937–1952* (New York: Simon & Schuster, 1968), p. 46.
3. A considerable literature has accumulated on this point, but the most famous expression of dissatisfaction with Twain's ending of the novel may be the comment of Ernest Hemingway (in *Green Hills of Africa* [New York: Charles Scribner's Sons, 1935], p. 22): "If you read it you must stop where the Nigger Jim is stolen from the boys. That is the real end. The rest is cheating." Bernard DeVoto wrote of the ending, "Mark was once more betrayed. He intended a further chapter in his tireless attack on romanticism, especially Southern romanticism, and nothing in his mind or training enabled him to understand that this extemporized burlesque was a defacement of his pure work" (*Mark Twain's America* [1932], excerpted in *Huckleberry Finn*, ed.

"modified frame story" because Tom Sawyer, instead of Huck, is the major character in these opening and concluding sections.[4] Technically, of course, the narration is still Huck's, but Tom's mind is omnipresent in these parts since the action is primarily dictated not only by what Tom does but also by his way of thinking, his version of life. And this version is now felt—as it is not so deeply felt in *Tom Sawyer*—decidedly to be a fiction, a viewpoint that consciously constructs reality into certain formal arrangements. The Tom Sawyer frame serves to prepare the reader to regard what it encloses as also structured by imaginative invention.

We say at once that Tom's imagination is "literary." He represents that side of Twain's own mind that was capable of absorbing a multitude of literary models. Twain recognized in himself, indeed, a tendency to "unconscious plagiarism" and approved the statement of Dumas, "The man of genius does not steal; he conquers; and what he conquers, he annexes to his empire."[5] *The Adventures of Tom Sawyer* has been shown to utilize suggestions and details from literature at every level—from the work of native Southwest or Yankee humorists, from dime novels and melodramas, and from the tradition of belles lettres. Among literary respectables from whom it borrows are Dickens, Charles Reade, Wilkie Collins, and Poe—the grave-robbing scene in the book can be related to an episode in *A Tale of Two Cities*, for example, and the digging for buried treasure to "The Gold Bug." The absorption of literary models and suggestions continues in *Huckleberry Finn*, which uses some of these same sources.[6]

Both works, in being openly imitative of known literary and popular models, tend toward parody, making comment not only on life directly but on other versions of life. In its earliest form as "The Boy's Manuscript," *Tom*

Bradley et al., pp. 302–3). Twain's denouement was defended, though only casually, by Lionel Trilling, who remarked in 1948 that it permitted Huck to "return to his anonymity, to give up his role of hero which he prefers, for he is modest in all things," and by T. S. Eliot in 1950: "Huck Finn must come from nowhere and be bound for nowhere . . . he is in a state of nature as detached as the state of the saint." In 1953 Leo Marx responded to both in an essay maintaining that Twain had "jeopardized the significance of the entire novel" by an ending in which Huck's search for freedom is surrendered and his growth of character denied (all three essays reproduced in *Huckleberry Finn*, ed. Bradley et al., pp. 318–49). To Marx there have been a number of important replies, among them those of Frank Baldanza ("The Structure of *Huckleberry Finn*," *AL* 27 [1955]: 347–55) and Richard P. Adams ("The Unity and Coherence of *Huckleberry Finn*," *TSE* 6 [1956]: 87–103), who argue for the coherence of the whole book including the ending as a result of rhythms of repetition and variation and patterns of imagery. My own argument for the meaningfulness of Twain's ending finds a start in the statement of James M. Cox that "after Huck reached his unknown destination, the Phelps farm, the only terms on which he could exist were Tom's terms." Cox sees the ending as a "sad initiation" into respectable society ("Remarks on the Sad Initiation of Huckleberry Finn," *SR* 62 [1954]: 389–405).

4. "The Relation between Point of View and Style in the Works of Mark Twain," *Style in Prose Fiction*, English Institute Essays: 1958 (New York: Columbia University Press, 1959), p. 165.

5. Compare Walter Blair, *Mark Twain and Huck Finn* (Berkeley: University of California Press, 1960), p. 60.

6. Blair, ibid., has demonstrated the relation of both novels to "the literary flux." Compare pp. 58–67, 111–30.

Sawyer began, probably, as a literary burlesque, suggested by David Copperfield's courtship of Dora.[7] The suggestion of parody reminds us that what we are reading is itself only another text, another fiction without absolute standing as a version of experience. But *Huckleberry Finn* goes further than *Tom Sawyer* in this direction, as I have said, partly because it also replicates and comments upon its own predecessor by the same author. It reproduces certain situations from the earlier novel—such as Huck's discussion with Tom about the lives of pirates and robbers or the behavior of prisoners—that particularly reflect the conventions of literature. In the context of Huck's narration these discussions become self-conscious references to the art of fiction as practiced by Tom himself as well as by his creator. More covertly than by the direct reference of the opening sentence but still significantly to the recognizing reader who knows the earlier book, the text of *Huckleberry Finn* informs one that it is a text and suggests the textuality of experience.

When we say that Tom Sawyer's imagination is "literary" we also remind ourselves that he is one of the great examples, like Quixote, of the mind saturated with literature almost to the point of delerium. This is true not only because Tom wants to make reality conform to literary models and consciously invokes those models as "authorities" but also because his concept of "style" is the governing principle that directs his actions. *Style*, after all, is a term only restrictedly applied to art; in a more general sense it is a way of describing human behavior as it approximates some ideal pattern. Tom's preoccupation with form, evident throughout *Tom Sawyer* and still more conspicuous in the portions of *Huckleberry Finn* in which he is present, persists in the "interior" parts of the book where Sawyerism is felt as a continuing presence even though Tom is gone, an element internalized sometimes in Huck himself.

Yet Huck's mind is fundamentally opposed to Tom's, as Sancho's is to Quixote's. Huck has only recently become literate, and his speech is still free of the elegancy or obfuscation induced by written models. Huck's moral imagination is also free, despite the "deformed conscience"[8] that seems to overwhelm it from time to time. His "primitive" responses to experience have no available justification or even name; they remain outside the patterns of approved social value and of language as well. Yet his personal speech, the governing voice of the book, is as near a literary equivalence of his existential ethic as it is possible to imagine, a miracle of the emergence of validity out of the unlearned powers of mind and the least refutable aspects of perception.

Huckleberry Finn's colloquial autobiographical mode effected, of course, an alteration in the relation between language and literature in our culture.

7. Henry Nash Smith, *Mark Twain: The Development of a Writer* (New York: Atheneum, 1967), p. 81.

8. In 1895 Twain wrote concerning Huck's decision in Chapter 16 not to betray Jim, "I should exploit the proposition that in a crucial moral emergency, a sound heart is a safer guide than an ill-trained conscience. I sh'd support this doctrine with a chapter from a book of mine where a sound heart and a deformed conscience come into collision and conscience suffers defeat" (Blair, *Mark Twain and Huck Finn*, p. 143).

It converted an oral-comic tradition, previously employable only in sub-literature or journalism, to the highest literary ends. After Twain, in fact, there is no longer any reason to distinguish between low and high styles at all. But the immediate impact of this novel derived from the fact that the distinction, at the time of its writing, was still a powerful one. Colloquial speech, the speech of a half-educated country person, was adapted in this unclassifiable prose to ends that proved serious, even "poetic" in an unprecedented way. Yet, because of its thrust against the traditional mode for such expression, it was felt to be subversive. This historic subversiveness had obvious objects: literary genteelism, to begin with—but literary genteelism was linked in Twain's mind with the social pretensions of aristocracies in general and with the self-justifications of a defunct Southern aristocracy in particular. Twain, connecting styles of life and language he judged equally dishonest, related the false dignity and claims of refinement of the slave-owners to their defensive rhetoric. He thought there were particular sources for both in literature itself, specifically in the novels of Sir Walter Scott, which he accused of poisoning literature with "wordy, windy, flowery 'eloquence,' romanticism, sentimentality" and with bringing on the Civil War.[9]

We only faintly sense this political motive in *Huckleberry Finn*'s stylistic innovation. But, a hundred years later, we can still perceive how the book opposes all aspects of *any* dominant culture with what Henry Nash Smith has called the "vernacular attitude."[10] Twain's skepticism seems wholesale and modernist. His suspicions that all social forms—not merely American Southern aristocratic ones—might be impositions had already begun to surface in this, his greatest work. Eventually they would reach that nihilism visible in the writings of his last years which belong so clearly to our own century. It is this total distrust of received values and meanings that earlier had energized his propensity to satire and burlesque of any and every propriety. Nor do Twain's biographers stress irrelevantly the fiasco of the *Atlantic Monthly* Whittier dinner in 1876,[11] when Twain was working on the early chapters of the novel. On this occasion, to his own chagrin, some inner demon caused him to hold up to ridicule those distinguished fellow guests and cultural idols, Longfellow, Holmes, and Emerson. Twain's mockery knew its own ultimate objects despite his "deformed" inner censor.

Huckleberry Finn expresses this same irreverence filtered through Huck's innocent humorlessness. To every cultural or social pretension, the novel's mode of narration opposes an anti-stylistic style. Scrupulously pruned of rhetoric, reduced in syntax and vocabulary to simple elements of plain statement, Huck's first-person retrospection appears, in the best passages of the book, to be artless. It is nothing of the sort, of course, but it was *designed* to seem so, to convey the effect of spontaneity because the spontaneous, the untutored, was a value to be set against that which surrounded it, the behavior patterns and language dominant in the culture and expressing its bad

9. *Life on the Mississippi* (New York: Signet, 1961), p. 267.
10. Smith, *Mark Twain*.
11. See ibid., chap. 5.

faiths. Devoid of literary and social preconceptions, this pseudo-oral style was made to seem the direct record of honest sensation and feeling.

This subversion of "style" as such is part of a general antiformal impulse in the work. We should, I think, take with utmost seriousness Twain's notice to the reader: "persons attempting to find a moral in it will be banished; persons attempting to find a plot in it will be shot" (p. [5]). Twain discarded quite deliberately the apocalyptic fictional form long dominant in the novel and drew instead on an early, looser model, the picaresque, with its license to disjunctive, open-ended narrative and to a hero who does not develop as his history progresses. The correspondences of *Huckleberry Finn* with *Don Quixote* are less fundamental than one might suppose, despite the obvious parallels.[12] Cervantes's view of Quixote is more complex than Twain's view of Tom; Huck is very different from the pragmatic Sancho. But the "open form" resulting from what Robert M. Adams calls an "unresolved tension" between Cervantes's pair[13] may have provided a suggestive design along with adapted details. Twain himself, we know, greatly approved the Spanish classic and contrasted it, in the passage in *Life on the Mississippi* already referred to, with Scott's *Ivanhoe*, because it "swept the world's admiration for medieval chivalry-silliness out of existence,"[14] while *Ivanhoe* restored it. In his own attack on the same delusions, he may even have identified himself with Cervantes but been influenced more than he was aware by the subtle rejection of resolution that makes the Spanish masterpiece so different from such a work as Scott's.

The title of Twain's book expresses the fact that Huck has "adventures," has, that is, engagements with chance, and that the incidents he relates are not caused by him and do not change him. Of course, we are tempted to think that something else is going on, despite the picaresque form, for *Huckleberry Finn* does more with its hero than conduct him, in the picaresque way, through the layers of his society, so revealing them to us. The work does not seem to be a comic journey without goal, for Huck appears to "grow," like the hero of tragedy, as he passes along the stages of his downriver voyage with Jim. We are even likely to see in his experience one of the standard patterns of the novel of character, the penetration of illusion, the coming to maturity through trial, of the youthful protagonist. But reading the book in this way brings us up (with a cry of critical anguish, generally) against the ending. For if Huck *has* changed and grown, if we have really gone somewhere with him, what is the meaning of that return, in the Phelps Farm chapters, to the exact conditions of the opening when he is enrolled in Tom Sawyer's band of make-believe robbers and Jim is merely the object of a boyish practical joke?

It is my contention that we must understand *Huckleberry Finn* in some other way than as a novel of development—and that still the book is "se-

12. The parallels with *Don Quixote* were pointed out by Olin H. Moore, "Mark Twain and *Don Quixote*," *PMLA* 37 (1922): 337–38.

13. *Strains of Discord: Studies in Literary Openness* (Ithaca: Cornell University Press, 1958), p. 73.

14. *Life on the Mississippi*, p. 267.

rious." It expresses not only Twain's view of his own society but also his understanding of human life in general as a condition of precarious continuity in which identity is maintained only by our willingness to accept definition of ourselves from the norms of society and the expectations of others. Huck's experiments with freedom, the sloughing off of old habits of thought and action, are the experiments of utopia, the utopia of the raft. That utopia cannot survive on the shore, which finally even invades and destroys the raft itself. Huck's adventures involve him in the greatest risk because of their continued invitation not so much to the discovery of a new self as to the loss of membership altogether in human society, the source of all role and all selfhood. It is no accident that the narrative is permeated by references to death and by the narrator's own death thoughts, lyric moments in which he seems ready to surrender selfhood altogether, to merge with the flow of natural forces that bear him onward, not to any landing where he and Jim can continue as they are, but toward a sea of silence.[15]

If indeed the plot of *Huckleberry Finn* can thus be described as an antiplot, a frustration of our expectations of development and consequence, it may suggest that life in general may not possess inherent design. Plot, character, formal closure, even "theme" are, after all, ways of saying that life has inherent form. If these can be seen as the inventions of the human imagination, we are reminded that life is not, after all, a coherent story and that we can only pretend that we know who we are. This, of course, is itself a statement, a theme, and perhaps *Huckleberry Finn*, while undermining more obvious themes, leaves this one on our hands.

The mark of such an intention is the obsessive stress in the book on the games literature plays in imposing its designs upon life and the interpretation of social forms as games perfectly analogous to the games of literature. The Phelps Farm coda is distinguished from what has gone before only because the emphasis on language and literature—present earlier too—takes over completely from the social and psychological interests that are finally revealed in all their desolating vacuity as make-believe. It is indeed a pessimistic reduction from the previous richness of Huck's moral effort and hope. His story-telling is over now, subdued to Tom's art-for-art's-sake view of life as an aesthetic opportunity. Huck escapes at the very end with a vow of silence, "If I'd a knowed what a trouble it was to make a book I wouldn't a tackled it and ain't agoing to no more" (p. 366): Tom's art prevails and survives, however; his is the unresting imagination forever generating roles for himself and others out of the conventions of society and the formulas of literature.

As I shall try to show, the literary imagination, chiefly identified with Tom at the start as at the end, comes to stand for all lies imposed by social life. But what forms of social life are not lies? The literary imagination is the enemy of Huck's existential freedom and yet, paradoxically, it is the only means of his survival. His adventures, even when he is separated from Tom—as he

---

15. I have elaborated this interpretation in "*Huckleberry Finn*: Journey without End," *VQR* 58, no. 3 (1982): 253–67.

is for most of the story—involve him in the play-acting, the charades and deceits of others, an assortment of characters who represent both the respectable and the disreputable in society. Only the private life established between Huck and Jim on the raft is free from such deceits, though Huck can play games that make "trash" out of Jim's feelings in the early stages of their relationship and though he subscribes to society's cruel fiction that a human being can be regarded as a piece of property. But even more benignly Huck is compelled in his contacts with a lying society to resort to life-saving fictions; Huck's own fertility of self-invention produces a succession of impersonations that both express, in a symbolic mode, his orphanhood and peril and combat the destructive designs of society. Thus, the descent in tone, the tedious burlesque of the ending with its emphasis on game-playing pure and simple, is anticipated in the whole of the work more than critics have been willing to admit. The Phelps chapters are not so much an anticlimax as consistent with much that has gone before.

The ending also implies a cyclicity rather than a linearity in experience, for though Huck initially resists the seductions and sleights of Tom's imagination, he submits to the forms of respectability, agrees to go to live with the Widow Douglas, as the price of that same membership in the gang, joining the make-believe of society and of the gang at the same time. It is clear that respectability, membership in societies, is the same in both the larger world of adults and the imaginative world of the boys. The final paragraph tells us that he will be joining Tom for new adventures over in the Territory but will somehow manage to evade Aunt Sally's intention to adopt and "sivilize" him. Yet we cannot help seeing here only the temporary rebellion and self-exile that had preceded his original submission in the first chapter. Tom's price will be the same as before. The whole narrative, indeed, exhibits a continuation of such resistances and returns, and anticipates the end. One may mention, for example, Huck's decision not to oppose the pretenses of the Duke and the Dauphin "'long as it would keep peace in the family" (p. 166), recognizing as he does that lies are somehow the very essence of social cohesion.

There is no real difference, it is plain at the start, between the making-up of reality by the gang and the Bible stories Huck is told by the widow. He loses interest in the latter when he learns that "Moses had been dead a considerable long time . . . because I don't take no stock in dead people" (p. 18). He finds that religion asks him to interest himself in either an imagined past or an imagined future, and Miss Watson's theology leaves him cold: "All I wanted was to go somewheres; all I wanted was a change, I warn't particular" (p. 19). Tom's preference for art over nature exhibits itself just as promptly and just as bewilderingly to Huck. On the night of their first escapade he wants to tie the sleeping Jim to a tree "for fun" until Huck points out that this would wake him, but still "nothing would do Tom but he must crawl to where Jim was, on his hands and knees, and play something on him" (p. 23). This "play" is the first of the three practical jokes inflicted on Jim during the course of the story, the first of the three impositions of fancy that become increasingly dangerous until Huck rejects all such games as a way of dealing with his friend. A staple of American humor that Twain him-self found detestable, the practical joke is essentially a fiction, a made-up explanation of appearances intended to deceive and when the deception is disclosed to embarrass the victim. Jim's own self-seduction by fantasy col-laborates here when he finds his hat hung on a tree to make him think that he has been acted upon by witches and is then tempted himself into extrava-gances of story-telling as he develops an account of what happened in more and more fanciful versions. Story-telling thus begets more story-telling.

The inspiration for Tom's robber-band is openly literary. Tom's "beautiful oath" to which all must swear comes, he admits, only in part "out of his own head," the rest "out of pirate books, and robber books" (p. 26). Tom—or Twain—draws, in fact, on sources as diverse as Carlyle's *History of the French Revolution*, Dickens's *A Tale of Two Cities*, and Robert Montgom-ery Bird's *Nick of the Woods* for details here.[16] The fidelity to formula is, indeed, compulsive: Huck is almost excluded because he hasn't a family to be killed if he tells the gang's secrets. The business of the gang is routine, "*only* robbery and murder" (emphasis mine), but it is no mere unimagina-tive burglary: "We ain't burglars. That ain't no sort of style," says Tom. "We are highwaymen. We stop stages and carriages on the road, with masks on, and kill the people and take their watches and money" (pp. 26–27). "Kill-ing people" is part of the prescription for proper style, except perhaps when the robbers hold their captives for ransom, a variation permitted by some "authorities," which is to say, by some texts. Tom doesn't really know what the word *ransom* means, and when Ben Rogers says, "Why can't a body take a club and ransom them as soon as they get here," he answers, "Because it ain't in the books so—that's why" (p. 67).

After a month of playing robber, Huck and the other boys resign from the gang. Realists, they tire of fancy: "We hadn't robbed nobody, we hadn't killed any people, but only just pretended" (p. 30). Tom alone retains the taste for calling things what they are not—only for him are hogs "ingots," turnips "julery." The attack upon a camp of Spanish merchants and A-rabs "warn't anything but a Sunday-school picnic, and only a primer-class at that" (pp. 31–32). When challenged about wonders the others fail to see, Tom refers Huck to *Don Quixote* and explains that "enchantment" had converted the A-rabs and elephants into picnickers. Tom is thus explicitly identified with Cervantes's hero, and the twist of logic that makes him argue that *appearances* are what is unreal suggests that the consequence of believ-ing in the reality of fantasy is, as Borges (in the remark quoted earlier) ob-serves, that one must suspect the fantasy of reality. So, Huck tries to work the enchantment himself by rubbing an old tin lamp, "calculating to build a palace and sell it," but he gets nowhere: "all that stuff was only just one of Tom Sawyer's lies" (p. 33). It is a famous deflation of the literary imagination at its game of reversing the relation between fancy and fact, a game more serious than it seems at this early point, for though we can laugh easily at the harmless nature of Tom's play-acting, more serious fictions upon which so-

16. Blair, *Mark Twain and Huck Finn*, p. 117.

ciety's very existence bases itself—such as racial inequality—will soon be posing as reality.

Huck himself is getting used to the artifices of society, though various signs tell him that Pap—the demon presence behind the fine appearance of the social world—is around. Then Pap appears, the destroyer, it would seem at first, of all civilized lies, with a particular hatred for literature; Huck is reading about George Washington when the old man whacks the book out of his hand and shouts, "First you know you'll get religion, too" (p. 40), correctly—from Twain's point of view—connecting the fictions of history and religious belief. But, of course, Pap is no real enemy of these things—he is the Master of Lies, expert in his own right in all pretenses and fabrications sanctified by social usage. Gaining the sympathy of the judge by enacting the convention of father-love, he takes him in further by his parody of "reform." Pap is really a subscriber to society's formulas, for all his seeming unregeneracy—as his drunken reproaches to Huck that he has been cheated of the due rewards of fatherhood and his denunciations of the state of Ohio for letting a "nigger" vote both illustrate. He is, in fact, the wicked soul of conventionality, his hypocrisy simply more blatant still than that of respectable society.

Huck makes his escape from both respectable and disreputable versions of constraint, from the Widow and Pap, by a device of make-believe, his own faked murder. On the one hand this is symbolically veracious and life-saving; Huck must "die to" an old life in order to reach for freedom, and this reaching must threaten to extinguish the sense of self by which one survives in society. It can be contrasted with the theatrics of Pap that precipitate it—Pap's drunken delusion that Huck is the "Angel of Death." But Huck is right to recognize, on the other hand, that he is engaging himself, out of necessity, in the very mode he is bidding farewell to, the mode of fiction-making. He acknowledges that his is an inferior achievement to what Tom might have devised: "I did wish Tom Sawyer was there, I knowed he would take an interest in this kind of business, and throw in the fancy touches" (p. 57). Yet henceforth such story-telling as Huck engages in will, for the most part, be enforced by the necessity, paradoxically, of keeping himself free from the world of social lies or of protecting Jim from its designs.

Only occasionally is he afterward tempted to regress to idle, mischievous make-believe. The second practical joke on Jim, the snakeskin laid at the foot of his bed, brings the dead snake's mate to bite Jim on the heel. Jim thinks that bad luck has been invoked, but Huck knows that the misfortune has been brought on not by handling the snakeskin as such but by his own undisciplined impulse toward "fun." Then directly, Huck must himself, again, needfully make-believe to find out the state of things in St. Petersburg, and he goes onshore as a girl, with a tale of a sick mother needing help. Detected as a boy, he is quick with another tale—this one of a runaway orphan bound to a mean, old farmer—and is believed, his story-telling thus having served the function of keeping him safe from discovery while truly, in this second case, representing his condition of orphanhood and flight.

He is tempted again by the lure of motiveless "adventure," the distractions so often offered him by Tom, who is, in this sense, still present within him when he goes aboard the wrecked steamboat despite Jim's misgivings. He is thinking of Tom, indeed, as he says to himself, "wouldn't [Tom] throw style into it?" (p. 97). His reproof is the harrowing sight of the murderers aboard the wreck and the loss, temporarily, of the raft—admonishment, as after the snakeskin trick, of the consequence of idle fancy. To do what he can for the murderers, now trapped on the sinking vessel, he resorts to another invented story to the ferryboat watchman, trying to rescue them by his tale as he had tried to safeguard himself and Jim by his tales to Mrs. Loftus, for, as he says, "there ain't no telling but I might come to be a murderer myself" (p. 103). But imagination cannot work its life-saving magic this time, and the vessel sinks before help can come.

She is called, of course, the *Walter Scott*, and with her, taking this opportunity to mock once more the novel's antimodel, Twain sinks Huck's appetite for romance. As for Jim, he "didn't want no more adventures," the word now signifying Tom Sawyer–style escapades, and Huck concludes, "he was right; he was most always right; he had an uncommon level head, for a nigger" (p. 109). Part of the "truck" they have carried off from the *Walter Scott* is, not surprisingly, "a lot of books," from which the recently literate Huck reads to Jim—"about kings, and dukes, and earls, and such" (p. 109)—and they discuss the ways of such fabulous beings. They also discuss the ways of the greatest of Old Testament kings, Solomon, who wanted to cut a baby in half, and Jim thinks him plagued by the "dad-fetchedes' ways" (p. 111) he has ever seen. Jim scores, too, over Huck's book-learning by "proving," with irrefutable logic, that although cats and dogs "talk" differently, Frenchmen and Americans must talk alike. All this conversation may seem simply a comic interval between significant action unless we realize its import—Jim, the illiterate and even more alienated refugee from society, must teach Huck the futility of the "truck" of notions he has rescued from the sinking vessel of his social membership.

It is at this point, however, when the raft and the canoe are separated in the fog, that Huck loses Jim, his instructor in pragmatic wisdom. When he finds him again, he has forgotten what he learned about idle story-telling and plays the third of his practical jokes on Jim, pretending never to have been gone at all, even though Jim has worried solely about him. Jim's reproach, his reduction of cruel fantasy to truth, is telling: "Dat truck dah is *trash*; en trash is what people is dat puts dirt on de head er dey fren's en makes 'em ashamed" (p. 121). Again the word *truck* stands for the useless—and sometimes dangerous—freight of lies that even the raft is carrying, as the *Walter Scott* had, something that is no better than "trash." Huck's apology, as every reader notes, is a giant step in his moral progress. It also represents his resolution to dispense with Tom-Sawyer-foolery. He will tell no more false tales, unless he has to, to save life. So, he immediately lies again, but only for this reason, with a lie that is better than the truth he intended to tell the men with guns who are on the lookout for runaway slaves. Not even Tom could have improved upon his suggestion, by implication, that his family is afflicted with smallpox. That he does not actually say this—but leaves the specification to the imagination of the bounty-hunters, is probably significant; Huck's restraint is more than strategic, for it may represent his disinclination, now, for elaborating even necessary fictions.

Again separated from Jim when the steamboat collides with the raft, Huck must once more reinvent himself as "George Jackson," just fallen off the steamboat, a fiction of orphaning symbolically justifiable. But it is not Huck who is the source of the engulfing and ultimately murderous fiction of the Grangerfords, whose adopted son this orphan becomes. At first he is delighted to find himself in such a fine family, one so completely equipped with all the standard appurtenances and practiced in the appropriate rituals of gentility. Huck has never before seen a house that has "so much style" (p. 136), so many objects too elegant to function, like the mantel clock, with the picture of a town painted on it and a beautiful tick, which would "start in and strike a hundred and fifty before she got tuckered out" (p. 137) after a traveling peddler repaired it, or the crockery basket filled with painted plaster fruit. Indeed, the house is *all* style without substance, filled with what might be called stage-props rather than realities.

Of course, the Grangerfords possess books. There is *Pilgrim's Progress*, which Huck summarizes, in his ignorance, as "about a man that left his family it didn't say why" (p. 137), a Bible, a gift-book annual full of poetry, a home medical manual, Henry Clay's speeches, and a hymn book. The collection is ironically significant, as Walter Blair has pointed out, enforcing "the evidence of fraudulent pretense"[17] in the Grangerford way of life. Though they subscribe to "Friendship's Offering," though they possess the religious texts that instruct one to love one's neighbor, though they can learn from the medical volume how to treat the injured and save life, the Grangerfords inhabit a house of hatred and death where the most powerful feeling is enmity for one's neighbor and a desire to injure and destroy him. And in this family of fictionizers there has even been one literary creator, the lamented Emmeline, whose grotesquely sentimental verses and drawings not only parody a tradition of false art but also demonstrate the falsifying artifice of Grangerford being.

For in this House of Fiction, the greatest fiction of all is the Grangerford family itself. At the Grangerfords', social behavior is as ritualized as the ceremonies of Tom Sawyer's band, got up from the best authorities. The fine manners and high principles, like the accumulations of artifacts in their house, are as much a fiction as are the practices of the make-believe boy-robbers, as much a structure of the imagination unrelated to reality. But, unlike the boys' games, the Grangerfords' pretenses are not for fun; the feud will become murderous and cost the lives of all the male members of the clan, even down to young Buck. Buck, save for a letter of his name, is Huck himself, who is nearly dead with horror as he witnesses the slaughter of his twin. But Buck, because of his implication in the gang-war of the adults, is also that other brother to Huck, his friend Tom, the young knight of pretenses and the willing collaborator in the social game.

17. Ibid., p. 229.

Huck escapes this death of self and the imagination by the narrowest squeak and reaches the eden, once more, of the raft. But it is soon invaded by those final virtuosi of story-telling, the Duke and the Dauphin. They are, even more obviously than the Grangerfords, literary fabricators, conscious tellers of tales, inventors of false identity. These scoundrels perpetrate frauds that are parodies of social roles, dramatic impersonations behind which no definable selfhood or meaningful history exists. When first encountered each has got into trouble for a false tale—one for vending a dentifrice that really melts the enamel off teeth, the other for running a temperance revival while swigging the jug on the sly. The first soon tells his story of his descent from the Duke of Bridgewater, only to have it immediately topped by the other's claim to be Louis the Seventeenth, the lost Dauphin. It doesn't take Huck long to discern that the liars "warn't no kings nor dukes at all, but just low-down humbugs and frauds," but he raises no fuss, understanding by this time that society is sustained, peace is kept in the family, by lying tales. "If I never learnt nothing else out of Pap," Huck observes, "I learnt that the best way to get along with his kind of people is to let them have their own way" (p. 166). The Duke and the Dauphin, then, are replications of his own terrible father, representatives of the deceitful, pretending, and enslaving parent-culture to which, for the sake of family peace, Huck has learned to accommodate himself.

To protect Jim, whom the scoundrels immediately suspect of being a runaway slave, Huck must still another time subdue himself to the mode of pretense and tell his false identity tale (in which he is again, so *truly*, the orphan with no one but Jim to cling to). But the Duke soon devises new identities for Jim, supposedly also meant for protection but really bringing him into closer correspondence with the endangering condition of criminal and racial outcast, printing his picture on a "Reward" poster to be used when they want to claim him as their captive or making him up to represent a "sick Arab." None of the Duke and the Dauphin's lies can have any effect, in the end, but destruction—it is they who soon enough will collect a forty-dollar reward for turning Jim in.

The inventions of the Duke and the Dauphin elaborate Twain's ridicule of the formulas of society. Religion, the object of satiric contempt in almost everything Twain wrote from *Innocents Abroad* to *The Mysterious Stranger*, is immediately represented not only by the campmeeting sermon but also by the King's pose as repentant pirate, itself reminiscent of Pap's earlier posturing as repentant sinner. At the Wilks funeral, again, the false piety of society at large is only echoed by the hypocrisy of the King posing as the preacher uncle from Sheffield. The funeral sermon of the Reverend Hobson is less significant to his audience than the racket of the dog who has caught a rat in the cellar of the house, and at the auction of the Wilks property the King is on hand, "looking his level piousest . . . chipping in a little Scripture, now and then, or a little goody-goody saying" (p. 249) to the general edification.

But the most significant pretenses of the Duke and the Dauphin are parodic of language itself. The garbled Shakespeare speeches may seem tedious unless we realize that Twain has undercut the dignity of the most profound passages by mixing lines that almost coalesce; all coherence is mocked when one's ear is lulled into accepting the false connectedness of "To be or not to be; that is the bare bodkin / That makes calamity of so long life," (p. 179) and so on. Similarly, the coherence of history is a little later made ridiculous by Huck when he undertakes to explain to Jim that "kings is mostly rapscallions" (p. 199), mixing the Doomesday Book and the Arabian Nights, the lives of Henry VIII and the Duke of Wellington, and conflating the mistresses of Henry II, Edward IV, and Charles II.

The question of language as the source of deceits and fictions is crucial, and Twain seems willing to turn even upon the colloquial style he has reserved for Huck's monologue and to show that it, too, can be the container of corruption and conventionality. At Bricksville, that devastating second look at St. Petersburg, the common men who exchange their banalities as they lounge along the filthy main street are quite deserving of the contempt of Colonel Sherburn who, like another Grangerford, has shot down the drunken lout Boggs out of offended dignity. The lecture he delivers to the crowd that thinks it wants to lynch him is couched in a style as formally correct as it is coldly superior in logic and truth to that of his hearers. But the Duke and the Dauphin are capable of parodying all styles, high and low. Their final caper, the attempt to fleece the Wilks family, exhibits them as polite gentlemen from the birthplace of the idea of the gentleman, old England, while constantly revealing, as though through the rents in their shoddy costumes, their true coarseness. The speeches of the King—"tears and flapdoodle" (p. 212), as Huck says—are never more deliciously comic versions of the rhetoric of high occasions than when they focus on a malapropism, his use of the word *orgies*. When he even offers a pseudo-etymology to justify it, Huck declares, "He was the *worst* I ever struck" (p. 217). Yet their imperfect command of their roles proves their undoing, for it is their speech that distinguishes them from the genuine English relatives and gives the cue to Doctor Robinson.

To foil the plotters Huck must rouse himself from his customary passivity and, devising a plot himself, make a confidante of Mary Jane so that she may witness to the truth after he has escaped. He knows that his plot is in the Tom Sawyer mode, but beneath Tom's purity of impracticality and superfluous style. "I judged I had done it pretty neat—I reckoned Tom Sawyer couldn't a done it no neater himself," says Huck, though he admits, "Of course he would a throwed more style into it, but I can't do that very handy, not being brung up to it" (pp. 248–49). His strategem has rested on truth rather than falsity, an unorthodox procedure indeed. As he reflects after his revelation to Mary Jane:

> I reckon a body that ups and tells the truth when he is in a tight place, is taking considerable many risks, though I ain't had no experience, and can't say for certain; but it looks so to me, anyway; and yet here's a case where I'm blest if it don't look to me like the truth is better, and actuly *safer* than a lie. I must lay it by in my mind, and think it over some time or other, it's so kind of strange and unregular. I never see nothing like it. Well, I says to myself at last, I'm agoing to chance it; I'll up and tell the truth this time, though it does seem most like set-

ting down on a kag of powder and touching it off just to see where you'll go to. (P. 240)

To tell the truth—not to "make up a story"—is, of course, to deny the superiority of fiction to fact, to deny the validity of pretense, to deny Tom Sawyer. Huck's resolution to dispense with falsehood this time fills him with misgiving, goes against his sense of what he *ought* to do, and is a crisis in which his heart triumphs over his conscience, anticipating the more famous crisis that immediately follows. Before this happens he turns, ineptly, to lying again, trying to describe life in the pretended English home of the fake Wilks uncles and himself, and Levi Bell, the lawyer, observes, "I reckon you ain't used to lying, it don't seem to come handy; what you want is practice. You do it pretty awkward" (p. 254).

He makes his most famous repudiation of lying when he discovers that he cannot pretend to himself that he wants to turn Jim in: "You can't pray a lie" (p. 270), he observes, and, though he proceeds to write the letter to Miss Watson, he decides to damn himself and "steal Jim out of slavery again" (p. 272), and so tears up the letter. Paradoxically, he is full of inventive ingenuity on behalf of the truth to which he has committed himself and successfully talks his way out of obstruction by the two knaves as he makes his way to the Phelps Farm—he must still resort to life-saving fiction to combat a world of lies.

When he arrives at the Phelps Farm in Chapter 32, he is once again in one of those moods of melancholy trancendence to which I have referred and even wishes himself dead as the breeze whispering of dead spirits quivers the leaves. And he is ready for his last relapse into the character of Tom Sawyer, ready to accept Tom's name and serve Tom's imagination. His own existential truthfulness, his independence of the lies and the fictions of the social world, must be surrendered. But if what I have been maintaining is true, we should not be surprised. The last ten chapters are no reversal, after all. If Huck is to survive he must reattach himself to his world and to its lies, fabricate the self out of them. At this moment, indeed, Huck is, for once, without a prepared selfhood. He is a ghost without a name, listening to the words of others for a cue to his identity: "I wanted to get them [the children] out to one side, and pump them a little, and find out who I was" (p. 281). When he is at last "recognized" as Tom, he is overjoyed: "if they was joyful, it warn't nothing to what I was; for it was like being born again. I was so glad to find out who I was. . . . Being Tom Sawyer was easy and comfortable" (pp. 282–83). The exhausting struggle for free formlessness of being is over, and he is easy and comfortable in the role of the inventor of fictional selves and stories, Tom Sawyer.

Tom himself greets Huck as an impersonating ghost and warns him, "Don't you play nothing on me, because I wouldn't on you" (p. [284]), which is a joke, we will realize, for Tom *is* about to "play" a joke on Huck—one of those practical jokes that hurt—to pretend to be a "nigger-stealer," willing to help him free Jim. It is Tom's deception underlying all the deceptions the boys will now practice together upon others. Meanwhile, he welcomes

Huck back, in effect, to the robber-band. He is full of praise when he hears how Huck made his escape from Pap by the faked murder: "I warn't ever murdered at all—I played it on them," says Huck with some pride, suggesting by "them" some vaguely general social audience. Tom calls Huck's story, "a grand adventure, and mysterious" (p. 285). As Huck says, "it hit him where he lived" (p. 285).

So, under the rule of Tom's imagination, made-up history, appearance as costume, and theatrical improvisation all flourish. Tom pretends to be someone else before he assumes the "true" (but really still false) identity of Sid. When the Phelpses see him at their door, says Huck, he has "his store clothes on, and an audience—and that was always nuts for Tom Sawyer. In them circumstances it warn't no trouble to him to throw in an amount of style that was suitable" (p. 286). So, first he claims to be William Thompson, a young traveler from Hicksville, Ohio—which then appears to be one of those practical jokes so relished by the Sawyer imagination when he "reveals" himself to Aunt Sally as Sid. She declares, "I'd be willing to stand a thousand such jokes to have you here. Well, to think of that performance" (p. 289), not realizing that "Sid's" disclosure is but another layer of performance. Unlike Huck's disguises, Tom's are prompted not by need but by his insatiable appetite for histrionics.

Sleights and disguises are all, indeed, that we will ever get from Tom, who is not, even when finally revealed as himself, ever reduced to a final essence, an unalterable core, since he is always precisely no more than what he appears. Huck is awed as Tom begins to develop schemes for the liberation of Jim, and he yearns to complete his own submergence in the mode of the protean imagination, already signaled by the adoption of Tom's name: "if I had Tom Sawyer's head, I wouldn't trade it off to be a duke, nor mate of a steamboat, nor clown in a circus, nor nothing I can think of" (p. 294). No particular role can offer more delight than the artist's, for his is the capacity to impersonate all roles. For the artist there is, really, no "authenticity."

Huck realizes that his own capacity for creating plot is rudimentary compared to Tom's. His plan for freeing Jim has the defect of mere functionality (as Tom says, "it's *too* blame' simple; there ain't nothing *to* it"), whereas Tom's own, Huck says, "was worth fifteen of mine, for style, and would make Jim just as free a man as mine would, and maybe get us all killed besides" (p. 294). The fantasy that entails *real* danger, even the threat of death, is the best of all, as Tom had long before pointed out to his boy-robber companions when he insisted that they were highwaymen who "killed people" and could get killed themselves, and not mere burglars. The Grangerford fantasy proved its excellence by its murderous—and suicidal—consequences. And this elegant plan of Tom's will nearly get Jim and themselves killed, as it turns out.

When Huck suggests with plain practicality that Jim escape through the cabin window, Tom reproaches him, "I should *hope* we can find a way that's a little more complicated than *that*, Huck Finn," and proposes that they dig the prisoner out. At the house, the back-door fastened by a latch-string "warn't romantical enough for Tom Sawyer: no way would do him but he must climb up the lightning-rod" (p. 297). Tom is actually distressed by the altogether too "easy and awkard" conditions they confront—"It makes it so rotten difficult to get up a difficult plan. There ain't no watchman to be drugged—now there *ought* to be a watchman. There ain't even a dog to give a sleeping-mixture to. And there's Jim chained by one leg, with a ten-foot chain, to the leg of his bed: why, all you got to do is lift up the bedstead and slip off the chain" (p. [300]).

The absence of the conventional plot ingredients enforces artistic creation: "You got to invent *all* the difficulties." But the more to be invented the more honor to the artistic imagination: "there's more honor in getting him out through a lot of difficulties and dangers, where there warn't one of them furnished you by the people who it was their duty to furnish them, and you had to contrive them all out of your own head" (p. 301). Of course, getting them out of one's own literary head means getting them from the "best authorities" and examples—among whom Tom names Baron Trenck, Casanova, Cellini, King Henry IV of France, and Dumas's *The Man in the Iron Mask* and *The Count of Monte Cristo*, getting the idea for titling his escapade on "evasion" from Dumas's *L'Évasion du Duc de Beaufort*. Tom is proud to claim an authority for everything—the rope ladder that Jim has to hide in his bed, the "journal" that Jim must write on his shirt, though he can't write, and so on.

When Tom finally agrees to use pick and shovel instead of case knives to dig Jim out, he admits it isn't moral, reversing the sense of *morality* to make it mean aesthetic impracticality, inefficacy. Huck's stubborn anti-aesthetic *im*morality (as Tom would judge it) makes him insist, "Picks is the thing, moral or no moral; and as for me, I don't care shucks for the morality of it, nohow. When I start in to steal a nigger, or a watermelon, or a Sunday-school book, I ain't no ways particular how it's done so it's done. What I want is my nigger; or what I want is my watermelon; or what I want is my Sunday-school book; and if a pick's the handiest thing, that's the thing I'm agoing to dig that nigger or that watermelon or that Sunday-school book out with; and I don't give a dead rat what the authorities thinks about it nuther" (p. 310). *Morality* here is absolutely synonymous with *conscience* as Huck has used the latter word, the "deformed" conscience of social modes that reproves the instinctive promptings of his heart.

Even Tom must yield, somewhat, to the practical, though in that case the pretense of impracticality must be maintained. Picks must be thought of as case knives and stairs as the lightning rod it is really too difficult to climb. But wherever possible the complications of imagination are to be preferred to the merely efficacious, especially if the former are *less* efficacious. Jim, who could be freed by the quick application of a cold chisel to his shackles, must be subjected to the tedious, the distressing, even the dangerous devices of Sawyerism. "Tom was in high spirits. He said it was the best fun he ever had in his life, and the most intellectural; and said if he only could see his way to it we would keep it up all the rest of our lives and leave Jim to our children to get out" (p. 313). Jim must be a proper literary prisoner, with tools or rope ladders smuggled to him in a pie, must scratch inscriptions and a coat of arms on the wall, and must adopt a pet rat and plant a garden, however incomprehensible these things are to him. And the Phelps household must be thrown into confusion by the disappearance of sheets and shirts and spoons and the escape of the rats and snakes the boys have collected. It is all almost as tiresome to the reader as it is to Jim himself, and even to Huck.

The warnings and anonymous letters that Tom now insists upon prove, however, the source not merely of "style" but of near disaster, though perhaps one should say that high style requires a flouting of the utilitarian to the point of a deadly indifference. Jim and his two liberators make it to the raft despite the real pursuit they have generated, and even Jim must admit, "It 'uz planned beautiful, en it'uz *done* beautiful; en dey ain't *nobody* kin git up a plan dat's mo' mixed-up en splendid den what dat one wuz." Tom himself is positively delighted that make-believe has almost had fatal consequences: "Tom was the gladdest of all, because he had a bullet in the calf of his leg" (p. 344). "Boys," he says, "we done it elegant!" (p. 344). Tom is consistent enough to instruct that the doctor now needed must be kidnapped and brought blindfolded, but Huck is practical enough to employ his own lower kind of make-believe in a story about a brother hurt in a hunting accident. This tale, though not very convincing, is a correct and consistent summary of what actually happened: "He had a dream," Huck tells the doctor, "and it shot him." And the doctor comments, "Singular dream" (p. [347]). Indeed, dreams or fictions play real and sometimes dire roles in our lives, as the dreams of the Grangerfords and Shepherdsons have already done in the novel, or, as Twain probably thought, the dreams of North and South had done in the country's recent history.

Yet, now that the Evasion is ending, Huck is ready to be reconciled to the dreams by which life sustains itself. Aunt Sally, it seems, is much nicer than the widow, though the cyclicity of the plot tells us that she is really a duplication of that matriarchal authority from which he has been in flight. Huck cannot stand any longer the deception he has practiced on her and swears to himself that he "wouldn't never do nothing to grieve her any more" (p. 354). Society now offers him its most self-flattering versions of itself. Though Jim is put back into chains, he is acknowledged, after the doctor's report, to be "a nigger . . . worth a thousand dollars—and kind treatment, too," and the Phelpses take one or two of his chains off and let him have meat and greens with his bread and water. Huck no longer thinks of Jim's freedom— or of his own.

So it is time for Tom's revelation that Jim has been free all along because of Miss Watson's will. It does not matter that her death-bed repentance for her resolution to sell him downriver is blatantly improbable, a formula of cheap romance. As for Tom's commitment, even temporarily, to the project of setting a free nigger free, it is clear, now, that this has been only another of his make-believe adventures, a fiction. If it had succeeded it would only have been the start of further adventures; the three would have continued downriver on the raft and had "adventures plumb to the mouth of the river," and only then, perhaps, would Tom and Huck tell Jim that he was a free man and take him "back up home on a steamboat, in style, and pay him [forty dollars] for his lost time" (p. [364]). Tom does give Jim forty dollars for being a patient prisoner. Is it only an accident that this is the same sum for which the Duke and the Dauphin had sold him back into slavery? Huck, at any rate, is ready for "more howling adventures," and he will even be member enough of respectable society to be able to purchase the necessary outfit, his six thousand dollars having been kept safe for him all this while by Judge Thatcher.

With deliberate irony the last chapters overturn any expectations we have cherished, despite Twain's numerous hints and warnings, that the search for a meaningful design in experience is anything but a game. That Jim was free all along makes Tom's Evasion properly titled. His plan has been, as he would claim, "beautifully" purposeless, an evasion of the whole issue of personal freedom. And all Huck's efforts, earlier, to help Jim gain freedom, those struggles, even against conscience, to stand by his friend, to protect him from those who would keep him a slave—these too, in retrospect, become plot without motive, pure art or adventure in the Tom Sawyer sense. Huck has risked social selfhood, the only identity society allows, in his passage down the river, but now he accepts once more his role as Tom Sawyer's lieutenant, becomes the willing accomplice in the sleights of the imagination.

III

Contexts and Conventions

T HE exploration of the literary traditions and conventions available to Twain in composing *Adventures of Huckleberry Finn* has been painstaking and thorough, but this realm of sources, analogues, contemporary influences, popular traditions, and the like has not by any means been the province of sub-sub-librarians. As the exchange of views between Van Wyck Brooks's *The Ordeal of Mark Twain* and Bernard DeVoto's *Mark Twain's America* dramatized, Twain's work, and *Huckleberry Finn* in particular, has been a high point of reference in the long debate between literary dandies and squatters in America, between those who lament the thinness and the poverty of American materials and society and those who point to the enrichment to art offered by indigenous resources. All the essays in this section comment, whether directly or obliquely, on this issue, and it seems inevitable to conclude that both the strengths and the weaknesses of *Huckleberry Finn* are bound up in the obligations Twain incurred to his cultures (antebellum Missouri and the East of the Gilded Age) and the traditions and conventions that circulated within them.

One of the most obvious of the contemporary contexts of *Huck Finn* is the subgenre Twain helped to create and define, the "boy book." Alan Gribben traces the influence on Twain's Hannibal boy books of Thomas Bailey Aldrich's landmark *The Story of a Bad Boy* (1869), showing how extensively Twain used its example in the creation of his boys' world, and also advancing modestly but courageously (given the current tenor of criticism) a defense of Tom Sawyer's role and character in *Huckleberry Finn*. From small boys to their mothers and other female keepers is but a small step, and Nancy Walker's essay describes what might be termed the morphology of women characters in *Huck Finn*. It is, expectedly, a short list with but narrow variation, and one that dramatizes the extent to which Twain was hobbled in his creation of female characters by the Victorian stereotypes he accepted. Much more remains to be said, it would seem, on the roles of women and the family in the novel. The relative lack of essays with a feminist perspective submitted to this volume makes one wonder if the novel, embracing as it does quintessentially masculine myths and rituals, simply fails to register as deeply—except as negative example—to female as it does to male readers.

William Lenz's essay takes up the novel from the angle of a character type—the confidence man—who appears in it frequently and who has been much studied recently as a phenomenon of American literature. Lenz enlarges what others have shown in identifying Twain's debts to earlier avatars of the type, but his essay might just as well have been placed in the last section of this volume—on the novel as document of American culture—for its subject widens to a consideration of the cultural weaknesses exposed in both the prewar "flush times" of the original confidence man and the postwar era of widespread corruption that Twain's first novel has named.

David Sewell's essay is an acute and intricate analysis of the various forms of speech and linguistic behavior that inform the central moral values in the novel. Insisting that the dynamics of the book reside not in a simple bipolar opposition between "genteel" and "vernacular" language but in the interplay of a variety of intentions governing both these modes of speech, Sewell places the brilliance of Huck's unwashed language in the context of Noah Webster and "our great nineteenth-century educational enterprise of prescriptive language teaching." His is a major clarification of the power and beauty of Huck's "unfallen, Adamic dialect" that remains incapable of speaking evil.

George C. Carrington, on the other hand, having had his longer say in *The Dramatic Unity of Huckleberry Finn*, restricts his analysis of the novel to some considerations that follow upon our recognizing the importance of the elements of farce it contains. That this analysis has not been undertaken before is curious, given Twain's addiction to burlesque and the hoax, and Carrington's thesis will be perhaps even more curious to those who view Huck as a hero, for in this challenging reading Tom Sawyer emerges as the central character, Jim as a fool, and Huck himself as a mere "fumbler."

One of the most obvious contexts in which a literary work lives is the one provided by the writer's earlier works, especially if, as was the case with Twain, the writer was a household name and might reasonably expect readers to be familiar with his previous books. As Robert Regan demonstrates in "Huck Finn in the Wake of the *Quaker City*," Twain seems to have made this claim on his immediate audience, and we risk errors today if we fail to recognize the "polyvalence" these earlier works (especially the seminal *Innocents Abroad*) establish in contrast to the "monovalence" of Huck's uneducated voice. The anterior discourses that are evoked in *Huckleberry Finn* should qualify our strictures about the beginning and the ending of the novel. As the former looks backward to *Tom Sawyer*, and the latter looks ahead to sequels, we should be reminded that *Huck Finn*, like the Territory its hero hopes to escape to, is not yet closed.

9 ALAN GRIBBEN

"I Did Wish Tom Sawyer Was There": Boy-Book Elements in *Tom Sawyer* and *Huckleberry Finn*

Tom Sawyer sorely tried the patience of the fictional villagers of St. Petersburg, and more than a century after his first impudent appearance he proves to be equally disturbing to literary critics. In contrast with that of his universally acclaimed companion, Huckleberry Finn, Tom Sawyer's reputation has noticeably sagged over the years. For some modern-day readers, in fact, the very presence of Tom—vainglorious, prevaricating, exhibitionistic, insincere, manipulative—"ruins" Huck Finn's marvelous narrative.[1]

Of course Tom Sawyer will always be at a disadvantage in any comparison with his subsequently invented playmate, for their creator endowed Tom with the trite sensibilities and grandiose visions of a declining Romantic tradition, burlesquing in this childish literary figure the books that Sam Clemens himself had relished as a boy. Most reasonable commentators will allow Tom Sawyer the right to play pranks in his own book, but Jesse Bier is typical in declaring, "If Samuel Clemens loved Tom Sawyer, Mark Twain in his masterpiece had his alternative view of this biggest little con man of them all. For in *Huckleberry Finn* Tom is an ambiguous charmer at best, for all his fetching outlawry. At his worst, which he is in this book, he is a self-deceiver, over-romanticizing and falsifying all experience, bathing in sentimentality, and living a constant lie of style and substance."[2] Judith Fetterley asserts that Tom Sawyer becomes "a creature of delusion" in *Huckleberry Finn*, in which "the action of the novel works to expose the hypocrisy of Tom Sawyer who . . . enacts cruelty after cruelty."[3]

It has almost reached the point where one is hesitant to discuss the character of Tom Sawyer in print, because to do so is to enter an arena where two

1. The characterization of Tom Sawyer has become all the more tiresome and irritating for many commentators since accurate texts of several sequels to *Huckleberry Finn* became available—"Huck Finn and Tom Sawyer among the Indians," "Tom Sawyer's Gang Plans a Naval Battle," "Tom Sawyer's Conspiracy" (*Mark Twain's Hannibal, Huck and Tom*, ed. Walter Blair [Berkeley: University of California Press, 1969]), and "Tom Sawyer Abroad" and "Tom Sawyer, Detective" (*The Adventures of Tom Sawyer, Tom Sawyer Abroad, Tom Sawyer, Detective*, ed. John C. Gerber, Paul Baender, and Terry Firkins [Berkeley: University of California Press, 1980]). I do not discuss these inferior works, but their contents generally corroborate my conclusions. The latter book contains the edition of *Tom Sawyer* consulted for this essay.

2. *The Rise and Fall of American Humor* (New York: Holt, Rinehart and Winston, 1968), p. 132.

3. "Disenchantment: Tom Sawyer in *Huckleberry Finn*," PMLA 87 (January 1972): 70, 73.

major disagreements in Mark Twain criticism have been contested for decades. The first is the question of whether Tom Sawyer "matures" discernibly
toward the end of the novel named after him,[4] and the second pertains to
whether Tom Sawyer's hijinks at the Phelps plantation desecrate beyond redemption the concluding chapters in *Huckleberry Finn*—which is another
way of asking whether Huck Finn is given an opportunity to "mature" satisfactorily in *his* novel.[5] Most of the critics who have taken any of the positions in the multiple permutations of these arguments can agree on at least
one matter: to dislike the "Evasion" episodes of *Huckleberry Finn* is to dislike Tom Sawyer, who is in most respects an embarrassment to the stature of
his originator and to the artistic work in which Tom interferes as a most
definite blemish.[6]

Can Tom Sawyer, at this late date, be exculpated even slightly? This essay
suggests—audaciously perhaps—that he can, but first some preliminary
sketching of related topics must be allowed. To understand Tom Sawyer as he
behaves in *Huckleberry Finn* it is necessary to recall his exertions in *Tom
Sawyer*, and to fathom the Tom Sawyer figure in that earlier novel it be-
hooves us to look at the state of the "boy book" in the 1870s. Mark Twain's
contributions to this type of juvenile fiction have never been in doubt. As
one critic has noted, "From the moment of Aunt Polly's first cry ["Tom!"] a
new spontaneity and vigor have entered into the boy-book."[7] Although *The
Adventures of Tom Sawyer* (1876) initially had a disappointing sale,[8] the
work gradually gained a hold on the American popular imagination. Twain

4. Walter Blair, "On the Structure of *Tom Sawyer*," *MP* 37 (August 1939): 75–88; Barry A.
Marks, "Mark Twain's Hymn of Praise," *EJ* 48 (November 1959): 443–49; Hamlin Hill, "The
Composition and the Structure of *Tom Sawyer*," *AL* 32 (January 1961): 379–92; Albert E.
Stone, Jr., *The Innocent Eye: Childhood in Mark Twain's Imagination* (New Haven: Yale Uni-
versity Press, 1961), pp. 78–89; and Robert Regan, *Unpromising Heroes: Mark Twain and
His Characters* (Berkeley: University of California Press, 1966), pp. 117–21, argue persuasively
in favor of Tom's maturity; Robert Bray entertainingly summarizes this and other debates about
Tom Sawyer in "*Tom Sawyer* Once and for All," *Review* 3 (1981): 77–83. Most commentators have based their arguments on Blair's seminal article, but in "The Sanctioned Rebel,"
SNNTS 3 (Fall 1971): 293–304, Judith Fetterley astutely challenges the entire thesis on which
these essays have depended.

5. This topic, launched by Lionel Trilling and T. S. Eliot, has become too involved to treat
fully in a note; in the avalanche of scholarly print that the issue has brought down upon the
novel, representative studies include Henry Nash Smith's *Mark Twain: The Development of a
Writer* (Cambridge: Harvard University Press, 1962), pp. 129–35; Pascal Covici, Jr.'s *Mark
Twain's Humor: The Image of a World* (Dallas: Southern Methodist University Press, 1962),
pp. 159–85; Richard Poirier's *A World Elsewhere: The Place of Style in American Literature*
(New York: Oxford University Press, 1966), pp. 183–95; James M. Cox's *Mark Twain: The
Fate of Humor* (Princeton: Princeton University Press, 1966), pp. 171–84; and George C. Car-
rington, Jr.'s *The Dramatic Unity of "Huckleberry Finn"* (Columbus: Ohio State University
Press, 1976), pp. 153–87.

6. See, for example, A. N. Kaul, *The American Vision: Actual and Ideal Society in Nineteenth-
Century Fiction* (New Haven: Yale University Press, 1963), p. 304: "Tom Sawyer is nowhere else
so unsympathetic, and his 'heroism' nowhere so meretricious, as in the concluding chapters of
this novel."

7. Jim Hunter, "Mark Twain and the Boy-Book in 19th-Century America," *CE* 24 (March
1963): 433.

8. Gerber, in "Introduction," *Tom Sawyer*, p. 29.

would later explain shrewdly: "I conceive that the right way to write a story for boys is to write so that it will not only interest boys but will also strongly interest any man *who has ever been a boy*. That immensely *enlarges the audience*."[9] The efficacy of this formula, suggestively phrased in exclusively male terms, is apparent in the public's abiding fondness for Tom Sawyer's "boyish" pranks, indulgent amusement that found its permanent reflection in the idealized series of Hannibal paintings by Norman Rockwell.

More than a commercially successful technique linked this novelist to his major characters and themes, however; Samuel Clemens's yearning for perennial youthfulness became a fetish in his personal life while beneficially stimulating his creative impulses. Brander Matthews, who left behind the most pithily accurate short sketch of Clemens ever published by one who knew him personally, recalled that in the summer of 1890 (when Clemens was nearing the age of fifty-five) he and Clemens joined a socially prominent group—many of them middle-aged women—vacationing at the Onteora Club in the Catskills. The people often passed their time playing card games, and Matthews noticed that his friend Clemens "was forever wanting to make over the rules of the game to suit his whim of the moment,—a boyish trait which I soon discovered to be entirely characteristic. But we were all boys together that summer; and we invented new ways for discharging our high spirits. . . . He was a hard worker at intervals. . . . But he liked to play, especially with his own children, making them accept him as of their own age; and he also could play with the grownups as if he were a child." The same author who enjoyed playacting with children and adults "as if he were a child" (free from inhibiting social expectations) talked with Matthews that summer about his method of writing, claiming that "he began the composition of 'Tom Sawyer' with certain of his boyish recollections in mind, writing on and on until he had utilized them all." In Matthews's opinion, "one reason why 'Tom Sawyer' and 'Huckleberry Finn' are to be ranked among the best of boys' books is because Mark had the rare gift of recovering the spirit of boyhood, with its eagerness and its assurance, its exuberant energy and its incessant desire to assert individuality,—in other words, to 'show off.' Until his dying day Mark retained the essentials of boyishness. It might almost be said that he never grew up. He had the effervescent irresponsibility of a boy, the impulsive recklessness. . . . It is not to be wondered at that the name given him by the one who knew him best, his wife, was 'Youth.'"[10] Nor is strange that a (too doctrinaire) exercise in psychobiography decided that Twain's "fiction is boyish and incomplete."[11] Tony Tanner,

9. *Mark Twain's Letters*, ed. Albert Bigelow Paine, 2 vols. (New York: Harper & Brothers, 1917), 2:566. The emphasis is Twain's.

10. "Memories of Mark Twain," collected in *The Tocsin of Revolt and Other Essays* (New York: Charles Scribner's Sons, 1922), pp. 260–61, 265, 290–91.

11. Irving Malin, "Mark Twain: The Boy as Artist," *L&P* 11 (Summer 1961): 78. Malin asserts that a writer "adopt[s] a literary tradition for . . . psychological reasons"—in Mark Twain's case, a tradition of "exaggeration, emphasis on violence and rebellion, fantasy." Twain "presents fragmented and immature images of the son in conflict with his parents; he fails to give a complete picture of the father" (p. 78).

pointing out that Twain was one of the writers who "had spent their childhood in the Eden of pre-Civil-War America," speculated that "dismay with
the harsh reality of post-war corruption and spoliation of the continent
thrust them back to the psychic reality of their youth," so that "youth, for
those who had spent it before the war, took on a paradisiacal, mythical
glow." Twain's character Huck Finn, according to Tanner, made it possible
for Twain to "recover, if only through writing, his innocent youthful intimacy with a lost past"; donning the mask of Huck, Twain "speaks and
thinks as a child." [12] Tom Sawyer, too, was an outlet for these longings—was,
indeed, Twain's first, absorbing connection with his uncomplicated Missouri
boyhood.

The achievement of *Tom Sawyer*, especially set against the reigning literature about boys, was immediately apparent to a reviewer for the *New York
Times* who commented in 1877 on salutary differences between Twain's
high-spirited youngster and the goody-goody characters drawn by Thomas
Day: "Had Sandford or Merton ever for a single moment dipped inside of
Tom Sawyer's pages, astronomy and physics, with all the musty old farrago
of Greek and Latin history, would have been thrown to the dogs. . . . Books
for children in former bygone periods were mostly constructed in one monotonous key. Was it not good old Peter Parley [Samuel G. Goodrich, 1793–
1860] who in this country first broke loose from conventional trammels,
and made American children truly happy? We have certainly gone far beyond Mr. Goodrich's manner." Though the reviewer went on dutifully to
express concern about "the decidedly sanguinary tendency in juvenile books"
that had followed these breakthroughs, he praised Mark Twain's ability to
re-create "that wild village life which has schooled many a man to self-
reliance and energy. Mr. Clemens has a remarkable memory for those pecu-
liarities of American boy-talk which the grown man may have forgotten, but
which return to him not unpleasantly." [13]

What that anonymous reviewer was heralding, we can see now, was the
rise of what has accurately been termed the *Bad Boy book*, a movement that
began by rebelling against the implausible portrayals of behavior in the
pages of its listless predecessors and that (some would say) proceeded to the
point of glorifying with nostalgic reverence the escapades of young village
hooligans. Whereas early Southern humorists such as J. J. Hooper and G. W.
Harris and literary comedians like B. P. Shillaber and James M. Bailey had
produced sketches depicting the shenanigans of two-dimensional, rascally
youths, most literary historians date the true advent of the Bad Boy book
with the appearance of Thomas Bailey Aldrich's aptly named *The Story of a
Bad Boy* (1869), whose well-known opening sentences announce: "This is
the Story of a Bad Boy. Well, not such a very bad, but a pretty bad boy; and I
ought to know, for I am, or rather I was, that boy myself." [14] As Judith Fet-

12. Chap. 9, "The Pond of Youth," in *The Reign of Wonder: Naivety and Reality in American Literature* (Cambridge: Cambridge University Press, 1965), pp. 147–49.

13. Unsigned review, 13 January 1877, p. 3; reprinted in *Mark Twain: The Critical Heritage*, ed. Frederick Anderson (New York: Barnes & Noble, 1971), pp. 70–71.

14. *The Story of a Bad Boy, The Little Violinist, and Other Sketches*, The Writings of

terley observes, the tradition that followed this example implied that "socially useful adults develop only from real boys who have shown some life as children"; moreover, "the Bad Boy is a rebel in that he temporarily flaunts and outrages the community, but he is a sanctioned rebel, because his rebellion . . . is a stage which has respectability at its other end." [15] Joining Aldrich in reacting against the Model Boy of such series as those manufactured by Jacob Abbott, Horatio Alger, Jr., and various Sunday school authors were, in addition to Mark Twain (whose debunking but undeveloped "Story of the Bad Little Boy Who Didn't Come to Grief" had appeared in 1865), writers like Charles Dudley Warner, Robert J. Burdette, Edward Eggleston, George W. Peck, William Dean Howells, Stephen Crane, Henry A. Shute, William Allen White, and Booth Tarkington. [16]

In terms of this small revolution in outlook and decorum, and particularly in regard to its impression on the fiction of Mark Twain, the contribution of Aldrich is due more appreciative analysis than it has been accorded. To look anew at Aldrich's accomplishment is in effect to reinvestigate several circumstances surrounding the gestation and birth of Tom Sawyer, and also to review why the humor of Tom's behavior is often thrown away on modern audiences. In an important sense, to lose our pleasure in Tom Sawyer's madcap antics is at once to lose sight of rewarding dimensions of *Huckleberry Finn* that Twain's contemporaries enjoyed more than we seem capable of doing and to miss the fullest reading experience that the novel affords. Certain explanations for Tom's characterization reside in literary sources available to Mark Twain, especially in the work of Aldrich, a man once immensely respected but now scarcely known. In fact, at the distance of a century from the national fame of Thomas Bailey Aldrich (1836–1907), whose birth and death dates nearly coincided with Samuel Clemens's, it is difficult to account for Aldrich's contemporary literary reputation, though he did produce, in 1873, a lauded short story ironically titled (after an imaginary girl) "Marjorie Daw." Aldrich's editorship of the *Atlantic Monthly* for nearly a decade, 1881–1890, presumably inflated the worth of the poetry and fiction of this droll, dapper, mustachioed man.

The Story of a Bad Boy, published by Fields, Osgood & Company in 1869, has long been associated with *Tom Sawyer*, mainly because both achieved wide popularity on the common theme of antebellum boyhoods passed idyllically in small towns, and also because Twain mistakenly informed Albert Bigelow Paine that Aldrich was writing *Bad Boy* at the time Twain was commencing *Tom Sawyer*, and recalled that they compared their works in progress. [17] Unless Twain erroneously meant his fragmentary "Boy's

Thomas Bailey Aldrich, 9 vols. (Boston: Houghton Mifflin, 1897), 7:3. This edition will be quoted elsewhere.

15. "The Sanctioned Rebel," pp. 299, 301.

16. For discussions of the Boy Book tradition, see Blair, "On the Structure of *Tom Sawyer*," pp. 375–79; John Hinz, "Huck and Pluck: 'Bad' Boys in American Fiction," *SAQ* 51 (1952): 120–29; Stone, *The Innocent Eye*, pp. 62–72 (especially useful); Hunter, "Mark Twain and the Boy-Book," pp. 430–38; and Fetterley, "Sanctioned Rebel," pp. 299–302.

17. Albert Bigelow Paine, *Mark Twain: A Biography* (New York: Harper & Brothers, 1912), p. 1456.

Manuscript," probably composed in 1870, the event is an impossibility; Twain began writing *Tom Sawyer* no earlier than the winter of 1872–1873.[18] Such an obvious slip is especially illuminating in view of Twain's professed disinterest in the Aldrich book when it first appeared; shortly before marrying Livy Langdon, Clemens explained why he had not annotated any books recently for her amusement: "I have read several books, lately, but none worth marking, & so I have not marked any. I started to mark the Story of a Bad Boy, but for the life of me I could not admire the volume much."[19] Significantly, too, *Bad Boy* was one of the few publications of Aldrich lacking in Clemens's personal library—in fact, aside from that disparaging remark to his fiancée, no trace of his ever owning a copy remains.[20]

Yet Aldrich's book unquestionably made a greater impact on Twain's imagination than many other books treated in scholarship. We know that Mark Twain, like many another writer, developed a habit of disingenuousness about his major literary influences—deprecating or sometimes even denying that he was familiar with some of his chief early reading experiences such as Dickens, Cooper, Scott, and various later books as well, like Doyle's Sherlock Holmes series and Carlyle's *Sartor Resartus*. What pique of jealousy, then, must have seized Mark Twain in 1869 as he held this small book, written by a man he did not yet know. Perhaps a sensation of disgust with himself surged through him as he read its pages. For within this work lay the incidents that apparently prompted Mark Twain to value at last the wealth of literary materials lying unclaimed in his recollections of prewar Hannibal. Pranks that would make Aldrich's Rivermouthian boys seem primly namby-pamby by comparison had been everyday occurrences in Hannibal, he now remembered. Here in this less-than-great work he suddenly came to terms with the powerful appeal of the materials that Henry Nash Smith called "the Matter of Hannibal." We can hardly blame him for hesitating to show Aldrich's book to the cherished woman who was to read and evaluate all future writings of Mark Twain.

Most literary histories refer to *Bad Boy* as a semi-autobiographical novel about Aldrich's boyhood in Portsmouth, New Hampshire, but it is less a novel than a collection of sketches, and though Portsmouth is the locale of "Rivermouth" in the book, the young protagonist Tom Bailey is constantly aware that he has moved there for his schooling from New Orleans and that his father and mother remain behind in the Deep South. Indeed, his father's business dealings sometimes take him up the Mississippi River to Natchez. Both this Southern background and the conclusion of the book—the early death of Tom's father, and young Tom's leaving school to enter business—paralleled Aldrich's own biography (and Clemens's, too, in a general way). Presumably the book contains fictional episodes, but it reads more nearly

18. Gerber et al., eds., *Tom Sawyer*, pp. 9, 504–5.
19. Clemens to Olivia Langdon, New Haven, Conn., 27 December 1869, in *The Love Letters of Mark Twain*, ed. Dixon Wecter (New York: Harper & Brothers, 1949), p. 132.
20. Clemens's library contained more than a dozen of Aldrich's books, one of his larger collections of works by a single author—see my *Mark Twain's Library: A Reconstruction*, 2 vols. (Boston: G. K. Hall, 1980), 1:15–18.

like autobiography than fiction: virtually plotless, the narrative simply introduces us to Tom's schoolmates, relates a few of their adventures, closes with Tom's giving up Harvard for a business career in New York City, and sums up the subsequent careers and deaths of Tom's Rivermouth relatives, friends, and teachers.

Fewer than half a dozen scholars have accorded passing notice to links they perceived between Aldrich's narrative and Mark Twain's boy books.[21] But these acknowledgments, valid as they are, barely hint at the inspiration Aldrich's book provided for *Tom Sawyer, Life on the Mississippi*, and *Huckleberry Finn*, or at its effect on Clemens's conception of the life he had lived as a youth. In the first place, Aldrich's narrative opens by identifying the adult persona with the author and the young boy, all in one: "I am, or rather I was, that boy myself." This is a long way from Huckleberry Finn's frank, vernacular address to the reader, but we are already close to the condescending adult narrator of *Tom Sawyer*, who in Chapter 1 compares Tom's new discovery about whistling to the elation of an astronomer who has discovered a new planet, adding, "the reader probably remembers how to do it if he has ever been a boy." The very landscape of Rivermouth must have reawakened Clemens's drowsing remembrances of Hannibal environs—Holliday's Hill, the broad brown river, Jackson's Island; Aldrich's narrator recalls in chapter 6 that "there was always some exciting excursion on foot—a ramble through the pine woods, a visit to the Devil's Pulpit, a high cliff in the neighborhood—or a surreptitious row on the river, involving an exploration of a group of diminutive islands, upon one of which we pitched a tent and played we were the Spanish sailors who got wrecked there years ago."

By midbook, Aldrich's Tom remains divided between two great ambitions: to be a great classical scholar like his teacher Mr. Grimshaw, "or a circus-rider." However, in a passage that notably reminds us of Twain's famous first chapter, "The Boys' Ambition," in the "Old Times on the Mississippi" series for *Atlantic Monthly* (1875), Aldrich records,

21. Blair initially doubted whether the "somewhat mild" story of Tom Bailey "can be thought of as a direct inspiration for Mark Twain's book about boys" ("On the Structure of *Tom Sawyer*," pp. 78, 79). But by 1960, he was terming Aldrich's book "another probable influence" on *Tom Sawyer*, noting that Twain met Aldrich and his wife in 1871, that William Dean Howells compared the two boy books in reviewing Twain's novel, and that "Tom Bailey acts out a childish burlesque of sentimental lovesickness" that reminds one of Tom Sawyer's yearnings for Becky Thatcher in Chapter 8 of *Tom Sawyer* (*Mark Twain and Huck Finn* [Berkeley: University of California Press, 1960], pp. 64–65). Hinz complained that Tom Bailey's tale is told in "tepid prose [that] gently laves away his grittiness, softens and blurs his features" ("Huck and Pluck," p. 124); however, Hunter reminded readers that *Bad Boy* was "the first of the line," a groundbreaking "childhood autobiography of an original kind" ("Mark Twain and the Boy-Book," pp. 432–33). By far the most discerning analysis of the relationship between Aldrich's book and Twain's subsequent novels is Stone's *The Innocent Eye*. Stone observes that *Bad Boy* "is the first of a whole line of boy's books written as much for adults as for the boys themselves"; as one result, "this shifting back and forth between boyish character and adult author becomes actually the underlying theme of the novel." According to Stone, Tom Bailey, "the immediate ancestor of Tom Sawyer," is Twain's "principal prototype." Tom Sawyer "possibly inherited" his bookishness from Tom Bailey, but the latter's speech "resembles more a boys' magazine version of British public-school lingo than the idiom of an American boy" (pp. 27–28, 30–31, 64–65).

every Rivermouth boy looks upon the sea as being in some way mixed up with his destiny. . . . He wanders by the sandy shore, . . . and he burns for the time when he shall stand on the quarter-deck of his own ship, and go sailing proudly across that mysterious waste of waters. . . . The shipyards, the wharves, and the tawny fleet of fishing-smacks yearly fitted out at Rivermouth—these things, and a hundred other, feed the imagination and fill the brain of every healthy boy with dreams of adventure. . . . He is born a sailor, whatever he may turn out to be afterwards. To own the whole or a portion of a rowboat is his earliest ambition. (Chap. 14)

Ultimately Tom Bailey and three friends do acquire a small boat, the *Dolphin*, and on a school holiday they undertake an expedition to Sandpeep Island, the last of the harbor islands. Tom, like the others, "quietly slipped out of the house without letting his estimable family know what he was up to." The boys row among the cluster of islands, seeking the mouth of the harbor, and Aldrich's language reminds one of the amused adult narrator of the dawn passage in Chapter 14 of *Tom Sawyer*: "The measured dip of our oars and the drowsy twitterings of the birds seemed to mingle with, rather than break, the enchanted silence that reigned about us. The scent of the new clover comes back to me now, as I recall that delicious morning when we floated away in a fairy boat down a river like a dream!" (*Bad Boy*, chap. 14).

But after the boys have set up their encampment on Sandpeep Island and have made seafood chowder (and Phil Adams has smoked his sweet-fern cigars), a tremendous storm overtakes them while they are swimming. "From these threatening masses, seamed at intervals with pale lightning, there now burst a heavy peal of thunder that shook the ground." When the smallest boy in Tom Bailey's group, Binny Wallace, attempts to secure their boat on the beach, he finds himself cast adrift helplessly and oarlessly in the *Dolphin*, and the boys watch in agony as the gale carries the tiny craft far out to sea. Even before Binny Wallace's body washes ashore at Grave Point—where the boys had once swum and frolicked—young Bailey experiences torments of guilt and remorse that remind us of Tom Sawyer's faints and slow recoveries in both of Twain's novels that feature him; we also recollect Mark Twain's repentance and distress over the drowning deaths of Lem Hackett and a boy named Dutchy, both tales told in Chapter 54 of *Life on the Mississippi* and both incidents associated by the narrator with storms and restless sleep. Tom Bailey recalls that after Binny Wallace's disappearance,

> I was in a forlorn state, physically and mentally. Captain Nutter put me to bed between hot blankets. . . . I was wandering in my mind, and fancied myself still on Sandpeep Island . . . and, in my delirium, I laughed aloud and shouted to my comrades. . . . Towards evening a high fever set in, and it was many days before my grandfather deemed it prudent to tell me that the Dolphin had been found, floating keel upwards. . . . Poor little Binny Wallace! How strange it seemed, when I went to school again, to see that empty seat in the fifth row! . . . How well I remember the funeral, and what a piteous sight it was afterwards to see his familiar name on a small headstone in the Old South Burying-Ground. (Chap. 14)

Twain's imaginative faculty supplied many fresh inventions in the account of Tom Sawyer's schemes to convince his gang to hide out on an island and then return to a heroes' welcome at their own funerals, but the congruence of so many elements—the adventurous expedition, the remote island, the group-swimming, the thunderstorm, the supposed drowning, the boy's remorse—make for suggestive parallels.

One striking passage in *Bad Boy* furnishes indications that Aldrich's creation stimulated Twain's processes of memory even earlier than the final composition stages of *Tom Sawyer*. Consider Aldrich's description of the bustle attending the approach of a ship toward the harbor:

> I joined Pepper at the end of the wharf. . . . He had formed a telescope of his hands. . . . "Look there! Isn't that a bark coming up the Narrows?" . . . Sure enough, it was a vessel of considerable size, slowly beating up to town. In a few moments more the other two masts were visible above the green hillocks. . . .
> Then the gleeful chant of the sailors at the capstan came to us pleasantly across the water. . . .
> In a neglected seaport like Rivermouth the arrival of a large ship is an event of moment. The prospect of having twenty or thirty jolly tars let loose on the peaceful town excites divers emotions among the inhabitants. The small shop-keepers along the wharves anticipate a thriving trade; the proprietors of the two rival boarding-houses . . . hasten down to the landing to secure lodgers; and the female population of Anchor Lane turn out to a woman, for a ship fresh from sea is always full of possible husbands and long-lost prodigal sons. (Chap. 15)

Could these be sentences that induced Mark Twain to pen the much-quoted passage in "Old Times on the Mississippi" (1875) that begins, "Once a day a cheap, gaudy packet arrived upward from St. Louis, and another downward from Keokuk"? In Twain's masterful version, "Before these events, the day was glorious with expectancy; after them, the day was a dead and empty thing," and he details how dramatically "the scene changes" when a Negro drayman announces that the steamboat has hove into view around the point that turns the river "into a sort of sea, and withal a very still and brilliant and lonely one"; ten minutes later, "the town is dead again."[22]

Mainly, however, Aldrich's book brings to mind Twain's boy books. Tom Bailey and Pepper Whitcomb form a friendship adumbrating Tom Sawyer and Huckleberry Finn's: they rig a twine telegraph between their houses; they share their pocket money and their secrets—"those amazing secrets which boys have. We met in lonely places by stealth, and parted like conspirators; we could not buy a jackknife or build a kite without throwing an air of mystery and guilt over the transaction." Before revealing one particular secret, Tom Bailey "dragged him for that purpose to a secluded spot in the dark pine woods outside the town" (chap. 15). There is even in Aldrich's story, as Walter Blair has noticed, a lengthy bout of puppy love that torments Tom Bailey, smitten by the older and unobtainable Miss Nelly Glentworth; learning that she is destined to marry another, Tom sulks in the manner of

22. Included in Chapter 4 of *Life on the Mississippi* (1883).

Tom Sawyer in Twain's novel, indulging in the same morbid fantasies about the advantages of an early death (*Bad Boy*, chap. 19).

Always the Southernness of Bailey's background obtrudes itself, drawing young Tom's thoughts back to New Orleans, where his mother and father remain. In recalling his days there, Tom remembers the fierce defiance of his old black nurse, Aunt Chloe, who prefigures in dialect and tone the spell-binding Aunt Rachel of Twain's "A True Story" (1874): "Dar ain't no gentl'-men in the Norf noway. . . . If any of dem mean whites tries to git me away from marster, I's jes' gwine to knock 'em on de head wid a gourd!" Had she added that she is one of the old blue hen's chickens, we might be convinced that Mark Twain had written this vow. Tom eventually decides to run away south to his parents' residence, shipping as a cabin boy from Boston. But Tom Bailey, unlike Huck Finn, is stopped before he can undertake this sea-board journey toward the mouth of the Mississippi River, and, upon his return to his grandfather's home, he finds a letter with a black seal announcing the death of his father from cholera; as with the body of Huck Finn's father in the floating house, the letter, in fact, "had passed [Tom Bailey] on the road by the down train" (chap. 21).

What, then, can be concluded from this glance at Aldrich's suggestive but decidedly minor classic book? That it showed Mark Twain how to make use of vivid autobiographical recollections of the camaraderie, mischief, and games of boyhood; that it emboldened him to attempt a story with a South-ern setting; that it tutored him in creating a sentimental, dignified, patroniz-ing adult persona; that it revealed the rich possibilities for including the superstitions and folkways of children among the quaint customs being ex-plored by local-color writers for the literary monthlies; that it reminded him of such promising material as the strict codes of juvenile fraternities like the Cadets of Temperance (Tom Bailey is initiated into the secret society of the Rivermouth Centipedes), the pangs of blind sexual adoration, the gratifica-tion of community acceptance. Truly *Bad Boy* has never been fully accepted as the model inspiriting *Tom Sawyer* and coloring *Life on the Mississippi* and *Huckleberry Finn* and as the standard work against which Twain per-haps unconsciously reacted and also tried to surpass. This dearth of schol-arly curiosity has prevailed partly because Twain mixed up the sequence of events in discussing his own work and Aldrich's book, and because he down-played his interest in, and admiration for, Aldrich's accomplishment in the realm of boy books.

Yet there is factual evidence that Twain thought rather well of *Bad Boy*; for instance, he included a portion of it, "How We Astonished the River-mouthians," in the compendium of comic sketches that he edited with Wil-liam Dean Howells and Charles H. Clark, *Mark Twain's Library of Humor* (1888).[23] That extract tells of the boys' most ambitious prank—the firing of

23. This may explain the disappearance of Clemens's personal copy of *Bad Boy* (see n. 20). There is evidence that Twain destroyed part of his library collection in the course of obtaining texts and illustrations for *Mark Twain's Library of Humor*; I described this process in "Mark Twain Reads Longstreet's *Georgia Scenes*," in *Gyascutus: Studies in Antebellum Southern Hu-*

a dozen abandoned cannons along the beach at the outskirts of the town. Because Tom Bailey is chosen to set the match to the trail of gunpowder, he refers to the cannons as "Bailey's Battery." Twain and his coeditors praised Aldrich's "peculiar vein of humor," which is manifest when the startled citizens rush from their homes with lanterns, excitedly conjecturing that their unoffending town is being attacked by spectral ships off the coast. This mass response of the frightened villagers conveys an image of crowd behavior comparable with those occurring in Twain's boy books about the Mississippi River (especially the alarm at the Phelps farm in *Huckleberry Finn* about an anticipated invasion), and these boys derive similar satisfaction from being the cause of so much commotion and speculation. In Notebook 40 (June 1898), Twain included Tom Bailey's name among the list of famous child characters he thought of assembling for a tale tentatively titled "Creatures of Fiction."[24] And when Aldrich added an epilogue of history and reminiscence in a book called *An Old Town by the Sea* (1893), Twain, beset by financial worries, took time to write to Aldrich on 6 December 1893 testifying that he had stayed up until 3 A.M. reading the slender volume: "Portsmouth was become the town of my boyhood," Twain wrote, "with all which that implies & compels. . . . I enjoyed it all—every line of it."[25]

Though there are instances where Mark Twain gave public credit to Bret Harte and a few other writers who improved the craftsmanship of his fiction, it is fair to say that he was generally reluctant to concede the role of specific books in demonstrating possibilities of plot, incident, and character. However understandable this tendency is, the literary historian may be forgiven, surely, if he notes such coincidences as the lightning storm to which the boys are subjected on their respective islands, Sandpeep and Jackson's. What Aldrich tried to express with heavyhanded sympathy, Twain would communicate with a less condescending, more colloquial tone, and a direct intimacy with his reader; and in *Huckleberry Finn*, of course, he would dispense with the intervening, interpreting adult voice altogether.

But if Twain partially relied on Aldrich's book as a model (and challenge) of sorts for his own boy book, Aldrich himself was equally indebted to a literary work that some critics have been puzzled to find Twain seemingly ignoring. Though Twain apparently owned a copy of Thomas Hughes's *Tom Brown's School Days* (1857),[26] he alluded to it only once in print—in Chapter 15 of *Following the Equator* (1898)—and there confused it with Hughes's less successful *Tom Brown at Oxford* (1861). Aldrich, on the other hand, openly acknowledged his debt to Hughes, even quoting from *Tom Brown's School Days* in *Bad Boy* (regarding the boys' universal code of fighting) and referring to it as "one of the best books ever written for boys" (chap. 10).

This cluster of *Tom*-boy books—Thomas Hughes's *Tom Brown's School*

---

morous and Sporting Writing, ed. James L. W. West III (Atlantic Highlands, N.J.: Humanities Press, 1978), pp. 103–11.

24. Notebook in the Mark Twain Papers, Bancroft Library, University of California, Berkeley.

25. Letter in the Houghton Library, Harvard University; photocopy in Mark Twain Papers.

26. *Mark Twain's Library*, p. 338.

Days, the chief influence on Thomas Aldrich's *Bad Boy*, whose hero Tom Bailey was a prototype for Tom Sawyer—seems worthy of remark. As a matter of fact, another commentator has posed an inviting question that is precisely relevant. In 1978, Leslie Fiedler, who possesses an indisputable knack for uncovering tantalizing issues in American literature, pondered a new puzzle he had located: Mark Twain "created fictional look-alikes, ranging from Tom Canty . . . to Tom X in 'Which Was the Dream?' Even Tom Sawyer and Huck Finn are utterly confused with each other toward the end of *Huckleberry Finn*, and the series culminates in the slave Valet de Chambre and the 'free' Thomas à Beckett Driscoll of *Pudd'nhead Wilson*. In each, one of the paired characters is called Tom for reasons nobody has ever convincingly explained, and in each a main theme is usurpation."[27] To this list might be added the cub pilot "Tom G———" of *Life on the Mississippi* (chap. 12), who wins the admiration of a lovely sixteen-year-old girl—to the disgust of the envious narrator—because Tom is nearly killed while "sounding" for the steamboat.

The answer to the part of this conundrum having to do with characters named "Tom" who are involved with themes of taking over someone's rightful place or heritage can be traced to the thrill of jealousy and competitiveness that pulsed through Twain's mind when he first read and grasped the epochmaking achievement of Aldrich's Bad Boy book. In joining the tradition forged by Thomas Hughes and Thomas Aldrich, Mark Twain calculatedly, defiantly retained the first name of the boy characters, but he produced a book that left Aldrich's in its wake and whose literary figures are today far better known on both shores of the Atlantic than the actors in Tom Brown's adventures. One might say that Mark Twain took the dare, by calling his fictional boy "*Tom* Sawyer" and thus placing him squarely in a familial relationship to his celebrated precursors in the boy-book field: if this new cousin was a hit, he would reap the advantages pioneered by his famous namesakes; if he flopped, Tom's very name would give the clue to the inspirations for this unworthy usurper.

Aside from brazenly labeling his new character with the already familiar tag-name *Tom*, Twain was highly inventive in naming his fictional boys. Even in the matter of these names, however, Twain vastly favored his outcast urchin, Huck. Tom took his last name from a potentially dangerous obstruction to river navigation, whose significance Twain well knew from his piloting days;[28] in other words, from the beginning Tom Sawyer's name suggested his (and his creator's) latent aggressiveness and powers of dissembling. *Saw-*

27. *Freaks: Myths and Images of the Secret Self* (New York: Simon and Schuster, 1978), p. 270.

28. OED, 9:147, and *Supplement to the OED*, 3:1505, quote allusions to *sawyer* from 1786 until 1882, most identifying it as a tree snagged in the mud, bobbing up and down. For example, Charles Dickens's *American Notes* (1842), reviling the Mississippi River, records how "for two days we toiled up this foul stream, striking constantly against the floating timber, or stopping to avoid those more dangerous obstacles, the snags, or sawyers, which are the hidden trunks of trees that have their roots below the tide." In *Life on the Mississippi* (1883), Mark Twain recalled the waterway through Louisiana as "the pilot's paradise: a wide river . . . and no bars, snags, sawyers, or wrecks" (chap. 40). Twain testified, " 'Tom Sawyer' was not the . . .

yer conceivably also bore in Twain's mind a connection with the sometimes unscrupulous wood sawyers who displayed their cords of logs along the river for sale to the wood-fueled steamboats—often stacked by "cheats," according to Huck, "so you can throw a dog through it anywhere" (p. 158). Twain was reminded of their insolence by a railroad conductor he encountered between New York City and St. Louis, "pompous and discourteous, as natural wood-sawyers in office are apt to be" (15 March 1867, letter to *Alta California*). More obvious is the rhyming link with the profession—both esteemed and disdained in that day, as in ours—of "lawyer," for which Tom seems destined; in Chapter 35 of *Tom Sawyer*, Judge Thatcher intends to reward Tom's enterprise and bravery by sending him to the National Military Academy and then training him "in the best law school in the country, in order that he might be ready for either career or both." Previous commentators have noted that Charles Dickens's *Pickwick Papers* (1836–1837) included a comical medical student named Bob Sawyer, a swaggering young gentleman who "looked, upon the whole, something like a dissipated Robinson Crusoe." In *Roughing It* (1872), Mark Twain assigned the name *Sawyer* to an unrelated "honest" man of "hearty countenance" whom Twain hired as a laugher to attend Twain's first comic lecture in San Francisco, an individual who enjoyed his job so much that Twain almost feared "Sawyer might choke himself" (chap. 78).

Huckleberry, in contrast, is the namesake of the beloved berry that is plentiful in Missouri as well as around Twain's adopted town of Hartford, Connecticut. Its nineteenth-century associations included "a person of little consequence."[29] Huck's family name, *Finn* (conveniently supplied by the Hannibal town drunkard, Jimmy Finn), suggests his associations with the river and the fish on which he and Jim would depend for sustenance; with its reference to a legendary Gaelic warrior and leader of the misty Irish past, it also implies that a former grandeur lies behind the family debased by a wretched, degenerate offshoot, Pap Finn.

A final link between *Bad Boy* and *Tom Sawyer* is crucial in establishing a better understanding of Twain's precedent and motive in constructing the framing "Tom Sawyer" sections of *Huckleberry Finn*. More than any other characteristic, it is Tom Bailey's fondness for literary classics that draws attention to him in Aldrich's story. As Tom Bailey listens to his friend Charley Marden call for more ice cream at Pettingil's confectionery shop in Rivermouth, he thinks that Marden has "the air of Aladdin ordering up a fresh hogshead of pearls and rubies" (chap. 8). When the Rivermouth boys are locked up by the night watchmen for burning an old stagecoach stolen from an abandoned stable, "it was only by thinking how the late Baron Trenck would have conducted himself under similar circumstances that I was able to restrain my tears" (chap. 7). Indeed, Tom Bailey's favorite books bear a distinct resemblance to the reading of the "authorities"-ridden Tom Sawyer:

---

name of any person I ever knew" (*Portland Oregonian*, 11 August 1895; quoted in Blair, *Mark Twain and Huck Finn*, p. 54).

29. *Supplement to the OED*, 2:179.

Over the head of the bed were two oak shelves, holding perhaps a dozen books—among which were Theodore, or The Peruvians; Robinson Crusoe; an odd volume of Tristram Shandy; Baxter's Saint's Rest; and a fine English edition of the Arabian Nights. . . .

Shall I ever forget the hour when I first overhauled these books? I do not allude especially to Baxter's Saint's Rest, . . . but to the Arabian Nights, and particularly to Robinson Crusoe. The thrill that ran into my fingers' ends then has not run out yet. Many a time did I . . . glide off into an enchanted realm, where there were no lessons to get. . . . In a lidless trunk in the garret I subsequently unearthed another motley collection of novels and romances, embracing the adventures of Baron Trenck, Jack Sheppard, Don Quixote, Gil Blas, and Charlotte Temple—all of which I fed upon like a bookworm.

I never come across a copy of any of those works without feeling a certain tenderness for the yellow-haired little rascal who used to lean above the magic pages hour after hour, religiously believing every word he read, and no more doubting the reality of Sindbad the Sailor, or the Knight of the Sorrowful Countenance, than he did the existence of his own grandfather. (*Bad Boy*, chap. 5)

Perhaps we can descry here the reasons that Aldrich's threadbare phrasing and situation have faded from public interest and that Mark Twain's novel, which depicts the absurd consequences of Tom Sawyer's taking literally the romances on which he feeds, has gained immortality. If we grant the likelihood that Tom Bailey's affection for *Don Quixote*, *The Arabian Nights*, and the other literary works served as a catalyst for Twain's portrayal of Tom Sawyer,[30] then we must also recognize the mocking malice behind Twain's selecting Aldrich's sappily sentimental, backward-looking adult as his target, for again and again Twain demolishes this sort of attitude in relating Tom Sawyer's sometimes hurtful and always pointless antics.

According to one critic, in fact, Mark Twain became "disenchanted with his boy hero," as evidenced by developments in *Huckleberry Finn*: "money has replaced pleasure as the currency of Tom's control" over the other boys, and "the entire final sequence of the novel is studded with instances of the pleasure Tom takes in other people's discomfort."[31] This interpretation astutely discerns that Tom Sawyer's character traits are enlarged and deepened in the second of the two novels, but that expansion principally occurs because Mark Twain was exploiting possibilities barely tapped in *Tom Sawyer*; Tom's reading (and misreading) representing one of the prospects Twain most wanted to explore. Indeed, in *Huckleberry Finn*, Tom's romance books dominate him completely, whereas in *Tom Sawyer* they had been only cursorily identified. The literary source for the Robin Hood play-acting of Tom and Joe Harper on Cardiff Hill is a good example: we have a vague sense that there is a specific text for their stage directions, but a measure of scholarly

---

30. *The Arabian Nights*, for example, permeates Twain's "Tom Sawyer Abroad" (1894), as for instance in Huck Finn's description of Egypt as the land of "a raft of other Arabian Nights folks, which the half of them never done the things they let on they done, I don't believe"—a reaction to Tom's intense excitement because Egypt "was so full of history that was in his line" (chap. 12).

31. Fetterley, "Disenchantment," pp. 69, 71–72.

investigation is necessary to discover the actual source.[32] Books in *Tom Sawyer* are no more than hazily influential, providing reassurance that Twain's "bad boys" know their standard juvenile library as well as dime-novels about buccaneers and outlaws.

The explicitness of Tom's references in *Huckleberry Finn*, by contrast, results in less inventiveness on Tom's part, and less fun for the members of his gang; the Romantic order of adventures turns out to be as stifling and confining as Huck Finn's adventure on the wrecked *Walter Scott* proves to be unbearably scary. Indeed, whereas Tom Sawyer had the lion's share of true-life chills in *Tom Sawyer*, especially in the cave, while Huck merely ran to the Welshman's house to get help for the Widow Douglas, in *Huckleberry Finn* Tom must content himself with an after-the-fact liberation of a black prisoner. (Mark Twain similarly had to settle for writing a story about an escaped slave two decades after a great war had freed Jim's race.)

The romances themselves become recurrent targets for burlesque in *Huckleberry Finn*, and a single example can illustrate Twain's technique of at once invoking and ridiculing a designated work of literature. In Chapter 38 of *Huckleberry Finn*, Tom insists that the captive Jim raise a flower (Tom eventually compromises on one of the "cat-tail-lookin' mullen-stalks") in the dark hut where Jim is kept. "We'll fetch you a little one, and you plant it in the corner, over there, and raise it. And don't call it mullen, call it Pitchiola—that's its right name, when it's in a prison. And you want to water it with your tears" (p. 331). Tom repeats this final instruction, adding, "It's the way they always do." When Jim protests this and Tom's other requirements, Tom disgustedly remarks that Jim "was just loadened down with more gaudier chances than a prisoner ever had in the world to make a name for himself, and yet he didn't know enough to appreciate them, and they was just about wasted on him" (p. 332).

Tom Sawyer's reference to "Pitchiola" is of course an allusion to the novel titled *Picciola*, and that phonetic representation of a reasonably good pronunciation reminds us that Huck Finn, the linguistic filter between us and Tom Sawyer, has merely *heard* these titles and authors rather than *read* them (which also recalls the humor in Tom's emphatic bookishness on the one hand and, on the other, Huck's dogged commitment to record all significant details in the narrative he has commenced and his resultant discovery of "what a trouble it was to make a book"). In *Tom Sawyer*, the adult narrator is only superficially interested in Tom's "authorities," but in *Huckleberry Finn* we are confronted with Huck's laborious transcription of Tom's speech, replete with specific book citations. Huck's version of these literary names, however, inevitably tends to undercut Tom's veneration for romantic figures. Searching for a way to convey names he has never seen in print, Huck seizes upon similarly pronounced words with which he is more familiar, even though he may not know *their* correct spelling, either. Thus, the Château D'If becomes "the Castle Deef" (chap. 35). *Picciola*, rendered as "Pitchiola," emerges as a homely sounding word that subliminally reinforces Jim's plea for the boys to allow him to water the stipulated flower with "spring water," and it fits with Tom's solution that Jim's crying over his flower be aided by an onion smuggled in his "coffee-pot" pitcher. But mainly "Pitchiola" simply makes the noble romance *sound* absurdly foreign in the situation, just as Huck turned another Italian word into an incongruous, "y"-ending name in his grapple with "Chelleeny" (chap. 35).

Few modern readers have occasion to look at a copy of *Picciola: The Prisoner of Fenestrella; or, Captivity Captive* (1836), the translated title of the romance by Xavier Saintine, actually Joseph Xavier Boniface (1798–1865), a French writer of fiction, plays, and vaudeville sketches. In a word, Saintine's story can be said to recount the imprisonment of Charles Veramont, Count de Charney, charged with political conspiracy and subversion during the reign of Napoleon. Deprived of every stimulation, Charney is sequestered in a cell in the fortress of Fenestrella. Taking pity on Charney's plight, the Italian jailer Ludovico spares a nameless plant in the walkway of Charney's cell, a mere "weed" upon which Charney lavishes all his attention in a desperate effort to forget the desolation of his prison. This solitary specimen of organic life becomes a source of strength and sanity for Charney; its symbolism is apparent when Charney, who has attributed medicinal healing powers to the plant's leaves, is nursed through a near-fatal illness by a broth made from them and administered by the humanitarian jailer. He is befriended by Girardi, another prisoner, and his comely daughter, Teresa. When the plant's health is threatened by stones in the prison floor that impede its growth, Teresa makes a tearful appeal to Napoleon and Josephine, pleading that Charney's life depends upon his cherished *picciola*, "flower of the captive." Josephine ultimately gains the emperor's permission to spare the plant. After Girardi serves his term, Napoleon grants a pardon to the once-proud Charney, who now lives solely for his plant and his prison friends. Teresa soon becomes the Countess de Charney. Her husband transplants the flower and takes it with him into the outer world, but the plant eventually dies unnoticed amid his "domestic happiness," since its "appointed task was over." [33]

The tale is a little less melodramatic and overwrought than this brief summary makes it appear—the scenes depicting Charney's utter isolation are effectively chronicled—but there is much for a later age to scoff at, nevertheless. Twice Charney does weep over his flower—once after it has healed him at the expense of its leaves (book 1, chap. 8), and again "tears rose in his eyes" when he watched helplessly as the prison commandant ordered the plant to be uprooted (book 2, chap. 8)—but neither time does he "water it with . . . tears," as Tom ridiculously insists that Jim do. Once more Tom has absurdly misconstrued the meaning of a literary passage. Writing almost

33. The edition quoted is *Picciola: The Prisoner of Fenestrella; or, Captivity Captive* (New York: D. Appleton and Co., 1895). Walter Blair briefly mentions this "specific source" in "The French Revolution and *Huckleberry Finn*," MP 55 (August 1957): 23–24, revealing that Twain deleted another *Picciola* reference from the manuscript of *Huckleberry Finn*.

half a century later, Twain could hardly take seriously this fervent, verbose narrative, though he himself had once attempted a similar story about a man, accidentally made captive in a castle vault, who is thrown upon his own resources to save his wits and his physical health.[34] Perhaps Twain has Charney's fate in mind when Tom Sawyer finds "a couple of shingle-nails that Tom said would be handy for a prisoner to scrabble his name and sorrows on the dungeon walls with" (p. [316]). The Count de Charney "at first . . . amused himself with scribbling with a morsel of charcoal on the walls of his prison the dates of every happy event of his childhood"; next he inscribes a "withering creed" on the wall: "CHANCE, THOUGH BLIND, IS THE SOLE AUTHOR OF THE CREATION"; and later he adds another blasphemy: "God is but a word!" (book 1, chaps. 2, 3, 11).

Maudlin, frequently tedious and pontifical, *Picciola* seemingly was an ideal target for Twain's burlesque. But this choice had a costly flaw. Recognizable at least by title in Twain's lifetime, the romance has now slipped from memory almost entirely. Today it requires an identifying footnote in the classroom editions of *Huckleberry Finn*, further estranging us from full contact with the novel; annotative elucidations can never be as satisfactory as a piece of literary knowledge that the reader personally brings into conjunction with the text. And this *Picciola* problem represents in miniature one of the greatest difficulties with the concluding chapters of *Huckleberry Finn* and with Tom Sawyer's book-bound notions of romance. Twain needed, in part because of his training on the writing staffs of Western newspapers and literary journals, a hyperbolic target from the genteel culture for his best burlesques; but he necessarily chose from time to time, as he did here, materials that proved to be dated in their basic appeal. If the original allure is defunct, then the burlesque is predictably moribund as well. The foolery of the King and the Duke still works, because their nonsense depends upon recognizable figures from the French Revolution and literary passages from the plays of Shakespeare; when Tom takes over the stage, however, his comic farce about prisoners' sufferings and escapes falls flat—the materials have died in the interval since 1885, were dying even then, in fact.

Yet for us to blame Tom Sawyer for this deficiency is to dismiss the opportunity for Twain to conclude the novel on the note of burlesque, thus stifling a dependable mode of Twain's original Western genius that found its forte in exaggeration and in playing with respected literary works and forms. Should he merely have chosen for his subject another, more current romance about imprisonment? A few were still in vogue in the second half of the nineteenth century; indeed, one was yet to be written—Anthony Hope's swashbuckling *The Prisoner of Zenda* (1894). But Twain sought literature about the mental and physical torture of political prisoners for this section of *Huckleberry Finn*, and Alexander Dumas's romances, levied upon heavily, would not answer all his purposes. Virtually any of the available sources would have met the same fate as *Picciola*. For our contemporary tastes, Twain considerably overdid this prison business, but his penchant for burlesque was always irre-

---

34. "The Mysterious Chamber," fragmentary manuscript, DV56, Mark Twain Papers.

pressible, and he habitually carried his humor further than Howells and many subsequent critics would have preferred. One of his potential liabilities as a literary artist was also one of his superlative comedic talents.

Twain's obligation to Aldrich's *Bad Boy*, on the other hand, was an unalloyed triumph. The book taught Twain the possibilities inherent in this emergent antigenre, and he was quick to start sifting his own boyhood for publishable incidents. Biographers have long linked Clemens's marriage in February 1870 to his discovery of the Matter of Hannibal, inferring that somehow the nuptials and his wedding trip to Elmira released into his conscious memory the recollections that would find fruition in his boy books. But Twain's perusal of Aldrich's story in December 1869 supplies another explanation for why Twain "rained reminiscences" in that famous letter to Will Bowen of 6 February 1870, written while the new bride was "lying asleep upstairs" and "the old life . . . swept before" Mark Twain "like a panorama." The lengthy list of boyish pranks cataloged in Twain's letter to Bowen—playing Robin Hood on Holliday's Hill, swimming in the river, making the town think he was drowned—was not only a rehearsal for episodes of *Tom Sawyer* and *Huckleberry Finn* but also (more immediately) a responsive tribute to Aldrich's evoking narrative. Even Mark Twain's benedictory tone in addressing Will Bowen ("keep your heart fresh & your memory green for the old days that will never come again") indicates his recent acquaintance with the best boy book he had ever encountered.[35] From Aldrich's example, Twain launched his lifelong glorification of youth and innocence as opposed to wisdom and age. Critics are often mistaken in writing about Twain's boy books without any reference to their historical and cultural context, as though Mark Twain invented the bad boy in literature. He did not—he just invented the bad boy *as hero*. Young Tom Bailey had many of the same experiences as Twain's boy characters, but Bailey generally seemed to be a victim—of his comrades' pranks, of adult authorities, of circumstances and fate—rather than a victor. Tom Sawyer vanquishes his enemies and reaps tangible rewards; this is fictional fantasy rather than autobiography.[36]

There are other commonly accepted fallacies in current Mark Twain studies, most of them detrimental in the college classroom to the beleaguered Tom Sawyer's status. Too seldom, for instance, are Twain's most famous Bad Boy books approached as he intended them to be read, as companion volumes. True, delays interrupted his narrative of *Huckleberry Finn* for nearly a decade after its inception, and true, the core of that novel, the Huck-and-Jim "raft" passages, rises above the artistic level of anything Twain had attempted in his earlier book. But it should always be pointed out that Huck's opening statement in his own novel—"You don't know about me, without you have read a book by the name of 'The Adventures of Tom Sawyer'"— dictates the ideal preparation for any student. Still, one gifted critic has argued that in the cave episode in *Tom Sawyer*, "Tom at last renounces his

---

35. Clemens's letter appears in *Mark Twain's Letters to Will Bowen*, ed. Theodore Hornberger (Austin: University of Texas Press, 1941), pp. 18–21.
36. Regan's valid thesis in *Unpromising Heroes* is applicable here.

Romantic aspirations and his equally Romantic defiance," [37] presumably meaning only *temporarily*, for Tom reappears in the subsequent novel more dreamily out of touch with everyday reality than ever. Another excellent commentator faults the ending of *Tom Sawyer* because Injun Joe dies by accident ("an ending with no resolution at all") and because Tom "has accommodated himself to the oddities of his environment and given over resistance. . . . He becomes that worst of all possible things—a 'Model Boy'—the voice of conformity in a genteel society." [38] But we have only to recall that Tom discards this passing aberration in the preliminary passages of *Huckleberry Finn* to recognize that Tom has mastered a useful adult trait—the ability to follow (for the sake of appearances) both paths, conformity and rebellion, simultaneously. If only there were more copies in existence of that rare binding of *Huckleberry Finn*—the first edition in blue cloth that matches the bright blue hue used for *Tom Sawyer*—then perhaps the works would naturally seem like a fictional unit, despite disparities in viewpoint and tone. [39] Jointly, these Bad Boy books envelop (and effectually frame) Huck's unsentimental, prudent flight downriver between the phantasmagoric conceits of Tom's immature perceptions of family and society.

It is therefore fallacious to surmise that Tom Sawyer has little or no purpose in appearing in *Huckleberry Finn*. The brotherless Huck explicitly yearns for (and *prefers*) Tom's company. Staging his own pretended murder at Pap Finn's cabin, Huck takes pride in his ingenuity in butchering a wild pig to provide a trail of blood; the scheme lacks a satisfying ingredient, however, for Huck writes: "I did wish Tom Sawyer was there, I knowed he would take an interest in this kind of business, and throw in the fancy touches" (p. 57). Is it any wonder that Huck Finn misses Tom, if one considers what Tom Sawyer does for his epistolary novel? When the book opens, Tom's presence provides one of the main points of continuity between the earlier book and its successor, helping the reader find his bearings in an unconventional perspective on St. Petersburg. And Huck would never be so appealing if the officious Tom were not there as an increasingly ludicrous foil. Tom's bluster provides a noisy static that establishes Huck's voice as identifiably authentic.

Eventually any discussion of Tom Sawyer's utility must come to terms with Tom's sudden reappearance in the much-maligned Evasion sequence at the Phelps plantation. Amid still-mounting publications on this issue, the concluding section of *Huckleberry Finn* has been seen as "a worthy finish" [40]

37. One of the few blemishes in Tom H. Towers's otherwise penetrating essay, "'I Never Thought We Might Want to Come Back': Strategies of Transcendence in *Tom Sawyer*," *MFS* 21 (Winter 1975–1976): 509–20; see p. 519. Towers manages to stay outside the debate over the "structure" of *Tom Sawyer* and the "maturation" of its hero.

38. Cynthia Griffin Wolff, "*The Adventures of Tom Sawyer*: A Nightmare Vision of American Boyhood," *MR* 21 (Winter 1980): 651.

39. The sales prospectuses for *Huckleberry Finn* offered customers the option of ordering the novel in either blue or green cloth; if no color was specified, the publisher shipped a green-bound copy. The implication was that some readers might wish to obtain a blue binding that matched their copies of *Tom Sawyer*.

40. Virginia Wexman, "The Role of Structure in *Tom Sawyer* and *Huckleberry Finn*," *ALR* 6 (1973): 1.

and as a series of episodes that "nearly destroyed" Twain's masterpiece,[41] with the latter view seemingly leading the vote. As even a sympathetic commentator remarks, "the ending . . . makes Tom Sawyer unpleasantly visible. . . . It is easy to make Tom look bad."[42] Yet in this instance, too, many readers are choosing to ignore a plain fact: Tom's presence is necessary for comic relief, now that the Duke and the King have departed (Huck sees them only once more, tarred and feathered by the townsfolk, in the same chapter [33] in which Tom Sawyer puts in his appearance).[43] After the strong medicine of these rascals' chicanery, Tom Sawyer's tricking of Jim and Huck looks relatively benign, emanating as it does from the character who picks up the same thread of burlesque humor that the less scrupulous Duke and King have exploited since Chapter 19. If nothing else, the disappointing conclusion of John Seelye's attempt to rewrite Huck's story—*The True Adventures of Huckleberry Finn* (1970), which endeavors to appease the "crickits" (critics) by omitting the entire Evasion sequence—ought to prove the indispensability of Tom Sawyer's serious frivolity at the Phelps farm.

When Tom reappears in *Huckleberry Finn*, he promptly resumes his search for idealized, spiritualized, "noble" romance in the material world; we leave behind Huck Finn's pragmatic, realistic viewpoint—a frankness that can include the odor of "dead fish laying around, gars, and such" (p. 158), in the otherwise nearly lyrical description of the stages of dawn on the river. Under Tom Sawyer's management, the tasks must be made harder, the odds must be raised higher, than life would normally arrange them. Tom is the epitome of Romantic, Byronic striving. The glory for him in an enterprise lies in the sheer effort of struggling against formidable, restricting barriers. From the standpoint of the structure of the novel (its geographical map, as it were), Tom's resurfacing certainly has advantages. As always when Tom enters the scene, Huckleberry Finn is abruptly immobilized, grounded; he cannot seem to travel (or even to flee perils) if Tom Sawyer is present. Enthralled by Tom's promises, he could not manage to leave St. Petersburg, even though frightened, until Pap Finn removed him forcibly from Tom's company. At the Phelps plantation he becomes equally stationary; he is stuck firmly there, enchanted and intimidated by turns with Tom Sawyer's flourishes and "style." The raft is neglected, the downriver journey brought to a melodramatic conclusion. Tom Sawyer has arrived to terminate Huck's drifting idyll, substituting a makeshift "pretend"-world imagination willing to "*let on*, to ourselves, that we was at it [Jim's liberation] thirty-seven years" (p. 307). Huck is so trans-

41. Bray, "Tom Sawyer Once and for All," p. 89, echoing Leo Marx—"Mr. Eliot, Mr. Trilling, and *Huckleberry Finn*," *ASch* 22 (1953): 423–40—and many other critics. Neil Schmitz, for example, holds that Twain "writes an unforgivable ending to *Huckleberry Finn*" because "he does not avoid Tom Sawyer's evasion" (*Of Huck and Alice: Humorous Writing in American Literature* [Minneapolis: University of Minnesota Press, 1983], p. 123).

42. Carrington, *Dramatic Unity*, p. 156. However, Carrington does defend the novel's conclusion, whose "internal qualities . . . serve to reinforce and reemphasize Twain's meanings" (p. 159).

43. Daniel G. Hoffman elaborates on the connections between Tom Sawyer and the Duke and the King in *Form and Fable in American Fiction* (New York: Oxford University Press, 1961), pp. 328–29.

fixed by Tom's prolix visions, it should be noted, that he merely *supposes* he will "light out for the Territory," assuming that Tom Sawyer and Jim will join him there; Huck's key phrase about this fantasy is "I reckon." Henry Nash Smith has decried the "apparently impregnable misreading" of the ending sentences that glibly assumes Huck has in fact left for the Far West, "intending if possible to stay there permanently, because he is revolted by the corrupt slave-holding society of the Old South."[44] Oddly, nearly every critic nowadays wants to hurry Huckleberry Finn on his way to that Indian Territory, wishing to believe that the novel actually concludes with the beginning of this journey.[45] The publication of Twain's fragmentary sequel, "Huck Finn and Tom Sawyer among the Indians" (1969), has made Huck's departure seem like an incontrovertible part of the original novel.[46]

A final, even more unfortunate misconstruction mars much of the commentary on Twain's boy books—the assumption that Huck Finn is completely, absolutely in thralldom to Tom's bidding. Yet an unjaundiced reading of the texts confirms quite the reverse: that Huck resists Tom at virtually every turn in their many colloquies. It is true that Tom usually wins his point, relying in extreme cases on his printed "authorities"—but he never gains Huck's acquiescence and cooperation until he has rephrased his argument in terms that suit Huck's notions of practicality and reason. Indeed, much of the comedy of Tom's outlandish claims derives from Huck's commonsensical querying of his exasperated chum's rationales. When Tom finally yields on the matter of spending thirty-seven years digging Jim out with "a couple of case-knives" (p. 306), Huck consents readily: "Now, there's *sense* in that. . . . Letting on don't cost nothing; letting on ain't no trouble; and if it's any object, I don't mind letting on we was at it a hundred and fifty year" (p. 308).

It might be well to review as a reference point the first, indifferent words

44. Smith, "Foreword," in Gribben's *Mark Twain's Library*, p. xii, repeating a point that Smith made in print as early as 1958. Kenneth S. Lynn's perceptive and courageous essay, "Welcome Back from the Raft, Huck Honey!," *ASch* 46 (1977): 338–47, warned, "In the classrooms of this country, students are being seduced . . . by an antisocial vision of human relations that Mark Twain himself did not formulate."

45. See, for instance, Cox's *The Fate of Humor*, "he departs" (p. 178) and "he went to the territory because he was true to himself and to his creator" (p. 183); Alan Trachtenberg's "The Form of Freedom in *Adventures of Huckleberry Finn*," *SoR* 6 (Autumn 1970): 962, "at the end of the book he again 'lights out,' this time for 'howling adventures amongst the Indians'"; and Towers's "'I Never Thought We Might Want to Come Back,'" p. 519, "in his own story, Huck renounces society and flees to the territory in order to preserve the selfhood he has found on the river"; Forrest G. Robinson, "The Silences in *Huckleberry Finn*," *NCF* 37 (June 1982): 70–71, "opting for flight," "leaving Tom and Aunt Sally," being "in flight."

46. For that matter, all of Twain's attempted sequels to *Huckleberry Finn* begin by placing Huck back in St. Petersburg, even "Huck Finn and Tom Sawyer among the Indians" specifies, "Aunt Sally took us off up home to Missouri." In this narrative, seemingly written in 1884, Tom Sawyer is more eager to run off to the Far West than Huck is, and when Huck finally departs for the Indian Territory he is in the company of Tom and Jim. If subsequent narratives are to be taken into account, Huck Finn opens "Tom Sawyer's Conspiracy" (written 1897–1902) by stating: "Well, we was back home and I was at the Widow Douglas's up on Cardiff Hill again getting sivilized some more along of her and old Miss Watson" (*Hannibal, Huck and Tom*, pp. 92, 163).

that Huck speaks in Mark Twain's fiction; in the novel of 1876, a work entirely centered on Tom Sawyer, "Tom hailed the romantic outcast: 'Hello, Huckleberry!'" and Huck nonchalantly replied, "Hello yourself, and see how you like it" (chap. 6). This outright insolence recedes in Huck's relationship with Tom, but Huck invariably retains a greater measure of his independence of action than critics have conceded. Huck may choose to stay around Tom, but this is because he finds Tom's stunts and rhetorical skills entertainingly riveting. Although few commentators have discerned much to praise in Huck's performance in the Evasion sequence, most insisting that he falls too deeply under Tom Sawyer's sway to remain an admirable figure, little notice has been taken of Huck's crucial decision in chapter 40, a deed that defies Tom's orders and shapes the course of the remaining chapters.[47] Having freed Jim and reached the raft safely, the boys and the black man ecstatically congratulate themselves on the success of their venture. But when Tom reveals that he has received a gunshot wound in the leg, Huck abruptly pauses as Tom tells him to "man the sweeps—man the sweeps!" The raft never leaves the riverbank again, for Huck, seconded by Jim,

> told Tom I [Huck] was agoing for a doctor. He raised considerable row about it, but me and Jim stuck to it and wouldn't budge; so he was for crawling out and setting the raft loose himself; but we wouldn't let him. Then he give us a piece of his mind—but it didn't do no good. (P. 345)

Huck characteristically gives the credit for this decision to Jim ("I knowed he was white inside"), but the paramount factor in the situation is Huck's implacable determination to seek medical assistance for Tom. It is noteworthy, too, that he utterly ignores Tom's romantic advice about blindfolding the doctor and confusing him about Tom's location; Huck straightforwardly informs the physician that Tom ("my brother") can be found on Spanish Island. This act—endangering Jim's newly won freedom, giving up another voyage down the river, inflicting the community's wrath on the boys, but saving Tom's life—by itself ought to exonerate Huck of the charges that he is too easily led by his more verbal companion. In this climactic scene, Huck never wavers in his determination to place a human life ahead of any potential adventures. Tom's most emphatic rebukes go unheeded. Like this pair of equally matched bad boys, their respective novels are inextricably fitted together. To elevate one character too grandly above the other, or to forget the balance, the elasticity, or the mortising in their relationship, is to leave behind some of the subtle effects that Twain achieved in linking their individual volumes. In the case of the boy book *Huckleberry Finn*, our vilification of Tom Sawyer's role has proceeded too far.

47. Hoffman does passingly cite this incident as evidence of "Huck's superior values" (*Form and Fable in American Fiction*, p. 347).

10   NANCY WALKER

Reformers and Young Maidens: Women and Virtue in *Adventures of Huckleberry Finn*

Mark Twain considered it "another boy's book." The Concord, Massachusetts, public library, in 1885, regarded it as "the veriest trash."[1] Daniel G. Hoffman has called it "the most universal book to have come out of the United States of America."[2] The object of praise, banning, and veneration during the hundred years since its publication, *Adventures of Huckleberry Finn* has not commonly been considered a novel about women in nineteenth-century American society. Men occupy center stage in *Huck Finn*; women stand toward the back and sides of the novel, nagging, providing inspiration, often weeping or hysterical. Indeed, Twain's masterpiece would seem a likely reference point for Judith Fetterley's blunt statement: "American literature is male. To read the canon of what is currently considered classic American literature is perforce to identify as male. . . . Our literature neither leaves women alone nor allows them to participate."[3]

As one of several novels commonly thought to address the formation of American attitudes and values, and therefore a "classic" part of the American literary tradition, *Huck Finn* is indeed a "male" novel in several senses. The narrative voice, the specific angle of vision from which the events of the novel unfold, is that of a young boy. Moreover, as a deliberate bildungsroman, the novel traces the moral development of Huck Finn: the traditional passage of the young man from youthful innocence to maturity. Most significantly, the thematic core of the novel embodies a dream of escape to freedom that is both peculiarly American and identifiably masculine. Historically, the political and physical experiences of exploring and settling a wilderness have required a power to initiate and lead social movements that has commonly been granted to men rather than to women. In mythic terms, the typical American hero has, like Huck, resisted the "civilizing" efforts of women and has struck out boldly, often iconoclastically, for a new "territory." For Fetterley, as for other recent critics, the exploitation of the land has come to be seen as analogous to the suppression of women, who are traditionally regarded as both desirable and dangerous. In Fetterley's terms, "America is fe-

1. Reported in the *Boston Transcript*, 17 March 1885, reprinted in Thomas Asa Tenney, *Mark Twain: A Reference Guide* (Boston: G. K. Hall, 1977), p. 14.
2. *Form and Fable in American Fiction* (Oxford University Press, 1961), p. 317.
3. *The Resisting Reader: A Feminist Approach to American Fiction* (Bloomington: Indiana University Press, 1978), p. xii.

male; to be American is male; and the quintessential American experience is betrayal by a woman."[4]

Although it would not be accurate to say that Huck Finn is "betrayed" by a woman, Miss Watson's decision to sell Jim down the river—certainly a betrayal of Jim—sets the novel in motion. Were it not for the relationship between the slave and the boy, much of Twain's social commentary would be impossible, and Miss Watson's action allows their relationship to develop, making her a vital element of the plot. Nevertheless, for most readers, the significance of *Huck Finn* requires the male characters to occupy the foreground, leaving the female characters as part of the scenic backdrop. Virtually all readings of the novel, from Leslie Fiedler's assumption of a homosexual relationship between Huck and Jim[5] to discussions of the novel's roots in Southwestern humor,[6] reflect its origins in a male-dominated culture. Even the controversy about the role Tom Sawyer plays in the last seven chapters of the novel centers on the conflict between Tom's romantic swagger and Huck's tenuous moral supremacy: a boy's games versus adult responsibility.

Without detracting from the central role that Huck Finn plays in the novel that bears his name, it is possible to re-view *Huck Finn* as embodying a basic tension between male and female values and roles—a tension that bears directly on Huck's moral growth. Most of the female characters are derived from traditional—usually unflattering—stereotypes of women common to nineteenth-century authors and readers; indeed, the novel could serve as an index to common attitudes toward women as reflected in these stereotypical images. Those few women in the novel who are not merely stereotypes, such as Judith Loftus and Mary Jane Wilks, have more to do with Huck's development than is normally acknowledged. Finally, Huck's ambivalence about women—whom he tends to view as either nagging moralists or paragons of virtue—demonstrates the limited nature of his maturity by the end of the novel. The virtues that Huck begins to develop—honesty, compassion, a sense of duty—are identified in the novel as female virtues. Yet Huck's maleness requires that he ultimately emulate men, that he see women as "other"; and in the end he tries to run from the civilizing presence of women, unable to make the distinction between essential humanity and what society incorrectly considers virtue.

Discussions of Twain's male characters' attitudes toward or relationships with women seem inevitably to address the attitudes of Twain—or, rather, Samuel Clemens—toward women in his own life. Clemens's relationships with his mother, Jane Clemens, and with his wife, Olivia, particularly as they appear to be sources for the female characters in his works (and, in the case of Olivia, to be a "censor" of his work), have been the subject of much biographical and critical study. Although such an approach can invite a confusion of character and author, it may be useful to consider briefly Clemens's

4. Ibid., p. xiii.
5. "Come Back to the Raft Ag'in, Huck Honey!" *PR* 15 (1948): 664–71.
6. See especially Walter Blair, *Mark Twain and Huck Finn* (Berkeley: University of California Press, 1960).

view of womanhood, since it is likely that, as the creation of a nineteenth-century male imagination, Huck mirrors some of Clemens's conceptions of the nature and role of women.

Mary Ellen Goad has defined the role that Clemens wished women to play in his own life in order to illuminate his creation of female characters. Goad contends that Twain created patterns of female behavior to which even the actual women in his life were expected to adhere, and that his fictional women were designed as models for the real women in his life:

> Twain viewed the role of the female in a particular, and, to the modern mind, strange way. He operated on the theory that the male of the species was rough and crude, and needed the softening and refining influence of a woman, or, if necessary, many women. The primary function of the women was thus the reformation of man.[7]

This view of woman as the reformer of inherently brutish man was not unique to Twain and had been enhanced by the Victorian insistence on female purity. Ann Douglas argues that between 1820 and 1875 middle-class women and Protestant ministers turned simultaneously to the promulgation of "the potentially matriarchal values of nurture, generosity, and acceptance."[8] Both groups felt powerless to exert influence in overt ways—women because of the removal of key economic activities from the household to the factory, and clergymen because of the legal disestablishment of the church—and therefore adopted the moral suasion of others as their sphere of influence. The fact that this position resulted in women remaining in a real sense powerless coincided with society's efforts to oppress them, according to Douglas, who states: "The cruelest aspect of the process of oppression is the logic by which it forces its objects to be oppressive in turn, to do the dirty work of their society in several senses."[9] The Victorian definition of woman's role as moral guide would account for such characters as Miss Watson and Aunt Sally, part of whose function is "civilizing" recalcitrant boys. In addition, the persistence of this figure in Twain's life and art is explained, Goad says, by the habit that Twain and some of his male characters had of not remaining long in a reformed state. "The business of reform became a game in which one made promises, then suffered periodic relapses, as a sort of recreation."[10]

When Goad discusses the female characters in Twain's work, however, she argues, as so many others have done, that they are merely flat and stereotypical—that in fact they represent one of Twain's failures as a writer. "Twain," she says, "was simply unable to create a female character, of whatever age, of whatever time and place, who is other than wooden and unrealistic." She continues:

7. "The Image and the Woman in the Life and Writings of Mark Twain," *ESRS* 19 : 3 (March 1971): 5.
8. *The Feminization of American Culture* (New York: Alfred A. Knopf, 1977), p. 10.
9. Ibid., p. 11.
10. Goad, "Image and Woman," p. 5.

He had evolved over the years a narrow, specialized role for women, and although none of the women he knew fit the ideal, Twain continued to hold it in the abstract. Livy refused to become the narrow, moralizing, reforming shrew that Twain seemed to want, and it is no doubt well that she did, for Twain could not have lived with such a woman. When he was creating a female character in a work of fiction, however, Twain was not troubled by either a refusal to fit a role or the problem of living with someone who did fit the role. He could make a character do exactly what he wanted her to do, and what he wanted was an idealization.[11]

In *Huck Finn*, however, the relationship between Huck and women is more complex and dynamic than a simple response to idealized figures. Changes in our perceptions of the realities of women's lives during the last one hundred years allow us to see that, although Twain may have used idealizations of women as the basis for many of his female characters, those characters play a vital if underrated role in the society of which they are a part; although they may be perceived by the male characters only as occasions for rebellion or opportunities for heroic action, they represent both positive and negative values of that society. For all Twain's mockery of middle-class "respectability," without the real human virtues represented primarily by the women in *Huck Finn* there would be little opportunity for Huck to grow.

With few exceptions, the male characters in the novel are far from admirable by the standards of either conventional or actual morality. They tend to be degenerate, selfish, greedy, and vengeful and are just as stereotypical as are many of the female characters. Pap is an exaggerated version of the "natural man" on the frontier, an illiterate alcoholic such as inspired the temperance movement of the nineteenth century. Though a figure of broad comedy at times, he lives outside society's rules and rejects even its positive values, such as education. Huck's description of Pap in Chapter 5 underscores his subhuman status:

> There warn't no color in his face, where his face showed; it was white; not like another man's white, but a white to make a body sick, a white to make a body's flesh crawl—a tree-toad white, a fish-belly white. (P. [39])

The Duke and the Dauphin are far more human; they are—initially, at least—rogues rather than bestial villains despite their dishonest schemes. Twain clearly admires their rascality; they are vehicles of satire rather than subjects of horror. Also satirically treated are the Grangerfords and the Shepherdsons, to whom a half-forgotten lawsuit and murder are sufficient to maintain a multi-generational feud. Though Huck describes Colonel Grangerford as a "gentleman all over" (p. [143]), we are meant to see the irony of the term "gentle," and Huck is eventually glad to leave his house. Similarly, Colonel Sherburn, for all his insight into the cowardice of a lynch mob, is the cold-blooded killer of the drunken Boggs.

Not all the men in the novel are this recklessly violent, but none except Jim exhibits maturity and virtue. Uncle Silas Phelps is the stereotype of the bumbling, absentminded man married to a woman with a tart tongue; the

11. Ibid., p. 56.

couple is in the tradition of Rip and Dame Van Winkle and Harriet Beecher Stowe's Sam Lawson and his wife. Tom Sawyer, the classic "bad boy," turns from youthful prankster early in the novel to cunning—if not malicious—torturer during the "freeing" of Jim at the end.

When Huck and Jim lie and steal, they do so to survive, and this behavior seems therefore excusable. Huck's numerous false identities and Jim's posing as a "sick Arab" are ways of avoiding detection and thus contribute to rather than detract from the moral thrust of the novel. The same is true of their habit of stealing, or "borrowing," as Huck prefers to call it:

> Pap always said it warn't no harm to borrow things, if you was meaning to pay them back, sometime; but the widow said it warn't anything but a soft name for stealing, and no decent body would do it. Jim said he reckoned the widow was partly right and Pap was partly right. (P. 95)

Jim's morality thus mediates between the socially unacceptable element, represented by Pap, and the acceptable behavior represented by the widow. Because Jim and Huck steal food and other necessities, rather than the Wilks girls' inheritance, as do the Duke and the Dauphin, this habit, like lying, seems justified to the reader. Huck's most flagrant "sin" is helping a slave to escape, just as Jim's is running away from his owner; ironically, of course, these acts are in Twain's view their greatest moral triumphs, even though they are not sanctioned by the society Twain describes. Only Jim, among the male characters in the novel, exerts a positive influence on Huck. Jim's position outside white society allows him freedom from—if nothing else—both the moralizers and the rascals of that society, and he teaches Huck morality by example rather than by precept.

In contrast to the male characters in the novel, the female characters largely conform to what society—and Mark Twain—expects of them, and this conformity is the source of their often flat, stereotypical presence. Whether stern moralizers, like Miss Watson, or innocent young girls, like Boggs's daughter, the women have been molded by social pressure into representations of several kinds of womanly virtue. As members of the gender responsible for upholding the moral and religious values of civilization, even when those values sanction slaveowning, the women make possible the lawlessness and violence of the men. If we accept the fact that Twain saw men as naturally "rough and crude," then women were either reformers one could tease by temporarily conforming to their rules, or innocent maidens who could restore one's faith in decency and goodness.

Including the deceased Emmeline Grangerford, there are twelve women in *Huck Finn* aged fourteen or older. Of these, some are merely walk-on characters; for example, Emmeline's sisters, Charlotte and Sophia, and Mary Jane Wilks's sisters, Susan and Joanna. Sophia Grangerford, who Huck says is "gentle and sweet, like a dove" (p. 144), is one-half of the Romeo-and-Juliet couple whose elopement triggers a renewal of the feud between the Grangerfords and the Shepherdsons. Twain describes her as the stereotypical young woman in love, blushing and sighing and always "sweet." With Charlotte Grangerford and the younger Wilks sisters Huck has little to do, and Twain seems to use them all merely as parts of his portrait of Southern gentility.

The most obvious "reformers" in *Huck Finn* are the Widow Douglas, Miss Watson, and Aunt Sally Phelps. The widow and Miss Watson are Huck's unofficial guardians at the beginning of the novel; it is their insistence on prayers and clothes that makes Huck feel "all cramped up" (p. 18), and it is from Aunt Sally that Huck runs at the end, with his famous concluding statement, "But I reckon I got to light out for the Territory ahead of the rest, because Aunt Sally she's going to adopt me and sivilize me and I can't stand it. I been there before" (p. 366). Huck's comment that he's "been there before" points to the pattern of reform and backsliding that Goad discusses and suggests that, having escaped the clutches of the Widow Douglas and Miss Watson at the beginning of the novel, Huck has, at the end, endured another period of civilizing at the hands of Aunt Sally. The repetition of the pattern of reform and escape might lead one to believe that all these women are instances of the same stereotype, whereas in fact they represent three different popular images of women in the nineteenth century. There is no doubt that Twain had different models in mind when he created these three characters, and Huck's responses to them emphasize their differences.

The key to the differences among these three female reformers is their marital status. No matter how devoutly some women of the time clung to a state of "single blessedness," marriage was the only widely sanctioned state for an adult woman. American humor in the nineteenth century is filled with satiric portraits of husband-hunting spinsters and widows, and both humorous and serious literature describes the older single woman as straight-laced and narrow-minded. The novelist Marietta Holley, for example, has her persona, Samantha Allen, describe her spinster neighbor, Betsey Bobbet:

> She is awful opposed to wimmin's havein' any right only the right to get married. She holds on to that right as tight as any single woman I ever see which makes it hard and wearin' on the single men round here.[12]

Widows had a somewhat better time of it than spinsters in the public eye, as was pointed out by another female humorist, Helen Rowland: "Even a dead husband gives a widow some advantage over an old maid."[13] The spinster, presumed to be unwanted, is presumed also to have ossified. The image of the widow, at one time a wife and probably a mother, is somewhat softer; even as a "reformer," she has a kinder heart. The married woman, assumed to be in her proper element, provides the most contented image of the three and thus is likely to be the mildest reformer of all. The three principal reformers in *Huck Finn* represent each of these three states.

Walter Blair has suggested that the prototype for Miss Watson might have been a spinster schoolteacher who visited the Clemens family in Hannibal. Twain remembered this woman, Mary Ann Newcomb, as being a thin woman and a strict Calvinist.[14] Miss Watson has both of these qualities. Huck de-

12. *My Opinions and Betsey Bobbet's* (Hartford: American Publishing Co., 1872), p. 27.
13. *Reflections of a Bachelor Girl* (New York: Dodge, 1909), p. 35.
14. *Mark Twain and Huck Finn*, p. 106.

scribes her as "a tolerable slim old maid, with goggles on" (p. 19), and she threatens Huck with hellfire for his sins. It is not surprising that when Huck, Tom, and the other boys are forming their gang, and Huck has no family to be killed if he reveals the gang's secrets, he offers to let them kill Miss Watson. Miss Watson is a constant nagging presence who is particularly concerned with Huck's manners and his education. It is she, Huck says, who "took a set at me . . . with a spelling-book" and "worked me middling hard for about an hour" (p. 19). She is eternally watchful of his demeanor: "Miss Watson would say, 'Dont put your feet up there, Huckleberry;' and 'dont scrunch up like that, Huckleberry—set up straight'" (p. 19). In the matter of religion she seems to Huck prissy and sterile. The heaven she describes to him is unappealing: "She said all a body would have to do there was to go around all day long with a harp and sing, forever and ever. So I didn't think much of it" (pp. 19–20). The subject of heaven is one of several on which Huck distinguishes between the Widow Douglas and Miss Watson:

> Sometimes the widow would take me one side and talk about Providence in a way to make a body's mouth water; but maybe next day Miss Watson would take hold and knock it all down again. I judged I could see that there was two Providences, and a poor chap would stand considerable show with the widow's Providence, but if Miss Watson's got him there warn't no help for him any more. (P. 30)

Dedicated to duty rather than pleasure in a life that apparently has given her little of the latter, Miss Watson imagines an afterlife inspired by her Calvinist background, one ill-suited to the imagination of an adolescent boy.

Although Huck resists Miss Watson's bleak vision, he recognizes that she merely wishes to make him a "good" person according to her definition of that concept, and Twain suggests that Huck understands that Miss Watson is filling a role determined for "old maids" in American society. Huck's offer to let the gang kill her if he betrays them may be read in two ways. On the one hand, she may be an expendable person in his world, but the gang members have specifically required that he have a "family" to kill, and, by naming Miss Watson, Huck suggests that he accepts her as such. More telling is the famous episode in Chapter 31 in which Huck wrestles with his conscience about helping a slave to escape and ultimately decides that he will go to hell. Jim is Miss Watson's property, and the morality he has absorbed—partly from her—tells him he is stealing from her. As his argument with himself gradually builds from practical to humanistic considerations, he fears sending Jim back to Miss Watson because "she'd be mad and disgusted at [Jim's] rascality and ungratefulness for leaving her" (p. 269). When his "conscience" overtakes him, however, he agonizes about "stealing a poor old woman's nigger that hadn't ever done me no harm" (p. 270). Despite the syntax of the sentence, it is clear that Huck means that Miss Watson has "done [him] no harm." Although the reader can easily see the harm done by the spurious morality of people like Miss Watson, Huck merely sees her as a "poor old woman," as indeed she is.

Twain makes a clear distinction between Miss Watson and the Widow

Douglas. The widow is a far more gentle reformer than her unmarried sister and often intercedes between Huck and Miss Watson to mitigate the latter's severity. Although Twain based the character of the widow on a popular nineteenth-century conception of widowhood, he omitted several of the least desirable characteristics of that image. The most negative presentation of the widow in American humor is Frances M. Whicher's Widow Bedott, a gossiping husband-hunter who was the pseudonymous author of sketches in *Neal's Saturday Gazette* in the 1840s. Despite her protestations to the contrary, she is always on the lookout for eligible men, whom she smothers with terrible poetry and home remedies.[15] Twain's notes about his immediate prototype for the Widow Douglas, Mrs. Richard Holiday, suggest that he originally regarded her as a target of similar satire:

> Well off. Hospitable. Fond of having young people. Old, but anxious to marry. Always consulting fortune-tellers; always managed to make them understand that she had been promised three husbands by the first fraud.[16]

Aside from the fondness for young people, the Widow Douglas is considerably modified from this model.

Huck does not resent or pity the widow as he does Miss Watson. He is quick to excuse her behavior toward him, as he does early in the first chapter: "The widow she cried over me, and called me a poor lost lamb, and she called me a lot of other names, too, but she never meant no harm by it" (p. 18). He finds her attitude toward tobacco hypocritical, but is more amused than angry:

> Pretty soon I wanted to smoke, and asked the widow to let me. But she wouldn't. She said it was a mean practice and wasn't clean, and I must try not to do it any more. . . . And she took snuff, too; of course that was all right, because she done it herself. (Pp. 18–19)

The widow's method of reforming is to request or explain rather than to scold or nag. Whereas Miss Watson's "pecking" makes Huck feel "tiresome and lonesome" (p. 20), he responds favorably to the widow's kind heart. When Huck stays out all night with Tom and the gang, the two women react quite differently:

> Well, I got a good going-over in the morning, from old Miss Watson, on account of my clothes; but the widow she didn't scold, but only cleaned off the grease and clay and looked so sorry that I thought I would behave a while if I could. (P. [29])

By Chapter 4, Huck has become accustomed to being civilized. When he slips into his old habits, such as playing hooky from school, he welcomes the ensuing punishment: "the hiding I got next day done me good and cheered me up" (p. [34]). He retains a fondness for his old life but is pleased by the widow's praise of his progress:

> I liked the old ways best, but I was getting so I liked the new ones, too, a little bit. The widow said I was coming along slow but sure, and doing very satisfactory. She said she warn't ashamed of me. (P. [34])

15. *The Widow Bedott Papers* (New York: J. D. Derby, 1856).
16. Quoted in Blair, *Mark Twain and Huck Finn*, p. 106.

Huck's response to the Widow Douglas's kindness is important to under-standing his later reaction to Jim's essential humanity. From the first pages of the novel, Twain presents Huck as a basically decent boy who is able to re-spond to loving discipline, and it seems likely that he altered the stereotype of the widow—removing her more laughable traits—in order to allow her to have a positive influence on Huck's moral development. Before Huck sets out on the raft with Jim, Miss Watson and the Widow Douglas are the only representatives of decency in his world. Despite her implicit approval of slav-ery, the widow has a coherent view of what Huck needs in order to be a "respectable" citizen—a view involving education, cleanliness, and Chris-tian virtues. Were it not for the events that propel Huck into his trip down the river with Jim, he could grow up in the mold of the Horatio Alger hero. The other two major models for Huck's development at this point are Tom Sawyer and Pap; Tom, as the eternal child, would have Huck remain irre-sponsible and unrealistic, and Pap, in his complete rejection of society's rules and forms, would have him descend into barbarism. It is, after all, from Pap and not from the Widow Douglas that Huck flees in Chapter 7.

The most important lesson that Huck learns from the widow is that it is possible—even desirable—to place another human being's welfare before one's own. Not only has the widow taken the unpromising Huck into her home; she has also demonstrated that she cares about him, that his esca-pades make her not so much angry as sad. When Huck responds favorably to the widow's efforts to alter his behavior and values, he does so because he realizes his actions have an effect on others. It is this same principle that motivates Huck's final decision to help Jim escape regardless of the conse-quences for himself. As he is struggling with his conscience, he recalls first the good times he and Jim have had, then the favors Jim has done for him, and finally "the time I saved him by telling the men we had small-pox aboard, and he was so grateful, and said I was the best friend old Jim ever had in the world, and the *only* one he's got now" (p. 271). In his realization of his re-sponsibility for another human being, Huck builds upon the example the widow has set for him; in fact, he surpasses the widow in moral integrity by recognizing a black man as a fellow human being.

Yet Huck's experiences with the third "reforming woman," Aunt Sally Phelps, show the limits of his maturation. The effectiveness of the final chap-ters of *Huck Finn* has been debated for decades. Those critics who find Huck's acquiescence to Tom's romantic game-playing disturbing in light of his previous maturation on the river probably have the stronger argument, and this objection is strengthened by the presence of Aunt Sally. If Huck ever needs a reformer, it is during the torture of Jim in these final chapters, but Aunt Sally, because of the particular stereotype upon which she is based, is an ineffectual reformer, though reforming is clearly her function.

Aunt Sally and Uncle Silas are a familiar pair in American humor: the harmless nag and the befuddled husband. Aunt Sally is a warm, gregarious woman who whirls around the still center of Uncle Silas. Hers is far from the strict, staid demeanor of Miss Watson; though Uncle Silas is a part-time preacher, Aunt Sally is untouched by the Calvinist gloom that characterizes Miss Watson's outlook. Apparently happily married to the good-hearted

Silas, and the mother of several children, she has a far sunnier disposition than the Widow Douglas and is more likely to be understanding of youthful pranks. When Tom Sawyer kisses her while she still thinks he is the stranger William Thompson, she calls him an "owdacious puppy" and a "born fool," but once she thinks he is Sid Sawyer, she enjoys the joke: "I don't mind the terms—I'd be willing to stand a thousand such jokes to have you here" (p. 289).

But when Huck and Tom—disgused as Tom and Sid—embark on the activities that Tom feels appropriate to freeing a prisoner and begin stealing sheets and spoons and filling the Phelps house with rats and snakes, Aunt Sally shows her temper. Twain's gift for comic exaggeration is nowhere more apparent than in some of these slapstick scenes, and the descriptions of Aunt Sally are strikingly similar to those of Livy, his own "reforming woman," that he included in letters to friends and relatives early in their marriage. In February 1870 he wrote:

> But there is no romance in this existence for Livy. She embodies the Practical, the Hard, the Practical, the Unsentimental. She is lord of all she surveys. She goes around with her bunch of housekeeper's keys (which she don't know how to unlock anything with them because they are mixed,) & is overbearing & perfectly happy, when things don't go right she breaks the furniture & knocks everything endways. You ought to see her charge around. When I hear her war whoop I know it is time to climb out on the roof.[17]

Just as the dignified Livy becomes a comic figure in such descriptions, so Aunt Sally becomes comic and nonthreatening even as she attempts to discipline Huck and Tom. To cover their theft of a spoon, the two boys confuse Aunt Sally as she attempts to count:

> Well, she *was* in a tearing way—just a trembling all over, she was so mad. But she counted and counted, till she got that addled she'd start to count-in the *basket* for a spoon, sometimes; and so, three times they come out right, and three times they come out wrong. Then she grabbed up the basket and slammed it across the house and knocked the cat galley-west; and she said cle'r out and let her have some peace, and if we come bothering around her again betwixt that and dinner, she'd skin us. (Pp. 320–21)

Most of the time Aunt Sally's threats are idle, but even when she punishes the boys it has little effect. When the snakes they have collected to put in Jim's cabin get loose in the house, Aunt Sally takes action:

> We got a licking every time one of our snakes come in her way; and she allowed these lickings warn't nothing to what she would do if we ever loaded up the place again with them. I didn't mind the lickings, because they didn't amount to nothing; but I minded the trouble we had, to lay in another lot. (P. 334)

Huck's response to Aunt Sally's discipline is to ignore it—it "didn't amount to nothing"—whereas his reaction to the Widow Douglas's disappointment in his backsliding early in the novel had been to try to "behave a while" if he

---

17. Dixon Wecter, ed., *Mark Twain to Mrs. Fairbanks* (San Marino, Calif.: Huntington Library, 1949), p. 123.

could. The widow touched Huck's humanity; Aunt Sally merely touches his backside with a hickory switch.

It is difficult, therefore, to take seriously Huck's fear of being "sivilized" by Aunt Sally at the end of the novel. Not a true "reformer," she is a harmless comic figure similar to the Livy of Clemens's letters. Given Twain's insistence on the conflict between Huck's innocence and the corruption of civilization, it is important that Huck thinks he can escape at the end and that the reader knows he cannot—knows, that is, that the "Territory" is simply another civilization. But it seems odd to posit Aunt Sally as a major representative of civilization—instead of, say, Miss Watson or the Widow Douglas—unless we understand that Twain's view of women as the reformers of young men was a product of his own youthful fantasy, formed in part by the Victorian culture in which he lived. In attempting to claim legitimate—if ultimately ineffectual—authority and self-esteem in a society that had made them powerless, Victorian women willingly acceded to a "cult of motherhood," which, as Ann Douglas points out, "was nearly as sacred in mid-nineteenth-century America as the belief in some version of democracy." Douglas quotes Lydia Sigourney, who, writing to young mothers in 1838, urged them to realize their potential influence on their children: "How entire and perfect is this dominion over the unformed character of your infant. . . . Now you have over a new-born immortal almost that degree of power which the mind exercises over the body."[18] All three of the women who attempt to make Huck conform to society's rules are derived from traditional stereotypes of women who may superficially be seen as mother figures from the same societal mold; but Huck's more complex and ambivalent relationships with them point up the different social realities they represent and his own boyish immaturity at the end of the novel. The fact that Huck can ignore Aunt Sally's female authority testifies to both his own lack of significant maturity and Mark Twain's awareness of the final ineffectuality of women in his society.

What growth Huck does achieve comes largely from his perception of qualities in others that he wishes to assume himself. With the exception of Jim, all of Huck's important models of decent human behavior are female. Though the "goodness" of both the reforming older women and the young girls in the novel is exaggerated for comic or satiric effect, several of the women display qualities that Huck begins to adopt as his character develops before the final chapters. In addition to the Widow Douglas, whose kindness and sincerity are apparent to Huck even as he chafes at the restrictions of his life with her, Mrs. Judith Loftus and Mary Jane Wilks are important influences on his self-definition. Both characters are more than mere stereotypes, and both demonstrate intelligence and courage that Huck does not find in most of the men he knows.

Mrs. Loftus, whom Huck encounters just before he and Jim begin their trip on the raft, is the shrewd, garrulous woman who sees through Huck's disguise as a girl. She shares with common stereotypes of women a love of

18. Douglas, *Feminization*, pp. 74–75.

gossip, but it is her common sense and kindness to which Huck responds. In terms of her age, Mrs. Loftus belongs to the category of "reforming" women; Huck thinks she is "about forty year old" (p. 83). But her advice at this point in the novel (unlike the moralizing of Miss Watson and the Widow Douglas) is the practical sort that Huck needs for survival, and Huck perceives her as strong and intelligent. His clumsy efforts to thread a needle and catch a lump of lead in his lap call forth Mrs. Loftus's scorn, but Twain also emphasizes her kindly attitude toward the boy she assumes to be a runaway apprentice:

> I ain't going to hurt you, and I ain't going to tell on you, nuther. You just tell me your secret, and trust me. I'll keep it; and what's more, I'll help you. . . . Bless you, child, I wouldn't tell on you. (P. 89)

Huck cautiously responds with another lie about his identity, but he is clearly impressed with Mrs. Loftus's perspicacity. When he returns to the raft and reports on his conversation with Judith Loftus, Jim says she is a "smart one" (p. 94).

More importantly, Mrs. Loftus confirms Huck in his maleness early in the novel. Not only does she quickly see through Huck's female disguise; she also outlines for him the male behavior that has betrayed him:

> Bless you, child, when you set out to thread a needle, don't hold the thread still and fetch the needle up to it; hold the needle still and poke the thread at it— that's the way a woman most always does; but a man always does 'tother way. And when you throw at a rat or anything, hitch yourself up a tip-toe, and fetch your hand up over your head as awkward as you can, and miss your rat about six or seven foot. . . . And mind you, when a girl tries to catch anything in her lap, she throws her knees apart; she don't clap them together, the way you did when you catched the lump of lead. (Pp. 90–91)

Instead of following Mrs. Loftus's advice, Huck never again pretends to be a girl. He rejects his female disguise after he leaves the Loftus house by taking off his sunbonnet, "for I didn't want no blinders on" (p. 91). A few paragraphs later, at the end of Chapter 11, he joins his fortunes to those of Jim when he says, "There ain't a minute to lose. They're after us!" (p. 92). The male identification forecasts the American male adventure, at the end of which Huck will assume Tom Sawyer's identity and his behavior.

Later in the novel, in anticipation of Huck's final capitulation to Tom's boyish romanticism, comes Huck's rescue of the "damsel in distress," Mary Jane Wilks. Huck's response to Mary Jane is not merely that of the gallant knight to the damsel, however; he is at this point (Chaps. 24–30) still on his way to the real moral stature he will achieve in Chapter 31, and Mary Jane is more complex than the traditional damsel. Twain makes her simultaneously weak and strong, so that she in some ways embodies the paradox that Ann Douglas points to in Victorian women who "lived out a display of competence while they talked and wrote of the beauties of incompetence."[19] Though Mary Jane in part matches the sentimental stereotype of the pure, innocent

19. Ibid., p. 93.

young woman, Huck's view of her includes admiration as well as protectiveness. She combines the piety of the older reforming woman with the absolute innocence of the ideal young girl, but it is finally her intelligence and
courage that Huck finds most appealing.

Twain was apparently fascinated with young girls, and he idealized them
in both his life and his art. His deep attachment to his daughter Susy and his
intense interest in Joan of Arc are only two examples among many of this
preoccupation, and portraits of young female characters in his fiction are
often suffused with reverence for their beauty and spotless virtue. Albert E.
Stone, Jr., explores Twain's devotion to "young maidens, hovering on the
edge of adult experience," and quotes from a fragment that Twain wrote in
1898, describing a recurrent dream of adolescent love:

> She was always fifteen, and looked it and acted it; and I was always seventeen,
> and never felt a day older. To me she is a real person not a fiction, and her sweet
> and innocent society has been one of the prettiest and pleasantest experiences of
> my life.[20]

Most of the young girls in *Huck Finn* are versions of this romantic ideal,
including such minor figures as Boggs's daughter, glimpsed grieving over her
father's body: "She was about sixteen, and very sweet and gentle-looking,
but awful pale and scared" (p. 187). Here an object of pity, the young girl
can also be an object of satire, as in the well-known portrait of Emmeline
Grangerford. Apparently modeled on Julia A. Moore, a sentimental poet
known as the "Sweet Singer of Michigan,"[21] Emmeline represents the common stereotype of the morbid female poet, and Twain uses her to satirize
sentimental art and the execrable taste of the Grangerford family.

However, it is precisely for her *lack* of sentimentality that Huck admires
Mary Jane Wilks. At nineteen, she is the oldest of the three Wilks sisters,
undoubtedly older than Huck. The only drawback to her beauty is her red
hair, but Huck forgives that: "Mary Jane *was* red-headed, but that don't
make no difference, she was most awful beautiful, and her face and her eyes
was all lit up like glory" (p. [211]). Mary Jane is indeed innocent and trusting. She gives the inheritance money to the Duke and the Dauphin to prove
her faith in them and defends Huck when her younger sister accuses him—
accurately—of lying:

> "It don't make no difference what he *said*—that ain't the thing. The thing is
> for you to treat him *kind*, and not be saying things to make him remember he
> ain't in his own country and amongst his own folks."
> I says to myself, *this* is a girl that I'm letting that old reptile rob her of her
> money! (P. 225)

Mary Jane's goodness bothers Huck's conscience sufficiently that he decides
to foil the Duke and Dauphin's scheme by recovering and hiding the money,
but he does not tell her what he has done until he realizes that she is upset

20. *The Innocent Eye: Childhood in Mark Twain's Imagination* (New Haven: Archon
Books, 1970), pp. 207–9.
21. See L. W. Michaelson, "Four Emmeline Grangerfords," *MTJ* 11 (1961): 10–12.

about the slave family being broken up. In his effort to comfort her, Huck inadvertently tells her the truth, and in a passage that closely prefigures his later decision to help Jim escape, he wrestles with the necessity for truth, still in Mary Jane's presence:

> she set there, very impatient and excited, and handsome, but looking kind of happy and eased-up, like a person that's had a tooth pulled out. So I went to studying it out. I says to myself, I reckon a body that ups and tells the truth when he is in a tight place, is taking considerable many resks, . . . and yet here's a case where I'm blest if it don't look to me like the truth is better, and actuly *safer*, than a lie. (P. 240)

The passage describing Huck's parting with Mary Jane in Chapter 28 marks the penultimate step in the moral development that culminates in his decision to risk his soul to help Jim. He is impressed by her willingness to go along with his plan to save the girls' inheritance—a plan that, though involving lies and deceptions, is a model of decency compared with Tom's plan to free Jim—and particularly by her offer to pray for him. Contrasting his sinful nature to her goodness, he thinks:

> Pray for me! I reckoned if she knowed me she'd take a job that was more nearer her size. But I bet she done it, just the same—she was just that kind. She had the grit to pray for Judas if she took the notion—there warn't no backdown to her, I judge. (P. 245)

By putting himself in a category with Judas and emphasizing Mary Jane's virtues, Huck is playing a game with his reformer: though drawn to the innocence and purity she represents, he simultaneously insists on his unregenerate nature. Mary Jane represents the female principle of virtue, always coupled with beauty. "And when it comes to beauty," Huck says, "and goodness too—she lays over them all" (p. 245). Huck, on the other hand, is the sinful male, unworthy of but longing for the redeeming power of the woman.

However, Huck is not merely playing a game at this point. His praise of Mary Jane Wilks is couched in terms that show he has an adolescent crush on her. She has, he says, "more sand in her than any girl I ever see," and though she disappears from his life at this point, Huck's memory of her testifies to her effect on his values: "I reckon I've thought of her a many and a many a million times, and of her saying she would pray for me; and if ever I'd a thought it would do any good for me to pray for *her*, blamed if I wouldn't a done it or bust" (p. 245). Twain combines here the terms of a boy's admiration—"grit" and "sand"—and the desire to help another person that marks the maturing human being. Given Huck's uncomfortable relationship with religion, his willingness to pray for Mary Jane Wilks is a true gift of love. Huck's feelings for Mary Jane and Twain's depiction of her strength and determination raise her above the level of stereotype and allow her, like other women in the novel, to be a significant influence on Huck's developing conscience. His offer to pray for her if it "would do any good" suggests that the idea of self-sacrifice is becoming natural to him and prepares for his ultimate "sacrifice" of his own soul to help Jim.

A close look at the part women play in Huck Finn's life thus makes clearer the extent of his moral regression at the end of the novel. In his relationships with his principal female mentors—the Widow Douglas, Judith Loftus, and Mary Jane Wilks—he has achieved an appreciation of those virtues that begin to separate him from the hypocrisy and violence of the society in which he lives. But his contact with these women has also confirmed that he is in fact male and must remove himself from what he perceives as a "female" world of conformity to certain standards of behavior. With the Widow Douglas and Miss Watson he plays the part of the unruly boy; with Judith Loftus he tries to be a girl and fails; and with Mary Jane Wilks he assumes the role of the male protector of female innocence. Finally, with Jim, he arrives at a mature friendship with another man, one for whom he is prepared to risk eternal damnation. But his acquiescence to the adolescent behavior of Tom Sawyer in the final chapters demonstrates just how tenuous and fragile his maturity has been, and his desire to "light out for the Territory" is youthful escapism rather than a mature rejection of a corrupt society.

Twain's use of nineteenth-century stereotypes of women as the basis of his female characaters in *Huck Finn* allows the reader to understand some of the ways a male-dominated culture perceived woman's place and function. Both the men and the women in the novel illustrate the values of a society that has little regard for human dignity, but the female characters also embody virtues that could redeem that society if the women were empowered to do so. The male characters, even the rascals and thieves, are allowed the freedom to accept or reject these values, whereas the women, as members of a subservient group, are obliged to preserve and transmit them. Whether as innocent young girls or as middle-aged reforming women, the female characters are for the most part creations of a male imagination that requires them to inspire men with their goodness or "save" them from their undesirable tendencies. Huck is both inspired and "saved" or "sivilized" in the course of the novel, but finally he exercises the male prerogative of rejection—not of the values of his society, but of the "female" virtues he has struggled so hard to attain. By accepting the limited roles for women that his culture promoted, Twain effectively limits the extent to which Huck Finn can be a moral force in his society. Though they are frequently inspirational or influential, the women in *Huck Finn*, viewed from the male perspective of the novel, are finally powerless—as Aunt Sally Phelps demonstrates—to change the adolescent dreams of the American male.

11 WILLIAM E. LENZ

Confidence and Convention in *Huckleberry Finn*

THE confidence man, a distinctly American version of the archetypal trickster, rises from the historical conditions of boom and bust during the "flush times" of pre–Civil War America and takes on a literary life of his own in the 1840s. Augustus B. Longstreet's Yellow Blossom, Johnson J. Hooper's Captain Simon Suggs, Joseph G. Baldwin's Ovid Bolus, Esq., and Simon Suggs, Jr., George W. Harris's Sut Lovingood, Herman Melville's Confidence Man, and Kittrell J. Warren's Billy Fishback loosely represent the early nineteenth-century tradition of shifty characters that has recently received increased critical attention;[1] Gary Lindberg, in fact, insists that the confidence man is neither peripheral nor aberrant but "a representative American, perhaps even our covert hero."[2] At the very least, the confidence man embodies contradictory responses to the frontier "flush times" and plays a part in shaping American attitudes toward the undefined or largely imaginative "new country." Prowling border states where appearance and reality seem interchangeable, where style often substitutes for substance, the shifty man trades on not only the territory's ambiguities but also the individual's ambivalence; he exploits the fluidity of identity and the rigidity of social conventions, the need for confidence and the suspicion of betrayal, and

1. This selection is more or less random and makes no pretense of completeness. For the Yellow Blossom, see "The Horse-Swap," in Longstreet's *Georgia Scenes, Characters, Incidents, &c., in the First Half Century of the Republic* (Augusta, Ga.: Printed at the S. R. Sentinel Office, 1835); Simon Suggs is the star of Hooper's *Some Adventures of Captain Simon Suggs, Late of the Tallapoosy Volunteers* (Philadelphia: Carey and Hart, 1845); Ovid Bolus, Esq. and Simon Suggs, Jr., are found in Baldwin's *Flush Times of Alabama and Mississippi* (New York: D. Appleton & Co., 1853); Sut Lovingood cavorts through Harris's *Sut Lovingood: Yarns Spun by a "Nat'ral Born Durn'd Fool"* (New York: Dick & Fitzgerald, 1867); *The Confidence-Man: His Masquerade* is available in many modern editions (1857; rpt. New York: W. W. Norton & Co., 1971); and Billy Fishback creates havoc in Watkins, ed., *Life and Public Services of an Army Straggler, By Kittrell J. Warren* (Athens: University of Georgia Press, 1961).

2. *The Confidence Man in American Literature* (New York: Oxford University Press, 1982), p. 3. For other useful studies of the confidence man, see Constance Rourke, *American Humor: A Study of the National Character* (New York: Harcourt Brace Jovanovich, 1931, 1959); Kenneth S. Lynn, *Mark Twain and Southwestern Humor* (Boston: Little, Brown, 1959); Victor M. Hoar, "The Confidence Man in American Literature" (Ph.D. diss., University of Illinois, 1965); Jesse Bier, *The Rise and Fall of American Humor* (New York: Holt, Rinehart & Winston, 1968); Richard Boyd Hauck, *A Cheerful Nihilism: Confidence and "The Absurd" in American Humorous Fiction* (Bloomington: Indiana University Press, 1971); Susan Kuhlmann, *Knave, Fool, and Genius: The Confidence Man as He Appears in Nineteenth-Century American Fiction* (Chapel Hill: University of North Carolina Press, 1973); and Warwick Wadlington, *The Confidence Game* (Princeton: Princeton University Press, 1975).

the conflicting claims of explicit public optimism and implicit private pessimism. Emerging from the informal genre of Southwest humor, the confidence man had by midcentury achieved the status of a popular literary and cultural convention.

Kenneth S. Lynn has demonstrated that Mark Twain was thoroughly schooled in Southwest humor and wise to the wiles of the confidence man.[3] From *Innocents Abroad* (1869) to *Roughing It* (1872) and *The Gilded Age* (1873), Mark Twain tested, deformed, and discredited the literary conventions of popular sentimentalists and literary comedians through narrative juxtaposition with those of Southwestern humorists. Attempting to unscramble this technique of stylistic conflation, James M. Cox admits, "It is often difficult to tell whether Twain is trapped in clichés or simply exploiting them."[4] In *Adventures of Huckleberry Finn*, Twain masterfully engineers collisions of Southwest humor, literary or platform comedy, and sentimental, romantic, and realistic fiction to question the contemporary bases of confidence and convention; to accomplish this he reconstructs the antebellum flush times, the source for Twain of cultural contradictions and irreconcilable attitudes that by the 1880s had created what one nineteenth-century analyst termed "American nervousness."[5] Twain uses the confidence man and the issues of confidence he raises to probe the shaky foundations of American optimism, which he perceived to be unfounded, delusional, and ultimately self-destructive. The nostalgic impulse informing the shifty Colonel Sellers in *The Gilded Age* becomes in *Huckleberry Finn* the innocent-seeming critical tool for exposing the violently restrictive cultural attitudes qua stylistic conventions of American society. To Huckleberry Finn all—with the exception of Jim—seem to demand and betray confidence almost randomly, a puzzling amalgamation of conscious confidence men and unconscious hypocrites. Huck subverts this apparent conformity, measuring their inconsistencies from his perspective as a figure marginal to all levels of society.

Huck Finn blends the vernacular language and posture of Southwest humor, the youthful protagonist of the sentimental novelist, and the convention of the good-bad boy popularized by Thomas Bailey Aldrich in *The Story of a Bad Boy* (1870). As the novel's self-deprecating narrator, he inspires the reader's trust and emphasizes the importance of language; language—in particular diction, syntax, point of view, and tone—defines character, as the author comically warns in an explanatory note on dialect, and is itself a way of perceiving and ordering reality.[6] Huck's description of sup-

3. *Mark Twain and Southwestern Humor*, esp. chap. 6. See also Rourke, *American Humor*; Bernard DeVoto, *Mark Twain's America* (Boston: Little, Brown, 1932); and Walter Blair, *Mark Twain and Huck Finn* (Berkeley: University of California Press, 1960).

4. "*A Connecticut Yankee in King Arthur's Court*: The Machinery of Self-Preservation," YR 50 (1960): 95.

5. George Miller Beard, *American Nervousness: Its Causes and Consequences* (New York: G. P. Putnam's Sons, 1881). In Beard's view Americans were the victims of rapid urbanization and technological advances.

6. See James M. Cox, *Mark Twain: The Fate of Humor* (Princeton: Princeton University Press, 1966), p. 160.

per with Widow Douglas, for example, reveals far more than two sets of eating habits.

> The widow rung a bell for supper, and you had to come to time. When you got to the table you couldn't go right to eating, but you had to wait for the widow to tuck down her head and grumble a little over the victuals, though there warn't really anything the matter with them. That is, nothing only everything was cooked by itself. In a barrel of odds and ends it is different; things get mixed up, and the juice kind of swaps around, and the things go better. (P. 18)

Huck stresses two styles of life—the widow's rigid culture and his easy anarchy—in these culinary techniques, tying the reader to the vernacular by silently including him on Huck's side of the table while disarming him with the humorous "barrel of odds and ends" language. In Huck's first-person narration, "things get mixed up . . . and the things go better"; beneath his vernacular is an energy at once comic in its rapid shifts and juxtapositions of styles and eager in its anxiously repetitive attempts to record accurately events the boy does not always fully understand.[7] Language serves Huck as a vehicle for apprehending experience, while the language of others serves him as an index to their intentions.

Jim's dialect and superstitions are refined versions of those commonly found in Southwestern sketches such as Henry Clay Lewis's "Day of Judgment" (1850);[8] his speculations—in a cow that dies, a bank that "busts," a raft that is stolen—stereotype him within the limitations of a "low" comic character, the bumbling Negro who placidly suffers as the butt of condescending, cruel jokes. Huck learns, however, that Jim's language is deceptive, concealing under a humorous veneer the complexity of an individual. Huck's own conventional language has proved inadequate to interpret Jim. After convincing Jim that their separation in the fog was only a dream (an inversion of the witch-ride prank Tom pulled in Chapter 2), Huck is startled by the depth of emotion Jim conveys in dialect.

> "When I got all wore out wid work, en wid de callin' for you, en went to sleep, my heart wuz mos' broke bekase you wuz los', en I didn' k'yer no mo' what become er me en de raf'. En when I wake up en fine you back agin', all safe en soun', de tears come en I could a got down on my knees en kiss' yo' foot I's so thankful. En all you wuz thinkin' 'bout wuz how you could make a fool uv ole Jim wid a lie. Dat truck dah is *trash*; en trash is what people is dat puts dirt on de head er dey fren's en makes 'em ashamed." (P. 121)

The complexity—and moral justice—of Jim's criticism, rendered in the same style as his superstitions, requires Huck to evaluate him anew, now as a friend, rejecting as inappropriate the stock figure of Jim as a harmless, humorous, nonhuman slave. Huck has apparently been confused by the discrepancy between his culturally conditioned expectations of Jim's comic response and the reality of Jim's sharp pain; in addition, Huck is taken aback

7. See Richard Bridgman, *The Colloquial Style in America* (New York: Oxford University Press, 1966), pp. 119–30.

8. "Day of Judgment" can be located in John Q. Anderson, *Louisiana Swamp Doctor: The Life and Writings of Henry Clay Lewis* (Baton Rouge: Louisiana State University Press, 1962).

by the contrast between Jim's style of speech and its substance. Style, an ambiguous word that as Warwick Wadlington notes assumes through countless repetitions "near-magical properties,"[9] may not be an accurate, immediate indicator of character or motivation but a conventional, limited mode of expression. Jim's sophisticated manipulation of the culturally loaded word *trash* strikes Huck with the force of a slap in the face; as Lionel Trilling contends, at this point "Huck's one last dim vestige of pride of status, his sense of position as a white man, wholly vanishes."[10] Jim securely asserts his own superiority to "white trash" folks and their malicious tricks while offering Huck the opportunity to transcend the boundaries of Huck's own limiting stereotype; to the son of Pap Finn, Jim holds out the offer of concern, companionship, respect, and responsible, reciprocal love.

Huck questions the language of Widow Douglas, Tom Sawyer, Miss Watson, and Pap Finn in a similar fashion, exposing the "love" each appears to extend as self-serving illusion. Although the widow claims self-righteously that smoking tobacco "was a mean practice and wasn't clean, and I must try to not do it any more," "she took snuff too; of course that was all right, because she done it herself" (pp. 18–19). Language must be measured against the actions and values it often hides; the style of love the widow is willing to give is restrictive and is based on her self-satisfying design to "sivilize" Huck. Richard Poirier argues, "It is metaphorically suggested that Tom Sawyer and Widow Douglas are in tacit alliance, and both are indicted by the further suggestion that to be 'respectable' in her terms is the necessary condition for membership in his gang. 'Respectable' society as represented by the widow is equivalent to a 'band of robbers.'"[11] Without putting undue pressure on this assertion, we can agree that both the widow and Tom insist on remaking Huck, the widow with her Bible and Tom with his romances. That Huck recognizes identical attempts to imprison him becomes clear in the language he uses to reject Tom's tiresome adventures: "It had all the marks of a Sunday school" (p. 33). David E. E. Sloane widens this conspiracy against Huck to include Miss Watson and Pap Finn, both of whom desire "to exploit Huck for . . . egotistical satisfaction."[12] Both demand that Huck behave in a proscriptive manner and assure him, not of forgiveness and love, but of judgment and punishment for disobedience. Pap's "love" seems at best a device to keep Huck from acquiring what he perceives to be a superior style of culture and at worst a ploy to get for himself Huck's fortune while brutalizing his son physically and emotionally because of his own frustrations. Beneath all these languages lies a threat of violence absent from the relationship Huck develops with Jim. In abstract terms, Jim alone offers

9. *Confidence Game*, p. 247.

10. "Huckleberry Finn," in *The Liberal Imagination: Essays on Literature and Society* (Garden City, N.Y.: Doubleday & Co., 1953), p. 107. See also Wadlington's fine analysis of social hierarchy in *Confidence Game*, pp. 261–62.

11. *A World Elsewhere: The Place of Style in American Literature* (London: Oxford University Press, 1966), p. 182.

12. *Mark Twain as a Literary Comedian* (Baton Rouge: Louisiana State University Press, 1979), pp. 135, 141.

Huck the chance to rise above conventional limitations to become a responsible partner in an unconventional relationship based not on upbringing, age, race, or economic class but solely on mutual trust and respect.

The violence in the widow's style is so implicit that it usually passes without notice, the reader confidently accepting at face value Huck's conventional assurance that "she never meant no harm by it" (p. 18). Her hypocrisy over tobacco, however, coupled with her socially condoned intentions, demonstrates how even a good woman can internalize and rationalize official values that she unconsciously imposes on Huck. Each woman Huck holds up as a paragon of virtue—Widow Douglas, Miss Watson, Mary Jane Wilks, Aunt Sally Phelps—silently supports in broad terms the slave system and propagates it in her efforts to "sivilize" Huck. That readers do not question Huck's adoration illustrates the intention and the success of Twain's narrative point of view: to Huck, their attempts to improve him are in no sense equivalent to enslavement but appear beneficent Franklinian programs to help him achieve a desirable and wholly conventional moral perfection.

Tom's style veils two forms of violence. First, Tom is infected by what Twain tagged in *Life on the Mississippi* the "Sir Walter Scott Disease." [13] By insisting on the fulfillment of his literary romantic fantasies (especially in the novel's closing chapters), Tom literally threatens life and earns a bullet for his adventuring. Second, and more pernicious, Tom enforces conformity to exclusionary social conventions that dehumanize the individual—Huck, Jim, even Tom himself. In this view Tom is, as Poirier contends, the widow's accomplice.

The danger posed by the discrepancy between language and act is most obvious in the behavior of Pap Finn. Echoing Johnson Jones Hooper's shifty Simon Suggs at a campmeeting (as do the King and the Duke), Pap pretends to have seen the light; like Pap, Simon testifies to rebirth and receives congratulation all around.

> "Come up, come up; thar's room for all!" cried brother Bugg, in his evening exhortation. "Come to the 'seat,' and ef you won't pray yourselves, let *me* pray for you!"
>
> "Yes!" said Simon . . . "it's a game that all can win at! . . . No matter what sort of a hand you've got," added Simon in the fulness of his benevolence; "take stock! Here am *I*, the wickedest and blindest of sinners—has spent my whole life in the sarvice of the devil—has now come in on *narry pair* and won a pile!" [14]

Pap's dramatic performance mimics the pieties of popular reform repeatedly satirized by Southwest humorists. [15]

13. *Life on the Mississippi* (Boston: Osgood, 1883), chaps. 38 and 46. See also Blair's discussion in *Mark Twain and Huck Finn*, pp. 285–99.

14. *Some Adventures of Captain Simon Suggs* (1845; rpt. Upper Saddle River, N.J.: Literature House/Gregg Press, 1970), p. 129. Subsequent references will be to this edition and will be abbreviated in the text as *SS*.

15. In addition to Hooper's "The Captain Attends A Camp-Meeting" and Lewis's "Day of Judgment," the most memorable sketch is George Washington Harris's "Parson John Bullen's Lizards" in *Sut Lovingood*.

> "Look at it gentlemen, and ladies all; take ahold of it; shake it. There's a hand that was the hand of a hog; but it ain't so no more; it's the hand of a man that's started in on a new life, and 'll die before he'll go back. You mark them words— don't forget I said them. It's a clean hand now; shake it—don't be afeard."
>
> So they shook it, one after the other, all around, and cried. The judge's wife she kissed it. Then the old man he signed a pledge—made his mark. The judge said it was the holiest time on record, or something like that. (P. 43)

In the tradition of Simon Suggs and Sut Lovingood, Pap counterfeits the conventional sentimental rhetoric of nineteenth-century revelation and consolation characteristic of writers from Mason Locke Weems to Henry Ward Beecher and Elizabeth Stuart Phelps. Just as Jim's low dialect could not long hide his full nature, so Pap Finn's pretense of repentance quickly collapses.

> In the night sometime he got powerful thirsty and clumb out onto the porch-roof and slid down a stanchion and traded his new coat [given him by the credulous reforming judge] for a jug of forty-rod, and clumb back again and had a good old time; and towards daylight he crawled out again, drunk as a fiddler, and rolled off the porch and broke his left arm in two places and was most froze to death when somebody found him after sun-up. And when they come to look at that spare room, they had to take soundings before they could navigate it.
>
> The judge he felt kind of sore. He said he reckoned a body could reform the ole man with a shot-gun, maybe, but he didn't know no other way. (Pp. 43–44)

Pap's destruction of the room reveals the violence lurking just below the surface of his language and prefigures his drunken antigovernment, anti-Negro tirade, which culminates in his attempt to murder Huck (Chap. 6). The conventional piety and self-serving racist politics Pap mouths suggest that language is not a substitute for violence but a prelude to it; even the Judge's language contains a threat. Words can be used to hide violent truth. The ease with which the widow, Pap, and the Judge shift styles indicates that language is part of a conventional pose that may both reveal and conceal values and intentions. Although Miss Watson preaches to Huck about the horrors of blasphemy and says "*she* was going to live so as to go to the good place" (p. 19), she betrays Jim's confidence in her: she "awluz said she wouldn' sell me down to Orleans. . . . Well, one night I creeps to de do', pooty late, en de do' warn't quite shet, en I hear ole missus tell de widder she gwyne to sell me down to Orleans, but she didn' want to, but she could git eight hund'd dollars for me, en it 'uz sich a big stack o' money she couldn' resis'" (p. 69). Miss Watson completes the process of rationalization, betrayal, and hypocrisy by attending a campmeeting. At this point in the novel Huck and Jim inhabit a world endangered by an entire society that seems to have assimilated the confidence man's methods and ethics. The threat is all the more frightening because it parades the streets in the guise of respectability.

The discrepancy between language and act is nowhere more apparent than in the chapters on the Grangerfords and their feud with the Shepherdsons (17–18). Their house, which has "so much style" (p. 136), is ruled by the equally impressive Colonel Grangerford: "Col. Grangerford was a gentleman, you see. He was a gentleman all over; and so was his family. . . . He was as kind as he could be—you could feel that, you know, and so you had confidence" (pp. [143]–44). Huck misplaces his confidence, for the colonel's impeccable manners, like his emblematic white linen suit, mask the soul of a madman. The Grangerfords appear to have refinement, religion, and respectability, but it is the forms—the style—the family truly cherishes. The religion of this "handsome lot of quality" is little more than a sentimental cult of death, consecrating the irrational feud and hallowing the "spidery" crayon masterpiece of Emmeline as if it were a death-bed self-portrait. Despite the comfort, kindness, and generosity Huck shares in the Grangerford home, the realities of their feud make him sick and reveal to the reader how bankrupt of ultimate moral values is their natural aristocracy. Huck detects an underlying kinship, moreover, between Emmeline's speedy tributes for the dead and Buck's monomaniacal haste to kill a Shepherdson; both illustrate the obsessiveness that has become normal. Emmeline's pictures always give Huck the "fan-tods" in part because they indicate an unhealthy preoccupation with death as an aesthetic, idealized experience.

> Every time a man died, or a woman died, or a child died, she would be on hand with her 'tribute' before he was cold. She called them tributes. The neighbors said it was the doctor first, then Emmeline, then the undertaker—the undertaker never got in ahead of Emmeline but once, and then she hung fire on a rhyme for the dead person's name, which was Whistler. She warn't ever the same, after that; she never complained, but she kind of pined away and did not live long. (P. 141)

The central place death has assumed during the long years of the feud has blinded everyone (with the exception of Harney Shepherdson, who spares Buck and Huck before he elopes with Sophia Grangerford) to the corrupting influence this unexamined, obsessive focus has on basically good people. The highly stylized graveyard portrait of a distraught lover—"And Art Thou Gone Yes Thou Art Gone Alas"—suggests that the cultural trappings highly visible in the house's style license the feud's code of violence. Death is either casually dismissed or emotionally applauded. In response to Huck's question "Has anybody been killed this year, Buck?" the boy replies, "Yes, we got one and they got one" (p. 147). And when Huck accuses Baldy Shepherdson of cowardice, Buck immediately rallies to his defense: "I reckon he *warn't* a coward. Not by a blame' sight. There ain't a coward amongst them Shepherdsons—not a one. And there ain't no cowards amongst the Grangerfords, either. Why, that old man kep' up his end in a fight one day, for a half an hour, against three Grangerfords, and come out winner" (p. 148). Reminiscent of sentimental rationalizations of death common in Civil War fictions such as the popular *Norwood* (1867, 1868) by Henry Ward Beecher, the Grangerfords' conciliatory program encourages murder, though the causes of the "war" are at best dimly understood by individuals. Violence has become so ingrained in their minds that it dominates their lives, warping their love for the dead Emmeline and the eloped Sophia. The slaughter at the river, punctuated by shouts of "Kill Them! Kill Them!," strips away the last shreds of respectability for the reader and for Huck: "It made me so sick I most fell out of the tree" (p. 154).

Huck also voices Twain's disgust at the antebellum cult of sentimentality that linked honor with violence. In *Life on the Mississippi* he argues that stylistic affectations—castles, false culture, Sir Walter Scott, and duels— caused the Civil War. This self-deluding, self-authenticating "Sir Walter Scott disease" made violence a national virtue and, dissociating death from reality, swept historical (and literary) alternatives aside. Families, individuals, and mobs are encouraged to prove themselves through rites that are socially sanctioned forms of murder. Thus the drunken Boggs, a comic figure lifted from Southwest humor, is honorably gunned down by the aristocratic Colonel Sherburn; honorably, for though Boggs is not armed, he ignores Colonel Sherburn's gentlemanly warning. In like manner, the nation ignored warnings of impending war and accepted the violence of the Colonel Sherburns as heroic. Boggs, the focus of the delighted crowd, poses an institutionalized comic threat; Colonel Sherburn, either taking Boggs at his word or simply bored by him, changes the traditional comedy of the Old Southwest—the boasting or bluffing contest that is often a substitute for violence [16]—into a sentimental tragedy. To this the crowd reacts by threatening to lynch Colonel Sherburn, but their threat, like Boggs's, is all bluster. Twain documents the manner in which sentimental forms of aristocratic pretension come to dominate the humorous tradition of Southwestern humor—kill it, in fact—and the manner in which these idealizations—represented by Colonel Sherburn—retain their power. Once Sherburn has been recognized as heroic, an epitome of American culture, and has been awarded a title of public respect ("Colonel"), he has been given the authority to command respect, though he publicly commits murder. Obeying the very forms the people have chosen to elevate, Colonel Sherburn triumphs over the lynch mob stylistically:

> "The idea of *you* lynching anybody! It's amusing. The idea of you thinking you had pluck enough to lynch a *man*! Because you're brave enough to tar and feather poor friendless cast-out women that come along here, did that make you think you had grit enough to lay your hands on a *man*? Why, a *man's* safe in the hands of ten thousand of your kind—as long as it's day-time and you're not behind him." (P. 190)

Huck doesn't wish to dwell on the implications of Colonel Sherburn's evaluation of American manhood, for the colonel seems a cold-blooded killer who successfully defends himself from the crowd by demonstrating the qualities Americans most admire—confidence, individualism, and bravado. Categories of experience break down as a comic drunk becomes a tragic victim and a cowardly murderer seems suddenly a towering hero. These paradoxical transformations indicate a radical disorder at the center of American culture, one that threatens to wrench Huck from the normative context of referential language and deed and throw him headfirst into a morally chaotic world of violent and ambiguous action.

16. See Walter Blair, "Americanized Comic Braggarts," *CritI* 4 : 2 (1977): 331–49.

To define this aberrant society Twain turns directly to the flush-times confidence man. At the center of *Huckleberry Finn* spring up the King and the Duke, a counterforce to the violent sentimentality promulgated by Colonels Grangerford and Sherburn. The King and the Duke are at first Suggsian confidence men who recapitulate the entire Southwestern humorous tradition; in addition to selling teeth cleaner and running temperance revivals, their repertoire of "snaps" includes, according to them, the following:

> "Jour printer, by trade; do a little in patent medicines; theatre-actor—tragedy, you know; take a turn at mesmerism and phrenology when there's a chance; teach singing-geography school for a change; sling a lecture, sometimes—oh, I do lots of things—most anything that comes handy, so it ain't work. What's your lay?"
>
> "I've done considerable in the doctoring way in my time [replies the King to the Duke]. Layin' on o' hands is my best holt—for cancer, and paralysis, and sich things; and I k'n tell a fortune pretty good, when I've got somebody along to find out the facts for me. Preachin's my line, too; and workin' camp-meetin's; and missionaryin' around." (P. 152)

In language, physical appearance, and profession these rogues recall the confidence men of Hooper, Baldwin, Harris, Melville, and a dozen of their cronies from the *Spirit of the Times*. Their games are designed to fleece hypocrites, pretenders, and fools and as such serve as chastening antidotes to the virulent poisons of the self-righteous society of murdering heroes. Insinuating themselves with Huck and Jim, they create humorous identities for themselves in a ritual ceremony of mock-revelation.

> "Gentlemen," says the young man, very solemn, "I will reveal it to you, for I feel I may have confidence in you. By rights I am duke!"
>
> Jim's eyes bugged out when he heard that; and I reckon mine did, too. Then the baldhead says: "No! you can't mean it?"
>
> "Yes. My great-grandfather, eldest son of the Duke of Bridgewater, fled to this country about the end of the last century, to breathe the pure air of freedom; married here, and died, leaving a son, his own father dying about the same time. The second son of the late Duke seized the title and estates—the infant real duke was ignored. I am the lineal descendant of that infant—I am the rightful Duke of Bridgewater." (P. 163)

His companion, however, will not be outdone in invention.

> "Bilgewater, kin I trust you?" says the old man, still sort of sobbing.
>
> "To the bitter death!" He took the old man by the hand and squeezed it, and says, "The secret of your being: speak!"
>
> "Bilgewater, I am the late Dauphin!"
>
> You bet you Jim and me stared, this time. Then the duke says:
>
> "You are what?"
>
> "Yes, my friend, it is too true—your eyes is lookin' at this very moment on the pore disappeared Dauphin, Looy the Seventeen, son of Looy the Sixteen and Marry Antonette." (P. 164)

These caricatures parody the convention of concealed royal birth gracing innumerable sentimental fictions and "Wild Western" Beadle novels. Twain sets up and satisfies comic expectations, using the King's rechristening of

Bridgewater as "Bilgewater" to deflate the pretensions of both impersonators and to burlesque the posturing of real kings and dukes.

Sharing Huck's point of view, the reader recognizes with him "that these liars warn't no kings nor dukes, at all [though they give Huck a moment's pause], but just low-down humbugs and frauds." Huck's instinct, however, is to play along.

> If they wanted us to call them kings and dukes, I hadn't no objections, 'long as it would keep peace in the family; and it warn't no use to tell Jim, so I didn't tell him. If I never learnt nothing else out of pap, I learnt that the best way to get along with his kind of people is to let them have their own way. (P. 166)

Huck characterizes these four as a "family," asserting and extending the complex relationship he has developed with Jim to include two humorous confidence men. They too must be seen as more than mere stereotypes; they are individuals speaking discrete languages, personalities with human emotions and motives. Yet in lumping the King and the Duke with Pap in the phrase *his kind of people*, Huck foreshadows a sinister side to these comedians not immediately apparent: the King and the Duke are akin to Pap in having the capacity for violence, and they too interpret selfishly the meaning of the word *family*.

There is little evidence of their violence at the Pokeville campmeeting; only the emotions of the congregation are violent.

> You couldn't make out what the preacher said, any more, on account of the shouting and crying. Folks got up, everywheres in the crowd, and worked their way, just by main strength, to the mourners' bench, with the tears running down their faces; and when all the mourners had got up there to the front benches in a crowd, they sung, and shouted, and flung themselves down on the straw, just crazy and wild. (P. 173)

Critics including Bernard DeVoto and Walter Blair have proved that Twain's campmeeting owes more than a nod to Hooper's in style, tone, and action.[17]

> The rest were walking to and fro, (engaged in the other exercises we have indicated,) among the "mourners"—a host of whom occupied the seat set apart for their especial use—or made personal appeals to the mere spectators. The excitement was intense, Men and women rolled on the ground, or lay sobbing or shouting in promiscuous heaps. More than all, the negroes sang and screamed and prayed. Several, under the influence of what is technically called "the jerks," were plunging and pitching about with convulsive energy. (*SS*, pp. 119–20)

Simon Suggs and the King exploit the communal desire for religious ecstasy, which the *North American Review* called in 1862 "aesthetic religionism": "It is sought for its emotions. . . . but when emotion is sought for its own sake, it may become as selfish as the love of money, or the love of fame. We desire the spiritual luxury, and, if it comes not otherwise, it must

---

17. DeVoto, *Mark Twain's America*, p. 255, and Blair, *Mark Twain and Huck Finn*, pp. 279–84. I disagree with Lynn's conclusion that "in Hooper's story, the Confidence Man is a symbol of the age; in Chapter XX of *Huckleberry Finn*, he is a freak" (*Mark Twain and Southwestern Humor*, p. 225).

be got up." [18] This "sentimental pietism" is false, a perverse elevation of style over substance suitable for attack in 1845 (*Simon Suggs*), in 1862 (the *North American Review*), and in 1884 (*Huckleberry Finn*); it defines one variety of religious experience that continues to haunt the American mind, manifesting itself in William Dean Howells's *Leatherwood God* (1916), Sinclair Lewis's *Elmer Gantry* (1927), and Nathanael West's *Miss Lonelyhearts* (1933) and *The Day of the Locust* (1939), to list only a sample from the early twentieth century.

Mark Twain plays the campmeeting in Hooper's style. The King's counterfeit of a pious conversion imitates that of Simon Suggs, though the King's harangue is narrated by Huck while Simon speaks for himself. The King pretends to be a reformed pirate of the Indian Ocean while Simon—though he pretends to have "got" religion—delights in manipulating the brethren without benefit of masquerade. The reader's enjoyment of the King's snap is limited by the fact that Twain renders it in the third person; although the congregation may deserve fleecing, Twain wishes the reader to withhold complete approval of the King's actions. While the reader responds directly to Simon Suggs, Twain desires the reader to respond with laughter to his scene but maintains enough critical distance from the King to discourage reader-character identification. For this reason the King takes on the self-consciously literary identity of a pirate: he remains at this point a two-dimensional comic character within a larger, conventional, comic structure and does not make the personal demand of empathic approval that Simon Suggs (or Huck Finn) does of the reader. Both confidence men bilk the campmeeting so that they can purportedly begin the good works of the missionary preacher, and as the King concludes (in his one bit of direct discourse), both find the preacher "the truest friend a pirate ever had" (p. 174).

The King and Duke's burlesque "Shaksperean Revival" follows the popular tradition of butchered classics [19]: "They laughed all the time, and that made the duke mad; and everybody left, anyway, before the show was over, but one boy which was asleep" (p. 194). The revival, an analogue to the campmeeting, sets the stage for the drunken entrance of Boggs. Twain juxtaposes frontier comedy and frontier violence, suggesting that the inflamed aesthetics of the Arkansas townsfolk encourage Colonel Sherburn to kill Boggs: their "sentimental pietism" casts aside fineness of emotion for intensity of emotion. In the Duke's words, "What they wanted was low comedy—and may be something ruther worse than low comedy" (p. 194).

What they get, first of all, is the spectacular murder of Boggs. It is clearly

18. "Moral Types of Mankind," review of *Undercurrents of Wall Street. A Romance of Business*, by Richard B. Kimball, *NAR* 95:196 (July 1862): 123.

19. For this tradition, see Oscar G. Brockett, *History of the Theatre* (Boston: Allyn & Bacon, 1968), p. 498, and David Grimsted, *Melodrama Unveiled: American Theater and Culture, 1800–1850* (Chicago: University of Chicago Press, 1968), pp. 48–49. Other useful treatments of Shakespeare and frontier theater include Ray Allen Billington, *America's Frontier Heritage* (New York: Holt, Rinehart & Winston, 1966), pp. 85–87; and William G. B. Carson, *The Theatre on the Frontier: The Early Years of the St. Louis Stage* (New York: Benjamin Blom, 1965), esp. pp. 246–306.

intended to be "worse than low comedy," as is Colonel Sherburn's parallel cowing of the mob. Yet the Duke has something different in mind; this town deserves not garbled Shakespeare but his revived revival, "The King's Camelopard or The Royal Nonesuch." The Duke packs the house by printing handbills concluding with the line, "LADIES AND CHILDREN NOT ADMITTED" (p. 195), which the men swallow as the euphemistic promise of obscenity.[20] They eagerly pay up for three nights, filling the theater as they had filled the street around Boggs, as they had listened to the story of his murder with rapt attention, and as they had rushed to the house of Colonel Sherburn.[21] The Duke "said he could size their style"; what they desire is a dehumanizing show.

> And at last when [the Duke had] got everybody's expectations up high enough, he rolled up the curtain, and the next minute the king come a-prancing out on all fours, naked; and he was painted all over, ring-streaked-and-striped, all sorts of colors, as splendid as a rainbow. . . . The people most killed themselves laughing; and when the king got done capering, and capered off behind the scenes, they roared and clapped and stormed and haw-hawed till he come back and done it over again; and after that, they made him do it another time. (Pp. 196–97)

They are sold in the finest Suggsian tradition. Twain dramatizes a momentary victory of Southwest humor over the cult of emotion and style, which demands that the performance be repeated, like the retelling of Boggs's murder, again and again. In a gesture of poetic justice, the confidence men give the townspeople what they demand. At the Royal Nonesuch, as at the campmeeting, the comic actions of the confidence men offer a corrective to violent sentimentality. In *Simon Suggs* and *Huckleberry Finn* confidence men boil hypocrites in laughter.

Since Chapter 19 the novel has been humorously directed by the King and the Duke; however, the heart-wrenching yet conventional sentimental story of Jim's deaf and dumb daughter 'Lisbeth (pp. 201–2) ushers Huck and Jim into a nightmarish reality. The King and the Duke, at first able to exploit the falseness of language and social convention for profit, at last become trapped themselves in the flush-times dream of instant wealth; whereas at the campmeeting or the Royal Nonesuch they had consciously manipulated the forms of society, in the Wilks adventure they succumb to its substance, no longer mimicking but embodying the fantasies of Pap Finn and the violence of Colonel Sherburn. When the King and the Duke rationalize selling Jim, they have become part of the culture whose pretensions they had humorously counterfeited. Although they con the naive Wilks girls, Gary Lindberg argues that at this point the King and the Duke "must be seen not as peripheral freaks but as stylized exemplars. They help characterize the suckers

---

20. Blair traces the possible evolution of this incident in *Mark Twain and Huck Finn*, pp. 316–21. An oral version of the episode that makes its obscene character obvious is reported by Wallace Graves, "Mark Twain's 'Burning Shame,'" *NCF* 23 (1968): 93–98.

21. An excellent discussion of the people of Bricksville and their entertainments is found in Lindberg, *Confidence Man*, p. 194.

they exploit, for their methods depend on a massive public willingness to settle for trumpery."[22] Their poor performance, which "was enough to make a body ashamed of the human race" (p. 210), reveals a shift in their function and effect. Confidence art, so important to the comedy of Longstreet's Yellow Blossom, Hooper's Simon Suggs, Baldwin's Ovid Bolus, Harris's Sut Lovingood, and Melville's Confidence Man, is made subservient to what Whitman called the "magician's serpent" of moneymaking; with a wriggle the King and the Duke assume the position and the imperative of Baldwin's Simon Suggs, Jr., and Warren's Billy Fishback: "By-and-by the thing dragged through, and everything was sold. Everything but a little old trifling lot in the graveyard. So they'd got to work *that* off—I never see such a girafft as the king was for wanting to swallow *everything*" (p. 249).

The desire to reduce everything to sacks of gold marks the absorption of the King and the Duke into the heart of society. In contrast to Simon Suggs, they cease to be marginal characters of the frontier and come to represent the direction in which the new country as a whole is headed: all will be assimilated into a modern age of hypocrisy, violence, and greed. Although the gradual souring of the confidence man's humor is present throughout the nineteenth century, the King and the Duke cause an especially bad taste to linger: not only is the reader made to sympathize with the victimized Huck, Jim, and the Wilks girls, but the sale of Jim defeats the entire imaginative—and moral—journey of the novel. Even Tom Sawyer, who seems to take up the role of comic confidence man at the end of *Huckleberry Finn*, betrays Huck and Jim to a figurative ride on a rail. Tom obeys the dehumanizing forms of sentimental culture defined by the King and the Duke, Pap, Widow Douglas, Miss Watson, the Grangerfords, Colonel Sherburn, and even the good Phelpses. He supports its style, perpetuates its violence, and cherishes its emblem—a totemic bullet. Yet Tom's prank is but a romantic shadow of the Southwestern confidence man's art, a betrayal that he attempts to ignore by reversing the traditional Suggsian exchange of cash: "We had Jim out of the chains in no time. . . . and Tom give Jim forty dollars for being prisoner" (pp. 364–65).

Mark Twain reimagines the confidence man, a convention representative of the frontier flush times, to reveal the bankruptcy of the twin traditions of sentimental and humorous consolation that inform his contemporary culture. In *Huckleberry Finn* he contrasts Southwestern and sentimental fiction, juxtaposing and conflating the confidence man's conscious manipulation of fraudulent social forms with the sentimental character's unconscious acceptance of them as genuine to create a radical new paradigm of American society. The horror at the center of antebellum culture, the cause of the Civil War and the source of the corrupt Gilded Age, is an infinite capacity for confident self-delusion visible in the history of the confidence man; preaching equality, opportunity, and freedom, society enforces submission to its self-serving, self-destructive conventions. Huck Finn recognizes—as the King and the Duke (and Tom) do not—that the confidence man is no longer a

22. Ibid., p. 195.

marginal predator but a national symbol of American culture. Forsaking mastery of the frontier flush times and betraying the heritage of Southwest humor that spawned him, the confidence man stands self-deceived. Twain's variations on the convention suggest that unlike Huck, who can potentially "light out for the Territory," the confidence man loses much of his flexibility and many of his humorous characteristics as he willingly submits—like the new country itself—to Aunt Sally's attempts to "sivilize" him.

Huck Finn should not be seen as yet another confidence man, though as Gary Lindberg notes he "can disengage principle from practice by his dexterity."[23] He does tell lies, assume false identities, and manipulate morality as easily as persimmons. Yet with the exception of the early tricks he plays on Jim in the style of Harris's Sut Lovingood, Huck's deceptions have an implicit consecration of their own. "All of Huck's freely chosen commitments to one face or another of his varied masquerade," claims Daniel G. Hoffman, "are given with the ultimate end of protecting Jim and himself from the world."[24] Struggling to survive in what Richard Poirier terms "a whole society built on games, tricks, and illusions,"[25] Huck spontaneously adopts when necessary the colors of the enemy—the language of the confidence man. Warwick Wadlington aptly remarks that "the benign, defensive trickster Huck discovers that he cannot pray a lie,"[26] while Richard Boyd Hauck correctly contends that Huck "never develops a conscious knowledge of what lies are for. . . . His beautifully constructed defensive lies succeed in keeping Jim safe, but their success does not help expand Huck's vision."[27] Huck must be seen as distinct from the King and the Duke, who acquire from the success of their early tricks the confidence to expand their operations past the breaking point in the Wilks episode. On the raft Jim teaches Huck that the confidence man's grammar of humor masks a language of cruelty and betrayal, and it is this lesson that makes Huck uncomfortable with Tom's romantic charade in the novel's closing chapters. His resistance to Tom's shenanigans, through which Jim must suffer as a literal and figurative "prisoner of style" (p. 337), supports Lionel Trilling's assessment that, although Huck may be a skillful liar, he never lies to himself.[28] Self-delusion ultimately delimits the convention of the confidence man. Huck's appeal resides in his uncanny ability to transcend literary and cultural stereotypes, even such a protean and practical form as that of the confidence man.

In Twain's later fiction, Hank Morgan is a Franklinian pragmatist whose confident manipulations result in massacre, while the switched infants Pudd'nhead Wilson never satisfactorily sorts out suggest a vision of fate not entirely subject to the confidence man's legerdemain. In the fragments that Albert Bigelow Paine collected and revised as *The Mysterious Stranger* in 1916, the confidence man has become a fantastic being operating in an ab-

---

23. Ibid., p. 197.
24. *Form and Fable in American Fiction* (New York: Oxford University Press, 1961), p. 345.
25. *World Elsewhere*, p. 185. See also Lindberg, *Confidence Man*, p. 197.
26. *Confidence Game*, p. 252.
27. *Cheerful Nihilism*, pp. 148, 150.
28. *Liberal Imagination*, p. 101.

stract realm of mythic forces. The confidence man emerges from these pages as Satan, a recombination of the convention with larger traditions. Although Twain himself never finished the manuscripts, Satan's dramatic revelation—that all is "a grotesque and foolish dream"[29]—suggests that to resolve the issues of confidence and convention his fictions raised, Twain was forced to resort to sleight of hand. As Huck Finn concludes, "I been there before."

29. William M. Gibson, ed., *Mark Twain's Mysterious Stranger Manuscripts* (Berkeley: University of California Press, 1969), p. 405.

12 DAVID SEWELL

We Ain't All Trying to Talk Alike: Varieties of Language in *Huckleberry Finn*

> In this book a number of dialects are used . . . I make this explanation for the reason that without it many readers would suppose that all these characters were trying to talk alike and not succeeding. (P. [7])

I. Standards and Vernaculars

CONVENTIONAL wisdom makes *Adventures of Huckleberry Finn* a declaration of linguistic independence, and Mark Twain the Dante of the American vernacular. In the novel's opening sentence, one critic has said, "the American language was first used as the medium of great fiction."[1] Mark Twain might have written, "You don't know about Huck Finn unless you have read a book called 'The Adventures of Tom Sawyer,' but that is unimportant." Instead he let Huck tell his own story, in his own language: "You don't know about me, without you have read a book by the name of 'The Adventures of Tom Sawyer,' but that ain't no matter" (p. [17]). Viewed from the perspective of standard or formal English, Huck's speech is riddled with errors. But it is impossible to maintain that perspective while reading *Huckleberry Finn*; since Huck is the narrator, his speech becomes normative for the duration of the novel. Read his narrative aloud, and only with difficulty can you resist modifying your speech toward your best approximation of Missouri dialect. Indeed, the only successful resistance is to close the book and retreat into silence. Such a narrative strategy has as its implicit program the assertion that the narrator's language is a valid literary dialect. It is one thing, however, to claim with Michael Egan that Mark Twain's novel teaches us to "speak Finnian," quite another to infer that Huck's "depart[ure] from the polite cadences of educated grammar" makes us "co-conspirators in his subversion of our language."[2] In fact, Huck Finn's vernacular proves in the end a staunch if unlikely ally of educated grammar. After Robin Hood's fashion, Huck's verbal outlawry victimizes only those who usurp authority unjustly; it is ever ready to bow the knee to a linguistic Richard the Lionhearted.

---

1. Bernard DeVoto, *Mark Twain at Work* (Cambridge: Harvard University Press, 1942), p. 51.
2. *Mark Twain's "Huckleberry Finn": Race, Class, and Society* (London: Published for Sussex University Press, by Chatto & Windus, 1977), p. 73.

Henry Nash Smith has taught a generation of critics to perceive a bipolar opposition in *Huckleberry Finn* between "vernacular" and "genteel" language. By "vernacular," Smith tells us, he means "not only the language of rustic or backwoods characters but also the values, the ethical and aesthetic assumptions, they represent."[3] This quasi-Whorfian conjoining of thought or values and language runs into immediate difficulty when applied to the novel, however. Surely, to take the most striking case, Huck and Pap Finn do not share identical "vernacular" values, although they speak roughly the same language. George C. Carrington, Jr., observing this paradox, has suggested that the vernacular-official distinction, while "good as taxonomy, is inadequate in terms of the dynamics of the novel."[4] Carrington's structuralist approach to the novel has led him to the essential insight that good grammar and bad grammar do not correspond rigidly to good and bad morality, that the force of an *ain't* depends upon context. But his criticism of Smith needs to be inverted: the problem with the vernacular-genteel dualism has less to do with narrative dynamics than with the fact that it is not an ideal taxonomy, that a better one can be devised. There are, in fact, two very different "vernaculars" and two "standard languages" in the novel. Twain created a linguistic universe in which the purpose and moral coherence of varieties of speech are more important than their objective form.

In *Tom Sawyer*, where the "shadings" of dialect are much lighter, the normative standard language is the dialect of St. Petersburg's ruling institutions: the church, the law courts, and the public school. In *Huckleberry Finn*, however, the standard is virtually absent. Almost nobody speaks what linguists today politely call Standard American English, what the nineteenth century more bluntly called "good English." Nevertheless, standard English remains, for both Twain and his narrator Huck, the understood symbol or outward sign of social authority. In Twain's linguistic economy, Standard English, like paper money, has no inherent value: it is worthless if its issuer does not possess the fund of social authority that his or her language promises. A character like Judge Thatcher is literally "as good as his word"; his verbal currency is backed by moral gold, authentic social worth. A Tom Sawyer or a Colonel Sherburn issues words that look the same but are like notes on a wildcat bank: when we try to redeem them for specie, we find that there is no gold in the vault.

Several of the novel's characters speak what I call "authentic Standard English," which indicates merited social, moral, and intellectual position. Chief among these is Judge Thatcher, the sole character in *Huckleberry Finn* whose represented speech is entirely free from grammatical error or regionalism. Properly speaking, Judge Thatcher is not so much a "character" as a function: he serves as a polar opposite to Pap Finn, with whom he disputes

3. *Mark Twain: The Development of a Writer* (Cambridge: Harvard University Press, 1962), p. 20.
4. *The Dramatic Unity of "Huckleberry Finn"* (Columbus: Ohio State University Press, 1976), p. 23. Smith himself had recognized that "speaking in dialect does not in itself imply moral authority" (*Development of a Writer*, p. 122), but the terms of his argument restrained him from exploring the implications of the observation.

the fate of Huck and Huck's money. Where Pap's heavily shaded dialect and scorn for literacy mark him as "ornery," an occupant of the lowest rung of white society, the Judge's correct and colorless speech guarantees his respectability. The opening of the novel sets up a sharp distinction between civilized and uncivilized modes of behavior, and the Judge's language is convenient shorthand for "civilized." The need for precise expression of social relationships explains the inconsistencies in the speech of another minor character, Doctor Robinson of the Wilks episode. When he first appears in Chapter 25, where his function is to debunk the King's imitation of an Englishman, his speech is eloquent standard American except for a lone colloquial "somewheres" (p. 218). His command of the standard dialect here symbolizes social and intellectual superiority to his more gullible fellow citizens. In Chapter 29, however, when the whole town is morally outraged and the Doctor's position is no longer unsupported, he slips back into a comfortable Pike County dialect: "Neighbors, I don't know whether the new couple is frauds or not; but if *these* two ain't frauds, I am an idiot, that's all" (p. 252). From the point of view of mimetic realism Twain has erred, but the doctor's language is in each case contextually appropriate. Other members of the professional classes consistently speak the heavily shaded dialect that Twain had found even among the "college-bred" in the West and South.[5] Twain's reproduction of their speech does not indicate unqualified approval: *Huckleberry Finn* is the product of an author for whom correct speech is still a moral norm.[6]

The use of "correct English" to indicate moral authority explains what is otherwise a flagrant inconsistency in the speech of a major character, Mary Jane Wilks. At first she shares the dialect of her younger sisters. Redheaded and "awful beautiful," she appears conventionally genteel, but her speech betrays her origins: "Take this six thousand dollars . . . and don't give us no receipt for it" (p. 219); "It ain't right nor kind for you to talk so to him, and him a stranger and so far from his people" (p. 224). For three chapters Mary Jane is kindly and sympathetic, but she is not yet a heroine. When, in Chapter 28, she assumes the moral stature of Twain's beloved Joan of Arc, she undergoes an instantaneous linguistic transformation. As the chapter opens, Mary Jane is sobbing over the fate of the household slaves, separated when the King sold them in opposite directions. While she remains an object of pity she is allowed to keep an index of her vernacular: "Oh, dear, dear, to think they ain't *ever* going to see each other any more!" (p. 240). As Huck reveals the details of the King and Duke's con game, sorrow is replaced by righteous indignation, marked physically by "eyes a blazing higher and higher all the time" and a face "afire like sunset" (p. 241). Her speech becomes that of a dramatic heroine and loses all trace of grammatical impurity: "The brute! Come—don't waste a minute—not a *second*—we'll have them tarred and feathered, and flung in the river!" (p. 241). More than pure, it is

5. See Twain's criticism of the execrable grammar of a "college-bred" country gentleman in Chapter 26 of *Life on the Mississippi* (New York: Harper, 1917), p. 222.

6. See David Sewell, "'A Lot of Rules': Twain and Grammar," in "Varieties of Language in the Works of Mark Twain" (Ph.D. diss., University of California, San Diego, 1984), pp. 9–43.

elegant: "Stand by you, indeed I will. They sha'n't touch a hair of your head!" she says, "and I see her nostrils spread and her eyes snap when she said it, too" (p. 242). Mary Jane has deftly navigated the modal waters of "shall" and "will," thus escaping the confusion judged in *Life on the Mississippi* to be endemic among Southerners.[7]

Dr. Robinson's protean dialect and Mary Jane's sudden grammatical purgation result from conventional, as opposed to naturalistic, handling of character. It is not an error but a deliberate strategy, one that Twain would have discovered in English novelists from Fielding to Dickens. In the British novel, as Norman Page has shown, "dialect is a variable dependent on the demands of fictional situation rather than on the probable behavior of an actual speaker."[8] Oliver Twist speaks like a young gentleman despite his origins; Lizzie Hexam in *Our Mutual Friend* rapidly loses dialect features as her moral education progresses. In general, Dickens follows a "convention of dialogue which deliberately sacrifices realism to moral appropriateness."[9]

For the virtuous characters in *Huckleberry Finn*, then, the standard language is a sign of affiliation with a natural aristocracy whose membership qualifications are primarily moral. There is another set of characters who use, or who attempt to use, correct or elevated speech in support of claims to an aristocratic station for which they are not morally qualified. I accordingly classify their deceptive language as "misappropriated Standard English"; it corresponds to what Henry Nash Smith calls "genteel English." The misappropriated standard is language as sheer instrumentality, a commodity valued entirely for what it can accomplish.

To the Duke, for example, standard English is merely the sine qua non of the professional confidence man. As an experienced actor, he can modify his lightly shaded Pike County speech to achieve a reasonable facsimile of hypergenteel sentimental diction. He shifts into his formal register in order to establish his "aristocratic" credentials shortly after he meets Huck and Jim. His performance is flawed by an "ain't" here (p. 162) and an "I reckon" there (p. 178), but on the whole he is convincing: he can fabricate the high style as easily as he can a patent medicine. Thus he represents the threat to the reliability of social indicators that Erving Goffman has called the essence of the confidence man: "Perhaps the real crime of the confidence man is not that he takes money from his victims but that he robs all of us of the belief that middle-class manners and appearance can be sustained only by middle-class people."[10]

We ordinarily think of dialect imitation as a unidirectional phenomenon: a performer of higher social status mimics a dialect with low prestige for comic effect. The Duke reminds us that so far as mimicry is concerned, standard English is as legitimate an object as any other. Twain observed in the

---

7. *Life on the Mississippi*, p. 313.
8. *Speech in the English Novel* (London: Longman, 1973), p. 55.
9. Ibid., p. 98.
10. *The Presentation of Self in Everyday Life* (Garden City, N.Y.: Doubleday, 1959), p. 18n.

minstrel shows of his boyhood the capacity of the professional showman to imitate in either direction:

> The minstrel used a very broad negro dialect; he used it competently and with easy facility. . . . However, there was one member of the minstrel troupe of those early days who was not extravagantly dressed and did not use the negro dialect. He was clothed in the faultless evening costume of the white society gentleman and used a stilted, courtly, artificial, and painfully grammatical form of speech, which the innocent villagers took for the real thing as exhibited in high and citified society, and they vastly admired it and envied the man who could frame it on the spot without reflection and deliver it in this easy and fluent and artistic fashion.[11]

This description of the manners and speech of the minstrel show straight man is a coat that will fit Colonel Sherburn with little alteration. He "was a heap the best dressed man in [the] town" (p. 185); his speeches to Boggs and to the lynch mob are courtly and artificial; and the ignorant villagers of Bricksville are cowed and impressed by what is essentially a set piece. Sherburn's speech to the mob is, in fact, a dramatic performance, no less theatrical than the "Balcony Scene" from *Romeo and Juliet* that the Duke and the King have just advertised.[12] Some critics are disturbed by Sherburn's denunciation of mob violence and human cowardice because they feel that we obviously hear the voice of Mark Twain speaking ex cathedra. Twain's language it is, but Sherburn has misappropriated it, his cold-blooded murder of Boggs having eliminated his right to pretend to any degree of normative speech. His address to the mob is the supreme example of the misappropriated standard in *Huckleberry Finn*: the heroic ethos he means to project is in truth a persona, a mask, a role. The veneer of *Murray's Grammar* that covers his Southern village speech is the verbal equivalent of whitewash on a sepulcher.

If standard or "genteel" speech in *Huckleberry Finn* is not inherently "bad," neither is the vernacular inherently "good." I will identify three varieties of vernacular speakers, distinguished not so much by the form of their speech as by the purposes it serves. First there are figures like Huck, Jim, Judith Loftus, Aunt Sally, and the raftsmen, whose vernacular functions as part of a positive characterization. These are the characters critics have in mind when they speak of the "vernacular values" of the novel. I will call their language *folk speech*, a term from folklore studies that suggests appropriate parallels with an entire series of terms like *folk art, folk music*, and *folk narrative*. The second category may be called *speech of pretentious ignorance*. (The phrase is borrowed from Richard Grant White; I discuss his importance below.) This is the speech of characters who attempt to assert the authority of an elevated social class but are not skilled enough to mimic the genteel style, so they superimpose a few learned borrowings upon a sub-

11. Bernard DeVoto, ed., *Mark Twain in Eruption* (New York: Harper, 1940), pp. 111–12.
12. To Carrington, Sherburn is a "dramatist's dramatist" whose speech to the mob "is actually double-talk, impressive gibberish, a verbal drama of pure 'style'" (*Dramatic Unity*, pp. 98, 138).

stratum of the vulgate. Such is the speech and manner of the King, the Grangerfords, and Tom Sawyer. Third is "ornery speech," defined by the depravity of its users, their low social position, and their active hostility or passive indifference to rungs higher up on the social ladder. Pap and the Bricksville loafers are clear examples. While the linguistic unconcern of folk speakers proceeds from childlike innocence, ornery speakers are adults who knowingly choose vicious language. The claim for a three-way structural division of vernacular speech in the novel is supported by the fact that similar distinctions can be found in the writings of nineteenth-century observers of language, in both England and the United States.

"Folk speech" is a product of the Romantic movement. It is a thoroughly idealized version of genuine vernacular, understood to be morally and aesthetically superior; rural rather than urban, it is the Adamic language away from which civilized society has fallen. Had Twain been pressed to explain why his greatest novel should be narrated by an ignorant runaway, he could have done no better than to cite Wordsworth on the "language really used by men" in rural life:

> [Their] language . . . has been adopted (purified indeed from what appear to be its real defects, from all lasting and rational causes of dislike or disgust) because such men hourly communicate with the best objects from which the best part of language is originally derived; and because, from their rank in society and the sameness and narrow circle of their intercourse, being less under the influence of social vanity, they convey their feelings and notions in simple unelaborated expressions.[13]

From this conception of folk speech comes the lyricism of many passages in Huck's narrative discourse, such as the long description of morning on the river that opens Chapter 19. Romantic as well is Huck's innate sense of linguistic propriety; as narrator, he is his own purifier, careful to avoid occasion for "dislike or disgust." Folk speech is the natural language of the family, an androgynous language that gives force to women's speech while tempering male discourse. The women characterized by folk speech—Judith Loftus, Aunt Sally Phelps, Aunt Polly (to whose brief appearance here may be added her role in *Tom Sawyer*)—are matrons who serve as stable centers of households that actually or symbolically lack men. (Aunt Polly is a widow; Silas Phelps is an absentminded, ineffectual man; Judith Loftus's husband is gone when Huck arrives.) Their ungrammatical, coarse-hewn speech extends a promise of strength and protection that is absent from the sentimental dialogue of their genteel sisters:

> [Judith Loftus to Huck] "Set down and stay where you are. I ain't going to hurt you and I ain't going to tell on you, nuther. . . . You see, you're a runaway 'prentice—that's all. It ain't anything. There ain't any harm in it. . . . Bless you, child, I wouldn't tell on you." (P. 89)

Similarly, the violence of little Davy's raftsmen's slang is directed, in a parental way, against anyone who would unjustly harm Huck:

13. "Preface to the Second Edition of 'Lyrical Ballads,'" in E. De Selincourt, ed., *The Poetical Work of William Wordsworth*, 2d ed. (Oxford: Oxford University Press, 1952), 2:387.

> "'Vast there. He's nothing but a cub. I'll paint the man that teches him!'" . . .
> "Come, now, tell a straight story and nobody'll hurt you, if you ain't up to any-
> thing wrong." [14]

An oath in form only, Davy's "blast it, boy" is identical in emotional force to Judith Loftus's "bless you, child." Beneath the gruff exteriors beat hearts of gold; Twain owed more than he cared to admit to Bret Harte's benevolent gamblers and harlots. The fact that Twain's slave Jim does not speak the exaggerated farcical dialect of the blackface minstrels had misled critics into describing his speech as "realistic" black dialect. It is, in fact, romanticized folk speech, purified of any forceful hostility that might, coming from a black speaker, have seemed threatening to a white readership even in the postwar North.

The distinction between folk speech and ignorantly pretentious speech is stressed frequently in Richard Grant White's guide to stylistic etiquette, *Words and Their Uses* (1870), a copy of which Twain owned.[15]

> Simple and unpretending ignorance is always respectable, and sometimes charming; but there is little that more deserves contempt than the pretence of ignorance to knowledge. The curse and the peril of language in this day, and particularly in this country, is, that it is at the mercy of men who, instead of being content to use it well according to their honest ignorance, use it ill according to their affected knowledge; who, being vulgar, would seem elegant; who, being empty, would seem full; who make up in pretence what they lack in reality.[16]

White's categorization helps explain the relation of language use to moral evaluation of characters in *Huckleberry Finn*. The birthright use of correct English by members of the natural aristocracy provides one standard, and "simple, unpretending" use of the vernacular the other. But woe to those who presume to a cultural authority they do not merit. Twain reserves his special scorn for social climbers of all colors who attempt to pass off flawed and inflated language for genuine merchandise, relying on a mannered style to cover hollow thoughts. (White's attack on the English of journalists, politicians, and social parvenus is paralleled most closely in Twain's portions of *The Gilded Age*. The dialogue Twain wrote to illustrate the language of the "Aristocracy of the Parvenues" in Washington is a fictional expansion of White's jeremiad.)[17] In *Huckleberry Finn* the line between the vernacular of pretentious ignorance and misappropriated Standard English is not drawn with absolute sharpness. Instead, characters can be ranked along a continuum, according to their success in imitating prestige forms: the Duke and Sherburn at the top, followed by Tom Sawyer and the Grangerfords, with the King at the bottom. I group together the latter three because their speech

14. *Life on the Mississippi*, pp. 30–31.

15. Alan Gribben, *Mark Twain's Library: A Reconstruction* (Boston: G. K. Hall, 1980), 2:762.

16. Richard Grant White, *Words and Their Uses, Past and Present. A Study of the English Language*, 20th ed. (Boston: Houghton Mifflin, 1892), p. 28.

17. Indeed, it is possible that White's book directly influenced the novel's composition. See Sewell, "Varieties of Language," pp. 44–46.

is essentially a colloquial over which fragments of the genteel style are pasted at irregular intervals. Much of the humor in the treatment of Tom and the King derives from their half-educated misuse of the terms that they employ in order to make an impression. Speakers of the misappropriated standard are too dangerous to be funny, but the vernacular of pretentious ignorance continually deflates itself with needles borrowed from Mrs. Malaprop: the King, eulogizing his dead "brother," will try to cover up his reference to "funeral orgies" by insisting that "orgies is the right term. . . . it means the thing you're after, more exact," supporting his claim with a ludicrous mock-etymology (p. 217). Half-assimilated Latinate vocabulary exists in English comedy at least as far back as Shakespeare's constable Dogberry, but the King's discourse probably derives more immediately from the grotesquely error-laden stump speeches of the minstrel show.[18]

For the pretentious ignorant, linguistic and cultural phenomena are ways of displaying status; for the "ornery" these objects do not possess even display value. "Correct English" is a foreign language to this class of speakers, an alien regarded with all the xenophobia of Know-Nothingism. Moreover, the compactness, energy, and penchant for metaphor characterizing folk speech are absent from this brand of the vernacular. Instead, ornery speech is marked by its tedious repetition; it is the language of the verbally damned, condemned to walk forever in the same conversational circles:

> [The Bricksville loafers] talked lazy and drawly, and used considerable many cuss-words. . . . What a body was hearing amongst them, all the time was—
> "Gimme a chaw 'v tobacker, Hank."
> "Cain't—I hain't got but one chaw left. Ask Bill." (P. 182)

The loafers' language is entirely formulaic. Their social lies are so old and worn out that they "don't fool nobody but a stranger"; their insults and complaints never vary. Pap Finn's dialogue is comparatively animated, but it, too, displays an abundance of the reiterated formulas typical of authentic vernacular speech: "I never see such a son" (two times); "Hey?" (three); "You hear?" (two); "Looky here" (three). All of these occur in the space of two pages (pp. 40–41). Pap's "Call this a govment!" monologue (pp. 49–50) is marked by similar formulas, this time in a narrative context. He stresses his reported dialogue with a constant "says I" and a defiant "them's the very words." While it is true, as Richard Bridgman has stressed, that repetition is integral to the narrative poetics of colloquial prose, the purely phatic repetition in the speech of Twain's lowest characters is meant to be read as a structural weakness.[19]

David Carkeet has pointed out an important fact about ornery speech: it

18. For an example, and a discussion of the burlesque stump speech as a genre, see Robert C. Toll, *Blacking Up: The Minstrel Show in Nineteenth-Century America* (New York: Oxford University Press, 1974), pp. 55–58.

19. *The Colloquial Style in America* (New York: Oxford University Press, 1960), pp. 32–39. In a "Comment on Tautology and Grammar," written in 1898, Twain distinguished between justifiable and careless tautology (*Mark Twain's Autobiography*, ed. Albert Bigelow Paine [New York: Harper, 1924], 1:172).

shares several traits with the "negro dialect" of *Huckleberry Finn*. "In *Huckleberry Finn*, *gwyne*, palatalization, and *r*-lessness are—for both blacks and whites—physical signals of low social status, and—for whites only—physical signals of 'substandard' morals." [20] The reason is not far to seek: slaves are not responsible for their low social status and marked speech, while whites are not only allowed but obligated to educate out the "infelicities" of their language. The variable significance of "negro dialect" in the novel is a good example of what Meir Sternberg has recently called the "Proteus Principle" in discourse theory: "In different contexts . . . the same form may fulfill different functions *and* different forms the same function." [21] Standard English and vernacular English do not possess value independent of context; their meaning depends on their structural function in a series of oppositions. What we have in *Huckleberry Finn* is a schema like this:

Virtue:	Authentic standard (natural aristocracy)	Folk speech (idealized vernacular culture)
Corruption:	Misappropriated standard (sham aristocracy)	Pretentious ignorance (social climbers)
	(tendency)	Ornery speech (debased vernacular culture)

The contradictions and oppositions among these categories suggest the traditional logic square for modal propositions. Indeed, we can redefine the categories to fit it precisely (*SE* stands for *Standard English*):

SE must be spoken	SE cannot be spoken
SE can be spoken	SE need not be spoken

Each group of speakers can then be described in terms of its relation to the deontic statement "Standard English must be spoken." Huck and his fellows do not defy the linguistic code; they are merely incapable of following it, speaking as they do a language ordered by entirely different rules. Their failure thus carries no moral opprobrium. Far more severely judged are those who are able but unwilling to follow the normative code and those who follow it for self-serving reasons rather than out of a sense of obligation. The world of *Huckleberry Finn* is one in which logical contraries ("must be" versus "cannot be") can coexist, where Judge Thatcher and Mary Jane Wilks, bearers of the authoritative culture, can form common cause with the innocent outcast Huck.

These schemata help clarify the nature of the vernacular-genteel confrontation in the novel. Neither Twain nor Huck is mounting a demotic attack on genuine high culture. Instead, the major conflict is between an idealized folk, better than its real prototype, and a debased pseudo-gentility, parasitic upon its prototype. The model also explains why Mary Jane can jump instantaneously from folk speech to standard without inconsistency:

20. "The Dialects in *Huckleberry Finn*," *AL* 51 (1979): 332.
21. "Proteus in Quotation-Land: Mimesis and the Forms of Reported Discourse," *PoT* 3 (1982): 148.

the varieties share a positive moral component that sets them together against the other two. Moreover—and most importantly—the only "characters" in the novel who simultaneously understand the systems of both the ideal standard and the ideal vernacular are the author and his implied reader. As a naive narrator, a folk speaker who is outside the standard system and the values it symbolizes, Huck is likely to mistake what Emerson called the "paper currency" of "rotten diction" for the "good writing and brilliant discourse" that make words one with things. Although he can see through the "tears and flapdoodle" of the King's oratory, he stands for the uncritical mass reading audience when he is impressed by the sentimentality of Emmeline Grangerford's funerary poems. Only the intelligent, sophisticated adult reader, who imports into the novel the entire complex of values belonging to the high culture, will be able to evaluate correctly the inflated and pretentious language of a Grangerford, a Sherburn, a Tom Sawyer.

II. Conventions and Anticonventions

I want to return to the second paragraph of Twain's "Explanatory" note, a passage that has received comparatively little attention: "I make this explanation for the reason that without it many readers would suppose that all these characters were trying to talk alike and not succeeding." Why, even in jest, would Twain suppose his readers might think his characters were "all trying to talk alike"? Overtly, of course, he is defending himself against the charge of having mishandled literary dialect—a charge he himself leveled against Bret Harte in public and in private. Covertly, I think, Twain is alluding to the great nineteenth-century educational enterprise of prescriptive language teaching, which took for its text Noah Webster's pronouncement that our "political harmony is concerned . . . in a uniformity of language." [22] Linguistic prescriptivism ruled over three domains—orthography, orthoepy, and grammar proper. But "talking alike" involves as well a vast region of unwritten rules or conventions governing larger and less easily formalized types of discourse. In these realms "uniformity of language" is necessary not merely to a political democracy but to the existence of any cohesive society, indeed to the existence of dialogue itself. Rules governing paralinguistic behavior, conversational turn-taking, the cases when truth should or should not be told: this is the bulk of the iceberg of language that lies below the visible mass charted by formal grammars. Throughout his life Twain was interested in strategies and rules governing oral speech-events like the tall tale, backwoods boasting, after-dinner speeches, swearing, "How to Tell a Story," and so on. The "grammars" governing such events are highly context-sensitive: for example, the pause that made the "nub" of Twain's "Golden Arm" story so effective would have been death to a dinner-table conversation. The conventions and rules that govern dialogue and speech in the world of *Huckleberry Finn* are no less important than the "number of dialects" to which Twain draws the reader's conscious attention. It turns out

22. *Dissertations on the English Language* (Boston: Isaiah Thomas, 1789), pp. 19–20.

that his characters are *not* all trying to talk alike, because the conventions by which they operate are mutually exclusive. Characters ignore, misinterpret, or else seek to manipulate each other's conventions. It is no coincidence that among the dialogues we remember best from the novel are Huck's lies; arguments among the raftsmen, Huck and Jim or Tom, the Duke and the King; and the exaggerated oratory of the King and Colonel Sherburn. We remember Huck and Jim on foreign languages: "'Spose a man was to come to you and say *Polly-voo-franzy*—what would you think?' 'I wouldn' think nuff'n; I'd take en bust him over de head'" (p. 113). The violent legacy of Babel, whether in the form of farce (as here) or in the form of tragedy (as in the Boggs-Sherburn confrontation), governs the frequent misunderstandings that occur along the Mississippi. On the few occasions when there is perfect understanding between characters (notably Huck and Jim, and Huck and Mary Jane Wilks), we are in a realm of idealized convention, like that of the ideal vernacular, that verges perilously close on sentimentalism.

Huck Finn is in every sense an *unconventional* character. His rebellion against the conventions of polite adult society is the kernel around which other layers of his personality have accreted, as critics of the novel have observed.[23] In an important early passage, we are shown that middle-class conventions of language, physical etiquette, and religion merge almost without boundaries as they are wielded against Huck's behavior:

> Miss Watson . . . took a set at me now, with a spelling-book. She worked me middling hard for about an hour. . . . Then for an hour it was deadly dull, and I was fidgety. Miss Watson would say, "Dont put your feet up there, Huckleberry;" and "dont scrunch up like that, Huckleberry—set up straight;" and pretty soon she would say, "Don't gap and stretch like that, Huckleberry—why don't you try to behave?" Then she told me all about the bad place, and I said I wished I was there. (P. 19)

Huck's "bad" rebels against the "good" or "right" conventions Miss Watson is imposing—literally, ortho-graphy, ortho-pedics, and ortho-doxy. Appropriately, Huck's language is thoroughly unconventional, breaking rules of discourse at all levels. His "bad" grammar and pronunciation, markers of a traditional literary vernacular, are finally less important than his refusal to follow or to understand the conventions of ordinary speech and of speech genres like riddles and playful make-believe.

In Huck's speech, for example, the limitation in range of styles typical of uneducated speakers is exaggerated beyond the bounds of realism.[24] Huck is virtually incapable of altering his speech in the direction of a prestige dialect; moreover, he seems to lack a formal/informal distinction. The limitation has a clear literary purpose: folk speech in Twain is characteristically

23. James M. Cox, for instance, has said that Huck's role is to invert "all [the] controls, which are really *conventions*, [that] exist outside the novel" (*Mark Twain: The Fate of Humor* [Princeton: Princeton University Press, 1966], p. 169). My only disagreement is that I find important traces of normative convention *within* the novel.

24. Drawing from a wide variety of informants, sociolinguist William Labov has concluded, "There are no single-style speakers" ("The Study of Language in its Social Context," in *Sociolinguistic Patterns* [Philadelphia: University of Philadelphia Press, 1972], p. 208).

innocent, averse to the role-playing that goes along with the shifts in style adopted easily by the Duke or Tom Sawyer. To a large extent the nature of Huck's language is dictated by his long-recognized role as an "innocent eye," a naive narrator whose perceptions of social hypocrisy create ironies that he misses but the reader is meant to catch:

> The widow rung a bell for supper, and you had to come to time. When you got to the table you couldn't go right to eating, but you had to wait for the widow to tuck down her head and grumble over the victuals, though there warn't really anything the matter with them. (P. 18)

Literal Huck does not understand the concept of "saying grace"—objectively, the utterance sounds like grumbling. The humor resulting from such gaps between literal and conventional readings of words and events is part of the "making-strange" that is a fundamental technique of satire.

But Huck's lack of socialization extends far beyond the structure of his lexicon. In general, Huck does not or will not understand linguistic processes that permit a dissimilarity between content and form. To use J. L. Austin's terms, the widow at the dinner table performs the locutionary act of uttering mumbled words. The illocutionary (or meaningful) force of the act, however, is "prayer" or "thanksgiving," a conventional significance that is independent of the content or even the intelligibility of the words. (A standard illustration of illocutionary force is the question, "Can you pass the salt?"—not a query about capability, but a request for action. Huck's reluctance to understand Tom's "'Gimme a *case-knife*'" [p. 310] as the encoded form of "give me a pick-axe" plays on a similar relationship.) Huck commonly rejects the mechanism whereby a statement is made to carry a force different from that of its propositional content:

> Mary Jane she set at the head of the table, with Susan along side of her, and said how bad the biscuits was, and how mean the preserves was, and how ornery and tough the fried chicken was—and all that kind of rot, the way women always do for to force out compliments; and the people all knowed everything was tip-top, and said so—said "How *do* you get biscuits to brown so nice?" . . . and all that kind of humbug talky-talk, just the way people always does at a supper, you know. (P. 221)

Far more tolerant than Molière's misanthrope Alceste, Huck nonetheless shares his disapproval of the minor insincerities that make society go.

Huck's dialogue with Tom demonstrates his hostile unfamiliarity with several oral and literary genres. At both the beginning and the end of the novel, Huck fails to comprehend Tom's make-believe; he does not care to perform the willing suspension of disbelief required for the success of both children's fantasy-play and the literary "play" of the romances Tom enjoys. The opposition between literal Huck and Quixotic Tom has long been a topic of critical commentary. What I suspect may not have been stressed, though, is that Huck's pragmatism is "vernacular" only in the sense of the idealized folk-speech I have previously described. Tom's enthusiasm for varieties of make-believe is "realistic" insofar as it exaggerates in degree but not in kind children's actual behavior. Huck, on the other hand, shows that he is an outcast not only from adult society but from the subculture of childhood as well. He has no idea how to respond to a favorite children's riddle:

[Buck] asked me where Moses was when the candle went out. I said I didn't know; I hadn't heard about it before, no way.

"Well, guess," he says.

"How'm I going to guess," says I, "when I never heard tell about it before?"

"But you can guess, can't you? It's just as easy."

"*Which* candle?" I says.

"Why, any candle," he says.

"I don't know where he was," says I; "where was he?"

"Why he was in the *dark*! That's where he was!"

"Well, if you knowed where he was, what did you ask me for?"

"Why, blame it, it's a riddle, don't you see?" (P. 135)

Huck *doesn't* see, because he does not understand the conventions governing the genre *riddle*. For Huck, a question ought to be a question; the sheer gratuity of riddling is beyond him, as is the ludic potential of language in general. His comments and his speech demonstrate that he thinks language ought to be instrumental. This is why he (like Jim) understands magic but not religion. Spells work automatically so long as proper ritual is observed, but when praying for fishhooks fails to produce fishhooks, Huck rightly— according to his logic—discards prayer as useless.

If Huck's unconventional variety of language prevents him from participating fully in the discourse of his society, it paradoxically liberates him to move more freely in the domain of language itself. If we take Roman Jakobson's six functions of language as a convenient typology, Huck's discourse would seem to be limited to the referential and the conative functions: he is interested in the content of his speech and its pragmatic effect on a listener (particularly when his speech is a lie).[25] Tom, with his interest in "style," presumably values the poetic function of language, "focus on the message for its own sake." I would suggest, however, that Huck's beliefs about his own use of language are as inaccurate as those about his "guilt" as a proto-abolitionist. In fact, Huck and Jim are the only characters in the novel who freely and joyously embody all six of Jakobson's functions. Huck thinks he is merely pragmatic and literal, but we who read both his reported dialogue and his narrative know better. His descriptions of the river and his account of his attitude toward Jim are fully "emotive" and "poetic"—that is, Huck's own feelings and the texture of his language are foci of attention. Huck is sometimes even "metalingual," as when he evaluates the King's imitation of

25. Jakobson's six functions of language are based on the communication-theory model of addresser, addressee, and message. Each of the six functions is oriented toward a corresponding linguistic "factor." (1) The referential function is the denotative orientation to the context of the message; (2) the emotive or "expressive" function focuses on the attitude and feelings of the addresser; (3) the conative or rhetorical function seeks response or action from the addressee; (4) the phatic function is concerned with mere contact between the interlocutors; (5) the meta-lingual function is focused on the linguistic code itself; and (6) the poetic function is the "focus on the message [*form* rather than content] for its own sake" ("Closing Statement: Linguistics and Poetics," in Thomas A. Sebeok, ed., *Style in Language* [Cambridge: M.I.T. Press, 1960], pp. 353–57).

an Englishman, or condemns the graffiti in the floating house as "the igno-rantest kind of words" (p. 78).

Other characters are limited in ways that can be related to Jakobson's cate-gories, although his basic six-way division of language functions must be elaborated by combining it with some sort of moral axis. (Referential lan-guage can be true or false; emotive language sincere or insincere; conative language manipulative or empathetic; phatic language perfunctory or en-thusiastic.) The speech of the Bricksville loafers is language stripped of all but its phatic function. "We exist" is the sum of its referential content. Tom values the emotive and poetic functions to the exclusion of the conative: his delight in the "Evasion" derives from a self-centered aesthetic, for he lacks Huck's concern about the effect of his words on his hearers. Tom is thus in-capable of an apology, particularly one directed to Jim. The best he can do is offer a payment that substitutes for words ("Tom give Jim forty dollars for being prisoner for us so patient," p. 365). The Duke and the King, on the other hand, value only the conative function, which allows them to manipu-late others. For the Duke, Hamlet's soliloquy signifies money; if he can only "fetch the house" (p. 178) it does not matter how Shakespeare's words are mangled.

We ain't all trying to talk alike: Mark Twain's central linguistic insight in *Huckleberry Finn* is that the heterogeneity of language goes beyond surface features like pronunciation and morphology. Take, by way of contrast, the defense of the use of vulgar slang with which Émile Zola prefaced *L'As-sommoir* in 1877: "My crime is to have had the literary curiosity to collect and pour into a carefully worked mold the speech of the people. . . . No-body saw that my desire was to perform a purely philological work, one that I believe to be of lively historical and social interest." [26] As a self-styled natu-ralist, Zola wanted to transfer unchanged to his literary work speech that existed objectively in the working-class districts he wrote about. Despite the apparent empirical pretensions of the "Explanatory" note to *Huckleberry Finn*, Twain's project was different: he created a literary simulacrum of lin-guistic diversity that exaggerates and stylizes the heteroglossic interweaving of speech types found in real societies. In the process he created several pure types that never exist in the world in unadulterated form. Huck Finn, in par-ticular, is a linguistic impossibility. What he speaks is an unfallen, Adamic dialect, which names objects as if they had never been named before. [27] His language is logically impossible, for it is a plenum, a fully functioning sys-tem, that is nevertheless innocent of the conventions imposed by the social roles language must play. It is not, like that of Swift's Houyhnhnms, an idiom incapable of "saying the thing that is not," but it is one that speaks no evil. Roy Harvey Pearce has written of Huck as a boy who "exists not as

26. In *Oeuvres complètes*, ed. Henri Mitterand (Paris: Cercle du Livre Précieux, 1967), 3 : 599; my translation.

27. Richard Bridgman has observed that whereas an adult is "tainted with stylistic original sin," Huck's style is "prelapsarian in its innocence and single-minded directness" (*Colloquial Style*, p. 10).

an actuality but a possibility. . . . [an] ideal perhaps never-to-be-attained type."[28] Huck is, in fact, an infinitely more human and humorous version of the Mysterious Stranger who haunted Mark Twain's later imagination, a figure whose transcendent nature makes him incapable of understanding ordinary human behavior. Huck's speech serves to remind us that language, like any social institution, progresses only through the dialectic interplay between the fixed standard that crystallizes old visions and old voices, and the grammarless voices, undergoing constant growth and flux, of the present historical moment.

28. "Yours Truly, Huck Finn," pp. 313–24 of the present volume.

13 GEORGE C. CARRINGTON, JR.

Farce and *Huckleberry Finn*

The stage, which was not for low farce designed,
But to divert, instruct, and mend mankind.

W HEN Fielding wrote these lines,[1] he struck a note of contempt for farce that has long endured, but at the same time he pointed the
way toward a hospitable view of farce—the idea that farce, as a mode or
genre, does have serious artistic functions. Evolving slowly from a Field-
ingesque distress with the farce in *Adventures of Huckleberry Finn*, my
own view of the novel now is that most of its elements are indeed farcical
and add up to serious farce that not only diverts but also painfully instructs and may mend mankind. Combining traditional methods of farce
with a modern tragifarcical outlook, Mark Twain created a fictional world
in which Tom Sawyer emerges as a dominating knave and the true central
character, Huck as a weak fumbler, and Jim as a helpless victim. Such a seriously farcical reading of *Huckleberry Finn* can only be justified by an examination of the novel in terms of a theory of farce. Before that examination, it is necessary to define what farce is and does.

Grappling with one farce and its meaning, a reader must become aware
that critical theory itself is still groping toward a coherent theory of the
genre. Shaw said, "To laugh without sympathy is a ruinous abuse of a noble
function; and the degradation of any race may be measured by the degree of
their addiction to it," that is, to "the deliberate indulgence of that horrible,
derisive joy in humiliation and suffering which is the beastliest element in
human nature," and which evokes laughter that is "purely galvanic" rather
than edifying.[2] This is a classic statement of the stern platonic objection to
farce that recent students of farce such as Eric Bentley, Walter Kerr, and
Jessica Milner Davis have tried to counter.[3] Turning to Freud does not help
clarify matters. His work that seems closest to the subject, *Der Witz und*

1. Henry Fielding, "Prologue," *The Modern Husband* (1732), in *The Complete Works of
Henry Fielding, Esq.*, ed. William Ernest Henley, 16 vols. (New York: Barnes and Noble, 1967),
10:10.
2. "The Farcical Comedy Outbreak," in *Dramatic Opinions and Essays*, 2 vols. (New
York: Brentano's, 1906), 1:413, 414, 415.
3. Bentley, *The Life of the Drama* (New York: Atheneum, 1965), pp. 219–56; Kerr, *Tragedy and Comedy* (New York: Simon & Schuster, 1968), pp. 309–15; Davis, *Farce* (London:
Methuen, 1978), pp. 22, 102.

seine Beziehung zum Unbewussten (1905), deals only with brief jokes, or with witticisms, if one translates *der Witz* as "wit" rather than "joke." Farce is a great deal more than jokes. In the serious novel, farce devices such as mechanical repetition have until recently been associated with sloppy characterization—quick, shallow rendering of minor, "humorous" characters like Thwackum and Barkis—so that *farce* and *trivial* are automatically associated.[4]

Even when critics approach farce seriously, they find it slipping away from them and blending into other genres. In his 1899 series of articles collected as *Le Rire* (1900), Henri Bergson thought that he was defining comedy and the comic, and no one can argue that his favorite exemplary author, Molière, is not comic; yet Bergson's elaborate analyses of such techniques as absurd mechanical repetition are a *vade mecum* for a student or writer of farce, and the examples Bergson gives from Molière are unquestionably farce. Wylie Sypher, a student and editor of Bergson, writes on "comedy" but talks about such farce elements as puppetlike characters and argues for the importance of "low" comedy, meaning farce.[5] George McFadden has presented a strong argument for the loftiness of the spirit of comedy, but he turns his major example, James's *The Pupil*, into a farce, in which most of the characters are reduced to fools and the child Morgan Moreen schemes slyly and desperately for survival and escape, rather like Huck Finn in numerous crises.[6] In an essay generally sympathetic to farce, George Stephenson finds it "less *genre* than tone or method" and labels it "inchoate *vis comica* in search of a body"; when it finds that body in comedy, it disappears.[7] Even Eric Bentley, one of the first to take farce seriously and define it carefully, finds its greatest significance when it blends into tragedy and comedy in works such as *Waiting for Godot*.[8] In another recent book friendly to farce, Jessica Milner Davis carefully establishes that farce is indeed a serious form, although her final sentence is loaded with caveats and conspicuously omits any reference to fiction: "Despite its gaiety, despite its cruelty, farce is a serious theatrical genre."[9]

These earnest studies identify several senses of farce that show it to have common qualities and serious functions helpful to the student of *Huckleberry Finn*. For critics since Bergson, the forms and functions of farce lie along a spectrum from "low farce" or "low comedy" to what is variously called *farce tragique, farce noire*, tragifarce, absurd comedy, or black humor, the functions of these forms running from simple relief of psychological tensions all the way to revelation of the nightmare horror of life.[10] At one end of the spectrum lie aggression, violence, and wisecracks lumped to-

4. Robert C. Stephenson, "Farce as Method," in *Comedy: Meaning and Form*, ed. Robert W. Corrigan (San Francisco: Chandler, 1965), pp. 318–19.

5. "Appendix: The Meanings of Comedy," in *Comedy*, ed. Wylie Sypher (Garden City, N.Y.: Doubleday, Anchor Books, 1956), pp. 201, 207–8.

6. *Discovering the Comic* (Princeton: Princeton University Press, 1982), pp. 246–54.

7. "Farce," pp. 324, 318.

8. *Drama*, pp. 340–53.

9. *Farce*, p. 102.

10. Bentley, *Drama*, pp. 340–46; Davis, *Farce*, p. 93.

gether in the crude plots of, for example, the Three Stooges or very early Chaplin. Here characters are so stylized and unreal that we cannot worry about what happens but only release our inhibitions for a moment in outbursts of the "purely galvanic" laughter that Shaw detested. In the middle are the vast body of conventional farces, mostly plays with stylized characters (knaves, fools, and victims), fast-moving complex plots, casual violation and ultimate restoration of social taboos, and ironic, indulgent acceptance of the messy human condition.[11] Occasionally, when the mood and the jokes become gentler, the audience sympathetic, and the characters somewhat aware of what they are doing, we have "farce en rose," blending into romantic comedy and characteristic of much farce from the eighteenth-century age of sentiment up to the mature Chaplin.[12] At the dark end of the spectrum the genre becomes harsher, and we are in the world of contemporary tragifarce, with existence a dreadful joke, and the characters helpless victims or tireless torturers locked together in a closed world. All this is not necessarily far from conventional farce. Ionesco himself recognized the similarities between his "absurd" dramas and the abrasive farces of Feydeau.[13]

There is, however, an important difference between farce and "farce noire" or tragifarce. In the one, the characters are unaware of the implications of what they are doing; in the other, the knaves know that they are cruel and the victims know that they are suffering. Conventional farce characters are too busy plotting and acting to figure out the implications of what they do. In any case, as Bergson points out, human potentialities and plasticity often harden into "comic rigidity," blind narrowness, and unconscious callowness as a result of prolonged membership in cultural, social, and professional groups.[14] In tragifarce realization is of the essence. "As long as the clown is imperturbable in defeat and disaster, laughter remains broad and uncomplicated; but when his terror begins to show, it renders our laughter more and more alarming."[15] And alarmed, when we become aware of the malicious pleasure of the knave in tormenting his victims and realize that in this kind of knave the malignancies of life are personified. Redeeming the "extreme virulence of modern tragi-comedy" is the important artistic function of the genre. It "not only gives a somber account of the world, it gives the public a shaking"; the audience becomes aware and undergoes a special catharsis.[16] In low farce one feels not pity and fear (however defined) but at the most a mild sympathy for the fools and casual contempt for the knaves.[17] The catharsis of tragifarce approaches strong pity for the victims and true fear for the malevolence that crushes them. Through this strong awareness, the audience gains a kind of triumph. It is made better able to understand and cope

11. Davis, *Farce*, p. 85.
12. Ibid., pp. 87–90.
13. Ibid., p. 98.
14. Bergson, "Laughter" (1900), in *Comedy*, ed. Wylie Sypher, pp. 174–77.
15. Davis, *Farce*, p. 94.
16. Bentley, *Drama*, p. 344.
17. Ibid., p. 246.

with what it cannot defeat, the grimness of life. The artist, of course, has his triumph in transcending despair through art.[18]

These modern ideas about farce illuminate *Huckleberry Finn* without affecting other interpretations from different perspectives. From Twain's skilled use of many elements of farce arise points of significance about humanity and the world it must willy-nilly inhabit. Seen in terms of farce, *Huckleberry Finn* is a tragifarce or "farce noire," the major members of the cast being: a dimly comprehending fumbler and stooge, Huck Finn; a dominating knave, Tom Sawyer; and a victim, Jim.

This novel is so richly farcical that even the potentially tragic episodes are moved into the domain of tragifarce. Pap's death could easily be made tragic, or sentimental, if Twain were in his *Prince and the Pauper* mood, but the event is reported, by Jim, long after the fact and in such euphoric circumstances that its impact is muted. In fact, Huck does not comment on his father's death at all. In any case, Pap's death is simply that of a type-fool, an unperceptive braggart casually murdered by type-knaves, the "mighty hard looking strangers" that Mrs. Loftus tells Huck about (p. 86). In the Wilks episode, Twain seems to be working up a standard Victorian sentimental melodrama of wronged innocence, but the episode dissolves into farce: coincidences, confusion, wildly fast action, and flight and pursuit, ending with the tragifarce of Huck's apparent escape from the King and the Duke turning into further bondage on the raft.

Likewise, the Grangerford episode seems at first to be moving toward tragedy, with the slaughter of the two families and the wretched death of Buck and his cousin. But the episode is, internally, the typical farce episode of this novel and, externally (to the reader), a tragifarce, ridiculous yet moving, moving yet ridiculous. In this episode Twain uses several of the classic devices of farce: snowballing, that is, the widening of farce to include more and more people (all the members of both families and Huck, too); acceleration, the speedup of action, from one or two killings a year to the butchery of both feuding families in a few hours; mechanical, repetitious, illogical behavior defeated by natural human behavior (the insane mechanism of the feud neatly outwitted by the two lovers); and the heartless cruelties of knaves inadvertently helped by the obtuseness and woolgathering of a type-fool. The last is especially important for the advancement of the plot and the characterization of Huck, because it is Huck who brings the note to Miss Sophia and thus not only helps her escape but also precipitates the slaughter, and it is Huck whose faulty watchkeeping allows the Shepherdsons to kill Buck Grangerford and his cousin.

To these materials of farce and tragedy Twain adds Huck's narration, which mixes perceptiveness and denseness in a tragifarcical way. It is funny when Huck describes the Grangerfords' pretentious furnishings and Emmeline's outlandish artworks with wide-eyed seriousness. It is not funny, however, when Huck can only vaguely realize his responsibility for the gen-

18. Ibid., pp. 345–53.

eral disaster ("I reckoned I was to blame somehow. . . . I judged I ought to told her father about that paper") and can never realize, even months later, his partial responsibility for the death of the two Grangerford boys. Watching the final battle at the steamboat landing from a tree, he is told by Buck Grangerford "to watch out sharp and let him know when the [Shepherdson] men come in sight again; said they was up to some devilment or other—wouldn't be gone long" (p. 154). Anxious to be "out of that tree," and absorbed in Buck's story of the deaths of the Grangerford men, Huck fails to watch out. "All of a sudden, bang! bang! bang! goes three or four guns—the men had slipped around through the woods and come in from behind without their horses!" (p. 154). Huck's jerky, exclamatory style here reflects his amazement and horror but no awareness of his failure to keep watch for just such "devilment." In narrating the deaths of the boys Huck further mutes, while unwittingly emphasizing, the tragic element. First Huck suggests the brutality of the berserk Shepherdsons: "the men run along the bank shooting at them and singing out, 'Kill them, kill them!'" Then Huck becomes reticent: "I ain't agoing to tell *all* that happened—it would make me sick again if I was to do that" (p. 154). He goes on, though, obsessively brooding over his memories of the scene and his inability to "get shut of them." We are left to infer that the boys were tortured to death, or mutilated after death, in ways that Huck can neither speak of nor forget. Thus the Grangerford episode balances its devices and effects, and for the reader leaves a bitter quality appropriate for tragifarce—some of the barbaric quality of *Lear* without the forgiveness and reconciliation, and some of the family-uniting and love-conquers-difficulties elements of romance in *Romeo and Juliet* and "The Eve of St. Agnes" without the tragic elements of the one or the fantasy elements of the other.

Most of the other scenes of *Huckleberry Finn* are in large part made of farce-elements. Several of the scenes with little or no farce dramatize flashes of awareness: Huck realizing Jim's dignity after the storm (Chap. 15); Huck amazed that Jim loves his family (Chap. 23); Huck becoming aware, visually if not verbally, of Jim's full humanity and vowing to steal him (Chap. 31). Such scenes as these stand out so vividly against the farcical background that critics have naturally singled them out for attention and have often seen them as the true core of the novel. But in the light of the overall pattern of the book as I see it, the realization scenes are literally comic relief, comedy being farce plus realization by a character of a truth or truths in the situation.[19] These scenes are not the intrusion of realistic farce into tragedy, but the intrusion of flashes of high comedy into farce. In each scene the brief moment of awareness serves to emphasize the force of the major, dominating element. And several of the moments of awareness are offset by distorted thoughts that are a kind of negative awareness: Huck being disgusted by Jim's hope of stealing his wife and children (Chap. 15); Huck almost accepting his conscience as authority for betraying Jim (Chaps. 15, 31). This balancing of good and bad is epitomized in the scene discussed above in which Huck re-

19. Davis, *Farce*, p. 88.

alizes one part of his responsibility in the Grangerford debacle but not the other part. As Huck says of his failure to realize that Jim is in the Phelpses' little cabin, "It shows how a body can see and don't see at the same time" (p. 293).

The farce elements available to Twain, most of them well defined in Bergson's *vade mecum*, can be divided into elements of language, structure, characterization, and world. Language as an instrument of wit, jokes, and distortion is of course an important part of Bergsonian "comedy," given his emphasis on Molière, but language contributes little to the farce in *Huckleberry Finn* because Huck is not a wit or a joker or a Malaprop. Aside from a few ironic remarks, such as his out-of-character comment on the fate of the *Walter Scott* ruffians—"I reckoned if they could stand it, I could" (p. 107)—Huck is not a humorous narrator. The humor and perception in his narration are largely unconscious. As befits Tom Sawyer's tirelessly active and dominating nature, he is a fountain of what he thinks are devastating witticisms: "It's as mild as goose-milk. Why, Huck, it wouldn't make no more talk than breaking into a soap factory" (p. 294), and so on. But if Tom dominates the chatter and much of the action, Huck dominates the narration, and that fact puts at a distance the wit of the other characters, such as it is.

Fitting the timeless rules of farce, everything else in the novel is abnormal, artificial, unreal, bizarre. Bergson says, "Comic absurdity is of the same nature as that of dreams." [20] To "dreams" one can add "nightmares," the medium of "farce noire" and tragifarce. Bringing Bergson's theory of "comedy" (farce) up-to-date, Wylie Sypher points out,

> the comic artist begins by accepting the absurd, "the improbable," in human existence. Therefore he has less resistance than the tragic artist to representing what seems incoherent and inexplicable, and this lowers the threshold of artistic perception. After all, comedy, not tragedy, admits the disorderly into the realm of art; the grotesque depends upon an irrational focus. Ours is a century of disorder and irrationalism. [21]

So was the century of Mark Twain and Huck Finn. Twain admits everything into his novel, and distorts it, from the beginning. Other critics tell us that farce is "extravagance," broad and hospitable; that farce is wild and maniacal; that farce is everywhere extravagant. [22] Huck and the reader enter such a world at once, and stay there. After two paragraphs of exposition in Chapter 1, Huck finds himself in the clutches of the demonic Miss Watson, flees her only to expose himself to the malignant energies of nature ("the wind was trying to whisper something to me"), and flees that threat for Tom Sawyer. In Chapter 2, as the boys tiptoe around in the dark and hide from Jim, they seem to be free in a boyish world of adventure. Then Huck's ankle begins to itch.

20. "Laughter," p. 180.
21. "Appendix," p. 201.
22. Kerr, *Tragedy and Comedy*, pp. 309–12; Davis, *Farce*, p. 59; Bentley, *Drama*, p. 247; Bergson, "Laughter," p. 102.

With that itching ankle we are back in the world of farce, where low farce combines "the ordinary unenlarged environment" and "direct and wild fantasies."[23] Itching is ordinary, but nothing could be more extraordinary than Huck's suffering ("Seemed like I'd die if I couldn't scratch"), which seems to reach a peak when his ankle, ear, and back itch; but Twain piles on another climax ("My nose begun to itch") and another ("Then it begun to itch on the inside") and another ("Next I got to itching underneath"). Huck "dasn't scratch," though. He is trapped in a farcical condition of mechanical behavior by his own pointless but serious need to hide from Jim and to impress Tom by staying completely still. The misery seems to last forever, but finally Jim snores and Huck can move and scratch. Later, as Huck writes about the incident while at the Phelps farm, he adds, "Well, I've noticed that thing plenty of times since. If you are with the quality, or at a funeral, or trying to go to sleep when you ain't sleepy—if you are anywheres where it won't do for you to scratch, why you will itch all over in upwards of a thousand places" (pp. [22]–23). "That thing" is the power of farce, which seizes every possible occasion to turn reality into an exasperating dream and renders every one a victim. The more absurd the victimization, the better. In this scene Huck, the victim of his own ideas and his own body, is doubly ridiculous.

From the itching scene the action advances for one sentence ("we cut along the path"). Then Huck breaks in on himself with the extravagantly farcical tale that Jim made up, about being "rode by witches," in order to impress the fools among the slaves. After that comes the sometimes ridiculous, sometimes mad affair of Tom's robber-gang—and so on, to the end of the novel, with inexhaustible riches of extravagant farcical character and event, constantly edging toward tragedy and then drawing back. We have seen examples of this typical pattern already. One thinks also of Huck's being saved from his own father's murderous wrath. How? "The old man" falls asleep (p. 51). Or of the grim Boggs-Sherburn episode (Chaps. 21, 22), which does not end but is dropped, because Huck finds a farcical circus even more interesting than a tragifarcical murder and wants to tell us about it. At the end Twain creates a superfarce, Tom Sawyer's "Evasion," which turns mild Arkansas reality into a bad dream and ends by skirting tragedy by the closest of margins. If Tom had been killed rather than slightly wounded, the novel would have more than fulfilled the basic requirement of tragifarce, that reality be turned into nightmare.

Within each episode Twain uses skillfully the aged but always effective devices of farce. The hoax, so prominent throughout *Huckleberry Finn*, is a major form of pretense, and pretense is at the heart of farce.[24] The great farce-knaves manipulate and hoax others, use disguises, and are unmasked or unmask others.[25] Equally central and useful in *Huckleberry Finn* is the

23. Bentley, *Drama*, p. 241. For a similar idea, see Bergson, "Laughter," pp. 105, 148–49.
24. Bentley, *Drama*, p. 251.
25. Ibid.; McFadden, *Discovering the Comic*, p. 252. McFadden refers to Tom Sawyer in *Huckleberry Finn* as a "fabricator of 'boy's book' plots that commandeer adults for rather servile instrumental roles" (p. 252). Leo Hughes, *A Century of English Farce* (Princeton: Prince-

plot device of pursuit and flight, the classic chase. One advantage of the chase is that it allows unlimited openings for the small devices of farce.[26] As tabulated by Bergson, these devices include concealment and disguise, exposure, "jack-in-the-box," acceleration and snowballing, the "dancing-jack," repetition, reversal, the "talisman," absent-mindedness, acting at cross-purposes, and coincidence.[27] Most of these devices are familiar to modern audiences through classic film farce. Disguise, exposure, and snow-balling have been touched on. "Jack-in-the-box" is absurd mechanical repetition. Tom Sawyer uses this device in his torture of Aunt Sally in Chapter 37, when his theft and replacement of spoons and sheets drive her out of her orderly-housewife mind. Pointless, mindless repetition is inherently ridiculous and in farce commonly leads to trouble. The foolish repetition of the Royal Nonesuch leads inevitably to the exposure of the King and the Duke and their terrible yet ridiculous punishment by tarring and feathering. (Surely they die, while the yokels guffaw.) Although farce is inherently fast-paced, acceleration increases the pace and intensity to frenzy. The obvious example in *Huckleberry Finn* is the "Evasion," which begins quietly in the mood of deathlike inactivity that Huck finds when he approaches the Phelps farm (pp. [277]–78), and ends with spiders, snakes, pie plates and grindstones covered with strange messages, sheet-ladders, witch pies, hysterical farmers and their wives, Huck's brains dripping out from under his hat, a wild chase, recapture, Tom's delirium, the near lynching of Jim, the sudden arrival of Aunt Polly, and a farcical deceleration in the sudden resolution at the very end. Acceleration and snowballing are reciprocally linked. The faster the pace, the more people are involved, and vice versa. By the end of the Evasion the whole community seems caught up in the hysteria.

The "dancing-jack," says Bergson, is a character who thinks he is acting freely but is really "a mere toy," like the child's puppet, manipulated by another, often in an absurdly mechanical way.[28] What many readers find most objectionable in Huck's and Jim's behavior at the end of the novel is that the two seem to have become Tom's playthings. Our feelings about that painful fact determine, in part, our final sense of the novel. In general Twain prefers humor arising from varied action, with acceleration and snowballing, to the humor of these mechanical devices, which fit the stage and film better. Likewise Twain uses reversal—of roles, domination, and so on—more for plot complications than for laughs. Some tragifarcical effects do come from ruinous reversals. The Grangerfords are hoist by their own petard, the feud; Huck's prolonged effort to save Jim goes to smash in a moment when the King sells him; a bullet in Tom's leg reverses the advantage in the Evasion.

Twain uses other basic devices of farce to generate action. One such device is the talisman, an essential missing thing or person. The search for the talisman produces and sustains action, as in Labiche's classic *The Italian Straw*

---

ton University Press, 1956), pp. 35–43; Hughes discusses the "varied and complex . . . disguise motif" (p. 35) in eighteenth- and nineteenth-century farce. Bentley, *Drama*, pp. 242–43.

26. Hughes, *Century of Farce*, pp. 25–26.

27. "Laughter," pp. 104–27.

28. Ibid., p. 111; Bentley, *Drama*, p. 247.

Hat. *Huckleberry Finn* contains both ordinary and reverse talisman farce. After the brief search for the missing Huck in Chapter 8, Jim is the talisman. His imprisonment, a form of absence, gives Tom his chance to arrange the farcical Evasion, which can only continue, as Tom eventually realizes, as long as Jim is locked up. That awkward necessity produces one of the most farcical scenes in the novel. In order to roll the stolen grindstone into Jim's cabin, he is released from his chains, used to move the stone, and then locked up again. As a reverse talisman, Jim's presence causes complications during the raft voyage. The need to account for his presence results in his being tied up or painted blue by the Duke, whose smug satisfaction with these "solutions" is as farcical as Jim's unheeded misery is pathetic. Absent-mindedness—failure to focus on the immediate situation—lies at the heart of the farce-fool's character, as its opposite, shrewd awareness, is at the heart of the knave's. Both traits generate farcical plot elements.[29] In *Huckleberry Finn* a crucial example of the importance of absented-mindedness and awareness comes at the beginning of Chapter 34. Huck fails to notice that the food for the "dog" in the little cabin includes watermelon. Tom does notice, triumphantly deduces Jim's presence in the cabin, impresses Huck with his cleverness, and at once asks for Huck's suggestions for rescuing Jim. In the context Huck's simple, logical plan stands no chance against any plan of Tom's, even before Huck says a word. Given carte blanche, Tom turns the rescue into extreme farce.

Coincidence is central to farce and to *Huckleberry Finn* and the critical disputes over it. Farce is a world of coincidences, and a farce is a structure of coincidences. All critics agree on this rule.[30] From his earliest years as a writer Twain used convenient coincidences and accidents in his art and admired works that contained them. An admirer of Howells's many stage farces, which are full of outrageous coincidences, Twain called Howells's *The Parlor Car* "light and delicious."[31] In the ending of *Huckleberry Finn*, Twain confronts the reader with two major coincidences. In the first, the Phelps farm, from which Huck must rescue Jim, turns out to be owned by a man who married the sister of Tom Sawyer's Aunt Polly, who lives hundreds of miles away. In the second, Huck arrives at the plantation the day that Tom is expected for a visit, and a few hours before Tom actually arrives. Confronted with these blatant coincidences, central to all the low farce and tragifarce that follow, the reader must fish or cut bait—he must decide either that this novel belongs to a genre, farce, in which coincidence is acceptable and meaningful, or that the novel makes no sense. For many readers the second choice is the only one, the first being too much to swallow.

---

29. Bergson, "Laughter," pp. 67–68; Davis, *Farce*, p. 88; Bentley, *Drama*, pp. 295–97.

30. See, for example, Bentley, *Drama*, pp. 244–48; Kerr, *Tragedy and Comedy*, p. 201; Sypher, "Appendix," pp. 201–10; Davis, *Farce*, pp. 54–59.

31. Howells's dramatic method "was chiefly farce"; see Walter J. Meserve, "Introduction," *The Complete Plays of W. D. Howells*, ed. Walter J. Meserve (New York: New York University Press, 1960), p. xvii. On *The Parlor Car*, see S. L. Clemens to W. D. Howells, 23 August 1876, in *Mark Twain–Howells Letters*, ed. Henry Nash Smith and William M. Gibson, 2 vols. (Cambridge: Harvard University Press, 1960), 1:147.

The active characters of farce—the knaves and the fools—are dehuman-
ized, even manic, in their behavior. They are tirelessly aggressive, violent,
hostile, and contemptuous of others. They are conceited but lack true self-
awareness, and they often suffer from absence of mind, unless they are perfect knaves. These qualities describe most of the characters, most of the
time, in *Huckleberry Finn*, especially those aggressive power-seekers—rigid,
humorless, unreflective, and often self-destructive—Tom Sawyer, the King
and the Duke, the Grangerfords, Pap, Colonel Sherburn. The power they
seek—over a child, a muddy village, or a rural neighborhood—may be trivial to the reader, but not to them. They willingly reduce people to puppets,
even kill in cold blood, to achieve that power. The worlds they live in are,
as appropriate to farce, small and closed and isolated.[32] The world of the
raft, twelve feet square, is the epitome of those worlds, but Pap's cabin is
not much bigger, and the worlds of Bricksville and the Grangerfords are
cramped and claustrophobic. Most of these characters are confined, moreover, to single episodes or sections of the book, but even Tom and Huck and
Jim, though they move through the entire book temporally and spatially, live
in a closed world of permanent relationships. The presence of Aunt Sally in
Arkansas signals that we have circled back to St. Petersburg, and the reappearance of Tom clinches the matter. And because Tom is so tirelessly and
resourcefully aggressive, so dominates any world that he enters, "the Territory," the supposedly open world beckoning in Chapter the Last, will become the same world that the Phelps farm and the robber-gang's cave and St.
Petersburg became when Tom recast them in terms of his drive for power.

If we allow these strong, varied farce elements in *Huckleberry Finn* to illuminate our understanding of the novel, some disturbing points emerge:
Huck is not the true protagonist, Tom is; and the novel is farce if taken at
face value, but tragifarce if we reflect upon its meanings. In *The Dramatic
Unity of Huckleberry Finn* (1976), I took Huck to task for his errors and
inadequacies, which make it hard to see him as a "vernacular hero" or "picaresque saint." Here I am concerned with his limitations in a farce, a farce
taken to the borderline where it verges on tragedy. Unlike the greatest characters of comedy such as Falstaff, and unlike Tom Sawyer most of the time,
Huck generally lacks what Hazlitt called "*keeping*," "the quality in a character of always being himself or herself, despite dislocations of situation and
behavior."[33] Huck is seldom comfortable or in control of himself or his
world. The moments when he is are memorable, but they are brief and exceptional, and memorable for that reason. After escaping from Pap, Huck
lies on his back in the canoe in the moonshine as he drifts down to Jackson's

32. On dehumanization, see, e.g., Bergson, "Laughter," pp. 67, 79–85, 90–103, 105–19;
McFadden, *Discovering the Comic*, p. 36; Sypher, "Appendix," p. 209. On aggressiveness and
associated qualities, see, e.g., Davis, *Farce*, pp. 24–30, 85; Bentley, *Drama*, pp. 240, 243;
Sypher, "Appendix," pp. 201, 242. On lack of self-awareness, see, e.g., Davis, *Farce*, p. 88;
Bentley, *Drama*, pp. 295–99; Bergson, "Laughter," pp. 67–74, 104.

33. McFadden, *Discovering the Comic*, p. 90. "*Keeping*," quoted by McFadden, is from
Lecture I, "On Wit and Humour," *Lectures on the Comic Writers* (1818–1819), in *The Complete Works of William Hazlitt*, ed. P. P. Howe, 21 vols. (New York: AMS Press, 1967), 6:5.

Island; once there he feels "powerful lazy and comfortable" (p. [61]) and "boss" (p. 64) of the island. After escaping from the Grangerford massacre, he floats downriver with Jim as the days "slid along so quiet and smooth and lovely" (p. [157]). But on the island the discovery of Jim ends the placid interval, and those smooth-sliding days add up to "two or three" only, because the King and the Duke invade the raft. Huck's moments of desperate acting more than once enable him to control his world for a time, but only a short time in each case. The brilliant handling of the slave-hunters in Chapter 16 is followed the next night by proof that the raft has passed Cairo, and the night after that by the smashing of the raft by a steamboat. Neither trouble is Huck's fault, which simply reinforces the point that Huck, not Jim, is the one who is "snake-bit," fundamentally at odds with his world. The point is clinched at the Phelpses' when Huck's momentary satisfaction at being "born again" as Tom Sawyer is swept away by the "uncomfortable" realization that the real Tom Sawyer may walk in at any moment (Chap. 32). When Tom does arrive, Huck is second fiddle once again. As for Huck's gratuitously assumed disguises, they are more often ineffective than not and sometimes lead him to the edge of disaster. Huck can't help trying, though. This yearning to be something one is not "is universal in comic characters and normally involves an element of self-deception."[34] In a farce, such a character, especially if he is a fool, often finds himself in great trouble.

As if Huck didn't have enough trouble with his identity, he is taken for Tom Sawyer at the Phelps farm and finds himself locked into this role when Tom appears and takes the name of *Sid*. Sid is familiar to the readers of *The Adventures of Tom Sawyer*. As the opening paragraph of *Huckleberry Finn* shows, Huck expects his readers to know the earlier novel well and therefore to remember Sid. The role of Tom—that is, not simply being called Tom but acting like Tom—does not suit Huck at all. Twain takes pains to make that point in the *Walter Scott* episode, during which Huck's eagerness to imitate and even outdo Tom nearly gets Huck and Jim killed. Every time the Phelpses call Huck *Tom*, as they do for twenty chapters, they remind us that Huck is not Tom, literally or figuratively. The Phelpses call Tom "Sid," and of course Huck calls "Sid" Tom and Tom calls "Tom" Huck. Besides being confused by all this, we are reminded, if we need reminding, that Tom is no more a Sid, figuratively speaking, than Huck is a Tom.

These references to Sid are appropriate, in a deeply ironic way, because Huck's relationship with Tom, the key relationship of the Phelps episode, has something important in common with Sid's earlier relationship with Tom. The Sid of *Tom Sawyer* is a farce-fool. He is prissy, cowardly, and consistently ineffectual in his repeated malicious attempts to get even with Tom. Huck has none of Sid's meanness, certainly. What Huck does share with Sid is the mode of his relationship with Tom. Sid exists entirely in relation to Tom, as a weak and unwilling foil and satellite. Tom acts, Sid reacts. Like Sid, Huck is largely ineffectual in his relation with Tom. Huck sets out val-

34. McFadden, *Discovering the Comic*, p. 39. McFadden's major example of such a mistake is Falstaff's effort to become the official court jester in *Henry IV, Part 2*.

iantly to rescue Jim, but, as we have seen, Huck's best effort to plan the rescue is instantly crushed by Tom, who establishes permanent mastery over Huck and the situation. Never fully comfortable as Tom's "dancing-jack," Huck from time to time does try to protest some of Tom's crazier schemes, but Huck always fails and gives in. To the end he is Tom's satellite. The result is the classic farce of the last chapters. Another result is the exasperation, the sense of betrayal, of generations of readers. The noble Huck of Chapter 31, who vows to "*go to hell*" for stealing a slave, becomes a player in Tom's heartless game and joins Sid in the broad category of incompetent farce-fools.

Not just during the ending but during most of the novel, Huck must be put with the fools of farce. Impulsive, erratic, easily diverted, he lacks the tireless driving aggressiveness of the dominating knaves of farce. Rather like his fictional contemporary, Bartley Hubbard in Howells's *A Modern Instance* (1882), Huck is a "natural man," with no definite goal or goals beyond the negative one of avoiding bother. It is a bother to resist Miss Watson, so Huck goes to school and eventually gets so he can "stand it" (p. [34]). Later it is dangerous to stand up to Pap, so Huck reverses himself and learns to enjoy "laying off comfortable all day, . . . no books nor study" (p. 46). And after the King and the Duke take over the raft, Huck concludes that "the best way to get along" with these "low-down humbugs and frauds" "is to let them have their own way" (p. 166). A sensible and convenient solution, but not the solution of a dominating character such as Tom Sawyer.

Huck never sees the limitations of these reactions to trouble, or of his other actions and reactions. When Huck violates the raft-refuge with his cruelty to Jim (Chap. 15), Huck fails to see what he has done until Jim explains it to him in his moving speech about putting "dirt on de head er dey fren's" (p. 121). Although Huck has two chances to understand each experience, when it happens and when he writes about it later, he shows only too rarely, as we have seen, that he understands or has learned from experience. Huck sees the cruelty in the tarring and feathering of the King and Duke but cannot apply his admirable moral there ("Human beings *can* be awful cruel to one another") during his thoughtlessly cruel treatment of Jim beginning the next day or during his retelling of the cruelties a few weeks later. Thus Huck conforms to Bergson's idea of the absent-minded "comic" character, except that Huck's inability to put two and two together has results that go beyond comedy and, like so many other aspects of this novel, skirt tragedy and help make the book tragifarce. Huck's absence of mind even throws into doubt some of his few jokes. When Huck says of Tom's scheme to rescue Jim, "I see in a minute it was worth fifteen of mine, for style, and would make Jim just as free a man as mine would, and maybe get us all killed besides" (p. 294), we cannot be sure if the last seven words are a joke, even though Huck has had several weeks to reflect on the point. If Tom said those words, we would know that they were a joke, because Tom has what Freud calls "a judgment which produces a comic contrast."[35]

35. *Jokes and Their Relations to the Unconscious*, ed. and trans. James Strachey (Harmondsworth, Eng.: Penguin Books, 1960), p. 40.

From a discussion of Huck and *Huckleberry Finn* in terms of farce, Tom Sawyer emerges as the true central character, the ideal farce-knave and protagonist of a tragifarce. Tom has judgment in abundance. He almost always knows what he is doing, as he sharply reminds Huck during their crucial struggle for mastery in Chapter 34: "Don't you reckon I know what I'm about? Don't I generly know what I'm about?" (p. 295). Of course, what Tom is so knowledgeably "about" is pointless, even mad, often destructive, and almost self-destructive when it leads Tom to stop a bullet. But these objections are irrelevant in the sealed-off, mechanical world of farce, where action follows with consistent logic from mad premises. In this world Tom is entirely at home. He has complete "integrity and substantiality of self," as George McFadden defines Hazlitt's term *keeping*.[36] He is always himself, and always at ease. He doesn't enter the Phelpses' yard "like a sheep," as Huck does; "no, he come ca'm and important, like the ram" (p. 286). His almost never-failing presence of mind is best illustrated in the perception that turns the course of the rescue in Chapter 34. It is not remarkable that Tom notices the watermelon and realizes that Jim, not a dog, is in the cabin. What is remarkable, and sets Tom off as a great knave, is his realization that he has gained a fleeting moment of psychological advantage. Seizing that moment, he forces a hastily thought-out plan for rescuing Jim from the flustered Huck and reserves his own plan until he has demolished Huck's plan and Huck, too.

To these attributes Tom adds others. He has the authority of mystery. He is always seen from outside, through Huck's almost always admiring vision. In *Tom Sawyer*, Tom, presented by Twain's condescending adult narrator, is a boy until the last pages, where he seems somewhat older. In *Huckleberry Finn*, however, Tom seems and acts like an adult, treating his friends with the authority and sharp impatience of a nineteenth-century adult dealing with children. Huck refers to Tom as a boy only once, and then admiringly: "What a head for just a boy to have" (p. 294). Tom also gains strength and poise from the emotional security that he derives from his firm relationship with his adoptive mother, Aunt Polly. Surviving every test, this relationship is established in *Tom Sawyer* and revived at the end of *Huckleberry Finn*, when Aunt Polly suddenly reappears to scold and protect. Huck, in contrast, has no mother, real or adoptive, and never thinks about his mother or a mother; he is psychologically alone.

Operating with judgment from his secure emotional base, Tom can engage in actions that create the Action of the book, which Huck narrates and which is therefore his but not his, as *The Great Gatsby* is and is not Carraway's book. Here I work from George McFadden's definition of the comic, which applies equally to the world of farce:

> the comic resides in an hypostasis that is constantly asserted, frequently threatened with alteration, but always maintained. . . . What happens in comedy is the conservation of a state of affairs (not necessarily a character) that is aesthet-

36. *Discovering the Comic*, p. 90.

ically satisfying but not insistently good, bad, or great, so as to affirm its continued opportunity for existence and action.

The comic plot, McFadden adds, need not be logical as long as it has the rhythm of stasis-threat-stasis, sets a firm and usually brisk pace, and provides some kind of ending (any kind will do).[37] One notes that in a literal way Huck meets these requirements for the major comic character, but because Huck's "state of affairs" is generally little better than mere survival, because he often makes a poor job of that, and because he takes a subordinate stance in relation to Tom when they are together (and sometimes when they are not), Huck is not Tom's equal.

Tom's "state of affairs" involves the opportunity and the freedom to dominate and arrange (dramatize) reality, always in a certain social grouping: himself as leader and protagonist with one or more satellites. In *Tom Sawyer* that state of affairs is unchanging and uncontested, except for a few tussles with intruding boys and the shift from Joe Harper to Huck as number-one satellite. (Tom's conflict with Injun Joe is irrelevant to this plane of action.) In *Huckleberry Finn*, however, Tom begins in, loses, and then regains his natural state of domination, in a typical comic action with tragically farcical qualities. At the beginning of the novel Tom is the unquestioned authority figure. During the robber-gang episode (Chaps. 2 and 3) Tom at first reinforces his domination but then abruptly loses it because of his one major absent-minded action, an error of judgment of a kind fatal for any tyrant. He makes promises—about lamp-rubbing, praying, and robbing A-rabs—that he cannot possibly deliver on and whose collapse in the cold light of reality makes him look like a fool. "I judged that all that stuff was only just one of Tom Sawyer's lies" (p. 33), says Huck, sounding contemptuous of Tom for the only time in the novel.

His image badly tarnished, Tom can now appear only as just another boy, Huck's equal, but given Tom's position as protagonist and knave, he cannot possibly do that, so he vanishes from the book. During the "three or four months" (Chap. 4) that Huck remains in St. Petersburg, Tom never reappears. Pap does, and the story embarks on a new course to which Tom is irrelevant. Until the Phelps episode at the end, Tom reappears only once, as a face in the crowd on the steamboat looking for Huck's corpse in Chapter 8. Though Huck admiringly recalls Tom's style from time to time, he shows no consistent need for Tom, as a person or an inspiration. To regain his natural level of control Tom must reappear in person and must act firmly. Given the madly logical, coincidence-ridden nature of farce plots, there is nothing odd about Tom reappearing just as Huck is about to embark on the action, freeing Jim, that could establish Huck himself as a Tom Sawyer, a shrewd dominating figure. Methodically Tom bends first Huck and Jim and then the whole Phelps world to his will. At the very end Tom, now with two satellites, is about to embark on "howling adventures" in "the Territory"—meaning that he is in total command, with carte blanche to do what he wants.

37. Ibid., p. 36.

With this ending, narrated with happy incomprehension by Huck, we are in the world of "farce noire," tragifarce. This world belongs to the knaves with the skill and the "clout," the social prestige, to help them get what they want and avoid paying for their errors. Colonel Sherburn does not pay for his cold-blooded murder of Boggs, nor does Tom pay for breaking up the Sunday school picnic and the Phelps world. The erratic, ultimately ineffectual fools and would-be knaves—the King and the Duke, Pap, the Grangerfords—pay with their lives. When Huck is about to establish himself as competent by freeing Jim, an easy matter, fate intervenes, almost contemptuously, shoves Tom into the situation, and reduces Huck to a stooge. The moral is that crime pays, and the fools pay the criminals. *Huckleberry Finn* does not, however, give us the vision of extreme modern tragifarce, "*a vision of the world as an unmitigated horror*," the horror of Burroughs's novels or *Endgame.*[38] Tom's acts of domination are small and self-limiting. That robbergang might get Tom's friends into serious trouble, but it self-destructs before matters get beyond petty vandalism. Tom's behavior does no more than suggest the really dreadful knavery of extreme modern drama and absurdist fiction. Also, the acts of cruelty in the novel are so muted or reshaped in Huck's retelling that their potential for horror is limited. The fate of the King and the Duke even has an oddly aesthetic twist: tarred and feathered, they look like "monstrous big soldier-plumes" (p. 291). Huck's world muddles along in a way somewhere between the hard mechanistic quality of standard farce and the full horror of extreme "farce noire."

It is for us, the readers, that *Huckleberry Finn* is significant and tragic farce. The characters are unaware in their world of farce. The reader, in knowing that they live in such a world, brings meaning to it, thanks to Twain's subtle and suggestive art. It is the adding of meaning that makes farce into comedy in some cases, and into tragifarce in the case of *Huckleberry Finn*. During the Phelps episode, for example, Tom and Huck treat Jim with thoughtless cruelty, but we see Jim, as a victim, a scapegoat, almost a martyr or Christ-figure, who sacrifices himself, after his resurrection from his cabin-tomb, when he gives up his freedom to help the wounded Tom.[39] Seeing and sympathizing, we are still bound by farce, because the knaves still rule the roost, but we are moving from farce toward the worlds of tragedy and comedy, where human folly is displayed to us so that we may, as Hazlitt said, be "struck with the difference between what things are, and what they ought to be."[40] That *Huckleberry Finn* can still "give the public a shaking" one hundred years after its publication suggests the magnitude of Twain's skill and achievement.

38. Bentley, *Drama*, p. 337.
39. Sypher, "Appendix," pp. 220, 245, discusses the use of the comic scapegoat as Christ-figure.
40. Hazlitt, *Works*, 6:5.

14 ROBERT REGAN

Huck Finn in the Wake of the *Quaker City*

"YOU don't know about me, without you have read a book by the name of 'The Adventures of Tom Sawyer,' but that ain't no matter" (p. [17]). If Mark Twain had wanted Huck Finn to establish a reputation for scrupulous veracity, he could surely have found a better opening sentence for his *Adventures*. It matters—it matters quite a lot—that readers of *Huckleberry Finn* have read *Tom Sawyer*. But Mark Twain had no reason to fear that anyone would not already know about Huck and Tom. A "chromo" that once (I am not sure when) illustrated boxes of Mark Twain Cigars makes the point: a handsome picture of the author in his forties is flanked by illustrations of Huck fishing from a riverbank and Tom carrying his bucket of whitewash. The slogan in gold is intended, I suppose, to apply simultaneously to the cigars, the author, and the book illustrated: "KNOWN TO EVERYONE—LIKED BY ALL." *The Adventures of Tom Sawyer* had quickly and permanently established itself in the memory of Mark Twain's readers. Huck's ostensible disclaimer that we need not have read the earlier book serves actually to retrieve our recollections of it. It compels us to perceive the new work in the context of the old and as part of a new context that contains the old.

To what extent, Tzvetan Todorov invites us to ask, does a discourse "invoke an anterior discourse"? If a discourse could so utterly disregard the past as to echo nothing from it, even negatively, Todorov calls it "monovalent." But whenever a discourse "invokes an anterior discourse more or less explicitly"—whether one passage in a specific book or merely "a certain style, a particular tradition"—he calls it "polyvalent."[1] As Todorov recognizes, all literary texts, if not all discourses, are more or less polyvalent; but asking how much more or less a work calls to mind its antecedents and in what ways and to what ends it calls them to mind may yield revealing answers. This seems to me particularly true of Mark Twain's works, which are insistently monovalent in one sense (a fact I'll discuss later), insistently polyvalent in another.

They are polyvalent almost exclusively in invoking each other. Even before Huck's first sentence makes reference to Tom's *Adventures*, the last three words of the title of the book have established its context: *Adventures of*

---

1. *Introduction to Poetics*, trans. Richard Howard (Minneapolis: University of Minnesota Press, 1981), pp. 23–25.

Huckleberry Finn (Tom Sawyer's Comrade). When today's writers dare to say—to whisper, to hint—that it is our responsibility to read their earlier works, they risk addressing a much diminished audience. But as regards this issue Mark Twain was singularly privileged even for his time: he knew, if Huck did not, that he could ask his readers to do their homework, if they had not done it already, by reading all his earlier books. Indeed, to facilitate their compliance, he arranged to have the agents who were to sell *Huckleberry Finn* door-to-door offer all the other works for sale.[2] For not *Tom Sawyer* merely but all those earlier books constitute the "anterior discourse" that Huck's polyvalent voice invoked for the audience of 1885. The monovalence of Huck's voice is ineluctably a fiction, but it is a powerful one: Huck commences his adventures as an illiterate; he writes his *Adventures* in a semiliterate—albeit an inspired—language that reminds us sentence by sentence that he is innocent of books. But an examination of his book's polyvalence will lead us back to this quite central issue.

Mark Twain's titles frequently remind us of his assumption that his readers know his earlier works (and in his case we need not distinguish "actual" from "intended" or "ideal" readers: they are all one). The titles of *A Tramp Abroad* and of *Tom Sawyer Abroad* as well as the titles of two books he did not complete, "A Tramp Abroad Again" and "The Innocents Adrift,"[3] place them in a set initiated by *The Innocents Abroad*. And those particular titles suggest a relation between his two principal genres, narrative fiction and personal narrative: the autobiographical works he published are without exception cast as travel books, and almost all his novels (*The Adventures of Tom Sawyer* is a conspicuous exception) are dominated by travel motifs, each focusing on a stranger in a strange land whose problem is to discover both where he is and who he is. They are, with that notable exception, about displaced persons, innocents abroad. Abundant evidence in the novels indicates that Mark Twain expected and intended readers to recognize connections with the travel books—with all of them, but especially with *The Innocents Abroad*, the first, the most celebrated, and the most successful. As late as 1893, *Century Magazine* presented one of his shorter travel fictions, "The £1,000,000 Bank Note," as "By the author of 'Innocents Abroad,'" etc. "It sells right along just like the Bible," William Dean Howells reported Mark Twain's saying of *The Innocents Abroad*.[4] From time to time Huck Finn's discourse invokes the Bible; much more frequently it invokes *The Innocents Abroad* and the books that followed in its wake.

---

2. *Mark Twain's Letters to His Publishers, 1867–1894*, ed. Hamlin Hill (Berkeley: University of California Press, 1967), pp. 177–80. His arrangements, as the correspondence indicates, were not wholly successful.

3. "A Tramp Abroad Again" was the proposed title for a book to be developed from six travel letters Mark Twain wrote for S. S. McClure's syndicate in 1891–1892. "The Innocents Adrift" is his title for the work Albert Bigelow Paine published (in part) as "Down the Rhine" in *Europe and Elsewhere* (New York: Harper, 1923), pp. 129–68.

4. *My Mark Twain* (New York: Harper, 1910), p. 8.

II

A two-page Exxon advertisement in the 4 October 1982 issue of *The New Yorker* announced a series of "Great Performances" on television. One of these was to be "Innocents Abroad," billed as "Mark Twain's witty travel journal-turned-novel"; and there is an illustration: seated on a steamer-trunk between a valise and a hatbox is a very pretty young American woman. Wrong. Doubly wrong.

In 1870, Mark Twain "reprinted" an "English" review of *The Innocents Abroad* in the New York magazine *Galaxy*. The "English critic" refused to believe that Mark Twain had actually found among the rubbish of Rome's Colosseum a playbill for gladiatorial games and a review of the theatrical carnage in a "stained and mutilated copy of the *Roman Daily Battle-Ax*" (Chap. 26). The suspicious critic may have erred in his assumption that Mark Twain intended to deceive his readers, but he quite correctly understood that *The Innocents Abroad* presents its contents, with an exception here and there, as fact.[5] And fact, with an exception here and there, it is. This is no novel. (It would take Mark Twain some years to come to terms with the novel.) Perhaps *The Innocents Abroad* would have been a better book—a more consistent and sustained artistic achievement—if it had played fast and loose with the facts. But it did not. The point of the burlesque playbill and review, of course, is that "historical" documents themselves play fast and loose with the facts. They are fabricated to impress—to impress free Americans into involuntary servitude. The worst offenders are guidebooks. *The Innocents Abroad* distances itself from such books by insisting in the one-page Preface that

> This book is a record of a pleasure-trip. If it were a record of a solemn scientific expedition, it would have about it that gravity, that profundity, and that impressive incomprehensibility which are so proper to works of that kind, and withal so attractive. . . . I make small pretence of showing any one how he *ought* to look at objects of interest beyond the sea—other books do that, and therefore, even if I were competent to do it, there is no need.
>
> I offer no apologies for any departures from the usual style of travel-writing that may be charged against me—for I think I have seen with impartial eyes, and I am sure I have written at least honestly, whether wisely or not.

We will discover that books of "gravity," "profundity," and "impressive incomprehensibility" constitute the most cumbersome baggage the "pilgrims"—Mark Twain's antagonists—take with them on the excursion of the steamer *Quaker City*. These hidebound encumbrances constantly restrict their freedom of intellectual movement. Having read what a Lamartine or a nameless guidebook author has seen or felt, they can see or feel nothing else

---

5.   The real English review appeared in *Saturday Review* 30 (8 October 1870): 467–68. Mark Twain responded in *Galaxy* 10 (December 1870): 876–78, by "reprinting" the *Saturday Review* piece—actually by rewriting it and incorporating this preposterous misreading of Chapter 26 and similar misreadings. Although greatly exaggerated, Mark Twain's "review" reflects the dismissal of his "stupendous lies" (his phrase, of course).

(Chap. 55). "Our forty pilgrims" read, quote, and imitate their respected author-authorities; "the boys"—Mark Twain and his half-dozen scapegrace pals—travel light, bookless, and see and feel for themselves. Books and their venerated authors are Mark Twain's favorite target throughout *The Innocents Abroad*. He invokes them exclusively to repudiate them: the "Rev. William H. Neligan, LL.D, M.A., Trinity College, Dublin; Member of the Archaeological Society of Great Britain" puts Mark Twain's "credulity on its mettle every now and then" with assertions like "Here the heart of St. Phillip Neri was so inflamed with divine love as to burst his ribs." But for Father Neligan's resonant credentials, Mark Twain might have questioned "what Phillip had for dinner" (Chap. 27). And he finds the works of William C. Prime—Grimes, he calls him—representative of the travel books with which the "pilgrims" are loaded down. They present "ingeniously written descriptions, and well calculated to deceive." All the books Mark Twain cites are packed with lies—fictions—contrived to "scare the reader or excite his envy or his admiration" (Chaps. 48, 50). Travel books are as a class "calculated to deceive"; Mark Twain has "written at least honestly": he all but denies that his discourse belongs to the classification *book*. Thus *The Innocents Abroad* attains its winning kind of "monovalence."

As for the pretty young woman in the *New Yorker* ad, she is nowhere to be found in *The Innocents Abroad*.[6] The illustrations in the original edition occasionally remind the reader that the excursionists aboard the *Quaker City* were of both sexes; readers of editions lacking pictures might easily forget. We do not so much as learn the name of a single female passenger. By Chapter 7 we have encountered Dan and the doctor, Blucher, Moult, and Jack—the "boys"—and the General, the Judge, the Commodore, the Colonel, the Commissioner of the United States to Europe, Asia, and Africa, as well as the Interrogation Point, the Oracle, and the Poet Lariat—all of the "pilgrims." Later we learn the actual surnames of several male passengers, but not one woman is named or described. Yet if women are out of sight, they are not quite out of mind. Consider the case of Jack, the youngest of the "boys": Jack had been admonished by his father before the ship sailed that he should "never appear in public on those decks in fair weather, in a costume unbecoming your mother's drawing-room!" (Chap. 57). The mother is not present, but she is a presence, denying Jack his freedom to dress as himself. Similarly, first the Widow Douglas and then the Shepherdsons would dress Huck in "new clothes . . . too good to be comfortable" (Chaps. 1, 19). But neither Huck nor Jack submits: Huck goes naked on the raft, and Jack wears his "tasseled red fez" and his buckskin-bottomed pantaloons on the decks of the *Quaker City*.

6. In the PBS production of *Innocents Abroad*, broadcast on 9 May 1983, the actress Brooke Adams appears as Julia Newell, the doctor's romantic interest on the voyage. She made a brief appearance in the manuscript in a passage on Spain now in the Vassar College library, but Mark Twain wisely deleted the passage: this is a book about escaping the domination of women, if only temporarily. I acknowledge with pleasure my indebtedness here and in what follows to Ann Douglas's *The Feminization of American Culture* (New York: Alfred A. Knopf, 1977).

III

Lamartine's sentimental account of the Levant; Jack's mother's well-policed drawing room: Mark Twain perceives in both a threat to the freedom of his "boys." Respected writers and respectable ladies continue to menace liberty—indeed, liberty, equality, and fraternity—in *Huckleberry Finn*. The novel is in this respect a long exemplum pointing the moral of *The Innocents Abroad*. In Chapter 16 Huck undergoes one of his crises of conscience: Jim feels "all over trembly and feverish" because he is getting "close to freedom"; Huck feels equally "trembly and feverish" because he knows he has been instrumental in effecting Jim's escape:

> Conscience says to me, "What had poor Miss Watson done to you, that you could see her nigger go off right under your eyes and never say one single word? What did that poor old woman do to you, that you could treat her so mean? Why, she tried to learn you your book, she tried to learn you your manners, she tried to be good to you every way she knowed how. *That's* what she done."
> (P. 123)

Huck does not realize that he disapproves of slavery; nor is he aware that he disapproves of book-learning and manners and the piety that informs his conscience. Mark Twain knows; so do we.

The same Miss Watson who had "learned" Huck his "book" resolves to sell Jim down the river. The only heartless slaveholder we meet in *Huckleberry Finn* is a woman. But she is not the only threat to Huck's liberty, nor to Jim's. Why does Mark Twain present women as menacing freedom—Miss Watson and the kindly Widow Douglas, who, we learn on the first page, "allowed she would sivilize" Huck, and the equally kindly Aunt Sally, whose resolve to "sivilize" him brings the novel to its close? *The Innocents Abroad* may hint at an answer to this puzzle, but a clearer answer is accessible in the logic—or logical lapse—of a paragraph from George Santayana's 1911 lecture "The Genteel Tradition in American Philosophy":

> America . . . is a country with two mentalities, one a survival of the beliefs and standards of the fathers, the other an expression of the instincts, practice, and discoveries of the younger generations. In all the higher things of the mind—in religion, in literature, in the moral emotions—it is the hereditary spirit that still prevails. . . . The truth is that one half of the American mind, that not occupied intensely in practical affairs, has remained, I will not say high and dry, but slightly becalmed; it has floated gently in the backwater, while, alongside, in invention and industry and social organization, the other half of the mind was leaping down a sort of Niagara Rapids. This division may be found symbolized in American architecture: a neat reproduction of the colonial mansion—with some modern comforts introduced surreptitiously—stands beside the skyscraper. The American Will inhabits the skyscraper; the American Intellect inhabits the colonial mansion. The one is the sphere of the American man; the other, at least predominantly, of the American woman. The one is all aggressive enterprise; the other is all genteel tradition.[7]

7. In *Selected Critical Writings of George Santayana* (Cambridge: Cambridge University Press, 1968), 2:86.

We may extract from this famous and fascinating passage two lists of con-
catenated terms:

Younger generations' instincts	*fathers'* beliefs
practice	standards
discoveries	higher things of the mind
practical affairs	religion
invention	literature
industry	hereditary spirit
social organization	moral emotions
skyscraper	neat reproduction of the colonial mansion
American Will	American Intellect
American *man*	American *woman*
aggressive enterprise	genteel tradition

Santayana's associations "leap down a sort of Niagara Rapids" from the
"younger generation" to the "American man" and his "aggressive enterprise"; at the same time, they drift rudderless through a murky "backwater"
from the "fathers" and their "standards" to the "American woman" and her
"genteel tradition." Many, especially Freudians bent on finding an Oedipal
root in every rebellion, may be perplexed by the eddies in the stream of Santayana's thought. A precise logician would have trouble tracing the course
that leads the philosopher from "fathers" to "woman"—but not Jack, in his
fez and buckskin, and not Huck, in his nakedness. Both know that the
"higher things of the mind"—all the items in the second list I have extracted
from Santayana, but especially religion and literature—are the chief weapons in the arsenal of the genteel tradition, the weapons that American fathers (disguised as mothers) wield against American boys.

IV

The "boys" of *The Innocents Abroad* defend themselves by feigning ignorance, by pretending that they recall no discourse anterior to their own. Eu-
ropeans, especially European guides, playing the father/mother role, invoke
the "hereditary spirit" that demands that the present pay homage to the
past, that the New World confess its inferiority to the Old. A guide spreads
"a stained and aged document" before the "boys": "see! handwriting Christopher Colombo! write it himself!" The doctor, the chief wag of the group,
responds, "Why, I have seen boys in America only fourteen years old that
can write better than that." The guide displays "a royal Egyptian mummy—
the best preserved in the world, perhaps." The doctor demands to see "a
nice *fresh* corpse" or none at all (Chap. 27).

Taking Huck Finn as his narrator frees Mark Twain of this ironic pretense.
Huck is not constrained to feign ignorance. His ignorance is genuine. The
widow says grace before meals: "When you got to the table you couldn't go
right to eating, but you had to wait," Huck complains, "for the widow to
tuck her head and grumble a little over the victuals, though there warn't
really anything the matter with them." Later "she got out her book"—the

widow and Miss Watson pull books on poor Huck as if they were guns—
"and learned me about Moses and the Bulrushers." Huck is "in a sweat to
learn more about him: but by-and-by she let it out that Moses had been
dead a considerable long time." Like the doctor, Huck lives in the present:
"I don't take no stock in dead people" (p. 18). (Reading Huck's statement in
the context provided by the doctor's, we understand at once its political implications. That is what Mark Twain expects of us.) Here in the opening
chapter of his *Adventures*, Huck is proof against the pietism that maintained
the slavocracy because he is obliviously, invincibly ignorant of theology and
religious tradition. Readers may detect a typological significance in the reference to the foundling Moses: the widow, like Pharaoh's daughter, has
taken into her care a child abandoned in the "Bulrushers" of the Mississippi.
The widow seems to intend to implant that typology in Huck's mind: he is to
be her little Moses. By the end of his *Adventures*, Huck might easily have
connected himself with the grownup Moses: had he not, like the great Liberator, led a chosen people—well, a chosen *person*, anyhow—out of bondage? But he does not, early or late, recognize the connection. To do so would
be to confess belonging to the dead past. Huck does not, will not, learn the
widow's book or make it his book.

Huck's puzzlement over the widow's interest in Moses, "which was no kin
to her, and no use to anybody, being gone, you see" (p. 19), reminds us, and
must have reminded the original audience, of a much-cited passage in *The
Innocents Abroad*. Writing for an American audience that doted on seeing
itself as Adamic, Mark Twain jokes himself back into the present—or the
future-perfect—when he comes in Jerusalem upon the ostensible grave of
Adam, a "blood relation." Seeing the grave, he "burst into tears"—crocodile
tears—because Adam had not lived to see him, "to see his child" (Chap. 53).
Mark Twain ridicules typological connections. Huckleberry Finn ignores
them.

The last half of the title of Mark Twain's first book, *The Innocents Abroad,
or The New Pilgrim's Progress*, points to an ironic connection that, considering the status of Bunyan's classic in nineteenth-century America, can be
called almost typological. Mark Twain derisively refers to the sanctimonious
guidebook-toters-and-quoters he has to travel with as "our pilgrims," but
few readers will miss the point that the author himself plays—and only partially burlesques—the role of Bunyan's Christian. When Huck finds among
the Grangerford's books " 'Pilgrim's Progress,' about a man that left his family it didn't say why" (Chap. 17), readers can be expected to make a complex
set of associations. Huck, we are to sense, is playing the role Mark Twain
played in *The Innocents Abroad*: he is demonstrating that the apparent
reprobates are the true elect, the apparent elect the true reprobates. But,
even more to the point, he is playing, and not at all burlesquing, the role of
Bunyan's hero. This young Christian has fled his City of Destruction and
started his journey through Sloughs of Despond and Vanity Fairs toward the
Celestial Territory. And we should remember where Huck is when he takes
up Bunyan's book. He is in the Grangerfords' house, which Mark Twain has
already described—with penetrating ironies inaccessible to Huck—in Chap-

ter 38 of *Life on the Mississippi*, a chapter taking its title, "The House Beautiful," from *Pilgrim's Progress*. After reading "considerable" in Bunyan, Huck delivers his memorable critical dictum: "the statements was interesting, but tough." And that is all: Huck will not read himself into or out of any anterior discourse, for to do so would be to limit his freedom to shape his own history.

But we necessarily read his history into and out of the contexts supplied by Mark Twain's earlier books. For the properly prepared reader, Huck's catalog of the Grangerfords' library is as meaningful as it is funny: the properly prepared reader knows what the titles Huck mentions tell about the Grangerfords' morals and aesthetics and politics; such a reader even knows the titles of the books Huck fails to mention and what *they* tell about the Grangerfords. The properly prepared reader recalls the library of "The House Beautiful." *Life on the Mississippi* had been invoked earlier by the name of the wrecked steamboat Huck and Jim encountered in Chapter 12: the *Walter Scott*. The name calls to mind "the Walter Scott disease" that afflicted the South, making every "gentleman . . . a major or a colonel" and creating "rank and cast down there, and also reverence for rank and cast, and pride and pleasure in them." And led to the Civil War (Chap. 44), and to the prevalence of the particular kind of butchery that will terminate the Grangerford-Shepherdson episode—and the Grangerfords and Shepherdsons (Chap. 40, n. 1). What they read undid them. And Huck ignores yet another typological echo—one the Colonels Grangerford and Shepherdson and their families would have done well to heed. The names of the two families connect them with the figures in the archetypal blood feud between the first farmer (granger) and his shepherd brother, Abel and Cain.

Huck has the virtue of innocence: he alone can report all of these literary resonances without hearing one. In its general pattern and in its particulars, the Grangerford-Shepherdson feud reminds the reader, of course, of *Romeo and Juliet*. Harney Shepherdson's elopement with Sophia Grangerford is the occasion for the renewal of their families' vendetta. Shakespeare, following his sources, sacrifices his young lovers to save their elders from mutual destruction. Mark Twain, reversing the paradigm, conveys his young lovers across the river to safety and leaves their murderous families on the bank to exterminate one another. The young, who have not cast their lot with the dead past, who will not read their histories and identities out of books, live on; the elders, and all who honor them, perish by their own hands. The dead past is left without so much as a grave-digger to bury its dead. The reader knows that Harney and Sophia are cast in the roles of Romeo and Juliet; but Huck, their Friar Lawrence, does not know, nor do they: ignorance preserves these survivors. If the story had been *for them* polyvalent, they might have perished, sacrificial victims of reading.

V

Todorov's formulation asks us to ponder whether a work calls earlier works to mind. Any authorial discourse may invoke for the reader anterior discourses, but a narrative (particularly a fictional narrative, most particularly a first-person fictional narrative) will usually present a more complicated situation. Here we encounter an author and a reader, a narrator and an implied recipient (what criticism has fallen into calling a *narratee*), and characters who address their discourses to other characters. The situation demands a refinement and division of Todorov's question. Who invokes the anterior discourse? and to whose mind? Nabokov's Humbert Humbert thinks his passion for Lolita reminiscent of Poe's for Annabel Lee. Lolita is innocent of Annabel Lee; and we are better readers of Nabokov and of Poe than to acknowledge that Humbert's case resembles Annabel's inamorato's. Humbert stands discredited as a reader and therefore as arbiter of his own experience. Huck Finn cannot make such blunders. Having read next to nothing, Huck cannot view his experience in the light of his reading. That failing—and Mark Twain regards it as a failing even if one reads accurately—belongs in *Huckleberry Finn* to Tom Sawyer.

"The most important trait of Tom in this novel," Walter Blair observes, is "his love of books and his imitation of them."[8] In the harmless silly games that open the book and in the pernicious silly games that move it toward its conclusion, Tom imitates books; he restructures his experience to conform to the paradigms they supply. And he gets the paradigms wrong. We would, I suppose, be amused when Tom upbraids Huck for failing to understand that what appears to be a "Sunday-school picnic, and only a primer-class at that" is really "A-rabs . . . and elephants and things" (pp. 31–32) even if we had not read *Don Quixote*. But knowing the invoked text and grasping that Tom's problem is precisely that of the Knight of la Mancha, too much reading and too much credulity, saturates his complaint with irony: "He said if I warn't so ignorant, but had read a book called 'Don Quixote,' I would know without asking. He said it was all done by enchantment" (p. 32). It may be worth recalling—though here I doubt that Mark Twain expects us to recall—that Chapter 46 of *Life on the Mississippi*, which refers to "Sir Walter Scott with his enchantments," closes with this little paragraph:

> A curious exemplification of the power of a single book for good or harm is shown in the effects wrought by *Don Quixote* and those wrought by *Ivanhoe*. The first swept the world's admiration for the medieval chivalry silliness out of existence; and the other restored it. As far as our South is concerned, the good work done by Cervantes is pretty nearly a dead letter, so effectively has Scott's pernicious work undermined it.

Tom's mind, it appears, was a good deal too cluttered to be swept clean even by Cervantes. In Chapter 35 Tom again takes Huck to task: "Why, hain't you ever read any books at all?—Baron Trenck, nor Casanova, nor Benvenuto Chelleeny, nor Henri IV, nor none of them heroes?" (p. 301). Huck, innocent of the "best authorities," makes plans that are too simple, too direct, too goal-directed, for Tom. Readers of *The Innocents Abroad*, "etc.," will have been adequately rehearsed in the proper response of an independent American to such an appeal to the authority of books. Tom is merely masquer-

8. *Mark Twain and Huck Finn* (Berkeley: University of California Press, 1960), p. 118.

ading as one of the boys; under his costume he is one of them, not one of us. At one point, indeed, we see Tom not in disguise but in his proper attire: when he arrives at Phelps farm in Chapter 33, "Tom had his store clothes on, and an audience—and that was always nuts for Tom Sawyer" (p. 286). Not so for Huck Finn. The last two decades of criticism have freed us of the misconception that Huck is a tatterdemalion Tom. If we had all along read the book in the context it invokes, the critical labor would have been unnecessary.

VI

I have treated "The House Beautiful" chapter of *Life on the Mississippi* as an anterior discourse invoked for the reader by Huck's description of the Grangerfords' house; one could quite as accurately call it a posterior discourse invoked for Mark Twain by his writing of the Grangerford episode: in order of composition the Grangerford episode came first; in order of publication "The House Beautiful" came first.[9] When Huck encounters *Friendship's Offering* among the Grangerfords' books, we recall that it was also in the library of the House Beautiful; when Huck says that the Grangerford daughters sing "The Last Link Is Broken" and play "The Battle of Prague" (p. 141), we recall that both were among the fifteen titles of "music, bound and unbound," piled on and by the piano in the House Beautiful. On the Grangerfords' table, Huck finds—and admires—"a lovely crockery basket that had apples and oranges and peaches and grapes piled up in it which was much redder and yellower and prettier than real ones is, but they warn't real because you could see where pieces had got chipped off and showed the white chalk or whatever it was, underneath" (p. 137). We are reminded that Mark Twain had not admired the House Beautiful's "large basket of peaches and other fruits, natural size, all done in plaster, rudely, or in wax, and painted to resemble the originals—which they don't." These similarities and others are arresting enough to suggest that Mark Twain had his manuscript of Chapter 17 of *Huckleberry Finn* before him (or very freshly in mind) as he wrote Chapter 38 of *Life on the Mississippi*. In the latter, speaking *in propria persona*, he can comment on the aesthetic shortcomings of families like the Grangerfords and place their pretenses in the context of Southern culture and politics—the culture and politics of self-destruction. Huck is unqualified to venture such judgments, but by publishing *Life on the Mississippi* before *Huckleberry Finn*, Mark Twain precaptioned the image caught by Huck's "innocent eye."

The moral lesson of *Huckleberry Finn*, I venture at the risk of being banished, is that we should all read our personal histories monovalently: we must not ask books, not even *Huckleberry Finn*, to tell us who we are. But there is, I have been arguing, also a critical lesson here: we should read Mark Twain polyvalently, each of his books in the context it establishes with all the rest. If we do that, we will be spared many interpretative errors. If, for

9. See ibid., pp. 198–204, 285–99, for a summary of the chronology of composition.

example, we read *Huckleberry Finn* in a context that contains Mark Twain's one confrontation in all of *The Innocents Abroad* with a guide who makes *him* look silly, we shall not fall into the error of concluding that the depiction of Jim suggests that the author believed in the intellectual superiority of the white race: the learned, polyglot guide who inadvertently exposes Mark Twain's ignorance (he takes *Renaissance* to be the name of an artist) is an American black who, correctly believing that opportunity would be closed to him in his native land, makes Venice his home (Chap. 23).

One could argue that the opening and ending of *Huckleberry Finn* are not among its strengths: for critics who value frames, Chapter 1 may rely too heavily on our prior knowledge of *Tom Sawyer* and Chapter the Last may leave too much unsettled. But closure, containment, is not the goal Mark Twain strove for.[10] In his last paragraph, Huck tells us that he "ain't agoing to" tackle "no more" books. Huck is as unconvincing here as he was in the book's first sentence: as *Huckleberry Finn* looks back, it looks forward also. This is not a closed book.

10. The openness of Mark Twain's structures and the ways in which each book invokes others may contain a suggestion for textual editors. Cogent arguments have been advanced for restoring the Raftsmen's Passage, which Mark Twain removed from *Huckleberry Finn* and published as Chapter 3 of *Life on the Mississippi*. Editors should ponder the implications of Mark Twain's assumption that readers can and will bring their experience of his earlier works to bear on succeeding ones. Is it not probable that his decision not to restore the Raftsmen's Passage to Chapter 16 of *Huckleberry Finn* was influenced by that assumption? It would, for him, have been part of readers' total experience of his work, and repeating it might well have seemed to him indeed repetitious. Among the most compelling arguments for restoring the passage to *Huckleberry Finn* are those of Peter G. Beidler, "The Raft Episode in *Huckleberry Finn*," MFS 14 (Spring 1968): 11–20, and William R. Manierre, "On Keeping the Raftsmen's Passage in *Huckleberry Finn*," (1968): 118–22.

IV

Extensions and Transformations

O NE of the distinguishing features of a memorable novel is its capacity to renew its appeal to succeeding generations of readers. This quality often results in transformations—through media other than print and into other cultures and languages—as well as mere longevity, and surely few novels have had as lively and varied a centenarian's experience as *Adventures of Huckleberry Finn*. As John Gerber's Introduction documents, Huck's adventures are continuing ones, and his book has had a kind of protean vigor quite unlike anything else in American literature. One of the signs of this vitality after a hundred years is its unmatched eminence in the American school and among American students, from the elementary pupil who reads these adventures, as Thoreau says, "with saucer eyes, and erect and primitive curiosity," to the doctoral candidate stocked with the latest notions from Paris or New Haven, who sees (with considerable justification, it may be) the need to deconstruct the icon of this text. Eric Solomon's essay speaks to the novel's ability to endure and prevail in the classroom, where, despite Twain's injunctions to the contrary (injunctions many a student has doubtless wished the Chief of Ordnance would enforce), its motives, morals, and plot have been analyzed with more or less sophistication countless thousands of times since the study of American literature became academically respectable about fifty years ago. It would perhaps not be too much of a stretcher to suggest that the book has served its students much as the Mississippi served the young pilot Sam Clemens, as a beautiful and exacting discipline of the understanding and the imagination.

As an artifact of popular culture outside the classroom, *Huckleberry Finn* also assumes a dominant position in the American mind, for the story and the characters seem to "belong" to people who have not read the novel as much as to those who have been required to write a composition on its point of view or to discuss in a clearly organized essay the significance of the river. Allison Ensor's survey of the illustrating of *Huck Finn* provides, in this context, one index of the popular image of the novel and its characters and suggests the remarkable range of responses—from darkly tragic to saccharine—it continues to evoke. Suffice it to say that from the waggish engraver of the first edition who tried to make Uncle Silas an exhibitionist, to Norman Rockwell, whose renditions of Twain's characters might have appealed to Emmeline Grangerford had she been able to make them sufficiently "spidery," there has existed an almost perverse tendency to make the novel over in idiosyncratic and stylized ways. Regrettably, this collection contains no account of the various cinematic, theatrical, and television versions of the novel, for in these media, too, the underlying myths seem to have been cut loose from the text and to enjoy a sort of independent existence.

Foreign views and versions are equally suggestive, and although this volume contains no fresh appraisal of the novel's richly problematic history in Europe, it is especially intriguing in this day and age to consider Jan B. Gordon's account of the reactions of Japanese students to *Huck Finn*. The distinctive celebration of both youth and the sensuous perception of the passage of time that Stephen Gilman describes in his essay, and that an American reader tends to take for granted as healthy and restorative, may suggest to the Japanese only a culture profoundly out of synchronization with the fundamental rhythms of life. They, on the other hand, might respond for reasons obscure to us to the overwhelming "textuality" of this story told by a barely literate boy.

The subject of Hamlin Hill's essay on "Huck Finn's Humor Today" is of course an inevitable one for such a collection as this, for a persistent strain in criticism has attested to the novel's capacity to mirror changes in American society, the nature of humor, and even our view of the human condition. But, lest we consign ourselves to the obsolescence of that spate of essays on Huck and Holden Caulfield of a generation ago, it should be said that what tends to be of enduring timeliness about Huck Finn is his aloneness. It is perhaps appropriate that Huck, nowhere at home in his society or century, should be claimed by ours and find his place, as Hill shows, amid the dark irrational laughter of the present.

15   ERIC SOLOMON

My *Huckleberry Finn*: Thirty Years in the Classroom with Huck and Jim

IF William Dean Howells had his Mark Twain, I have had my *Adventures of Huckleberry Finn*. Those of us who have tried to explain American literature and culture to students, only too willing to heed Twain's initial warnings against the search for narrative motive, moral, or plot, have found the text itself to be our basic resource. In Matthew Arnold's phrase, the novel has been our touchstone; in John Barth's grandiloquent Professor's Prayer, from *Giles Goat Boy*, Twain's novel has vouchsafed "examples of the Unexampled, words to speak the Wordless . . . [so] . . . that upon the empty slates of these young minds I may inscribe, bold and squeaklessly, the Answers."[1] Indeed, one way to explain the weird adventures of such a postmodern American fictional creation as young Giles is to refer to Huck's passage to knowledge of a corrupt society through survival of his own wild adventures among moral savages. *Huckleberry Finn*, then, has been part of my teaching equipment for three decades among American undergraduates. To paraphrase the novel's third sentence, there will be things I will stretch, in this study of the novel's impact, but mainly I will tell the truth.

Early on, I learned that just as *Huckleberry Finn* may be all things to all critics of American literature, from Walter Blair to Leslie Fiedler, from Lionel Trilling to John Seelye, from T. S. Eliot to Ralph Ellison, so each student has a personal Huck Finn. Fresh out of four years of Harvard tutorials where I had explicated the rich symbolic implications of the RIVER in the novel, I stood before a class of freshman composition students at Ohio State and posed my favorite rhetorical question: "Who of us has ever traveled down the mighty Mississippi on a raft?" And a particularly dull young man from Chillicothe placidly raised his hand. The grandeur of Mark Twain's novel stems from the fact that it has spoken equally well to generations of scholars starting with Brander Matthews and to generations of students including the young man from Chillicothe. As Ralph Ellison, who certainly patterned many of his invisible man's adventures in the wildernesses of the rural South and the urban North on Huck Finn's archetypal journey from innocence to experience, raised the issue in a slightly different context—but one clearly applicable to Huckleberry Finn's vernacular description of his wars with truth, religion, and social mores—"Who knows but that, on the lower frequencies, I speak for you?"

1.   *Giles Goat Boy* (Garden City, N.Y.: Doubleday, 1966), p. 409.

II

Certainly, *Huckleberry Finn* allows the American literature commentator a significant reference point. Like Wallace Stevens's jar in Tennessee, Mark Twain's lyric novel changed its literary environment merely by virtue of its existence. When one professes American letters, one refers to many key elements such as the Puritan need to link dreams of guilt and hope in order to possess the land, Benjamin Franklin's rationalist drive played off against Jonathan Edwards's spiritual and intellectual frenzy, Edgar Allan Poe's detection of terror, or Thomas Paine's radical fervor. Before one approaches Twain in the classroom, one comments on the great days of American literary performance[2]: Nathaniel Hawthorne's moral romances, Ralph Waldo Emerson's insights into good, Herman Melville's into evil, Henry Thoreau's escape to the woods and the water, Walt Whitman's search for totality. Knowing *Huckleberry Finn*, American critics discover, if not forgiveness, at least further possibilities in Emily Dickinson's inner pain, Stephen Crane's youthful testing of war's horror, and Henry James's subtle combinations of wit and loss. But wherever one wanders in the realms of American achievement in literary form, from James Fenimore Cooper's forests to William Dean Howells's Back Bay houses, a basic image controls the imagination, the image that led Sherwood Anderson and Ernest Hemingway to agree that all American literature started with Twain's novel: the image of a white boy and a black man on a raft floating down the Big Muddy, the river that also fascinated T. S. Eliot and William Faulkner. As Eliot, himself creator of a hymn of praise to *Huckleberry Finn*, said in reference to *Ulysses*, myth (here the myth of a boy escaping a corrupt society and breaking free toward the Territory) provides "a way of controlling, of ordering, of giving a shape and a significance to the immense panorama of futility and anarchy which is contemporary history."[3]

Our *Huckleberry Finn* anticipates and summarizes most cultural and formal themes and approaches employed in the American novel since 1885. Whenever we discuss American fiction, we have this novel as our vital critical center.

Mark Twain wrote an improvisatory novel, as its sources, planning, and publication history make clear. Indeed, Twain's drive to discover language and situations that could show a world elsewhere, in Richard Poirier's term, gives us one more "Great American Novel," written as if the author must reinvent the form, one more work that fits the rambling, expansive, open form that defines American fiction from Melville through Thomas Wolfe to Thomas Pynchon. Here is a loose, baggy monster of a novel, the kind of American expression that would bother a formalist like Henry James as it

2. Obviously, English novels, from Charlotte Bronte's *Jane Eyre*, where Jane must trust her own way to salvation, through Charles Dickens's *Great Expectations*, where Pip must choose loyalty to his true benefactor, lay as much behind Mark Twain's creation of Huck as did the author's repudiation of Walter Scott.

3. "Ulysses, Order, and Myth," *Selected Prose of T. S. Eliot*, ed. Frank Kermode (New York: Harcourt Brace Jovanovich; Farrar, Straus & Giroux, 1975), p. 177.

has bothered generations of Twain's critics who try to fit the Phelps farm ending to the earlier great dramatic river passages. Mark Twain's novelistic form is indeed open; the ending stars Tom Sawyer, and the structure loosens as if Tom himself is the author of the last section. Yet the form is appropriate to the American novel, in a larger sense, as it moves between the polarities of documentary and dream. Huck the factualist and Tom the mythomaniac are encapsulated in, say, the double vision of Norman Mailer moving from the Novel as History to the American Dream. Like Mark Twain, writers as various as John Dos Passos, William Gaddis, and Gilbert Sorrentino have moved back and forth between masses of detail and auras of imagining.

Mark Twain's open form has demanded a communication with some basic idea of America: as wilderness, as seat of terror, as the last, best hope. Similar to Hawthorne's forest or Melville's ocean, Twain's river gives American literature a key double-edged symbol of freedom and doom. Chapter 19, with its lyric description of dawn over the river, with its equally forboding grasp of the dangers represented by the snags that can sink boats and men, is a touchstone for discussion of the wild river in Faulkner's "Old Man" or the escape from war's alarms threatened by the swamp in Hemingway's "Big Two-Hearted River." "As with Conrad," T. S. Eliot brilliantly insists, "we were continually reminded of the power and terror of Nature." [4]

Into this natural setting comes Huck, the essential American picaro, the slangy, visionary, orphaned wanderer, precursor even of Jewish wanderers in the cities, such as J. D. Salinger's Holden Caulfield or Saul Bellow's Augie March. To Frederick Karl, all American picaresque protagonists derive from Huck Finn—part pragmatist, part solitary—striving to master the vast American landscape by wandering freely. Ultimately, the existential anti-heroes of Robert Penn Warren or Walker Percy must, like Huckleberry Finn, seek an escape to the Territory, to the Midwest of F. Scott Fitzgerald's Nick Carraway, for example; but as with Huck, the permanence of their escape is dubious. They have all been there before, in the civilized parts, and they all know that the Territory is changing and, at best, they can only get there ahead of the others.

Huckleberry Finn resonates with themes and techniques fundamental to American novels. Like Crane and Faulkner, Twain muses on the nature of real courage as Colonel Sherburn defies a mob. Like Wolfe, Twain employs recurring symbols to diminish the size of his novelistic territory. Like Fitzgerald, whose Long Island Sound becomes the setting for past dreams of idealistic settlers, Mark Twain uses his symbolic imagination to ruminate on lyric possibilities. And when American novelists strive to cope with the immensity of our world, they, like Twain, sustain their viewpoints by a dependence on facts, on details; from Mark Twain we learn about a circus, from John O'Hara a speakeasy. So American writers from E. W. Howe to Sinclair Lewis can mock or praise a small town and its inhabitants in the terms Twain employs. One might argue that Mark Twain's ability to create in Huck

---

4. "Introduction to *Adventures of Huckleberry Finn*," in *Huckleberry Finn: Text, Sources, and Criticism*, ed. Kenneth S. Lynn (New York: Harcourt, Brace & World, 1961), p. 201.

and Pap a genuinely lower-class family demonstrates the seeds of proletarian fiction; even Mike Gold's *Jews Without Money*, in its young boy's brooding sympathy for whores and his need to escape to the territory of Central Park's mushroom fields, reflects some of Twain's understanding. Mostly, *Huckleberry Finn* prefigures what R. W. B. Lewis classified as fiction of Wrath and Laughter, the double reference to apocalypse and the ridiculous that defines such contemporary American novelists of the absurd as Ralph Ellison and Joseph Heller. And like those authors, as well as Hemingway, Fitzgerald, and Pynchon, Twain in *Huckleberry Finn* is his own best critic, parodying his combination of romance and realism, full of jokes and disguises in his nearly exhausted ending. Also he rejects, just as clearly as Hemingway does with Frederick Henry's words in the rain, abstract terms and religious generalizations.

Huckleberry Finn himself is the most American of heroes: he is the boy-man in a male world (my last reference to Fiedler) and solitary—alone even among others, a first-person narrator who is at home in nature and, like Cooper's Natty Bumppo, at a loss in towns, yet as able to cope with the venality and evil of knaves on the shore as any Dashiell Hammett or Raymond Chandler version of the Scout. As alienated as a James Baldwin youth, and as deeply engaged in the search for a proper father as a Faulkner boy, Huck Finn, an American orphan (indeed, is Orphan Huck very different from the female version in the great comic-adventure narrative of the 1930s, *Little Orphan Annie?*), is, above all, a lonely survivor, one who accommodates to his changing world as effectively as does Theodore Dreiser's Carrie Meeber.

In *Huckleberry Finn*, then, Mark Twain both summarizes the situations of American literary figures and prepares for generations of novelists to come. If American literature has always been experiential, the writing has also demanded a freshness, a vitality—"Make it New," exhorts Ezra Pound; "We need only realize our grandparents, and know ourselves, and our history is complete," states Gertrude Stein—that Twain in his finest novel sought and triumphantly achieved. It is manifest that *Huckleberry Finn* is subversive of accepted culture, politics, and morality; Huck himself is one of the great American refusers. He refuses to search for what William James termed the "bitch-goddess success," and Huck renounces comfort in favor of personal honor just as clearly as does Henry James's culture hero Lambert Strether. And if Mark Twain understands the nature of the American rebel-protagonist, Twain's comprehension of the major themes of American fiction has allowed generations of students of the American novel to employ *Huckleberry Finn* as an entry into the minds of American writers.

Violence as an act, an extreme gesture to cope with the sheer size, loneliness, and mobility of American experience, looms large in American fiction, and Mark Twain insists on its presence in what is only peripherally a boy's book. Most writers of the South continue to respond to the basic furious visions that mark Huck's imagination and experience. The slowly developed detail with which Huck describes the death of poor Boggs at the hands of Colonel Sherburn in Chapter 21 goes far beyond a Southwestern humor tradition and approaches the naturalism of Richard Wright or James

Farrell—"Bang! goes the first shot, and he staggers back clawing at the air—bang! goes the second one, and he tumbles backward on the ground, heavy and solid, with his arms spread out" (p. 186). Hating violence, Twain and Huck are fascinated by it, and the narrative is full of corpses—drowned and shot—and threats of murder.

Next, if American writers are trapped, in a near schizoid condition, between hope and despair ("Song of Myself" and "The Waste Land," the dream of success and the reality of failure), Twain gives us the homelike Phelps farm and the death-dealing—and Victorian parody of a genteel home—Grangerford house. While American fiction lurches forward trying to distinguish with Howells rises from falls, or with Edith Wharton ages of innocence from ages of guilt, *Huckleberry Finn* sustains throughout a double vision.

To approach any discussion of an American philosophy, the American literature teacher draws on Mark Twain's novel. If a pragmatic conceptualization remains our basic contribution to philosophical thought, then in the colloquial phrasings of Huck's ruminations exist the clear exemplifications of William James's expressed ideas: "For the philosophy which is so important in each of us is not a technical matter; it is our more or less dumb sense of what life honestly and deeply means."[5] Whatever works, is right, argues Huck, Tom Sawyer's more abstract, theoretical mind to the contrary. Additionally, the language of the novel's narration is itself inherently pragmatic; the vernacular is concrete, sensate, imagistic, objective. Twain insists that the vernacular in its irregularity must inform his text, just as ethnic novelists of all derivations depend on slang, the demotic, street talk, to illuminate practical truths. While Mark Twain is no innovator here, the literature teacher easily discovers in Huck's language the proper bridge to Ring Lardner and Philip Roth.

Somehow, magically, the open form Mark Twain discovers for his adventures of a youth with an escaped slave, down the great river, in pursuit of freedom and in flight from family, tradition, and the powers of pettifoggery and criminality, this form allows Twain to approach the dream of inclusiveness that often attracts American novelists. Like Melville or Mailer, the great bulk of our novelists seek to be definitive, to encompass all of society's failings in order to treat the artist's own guilt, in other words, to write that Great American Novel. *Huckleberry Finn* fails in that quest, as all American novels must. Yet the dream of catching the American spirit, of getting it *all* down, and correctly, informs the achievement—and the limits of the achievement—of Twain's novel. As W. H. Auden simply said: "Some think they're strong, some think they're smart, / Like butterflies they're pulled apart, / America can break your heart."[6]

For those who would employ a novel as a way of discussing America's racial polarizations, *Huckleberry Finn* has been paradigmatic and problem-

5. "The Present Dilemma in Philosophy," *The Writings of William James*, ed. John McDermott (New York: Modern Library, 1968), p. 362.

6. "Twelve Songs," *Collected Shorter Poems, 1927–57* (London: Faber & Faber, 1966), p. 157.

atic. For Concord librarians, the book was dirty; for De Land, Florida, blacks, the book is racist. Yet the complex relationship of Huck and Jim, built on condescension that becomes understanding, companionship that nears brotherhood, talk that becomes communication, grows steadily as Huck learns to hide with his black friend, to relax with him, more crucially, to apologize to him, to realize that he can feel remorse for his family, and, even in the diminished ending, to admire Jim's loyalty to the wounded Tom. The nightmare of racial prejudice has been an elemental part of the work of ethnic novelists, black and white, Toni Morrison and William Faulkner—and Mark Twain's own ambivalences make *Huckleberry Finn* a point of departure for fictional treatments of blacks and Jews, exiles and women, minorities who, as the then Le Roi Jones said, feel "the intellectual gulf that causes any serious man to be estranged from the mainstream of American life."[7] As Mark Twain well comprehended, this existential estrangement felt by Huck from the religiosity of Miss Watson, the bigotry of his father, the arrogance of the Grangerfords, the mendacity of the Duke and King, is even heavier for Jim, "only a nigger," who must add a racial estrangement to Huck's social and cultural resistance. In Lawrence Holland's view, Twain looked forward to the despair of Wright or Ellison, as the earlier author left his black man free but cut off from his family, with only forty dollars and the promise of a trip to the Territory awaiting him.

What about the Territory? Nostalgia, complains Wright Morris. Unreality, insists Bernard DeVoto, since the frontier was closing. Impermanence, I once wrote, since Huck was going there only briefly ahead of "the others." Still, that dream of escape, whether to sea, war, the West, or the city, continued to provide the closings for decades of American novels, and these endings were just as tenuous and fragile as Twain's. Sherwood Anderson sends his youths off to their territories with Huck Finn's mixture of hope and doubt; even Norman Mailer employs this ending for *Why Are We in Vietnam?*

An aspect of *Huckleberry Finn* often overlooked by professors but embraced by students is its status as a contribution to popular culture. While it might be simplistic to call Twain's information about rafting similar to Robert Coover's detailed compendium of baseball lore and statistics, and while comparisons to some popular forms like slave narratives or prison literature might be strained, Mark Twain's novel still hews quite closely to some basic American popular forms. He is both a local colorist in his vignettes of town life along the river and a brilliant parodist of romantic and sentimental fiction and poetry—from Tom Sawyer's fabrications to Emmeline Grangerford's verses. And the Mark Twain who would write detective stories featuring Tom Sawyer or Pudd'nhead Wilson supplies elements of mystery (Pap's death) or crime (the plot to steal the Wilkses' money) or escape. In a larger sense, *Huckleberry Finn* fits the popular genre of spy novel, when Huck dons his various disguises or lies about his past and his identity in order to enter behind enemy lines to gain information about pursuit and flight. Ultimately, all towns become enemy territory, and Huckleberry Finn

7. *Home* (New York: William Morrow, 1966), p. 186.

himself is a dangerous spy who would subvert religion, culture, and legal systems. Finally, like Raymond Chandler's Philip Marlowe, Huck Finn seems condemned to walk down America's mean streets to learn just how savage people can be to each other. Using his innocent eye, Huck views American culture as if it had never been described properly and gives a Dreiserian feel for detailed novelty in the descriptions of customs. The popular mode that the novel most clearly fits, set as it is in antebellum times, is that of the historical novel; it remains, with Margaret Mitchell's *Gone With the Wind*, one of the most persistent monuments to that form.

Most American, of course, is *Huckleberry Finn* as a monument, perhaps *the* monument, of American humor. After Walter Blair's and Hamlin Hill's work, little needs to be said about Mark Twain as a resource for American humorists. Southwestern humor, local color, *New Yorker* wits, bemused little men created by Robert Benchley and James Thurber, stand-up comedians rehearsing their childhood traumas—Twain looms over all. *Huckleberry Finn* bears close resemblance to the darkest strains of American humor, the black chaotic vision of Nathanael West or John Hawkes, the macabre ironies of Ellison's *Invisible Man* where the narrator understands how one can be free, like Huck himself, yet the man who is not free—Jim—is still free enough to realize an absence of freedom in Huck of which he, as a white, is unaware. Huck Finn, young and grim, sustains a typical American humorous stance. "Take up your cross and relax," he seems to say. To document the continuity of this role of darkly youthful commentator on Southern excesses, one has only to turn to Faulker's Ike, or Bayard, or Chick to discover the shadow of Twain's Huck.

Youth is the essential quality of *Huckleberry Finn*. As in the case of humor, the connections are very clear between Huck and Hemingway's boys trying to understand their old men, or Anderson's boys who want to know why, or Salinger's prep-school dropout; less clear, perhaps, but equally plausible, are the connections with James's Maisie and Fitzgerald's Basil. Huckleberry Finn moves through adolescence with fear and wonder, and much of the novel's greatness stems from his youthful encounters with reality, with a young American's dreams and nightmares. In *Huckleberry Finn*, Mark Twain attends seriously to the loss of innocence and the beginnings of wisdom, and Huck's voice is most authentic when introspective.

III

Once I was talking to a psychology professor in the university parking lot, and I broke off the conversation with, "I've got to go now and teach *Huckleberry Finn*." My colleague peered at me and wryly asked, "What are you going to teach him?" "Come *on*," I responded, "you know what I mean." His reply has remained with me, part of my professorial baggage: "No, I don't. Some day you'll say you're going to teach students, *about Huckleberry Finn*. Then, you'll be a teacher, my boy." What have I taught students, Harvard and Stanford and University of California students with literary sophistication they had not used yet, Ohio State and San Francisco State students to whom novels were mysteries to be unraveled, about *Huckleberry Finn*? All of the above, I guess, but, more fundamentally, five critical ideas about great moments in this most American of texts.

First, a crucial step in Huck's development is the same step shown by many American novelists in the 1930s, and it is indicated by a pronoun. American writing changed during the Depression years, says John Dos Passos, from discussions of *I* to *We*. And Ernest Hemingway at the end of *To Have and Have Not* evokes the absurdity of a man alone. As Chapter 11 of Mark Twain's novel ends, Huck, having learned that the slave-catchers are close on the trail, rushes to awaken Jim with the words, "Git up and hump yourself, Jim! There ain't a minute to lose. They're after us!" (p. 92). Only they weren't after *us*; they were after Jim, the escaped slave. But Huck's use of the pronoun is accurate: he has made, before he really knows it, his commitment to Jim, to man's fate, to the idea that no man is an island, to solidarity, to brotherhood. To me, those lines are among Twain's greatest, and to my students they give the true subtext of the novel.

Next, more obviously, we discuss Huck's basically pragmatic decision in Chapter 16 to tell a lie rather than to give Jim up, as Huck's society would dictate. A born liar, Huck is forced to come to a decision not about the act but about the issue he will lie about. "Well, then, says I, what's the use of you learning to do right, when it's troublesome to do right and ain't no trouble to do wrong, and the wages is just the same? I was stuck. I couldn't answer that. So I reckoned I wouldn't bother no more about it, but after this always do which ever came handiest at the time" (p. 128). The ability to eschew the Puritan ethic, to junk Edwards for Franklin, to judge practically, to make a distinction between a theoretical absolute and a real-life situation, represents, to many American students, Huck Finn's true intellectual position as an ad hoc moralist. Naturally, this passage leads to Huck's further development of a quintessentially American position of practical tinkerer and moral improviser (see Joseph Heller's Orr in *Catch-22* for a World War II version of Huck as survivor, complete with lies, fishing line, and raft) when in Chapter 31 he gives voice to the phrase that has echoed down to one hundred years of American readers. Faced with the choice between a heaven based on rigid ideas of Southern racism and a hell based on personal knowledge of a man's worth, Huckleberry Finn is free—"All right, then, I'll *go* to hell" (p. 272). When he tears up his letter that would have betrayed Jim—no matter that the action is anachronistic since, unknown to him, Jim has been freed—Huck turns away from written documents, accepts his oral tradition, and accepts also the nightmare of his choice, entering the Southern American's heart of darkness. Just as Faulkner's Ike McCaslin gives up the world of farms and banks for the wilderness of bears, Indians, and slaves, Huck Finn chooses true values. Like Lambert Strether, Nick Carraway, Niel Herbert, and Jack Burden, and like their creators, James, Fitzgerald, Cather, and Warren, Huckleberry Finn and Mark Twain are part of the American novel's panoply of innovators of moral commitment.

Thirdly, for a century of fiction that calls attention to man's inhumanity to man, Huck's dark, grotesque (how appropriate that in 1952 Flannery O'Connor, made an honorary member of the Mark Twain Society, sent two dollars "in memory of Mark Twain") death-obsessed imagination prepares students to confront murders and lynchings, death camps and atomic bombs. Young Huck can easily judge adult justice when in Chapter 33 the King and Duke, evil though they may be, are punished by a vengeful mob of ordinary citizens who use tar, feathers, and a rail: "Human beings *can* be awful cruel to one another" (p. 291).

Then as Huckleberry Finn in Chapter 15 brings himself to understand that his own cruel tricks have hurt Jim, for Jim is a person, not a thing, Twain prepares the way for Ike McCaslin's apology to all those black members of his family who were destroyed by his grandfather's dehumanizing acts of miscegenation and incest. Ike reads the ledgers and turns his maturity into one long, and fruitless, apology. Huck, equally capable of feeling shame and guilt, matures beyond racism to humanity: "It was fifteen minutes before I could work myself up to go and humble myself to a nigger—but I done it, and I warn't ever sorry for it afterwards, neither" (p. 121). But just as Ike fails to change the ways of his family and society, and becomes helpless at the end of the novel in which "The Bear" represents the moral center—and thus in "Delta Autumn" all that Ike has learned seems to be cheapened and parodied—so Huck fails to change the ways of Tom and the Phelps family, and during Jim's imprisonment at the novel's close all that Huck has learned about dignity and brotherhood seems to be mocked.

Finally, freedom. All of American literature, growls Hemingway, comes from this book, from Huck's ability to flow with the river, to light out for the Territory, to cover the American landscape along with the heroes of Thomas Wolfe, Jack Kerouac, Clancy Sigal. . . . East to West, or the reverse, South to North, or the reverse ("North Toward Home," says Willie Morris). The words need no explication for American students who encounter Cooper's Natty Bumppo in the forest, the folklore of Daniel Boone moving on, Thoreau at Walden Pond, Melville's Ishmael on the ocean, Hemingway's Nick Adams in the Big Two-Hearted River, Faulkner's Ike in the Big Woods. "We said there warn't no home like a raft, after all. Other places do seem so cramped up and smothery, but a raft don't. You feel mighty free and easy and comfortable on a raft" (p. 156).

It is a complex fate, remarked Henry James, to be an American. Lewis P. Simpson articulated clearly how well Mark Twain copes with this complexity in *Huckleberry Finn*, a book that in many ways calls for Matthew Arnold's stricture on Shakespeare—"Others abide our question, thou art free"—and transcends criticism. Twain's, says Simpson, was "a life dedicated at once to America as the idea of an unfolding revolutionary revelation, and redemption in human affairs; to the counter idea of America as an accomplished, a permanent, superior arrangement of existence."[8] And if Europe is approached by its novelists in an objective and historical mode, and America in a subjective, geographical mode, as Stephen Spender would have it, then there is no better way to explain America and Americans to our stu-

8. "Introduction to Mark Twain: Critical Perspectives," *SoR* 4 (1968): 492.

dents than through Mark Twain's enduring and revealing subjective "I" of Huckleberry Finn and geographical image of a boy on a raft on the river. American literature, continues Spender, shows "the identification of the single separate American with the other Americans and beyond the whole continent the whole earth and nature and the universe. . . . The unexplored continent spoke in the present tense."[9] That vision has never been more poignantly expressed than in Huck's words: "You feel mighty free and easy and comfortable on a raft."

Happy my former student who went down the river on a raft. For myself, the closest I came was to drive to Hannibal, climb over fences, cross railroad tracks, and finally gain a view of the Mississippi—narrow, brown, slow moving. Happier the professors and students who can share *Huckleberry Finn* in the realms of imaginative freedom given us by the author who has reached us all, for a century, by combining vernacular speech, dark visions, experiential knowledge, isolation and commitment, optimism and pessimism, romance and reality, and, best of all, freshness and lyricism that make the book as new today as in 1885. Huck Finn, in Mark Twain's vision, approaches his America just as an earlier American in Scott Fitzgerald's imagination faced the "last and greatest of human dreams; for a transitory enchanted moment man must have held his breath in the presence of this continent, compelled into an aesthetic contemplation he neither understood nor desired, face to face for the last time in history with something commensurate to his capacity for wonder."[10] For Huck Finn, America dawns with wonder in Chapter 19: "and you see the mist curl up off of the water, and the east reddens up, and the river . . . then the nice breeze springs up, and comes fanning you from over there, so cool and fresh, and sweet to smell, on account of the woods and the flowers" (p. 158). Then Huck recalls the smell of dead fish as well, to yoke lyric beauty to realistic ugliness. Teach *Huckleberry Finn*? Why, the book teaches itself; for a hundred years it has taught us all, students and professors alike, to share Mark's and Huck's last best hope in America.

---

9. *Love-Hate Relations* (New York: Random House, 1974), p. 15.
10. *The Great Gatsby* (New York: Charles Scribner's Sons, 1925), pp. 217–18.

16 ALLISON R. ENSOR

The Illustrating of *Huckleberry Finn*: A Centennial Perspective

W HAT did Huckleberry Finn look like? Since the novel is a first-person narrative, Huck gives no description of himself, and few if any clues are provided by what he reports the other characters as saying. We can, of course, use our imaginations, and there are those who would argue that this is best. One can do little else with the familiar Riverside, Bantam, Signet, Penguin, or Norton Critical editions used in so many classrooms, for they contain no illustrations beyond those on their covers. When the novel's text appears in an anthology of American literature, there are usually no pictures at all. But if one reads *Huckleberry Finn* in an illustrated edition, as everyone did one hundred years ago, then his imagination is directed, supplemented, by pictures revealing the artist's conception of Huck, Jim, Tom Sawyer, the Grangerfords, the King and the Duke, the Wilks girls, Aunt Sally and Uncle Silas Phelps. And in most instances the artist depicts these characters in action against the backgrounds of the places where that action occurred: St. Petersburg, the Grangerford house, the Wilks place, the Phelps farm, and, above all, the Mississippi River.[1]

Beginning with Edward Winsor Kemble (1861–1933), the illustrator chosen by Samuel Clemens and his publisher, Charles Webster, for the first edition, artist after artist has assumed the task of depicting the adventures of Huckleberry Finn. The approaches and techniques used have varied widely. Some have drawn a great many pictures, others relatively few. Some made black-and-white pen-and-ink drawings; others produced full-color oil paintings. Some pictures are highly realistic and vividly detailed; others are so impressionistic that out of context one would be unlikely to connect them with the novel at all. Some artists have worked with a good deal of knowledge of the

1.   I should like to acknowledge my debt to the Better English Fund of the University of Tennessee, Knoxville, for a grant that enabled me to do research for this essay in New York State. My thanks also to Mr. William Loos, curator of the Rare Book Room of the Buffalo and Erie County Public Library, Buffalo, N.Y., for his kindness in allowing me to examine the extensive collection of *Huckleberry Finn* editions there and for his assistance in obtaining copies of many of the illustrations from these editions. Ms. Lisa Browar was very helpful in providing me with access to the Jean Webster McKinney papers in the Helen D. Lockwood Library at Vassar College, Poughkeepsie, N.Y. The papers contain letters by Clemens, Webster, and Kemble, as well as a number of Kemble's original illustrations for the first edition of *Huckleberry Finn*. I have benefited from the comments of Prof. Paul Watkins of the Department of Art and Music Education at the University of Tennessee, Knoxville.

Mississippi valley; others have had none at all. Some artists have emphasized the darker, more violent moments of the novel; others have ignored these almost entirely. Even Clemens himself apparently wanted the illustrations to blink at some of the realities that the text portrayed.

How many illustrated editions of *Huckleberry Finn* have there been? It is not an easy question to answer. Michael Patrick Hearn lists forty-five "notable" editions of the novel;[2] of these, twenty-three were illustrated by eighteen different artists. One is illustrated with stills from a film version of the novel, a procedure that several publishers domestic and foreign have followed. The *Huckleberry Finn* collection at the Buffalo and Erie County Public Library contains about sixty editions in English, plus over seventy-five foreign-language editions.[3] Well over half of these are illustrated. Besides the standard editions of the novel, there have been profusely illustrated abridged and simplified children's editions, including a "Better Little Book" with pictures on every other page and two quite different *Classics Illustrated* comic books.[4]

Clearly, among artists who illustrated *Huckleberry Finn* the best known were Norman Rockwell and Thomas Hart Benton. Neither Howard Pyle nor N. C. Wyeth attempted *Huckleberry Finn*, though they did illustrate other books by Clemens. Certain of Rockwell's pictures are well known today, though more for their appearance in books devoted to Rockwell's work than for their presence in the original Heritage Press edition. The Rockwell paintings are almost certainly better known to the American public than any other illustrations of the novel. Benton's drawings are, in contrast, not widely known. They are seldom reproduced, and the limited edition in which they were published is not easily found. More accessible is his depiction of Huck and Jim in part of a mural for the Missouri state capitol; it has been reproduced several times. The original Kemble drawings have appeared in more editions, American and foreign, than any other and are still readily available, as in *The Annotated Huckleberry Finn*, the 1979 Franklin Library edition, and in the forthcoming Iowa-California edition of the novel.

To attempt to deal with every illustrated edition of *Huckleberry Finn* is clearly beyond the scope of this essay. What can be done is to look at some of the most significant illustrated editions—those of Kemble, Rockwell, Benton, and certain lesser-known artists—and to consider the various approaches they have taken as they tried to aid the reader in visualizing the characters and action of this major American novel.

The story of the illustrating of the first edition of *Huckleberry Finn* has

2. *The Annotated Huckleberry Finn*, ed. Michael Patrick Hearn (New York: Clarkson N. Potter, 1981), pp. 374–75.

3. These figures apparently represent only a small part of the total number of editions. Robert Rodney's *Mark Twain International: A Bibliography and Interpretation of His Worldwide Popularity* (Westport, Conn.: Greenwood Press, 1982), p. 264, states that between 1885 and 1976 there were 841 editions of *Huckleberry Finn*. Of these, 145 were domestic and 696 foreign. He states that the novel has been published in 47 countries in 53 languages.

4. Oddly enough, both issues of *Classics Illustrated* bear the same date, January 1945. Both are designated #19.

been told several times—by the illustrator himself, by his model, and by recent scholars.[5] Certain parts of it must necessarily be recounted here.

After brief consideration of an artist named Hooper whose services could
be obtained rather cheaply, Clemens turned to E. W. Kemble, son of the
founder and publisher of the *San Francisco Alta California*, the paper that
printed many of Clemens's 1867 letters from Europe and the Holy Land.
Kemble, now in the East, had done work for *Harper's Bazaar*, the *New York
Graphic*, and *Life*. He would later recall that Clemens's attention was attracted to him by a *Life* drawing of a little boy being stung by a bee, a boy
who matched Clemens's mental image of Huck Finn. Clemens's letter to his
publisher of 31 March 1884, however, mentions a different *Life* drawing:
"There *is* a Kemble on 'Life,'" he wrote, "but is he the man who illustrated
the applying of ,electrical protectors to door knobs, door-mats &c & electrical hurriers to messengers, waiters, &c, 4 or 5 weeks ago. *That* is the man
I want to try."[6] The drawing in question, "Some Uses for Electricity," had
appeared in *Life*'s issue of 13 March 1884 and included a picture Clemens
understandably failed to mention, of a book agent being shocked by an elec-
trified doormat.[7] Kemble was contacted and an agreement worked out
whereby he would produce about 175 illustrations for a fee of $1,200. In
some respects Kemble might have seemed poorly qualified: he was only
twenty-three years old, he had been drawing professionally for only two
years, he had never had a contract for book illustrations before, and he had
never seen the Mississippi River valley or the South. As he candidly admitted
latter, "I had up to that time, never been further south than Sandy Hook."

Undaunted by his lack of firsthand information concerning the setting of
the new novel, Kemble set about illustrating it as best he could from the
chapters of the manuscript he had been given. As his model for Huck Finn
he selected a sixteen-year-old boy named Courtland P. Morris but usually
called Cort. Young Morris was a native of New Jersey living in the Bronx at
the time Kemble asked him to pose, offering the boy four dollars a week. As
Kemble later recalled, Morris was "a bit tall for the ideal boy, but I could
jam him down a few pegs in my drawing and use him for the other characters." And that is just what Kemble did: Morris served as model not only for
Huck Finn but also for every character, male or female, white or black, in
the entire book. Kemble made use of a variety of costumes—an old sunbonnet and faded skirt for Mrs. Judith Loftus, an old frock coat and padded
waistline for the King.

Clemens was in the meantime getting impatient. "I sent the MS. to-day,"

5. E. W. Kemble, "Illustrating 'Huckleberry Finn,'" *The Colophon* 1, pt. 1 (February
1930): article 5; Courtland P. Morris, "The Model for Huck Finn," *MTQ* 2:4 (1938): 22–23;
Beverly R. David, "The Pictorial *Huck Finn*: Mark Twain and His Illustrator, E. W. Kemble,"
AQ 26 (1974): 331–51; Michael Patrick Hearn, "Mark Twain, E. W. Kemble, and *Huckleberry Finn*," *ABC* n.s. 2 (November–December 1981): 14–19. Hearn also discussed the Kemble illustrations in his *Annotated Huckleberry Finn*, pp. 11–16.

6. *Mark Twain, Business Man*, ed. Samuel C. Webster (Boston: Little, Brown, 1946),
p. 246.

7. This drawing is reproduced in *The Annotated Huckleberry Finn*, p. 11.

he wrote Webster on 12 April. "Let Kemble rush—time is already growing short."[8] Such pressure would not seem an ideal situation for an artist, and Kemble's predicament was worsened by conditions at his house. He wrote Webster on 1 May, "We all have the moving craze & are experiencing such little delights as eating our meals from off the mantle [*sic*] piece, bathing in a coal scuttle behind a fire screen &c &c. I have tried to work but cannot make it go." He included a sketch labeled "A faint idea of my condition," which depicts the artist seated on a barrel that is resting on a box, his pad leaned against a stepladder, as a passing worker casts an eye over Kemble's shoulder.[9] Another difficulty Kemble had to deal with was lack of access to the entire manuscript. At one point he asked Webster to "send me the manuscript from the XIII chapter on, as there are illustrations here & there which are described very minutely & I am afraid to touch them without the reading matter to refer to."[10]

Kemble did manage to get some of his illustrations finished, and they were passed on to Clemens. The author was not enthusiastic. "All right & good, & will answer," he told Webster on 7 May, after having seen the proposed cover for the book, "although the boy's mouth is a trifle more Irishy than necessary."[11] On 24 May, Clemens had a more detailed objection to make:

> Some of the pictures are good, but none of them are very *very* good. The faces are generally ugly, & wrenched into over-expression amounting sometimes to distortion. As a rule (though not always) the people in these pictures are forbidding and repulsive. Reduction will modify them, no doubt, but it can hardly make them pleasant folk to look at. An artist shouldn't follow a book too literally, perhaps—if this is the necessary result. And mind you, much of the drawing, in these pictures is careless & bad.
>
> The pictures will *do*—they will just barely do—& that is the best I can say for them.
>
> The frontispiece has the usual blemish—an ugly, ill-drawn face. Huck Finn is an exceedingly good-hearted boy, & should carry a good & good-looking face.
>
> Don't dishearten the artist—show him where he has *improved*, rather than where he has failed, & punch him up to improve more.[12]

The theory of illustration that Clemens espouses here is interesting and perhaps surprising: that an illustrator should not follow the text too closely, that the pictures should not tell as much truth as the text. Clemens made exactly this point again in a letter to Webster on 11 June. Now much better satisfied, he declared, "I *knew* Kemble had it *in* him, if he would only modify his violences & come down to careful, painstaking work. This batch of pictures is most rattling good. They please me exceedingly." Having said this, he went on to object to a particular picture. "But you must knock out one of them," he declared, "—the lecherous old rascal kissing the girl at the

8. *Mark Twain, Business Man*, p. 248.
9. Ibid., pp. 251–52.
10. Quoted in David, "Pictorial," p. 336. Corrected against original in McKinney Papers, Vassar College.
11. *Mark Twain's Letters to His Publishers, 1867–1894*, ed. Hamlin Hill (Berkeley: University of California Press, 1967), p. 174; *Mark Twain, Business Man*, p. 253.
12. *Mark Twain, Business Man*, pp. 255–56.

E. W. Kemble: Frontispiece of the first edition of *Adventures of Huckleberry Finn,*
1885.

campmeeting. It is powerful good, but it mustn't go in—don't forget it. Let's not make *any* pictures of the campmeeting. The subject won't *bear* illustrating. It is a disgusting thing, & pictures are sure to tell the truth about it too plainly." [13] One is reminded of Clemens's statement to Dan Beard, the illustrator of *A Connecticut Yankee*, about five years later: "I have endeavored to put in all the coarseness and vulgarity . . . that is necessary and rely upon you for all the refinement and delicacy of humor your facile pen can depict." [14] Accordingly, the offending illustration was omitted, and the only campmeeting picture that survives is one of two young people "courting on the sly." Kemble apparently needed no advice from Clemens to avoid portraying Huck and Jim in the state of nudity Huck says they were often in. And there is certainly nothing risqué about Kemble's picture of the King enacting the "Royal Nonesuch." Even so, the caption diverts our attention with the word *Tragedy*. [15]

The only further objection Clemens made to Kemble's pictures concerned a matter of riverboat knowledge. In drawing a wrecked steamboat, Kemble (who, we remember, did not always have as much of the manuscript as he needed) placed on it the name *Texas*, apparently assuming from mention of the texas deck that this was the boat's name. Clemens pointed out that "*every* boat" had a texas and that "that word had better be removed from that pilot house—that is where a boat's *name* is put, & that particular boat's name was, Walter Scott." [16] Clemens raised no objections to other errors that have been noted: the King was given a black hat in the Wilks episode, when the text specifically says he wore a white beaver hat; Joanna Wilks, according to the text about the same age as Huck, is shown considerably older. [17] Huck himself hardly looks a consistent fourteen throughout the book.

Clemens appears to have made no comment about what must appear rather striking to anyone studying the work of a variety of illustrators: Kem-

13. Ibid., p. 260. David, "Pictorial," stresses Clemens's desire that the illustrations not be too explicit, that they soften the harsher impressions created by the text.

14. Quoted in "Mark Twain, the Man, as Dan Beard Knew," *San Francisco Examiner*, 25 April 1910, p. 16.

15. The captions for Kemble's drawings are a unique feature of the first edition; while some of them are objective, others introduce a note of humor foreign to the rest of the book. Walter Blair attributed their authorship to Charles L. Webster (*Mark Twain and Huck Finn* [Berkeley: University of California Press, 1967], p. 360) as did I in "The Contributions of Charles Webster and Albert Bigelow Paine to *Huckleberry Finn*," *AL* 40 (1968): 222–27. Recently Beverly R. David has argued ("Mark Twain and the Legends for *Huckleberry Finn*," *ALR* 15 [1982]: 155–65) that Kemble wrote the original captions, which were put into final form by Clemens himself. David acknowledges, "There is no concrete evidence of Clemens's authorship" ("Legends," p. 162). Much of the question seems to turn on the proper interpretation of Webster's writing Clemens on 22 July 1884 that he had "inserted the titles of the *pages* and *pictures*" in "a batch of *paged* proof" that Clemens had already seen (quoted by David, "Legends," p. 156). To Blair this indicated that Webster was the author of the captions and running heads; David contends, "Clemens had received the original drawings with captions [by Kemble] and recaptioned them when necessary. Webster had then inserted these new 'titles' (headings for the separate pages and legends for the pictures). Now Webster was apparently requesting that his uncle double-check the accuracy of the titles before they went from paged proof into final print" ("Legends," pp. 156–57).

16. *Mark Twain, Business Man*, p. 262.

17. Hearn, "Twain, Kemble, and *Huck Finn*," p. 17.

ble's inclination to illustrate purely imaginary scenes. In only one instance do these scenes involve the main characters. At the beginning of Chapter 15, Kemble shows Huck and Jim in Cairo, Illinois, trying to sell their raft. Huck and Jim of course missed Cairo entirely; selling the raft there was something they only intended to do. Among the most capricious drawings are those showing the distressed parents of young Stephen Dowling Bots, the boy memorialized in Emmeline Grangerford's poem; the King as the pirate he claims to have been; Henry VIII tossing tea into Boston harbor, one of Huck's historical mistakes; Hanner Proctor with the mumps, which Huck claims she has; witches, apparently as imagined by the slave who brings Jim's food to him; a prisoner about to cut off his hand, as Tom says some of "the best authorities" have done in order to escape; and finally a picture labeled "One of His Ancestors," in which Kemble plays with the ambiguity of Huck's statement that Uncle Silas's warming pan "belonged to one of his ancestors with a long wooden handle that came over from England with William the Conqueror." Kemble depicts the ancestor with both a long-handled warming pan and a long wooden leg. Mention might also be made of the satirical drawing at the conclusion of the chapter in which the King and the Duke appear for the first time: in it the emblems of royalty intermingle with the whiskey bottle and satchel of the two frauds.

Most of the 174 drawings in the first edition are of a different nature, of course, for they simply depict the action of the book. Except for the frontispiece, none occupies a full page, and many are surrounded by text on three sides. Since there were to be so many drawings, it was necessary for Kemble to depict virtually every scene of importance in the book. Kemble did not decline to picture some of the novel's harsher realities: Jim Turner menaced by the men on the *Walter Scott*, the Grangerford-Shepherdson feud (though no dead bodies are shown), the shooting of Boggs by Colonel Sherburn (we see Boggs from the rear), the King and the Duke ridden out of town on a rail (the caption calls it "Traveling by Rail," thus inviting a laugh at what is for Huck a moment of pity and sadness). Nevertheless, as we will see, Kemble did miss certain scenes that have been great favorites with later illustrators. Kemble's pictures were considerably reduced in size for publication, as they were originally something like six and a half by eight inches. The originals are now scattered; Vassar College, Poughkeepsie, New York, has thirty-seven of them, plus the original design for the cover.

One of Kemble's illustrations was initially reproduced in a form different from that in which Kemble drew it. For the last picture of Chapter 32, Kemble showed Huck standing before an irate Uncle Silas and a grinning Aunt Sally, as the latter asks her husband, "Who do you reckon it is?" Apparently some mischievous person in the printing establishment found the expressions on the faces suggestive; it may have looked to him as if Huck had suddenly come upon some intimate scene. At any rate, he proceeded to alter the original drawing by adding a penis protruding from Uncle Silas's trousers.[18] The change was discovered before any books were issued, but one

18. Both David and Hearn discuss the "obscene" drawing at some length. For an earlier, important treatment of the matter, see Franklin J. Meine, "Some Notes on the First Editions of *Huck Finn*," *ABC* 10 (June 1960): 31–34.

would like to know what choice profanities escaped Clemens's lips when he first learned that this particular bit of mischief would cause his new book to miss the Christmas trade of 1884. The British and Canadian editions were able to appear in December, but the American had to wait until February of the next year.

On the whole Clemens seems to have been satisfied with Kemble's work, particularly in the last part of the book. "Kemble's pictures are mighty good, now," he wrote Webster on 1 July,[19] and in another letter later in the year he seems to take pride in the *Century*'s Richard Watson Gilder having described Kemble as "a gem of an artist."[20] It is not surprising that in August 1887, as he was planning his *Library of Humor*, he wrote Fred Hall and Webster: "I suggest that you get *Kemble* as artist; and that you get him right away, if he is getable."[21] Kemble was, in fact, paid $2,000 for the 204 illustrations in the *Library of Humor*.[22] In time, though, Clemens became disenchanted with Kemble's work; in reference to the illustrating of *A Connecticut Yankee*, he said:

> I prefer this time to contract for the very best an artist can do. This time I want pictures, not black-board outlines and charcoal sketches. If Kemble illustrations for my last book were handed me today, I could understand how tiresome to me that sameness would get to be, when distributed through a whole book, and I would put them promptly in the fire.[23]

It is scarcely surprising, then, that Clemens did not call upon Kemble to illustrate either of the sequels to *Huckleberry Finn* published in Clemens's lifetime, *Tom Sawyer Abroad* and *Tom Sawyer, Detective*.

Kemble may well have supposed that he was done with Huck and his adventures after 1884. In fact he was to produce eight more illustrations based on the novel. For the Autograph Edition of 1899 Kemble did four pen-and-wash pictures, and these were used as full-page illustrations in various editions of later years, including the widely available Author's National Edition, which used as a frontispiece Kemble's 1899 picture of Huck arriving at the Phelps farm to be met by a large black woman with three small children peeping out from behind her. Also in 1899 Kemble drew three illustrations for the *New York World* of 10 December, when its comic supplement ran a special Mark Twain number. Kemble's final drawing, made in 1932, the year before his death, shows Huck, Tom, and Jim reading about themselves in a copy of *Huckleberry Finn*. The drawing was done at George Macy's request and placed on the title page of the Limited Editions Club edition of the novel.[24]

Whatever second thoughts Clemens may have had about Kemble's ability

19. *Mark Twain, Business Man*, p. 263.
20. Ibid., p. 282.
21. *Mark Twain's Letters to His Publishers*, p. 223.
22. Ibid., p. 230, n. 4.
23. Ibid., p. 254.
24. All of the post-1884 Kemble illustrations are reproduced in *The Annotated Huckleberry Finn*: illustrations for the *World* appear on pp. 106, 205, 230; for the Autograph Edition on pp. 120, 182, 237, 290; and for the Limited Editions Club on p. 44.

as an artist, the verdict of posterity has been favorable. Thomas Hart Benton declared in 1942, "Kemble was a good illustrator and he did a particularly good job with Huck's adventures. . . . No illustrator who has tackled the book since has in any way approached his delicate fantasy, his pat humor, or his ability to produce an atmosphere of pathos."[25] Much more recently, Michael Patrick Hearn declared that no artist—Benton and Norman Rockwell included—has outdone Kemble. With perhaps some exaggeration, he found that "Huck Finn himself is remembered as much for Kemble's image of the good-hearted boy as for Twain's description."[26] It was, Hearn concludes, "a perfect marriage of author and illustrator."[27] There has, however, been some dissent about Kemble's ability as an artist. Joel Chandler Harris, some of whose work was illustrated by Kemble, commented, "For a man who has no conception whatever of human nature, Kemble does very well. But he is too doggoned flip to suit me."[28] Thomas Hart Benton complained that Kemble "was not much of a designer. . . . he didn't know how to lay out a space and set up a clean finished structure therein. His pictures came to no pictorial conclusion. They just ended." Benton also objected to Kemble's "monotonous pen-and-ink methods" and particularly to the fact that most of the Mississippi River characters looked like "Connecticut Yankees."[29]

The Kemble illustrations were used repeatedly in subsequent editions of the novel. Occasionally all of them appeared, but more often only a few were chosen. Leo Marx's edition for Bobbs-Merrill (1967), for instance, used only five and made them all into full-page illustrations. The Franklin Library edition (1979) used many of the Kemble drawings, with some as full-page illustrations and others printed the same size as in the first edition. Kemble's pictures have also appeared in a number of foreign-language editions, including Danish, Lettish, Russian, Swedish, and Ukranian. Furthermore, according to Kemble, his illustrations were used as a basis for the first (1920) film version of the novel. The director, Kemble recalled, "took a copy of the original edition and made his characters fit my drawings."[30]

Apparently the second American to illustrate *Huckleberry Finn* was Worth Brehm (1883–1928), an Indiana native whose pictures of life in that state were published in *Outing* magazine and thus came to the attention of Harper's. The firm commissioned Brehm to illustrate first *Tom Sawyer* and then its sequel. His *Huckleberry Finn* appeared in 1923.[31] Brehm's approach was entirely different from Kemble's. Instead of a great many drawings, Brehm prepared only nine, including a color frontispiece of Huck alone, fishing. Each picture occupied a full page and included much fuller detail than Kemble's

25. "A Note by the Illustrator," in *Adventures of Huckleberry Finn*, ed. Bernard DeVoto (New York: Limited Editions Club, 1942), pp. lxxi, lxxii–lxxiii.

26. *Annotated Huckleberry Finn*, p. 16.

27. "Twain, Kemble, and *Huck Finn*," p. 19.

28. Quoted in David, "Visions of the South: Joel Chandler Harris and His Illustrators," *ALR* 9 (1976): 198.

29. Benton, "Note," p. lxxii.

30. Kemble, "Illustrating," last page (unnumbered).

31. A British edition of the same year, published in London by Eveleigh Nash & Grayson, carried a color frontispiece of Huck and twelve stills from the 1920 silent film.

had. It was of course necessary for Brehm to choose as subjects scenes from various parts of the book, but he could leave out some sections, too, and consequently there is nothing of the Shepherdson-Grangerford feud or the Wilks family episode. There is no shooting of Boggs or punishment of the King and the Duke. The one scene of violence had been done by Kemble too: Jim Turner lying bound on the floor aboard the *Walter Scott* while two men stand over him, threatening his life. Brehm's picture is perhaps more ominous, more sinister. More realistic than Kemble's, it is also considerably darker. Brehm's other pictures frequently bear some resemblance to Kemble's: there is Huck being cussed by Pap at the Widow Douglas's (though Brehm has Pap outside, with his head in the window), Jim encountering what he believes is Huck's ghost on Jackson's Island, the King and the Duke fleeing their pursuers (almost a mirror image of Kemble's picture), the Duke's recitation of Hamlet's soliloquy on the raft (Brehm provides an audience missing in Kemble's version), Aunt Sally standing on her bed to escape the rats. Only two scenes appear to have no Kemble precedent: Huck's arrival at the Phelps farm, when he is surrounded by a large number of dogs, and the last picture of the book, in which Aunt Polly forces Huck to crawl out from under Tom's bed, while Aunt Sally looks on.

As Brehm's was the most notable illustrated *Huck Finn* of the 1920s, the most notable of the 1930s was an edition illustrated by A. S. Forrest.[32] This time there were seventeen illustrations, beginning with a frontispiece showing the by now familiar scene of Jim cowering before what he believes is the ghost of Huck Finn. As in Brehm's edition, the frontispiece was in color, while all the rest were black-and-white full-page drawings. Except for this frontispiece, Forrest seems to have sought to avoid following too closely in the footsteps of Kemble and Brehm. With the *Walter Scott*, for example, Forrest does not show us a scene onboard, but rather the sinking boat as Huck and Jim see it from their raft. The Shepherdson-Grangerford feud was the subject of two pictures illustrating passages separated by only one paragraph: the men running along the bank shouting "Kill them, kill them!" and then Huck's covering up the faces of the dead bodies. The Wilks episode is likewise represented by two pictures, both involving Mary Jane. In one, she puts the bag of money into the King's hands; in the other, she and Huck are in her room, with her partially packed trunk at hand, and Huck has just revealed the truth about her supposed uncles. Forrest's line drawings are somewhat fuller in detail, especially as to background, than Kemble's.

The 1940s brought to the illustrating of *Huckleberry Finn* both Norman Rockwell and Thomas Hart Benton.[33] Rockwell had already done *Tom Sawyer* for the Heritage Press edition of 1936, a task for which he must have seemed eminently suitable, in view of his many *Saturday Evening Post* covers depicting boys who might well have been characters in *Tom Sawyer* or *Huckleberry Finn*. To acquire a sense of the actual place where some of the

32. London: Thomas Nelson & Sons, 1935.

33. *The Adventures of Huckleberry Finn* (New York: Heritage Press, 1940); *Huckleberry Finn*, ed. DeVoto.

novels' adventures occurred, Rockwell made a trip to Hannibal, Missouri, where he visited all the appropriate sites and acquired a lot of old clothes to take back to the East with him.[34] It has been said that though Rockwell was "perfect" for the *Tom Sawyer* illustrations, he "failed to capture the bitter satire" of *Huck Finn*.[35] Others might argue that even in *Tom Sawyer* the darker atmosphere, the harsher realities are missing. The complete absence of Injun Joe from any of the eight color illustrations is indicative of this too-sunny view of *Tom Sawyer*. The same viewpoint continues in his 1940 *Huckleberry Finn*.[36] It can hardly surprise us, of course, given what we know about Rockwell's homey, nostalgic depiction of life from his hundreds of covers for the *Saturday Evening Post* and other magazines. Too, in 1940 the world was a rather dark place: World War II was on in Europe, Hitler was running rampant, the conquest of Britain seemed a real possibility, and one could only wonder how long the United States might remain uninvolved. People wanted something lighter, something that would amuse them or make them feel warmer inside. Rockwell did his best to oblige.

As in the companion *Tom Sawyer*, there were to be eight full-page color illustrations plus much smaller black-and-white pictures at the beginning of each chapter and on certain other pages. We need not concern ourselves with these smaller illustrations, which are usually of objects rather than people (though Huck takes a bow on the title page and looks out at us from the top of the page listing the illustrations), except to note that Jim's coat of arms at the beginning of Chapter 38 is virtually identical to that drawn by Kemble.

Rockwell did a remarkable job of avoiding almost all of the darker side of *Huckleberry Finn*, its terror, violence, and death. The Grangerford-Shepherdson feud was left out entirely, as were the scene on the *Walter Scott*, the shooting of Boggs, and the tarring and feathering of the King and the Duke. In fact, the frontispiece presents the only really frightening moment depicted: Huck comes into his room at the Widow Douglas's to find Pap reared back in his chair waiting for him. Yet even here Rockwell's treatment minimizes the sinister quality that Benton and others were to bring out very strongly. Two other illustrations deal with St. Petersburg happenings: Miss Watson praying with Huck in her closet, and Jim with Huck, as the former listens to his hair-ball oracle. After Jim and Huck begin their journey downriver, Rockwell shows us Huck pretending to be a girl and trying to thread a needle as Mrs. Judith Loftus observes him closely. We see the King and the Duke on the raft with Jim and Huck as the King reveals his royal heritage. A few yards of the Mississippi River are visible, the only glimpse of the river we

34. Somewhat contradictory accounts of Rockwell's visit to Hannibal appear in Arthur Guptill, *Norman Rockwell, Illustrator* (New York: Watson-Guptill Publications, 1946), pp. 101–7, and in Rockwell's *My Adventures as an Illustrator* (Garden City, N.Y.: Doubleday, 1960), pp. 302–6.

35. *Annotated Huckleberry Finn*, p. 15.

36. See my "'Norman Rockwell Sentimentality': The Rockwell Illustrations for *Tom Sawyer* and *Huckleberry Finn*," in *The Mythologizing of Mark Twain* (Tuscaloosa: University of Alabama Press, 1984), pp. 15–36.

Norman Rockwell: Then Miss Watson took me in the closet
and prayed but nothing come of it.

get in the sixteen color plates for the two novels. One may also observe that Jim is scarcely more than a boy, a comment that has also been made about Kemble's later versions of Jim.[37] The episode at the Wilks home gets two pictures: in the first we have the King and the Duke embracing and weeping, with Peter Wilks's coffin supported on two chairs behind them. No one else is visible in the room, though the text indicates it is crowded with people. But Rockwell avoided crowd scenes throughout his work in *Tom Sawyer* and *Huck Finn*. Most of his *Huck Finn* pictures have two people; none has more than four. A second Wilks picture shows Huck with Mary Jane and her partly packed trunk as he begins to tell the truth about the supposed uncles. Finally, out of all the possible moments at the Phelps farm, Rockwell chose to show us Aunt Sally's fright over one of the green snakes Tom and Huck collected. Two small children look on amused.

What Rockwell seems to have done, here and in *Tom Sawyer*, is to portray the novel most Americans think they remember—a novel full of boyish play and pranks with a few serious moments here and there, but nothing really frightening[38]—certainly not the deaths of the Grangerfords, or of Boggs, or the plight of Jim as a runaway slave. For all Rockwell's desire to be authentic, and of course his pictures are highly detailed, one can hardly say that his illustrations give us the authentic *Huckleberry Finn*.

Only two years later Thomas Hart Benton had his turn as illustrator. In a six-page note he explained to the reader his views on illustration and commented on the work of some of his predecessors. Perhaps with Rockwell in mind, he commented that most modern illustrators "tend to be too positive in the matter of characterization," that they "tend to overwhelm the reader's own imagination, and to take away from the suggestiveness of words with a too-bald literalness of representation." He went on to praise Kemble for his suggestiveness and for certain of his characters, especially Jim, Pap, and the King. Benton even explained that his own pictures of those characters are "borrowed" from Kemble, because he "couldn't work up the crust to put new faces on these characters." Again, with Rockwell surely in mind, Benton observed that some illustrators have failed "even with all the proper factual detail which Kemble didn't know about." He then assured us that he knows the river well and "was raised among people who talked the language of Huck Finn's people, who thought like them, and acted like them"; the whole project of illustrating the book had been "a big, slambang emotional indulgence."

Even without Benton's preface, one would have guessed that he would try for something radically different from Rockwell's work. Benton's pictures are much less explicit, more "suggestive," to use his word. They are not oil paintings, for one thing; they are ink and sepia wash, with some outlining in black. Typical of Benton's work, there is a kind of rumpled quality to the bodies and clothing, an exaggeration of facial features, an elongation of form.

37. This is one of the objections raised by David, "Pictorial," p. 337.
38. The Heritage Club advised its members (in *Sandglass*, 4D-R, p. 4) that the eight oil paintings were "certain to tickle your fancy as well as your ribs."

Thomas Hart Benton executed this lithograph of Jim and Huck
in 1936 in an edition of one hundred.

Benton prepared a great many drawings for his edition, though not nearly so many as Kemble. Each chapter begins with a small picture, and there are forty-five full-page illustrations. Having forty-five instead of Rockwell's eight, Benton obviously had more opportunity to illustrate different scenes from the book. Unlike Rockwell, Benton does not shrink from showing us some unpleasant moments: Pap chasing Huck with a knife and threatening to kill him, Jim's discovery of Pap's body (with several choice four-letter words partly visible on the wall of the floating house), some of the actual shooting in the Grangerford-Shepherdson feud. The killing of Boggs is dramatically depicted (Benton lets us see Boggs's face, as Kemble does not), and we see the King and the Duke being ridden on a rail. We have then a much closer look at the novel's harsh realities; we see life pretty much as it is, without any romantic coloring. Benton recognized, too, certain highly dramatic moments that his predecessors had not used. He was one of the first to make anything of the moment when Huck and Jim leap from their raft as it is about to be run down by a big steamboat. Many a later illustrator used this—Edward Burra and Richard Powers for their frontispieces—but Kemble, Brehm, and Rockwell had not. Another dramatic scene later illustrators have made much of occurs in the cemetery as Peter Wilks's body is being dug up. The rain comes down and lightning flashes across the sky as the crowd gathers around to see the opening of the coffin. Benton chose to show a moment while the digging is still going on. At least a dozen people are in sight, and one supposes that there are many more beyond the edges of the picture.

A final word about Benton's drawings: occasionally he followed Kemble in illustrating something that never actually happened. The second full-page illustration of the book shows a nude witch, broomstick in hand, her hair flying out behind, astride Jim, who is running on all fours. This is, of course, a representation of Jim's account of how he came to lose his hat when actually Tom had taken it and hung it on a tree limb. Benton shows the hat sailing along in the air behind the witch's head.

The late 1940s brought several illustrated editions that deserve some notice here. One was that of Baldwin Hawes,[39] the grandson of George Washington Cable, Clemens's partner in a lecture tour on which they were billed as the "Twins of Genius." Like Rockwell, Hawes did eight color illustrations but then added to these twenty full-page and forty-three half-page black-and-white illustrations (one for the beginning of each chapter). There was also an illustration on the title page, making a total of seventy-two. The color illustrations resemble Rockwell's in nothing but their number. The drawings are not detailed and show little facial expression. They seem rather primitive and childlike. Jim, with beard and pipe, might almost pass for a college professor. Violence is almost entirely absent from the color pictures, except that we see the King and the Duke astride their rail; it is present in some of the black-and-white illustrations. The steamboat runs down the raft again, but the drawing has little of Benton's sophistication or sense of drama.

39. Cleveland: World, 1947.

Donald McKay: There they all was, looking at me, and me at them.

Hawes does manage to show Huck jumping into the river stark naked, to join a Jim already conveniently immersed in the water. In his picture of the King acting the Royal Nonesuch, however, one would hardly guess that the old man is supposed to be nude.

A more satisfactory edition is that illustrated by Donald McKay for Grosset and Dunlap's Illustrated Junior Library.[40] (He had done *Tom Sawyer* for the same series.) Counting the frontispiece, there are ten full-page watercolors, all careful, detailed realizations. Most of the elements lacking in Rockwell's work are present here: the river, the crowds, the violent and sinister. The picture of Huck at the cabin menaced by Pap, with their larger-than-life shadows on the wall behind them, is sinister indeed. The shadow effect is used again in the picture of Huck confronted by several armed Grangerfords. McKay drew the shooting of Boggs, showing us his face just before Sherburn levels his pistol at him, and he did the tarring and feathering of the King and Duke, who appear at the rear of a large crowd. Other scenes have an ominous note to them too: in one the Duke seems about to strangle the kneeling King as Huck and Jim look on; in another, Huck, Tom, and Jim are running for their lives as the caption gives us the words ringing in their ears: "Who's that? Answer, or I'll shoot!" It would be a mistake, however, to fail to mention the lighter moments depicted: Huck fishing contentedly (McKay's frontispiece has the same subject as Brehm's, but here we see the great river beyond), Jim trying a dress on Huck—who is still smoking his pipe, Tom and Huck fooling Aunt Sally about the number of spoons she has. McKay's seems to be a balanced set of illustrations, skillfully done but not too photographic, showing both light and dark sides of the book. The cover itself has a fine view of Huck and Jim onshore talking, as we see the mighty river with rafts and steamboats in the background.

In marked contrast to McKay's work is the British edition of the same year illustrated by Edward Burra.[41] In Burra's hands the novel becomes dark and sinister. Beginning with a frontispiece showing a great steamboat about to smash the raft as Huck and Jim plunge into the river, Burra goes on to show in almost nightmarish style a series of terrible moments: Jim finding Pap's body, Huck crawling along the floor toward the place where Jim Turner lies at the mercy of the other two men onboard the *Walter Scott*, Boggs taunting Colonel Sherburn, the King and the Duke ridden out of town on a rail. In the end of the novel, where many illustrators (certainly Kemble and Benton) have provided a reasonably cheery picture, ᵇᵘᵣᵣₐs final drawing shows the wounded Tom Sawyer being brought to Aunt Sally's on a stretcher. Of particular note is the scene in the house where Pap lies dead. Burra followed Benton's lead in providing assorted obscene pictures and words on the walls, but he went still further by having Pap nude (as specified in the text) with playing cards still in his hand and a knife buried in his chest (the text has him shot in the back). Most of what Clemens did not want Kemble to show in pictures of the campmeeting appears in Burra's illustration: the

40. New York: Grosset & Dunlap, 1948.
41. London: Paul Elek, 1948.

Edward Burra: The opening of Peter Wilks's coffin.

King passes the hat as eager contributors come forth and a preacher declaims from the pulpit. Several whiskey jugs may be spotted, and at least three are lifted to the lips of thirsty members of the congregation. The "courting on the sly" emphasized by Kemble appears in the far background. Another striking illustration is that of the opening of Peter Wilks's coffin. Many illustrators have shown this moment, but none has portrayed it in quite this way. The wind and lightning are suggested, but at the center of the picture is the opened coffin, with the dead Peter's face (already like a skull) staring up at us; the bag of money rests on his chest. The spectators—at least fifteen of them—stare in amazement, as in the left foreground Huck is about to light out for safety. Throughout, the faces tend to be stark and grim. There is nothing pleasant here, nothing romanticized. It is one of the bleakest series of illustrations for *Huckleberry Finn*.

I will mention here only one American edition of the 1950s, that of Richard M. Powers.[42] He begins as does Burra, though in color, with a frontispiece showing a terrified Jim and Huck on their raft, with a tall steamboat coming at them from out of the darkness and fog. Later in the book a smaller black-and-white illustration shows the actual smashing of the raft, with the bodies of Huck and Jim in midair between raft and river. There are forty-four black-and-white drawings (as compared with Burra's seventeen), most of them occupying about half a page at the beginning of each chapter. Pap looks almost like a monster from a horror movie in one, and in another he vigorously pursues Huck while armed with a knife. Also shown are the menacing of Jim Turner, the feud, and the Royal Nonesuch (the nude King does a handstand). Powers takes a rather hard look at the violent side of the novel, but his treatment is not as stark as Burra's, and there are lighter moments. At the beginning of the final chapter, for instance, we see a convalescing Tom chatting happily with Huck and Jim, who are seated on opposite sides of his bed.

A notable British edition of the 1950s is that of C. Walter Hodges.[43] There are four full-page color illustrations, beginning with the frontispiece, a big crowd scene in which the "opposition line," the rival claimants to the fortune of Peter Wilks, arrives to confront the King and the Duke. The second color illustration, of Huck alone with a rifle on Jackson's Island, would have been a more traditional frontispiece. Other color scenes include the steamboat bearing down on Huck and Jim's raft (not nearly so frightening as Burra's or Powers's version) and an extensive river view in which we have the raft in the foreground, a steamboat in the middle distance, and then the river receding far into the background. In addition to the color plates, Hodges did fourteen black-and-white line drawings, none of them occupy-

42. Garden City, N.Y.: Doubleday, 1954. I have omitted the rather appealing drawings of Dave Mink for a 1953 edition of both *Tom Sawyer* and *Huck Finn* published by the Spencer Press of Chicago. Some are full page and others only half page. All appear carefully done, if not particularly original—both the steamboat approaching the raft and the raising of Peter Wilks's coffin appear.

43. London: Dent; New York: E. P. Dutton, 1955.

ing a full page. These in particular seem rather British and might well be illustrating a story by Dickens.

Also of note are the illustrations of Geoffrey Whittam.[44] His edition features eight color plates and a number of black-and-white pictures occupying about one-third of a page. The colors used are not brilliant but more pastel and gentle. The frontispiece—Huck finding Pap waiting for him in his room at the widow's—reminds one of Rockwell's, though here we see the scene from behind Huck, so that his face is hidden from us. Rockwell let us see Huck's frightened face illuminated by the candle he carries. Other Whittam color plates depict Jim and Huck taking their ease on Jackson's Island and standing on their raft as they see the steamboat coming toward them. Elsewhere Buck Grangerford and his cousin flee the Shepherdsons as Huck looks on from a tree, and the King, the Duke, and Huck walk toward Peter Wilks's house as a curious crowd surrounds them. Finally we see Huck and Tom finding Jim in the hut where he is held prisoner at the Phelps farm and then the wounded Tom brought on a stretcher to the Phelps house—a scene resembling Burra's, but less stark and grim. The Whittam illustrations are nicely done and judiciously chosen to show the various sections of the book. They do, however, shy away from depicting the more violent moments; if violence is involved at all, it has already happened or is about to happen.

Perhaps the most interesting American illustrations of the 1960s are those of John Falter.[45] Like Rockwell, Falter did a good deal of work for the *Saturday Evening Post* and at one time illustrated *Tom Sawyer* for a *Reader's Digest* volume of children's classics. Although the *Tom Sawyer* illustrations were done in color, here only the cover (Huck and Jim on their raft, headed downriver at night) is in color; there are fifteen black-and-white full-page pictures. The frontispiece (Huck on Jackson's Island, crouched behind a fallen tree as the steamboat passes) is repeated at its proper place in the novel—a highly unusual procedure. Some of Falter's detailed, quite realistic scenes are familiar: Jim before Huck when he thinks Huck is a ghost, Jim and Huck leaping overboard as the steamboat approaches the raft (Falter's picture is striking, as he makes the steamboat appear like a monster about to devour them), the Duke reciting Shakespeare on the raft, Huck about to reveal to Mary Jane the truth about the "uncles," and Aunt Sally besieged by the rats. All of these themes had been used time and again, though Falter does them very well. In some instances, Huck and Mary Jane, for example, a scene so much like Rockwell's, Falter is somehow more appealing, more convincing—despite the fact that the picture is in black and white and the background is not filled in.

One unusual British edition of the 1960s must be mentioned, that illustrated by Kamil Lhoták, a Czech artist.[46] Black-and-white pictures appear at the beginning of each chapter, but what catches our attention most are the sixteen full-page color illustrations. Lhoták has left all literal interpretations

44. London: Weidenfeld & Nicolson, 1958.
45. New York: Macmillan, 1962.
46. London: Paul Hamlyn, 1966.

John Falter: She failed on the first pies, because we didn't know how,
but she come up smiling on the last one.

to the Rockwells and the Falters. His approach is impressionistic, mood-creating, and has little concern with the real Mississippi valley. The frontispiece lets us know at once that this will be no ordinary set of illustrations. Here is Huck, his face and the upper part of his sweater occupying almost half of the page. The face, its expression, the cap he wears would be far more at home in some city of Continental Europe than in Missouri or Arkansas. And Huck continues to wear this distinctive cap throughout the novel. The only bit of local color in sight is a small section of a steamboat. Lhoták radically shifts his perspectives from picture to picture: sometimes the characters almost fill the page, while at other times they are only a very small part. In one we see Huck on Jackson's Island from a considerable distance. He stands solitary amid a vast landscape of land, river, and sky. Sometimes there are no people in the picture, as when we see a steamboat on the river from a distance. It is a somber, rather sinister scene. In another we simply see thick trees, perhaps a bit of the river beyond, a bird, and a little sky. Lhoták's is an unusual approach indeed. If British readers of the 1960s did not care for it, though, they could readily turn to a more conventional set of illustrations, such as those by Edward Ardizzone.[47] His numerous black-and-white drawings only occasionally occupy as much as a full page, as in the frontispiece, which shows not one scene but pictures of the main characters: the King, the Duke, Jim, Mary Jane, and of course Huck in the center. Immediately below Huck is a smaller picture of him and Jim on their raft making their way along the wide river. There are several violent moments (the feud, the shooting of Boggs), but there are comic ones as well (Aunt Sally and the rats). Some of Ardizzone's drawings are reminiscent of Kemble's (Jim before Huck on Jackson's Island, the King and the Duke shaking hands).

The late 1970s saw the appearance of two American editions that deserve attention here. Warren Chappell illustrated the novel for Harper and Row's "Centennial Edition" of *The Complete Adventures of Tom Sawyer and Huckleberry Finn* in 1978. Instead of doing full-page pictures, Chappell produced a series of smaller drawings in black and white, with some green added. More suggestive than realistic, the drawings provide little specific detail. A few squiggles often represent the background. The view of the King enacting the Royal Nonesuch is more explicit than usual, although he is not any rival to Uncle Silas in the "obscene" illustration in the first edition.

The Franklin Library issued in 1978 a volume of *Huck Finn* with twelve full-page black-and-white pictures by Barnett Plotkin.[48] The treatment is considerably more realistic than Chappell's and is indeed more like the work of John Falter, though there is more filling in of the background here. The frontispiece perhaps goes back to Worth Brehm for its inspiration, for it shows Huck alone, fishing. We get Huck and Pap, but in the hut in the woods, not at the widow's; Jim and Huck on the island; Huck and Jim

47. London: Heinemann, 1961.
48. There is also a 1979 Franklin Library edition that uses the Kemble illustrations, "reproduced from the original drawings and press cuts of the first edition." Some of the illustrations have been made into full-page pictures.

Kamil Lhoták: Huckleberry Finn.

Japanese edition: Huck flees the cemetery.

seeing the wreck of the *Walter Scott*. An unusual scene not often illustrated is that of Huck deceiving the men who are looking for runaway slaves. The Shepherdson-Grangerford feud is missing, but the King and the Duke turn up; we have, in fact, the King preaching at the campmeeting, one of those scenes Clemens would not allow Kemble to depict. Generally, one might say that Plotkin stays away from the violent and the unpleasant (though he does show Pap in the throes of the D.T.s). Perhaps the most dramatic scene is the often-used raising of the coffin of Peter Wilks as an eager crowd looks on and lightning streaks the sky.

A few words must be said about the foreign-language editions of *Huckleberry Finn*. There have been a great many, far more than there have been editions in English, and a high proportion of them have been illustrated in some way. Some have used movie stills; others have reprinted (sometimes rather poorly) illustrations from American editions; most have employed their own artists. These last have used a wide variety of techniques. There are Italian editions, for instance, with full-color, full-page plates almost like Rockwell's in their concern for detail (though one doubts that the artists spent much time in Hannibal, Missouri). Particularly notable in this regard is the work of Didone for a 1953 Milan edition. It is a little surprising, however, to see both Jim and the King completely bald and the King sporting a beard that extends downward to left and right from his mustache but does not cover his chin. More often the illustrations are in black and white, some-

Bulgarian edition: Huck and Pap.

Swedish edition: Huck surrounded by the dogs.

times covering an entire page, sometimes smaller. Many of the scenes most frequently found in editions in English appear here too. Thus, the German artist Horst Lemke depicts Huck and Jim standing on their raft a moment before jumping to escape the approaching steamboat, and a similar scene appears—far more impressionistically—in a Bulgarian edition of 1963. Huck flees from the cemetery where Peter Wilks's body has just been exhumed in Didone's Italian edition and in a full-page color illustration for a Japanese edition. Perhaps the main faults that American readers might complain of are that the characters often do not look American—the Huck on the title page of the 1963 Bulgarian edition looks almost Vietnamese—and foreign artists are more likely to resort to caricature, especially in regard to Jim. Most of the pictures in a Hungarian edition of 1956 look like cartoons, and Jim's huge eyes and lips dominate his face. In one scene, in Jim's cabin at the Phelps farm, he is surrounded by comical snakes, mice, and a spider hanging by a long thread from its web high above. The artist suggests that the reader need not take the situation of Jim's imprisonment seriously. Of course, many of the foreign illustrations are quite good; among the most praised are those of Eric Palmquist for a 1957 Swedish edition, which has many black-and-white illustrations and an occasional double-page illustration such as that of the King and the Duke tarred and feathered.

We have now considered the work of some fifteen artists who have wrestled with the task of illustrating one of the greatest works of American fiction. Presumably all had in mind a similar goal, to help readers visualize the characters and incidents of the book. No doubt many a reader—especially a young reader—has had his perception of the novel shaped by the illustrations, and no doubt many still visualize the characters in accord with how they looked in the pictures accompanying the edition in which they first encountered Huck, Jim, the King and the Duke, the Grangerfords, the Shepherdsons, and the Phelpses. To look at several sets of illustrations, one might find it hard to believe that all the artists are illustrating the same novel. While one finds it a sunny, happy story in which nothing too serious happens, another finds it a grim, bleak novel filled with unsavory characters and frightening incidents. Such differences occur for a variety of reasons: the intended audience (children or adults), the personality of the artist, the artist's interpretation of the novel. In Kemble's case, one has to add the personality and desires of the author as well. In the end, we perhaps ought to look at the illustrations as we would at printed critical interpretations, choosing those that most appeal to us, that seem to come closest to our own views of the text. That there can be so many varied interpretations in art as in written criticism is further testimony to the richness of *Huckleberry Finn*.

17   JAN B. GORDON

"Fan-Tods 'wid' de Samurai":
Huckleberry Finn in Japan

"Seventy five per cent of all baseball games in Japan are won by the team that scores first."[1]

ALTHOUGH there have been occasional departures from the success that allegedly accompanies "first strikes" in Japan, the Land of the Rising Sun is a country where "who does what, when" still matters. Among the most popular programs for children are the weekly animated cartoon adaptations of *Tom Sawyer*, *Huckleberry Finn*, and *Tom Sawyer Abroad*. These are among the longest-running programs on Japanese television, and the Huck who is presented to us has a similarly "long" duration—from his first "meeting" with Tom Sawyer to his "return" in the sequel. He has an existence beyond the boundaries of the book that bears his name. The serialized, cartoon format with its overlapping continuity prejudices the Japanese youth to see American literature as highly episodic—markedly different from the stillnesses and meditational silences that often punctuate his own literature. This first exposure to American "fiction," Sunday mornings at 10:30, conditions his response within a uniquely symbolic time. While his father may be playing a very expensive game of golf or his American counterpart is in church, the Japanese six year old is witness to an essentially foreign comic strip. It is the only American novel afforded such an honor in Japan, where the incredibly violent, often sadomasochistic comic book, distributed from street vending machines, is popular *adult* reading. In a country that discourages foreign imports by a variety of nontariff barriers, Huck and his companions have found a ready market, perhaps rivaled only by that other American import, baseball. The televised presence of Huck and Tom on Sunday mornings is as ritualized here in Japan as were *Kukla, Fran, and Ollie* in the early days of American television.

This initial encounter, at age five or six, with the American saga of male comradeship takes place typically in a crowded *tatami* room in company with the child's first pals. Many of these companions will progress with him through schools, university, job interviews, and perhaps, through the ritual of an *omiai* (arranged) marriage, a group honeymoon trip, and, still later, the noisy clusters of "sararimen" who populate after-hours watering holes.

1.   Robert Whiting, *The Chrysanthemum and the Bat* (Tokyo, 1977), p. 237.

Even on his way up the corporate ladder, the Japanese male is always in lock-step with his comrades. Although a number of observers of life in Japan have spoken ad nauseam of the group or herd instincts of the Japanese in provid-ing the strengths of consensual judgments and policy decisions, the Japanese themselves often do not view such an extended "family" so positively. Re-cently, the *Asahi Shinbun*, one of the respected English-language daily news-papers, complained of the great difficulty that Japanese have in making indi-vidual friendships.[2] The Japanese affection for "packaged" tours, for large and often unwieldy board meetings, and for "arranged" marriages, the ter-ror at exclusion from a group, the proliferation of "clubs" for everything— all speak of an inevitable fear of spontaneous friendships in favor of group affinity and allegiance. For the Japanese columnist, the very feature of Japa-nese life that appears most democratic to the west—group participation in decisions—is a disguise for the fear of losing face or potential friends.

Although any talk of *Adventures of Huckleberry Finn* in whatever coun-try seems always shaped by nostalgia, this harkening back to the occasion of first exposure is particularly acute in Japan, so acute, in fact, that the univer-sity student has real difficulty in taking the novel seriously. For it is not merely that the novel appears first to him as a cartoon, but that one of the themes of *Huckleberry Finn*—the enduring friendship between two people of different ages, ethnic groups, education, and outlook independent of com-pany or group loyalties—is possible at all. To the young Japanese student, this most classic example of American friendship with only the scantiest of shared goals, dreams, and interests between Huck and Jim belongs to the very world of fairy tales and cartoons that he is expected to grow out of. Perhaps the same thing happens in America to Japanese cultural emblems that have been made the objects of cartoons. It is indeed difficult for an older American to distinguish a comic-strip Emperor Hirohito, now the oldest monarch on the planet, benevolently strolling beside Mickey Mouse at Dis-neyland in a recent *Time* photograph, from those other propaganda cartoon leaflets dropped from B-29s on the eve of destruction. There is a sense in which the comic strip or the cartoon—on television or on an airborne warn-ing leaflet—always seems to exaggerate by flattening the perspective back to a time before the so-called "maturity" of youth, before the "maturity" of group loyalties, and before what diplomats call the "maturity" of the special friendship between the Japanese and the Americans. Historically, the Japa-nese have had to overcome unique hardships prior to the growth of special friendships, and Huck and Jim seem such easy friends after all. For the Japa-nese, as for Leslie Fiedler,[3] the friendship may in fact be so easy as not to be believed, except by children, or Americans.

Generalizations about cultures are always dangerous, but it is perhaps safe to say that most Japanese perceive of their lives as comprising distinctive but cumulative stages or niches. The child begins to acquire his language by

2. Editorial, *Asahi Shinbun*, 8 January 1982.
3. Leslie Fiedler, "Come Back to the Raft Ag'in, Huck Honey!" in *An End to Innocence* (New York: Stein & Day, 1972), pp. 142–51.

mastering two separate syllabary systems known as the Kanas (Hiragana and Katakana), which were originally used primarily by women. Later, he slowly begins to master the Chinese stroked characters, beginning with very simple ones, like ni (=), which comprises only two strokes. The schoolboy's writing book in Japan is carefully graded, so that in the first grade he learns characters number 1–48; in the second grade, 48–127; in the third grade, 127–340; and so on until he has mastered the two-thousand-odd characters that his government has approved for general use. The ideogram itself is composed of a radical that "keys" the meaning, surrounded by a cluster of satellites, and the student gains access to the language through step-by-step mastery of a combinatory system. If the child is withdrawn from a Japanese school at any point during this process of language acquisition, he suffers an almost irrecoverable gap in his "vocabulary" since he will have missed a range of ideograms upon which to build combinations. The ability to read a newspaper requires a special set of combinatory notation used only by newspapers, so that complete literacy is not obtained until the Japanese youth is fourteen or so. This acquisition of particular skills at particular times in fact pervades almost all of Japanese life.

Even more emphatically than the western tradition embodied in Ecclesiastes, the Japanese conceive of life and its activities as belonging to a particular season. The *ukiyo-e* woodcuts of the Edo period suggest that life's pilgrimage is a matter of fitting or synchronizing one's own pilgrimage with the movements of the spheres; in Hiroshige's woodcuts one must be at the right station along the Tokaido (the old Kyoto-Tokyo highway) at the right time, just as surely as today in the bullet train dining car, following the same route, the menu changes seasonally. The "marriage season" for the Japanese woman is between the ages of twenty-one and twenty-five; beyond that age, having not been chosen, she is regarded as a seasonal anachronism—akin to a late peach that no one wanted. There in fact seems to be an internal calendar in the country that prompts all men to celebrate the sartorial watershed of *koromogae*—a specific day on which every Japanese man changes from a summer-weight to an autumn-weight suit no matter what the actual weather is. Strikes, euphemistically translated as "industrial action" in Japan, have a specific season, *shuntou* (the third week in April), which corporations, assuming their workers will not have transport to their homes, prepare for by renting hotel rooms. All of these cultural idiosyncrasies, which provide amusement for so many foreigners living in Japan, actually suggest that life has a kind of rhythm here. Because lifetime employment contracts are a feature of so many Japanese corporations, all promotions tend to take place internally; the president or corporate director will have always come up through an internal system of progressive apprenticeships. He will have had a "season" each in accounting, marketing, personnel, and maintenance, acquiring both the skills and the knowledge of how those "seasons" fit together. It is the skill that *haiku* perfects. Yasunari Kawabata, quoting the fourteenth-century poet-priest Dogen in his Nobel Prize acceptance address, put his finger on the heart of Japan:

In the spring, cherry blossoms,
in the summer the cuckoo.
in autumn the moon, and in
winter the snow, clear cold.[4]

To teach *Huckleberry Finn* to university students, given all the emphasis upon the "appropriate" time for every activity—and hence the importance of timing in this country—is to teach it out of season. The phenomenon that I am imperfectly describing surely has its basis in the language itself. The Japanese character for *month* (gattsu) is the radical 月. But, combined with other characters, it indicates the organs of the human body. 心臓 would de- note *heart*, suggesting that every body, not just woman's body, is an inter- nalization of the movement of the moon. To be ill is to be suffering from a disorder of the moon's (month's) course, and, conversely one suspects, to be out of synchrony with heavenly movements is to be suffering from some so- cial dis-ease here, just as in Ch'ing Dynasty China an ill warlord was a sure sign that the mandate of heaven had been withdrawn in a quite literal sense. A student telling his college classmates that he is reading *Huckleberry Finn* would have the same impact here as a woman marrying at forty or one at- tending a baseball game in December.

The Japanese often see themselves as inhabiting a "floating world," where so many things are here today and gone tomorrow—hence the importance of synchronizing acts or utterances with settings. A natural history of earth- quakes, typhoons, and bomb blasts participates in the same metaphoric cluster as the sliding paper panels and doors of houses, the short-lived spring *sakura* (cherry blossoms), and the delicate lightness of *tempura*; the enjoy- ment of anything is only temporary, a brief season under the sun, after which all sinks under its own weight. The "floating world," so often a sub- ject of Japanese art, induces its corollary, "*aware*," the sentimental sadness of inevitable farewells. By contrast, the "floating world" inhabited intermit- tently by Huck and Jim, America's best-known fast friends, is shaped by dif- ferent cultural determinants that may, in fact, suggest substantive differences in what the two cultures expect of their literary heroes.

America's lack of emotional respect for its aged has always been matched by an enormous and exaggerated significance attributed to youth or pre- tenders to youth in the country's cultural life. If America lacks a distinctive tradition of children's literature equivalent to that of Perrault in France, the Grimm brothers in Germany, or the Dodgson-Potter-MacDonald axis in British literature, perhaps it is because our adult literature has always been populated by characters a bit out of season. For America's literary history is replete with those who cannot or will not grow up unless that act is accom- panied by rather unique physical, psychological, or spiritual threats. To grow up is often to risk death, exposure to European corruption, or a total compromise of the will. The country's literary heroes thus often live in a world of prolonged childhood, a stylized naiveté that is part of the *Reign of*

4. *Japan, the Beautiful and Myself* (Tokyo, 1981), p. 74.

Wonder: James's Isabel Archer, Fitzgerald's Jay Gatsby, Hemingway's impotent Jake Barnes, Faulkner's nameless convict in "Old Man," Salinger's Holden Caulfield, Norman Mailer's D. J., the spermatozoic narrator of Barth's "Lost in the Funhouse," and, until recently, John Updike's Rabbit Angstrum. The oft-heard allegations of reviewers in the staid pages of *TLS* that modern American literature is "immature" and the absence of American literature after 1920 from the Oxford syllabus are surely symptomatic of a problem in the international response to the kind of heroes that stalk the pages of America's classical novels.

America's children, fictional and real, seem to malinger in a prolonged adolescence like that in which Nick Carraway circumscribes his brief romantic idolatry of Gatsby. And it is inevitably an Indian summer that lasts too long, particularly for some cultural historians and sociologists who criticize institutions such as graduate schools and juvenile courts for artificially extending the season of childhood.[5] Although in terms of the duration of its Constitution, America is quite mature among the countries of the world, there is probably some merit in the international complaint that the country often projects itself as eternally youthful. If our politicians kiss babies and dye their hair and if our foreign policy often appears naive and vacillating to our allies, America's public life seems similarly to keep in touch with youth by prolonging it through a cast of characters that have difficulty acquiring permanent wisdom. Sensing the right moment to resign, retire, or even commit *hara-kiri* is always a credit in Japan (as in the recent resignation of Prime Minister Suzuki), but the careers of Muhammad Ali, Joe Namath, and Richard Nixon all suggest that Americans have difficulty in recognizing when they have lost the mandate of heaven—or its western equivalent.[6]

Huckleberry Finn, therefore, must, if it is to be taught in a university at all, justify itself as a worthy, "serious" American novel in a world that often faithfully believes America's carefully nurtured image as eternally youthful and always in the vanguard of new initiatives in science, art, and diplomacy. To teach *Huckleberry Finn* to a university student in Japan as America's serious paean to youthful freedom is to run the risk of being laughed at. The two children, one chronologically a child, the other forced to be a child by virtue of his race, may well become free at the novel's end, but it is a freedom that may be more exclusively American than we are willing to admit.

For growing up in Japan is a matter of mastering what to do at what time, so that education, whether of the Kyoto geisha or of the Sanyo executive, is conceived of as sequential. The entire culture, as Roland Barthes makes

5. Christopher Lasch, *The Culture of Narcissism* (New York: W. W. Norton & Co., 1978), pp. 185–220.
6. The tenure of Mike Mansfield as the current ambassador to Japan from the United States may be a case in point. Mansfield, one of the few holdovers from the Carter administration, is highly respected and valued by the Japanese (beyond the respect accorded most American political leaders) precisely because of his age, presumed wisdom, and ability to represent an administration whose ideology he clearly does not share. As the oldest active American ambassador, he is seen as a figure who sets aside his personal views in favor of a presumably harmonious consensus that is a sign of maturity in the "winter" of his career.

clear, is one that stores skills like a *tansu* (a Japanese chest of drawers) stores bedding or lacquered boxes fit one inside the other.[7] One is valued for the ability to bring disparate objects or opinions together in a harmonious package, rather than fleeing in an exclusionary gesture of defiance. It is nearly impossible for the Japanese student to perceive of the numerous episodes of Twain's masterpiece—the Grangerford feud, the Duke and the Dauphin, the Phelps farm imprisonment—as building upon one another in such a way as to enable Huck's sequential mastery and growth. And, of course, the genesis of *Huckleberry Finn* suggests that Mark Twain had similar difficulties in interlocking the episodes.[8] Although there is a critical industry in America devoted to finding motifs and patterns that link the episodes in *Huckleberry Finn*, such connections seem arbitrary. And as its easy adaptability for television serialization for six year olds reveals, the novel is incredibly and even defiantly episodic. The difficulty is in helping the student to perceive a difference between the adventures of Huck and Jim and those of, say, the Lone Ranger and Tonto, with whom they share a certain televised popularity and perhaps certain features of a mutual defense pact.

Americans teaching in Asia are beginning to recognize that the American critical response of the fifties and sixties was terribly parochial precisely because it participated in the very myth of America's perpetual immaturity that it was purportedly describing. In an attempt to discover an Adamic Man as an indispensable part of our ideals of literary heroism, many of our best critics exaggerated the myth of America's boundless energy and renewability. Rare were the literary heroes who did not become versions of D. H. Lawrence's potent snake, shedding its skin periodically to assume a new disguise. For Twain critics, the death represented by civilization onshore and the rebirth represented by the immersion of a prolonged childhood in the Father of Waters seemed ideally suited to our collective myth of "cycles" of American literature as well as to the endless death and rebirth of a nation through a sequence of New Deals, New Frontiers, and New Decencies. By participating in the same myths it sought to trace, postwar literary criticism enhanced the ideal of perpetual youth, notably in the image of the perpetual Birth of a Nation, recapitulated in each of its literary heroes. The Japanese, historically handicapped by a scarcity of raw materials, and perhaps because their nation was nearer the harsher realities of a phoenixlike rebirth in the postwar years, never bought the myth of infinite potentiality contained in the figure of America's Adamic Man. In fact, it might occur to the American teaching the book in Japan that Twain's novel may not sustain that myth. *Huckleberry Finn* incessantly points to its own provisional status, in part by its structure. The novel is itself "framed" both by the introductory disclaimer and warning from its author and by the valedictory "Yours truly, Huck Finn." This narrative frame creates a particularly arbitrary status for the novel insofar as

---

7. Roland Barthes, *The Empire of Signs*, trans. Richard Howard (New York: Hill & Wang, 1982), pp. 36–42. Although Barthes's interests typically are with the systemics of discourse in Japan, his occasional digressions into the proxemics of her cultural forms are brilliant.

8. Bernard DeVoto, "Noon and the Dark: *Huckleberry Finn*," in *Mark Twain's America and Mark Twain at Work* (Cambridge: Harvard University Press, 1967), pp. 45–104.

its beginning and ending belong not to some existential process but to an act of *writing*. For it is the ever-present awareness of its own textuality that all of my Japanese students take to be uniquely characteristic of the novel. *Huckleberry Finn* begins and ends with highly formalized boundaries that paradoxically enclose and contain highly spontaneous behavior, inducing in the novel the same provisional status as accrues to its hero. The whole question of freedom and slavery is recapitulated, as it were, in the text itself. In so arbitrarily formalizing the beginning and ending of his novel, Twain created for it the privileged status of "text" among many possible texts in a world that seems overpopulated with writing. One of my students remarked that the novel invites us to think of it as a *construction*, not as an *account* of experience. Elaborating this notion, she mentioned that each episode seemed entirely self-enclosed—usually having its own vernacular language—and independent of other experience, in the same way that the novel itself was rather neatly packaged with a "posted" warning as a greeting and a signature as a valedictory. When I offered the standard explanation, that the Mississippi River itself was the unifying element, she would have none of it. In Japan *Huckleberry Finn* appears as compartmentalized, as packaged, as a noontime lunchbox for a Toyota worker.

Japan is one culture with a peculiar affection for wrapping its products in such a way that the appearance is the reality: the layers of the kimono, the intricately wrapped seasonal confectionery, the television ads that arrest attention by an arbitrary superimposition of camera angles. In fact, Japanese paper sculpture, *origami*, is an art constructed from a wrapping that wraps nothing at all. At least one Japanese social psychologist has called attention to a proliferation of enclosing structures in this culture that turn out to harbor only a vacuum, an inner emptiness.[9] So many of the conventions in Japan—the two-word blessing upon finishing a meal or the universal removal of shoes prior to entering a house—do not really have a religious explanation in a country where 90 percent of the population has no readily identifiable religious affiliation. These gestures are enclosing forms that appear arbitrary because they have no historical rationale. One Japanese academic mentioned to me that their importance lies within their emptiness.

Containment effected by quite arbitrary boundaries, then, is the very feature of Twain's novel that drew the attention of my Japanese students. Illusions about the simplicities of childhood, the nostalgia involved in a drift to freedom, are constantly being undercut in *Huckleberry Finn* by the reminder that the book is, after all, but one more text, and one that explores the very nature of textuality. Thus the narrative proscribes and represses the very possibility of freedom that it expresses. The Japanese student, probably because of his earlier exposure to the serial comic film, is constantly aware, along with a sophisticated critic like John Seelye, that *Huckleberry Finn* is a sequel,[10] a supplementary text that sets limits by its very belatedness:

9. Takeo Doi, *The Anatomy of Dependence* (Tokyo, 1971), pp. 167–73.
10. Seelye, "What's in a Name: Sounding the Depths of *Tom Sawyer*," *SR* 90 (1982): 408–29.

You don't know about me, without you have read a book by the name of 'The Adventures of Tom Sawyer,' but that ain't no matter. That book was made by Mr. Mark Twain, and he told the truth, mainly. There was things which he stretched, but mainly he told the truth. (P. [17])

Huck, in the beginning, is already a vestige, a character left over, as it were, from another text. His derivative identity is vulnerable to recovery by textuality in much the same way that his early education at the hands of the Widow Douglas seems shaped by texts. The two texts, *Tom Sawyer* and *Huckleberry Finn*, are a "set" and hence companionable in the same way as are Tom and Huck themselves. The volume we read is part of a necessary succession in a sequential order, and the Japanese student sees Huck more as part of a continuity and thus a permanent order than does his American counterpart. The burden of so much American literary criticism, influenced by the hermeticism of New Critical aesthetics, is to isolate works of art in such a way that we forget that Huck's beginnings and endings are elsewhere, in *Tom Sawyer*, "Tom and Huck Among the Injuns," and *Tom Sawyer Abroad*.

Many critics have argued that Huck's flight is in fact a flight from books and the restrictive civilization that believes in the "word" and into "Jim's world," a different kingdom that mirrors the Book of Nature as an antitext. But the actual awareness of its own textuality, the self-conscious foregrounding of events that have a textual history, may in fact bring Twain's classic closer to the provisional status of, say, *Moby-Dick*, as a "draft of a draft," or even to the contemporary metafictions of Barth and Coover. The "beginning" of *Huckleberry Finn* is inherent in the "ending" of a predecessor: "Now the way that the book [*Tom Sawyer*] winds up, is this" (p. [17]). It is one of the few American novels that begins with the plot summary of an antecedent text whose relevance the narrator attempts to bring forward. In the very act of setting *Huckleberry Finn* apart as a unique achievement, its narrator binds it to a serial continuity. Hence the thematic interest in the recovery of an inheritance, in Jim's recovery of a presumably inalienable freedom, even in the nostalgic recovery of innocence is related at the outset to Twain's act of formal recovery.

In Japanese life, the self-consciousness of one's historical membership within a generic group is important. The history of *ukiyo-e* (eighteenth- and nineteenth-century woodcuts of the "floating world") is the history of students assuming the names of their drawing masters much as do contemporary students of Zen. There is a succession of discipleship in the history of Japanese art that is often mistaken in the West for blind imitation. Kuniyoshi is better known as Toyokuni III, and one way of understanding his achievement is to study the way in which he "extends" the line and therefore the school and the name of a predecessor. Art is in part an act of historical recovery. Far from being impaled on anxieties of influence, the Japanese artist thinks of his talent as heir to a generous tradition. There is such a high degree of self-referentiality in Japanese visual and verbal art that the creation of "societies" of artists (*geijyutsuka*) reflects not so much the *embourgeoise-*

ment of an art form as the societies' status as a historical reservoir of techniques. Little wonder that my Japanese students should want to know precisely what came before the opening sentence, what form preceded the novel we read.

Conditioned as children by the Sunday morning cartoon serialization with its emphasis upon framed boundaries and occasionally exaggerated "fillers" to effect continuity, my Japanese students come to a novel that they expect to be a *sequel*. And surely its status as a *sequel* shapes a meaning different from that perceived by most American students. Twain points to the very belatedness, not only of Huck himself, but of every attempt at writing with authority. No matter how much he gives the appearance of rebellion, Huck is a disciple, extending the boundaries of writing. He is part of a more pervasive tradition.

During the sixties, Huckleberry Finn was placed in the role of spiritual predecessor to more visible cult figures such as Jerry Rubin or Bob Dylan who similarly feigned an underground disguise in order to achieve a presumably idyllic freedom. The successive encounters with civilization on the shore were often seen as necessarily temporary sojourns with the counterfeit values of a decadent culture, from which, so such a reading had it, Huck returned to the counterculture of the raft. Twain's hero in fact was easily adaptable to what Kenneth Lynn has termed the "dropout" role.[11] He was the first of the free spirits, creating his own brotherhood by "moving on," to be followed by other mobile free spirits, for example, in Jack Kerouac's auto; on Robert Pirsig's motorcycle; in Ken Kesey's bus; and even by more static commune inhabitants who cheered the self-sufficiency of Huck and Jim. This interpretation of *Huckleberry Finn* appeals to an American generation nurtured on Dylan's "Rolling Stone" and alienated from violence on other shores, and it necessarily emphasizes Huck's alienation from society through a succession of progressively more elaborate rebirths. On the other hand, where the American student often reads Huck's story as one of youth's rebellion against convention, my Japanese students read of Huck's acceptance of conventions, in short, of membership.

Japanese students invariably read Twain's novel as parodic, as a caricature of the very process of writing. And they have some evidence on their side. Huck's existence has a kind of rhythm. He is tempted repeatedly to join "worlds" of *writing*, only to be persecuted or stultified when discourse eventually threatens him with boredom or routine. Upon fleeing the confinement of an existence that finds its basis in writing, he enters surrogate families who depend upon local vernacular speech (as opposed to writing) or into the long idyllic periods of comparative silence alone with Jim on the river. These experiences really constitute three separate modes of existence for Huck. And no matter how often he has intercourse with riverfront society and its noisy plethora of local nuance and dialect—so terribly difficult for the native Japanese speaker to come to terms with—Huck nonetheless comes to feel the pressure to acquire a more systemic discourse. One of my stu-

11. "Welcome Back from the Raft, Huck Honey," *ASch* 46 (1977): 338–47.

dents in Kyoto, struggling to accurately translate clusters of contractions, observed astutely that the novel always seems on the verge of collapsing back into speech.

For Mark Twain's introductory provisional *deference* is paralleled not only by the concluding, "The End. Yours truly, Huck Finn," but also by the attempted intrusion of other texts that have a bogus (in the sense of narrowly private) authority. The awful "mortality school" poetry of Emmeline Grangerford; a fake will; unnoticed tattoos on a dead man's chest; a broken hand that cannot sign; false advertisements for the Royal Nonesuch; Tom's "non-amous" letters; the demand that Jim, who cannot write, keep a diary—all represent the falsifying claims that writing makes over our civilization. Virtually anyone can become an author of something in *Huckleberry Finn* and, apparently, come to command some audience. It is as if Mark Twain, who invested heavily and unsuccessfully during his lifetime in a printing press, found a place for it to be perpetually useful. In almost every instance the act of writing is seen as an insult both to sensibility and to intelligence, yet writing remains the very basis of authority that creates plots and keeps them going:

> "Well, if that ain't just like you, Huck Finn. You *can* get up the infant-schooliest ways of going at a thing. Why, hain't you ever read any books at all?—Baron Trenck, nor Casanova, nor Benvenuto Chelleeny, nor Henri IV, nor none of them heroes? Whoever heard of getting a prisoner loose in such an old-maidy way as that? No; the way all the best *authorities* [italics mine] does, is to saw the bed-leg in two, and leave it just so, and swallow the sawdust." (P. 301)

Growing up beyond the "infant-schooliest ways" is obviously believed to be a function of acquiring the knowledge of manuals, almanacs, and the romances of imprisonment and escape. Answers to questions of moral right and wrong, so terribly askew in the novel, are a mere matter of citation, of mentioning the right authorities no matter what the application. And those authorities invariably have their basis in textuality. Although critics delight to talk of Huck's departure from the Widow Douglas and his brief tenure in Tom Sawyer's gang as evidence of his rejection of books and learning, he has in fact merely exchanged one textual order for another. For, in order to join Tom Sawyer's gang, he must sign an oath of allegiance in blood. Only then does Huck discover that the behavior and activities of the gang are prescribed by an antecedent text; departures from convention must be footnoted:

> "Because it ain't in the books so—that's why. Now Ben Rogers, do you want to do things regular, or don't you?—that's the idea. Don't you reckon that the people that made the books knows what's the correct thing to do? Do you reckon *you* can learn 'em anything?" (P. 27)

Tom Sawyer, like almost everyone else in the novel, betrays a respect for texts and what they do. The written word not only prescribes inappropriate behavior, even for a group of child thieves, but is in fact the visible bond of their community. Huck's agreement to return to his foster mother for education is a first recognition of the power of the *written* word, a recognition that any flight to freedom must inevitably confront texts that set conditions or severely restrict the enjoyment of that freedom. The spaces of potential freedom always bear the remnants of a WANTED poster in *Huckleberry Finn*.

Textuality in *Huckleberry Finn* has two potential limitations. In the first instance, texts have a tendency toward belatedness that always limits their effectiveness despite all pretenses to authority. It is often simply too late to be put to its intended use. Tom Sawyer's attempt to use historical romance to provide the paradigm for Jim's escape only postpones that escape. Books are being asked to do what they can never do, notably, to be invariably and reliably prescriptive. Secondly, there is a belief that people always believe what they read, that writing itself has an a priori authority. The Duke and the Dauphin believe that proper advertising will always produce an audience for their act. In effect both views constitute an overreliance on texts that results in a kind of tyranny; such self-conscious textualization gives every moral or political episode a markedly literary quality. This is but another way of saying that the episodic, picaresque quality of Twain's novel is not so much a part of the events that it relates as it is of the process of textualizing them, so that their deeds might be "read about" by others. The characteristic rhythm of *Huckleberry Finn* is either abundant preparatory advertisement (the notices for the performance of the Royal Nonesuch, "wanted" handbills for Jim, or Twain's "NOTICE" for his own novel) or, on the other hand, postponement in order to get the right book for the right recipe. Those who criticize both Tom's morality and his originality because, for example, his gang has its germination in "pirate books, and robber books" (p. 26), tend to ignore the fact that Twain himself has Huck locate his origin in another and prior text.

Perhaps the extreme example of this process of creeping textualization is the absentminded Reverend Uncle Silas's confusion over whether or not the disappearing spoons used to assist Jim's flight to freedom were not misplaced inside that other and prior Text that he glosses daily:

> "I reely don't know, Sally," he says, kind of apologizing, "or you know I would tell. I was a-studying over my text in Acts Seventeen, before breakfast, and I reckon I put it in there, not noticing, meaning to put my Testament in, and it must be so, because my Testament ain't in." (P. 319)

Under ordinary circumstances, the Bible has little in common with spoons, but in *Huckleberry Finn* texts have the ability to enclose and to circumscribe events and objects. The formation of communities, the determination of loss and gain, plans for future action, are all conditioned by the acceptance of a power vested in texts. The irony of course lies in the fact that the individual who has the most to gain or lose from written proclamation is beyond the reach of the word because he is illiterate.

The use and abuse of textuality in Twain's novel has a special appeal to the Japanese student who spends nine years merely acquiring his own language. The process of drawing all of these ideograms repeatedly until one not only recognizes them but is also able to write them places an extraordinary emphasis upon memory and recall. Where the child is in the course of acquiring his language is crucial, both to the formation of literacy and to his lifetime companions. If a Japanese child is pulled out of school or is forced to accompany his parents abroad for a year or two without the benefit of Japanese-language instruction, he has a permanent gap in his pictorial vocabulary. For an adult learning kanji, it is well-nigh impossible to find other adults at precisely the same level of literacy. This indicates again the importance given to affinity groups in Japan; one starts learning and progresses in lockstep with his classmates until all the necessary combinations and their variant readings have been learned. It is a process that strikes most westerners as tedious and mechanical, especially when one witnesses it applied to learning other skills such as tennis (in which young players at clubs, just learning the game, may spend four weeks hitting the same identical overhead shot projected from a ball machine). Everyone in the group perfects the skill in synchrony, so that literacy, group companionship, and quality control accrue at the same time. It is not merely, as Ezra Vogel believes, that the ability to think in very long runs accounts for Japanese industrial success, but rather that such patience may well be nurtured early on in the child's acquisition of literacy.[12] It is a tediously repetitive enterprise historically treasured through sumi art and calligraphy. One of my students told me, when I complained of my own problems remembering the stroking order for the ideograms, that she too practices writing once or twice a month so as not to lose the vocabulary of her own language.

Little wonder, then, that in this nation of 98 percent literacy, one of the highest in the world, my Japanese students should see Huck much as they see themselves—as controlled at virtually every turn in the river by the authority of some text and subjected to the demand to master it historically in order to achieve freedom. Huck's penchant for inventing tall tales just in time to free himself from yet another scrape is seen as binding him to a life of increasingly private codes that, however humorous, are ineffectual. For private codes and practical jokes, the part of Twain's achievement closest to the American grain, can never become an inherited and hence prescriptive part of a civilization. In removing himself from threatening situations by a verbal inventiveness that delights readers, Huck is condemned to live always ad hoc. Either he victimizes others or he is himself victimized in an endless cycle, but he can never become part of any community unless he accepts their texts, no matter how arbitrary they seem. Without texts—as even Miss Watson's belated will testifies—one is never free. Japanese students see Huck as a person bound to the episodic because he has not learned to control this arbitrary writing.

By emphasizing the way in which Huck's very existence is shaped by the demands of other texts, these Japanese students of American literature place him within a larger context. Whereas the American reader might see the concluding flight to Indian Territory as a last attempt to defy civilization, his Japanese counterpart views it as simply one more episode, no more likely to lead to genuine freedom or knowledge of the Indians than was the wigwam

12. Ezra Vogel, *Japan as Number One: Lessons for America* (Cambridge: Harvard University Press, 1979), pp. 108–12.

on the raft. And what finally happens to Huck, as anyone who has read *Tom Sawyer Abroad* understands, is not an escape into some unknown frontier but a return to the more mundane world of St. Petersburg with Jim in tow: "in glory. . . . from that long travel." Our youth returns home as a celebrity to a torchlight parade, applauded by the home folk who never expected so much. The return of the prodigal is of course a conservative ending, a tacit acceptance of the value of native community. It also tells us that in America the ease with which freedom is seduced by celebrity turns out to be, however perversely, as ineradicable in our national character as is our fabled quest for freedom. The need for an audience, for celebrated status, often compromises the sincerity of our arguments against the establishment. Like Jane Fonda after him, Huck finds his early complaint easily co-opted and his rebellion absorbed within the "life-style" of the country. Unlike the talented actress of our own day, however, he returns home a bit too late for a public celebration of reconciliation with a parent. Both "born actors" become writers of best-selling survival manuals—a Puritan solution to the crisis of aging.

Part of the complex process by which the celebrity is constituted—as any viewer of the *Tonight* show quickly understands—is through the publication of the autobiography or the confession. By having Huck bid his readers a temporary but belated farewell with the concluding "The End. Yours Truly, Huck Finn," Twain gave his hero the self-consciousness of the retiring celebrity-as-writer. Of course all of us know that it is not the end at all, just as in any Bugs Bunny cartoon the "That's All Folks" is only an arbitrary, temporary ending. As Bugs can be counted on to return again and again, so too can Huck, here in Japan, be counted on to return with an even greater frequency on Sunday mornings. In his last act, rather than seeking to rebel against all of the arbitrariness of bogus writing with a pretense to authority, Huck himself becomes a writer who authorizes his own text against which future generations will rebel. His concluding gesture involves accepting the writer's vocation, a grudging acknowledgment of the necessity of literacy in life's continuity that is just as conservative a gesture as is Stephen Daedalus's concluding diary. Given the dramatic nature of his opening defiance against Miss Watson's respect for books, Huck Finn's final signature, not in blood but in ink, authenticates a recognition of the power of texts to contain rebellion.

If writing is the repository of cultural values in *Huckleberry Finn*, it is a domain in which women, even those who wear goggles, have a vested interest. Although Widow Douglas and Miss Watson have been the objects of considerable ridicule over the years, their emphasis upon the disciplined acquisition of literacy in the early chapters of the novel is crucial to Huck's apprenticeship as the future author of his own text. For Huck is yet one more American hero of necessity bound to a household headed by a single female. He acquires authorial skills at the same time (and largely from the same Book) from which he acquires his more questionable puritan attitudes toward crime, punishment, and guilt. For the same woman whose posthumous will arbitrarily sets Jim "free at last" is also a devout believer in an equally arbitrary cycle of prayers and punishment. Puritanism and freedom paradoxically coexist in this novel, as in America itself, for both are inextricably bound to the very acquisition of literacy. In a recent survey, 95 percent of all Americans professed a belief in God: were that the sole criterion, we are the most religious nation on earth in spite of (or maybe because of) our professed separation of church and education, a separation Huck knows to be a fiction. In a novel where so many men have abandoned or contemplate abandoning their families for a freedom that in each instance is ephemeral, it is woman's writing and her interpretation of writing that enact freedom both for a slave and a hero-as-novelist. Although many American critics have lost sight of the contribution of women in *Huckleberry Finn*, none of my Japanese students did. For one of the four notational systems of modern written Japanese—hiragana or "flower writing"—was designed originally by women for use at court and today provides the "polite" endings that denote levels of familiarity and formality in everyday speech.

Huck's own authorized text—the "stretched" novel that we read, lapping aft into *Tom Sawyer* and fore into *Tom Sawyer Abroad*—has no more claim to truth than do any of the other counterfeit advertisements, wills, romances, biblical verses, schoolbooks, that he himself spends so much time circumventing. Yet, there are those who remain heedless of Mark Twain's prefatory admonition calling attention to the fragile nature of textuality:

> Persons attempting to find a motive in this narrative will be prosecuted; persons attempting to find a moral in it will be banished; persons attempting to find a plot in it will be shot.
>
> BY ORDER OF THE AUTHOR
> PER G.G., CHIEF OF ORDNANCE.

School boards both northern and southern persist in denying that advice and have been shooting the book instead by having it banished from high-school libraries. They rebel against the text by finding "hidden" meanings which, like so much of what is hidden in the novel, are diametrically opposite, as if *Huckleberry Finn* could simultaneously endorse Jim Crow and a nautical application of forced busing. Perhaps it is time for us to recognize that one outlandish reading, the one Twain himself advised, may in fact be necessary to "save" the text: to remain plotless, to possess no secret meanings at all, is to enjoy a kind of endurance, to survive in a very hostile land.

And the Japanese Sunday morning cartoon might be a first step in that direction. If *Huckleberry Finn* indeed describes the crisis of authority by textuality in which it has participated for these one hundred years, exposure to the novel is crucial to the map of misreadings that we superimpose upon all the other maps in a very topographic novel.[13] One does not have to subscribe to reader-response criticism to believe that our critical posture is often shaped by our collective exposure. The Japanese six year old watching a weekly animated cartoon whose overlapping "continuity" is carefully de-

---

13. One recent essay suggests that the misreadings of *Huckleberry Finn* by many American critics stem from Twain's own problematic attitude in regard to Jim's "freedom." See the marvelous piece by the late Laurence B. Holland, "A 'Raft of Trouble': Word and Deed in *Huckleberry Finn*," *Glyph* 5 (1979): 69–87.

signed to allow him to miss a week without really missing very much has a different "first" exposure from that of the American high-school senior about to be shoved out of the family nest. Because the Japanese, if he watches long enough, sees both Huck's flight *and* his return, he honors a different Huck Finn.

The celluloid cycle on Sundays is part of the rhythm of eternal return in a land of so many seasonal celebrations, a land where life itself is perceived to have a seasonal composition. Reading *Huckleberry Finn*, the American high-school student, guided by one or more of us trained in one or another "schools" of interpretation, sees this book, and perhaps every book, much as our Puritan forefathers saw another Book: as a plot, a conspiracy to be unraveled by successive interpretations. And if we educated critics see the novel as a plot, why should not others, with other motives, also see it as a plot?

On the eve of Huck's centennial, Peter Townsend, formerly of the rock group Who, has released an album entitled *Only the Best Cowboys Have Chinese Eyes*. As I study the animated cartoon in a Sony-equipped Japanese language laboratory with the latest in sophisticated instrumentation, I note that Huck Finn does have oriental, slanted eyes in their version. It is a fitting reminder that all of our meanings are very arbitrary indeed and conditioned by the circumstances and conditions of our contact with the text. But Huck, part huckster that he was and is, having played the best joke upon the critic, would appreciate that. On his one-hundredth birthday, he, like anyone else who hungers after celebrity, cherishes acceptance even on nonnative grounds.

18 HAMLIN HILL

Huck Finn's Humor Today

No one ever reads the same book twice: as our lives change and our perspectives alter, the same sentence, chapter, or book alters with us, like a patina on the surface of silver. We bring ourselves to literature, in spite of all that critics say about the purity of the text itself. This truism is perhaps more true of *Huckleberry Finn* than any other familiar work of fiction: We are saturated with the book through school and university, we are familiar with the movie versions, television adaptations, even comic-strip transmutations of the plot and characters. And as we change, the book changes along with us.

That same truth applies to generations of readers as well as to individuals. Books like *Walden* and *A Connecticut Yankee in King Arthur's Court* seem prophetic, now that we have a hindsight their contemporary readers lacked. Millennial texts from the past now seem naive; apocalyptic ones seem especially trenchant. And the same formula that changes *Huck* for the individual also operates for generations of readers.

When *Huck* first appeared, it was labeled a children's book—and a dangerous one at that. *Life* magazine condemned it; the Concord Public Library banned it, because, as the *Boston Transcript* reported, it was "rough, coarse and inelegant, dealing with a series of experiences not elevating, the whole book being more suited to the slums than to intelligent, respectable people."[1] Louisa May Alcott, who had emitted *Little Women* a decade and a half earlier, announced, "If Mr. Clemens cannot think of something better to tell our pure-minded lads and lasses, he had best stop writing for them."[2] *Huck* became something of an "underground" book, partly because of its subscription marketing, which kept it out of bookstores as dramatically as it is now kept out of high-school libraries. Joel Chandler Harris praised it—privately—and Andrew Long labeled it a historical novel "more valuable than *Uncle Tom's Cabin*."

At the end of the nineteenth century, even though the novel had gone through seven American and five English editions,[3] critical commentators praised in safely impressionistic terms its "epic" panorama, its characteriza-

---

1. *Boston Transcript*, 17 March 1885, reprinted in Thomas Asa Tenney, *Mark Twain: A Reference Guide* (Boston: G. K. Hall, 1977), p. 14.
2. Quoted in Thomas Beer, *The Mauve Decade* (New York: Vintage Books, 1961), p. 9.
3. Walter Blair, *Mark Twain and Huck Finn* (Berkeley: University of California Press, 1960), pp. 373, 376.

tion, its "Americanness," all the while neglecting those aspects of complexity, moral paradox, and ironic subtlety that more recent serious criticism has found in the book. Discussions of The Great American Novel included it as a possible dark horse. At the time of Mark Twain's death in 1910, two eulogists declared that *Huck* was "of quite inferior quality" as a work of art and that it would "remain [in print] for perhaps two decades." [4]

During this century *Huck* climbed his way to social acceptance. [5] As early as 1901, Barrett Wendell proposed in *A Literary History of America* that *Huckleberry Finn* was "a book which in certain moods one is disposed for all its eccentricity to call the most admirable work of literary art as yet produced on this continent." [6] By 1950, Lionel Trilling had called Huck and Jim "a community of saints"; Hemingway had announced, "All American literature begins with *Huckleberry Finn*"; and even T. S. Eliot had managed to restrain his fastidiousness long enough to call it "a masterpiece." Reassured, scholars and critics began to consider the book fair game and during the next decade built up a body of secondary material about its structure, its irony, its unreliable narrator, which they claimed to be unrivaled by any other American book.

Almost without exception, this segment of critical commentary was ecstatic. Because he achieved a freedom that transcended his society and his own training, Huck himself was labeled a "Liberator." His decision, "All right, then, I'll *go* to hell," was called the finest moment in all American literature. And his enlightenment as a result of his journey on the raft was hailed, repeatedly, as the victory of instinctive "right" over cultural suppression and coercion. He became by midcentury, at least in high-school classes and on college campuses, the literary symbol for the democratic spirit: the triumphant common American who reached heroic dimensions by following the egalitarian instincts of his own heart.

Since the 1960s, Huck has slowly changed again, not as quickly as Lon Chaney turning into the Wolfman, but just as dramatically. The book we now discuss is not the one that was published by subscription in the mid-1880s, peddled door-to-door like an Avon lipstick and barred from sale in metropolitan bookstores. Nor is it the book the first two-thirds of this century thought it was. We continue to laugh, but for reasons that would have shocked and puzzled readers during its first seventy-five years of existence. I would like to explore how and why *Huckleberry Finn* has been transformed by its audience to accommodate modern (and possibly postmodern) notions of what literature should be. [7]

4. Arnold Bennett and Harry Thurston Peck, both in Frederick Anderson, ed., *Mark Twain: The Critical Heritage* (London: Routledge & Kegan Paul, 1971), pp. 285, 292.
5. See Jay B. Hubbell, *Who Are the Major American Writers?* (Durham: Duke University Press, 1972), pp. 135–44, for a detailed account of the shifts in Mark Twain's reputation.
6. Quoted in Tenney, *Mark Twain*, p. 36.
7. The debate that began the slow change in Huck's reputation focused originally upon disagreement over the ending of the novel, most auspiciously with Leo Marx's "Mr. Eliot, Mr. Trilling, and *Huckleberry Finn*," *ASch* 22 (1953): 423–40. That debate has continued for thirty years; in addition, it has stimulated an increasingly large segment of "negative" commentary on the novel.

II

James E. Miller has attempted to define the basic ingredients of our contemporary novels. He proposed,

> For the first time in our literature, after World War II, the world that dominated our fiction was sick, hostile, or treacherous, and . . . the recurring stance of the modern fictional hero reflected some mixture of horror, bewilderment, and sardonic humor—or, to use the popular term, alienation. The common pattern of action which recurred was the pattern of the quest, the quest absurd in a world gone insane or turned opaque and inexplicable, or become meaningless. . . . The nightmare world, alienation and nausea, the quest for identity, and the comic doomsday vision—these are the four elements that characterize recent American fiction.[8]

They are, I would like to argue, also the qualities in *Huck Finn* that make it popular in the late twentieth century, subject it to continuing debate and re-evaluation, and keep it alive while the works of almost all of Mark Twain's contemporaries seem like curious museum-piece anachronisms.

First, Huck himself lives in a nightmare world. He learns to settle in to Miss Watson's "sivilized" routine in the early chapters, but that world makes no sense to him. Its rules are not his, and he cannot understand why "when you got to the table you couldn't go right to eating, but you had to wait for the widow to tuck down her head and grumble a little over the victuals, though there warn't really anything the matter with them" (p. 18). He states his suspicion of the widow's altruistic theology:

> I says to myself, if a body can get anything they pray for, why don't Deacon Winn get back the money he lost on pork? Why can't the widow get back her silver snuff-box that was stole? Why can't Miss Watson fat up? No, says I to myself, there ain't nothing in it. I went and told the widow about it, and she said the thing a body could get by praying for it was "spiritual gifts." This was too many for me, but she told me what she meant—I must help other people, and do everything I could for other people, and look out for them all the time, and never think about myself. This was including Miss Watson, as I took it. I went out in the woods and turned it over in my mind a long time, but I couldn't see no advantage about it—except for other people. (Pp. [29]–30)

None of Huck's other touchstones to reality—Tom's elaborate subterfuges, depending on a debased version of Romanticism; or Jim's superstitiousness, in which most omens portend unavoidable evil; or Pap's bigoted pragmatism—finally serves Huck as a method for dealing with his world.

He must surrender passively as the river determines his course to freedom; but, ironically, as the King and the Duke commandeer the raft, and as Tom reappears to manipulate the terms of Jim's escape in the final chapters, he is carried in a direction diametrically opposite to the one he and Jim desire. Huck's plans are constantly frustrated or reversed by unexpected circumstance.

History and language, too, assume an unreliable and nightmarish quality.

---

8. *Quests Surd and Absurd* (Chicago: University of Chicago Press, 1967), pp. 3–30, elaborates the malaise in the works of modern novelists.

Huck attempts to catalog English history from Henry VIII to the American Revolution for Jim:

> My, you ought to seen old Henry the Eight when he was in bloom. He *was* a blossom. He used to marry a new wife every day, and chop off her head next morning. And he would do it just as indifferent as if he was ordering up eggs. "Fetch up Nell Gwynn," he says. They fetch her up. Next morning, "Chop off her head!" And they chop if off. "Fetch up Jane Shore," he says; and up she comes. Next morning "Chop off her head"—and they chop it off. "Ring up Fair Rosamun." Fair Rosamun answers the bell. Next morning, "Chop off her head." And he made every one of them tell him a tale every night; and he kept that up till he had hogged a thousand and one tales that way, and then he put them all in a book, and called it Domesday Book—which was a good name and stated the case. . . . Well, Henry he takes a notion he wants to get up some trouble with this country. How does he go at it—give notice?—give the country a show? No. All of a sudden he heaves all the tea in Boston Harbor overboard, and whacks out a declaration of independence, and dares them to come on. . . . He had suspicions of his father, the Duke of Wellington. Well, what did he do?—ask him to show up? No—drownded him in a butt of mamsey, like a cat. (Pp. 199–200)

The past, indeed, is unreliable and as unpredictable as the future in Huck's world.

Huck has five opportunities to deny history and reality and to invent a universe more to his own preference. When Mrs. Judith Loftus asks Huck his story in Chapter 11, he responds, "I told her my father and mother was dead, and the law had bound me out to a mean old farmer in the country thirty mile back from the river, and he treated me so bad I couldn't stand it no longer; he went away to be gone a couple of days, and so I took my chance and stole some of his daughter's old clothes, and cleared out" (p. 89). Next in Chapter 13, Huck tells the ferryboat keeper that "pap, and mam, and sis" and Miss Hooker are all stranded on the sinking *Walter Scott*, while three others have drowned. In Chapter 16, a fictional pap and mam and sister Mary Ann are stricken with smallpox and unable to get help from anyone onshore. When Huck is stranded at the Grangerfords, the invention becomes even more catastrophic: "I told them how pap and me and all the family was living on a little farm down at the bottom of Arkansaw, and my sister Mary Ann run off and got married and never was heard of no more, and Bill went to hunt them and he warn't heard of no more, and Tom and Mort died, and then there warn't nobody but just me and pap left, and he was just trimmed down to nothing, on account of his troubles; so when he died I took what there was left, because the farm didn't belong to us, and started up the river" (pp. 135–36). Finally, when it is necessary for Huck to invent a background for the Duke and the Dauphin, in Chapter 20, he recites what is by now a familiar ritual:

> My folks was living in Pike County, in Missouri, where I was born, and they all died off but me and pa and my brother Ike. Pa, he 'lowed he'd break up and go down and live with Uncle Ben, who's got a little one-horse place on the river, forty-four mile below Orleans. Pa was pretty poor, and had some debts; so when he'd squared up there warn't nothing left but sixteen dollars and our nig-

ger, Jim. That warn't enough to take us fourteen hundred mile, deck passage nor no other way. Well, when the river rose, pa had a streak of luck one day; he ketched this piece of a raft; so we reckoned we'd go down to Orleans on it. Pa's luck didn't hold out; a steamboat run over the forrard corner of the raft, one night, and we all went overboard and dove under the wheel; Jim and me come up, all right, but pa was drunk, and Ike was only four years old, so they never come up no more. (Pp. [167]–68)

The total: four dead fathers and one with smallpox; three dead mothers and one marooned on a steamboat sinking in the Mississippi; three dead brothers and one disappeared; ubiquitous sister Mary Ann "married and never . . . heard of no more," bepoxed, and very possibly also on the *Walter Scott*; other family members, too numerous to mention, simply died off. Huck's imagination is fertile but lethal. It allows him no escape from the carnage, the misery, and the unpredictability of the world in which he actually lives. It provides no escape, offers no possibility of waking up in better circumstances. Huck is, to use his own word, too "ornery" to believe in an idealistic universe.

Nor does language provide a reliable means of communication. Huck's attempt to explain in a warped syllogism why Frenchmen do not speak English founders before Jim's common sense:

"Spose a man was to come to you and say *Polly-voo-franzy*—what would you think?"

"I wouldn' think nuff'n; I'd take and bust him over de head. Dat is, if he warn't white. I wouldn't 'low no nigger to call me dat."

"Shucks, it ain't calling you anything. It's only saying do you know how to talk French."

"Well, den, why couldn't he *say* it?"

"Why, he *is* a-saying it. That's a Frenchman's *way* of saying it."

"Well, it's a blame' ridicklous way, and I doan' want to hear no mo' 'bout it. Dey ain' no sense in it."

"Looky here, Jim; does a cat talk like we do?"

"No, a cat don't."

"Well, does a cow?"

"No, a cow don't, nuther."

"Does a cat talk like a cow, or a cow talk like a cat?"

"No, dey don't."

"It's natural and right for 'em to talk different from each other, ain't it?"

"'Course."

"And ain't it natural and right for a cat and a cow to talk different from *us*?"

"Why, mos' sholy it is."

"Well, then, why ain't it natural and right for a *Frenchman* to talk different from us? You answer me that."

"Is a cat a man, Huck?"

"No."

"Well, den, dey ain't no sense in a cat talkin' like a man. Is a cow a man?—er is a cow a cat?"

"No, she ain't either of them."

"Well, den, she ain' got no business to talk like either one or the yuther of 'em. Is a Frenchman a man?"

"Yes."

"*Well*, den? Dad blame it, why doan' he *talk* like a man? You answer me *dat!*"

As Huck points out, meaning more than he realizes, "I see it warn't no use wasting words" (pp. 113–14).

Later, the King does some fancy footwork with etymology when he mistakenly uses the word *orgy* for *obsequies*:

> "I say orgies, not because it's the common term, because it ain't—obsequies bein' the common term—but because orgies is the right term. Obsequies ain't used in England no more, now—it's gone out. We say orgies now, in England. Orgies is better because it means the thing you're after, more exact. It's a word that's made up out'n the Greek *orgo*, outside, open, abroad; and the Hebrew *jeesum*, to plant, cover up; hence in*ter*. So, you see, funeral orgies is an open or public funeral." (P. 217)

In the same episode at the Wilkses' town, the Duke protects his disguise by pretending to be a mute.

It would be wrong to impute more to these comic techniques than they deserve. Mark Twain constantly exploited the humorous values of the incongruity of mixed historical references and, even more often, of speakers who cannot communicate to one another (as he had done, say, in "Buck Fanshaw's Funeral" in *Roughing It*). But if we are not in the world of Barthelme's *dreck* and many modern novelists' private languages, we are not far from it in *Huckleberry Finn*.

III

To discuss Huck's sense of alienation in the world he did not create, cannot control or command, and attempts to outgrow and reject would simply be to summarize the last several decades of criticism of the novel. We are aware that Huck cannot live comfortably in any of the worlds he inhabits. He searches for a father he cannot find, having killed, at least symbolically, the legal one. He cannot find a home, at Widow Douglas's, in Pap's cabin, on Jackson's Island, at the Grangerfords, on the raft, or at the Phelps plantation, either because none of his worlds is insulated from outside interference or because he loses them to circumstance or expediency. The entire structure of the novel is one of frustrated attempt to escape from restrictions only to find the refuge susceptible to invasion and destruction. Judith Loftus's husband is "after us"; the slave-hunters and the Duke and Dauphin violate the pastoral immunity of the raft; Tom Sawyer appears at the Phelpses to orchestrate an attempt at freedom.

What has not been noticed sufficiently, however, is that Huck's response to the events he chronicles is frequently one of sickness—the nausea of Miller's catalog. When he attempts to turn Jim in to the slave-hunters in Chapter 16, "I just felt sick." When Buck Grangerford is murdered, "It made me so sick I most fell out of the tree. I ain't agoing to tell *all* that happened—it would make me sick again if I was to do that" (p. 154). When the Duke and the Dauphin pretend to be the English Wilks heirs, "It was enough to make a

body ashamed of the human race" (p. 210); and when the King feigns be-
reavement, "I never see anything so disgusting" (p. 212). At the end of
Chapter 29, when the King and Duke manage to escape the Wilks mob and
reach the raft, "I wilted right down onto the planks, then, and give up;
and it was all I could do to keep from crying" (p. 260). But when the King
and Duke are tarred and feathered (in Chapter 33), "Well, it made me sick to
see it. . . . It was a dreadful thing to see" (p. 291). Huck's reaction to the
events of the novel tends toward exactly the sickness that takes physical form
in Miller's definition.

Huck's quest for identity, or his success in finding it, is the subject of major
controversy among critics. But, more and more, the tendency is to view that
quest as abortive and absurd. Huck attempts to outgrow his society—its
slaveholding mentality, its morality, its theological beliefs. Ultimately, in order to achieve the transcendence for which we all hope as readers, he must
outgrow his own conscience as well. As we watch, Huck appears to make a
move for geographical freedom (ironic because of the direction in which he
is propelled), from his society's economic sanctions, and finally in Chapter
31 from the underlying religious code. We cheer, and if we are optimistic
ourselves we believe Huck has succeeded. But his "identities" throughout
the novel are constantly devious strategies that invent dead parents and
tragic circumstances; and finally, after the triumph of Chapter 31, he becomes Tom Sawyer—the nemesis of his attempt to free himself from external
control.

The concluding chapters of *Huck Finn* have probably produced more al-
ibis, explanations, and defenses than any other passage of similar length in
American literature. In spite of them, we cannot help feeling that the tone of
the novel has lowered to burlesque, that the stature Jim had achieved earlier
has been sacrificed to make him a minstrel-show straight man, and that
Huck—if, indeed, he has surmounted all his background and training—has
acquiesced too willingly and complacently to the real Tom's grandiose foolishness. But the serious absurdity of Huck's attempt to find his identity
should not blind us to the hilarity of the final chapters themselves. It is *only*
because we have hoped for so much from Huck that we react with depression to the Evasion. The last chapters present the reader with a cosmic
custard-pie response to Huck's quest for his identity probably unmatched
until *Miss Lonelyhearts* or Vonnegut.

Tom's schemes foreshadow the zaniness of the Marx Brothers at their best.
His suggestion that Jim play music on the jew's-harp to the rats and snakes
illustrates the quality:

> "You want to set on your bed, nights, before you go to sleep, and early in the
> mornings, and play your jews-harp; play The Last Link is Broken—that's the
> thing that'll scoop a rat, quicker'n anything else: and when you've played about
> two minutes, you'll see all the rats, and the snakes, and spiders, and things begin
> to feel worried about you, and come. And they'll just fairly swarm over you, and
> have a noble good time."
>
> "Yes, *dey* will, I reck'n, Mars Tom, but what kine er time is *Jim* havin'?"
> (P. 330)

Consider, too, Huck trapped with a stick of butter under his hat in a warm room until "a streak of butter come a trickling down my forehead, and Aunt Sally she see it, and turns white as a sheet, and says: 'For the land's sake what *is* the matter with the child!—he's got the brain fever as shore as you're born, and they're oozing out'" (p. 342). This is the result of Tom and Huck's storing two dozen garter snakes in the attic:

> We didn't half tie the sack, and they worked out, somehow, and left. But it didn't matter much, because they was still on the premises somewheres. So we judged we could get some of them again. No, there warn't no real scarcity of snakes about the house for a considerable spell. You'd see them dripping from the rafters and places, every now and then; and they generly landed in your plate, or down the back of your neck, and most of the time where you didn't want them. Well, they was handsome, and striped, and there warn't no harm in a million of them; but that never made no difference to Aunt Sally, she despised snakes, be the breed what they might, and she couldn't stand them no way you could fix it; and every time one of them flopped down on her, it didn't make no difference what she was doing, she would just lay that work down and light out. I never see such a woman. And you could hear her whoop to Jerico. (P. 334)

Similarly surreal is Huck's explanation to the doctor about Tom's leg wound: "He had a dream and it shot him." Finally, Sister Hotchkiss's monologue in Chapter 41 is a cameo vignette of empty-headed inanity.

In fact, then, even if Huck's search for independence and freedom is doomed to failure, the failure itself is rendered in a context that cannot help provoking laughter.

IV

In 1941, V. S. Pritchett shrewdly observed, "Everything really American, really non-English, comes out of that pair of spiritual derelicts, those two scarecrow figures with their half-lynched minds," Mark Twain and Edgar Allan Poe. "The peculiar power of American nostalgia," Pritchett went on, referring specifically to *Huckleberry Finn*, "is that it is not only harking back to something lost in the past, but suggests also the tragedy of a lost future."[9] And in Huck's "future" we sense apocalypse, Miller's "comic doomsday vision" as drastically as at the end of the movie *Dr. Strangelove* or the conclusion of *Cat's-Cradle*.

Whatever else the circularity of the novel does for its form, it returns us to the opening—Tom in charge, Huck as a servile sidekick, society settled back into its normal ruts, and the game of "Let's Pretend" the model for behavior. Huck has traveled eleven hundred miles only to find that he has gone nowhere. If his trip has moved him southward in linear progression, it has also been a treadmill with only the illusion of movement.

Huck's "Providence" is synonymous with Luck, not with a benevolent deity; and putting his trust in it suggests the chanciness of his future. The Territory to which he plans to light out is no less vicious and anarchistic than

9. "Books in General," *New Statesman and Nation* (London) 22 (3 August 1941): 113.

the society along the Mississippi. It morality, as Mark Twain himself had accurately presented it in *Roughing It*, is even more brutal than the one that guides the shore folk in *Huck*. Depravity is universal: as Huck says, "human beings *can* be awful cruel to one another." Even after presumably freeing himself from the constrictions of "conscience" in Chapter 31, when he decides to go to hell, Huck admits (in Chapter 33), "it don't make no difference whether you do right or wrong, a person's conscience ain't got no sense, and just goes for him *anyway*." We have no reason to believe that Huck is still not chained to his own conscience as firmly as he was at the beginning of the novel.

All this is to ask how, with so bleak a vision, can the apocalyptic forecast of *Huckleberry Finn* be called "comic"? The answer lies in a series of sardonic ironies that permeate the novel and to which we have become accustomed in recent fiction in ways that the nineteenth-century reader was not. For instance, when Tom learns at the conclusion that Jim has been reincarcerated, he melodramatically rises from his bed and announces, "Turn him loose! He ain't no slave; he's as free as any cretur that walks this earth!" (p. 360). But, given the movement of the entire novel, that is a mordantly ironic statement. None of the creatures who populate the novel is free. Each one is bound to convention, to self-interest, to some external pressure that controls his actions and behavior. Even in the act of speaking the line, Tom Sawyer strikes his typically authoritative and sensational pose, "his eye hot, and his nostrils opening and shutting like gills."

In the same way, Huck's decision in Chapter 31 to go to hell as a consequence of helping Jim escape has been comically foreshadowed early in the novel, when Miss Watson "told me all about the bad place, and I said I wished I was there. . . . She said it was wicked to say what I said; said she wouldn't say it for the whole world; *she* was going to live so as to go to the good place. Well, I couldn't see no advantage in going where she was going, so I made up my mind I wouldn't try for it" (p. 19). His heroic desire to avoid being "sivilized" at the conclusion is comically deflated when compared with his definition of that word in the early part of the book: in context, what he wishes to escape is, as he summarizes it, saying blessings at meals, wearing shoes, not smoking, being "dismal regular and decent."

The words upon which a heroic interpretation of *Huckleberry Finn* depends—hell, Providence, "sivilization," and freedom—are in fact comic words in the book, ones whose value to Huck is much more trivial than their value to the postmodern reader. We are, in fact, according to one interpretation of the novel, strung along on a grand hoax, willing ourselves to believe in a nobility unjustified by the action of the story or the personalities of the characters. Huck sees himself more clearly in the final chapters than readers anticipate; his unmasking reveals the same character who began the action—"brung up to wickedness" himself but aware that Tom Sawyer could never "help a body set a nigger free, with his bringing-up."

As a result, Huck's unreliability as a narrator extends only to the surface. His admiration of the Grangerfords' home furnishings is sincere:

> Well, there was a big outlandish parrot on each side of the clock, made out of something like chalk, and painted up gaudy. By one of the parrots was a cat made of crockery, and a crockery dog by the other; and when you pressed down on them they squeaked, but didn't open their mouths nor look different nor interested. They squeaked through underneath. There was a couple of big wild-turkey-wing fans spread out behind those things. On a table in the middle of the room was a kind of a lovely crockery basket that had apples and oranges and peaches and grapes piled up in it which was much redder and yellower and prettier than real ones is, but they warn't real because you could see where pieces had got chipped off and showed the white chalk or whatever it was, underneath. (P. 137)

For Huck's adjective *gaudy*, we would substitute *shabby*, but there is no justification for questioning the validity of his aesthetic judgment. When Huck philosophizes, "If you notice, most folks don't go to church only when they've got to; but a hog is different," we see the ironic implication, but Huck plays it sincerely straight. He records his personal opinion and comprehension of the events he witnesses, and readers are left to read more into those comments and circumstances than Huck possibly can. In that light, the famous passage in Chapter 32 becomes especially significant.

> "We blowed out a cylinder-head."
> "Good gracious! anybody hurt?"
> "No'm. Killed a nigger."
> "Well, it's lucky; because sometimes people do get hurt." (P. 280)

Clearly, Aunt Sally does not view a black as a person; but does Huck, even after his debate with his conscience a chapter earlier, provide any evidence that he views racial matters differently? Is he devious, is he even capable of such instant duplicity?

What exists in the novel, then, are its audience's high hopes, which Mark Twain consistently undercuts, thwarts, and batters in a complex strategy that he was to lose in his old age. As with so many modern novelists, so with Mark Twain: the reader is the writer's prey. The text itself becomes a battleground between author and audience, the goal of the former being to strip away the latter's idealistic delusions and replace them with a soberer notion of Huck's and the reader's own imperfectibility. That Twain does so in the context of a range of humor from broad slapstick to razor-honed irony fulfills the very modern requirement of "comic doomsday vision."

And so *Huckleberry Finn* evolved over nearly a century of reading and interpretation. Huck is no longer the inexcusably unsatisfactory teenager in a world of exaggerated brutality and violence, as the Brahmin reviewers saw him. Nor is he the outcast hero, whose decision to go to hell represents moral victory over injustice and slaveries of any kind, as the first half of the twentieth century saw him. Because the world has changed radically in the past hundred years, we are not shocked at lynchings or duels or tarrings and featherings. The world we see reflected in *Huckleberry Finn* is our own—and ours, incidentally, is one that would not surprise Mark Twain. It is the one he predicted incessantly in the last third of his life and one he believed represented the true characteristics of the damned human race. It would not disturb him to know that, for us, Huck represents the typically helpless victim of a world in which nightmare, absurd quests for identity, alienation, and apocalypse are the facts of daily life.

V

A Document of American Culture

"Nothing conceivable is so petty, so insipid, so crowded with paltry interests, in a word, so anti-poetic, as the life of a man in the United States. But amongst the thoughts which it suggests, there is always one which is full of poetry, and this is the hidden nerve which gives vigor to the whole frame. . . . Man remains, and the poet needs no more." So stated Alexis de Tocqueville, writing in the 1830s, about the singular sources of poetry in democratic ages. One ventures that even he, however, with all his powers of shrewd observation and prophecy, could not have foreseen the extravagance of the terms with which Twain drew upon those sources. There is, to be sure, the Tocquevillian Huck, fabulous and fabular when registered especially in those rare lyrical and meditative passages on the raft: the mythical Huck, the boy as "Man [who] springs out of nothing, crosses time, and disappears forever in the bosom of God; he is seen but for a moment, wandering on the verge of two abysses, and there he is lost." This is the Huck who has the mythmaking presence of "man himself, taken aloof from his country and his age, . . . standing in the presence of Nature and of God, with his passions, his doubts, his rare prosperities and inconceivable wretchedness." But if there is the Huck who creates his own such mythic space, there is also the Huck whose story insinuates the density and complexity of American history, much of it so beautifully and powerfully precisely because Huck is all unawares.

The essays in this concluding section are concerned generally with placing Huck in time, in history, and with illustrating the ways in which his story and the life of his book constitute one of those abiding Scrolls of American culture and history.

Roy Harvey Pearce's essay, like those of Oehlschlaeger and Bell in a previous section, addresses the question of the coherence of the Evasion episode, but his purposes, unlike their formalist intentions, are historicist, designed to demonstrate the dramatic conflict between Huck's and Tom's separate decisions to light out for the Territory. In Pearce's view, Twain, having created Huck as a character with no sense of history, immersed him nevertheless in the so-called Boomer movement that by the early 1880s had become a sociopolitical force—of which Tom Sawyer is the very epitome—bent on civilizing and commercializing the Indian Territory. In Twain's despairing view of American history, then, Huck's flight and his future are doomed; and in Pearce's intricately paradoxical reading, the boy is ours by virtue of being lost to us.

Interest in Huck as orphan, at once in deliberate flight from the "false" families of Pap and Miss Watson and unconsciously in search of an idea, a fact of family that would square with his joyful and intuited self, has been a steady motif of modern criticism on the novel. Robert Shulman's "Fathers, Brothers, and 'the Diseased': The Family, Individualism, and American Society in *Huckleberry Finn*" examines the book's power as a social and symbolic history of the way in which cultural fragmentation threatened and violated the possibility of authentic family that, Shulman claims, Twain regarded as "the most intimate institution of social order." The novel comes to be seen as a metaphorical fabric of the debased families of the Duke and King's "diseased" world, all of these countered, for as long as Twain could manage, by his myth of the cohesive family of Huck and Jim.

Huck's capacity for being shifty in a new country, his protean readiness to assume different identities and accept roles assigned him both in and outside the book, has been, from the beginning, a staple of the criticism. Relatively little attention, however, has been given to the function assigned Huck in Paul Taylor's "*Huckleberry Finn*: The Education of a Young Capitalist," which argues persuasively that Huck's increasing understanding of money and the right uses of money is an index to his growth and maturity. Taylor comments deftly on the motif of money-amounts—the six thousand, the eight hundred, the forty dollars—and makes them integral to the elemental design of Huck's adventures. His is a ranging and allusive essay in which he creates—in what he calls a "mythological narrative" of real historical facts— a lively overview of the shifting ethos of money, not only in Twain's Gilded Age but also in American cultural history generally.

Twain, having discovered the voice of Huck in 1876, seems to have grown up into the decision of what raw materials Huck was to spend that voice on. Two essays here, Robert Sattelmeyer's "'Interesting, but Tough': *Huckleberry Finn* and the Problem of Tradition" and Stanley Brodwin's "Mark Twain in the Pulpit: The Theological Comedy of *Huckleberry Finn*," take up the question of how Twain used biblical and Bible-related stories to create a vision at once comic and homiletic, a "countertheology," as Brodwin calls it, that Americanizes and subverts those original materials. Sattelmeyer charts Twain's religious allusions throughout Huck's story and, showing that they disappear in the 1883 portion of the adventures, suggests that this "disjunction of imagery" represents an abrupt shift not only in Twain's thought but in the deepest currents of American culture as well. Brodwin, placing *Huckleberry Finn* in the tradition of spiritual autobiography and providential literature, defines the book as Twain's "lay sermon," a jeremiad, as it were, subtle, quiet, comic, which "stands as a unique Protestant-American epic." Such, therefore, is what Twain made of raw materials "so petty, so insipid, so crowded with paltry interests."

No wonder, then, that *Adventures of Huckleberry Finn* has appeared to enjoy that unique twin success in American history: canonized by the literary and academic establishments and fixed alike in the public mind as an enduring part of our cultural baggage. Still, as James M. Cox points out, the book is the only nineteenth-century classic in American literature threatened now and again with censorship and banishment. With all its success, it still falls short of what Whitman called "the proof of the poet"—"that his country absorbs him as affectionately as he has absorbed it." For the country has been quicker to absorb Lenny Bruce and the four-letter-word become cliché than it has Huck's use of the word *nigger* and the brutalizing roles Jim is forced to play. The book, Cox contends, causes public embarrassment and has an even greater power to offend today when American blacks are integral rather than token presences in higher education; and the objections of the new black audience, Cox says, are assurance that the book is not so much canonized text as it is "alive in a living society." In an intense and ranging reexamination of the novel's motive, moral, and plot, he shows us how we have still not got used to the book and then goes on to teach us, readers all, how we might all read better this book, "A Hard Book to Take."

19 ROY HARVEY PEARCE

"Yours Truly, Huck Finn"

Huck Finn's closing words, as he is about to light out for the Territory, pose a dilemma not for him but for his reader.[1] Huck has been throughout a liar aspiring to be a shape-shifter, or vice versa. And he has not been altogether successful in either role. Moreover, as if his failure weren't enough, he is burdened—so one interpretive line has it[2]—with the failure of Mark Twain to invent for him in the final, the Evasion, chapters an action and a demeanor that will, from a reader's perspective, justify his special mode of credibility, his own way with the truth.

The problem centers on the ending of *Adventures of Huckleberry Finn*, to which in the end I shall come, in the hope of demonstrating that Huck has in fact, in the ironic rendering of his very factuality, wholly deserved that "Yours Truly," although at a great cost to us; and surely at a greater cost to Mark Twain. (Understanding this last would entail understanding the relationship between Samuel Clemens and Mark Twain—something beyond my competence.) For we must come to realize that rather than being possibly one of us—someone with whom, according to the canons of nineteenth-century realism, we might "identify"—Huck is exclusively a project of his own, Mark Twain-given possibility: in the end we must acknowledge the impossibility of his truth—all of it, and on its own terms—being ours. In the end we discover that we belong "realistically" at best with the Tom Sawyers of Huck's and our world, at worst with the Colonel Sherburns and the Dukes and the Dauphins—and, in a kind of merciful artistic transcendence, with the Mark Twains. But we also discover in the end that we are only possibly Tom Sawyers, Colonel Sherburns, Dukes and Dauphins, Mark Twains. Hope for something better, defined with high irony, does remain. But not for those interpreters among us who want guarantees beyond hope. The hope of *Huckleberry Finn* is the hope of utopianism, but necessarily (because ours is the way of the world of Tom Sawyer, of Colonel Sherburn and the Duke and the Dauphin, of Mark Twain) a failed utopianism. *Huckleberry Finn* teaches

1. This essay is a conflation and development of two previously published: "'The End. Yours Truly, Huck Finn': Postscript," *MLQ* 24 (1963): 253–56; and "Huck Finn in His History," *EA* 24 (1971): 283–91. I am grateful to the editors of those journals for allowing me to reprint material they have published. I dedicate this essay to Robert Elliott and John Isaacs: In Memoriam.

2. The major critique, of course, is Leo Marx, "Mr. Eliot, Mr. Trilling, and *Huckleberry Finn*," *ASch* 22 (1953): 423–40.

us (we should not flinch at the phrase) that whereas utopianism is possible, utopians are not.

Huckleberry Finn, then, is the sort of book that becomes absolutely central to the experience of a reader, American or otherwise, who would try to understand his sense of himself as against his sense of his culture. Its domain is Western America, but its purview, as in its art it universalizes Huck's experience, is the whole world. Through Huck's account of his world and those who inhabit it, Mark Twain renders Huck for us too—Huck at once in his world and apart from it. This of course is the abiding pattern of most of the masterworks of nineteenth-century American fiction, which project for our experience and understanding the central problem for the American in the nineteenth century, and also in the twentieth: How, in Emerson's words, satisfy the claims of the self as against those of the world? How, in Whitman's words, conceive of the person who must exist simply and separately and also as part of the mass? The mass protagonists of nineteenth-century fiction before Mark Twain are put through trials and tribulations whereby they are readied for a return to a society whose integrity they, in seeking too fiercely to discover their own private identities, have somehow violated. At the end Hawthorne's Hester, Melville's Ishmael, and many others of their kind are ready to accommodate themselves to their society, and in their newfound knowledge of the complexities of relations between self and society are perhaps capable of contributing to the "improvement" of both. The tales told of them are open-ended, finally ambiguous, and problematic. Under such terminal conditions, they have earned their right to try out the future. They have come to be endowed with a sense of their own history.

None of this is true of Huck. Return and accommodation—above all, the capacity to be an agent of "improvement"—are quite beyond him. His function, it turns out, is to demonstrate the absolute incompatibility of the sort of self he is and the sort of world in which he tries so hard to live. He gains no sense of his own history and has no future. Nor, as I shall show, need he have. Unlike Hester, Ishmael, and their kind, unlike the kind of committed person whom Emerson and Whitman envisaged, Huck neither could nor should be one of us. He exists not to judge his world but to furnish us the means of judging it—and also our world as it develops out of his.

The means to the judgment are the superb comedy and satire deriving from Huck's quite immediate and lyrical accounts of his own person and from his resolutely deadpan rendering of the doings of those among whom he has his adventures. The lyrical accounts abound and almost always establish his consonance with the natural world, as opposed to the civilized:

> Miss Watson she kept pecking at me, and it got tiresome and lonesome. By-and-by they fetched the niggers in and had prayers, and then everybody was off to bed. I went up to my room with a piece of candle and put it on the table. Then I set down in a chair by the window and tried to think of something cheerful, but it warn't no use. I felt so lonesome I most wished I was dead. The stars was shining, and the leaves rustled in the woods ever so mournful; and I heard an owl, away off, who-whooing about somebody that was dead, and a whippowill and a dog crying about somebody that was going to die; and the wind was try-

ing to whisper something to me and I couldn't make out what it was, and so it made the cold shivers run over me. (P. 20)

Against this tone, there is that of the witness to civilized falseness, foolishness, and cruelty to others. Here, Huck and Jim have taken on the Duke and the Dauphin and Huck has listened patiently to their outrageous stories about themselves:

> It didn't take me long to make up my mind that these liars warn't no kings nor dukes, at all, but just low-down humbugs and frauds. But I never said nothing, never let on; kept it to myself; it's the best way; then you don't have no quarrels, and don't get into no trouble. If they wanted us to call them kings and dukes, I hadn't no objections, 'long as it would keep peace in the family; and it warn't no use to tell Jim, so I didn't tell him. If I never learnt nothing else out of pap, I learnt that the best way to get along with his kind of people is to let them have their own way. (P. 166)

The range in style—from lyrical to matter-of-fact—delineates Huck's character. In the latter style, he can make judgments, but no judgments that lead to significant action. Above all, he is not one to change the world. What is important is that he be allowed at critical moments to be himself, so as to combine in that self the directness, naiveté, and often helplessness of a boy with the practical wisdom of a man, clever in the ways of surviving in towns and woods and on the river. His authentic self as Mark Twain develops it makes him essentially a witness, even when he is a participant. His is a vital presence. In the long run, what he does is altogether secondary to what he is.

It was, as we now know, Mark Twain's original intention to involve Huck all the way in the practical—and in effect radical—action of helping Jim achieve his freedom. Hence the opening words of Chapter 15 consolidate the action thus far: "We judged that three nights more would fetch us to Cairo, at the bottom of Illinois, where the Ohio River comes in, and that was what we was after. We would sell the raft and get on a steamboat and go way up the Ohio amongst the free States, and then be out of trouble" (p. [115]). It is in this chapter, too, that Huck's instinctive sense of Jim as a person becomes clear; he can even bring himself to "humble [himself] to a nigger" and not be sorry for it. In the next chapter, although he is conscience-stricken at realizing what helping Jim means, still he protects him. And then they discover that they have gone by Cairo, are still on the Mississippi in slave territory. If Mark Twain had let Huck and Jim find Cairo and the Ohio River, he would have realized his original intention and made Huck into the moderately "activist" type he first conceived him to be. Likely the story would have ended there. In any case, Mark Twain knew little or nothing about the Ohio River and almost everything about the Mississippi and would have been hard put to find materials with which further to develop the story. In his plotting he seems to have come to an impasse. For he stopped writing at this point, in 1876, not finally to complete *Huckleberry Finn* until 1883.[3] At the end of

---

3. See Henry Nash Smith, *Mark Twain: The Development of a Writer* (Cambridge: Harvard University Press, 1962), pp. 113–37, and Walter Blair, *Mark Twain and Huck Finn* (Berkeley: University of California Press, 1960), for basic accounts.

Chapter 16, a steamboat smashes the raft, and Huck and Jim, diving for their lives, are separated.

In the context of the Evasion episode, the fact of Mark Twain's impasse is worth pointing out, because the Huck of the rest of the book, although continuous with the Huck of the first sixteen chapters, is not confined to his own small world and the river, not just dedicated (but in an agonized way) to helping Jim achieve his freedom, but also made witness to the full panoply of people and institutions that, as we see even if he does not, would deny freedom not only to Jim but to themselves.

Between October 1879 and June 1883, while he finished *A Tramp Abroad* and *The Prince and the Pauper*, Mark Twain was able to write only Chapters 17–21 of *Huckleberry Finn*, for he still had not discovered the means of turning Huck's adventures with Jim into something of a wider compass. During the winter of 1882–1883, he was writing *Life on the Mississippi*, developing it out of a series of magazine articles, "Old Times on the Mississippi," published in 1875. In preparation for that development he had revisited the Mississippi River and was depressed to see how much of all that he had so lovingly recalled in the magazine articles was disappearing. Indeed, his life during the period 1876–1883 had been difficult and too often personally disappointing. Traveling to Europe, he despaired of the development of those traditional free institutions that most of his contemporaries had persuaded themselves had been Europe's glorious gift to the world. Reading Dickens's *Tale of Two Cities*, Carlyle's *History of the French Revolution*, and Lecky's *History of European Morals*, he began to think of man's history as only confirming the view he (and his collaborator, Charles Dudley Warner) had taken of corruption in government and business in *The Gilded Age* (1873). Thinking about the Mississippi again, meditating the downward path from past to present, finding his increasingly desperate view of the human situation confirmed by his reading, he discovered his imagination empowered and vivified. It was as though he were compelled to finish *Huckleberry Finn*. He finished a draft of the book during the summer of 1883, spent seven months revising it, and saw it published in England in December 1884 and in the United States in February 1885.

Despair, then, is, as antecedent and consequence, a prime characteristic of *Huckleberry Finn*. But in the book itself it produces mainly comedy and satire of a superb order. For counterbalancing the despair that went into the writing of the book, there is the abounding joy of Huck when he is most fully himself. In all his cleverness and dexterity, he is—except for what he does for Jim—essentially passive. He lives in the midst of violence and death; yet his only violence, if it can be called that, is the mild, ritualistic sort whereby when necessary he feeds himself. He hunts and fishes only when he has to. His joy is virtually private—to be shared, because instinctively understood, only by Jim. He is of course given no comic or satiric sense. He is given only his own rich sense of himself—richest when he is alone with Jim, on the river.

Comedy and satire derive from Huck's conviction that he must report fully what he sees—and further from the fact that it is he, capable of such joy, who does the reporting. Irony, a product of a tightly controlled point of view, is everywhere enforced for us by the fact that Huck, all unknowing, is its agent. He does not understand much of what he sees. Mark Twain's irony, however, lets us understand. What Huck is witness to again and again are doings of people who have contrived a world that distorts the public and private institutions—ranging from forms of government to forms of play—that just might make his sort of joy possible for all. His relationship with Jim—gained through his acceptance of the private guilt entailed by refusing to accept the injunction called for by public tradition and law—stands as a kind of utopian pattern for all human relationships. And we judge those in the book accordingly. Still, it is an appropriately primitive, even precivilized relationship; for Huck sees Jim not as a man with the responsibilities of a man but as one essentially like himself. This is his fundamental limitation, and yet the source of his strength. So long as that strength exists, so long as he exists, he can participate in the world only as a role-player, willing to go along with all the pretensions and make-believe that he witnesses. He accepts other names, other identities almost casually. Living them, he seems to "belong" in his world. But not quite. For always there is a certain reserve. Always there is the joy of his simple, separate self, to which he returns again and again as though to renew himself. Set against that self, the world in which he has his adventures can be constituted only of grotesque, marvelously distorted beings who are the stuff of comedy and satire.

In 1895, planning to "get up an elaborate and formal lay sermon on morals and the conduct of life, and things of that stately sort," Mark Twain defined Huck's situation in his world:

> Next, I should exploit the proposition that in a crucial moral emergency a sound heart is a safer guide than an ill-trained conscience, I sh'd support this doctrine with a chapter from a book of mine where a sound heart and a deformed conscience come into collision and conscience suffers defeat. Two persons figure in this chapter: Jim, a middle-aged slave, and Huck Finn, a boy of 14, . . . bosom friends, drawn together by a community of misfortune. . . .
>
> In those slave-holding days the whole community was agreed as to one thing—the awful sacredness of slave property. To help steal a horse or a cow was a low crime, but to help a hunted slave . . . or hesitate to promptly betray him to a slave-catcher when opportunity offered was a much baser crime, and carried with it a stain, a moral smirch which nothing could wipe away. That this sentiment should exist among slave-holders is comprehensible—there were good commercial reasons for it—but that it should exist and did exist among the paupers . . . and in a passionate and uncompromising form, is not in our remote day realizable. It seemed natural enough to me then; natural enough that Huck and his father the worthless loafer should feel and approve it, though it now seems absurd. It shows that that strange thing, the conscience—that unerring monitor—can be trained to approve any wild thing you *want* it to approve if you begin its education early and stick to it.[4]

4. Quoted in Blair, *Mark Twain and Huck Finn*, pp. 143–44, copyright 1960 by the Mark Twain Co.

Not only the distinction between heart and conscience but also the quite sophisticated notion of how culture, or society, or the world, forms conscience and so makes possible the death of the heart—these conceptions are central to the very structure of *Huckleberry Finn* as Mark Twain finally developed it, as is the fact that he gives Huck a sense of his own heart which, at however great a cost, persuades him that he can be in the great world only a player of roles.

At the beginning Huck tells us that this time, unlike the occasion of *Tom Sawyer*, he is going to speak out on his own and so correct Mr. Mark Twain in a few matters. His truth, in a consummate irony, is to be set against the conscience of even his creator. Huck now is letting himself be civilized and reports mildly on how it is. Yet at the end of the first chapter (in the the first passage cited above), we know that he is in full possession of his truthful self. Assured of that fact, we can rest easy while he goes along with Tom Sawyer's complicated make-believe and even plays a trick on Jim. His sojourn in the Widow Douglas's world, as in Tom's, is throughout marked by role-playing and make-believe. And he can as easily adjust to his father's world, play his role there and sustain the make-believe, as he can to Tom's and the Widow Douglas's. Perhaps the patterns of make-believe in *their worlds* are harmless; no one is hurt much; everyone can make himself out to be aspiring to something better or nobler. But the pretenses and distortions of his father's world are dangerous and frightening; and Huck suffers accordingly—still managing, however, to record, in his frankness, his sense of his own truth. The make-believe and role-playing of Tom's boy's world are Huck's way into the make-believe and role-playing in the world of adults. The formal design is surely carefully contrived, allowing us easily to move with Huck from one world to the other, and demanding of Mark Twain that at the end of the adventures he arrange things so that Huck attempts to come back to his proper world, which, according to a proper pattern of conscience-directing institutions, must be a boy's world.

Indeed, the episodes of *Huckleberry Finn* evolve one into the other on Huck and Jim's trip downriver as so many exempla of the nineteenth-century American "conscience—that unerring monitor"—as it "can be trained to approve any wild thing you *want* it to approve if you begin its education early and stick to it." The murder of Pap, Jim's running away, Huck's information-seeking visit with Mrs. Loftus, their finding the wreck of the *Walter Scott*, Huck's cruel joke on Jim and the beginning of his sense of dedication and obligation to him, the separation, Huck amid the Grangerfords in all their distorted pride and nobility, his escape from the feud and reunion with Jim—these opening episodes, as we recall them, regularly involve Huck as either role-player or witness, or both. At their conclusion (at the end of Chapter 18 and the beginning of Chapter 19), Huck with Jim on his own, is his truest self:

> We said there warn't no home like a raft, after all. Other places do seem so cramped up and smothery, but a raft don't. You feel mighty free and easy and comfortable on a raft. (P. 156)

> Two or three days and nights went by; I reckon I might say they swum by, they
> slid along so quiet and smooth and lovely. (P. [157])

So it goes for the time being; and we are reassured. But almost immediately Huck and Jim are with the Duke and the Dauphin, consummate artists in those forms of make-believe that fool all of the people most of the time, possessors of consciences distorted enough to make them (most of the time) masters of all whom they survey—including Huck and Jim. Again (in the second passage cited above), Huck is willing to go along. Or rather, he has no option but to go along.

The point is that he knows what he is doing, and accordingly we are reassured that his sense of his authentic truth will sustain him. He stands by—what else can he do?—while the Dauphin bilks a Pokeville campmeeting and the Duke takes over a print-shop and while they fleece the public with their promised obscene "Royal Nonesuch" show. Too, he is witness to Colonel Sherburn's denunciation of a small-town mob and his shooting-down of the town drunkard. There is no impulse to prevent any of this; this is beyond his capacities; and, after all, like the rest of the townspeople he too is fooled by the act of the comic drunk in the circus. Make-believe, all of it, and constant role-playing. Only with the attempt to fleece the Wilks girls does Huck's truth come to be powerful enough to bring him to act. Here, too, he acts by role-playing, but this time his role is set according to his truth. The failure of this attempt of the Duke and the Dauphin brings them to sell Jim. And there comes Huck's great crisis, in which truth once and for all triumphs over conscience, instinct over training, the self over society and all the good and needed things it offers.

The famous passage (in Chapter 31) begins:

> Once I said to myself it would be a thousand times better for Jim to be a slave
> at home where his family was, as long as he'd *got* to be a slave, and so I'd better
> write a letter to Tom Sawyer and tell him to tell Miss Watson where he was. But I
> soon give up that notion, for two things: she'd be mad and disgusted at his rascality and ungratefulness for leaving her, and so she'd sell him straight down the
> river again; and if she didn't, everybody naturally despises an ungrateful nigger,
> and they'd make Jim feel it all the time, and so he'd feel ornery and disgraced.
> And then think of *me*! It would get all around, that Huck Finn helped a nigger
> to get his freedom; and if I was ever to see anybody from that town again, I'd be
> ready to get down and lick his boots for shame. That's just the way: a person
> does a low-down thing, and then he don't want to take no consequences of it.
> Thinks as long as he can hide it, it ain't no disgrace. (Pp. 269–70)

This is the voice of conscience, and it torments Huck. He tries to pray but realizes he "can't pray a lie." For he knows he will sin against his conscience by continuing to try to help Jim. He goes so far as to write a letter to Miss Watson, telling her where Jim is, and feels "all washed clean of sin" (p. 271). But then he recalls his relationship with Jim and makes the great decision—to "steal Jim out of slavery again." And so he says, "All right, then, I'll *go* to hell" (p. 272).

But stealing Jim out of slavery, it turns out, is yet a matter of role-playing.

At the Phelpses, Huck is taken for Tom Sawyer and thereupon enters the last of his adventures—once more by assuming the name and, in part, the conscience of another. Tom comes, assumes his brother's name, and plunges them both into the work of the Evasion. Fittingly, necessarily, Huck must be brought back into that segment of the society that is, by the world's standards, appropriate to him—a boy's world.

The complications of the Evasion episode, and also its detail and length, tend to put off many readers of *Huckleberry Finn*. They see it as Mark Twain's evasion of the moral implications of his story, especially when they learn that Jim has been free all along. Huck, they say, should have seen Jim all the way to freedom. It might well be that the episode is in fact too complicated and too long, overbalancing the end of the story. Still, in the necessary scheme of the novel, in the necessary contrast between Huck's assumption of various forms of conscience and the truth he constantly has within him—in that scheme, it is imperative that the book begin as it ends: in effect, with a grotesque and sardonic comment on the nature of the forms of make-believe, pretense, and distortion that set the life-styles of those whose consciences they shape. It is all in the end very stupid. Men have given up the authentic truth they might well have had as children for the falsifying forms of conscience that lead to the violence, destruction, and predation that transform their society into the enemy of the very men it should sustain and preserve. Tom Sawyer here as earlier patterns his play principally after the romances of Sir Walter Scott. For boys it is moderately harmless play, although Tom is slightly wounded in the final scuffle. Yet we recall the episode of the wrecked steamboat, itself called *Walter Scott*, and are forced to realize what will necessarily ensue when boyish make-believe and role-playing become the mode of life of mature men and women. Conscience will not let truth survive.

Indeed, in this world Huckleberry Finn cannot continue to exist. He says at the end that he will not return to St. Petersburg: "I reckon I got to light out for the Territory ahead of the rest, because Aunt Sally she's going to adopt me and sivilize me and I can't stand it. I been there before." The plan to go to the Territory is Tom's, of course, for whom it is another opportunity for "howling adventures," this time "amongst the Injuns." Huck will survive, that is to say, by playing yet another role in this make-believe, conscience-stricken world. Here, however, he speaks only as witness.

II

In the last chapter of *Huckleberry Finn*, Huck in fact speaks twice of going to "the Territory." The first time he is reporting Tom's plans, now that the Evasion has been managed successfully, "to slide out of here, one of these nights, and get an outfit, and go for howling adventures amongst the Injuns, over in the Territory." The second time he is speaking of his own plans: "I reckon I got to light out for the Territory ahead of the rest, because Aunt Sally she's going to adopt me and sivilize me and I can't stand it. I been there before" (p. 366).

I suppose that the obvious irony of the two passages has not been pointed out precisely because it is so obvious. The Territory is, of course, the Indian Territory, which was to become Oklahoma. From the 1820s on, it had been organized and developed as a region to which Indians could be safely removed away from civilized society, since their lands were needed for higher purposes than those to which they could put them. The cruelty and deprivation of removal were generally taken to be the inevitable price American society had to pay as it passed through its God-ordained stages of development. One part of this price was said to be the yielding of a certain amount of freedom or, to put it as an article of faith in Manifest Destiny, the surrendering of a "lower" for a "higher" freedom.[5] It seems fairly evident that the man who was to write "To the Person Sitting in Darkness" and other such pieces would be fully aware of the removal episode, with its justifications and consequences, and that he intended his readers to be aware of it too. Read in this light, what for Tom is yet another willful adolescent fantasy becomes for Huck a compelling actuality. Tom's willfulness effects a parody that points up some of the grotesqueness of the historically authentic pioneering, civilizing spirit. Huck's compulsion effects a satire that simply denies that that spirit is authentic, despite its historical actuality. Huck will seek the freedom of the Territory just because it is an uncivilized freedom. (A better word, perhaps, is *noncivilized* freedom.) It is, indeed, the only true freedom for the authentic human being Huck eventually comes to be—in spite of himself.

Yet there is more to the passages, particularly the second, than this. Huck, we recall, speaks of lighting out for the Territory "ahead of the rest." Here, at the end, Mark Twain introduces his own point of view, which, of necessity, is more encompassing than Huck's; as a result Huck is given more to say than he could possibly know.[6] From Huck's simple point of view, the allusion is to Tom's vague plans to go to the Territory; for Mark Twain, it is to the Boomer movement that was a prime factor in the taking over of Indian lands, "sivilizing" the Territory, and creating another American state. The effect is that Huck, all unknowing, is given a kind of prescience that his adventures at this point surely justify. No matter where he goes, he will be one step ahead not only of the Tom Sawyers of his world but also of the sort of people into whom the Tom Sawyers grow.

After the Civil War, there was constant agitation in Kansas and Missouri to open up the unsettled parts of the Indian Territory to whites. To this end, bills were repeatedly, if on the whole unsuccessfully, introduced in Congress. Pressures were put on the so-called Five Civilized Nations (Cherokees, Creeks, and Choctaws principally) to cede part of their lands in the Territory

5. See my *Savages of America* (Baltimore: Johns Hopkins University Press, 1965), pp. 56–61.

6. Smith, *Mark Twain*, pp. 134–37, points out that the Colonel Sherburn episode derives from Mark Twain's point of view and thus is intrusive, a "flaw" in the structure of *Huckleberry Finn*. I think, however, that one must argue for Huck as a "reporter" and in this and other episodes (particularly that of the Evasion) wherein he is in no position to participate in, or at least dominate, the action and so render it in terms wholly congruent with his sensibility and understanding. The question is: How much irony are we to allow Mark Twain? An incidental burden of this interpretation is that in the end we must allow him enough and demand only of his novel that it "contain" its elements of irony.

to be used as reservations for other Indians and, for due payment, to make them available for settlement by whites. In the late 1870s and into the 1880s, white incursions into the Territory were numerous enough to call for the use of troops to defend Indian rights. Moreover, in 1879 a court decision found that even those lands in the Territory that had been ceded to the government by Indians could not be settled by whites, since such lands had been ceded conditionally for future settlement by other Indians.

Inevitably, however, white incursions—by groups who came to be known as Boomers—increased in tempo and number. Invaders were not jailed but fined. When they could not pay the fines, they were simply escorted to the territorial border by soldiers. The economics of the situation were complex: railroads encouraged and propagandized Boomers; cattlemen, wanting to use the lands for grazing, opposed the Boomers, who were farmers, and defended Indian rights, which included the right to rent their lands for grazing. The story (one of confusion, broken promises, and violence—all in the name of "civilization") moved toward its resolution in 1889, when the government bought certain lands from Indians and opened them to settlement as the Territory of Oklahoma.[7]

Boomerism, then, was the most recent expression of the westering American spirit. In the words of an 1885 petition to Congress, drawn up by B. L. Brush and John W. Marshall in Howard, Kansas, on behalf of Boomerism:

> Resolved, That we are opposed to the policy of the Government in using the army to drive out or interfere with actual settlers upon any of the public domain, as being foreign to the genius of our institutions. . . .
> Resolved, As this selfsame, bold spirit, that is now advancing to the front, has ever existed since the Pilgrim Fathers set their feet on Plymouth Rock, and will ever exist so long as we remain citizens of this grand Republic, that we, the citizens of Howard and vicinity, pledge ourselves to firmly support this grand element—the vanguard of civilization. . . .
> Resolved, That we are opposed to the settlement of any more bands of wild Indians on the Indian Territory.[8]

Although I know of no direct allusion in Mark Twain's writings to the troubles in the Indian Territory, I think it likely that he was well aware of them, for they were widely publicized and debated and of great interest to Congress. A considerable amount of Boomer ferment developed in Mark Twain's—and Huck's—Missouri, although Kansas was a more important center. The summer of 1883, when Twain was writing the last part of *Huckleberry Finn*,[9] David Payne and his Boomers were particularly active in promoting their cause. One historian of Oklahoma reports that the general whose responsibility it was to turn Boomers back declared that in 1883 "the whole affair had become simply a series of processions to and from the Kansas line."[10]

7. The story is best outlined in Roy Gittinger, *Formation of the State of Oklahoma, 1803–1906* (Norman: University of Oklahoma Press, 1939), pp. 68–157. On the Boomers, see Carl Coke Rister, *Land Hunger: David L. Payne and the Oklahoma Boomers* (Norman: University of Oklahoma Press, 1942).

8. Gittinger, *Oklahoma*, pp. 272–73.

9. Walter Blair, "When Was *Huckleberry Finn* Written?" *AL* 30 (1958): 1–25.

10. Gittinger, *Oklahoma*, p. 131.

Thus it would seem that in 1883, Mark Twain, now finally committed to a conception of Huck Finn whose fate it must always be to seek a freedom beyond the limits of any civilization, ended his novel by contrasting Tom's and Huck's sense of the Territory. Note that Huck is willing to go along with Tom, if he can get the money to outfit himself for those "howling adventures amongst the Injuns." Jim tells Huck that, now that his father is dead, he does have the money. However, he will have to claim it himself. The matter of the money and the "howling adventures" is then dropped. Since Tom is "most well" now, Huck says, there "ain't nothing more to write about." He will "light out for the Territory ahead of the rest." In one sense, perhaps, he simply means ahead of Tom and Jim; in a larger sense (so I think we must conclude) he means ahead of all those people whose civilizing mission Boomerism actualized in fact. The realities of the case are, as ever, contrasted with Tom's fantasies.

The Huck who seems willing to go along with Tom is, of course, not the Huck who, against the dictates of his conscience, has helped Jim in his quest for freedom. It is altogether necessary that this latter Huck must, alone, "light out for the Territory ahead of the rest." With the curious prescience that Mark Twain gives him, he knows that in antebellum days (as Mark Twain surely knew that summer of 1883), even in the Territory, he will be only one step ahead of the rest: Boomers, Dukes and Dauphins, Aunt Sallies, Colonel Sherburns, and Wilkses—civilizers all. Certainly we are not to assume that Huck self-consciously knows the full meaning (even the full moral meaning) of what he says here. Yet we cannot conclude that this allusion is simply a matter of Mark Twain speaking out in his own person. Huck's view and Mark Twain's, in a culminating irony, here become one. Huck's prescience is, within the limits of the narrative, a matter of intuition, forced into expression by his hardheaded sense that he has almost always been one step "ahead of the rest." He can say his final "Yours Truly" and yet must be willing to go to hell for saying it.

III

I think we must conclude that Huck is not meant to survive. He is so powerfully a being of truth as against conscience, self as against society, that he exists not as an actuality but as a possibility. In him Mark Twain projects the American's sense that somewhere, at some point—even if only in the imagination—it would indeed be possible to regain access to the truth, if only we could cut through the shams of conscience and of the institutions that form and justify it. But in the present situation, Mark Twain despaired of that possibility and in Huck, his nature, and his history saw it only as impossible. Huck, then, is that ideal, perhaps never-to-be-attained type— in Wallace Stevens's phrase, an "impossible possible philosopher's man." Huck, then, stands as witness to his experience, totally unaware of the irony whereby it becomes at once an aspect and a function of our experience. In rendering the witnessing, Mark Twain makes us, if we but grasp the irony, the judge of that experience—Huck's and our own—and the world in which it is shaped. It is inappropriate to regret that Huck does not follow through on his own to free Jim. That is not Huck's proper role; for it would be the role of someone in whom conscience and truth were to a significant degree harmonious. Huck, for whom conscience always means role-playing, in whom the naked truth must finally be overpowering, stands, as I have said, not as possibly one of us but rather as our means of judging his world and Mark Twain's—and, along with it, ours.

We can take Mark Twain's preliminary "Notice" to *Huckleberry Finn* with the deadly serious levity with which it is meant: "Persons attempting to find a motive in the narrative will be prosecuted; persons attempting to find a moral in it will be banished; persons attempting to find a plot in it will be shot." "Motive" and "plot" are, however, not so much absent as negative. Huck's motive is to survive; and we know that the conditions of his life and of his society are such that survival is impossible. The plot of his *Adventures* lays out the pattern of the impossibility; Huck's is a history of whose meaning he cannot be conscious and still be his truest self. Above all, the story has no "moral." Rather it is an exercise in the use of such moral sensibility as remains with us. Knowing what Huck is, we can know what we have become and measure the cost and the worth.

F. Scott Fitzgerald wrote in 1935,

> Huckleberry Finn took the first journey *back*. He was the first to look *back* at the republic from the perspective of the west. His eyes were the first eyes that ever looked at us objectively that were not eyes from overseas. There were mountains at the frontier but he wanted more than mountains to look at with his restive eyes—he wanted to find out about men and how they lived together. And because he turned back we have him forever.[11]

The condition of his turning back, however, is that we cannot demand that he be one of us. He stands as witness, bound to his own truth, so that we might go forth and be likewise.

---

11. I quote the statement from the original typescript, with the kind permission of its owner, Prof. Matthew Bruccoli. It has been previously printed in *Fitzgerald Newsletter* 8 (Winter 1960).

20 ROBERT SHULMAN

Fathers, Brothers, and "the Diseased": The Family, Individualism, and American Society in *Huck Finn*

EARLY in the nineteenth century Alexis de Tocqueville diagnosed the restlessness of Americans who, he observed, are chronically striving and dissatisfied in the midst of their prosperity. Tocqueville's American, freed from traditional restraints and ties, pushes his way through a crowd of equally striving men, equally free and equally on the move. But with everyone moving, Tocqueville recognized, each individual finds his own way blocked by others, so that, although his expectations are of limitless freedom, his actual freedom is restricted. The striving individual also encounters the limits of personal ability, which for Tocqueville are intrinsic and cannot be altered by any social system, however egalitarian. Even more important, no matter where a person is in an open society, someone else is always in a position slightly higher, looking down on and in a way devaluing his achievement. On all these counts, Tocqueville defined a basic conflict between the American's expectation of limitless mobility and equality and his experience of restraints and inequality.[1]

As a result, Tocqueville's Americans are never satisfied. They restlessly strive to demonstrate to themselves and others that they are the equals of men similarly striving. The process is endless and insatiable. Tocqueville perceptively realized that the American's notorious pursuit of money conceals a more basic problem, a problem of the self. For Tocqueville, what drives people in the new world is a need to establish a sense of self-worth in a competition with men similarly driven to achieve in a changing world where traditional ties, supports, and restrictions have been left behind along with their assurances about a person's self-worth and identity. Competitive people thus accumulate great wealth and are powerfully motivated to accumulate even more. They are perpetually disappointed, however, because their underlying hunger is for a sense of self-worth that material possessions cannot satisfy. For those who fail in the competitive struggle, the results are even more demoralizing.

For Tocqueville the restless, acquisitive American withdraws from a stable, communal world and faces the final threat of isolation. Tocqueville's American individualist "severs himself from the mass of his fellows and draws apart with his family and his friends, so that after he has thus formed a little circle

---

1. *Democracy in America*, ed. Phillips Bradley (New York: Vintage Books, 1945), 2: 144–47. Subsequent quotations will appear in the text.

of his own, he willingly leaves society at large to itself" (2 : 104). However, these family ties prove inadequate; they cannot hold an entire society together. Tocqueville pointedly observes, "Aristocracy had made a chain of all the members of the community, from the peasant to the king; democracy breaks that chain and severs every link of it." For Tocqueville *democracy* is shorthand for the individualism, competitiveness, and restless mobility of an open, egalitarian, nontraditional society. He associates democracy with the American belief that as competitive individuals we are self-made. For Tocqueville, Americans thus tend to cut their ties with their fellows, their ancestors, and their descendants. "They owe nothing to any man," and "they expect nothing from any man; they acquire the habit of always considering themselves as standing alone, and they are apt to imagine that their whole destiny is in their own hands." Under the impulses of democratic individualism, separated from ancestors, descendants, and contemporaries, the American is thus thrown "back forever upon himself alone." The threat is that in the end he will be confined "entirely within the solitude of his own heart" (2 : 105).

In Tocqueville's America, men cut their ties with each other and with the land (2 : 166), restlessly pursue material advantages that, even when attained, fail to satisfy them, and confront the ultimate prospect of total, dehumanizing isolation. If cohesive values exist at all, they are under extreme pressure. The tendencies Tocqueville had accurately analyzed in the 1830s, far from being diminished, became even more pervasive in post–Civil War America. The accelerating changes of industrialization, urbanization, and immigration intensified the sense of rootlessness. More and more people experienced the loneliness of urban life in a society that continued to define people on the basis of their acquisitions. At least in Tocqueville's period, people had the relative cohesion of their village communities; after the Civil War they increasingly cut their ties and moved to the new, impersonal, industrial-commercial cities. The extremes of wealth and poverty became even more apparent and disturbing. For an increasingly large number of Americans, the pressures of this new life resulted in an experience of weightlessness, "a vapid, anonymous existence—a death-in-life." [2] This sense of weightlessness was an intensified version of the strains Tocqueville had perceived. On the surface Americans were self-assured and confident. Internally, as in Tocqueville's period, they drove themselves relentlessly, made and lost fortunes, and continued to face the threat of isolation.

At first glance *Adventures of Huckleberry Finn* seems remote from the new post–Civil War world, but in his masterpiece Twain in fact engages the basic tendencies of his contemporary America. The rootlessness and striving, the unsettling impact on the self, and the threats to community are deeply rooted in the earlier America that Tocqueville had examined and that Twain had grown up in. After the Civil War these tendencies became even more pronounced. Twain's concern with cohesive values and the threats to

2. T. J. Jackson Lears, *No Place of Grace: Antimodernism and the Transformation of American Culture, 1880–1920* (New York: Pantheon Books, 1981), p. 33.

them reflects his sensitivity to, and acute understanding of, the most important human and social problem of his period. By concentrating on his treatment of the family and individualism in *Huck Finn*, we can deepen our own understanding of both his novel and the American society it emerges from and illuminates.

At its best, the late nineteenth-century American family embodies those possibilities of community and security the larger society undermines. In *Huck Finn* the actual families—Pap's, the Grangerfords', the Phelpses', and the widow and Miss Watson's—fall revealingly short of this cohesive ideal. As Kenneth S. Lynn first showed, however, Huck and Jim create a family.[3] Their family embodies an ideal of community that highlights the shortcomings of the actual families and society in the novel. Considering the family and the issue of community also obliges us to examine the individual. In traditional societies the family has a history and a future that transcend any one individual. From an American point of view these traditional societies are restrictive, because Americans find it difficult to imagine that individuality can develop fully in the context of a community or group like the family. As Americans, we usually think of the self opposed to society, the individual versus the community, the emerging person in conflict with the family. Twain's satiric treatment of the actual families and society in *Huck Finn* shows the considerable extent to which such opposition is necessary. Through the relation between Huck and Jim, however, Twain also suggests the possibility of an individualism not at odds with community. On the old world model, people gain security and identity at the price of their individuality. Twain suggests an American individualism appropriate to the new world. This individualism differs both from the restless, acquisitive individualism Tocqueville characterizes and from the traditional subordination of the individual to the family or society. Inevitably, this alternative individualism is not easy to sustain.

In *Huck Finn*, the relation between Huck and Jim is basic; self-fulfillment is a necessary but not sufficient condition for achieving a real individuality. James M. Cox has reoriented Twain criticism by showing the importance of satisfying a boy's need for pleasure, fun, and the expression of his own nature in opposition to the social conventions Tom Sawyer and the widow and Miss Watson represent.[4] What has not been shown, however, is that Huck thus embodies a style of individualism different from the debased romantic individualism of Tom Sawyer, the anarchic individualism of Pap, and, most especially, the acquisitive individualism of the Duke and the Dauphin. Equally important, in the great, idyllic moments on the river, Huck fully if briefly realizes his individuality in the context of a human community with Jim and a natural community with the surrounding world. Since in American thought "self" and "society" are usually opposed, it is worth stressing Twain's intuitive understanding of the possibility of an individualism insep-

3. "Huck and Jim," YR 47 (1958): 421–31. See also A. N. Kaul, *The American Vision: Actual and Ideal Society in Nineteenth-Century Fiction* (New Haven: Yale University Press, 1963), p. 293.
4. *Mark Twain: The Fate of Humor* (Princeton: Princeton University Press, 1967).

arable from rather than opposed to or threatened by community. In practice, the dominant acquisitive individualism of the Duke and the Dauphin under- cuts both the ideal community and the alternative individualism Huck and Jim develop.

In *Huck Finn*, the family is the focus for these concerns about differing versions of individualism and community. *Father, child, family, brother, friend*—in the novel these related words come to form a core of values cen- tering on Huck and Jim's relation. These cohesive family values are as basic to the human world of the novel as the river is to the natural world. Genuine feelings of joy and grief, real laughter and tears, the authentic language of the heart all contribute to the value of the family Huck and Jim create. Huck and especially Jim use a verbal and nonverbal language of the heart to ex- press their feelings for each other. These feelings and the way Huck and Jim express them are exceptionally important in a world dominated sometimes by the suppression of compassion, as with Miss Watson, and sometimes by the calculated expression of false compassion, as with the Duke and the Dauphin. The human ties and repsonsibilities centering on Huck and Jim's family similarly counter powerful tendencies toward a fragmented isolation.

Because of the family Huck and Jim create, and because of Jim's feelings for his wife and children, the novel, however precariously, gives substance to the idea of the larger family of man, not as an empty abstraction but as an endangered value without which modern life is reduced to the barrenness Tocqueville foresaw. To dramatize the danger and to highlight the value, Twain imagines a sequence of fragmented families, culminating in the Duke and the Dauphin's. These two frauds, in their vitality, inventiveness, and merciless pursuit of self-interest, provide a deeply comic, realistic counter- balance to Huck and Jim as family. The novel is organized around the ten- sion between these two created families' and their values as much as it is around the tension between the river and the shore.

At the outset of the novel Huck is part of a fragmented family. There is no father or husband at the widow and Miss Watson's, and this incompletion is symptomatic. The widow and her sister treat Huck differently, but even the kindly widow thinks she knows what is best for Huck and, without taking his needs, feelings, or nature into account, tries to fit him into the mold of respectability, to "sivilize" him (p. 17). For her part, Miss Watson, impatient with a boy's need to move about and implacable in her religion of prayers and guilt, represents a debased form of what Philip Greven described as an "evangelical" parent.[5] From the seventeenth into the nineteenth centuries these authoritarian fathers and mothers trained their children to love and fear them, to hate pleasure and their bodies, and to subordinate their wills and selves to their parents. Later such children did assert themselves, only to experience guilt and to be reborn, to become again as children and to relate to God as they had to their parents, loving and fearing an all-powerful God to whom they subordinated themselves. The widow is a more attractive ver-

5. *The Protestant Temperament: Patterns of Child-Rearing, Religious Experience, and the Self in Early America* (New York: Alfred A. Knopf, 1977), esp. pp. 21–48. Subsequent ref- erences will be noted in the text.

sion of the "moderate" parents Greven analyzes, authoritative rather than authoritarian parents who strove to bend rather than break the will of their children. Moderate parents exercised careful supervision and control over their children and sought through love to bring their children to God and a restrained, disciplined, useful life (pp. 151–261).

The widow and Miss Watson reveal the decline or weaknesses of both the "evangelical" and the "moderate" parent. In the opening episodes of *Huck Finn* both types of parent, and by extension the middle-class family as an instrument of socialization, are effectively satirized. Even well-meaning adults like the widow impose a code of social respectability at odds with Huck's real needs. In the widow and Miss Watson's family, Huck's genuine individuality is stifled, not developed. Religion, moreover, is not a life-giving force but is comically reduced to the level of manners and dress. It is no wonder that Huck, estranged from his adopted family and under the pressure of social and religious demands he can live with but that fail to satisfy his needs, "felt so lonesome I most wished I was dead" (p. 20). Ideally, families provide a sense of belonging, of cohesiveness, and they encourage the individual to develop his unique potentialities as part of the family and society. At best the family is also a counterforce to those feelings of loneliness and isolation Tocqueville showed to be especially American. The families in Huck's early experience, however, intensify rather than mitigate these feelings.

In the design of *Huck Finn* the fragmented family life and anarchic individualism Pap represents are at the opposite extreme not only from Huck and Jim's natural individualism and cohesive family but also from the widow and Miss Watson's declined Protestant individualism and feminine world of middle-class respectability. Ann Douglas has shown that during the nineteenth century women and ministers created a counterideology as an alternative to the masculine-dominated world of power.[6] This domestic ideology celebrated the "feminine" values of the family, motherhood, and religion. Unfortunately, as Douglas demonstrates, these values formed a sentimental culture integral to the genteel tradition. In his treatment of the widow and Miss Watson and of Emmeline Grangerford's sentimental poetry and painting, Twain reacts against the prevailing "feminine" sentimentality and religiosity. In imagining Huck and Jim as a family, Twain makes authentic family values an alternative to the "feminized" families of the widow and Miss Watson and Aunt Sally as well as to the "masculine" extremes Pap and the Duke and the Dauphin represent.

From another point of view the contrast between Pap and the widow and Miss Watson is not between nature and civilization, as might first appear, but between a decayed civilization viewed from the bottom and the more genteel version of the widow and Miss Watson. In the swamp of Pap's life, because he feels none of the positive ties of family and affection, he is cut off from civilization's most basic force of human cohesion. Pap embodies a nightmare version of what can happen to the American individualist cut off

6. *The Feminization of American Culture* (New York: Alfred A. Knopf, 1977).

from sustaining family ties and from any positive involvement in the larger society. Instead, Pap tries to acquire money without working and to satisfy himself through the most self-destructive drinking he can manage. He is a caricature of Tocqueville's acquisitive individualist, but lacking the prototypical restless striving and energy. The broken family life with Pap is a main source of Huck's alienation. Paradoxically, however, Pap's situation on the edges of society leaves Huck free to develop in his own way.

But when Pap takes Huck away from town into the woods, instead of freeing his son he confines him even more than his genteel counterparts did. The cabin in the woods becomes a prison, and Huck, though he likes losing the trappings of civilization, is not really free or natural. In the throes of delirium tremens, Pap tries to murder his son. This terrifying scene brings to life the full reality of Huck's loneliness and danger, his separation from sources of security and his unnatural condition of imprisonment. Through the immediacy of dramatic action, Twain conveys the same threatening sense of isolation that Tocqueville more abstractly shows as the ultimate danger in the American situation. Huck's relation with Pap, however, provides the impetus for him to escape; and thereafter Huck moves gradually, unintentionally, precariously toward a world of genuine freedom and life-giving ties with Jim on the journey down the river.

In the opening chapters of the novel, though, Jim is not a father either to his family or to Huck but is instead an object, a stage figure for Tom Sawyer to play tricks on and for Twain to exploit for his comic superstitions. When Jim first appears, Huck refuses to play along with Tom's trick of tying him up, not because he respects Jim's humanity but because he is worried that Jim "might wake and make a disturbance, and then they'd find out I warn't in" (p. 23). But later, on the island, "I was ever so glad to see Jim. I warn't lonesome, now" (p. 67). Thereafter, the human ties between Huck and Jim deepen. Like a father initiating his son, Jim almost immediately passes along to Huck what he knows about the mysteries of nature. As Daniel Hoffman has shown, this marvelously nonscientific lore constitutes a valuable alternative to the rationalistic outlook of the middle-class white world.[7] What has not been stressed, however, is that Jim also comically outlines his failure as a speculator, as a man involved with money, investment, and financial manipulation. Recall the way Balum's Ass conned Jim and made an ass of him for playing the investment game, an episode that comically calls to mind both the general atmosphere of financial speculation in the Gilded Age and Twain's own penchant for pouring his money into bad investments. But Jim has learned his lesson about making money through financial speculation, a basic enterprise of an acquisitive society. Later, when the Duke and the Dauphin appear, a restless pursuit of money and property contrasts with Jim and Huck's nonacquisitive relation to each other and the world around them. In Chapter 4 Huck gives the Judge his money when Pap shows up, and, more ominously, he later hides the money in the coffin in the Wilks episode, a revealing, unconscious association of money and death. Huck thus

7. *Form and Fable in American Fiction* (New York: Oxford University Press, 1961), pp. 322–42.

basically agrees with Jim about money and property. But in Chapters 16 and 31 Huck also feels he should turn Jim in because Jim is someone else's property. These contradictory feelings about money and property give urgency to Huck's central moral choice. In *Huck Finn*, Twain probes deeply along a major fault line of his society, its contradictory feelings about both property values and human values.

Jim embodies this conflict. Legally he is a piece of property worth $800. In contrast to the compelling, impersonal values of money and property, however, Jim's quality as a human being emerges subtly and convincingly. Jim, for example, refuses to let Huck look at the dead man who turns out to be Pap. Jim is again more a true father than the father who is now literally dead. After Huck puts the snakeskin in Jim's bed, however, they both suffer the consequences. Huck has still not fully realized Jim's humanity and the human responsibilities their relation entails.

Twain has Jim and Huck develop these issues unpretentiously in their comic argument about Solomon. Jim wins the first round by seeing clearly that what is at stake is not a half-child but "a whole chile," a whole person, alive and functioning, "en de man dat think he kin settle a 'spute 'bout a whole chile wid a half a chile, doan know enough to come in out'n de rain" (p. 112). Jim loses the second round, however, because he cannot understand why a Frenchman does not talk like a man. To counter Huck, Jim piles up a series of examples to show that cats and dogs and cows aren't men, but a Frenchman is a man, so "Dad blame it, why doan' he *talk* like a man? You answer me *dat*!" (p. 114). But Huck, who speaks for pluralism, reminds us that, just as cats and dogs and cows talk different from each other, "then, why ain't it natural and right for a *Frenchman* to talk different from us? You answer me that" (p. 114). The joke is intensified because Jim has just argued for the importance of the whole child, the whole man, and has accused Solomon of being limited by his upbringing; but because Jim also has his provincial limitations, the joke turns against him.

The argument between Huck and Jim centers on an idea of man. Huck and Jim raise the issues of the whole child, talking "like a man," and, to use Huck's words, what is "natural and right." Huck gets the better of the argument when he speaks for an idea of man large enough to include foreigners. Twain, however, knows that actual men often fail to live up to their best insights, as he has both Huck and Jim demonstrate in this episode, Huck at the very end when he says, "I see it warn't no use wasting words—you can't learn a nigger to argue. So I quit" (p. 114). The final twist on the joke is that, because of his view of "a nigger," Huck contradicts the basic argument that everyone is "a man."

In the fog scene and its sequel these issues about what is "a man" and what is "natural and right" are basic to the central choices of the characters and the full human and social implications of their dramatized relation. Huck and Jim have been close and in the fog they are separated. In this nightmarish, almost surreal episode Twain renders what it means to Huck to be separated, to have lost his bearings, to be alone again, this time in "the solid white fog" and "tangled good, now," totally confused and disoriented.

"If you think it ain't dismal and lonesome out in a fog that way, by yourself, in the night, you try it once—you'll see" (pp. 116, 117). The episode has the power of a disturbing dream. It brings alive the extreme Tocquevillean condition of being absolutely alone and separated, and it is also a metaphor for the dislocation of Huck's moral sense after his return, a wrenching the experience in the fog both provokes and represents.

When they are reunited, Jim responds to Huck's return like a father to a lost, loved "chile" (p. 119). But instead of telling Jim how relieved he is, Huck thoughtlessly belittles Jim by playing a Tom Sawyer–like trick on him. In one of the novel's most crucial passages, Jim then lets Huck know what real feelings are and what real friendship involves. Jim speaks the language of the heart—"my heart wuz mos' broke" (p. 121)—a language of genuine feeling and concern that expresses in tears the depth of his friendship for his "chile." *Friend*, *father*, and *child* lose their distinction in Jim's language of the heart. Huck gradually learns its rules and inflections, and the Duke and the Dauphin exploit it for ends that threaten the very life of that society whose cohesive values they pretend to speak for, even as they act out its dominant and divisive individualism. In contrast to the destructive self-interest of the Duke and the Dauphin, Huck develops through his choices and grows closer to Jim. After the trick with the snakeskin, Huck feels bad but keeps quiet; after he tricks Jim in the fog scene, Huck begins to speak Jim's language of feeling, humbles himself to his friend, and resolves not to "do him no more mean tricks, and I wouldn't done that one if I'd a knowed it would make him feel that way" (p. 121).

But Twain immediately puts Huck to the test. Jim keeps talking about being "a free man" (p. 123) and thus brings into sharp focus the novel's concern with what it means both to be free and to be a man. As an exemplary "free man," in the full normative sense of these key words, Jim wants to be reunited with his family. For Jim, to be a free man is to be fully human, a condition that for him is inseparable from the intimate, cohesive ties of the family. But his proposal to buy his wife and steal his two children shocks Huck, who is on the verge of turning Jim in. Although Jim's basic humanity is inseparable from his feelings for his family, Huck also sees Jim as property, as someone who "would steal his children—children that belonged to a man I didn't even know; a man that hadn't ever done me no harm. I was sorry to hear Jim say that, it was such a lowering of him" (p. 124).

Because Huck is both Jim's friend and metaphorically his child, the comic inversions illuminate basic values and reveal deep contradictions in Huck's consciousness and his American society. The novel is set in the 1840s, and the specific issue is Jim's status as a slave. But the implications of this conflict between human values and property values, it should be stressed, go beyond the issue of slavery in the 1840s. More significantly, they involve a fundamental division in American capitalism. Twain has brilliantly contrived the novel so that Jim is a commodity as well as a human being, a salable object as well as a free man and a true friend. As a piece of property he is worth $800 and his children belong to someone else. Jim, however, emerges as a whole man, not as a divided person who has accepted the dominant society's definition of him as a commodity. He has freed himself of his involvement in the money world, and during the central episodes of the novel he acts and sees himself as a free man. He is intimately related to the natural world and, though he is separated from his family, he is intimately related to them, too.

Huck, not Jim, is divided because of the dominant society's views about property. Huck is torn between the human claims of friendship and the impersonal but compelling values of property and social convention. His consciousness is polarized. Huck's conflict and divided consciousness are ones most people experience but usually in a less polarized and dramatic form. What is equally important, Twain has the genius to expose not only the social sources but also the personal, human consequences of this conflict. It is no accident, then, that Huck "just felt sick" (p. 125). The sickness he feels is the alienated consciousness that results from a split that dominates his culture. Huck has taken inside himself the central division of his market society. This division within the self, its social, economic, and racial causes, and its disturbing human results constitute, to apply the Dauphin's words in a new but related context, the most damaging illness in the world of "the diseased" (p. 213).

The imagery of disease occurs in key episodes involving alienation and the violation of humanity. Elsewhere in the novel Huck feels sick when his sense of humanity is violated by acts of cruelty, inhumanity, or injustice, acts originating from the outside, as when he sees Buck Grangerford murdered or the Duke and the Dauphin tarred and feathered. In the present episode, however, the alienation is inside Huck; rather, his basic humanity is at odds with his internalized social values. The conflict makes Huck feel sick. Although he has lived on the margins of society, Huck carries inside him the source of the sickness, the divisions generated by a society whose racism and commitment to property and property values conflict with the best of its own religious and humanistic values as well as the intuitively realized humanity Huck embodies. Racism, of course, is not peculiar to capitalism. But in practice the racism reinforces and is reinforced by the commitment to property.

The classic market society form of alienation involves the person who sells his labor as a possession, whose self is then separated internally, and who engages in work dictated by external demands. Twain renders another, related form of alienation. He shows that the self in conflict protests from the depths of its humanity against the violation of its humanity. Huck is not directly involved in the selling of his alienated self as a commodity, but indirectly he experiences the consequences, since he accepts the dominant class view of Jim as "nigger" and as property. As a black slave Jim brings into intense focus the contradiction between humane views of the whole self and the market society view that part of the self can be alienated and as a commodity can be sold for what it will command as labor. The irony is that Jim is whole, Huck and the dominant society are divided.

In the world of the diseased, we cannot expect permanent cures. But the vital ties Huck establishes with Jim and the river at least temporarily heal the divisions and, for a memorable interlude, cure the sickness of alienation. However briefly, this family idyll with Jim on the raft also makes us forget the friction and hostility that in the real world always accompany family love and affection. Far from being a deficiency, this precariously sustained interlude enhances the credibility of Twain's vision of freedom, cohesion, and the fusion of individuality and community. But a reader may grant that Twain has created a compelling myth of what we desire and nonetheless feel it is too remote from any possibility of realization to warrant our assent. Although the interlude is powerful in its claims on our imagination and in its ability to generate significant comedy in the novel, it is also vulnerable to the assaults of reality, most literally, to the assaults of the Duke and the Dauphin. Perhaps, like any vision of a green world or golden age, it is simultaneously indispensable as a reminder of human possibility perennially beyond our grasp.

It does not discredit Twain's goals to see them as tantalizingly beyond reach. In striving toward such indispensable, perhaps unattainable goals, however, we do need to sustain a precarious tension. We need to feel that our ideals have genuine roots and at least some chance of being realized. In the concluding chapters of *Huck Finn*, however, Twain shifts the focus back to Tom Sawyer and away from Huck's developing sense of freedom, community, and identity. Quite aside from its explicit content, this shift in itself constitutes an indirect form of social criticism, too indirect to be fully effective but nonetheless rooted in Twain's very genuine social disillusion. For many readers the episodes with Tom and the Phelpses represent an imaginative failure, a falling off from the promising themes Twain had been exploring. One explanation is that when he came to write the last third of *Huck Finn*, Twain had finally become too aware of the fragmenting power of his society to be willing or able to keep alive his vision of freedom and community. He apparently came to feel that his most precious ideals were too far removed from their roots in a vital social world.

If the secure good family exists anywhere in the novel, it ought to be at the Phelpses. The Phelpses are a family in the usual sense of having a mother, a father, children, nephews, aunts, and a network of family relations. This large family centers around Aunt Sally. The treatment of the Phelps family in the final episode rounds out a sequence that began with another, more obviously "feminized" family, the widow and Miss Watson's. In a low-keyed way, moreover, Twain's treatment of the Phelpses at once partakes of and undercuts nostalgia about the American rural family. The Phelpses' generosity and hospitality, the abundance of food and children, Aunt Sally's concern and Uncle Silas's absent-mindedness play off against their irritability and a recognition of the intolerance and ineptitude that exist along with their affection. For Twain, rural life includes the mob that joins the Phelpses to hunt the escaped slave. But the Phelpses also bring Jim special food, even as they imprison him.

Tom Sawyer conditions our view of the Phelps family. Tom controls events—the petty thefts of shirts, spoons, candles, and sheets; the ratholes filled and the escape hole dug. The turmoil he causes brings out Aunt Sally's irritability and repeatedly makes her and Uncle Silas look foolish. Partly because interest centers on the tricks and on the taking in of the adults, the relation between husband and wife consists mainly of Aunt Sally's yelling at Uncle Silas for oversights he did not really commit. Kind as they are, Aunt Sally and Uncle Silas do not instance a web of affectionate relations between husband and wife. Contrary to stereotypes about the authoritarian husband, moreover, Aunt Sally is the main authority in the Phelps family. Uncle Silas is gentle and absent-minded and provides openings for jokes about preaching and religion. The children are in the background to be smacked, hugged, and well fed.

Aunt Sally is at the center of the family. Like Jim, she has real feelings. She tucks Huck in "and mothered me so good I felt mean, and like I couldn't look her in the face" (p. 353). She cries when she thinks Tom is missing and in trouble. But unlike Jim, her tears and concern confine rather than free Huck. "The door ain't going to be locked," she tells him, "and there's the window and the rod; but you'll be good, *won't* you? And you won't go? For *my* sake" (p. 353). Huck wants to go "but after that, I wouldn't a went, not for kingdoms" (p. 354). Aunt Sally's compassion keeps Huck in line; it locks him up without keys. Huck reacts against this compassionate pressure to make him good in a way society approves. As with the widow and Miss Watson, to satisfy Aunt Sally, Huck must give up his individuality. Lighting out for the Territory may not be the answer, but Huck is going to try it "because Aunt Sally she's going to adopt me and sivilize me and I can't stand it. I been there before" (p. 366).

In contrast to Aunt Sally's family, the relation Huck and Jim develop on the river brings to memorable if temporary life a myth of cohesion and individuality. The Duke and the Dauphin provide the most basic contrasts to the sustaining ties Huck and Jim create. Aside from the Duke and the Dauphin and Huck and Jim, Twain's comic probing of the family ranges from Pap's at one extreme of the class ladder through the widow and Miss Watson's and the Phelpses' in the middle to the Grangerfords' at the other extreme. With the Grangerfords, though, the comedy turns on our perception that these aristocrats are not far removed in position and bad taste from the rest of their rural countrymen. The fact that Huck and Jim are outside this conventional scheme suggests both their value and their vulnerability.

In contrast to Huck and Jim's informal rituals, the Grangerfords have a formalized code of respect and dignity. In the idyll on the Mississippi, Huck and Jim take off their clothes and are at one with each other and the river. The Grangerfords, in splendid contrast, "dressed in white linen from head to foot, . . . and wore broad Panama hats" (p. 144), and they express their regard for each other in elaborate ceremonies with the decanter and the order of seating. Women and their honor are important in this set of conventions, but when Miss Sophia falls in love with a Shepherdson, her feelings and interests are ignored. The conventional values of the clan or family honor take empty precedence over her personal feelings and best interests, so that this "aristocratic" family reenacts the same pattern that characterizes Huck in his relations with Pap, Tom, the widow and Miss Watson, and Aunt

Sally. If Pap cares too little for the family, however, the Grangerfords care too much, and in the wrong way. Despite the Sunday values they pay lip service to, the Grangerfords separate brotherly love and positive family feeling from what they are really committed to: killing in the name of conventional honor. The split has gruesome results: the family is destroyed, and Huck feels "sick" (p. 154). When he feels sick about turning Jim in, Huck shares the alienation of his society. At the Grangerfords, though, the alienation is not inside Huck but in the world of the diseased; his sick feeling is his human response to the senseless violence and divisions of the culture.

After the violence and divisiveness of the Grangerfords' conventional society, Huck and Jim are reunited, "free and safe once more" in the "home" they have made together (pp. 155, 156). The cohesive family idyll on the river comes briefly and unforgettably alive. Huck describes his harmony with Jim and with the natural world. They are at one with each other and with the universe around them. They light up their pipes, dangle their legs in the water, and talk "about all kinds of things—we was always naked, day and night, whenever the mosquitoes would let us" (p. 159). They shed the clothes that symbolize the Grangerfords' civilization: "the new clothes Buck's folks made for me was too good to be comfortable, and besides I didn't go much on clothes, nohow" (p. 159). Open to each other and to nature, including the mosquitoes, they speculate about the origins of the vital universe they inhabit. "We had the sky, up there," Huck says, "all speckled with stars, and we used to lay on our backs and look up at them, and discuss about whether they was made, or only just happened." Their explanations, their canons of reason and probability, align them not with rationalistic scientists or theologians but with the ancient mythmakers. "Jim he allowed [the stars] was made, but I allowed they happened; I judged it would have took too long to *make* so many. Jim said the moon could a *laid* them; well, that looked kind of reasonable, so I didn't say nothing against it, because I've seen a frog lay most as many, so of course it could be done" (p. 159).

The Duke and the Dauphin, however, immediately bring civilization and its dissonances into this world of natural relations. The Duke and the Dauphin are a parody of the positive family Huck and Jim create. Instead of developing ties of real affection and concern, the two con men in the end fight each other. The younger one, who trusts no one, says to his old, bald-headed partner, "and I a trusting you all the time, like you was my own father" (p. 264). This final, comic reminder underscores the basic differences between these two created families, differences that define structure and values in the central sequences of *Huck Finn*. What holds the Duke and the Dauphin's family together is not trust, affection, or a journey toward community, freedom, and identity but rather the prospect of profit. The Duke and King are out for themselves at the expense of victims, primarily along the shore and finally on the raft itself. But since these acquisitive motives and values are central to American society, the Duke and the Dauphin also comically image the society they fleece.

As representatives of the larger society, they immediately introduce rank and social differences into the harmonious relation Huck and Jim have developed. Their fake genealogies and demands for deference satirize the fascination with rank and inequality of our supposedly egalitarian society. On a raft, however, conflict over status "would have been a miserable business," and Huck speaks for the precarious, resonant countervalue of "peace in the family" (p. 166). Although the acquisitive restlessness and greed of the Duke and the King finally destroy Huck's peaceful family, they highlight rather than diminish the need for the values Huck celebrates.

They do so most interestingly through a series of roles and identities they invent. We never know the real names of the Duke and the Dauphin. We know only their style, the parts they play, and the fact that they are constantly acting, performing. They embody the energy, resourcefulness, and greed of a culture in which men are cut off from fixed social and moral ties and are free to move and exploit. Because the society they emerge from is fluid and unstable, it does not provide the Duke and the Dauphin with stable identities, so they are constantly creating themselves. Instead of fixed identities, they have only their socially generated restlessness, inventiveness, and eye for the main chance. In their unlikely costumes, they come to assume mythic proportions. They bring to imaginative life essential tendencies of modern America and a familiar style of acquisitive individualism, certainly one Tocqueville would recognize.

Huck and Jim embody a cohesive family and an individualism compatible with community. Their individualism also leads to personal growth, not to the exploitation of other people. For insight into the contrasting world of the Duke and the Dauphin, consider the series of performances that culminates in one of the novel's funniest and most suggestive episodes, when the King plays the part of a pirate who wants to return to do good in the Indian Ocean. The King brilliantly satirizes and exploits "them dear people in Pokeville camp-meeting, natural brothers and benefactors of the race—and that dear preacher there, the truest friend a pirate ever had" (p. 174). Huck and Jim show that natural brotherhood and true friendship are at the heart of the novel, but again and again Twain also shows that these values are easily sentimentalized and drained of their real meaning. The King "busted into tears," a collection is taken up, and this pirate puts the cohesive values of brotherhood and friendship to the uses of private gain.

Because of its insights into the audience, its counterpoint of true and exploitative brotherhood, and its awareness of self-interest masked by religious pretense, the campmeeting scene provides an intensifying mirror for the performances that follow. The exposure of Bricksville and the loafers, the performances of Boggs and Sherburn and the acting out of the murder, the circus performance and Huck's response, and finally the Royal Nonesuch act—all are played out against the backdrop of the campmeeting. Each episode develops one or another of the themes that the King brings into comic focus.

What is particularly significant is that the organizing metaphor of acting, shows, and performances emerges from and illuminates the instability and fluidity of a society whose members are bored, rootless, and hungry for entertainment. For them improvisation is important, and the difference between the real and sham is difficult to establish. It is worth stressing that the traditional, old-world imagery of shows and performances—Shakespeare is only the most famous practitioner—thus gains new meaning in *Huck Finn* specifically because of the American social setting. Twain's imagery of duplicity and role-playing is also rooted in and exposes the fragmentation of his society, particularly when the Duke and the Dauphin play the parts of Peter Wilks's loving brothers. Cumulatively, Twain's handling of the organizing imagery of acting and performances thus provides a major instance of the intimate relation between an important formal pattern and its social origins and implications.[8] The related imagery of sickness and decay powerfully reenters the novel in the description of the town eaten away by the river and its inhabitants wasting away in a boredom broken by spasms of cruelty.

To contrast with the degradations of "the diseased" and to prepare for the Wilks episode, his most intense exploration of true and fake families, Twain has Jim again bring real family feelings, real grief and tears, to the fore. He is stricken, "moaning and mourning," as he thinks "about his wife and his children, away up yonder, and he was low and homesick; because he hadn't ever been away from home before in his life" (p. 201). Jim's natural feelings for his family emerge even more intensely as he recalls that he once hit his daughter for not minding him. In one of the most touching examples of the language of the heart, he then says, "Oh, Huck, I bust out a-cryin' en grab her up in my arms, en say, 'Oh, de po' little thing! de Lord God Almighty fogive po' ole Jim, kaze he never gwyne to fogive hisself as long's he live!' Oh, she was plumb deef en dumb, Huck, plumb deef en dumb—en I'd ben a-treat'n her so!" (p. 202).

Jim is not acting. He feels deep love for his daughter and genuine remorse for what he has done. His tears and words mean what they say. Continuing Twain's imagery of performance, however, the Duke and Dauphin immediately disguise Jim "in King Lear's outfit" (p. [203]), the most inappropriate choice imaginable given Jim's feelings for his family. The two con men then put on their own costumes and, in an orgy of acting, begin to play the roles of Peter Wilks's brothers. They fake the feelings of grief and concern Jim has shown naturally. Further underscoring the contrast with Jim, one of them even plays the "deef and dumb" brother.

Like Jim, the Duke and King "bust out a-crying" (p. 210), and in this and other ways they systematically parody and deprave the language of the heart. The King takes in his audience and tearfully "slobbers out" his speech "about its being a sore trial for him and his poor brother to lose the diseased, and to miss seeing diseased alive." The King also exploits "this dear sympathy" he pretends to feel and gives thanks "out of his heart and out of his brother's heart . . . till it was just sickening" (p. 213). Throughout Huck's report of the speech, the imagery of disease, of sickness, has the force of the imagery of corruption in *Hamlet*. In the presence of death, which calls for human

---

8. For another view of the theme of acting and performing, see George C. Carrington, Jr., *The Dramatic Unity of "Huckleberry Finn"* (Columbus: Ohio State University Press, 1976), pp. 47–108.

honesty and a community of the living, these false brothers violate and exploit the claims of human sympathy and the ties of family. The family, however vulnerable and fallible in practice, is also the most basic force of social cohesion in the world of the novel. To convey the intensity of his reaction against this violation of family ties and the language of the heart, Twain invents the malapropisms of "the diseased" and "his funeral orgies" (p. 217), and he has Huck emphasize "the rot and slush." For Huck "it was just sickening," and at the end the doctor says, "you're going to feel sick whenever you think of this day" (p. 219). Part of the illness is that the townspeople lack the resources to see through the act, to detect the fake language, to tell true from false feeling, real from sham brothers and brotherhood. More basically the sickening disease is the abuse of the bonds of family feeling and of the brotherhood of man in the interests of personal gain. The resulting alienation is the most basic disease of Twain's America.

During Twain's formative years, as Robert Wiebe wrote, "American institutions were still oriented toward a community life where family and church, education and press, professions and government, all largely found their meaning by the way they fit one with another inside a town or a detached portion of a city. As men ranged farther and farther from their communities" after the Civil War,

> they tried desperately to understand the larger world in terms of their small, familiar environment. They tried, in other words, to impose the known upon the unknown, to master an impersonal world through the customs of a personal society. They failed, usually without recognizing why; and that failure to comprehend a society they were helping to make contained the essence of the nation's story.[9]

But in telling his and his nation's story, Twain did comprehend. The violation of family ties is crucial to Twain, is a sickening disease, because, rooted as he is in "the customs of a personal society," he is especially well situated to sense and judge the divisive power of self-interest and the accelerating fragmentation of the culture, tendencies he knew from observation and his own painful experience. For Mark Twain, the debasing of the language of the heart and attacks on the family, the most intimate institution of social order, threaten to leave people with no other supports or ties, to leave them with no possibility of human community.

Adventures of Huckleberry Finn is poised between this vision of "the diseased," an alienated world presided over by the Duke and the Dauphin, and the myth of Huck and Jim's cohesive family. In America we usually see the individual opposed to society, the self versus the community, the person distinct from the group. Huck and Jim, however, are able to develop as individuals within and not opposed to the community they create. Huck, though, is also subject to the divisions of his culture; he carries as well as counters the sickness. Until the Phelps episode, Twain kept the contest even. Although the Duke and King are run out on a rail in Chapter 33, no one, least of

---

9. *The Search for Order, 1877–1920* (New York: Hill & Wang, 1967), p. 12.

all the Twain of the final chapters, believes that the style of individualism and the sense of community Huck and Jim develop has triumphed, either in the novel or in the restlessly changing society it grows from and illuminates. The triumph is that, knowing as intimately as he did the divisive power of acquisitive individualism, Twain nonetheless managed to sustain for as long as he did a life-affirming myth of cohesion and genuine individuality undercut by the dominant tendencies of that world of the diseased he both exposed and continued to live in.

21 PAUL TAYLOR

Huckleberry Finn: The Education of a Young Capitalist

When Huckleberry Finn announces his decision to "light out for the Territory ahead of the rest," he says he is doing so, as everyone knows, to avoid Aunt Sally's attempt to "sivilize" him. Huck's "escape" from that civilization has been the subject of considerable debate, but the criticism largely ignores one important element of Huck's decision: money.[1] When Tom Sawyer first proposes the trip, Huck responds, "all right, that suits me, but I ain't got no money for to buy the outfit, and I reckon I couldn't get none from home, because it's likely pap's been back before now, and got it all away from Judge Thatcher and drunk it up" (p. 365). This statement is remarkable for a variety of reasons. Huck has assigned a certain, though unspecified, value to the "outfit"—something that he cannot acquire without spending money. Though Huck has determined that the outfit has value, equivalent to the importance of his "escape," he believes that he does not possess the means necessary to purchase that escape, since Pap has "drunk up" his means. Huck's statement also prompts Jim to tell Huck about Pap's death. Pap's death—specifically, Jim's finally telling Huck of Pap's death—provides Huck with the money necessary to escape, and so concludes a story that came into being at the end of another story in which Huck suddenly becomes rich.

> Now the way that the book winds up, is this: Tom and me found the money that the robbers hid in the cave, and it made us rich. We got six thousand dollars apiece—all gold. It was an awful sight of money when it was piled up. Well, Judge Thatcher, he took it and put it out at interest, and it fetched us a dollar a day apiece, all the year round—more than a body could tell what to do with. The Widow Douglas, she took me for her son, and allowed she would sivilize me; but it was rough living in the house all the time, considering how dismal regular and decent the widow was in all her ways; and so when I couldn't stand it no longer, I lit out. I got into my old rags . . . and was free and satisfied. But Tom Sawyer, he hunted me up and said he was going to start a band of robbers, and I might join if I would go back to the widow and be respectable. So I went back. (Pp. [17]−18)

1. There have been, of course, studies that treat money in general as an important element of the novel, but few that note Mark Twain's use of specific sums of money as a recurring motif. An exception is the forty-dollar motif I mention later. See, for example, Victor A. Doyno, "Over Twain's Shoulder: The Composition and Structure of *Huckleberry Finn*," *MFS* 14 (Spring 1968): 3−9.

Huck has become a capitalist; his money is earning interest in Judge Thatcher's hands. However, instead of being liberated, as the strike-it-rich myth would suppose, Huck ironically loses his freedom almost at the moment he comes into possession of a large sum of money. Both Huck and his money are "taken" ("Judge Thatcher, he took it"; "The Widow Douglas, she took me") into captivity by a "regular and decent" civilization. He is "free and satisfied" only when he escapes and abandons the money. Later, the gold attracts Pap, who also confines Huck because of his money. If it were not for the gold Huck took out of a hole in the ground, there would have been no need for him to escape from both Pap and the widow and thus no adventures and no story. This situation, in which having money is antithetical to being "free and satisfied," is reversed at the novel's conclusion when Huck needs his money in order to escape. Thus, Huck's relationship with his newly acquired wealth undergoes a marked transformation during the course of the novel. That transformation begins immediately, since as soon as he gets the money, "Judge Thatcher, he took it and put it out at interest."

Judge Thatcher is not the only "robber" mentioned at the beginning of the novel. Significantly, the second paragraph begins and ends with robbers. The first robbers are the adults who hid the gold in the cave; the second robbers are the boys of Tom Sawyer's gang. This textual play between "real" robbers and "pretend" robbers is an example of the subtle irony with which Huck's narration of this "money-determined" story conjoins the worlds of boyish fantasy and adult fact. Tom Sawyer will allow Huck to join his band of robbers only if he is a "respectable" part of the widow's civilization. As part of that civilization, the judge who "took" Huck's money is a spokesman for the respectable robber: the "robber baron" of the American Gilded Age. The respectable robber emphasizes the production and accumulation of wealth. He has a morality of production—making money is good—but he has no equivalent morality of consumption. He makes more money "than a body could tell what to do with." When Huck runs to the judge in order to hide his money from Pap, the judge responds: "Did you come for your interest? . . . Quite a fortune for you. You better let me invest it along with your six thousand, because if you take it you'll spend it" (p. 35). For the "sivilized" robber-capitalist, money is not for anything as foolish as spending. Similarly, he does not simply give it away; since the ownership of money defines him as a capitalist, he must sell it: "You want to *sell* all your property to me—not give it. That's the correct idea" (p. 36). Whatever the judge's conscious motivation, the specific terminology of his redefinition—sell, not give—expresses both Huck's lack of control over his money and the "correct idea" of money as property, that is, as capital.

The judge's control over Huck's money is opposed by Pap. Almost the exact opposite of the respectable robber, Pap, having little to do with production and nothing to do with accumulation, has a genius for consumption. Huck is very much aware of the nature of Pap's genius. When a nine-log raft floats by early in the day, Huck realizes that he has an opportunity to escape: "Anybody but pap would a waited and seen the day through, so as to catch more stuff; but that warn't pap's style" (p. 55). Since he is a captive as a consequence of Pap's desire to "drink up" his money, it is ironic that Huck's escape is a consequence of Pap's fiscal "style." If Pap had stayed to accumulate more "stuff," Huck would not have had the time to plan and "execute" his escape. Moreover, the time Huck expected to have while Pap took the raft to town is not entirely a function of what might be called the "spendthrift" aspect of Pap's fiscal style; Pap's drink-it-up attitude toward money is not simply a matter of immediate consumption versus production and accumulation. Huck defines Pap's fiscal style in terms of consumption as intoxication: "Every time he got money he got drunk" (p. [45]), the most dramatic expression of this equation being Huck's metaphorical "drunk it up," quoted above in reference to his belief that Pap had gained control of his money.

Pap did not wrestle the money away from Huck; if he got it, he took it from the judge's control. In between the first and the last chapters of the novel, Huck never has control of his own wealth. The six thousand becomes the object of a struggle between two opposed "definitions" of wealth, neither of which represents an acceptable alternative for Huck. Huck's story resolves this dilemma by manipulating the specific sum of six thousand dollars. The initial appearance of that sum establishes the problem; the reappearance of that same sum in the Wilks episode allows Huck to reformulate the dilemma in a way that makes possible its resolution in the conclusion.

The adventures of Huckleberry Finn come into being as a consequence of unearned wealth: money taken from a cave, a hole in the ground. Coming from Injun Joe's grave, and being like any buried treasure worthy of its place in romantic or anti-romantic fiction, Huck's stolen money is dead man's gold, and Tom and Huck are grave robbers. Because it is both gold ore and cave loot, the six thousand is also doubly "earth-money." In the context of American economic life in the 1880s, the "stolen" nature of this earth-money can be associated with two distinct anxiety-inducing facts: the enormous wealth being taken from the natural resources of America by the "respectable" robber baron is largely unearned; and the exploitation of this natural wealth is an immoral act, a rape of mother earth. While the latter may be the dominant anxiety of the modern American, the late nineteenth-century American, closer to the Puritan morality requiring that all wealth be earned, may have been more anxious about the former. For the Puritans, only earned material success could be taken as a sign of favor for the man who works hard at his "calling." Thus, unearned wealth is also stolen wealth, necessarily taken from someone who earned it. For their heirs in the nineteenth century, unearned wealth was still suspected of having been stolen. Wealth taken from the earth, or robbed from the grave, like Huck's cave loot, creates a dilemma because it is free and easy, on the one hand, and unearned and immoral on the other.

In this formulation of Huck's money problems, the dead man's gold represents both unearned wealth and earth-money. The anxiety created by Huck's unearned wealth focuses on the dead man's claim, a claim represented by Pap, who is a dead man throughout most of Huck's story—though Huck either does not know it or does not believe it. When Huck sees a sign that the dead man, Pap, has come back, he races to Judge Thatcher's. The immediacy of his reaction indicates that the money is very much on his mind. Even though Huck seems willing to lose his money by giving it to the judge in order to preserve his freedom from Pap, he is not willing to lose it by simply letting Pap have it. He hides the money from Pap and "sells" it to the judge: a single transaction that expresses the two horns of his dilemma. Huck's ability to resolve that dilemma is complicated by the fact that Pap "stands for" both the money-drunk and the dead man. The reappearance of the six thousand dollars in the Wilks episode allows Huck to reformulate the dilemma and to separate the money-drunk/respectable robber opposition from the unearned/immoral anxiety.

Recapitulating the original transaction (taking the money robbers hid in the cave), Huck once again takes six thousand dollars from robbers—the Duke and the King, who are just as money-drunk as Pap. For all their money-making schemes, all they ever really do with money is get drunk on it. Moreover, the Duke and the King imitate Pap's ability to equate consumption with intoxication, because gold can intoxicate them without having to be turned into liquor—consider the excited state that the mere physical appearance of the gold induces in the Duke and the King: "They pawed the yaller-boys, and sifted them through their fingers and let them jingle down on the floor" (p. 214). Unlike Pap, however, they are not representatives of the dead man's claim on the gold. In fact, because they are trying to steal Peter Wilks's money, they are exactly opposed to the dead man's claim. Imitating the bifurcating structure of the second transaction (hiding the money from Pap and selling it to the judge), Huck hides the money from the Duke and the King and gives it to the dead man. Hiding it in Wilks's coffin, Huck returns the dead man's gold to the earth, thereby separating the anxiety imposed by the stolen nature of the earth-money from the dilemma concerned with the control of wealth. Near the conclusion of the Wilks episode, Huck escapes, this time from Hines and the other men surrounding Wilks's grave. Once again, just as he was given an opportunity to escape from Pap as a consequence of a money-drunk attitude toward wealth, Huck escapes because Hines and the others, intoxicated by the gold on Wilks's chest, all rush toward the grave.

The six thousand is now "free" to be spent by Peter Wilks's heirs. Since Pap is already dead in terms of the story material (the events out of which the narrative is constructed), the six thousand is also free to be spent by Huck. Why, then, does it take so long for Huck's narrative to "catch up" to the story material? In both the episodes involving six thousand dollars, Huck rids himself of the money in order to rid himself of the problems created, or so he believes, by that money. Before the money can be really free— and aligned with Huck's freedom instead of opposed to it—Huck must replace the abandoned respectable-robber and money-drunk attitudes with an attitude of his own. In order to do so, Huck must "narrate" himself into greater maturity. He must learn more about himself and what he values; he must also learn that it is not money itself but unhealthy attitudes toward money that created his dilemma. Those unhealthy attitudes were a dominant aspect of the Gilded Age, the setting for a particularly American drama about money. Samuel Clemens was both a critic of and an actor in that drama. It is perhaps not too much to say that Clemens, in slowly, haltingly constructing Huck's story, was recapitulating dramatically some of the hard lessons about accumulated wealth that he thought Americans of the Gilded Age were in need of learning, hard lessons that his own business experiences were teaching him.

Clemens's adventure with the Paige typesetter was, of course, the occasion of his sad initiation into a world of investment capitalism that had an appalling capacity to "drink it up." His acquaintance with the machine began in 1880, and, though in 1881 he could call his five-thousand-dollar stake "Very much the best investment I have ever made," by December 1887, according to Justin Kaplan, "the typesetter had already cost Clemens about fifty thousand dollars, which was twenty thousand dollars more than Paige's top estimate, and it was feeding fast and strong.[2] Clemens's business misfortunes grew until, finally, in 1893 he pleaded with Fred Hall, his partner in the publishing house, "Get me out of business! and I will be yours forever gratefully." [3] In that same year, Clemens met an important new friend, Henry Rogers, a prime mover in the development of the Standard Oil trust, who was to guide him through bankruptcy to a renewed prosperity. Clemens's problems with money in the 1880s were by no means unique. That decade was a pivotal one, representing both the culmination of an economic evolution of a particularly American type and the beginning of a transition to the national-market, corporate capitalism of the twentieth century.

The development of the Standard Oil trust, like Samuel Clemens's adventures with the Paige typesetter, can be read as an expression of the unique economic environment of the United States in the 1880s. *Huck Finn* can be read in the same way. Among the multitudinous identities and roles that Huck has been assigned—picaresque hero, social critic, anti-Romantic, and Everyman—or has taken on himself—damned abolitionist, various George, Tom, Dick, and Marys—Huck is also a young capitalist. Like many Americans in the Gilded Age, he is neither familiar with nor comfortable in that role. His individual discomfort is recapitulated by the country as a whole. In the following pages, I intend to create a "mythological" narrative composed of the historical events (names, places, dates, commonly held beliefs, and certain literary texts written during the 1880s) associated with that economic discomfort. It is a mythological narrative because, even though it is made up of real events, those events are combined according to the necessities of symbolic rather than historical verity. For example, the year 1893 is a symbolic fulcrum, giving events that occur in or are associated with that year an added significance. Thus, in the mythological narrative, it is important that the year in which Samuel Clemens meets Henry Rogers is also the year that Frederick Jackson Turner announces his frontier thesis—at the

2. *Mr. Clemens and Mark Twain: A Biography* (New York: Simon & Schuster, 1966), pp. 285, 288.

3. Albert Bigelow Paine, ed., *Mark Twain's Letters*, 2 vols. (New York: Harper & Brothers, 1917), 2:584.

same Chicago World's Fair that Henry Adams uses as the occasion for his comments concerning what he saw as a "watershed" event, the 1893 decision regarding the single gold standard. In this narrative, 1893 also "signifies" the end of a boom period and the beginning of a depression that provides a further shock to the consciousness of the American nation, intensifying the belief that an important transition has occurred. In a sense, then, both the development of the Standard Oil trust and the creation of *Huck Finn*, as well as the other literary texts I discuss later, are alike in being an anticipation of the year 1893 and all that it symbolizes.

The mythological narrative begins with an 1880s perspective on American history. Henry Adams, as the historian of the Jefferson and Madison administrations, looks into the future of Americans in 1817 and pronounces, "The continent lay before them, like an uncovered ore-bed. They could see, and they could calculate with reasonable accuracy, the wealth it could be made to yield."[4] Prior to 1817 the ore-bed did not "lay before" the American; in a sense, the four terms of the Jefferson and Madison administrations served to uncover its existence: "These sixteen years set at rest the natural doubts that had attended the nation's birth."[5] Digging did indeed commence immediately, but the miner could not devote his undivided attention to the task until after the Civil War.

The Gilded Age, by contrast, was a period of such unparalleled growth that it is difficult to avoid cliché when describing it. Richard Heffner sketches the economic environment that put the gild on this age: "Investment capital was readily available, for numbers of entrepreneurs had made large profits in the war years. Incredibly rich natural resources in timber, fertile lands, metals, coal, iron, and oil were at the disposal of business. A practically unlimited supply of cheap labor, increased yearly by an ever-growing stream of immigrants from distant shores, waited to serve the industrial colossus. An enormous continent guaranteed a profitable and seemingly insatiable domestic market."[6] The keynote of the age was expansion, understood as the ability to assert forward movement without having to worry about its direction.

The American mind of the Gilded Age was not only cleared suddenly of distractions but also inherited a theology particularly well suited for the miner who would be rich. Max Weber maintains that Calvinism altered the medieval notion of a man's "calling" and prepared the way for the rise of capitalism. The New England Puritan made a further improvement on the material/spiritual value of hard work. According to Perry Miller, the Puritan saint was expected to acquire property—without being affected by materialism—in order to demonstrate, by indirection, the Covenant of Grace. By the 1880s, the Puritan work ethic had undergone a marked evolution as a result of two main causes: the old reliable, theological underpinning for moral behavior was, for a variety of reasons, being cut away; and the Ameri-

4. *History of the United States* (New York: Antiquarian Press, 1962), 6:173–74.
5. Ibid., p. 172.
6. *A Documentary History of the United States* (Bloomington: Indiana University Press, 1952), p. 158.

can who struck it rich was acquiring wealth out of proportion to his sweat. As a consequence of the former, the Puritan work ethic was displaced by Andrew Carnegie's "Gospel of Wealth." [7] As for the latter, the example of Americans who "struck" wealth, even if those examples were often apocryphal, frustrated the belief that there was something demonstrably moral about the acquisition of such wealth, especially when that wealth was laying "uncovered," as Adams's metaphor has it, waiting for someone to fall into it.

The circumstances in which a man's wealth exceeds the value of his labor, then, refer not to a sudden increase in the wages of the working class but to the myth of striking it rich. Living on an uncovered ore-bed, the strong or smart American had no excuse (according to the myth) for not acquiring the riches of a lifetime with the sweat of a single day. It is not surprising that Mark Twain, armed with the graphic example of California and Nevada, would express the myth of suddenly acquired wealth in terms of mining metaphors: in Roughing It, a blind lead, a gold ore deposit, made Mark Twain a millionaire for ten days. As is the case with the image of the uncovered ore-bed, the American's wealth or potential wealth is often metaphorically equated with the frontier in the broadest sense, as an expression of total national resources. It is not merely the frontier's wealth that makes it a powerful image, but also its purported effect on the economic growth of the industrial East. According to Vernon L. Parrington, "It was this energetic East, with its accumulations of liquid capital awaiting investment and its factories turning out the material needed to push the settlements westward, that profited most from the conquest of the far West." [8]

Expansion and the conquest of the Far West were important aspects of Frederick Jackson Turner's frontier, or "safety valve," thesis. Although Turner's model has not fared well among historians, it does seem to reflect a powerful and widely held belief. Prior to beginning his post mortem on Turner's thesis, Fred Shannon remarks: "Long before Frederick Jackson Turner tacitly admitted the validity of the theory, even the name 'safety valve' had become a middle class aphorism. The idea was so old and so generally held that it was commonly repeated without question." [9] Though an unquestioned "middle class aphorism" may not make very good history, it may make good mythology; or, to paraphrase a well-known student of myth, it is not good to eat but good to think. [10] What if there had been no myth of the free land of opportunity, no myth of striking it rich in the uncovered ore-bed? If Americans of 1865–1893 had conceived no notion of possible "escape" to a frontier of opportunity, would a government policy of laissez faire have been possible for long? Frederick Lewis Allen has created a larger myth

7. Andrew Carnegie, "Wealth," NAR 148 (June 1889): 653–64.

8. The Beginnings of Critical Realism in America (New York: Harcourt, Brace, 1930), p. 8.

9. "A Post-Mortem on the Labor-Safety Valve Theory," in Turner and the Sociology of the Frontier, ed. Richard Hofstadter and Seymour Lipset (New York: Basic Books, 1968), p. 173.

10. Claude Levi-Strauss, Totemism, trans. Rodney Needham (Boston: Beacon Press, 1963), p. 89.

out of the relationship between the frontier thesis and laissez faire: "In the eighteen-seventies and eighteen-eighties the accepted principle of American business was free competition. Almost everybody believed in *laissez faire.* . . . if a competitor became crippled in the game, there were always other fields in the west where he could begin again unhandicapped." And he concludes, almost anticlimactically, "The standards of fair play were low." [11] As long as undirected expansion continued, and as long as the players believed that the safety net would bounce them out West where they could land on their feet, the governmental referee could stand on the sidelines and not blow his whistle.

Setting out to make "more money than a body could tell what to do with," the respectable-robber economics of the Gilded Age helped to create the dilemma it had to confront in 1893. Once the American has made his money, what will he buy? At the Chicago Exposition in 1893 where Turner announced his frontier thesis, Henry Adams pondered the nation's first decision regarding direction: "Chicago asked in 1893 for the first time the question whether the American people knew where they were driving." [12] Once the frontier closes, competitors must battle and co-exist in circumscribed quarters; Americans can no longer merely move outward, calling any movement "expansion." They must decide on a particular direction, and that decision necessitates a value judgment—whether economic or moral. Adams sketches the parameters of that decision:

> For a hundred years, between 1793 and 1893, the American people had hesitated, vacillated, swayed forward and back, between two forces, one simply industrial, the other capitalistic, centralizing, and mechanical. In 1893, the issue came on the single gold standard, and the majority at last declared itself, once for all, in favor of the capitalistic system with all its necessary machinery. [13]

Commenting on the Gilded Age, Howard Mumford Jones says, "It is significant that most financial tycoons wanted a gold currency." [14] Adams sided with silver, but he also realized that his position was anachronistic. The Americans "alighted on the single gold standard and the capitalistic system with its methods; the protective tariff; the corporations and trusts; the trades-unions and socialistic paternalism . . . which created monopolies capable of controlling the new energies that America adored." [15] Huck's struggles in adjusting to his new capitalistic nature constitute Mark Twain's condensation of an economic and moral adjustment confronting the American era that produced both his story and businessmen such as Henry Rogers and John D. Rockefeller who looked ahead to see that unfolding events would result in a shift from expansion to consolidation and control.

Like the Standard Oil trust and *Huck Finn*, certain literary texts written during the 1880s were in their own way responses to and comments upon

11. *The Lords of Creation* (New York: Harper, 1935), p. 4.
12. *The Education of Henry Adams* (Boston: Houghton Mifflin, 1918), p. 343.
13. Ibid., p. 344.
14. *The Age of Energy* (New York: Viking Press, 1970), p. 17.
15. Adams, *Education*, p. 345.

problems confronting suddenly wealthy Americans. The main protagonists in Henry James's *The Portrait of a Lady* (1881) and William Dean Howells's *The Rise of Silas Lapham* (1885) face the same dilemma Huck confronted as a young capitalist. James's novel is "about" a young American girl who does not know yet how to spend money or how to behave as a capitalist. The main crisis of the novel is, in fact, a direct consequence of Isabel's problems with her sudden wealth. One of the main reasons Isabel knows so little about money is that her father was not a successful capitalist. According to Ralph Touchett, Mr. Archer "gave her everything, because he used to spend his capital." [16] Mr. Archer obviously needed to follow Judge Thatcher's advice to Huck. Ralph compounds Isabel's problems when, not wanting to see her have to marry for money, he persuades his father to leave her sixty thousand pounds. Of course, in a wonderful example of Jamesian irony, Isabel is married for money precisely as a result of her inheritance. Even though the narrative does not dwell upon it, the sudden possession of unearned wealth can be viewed, in both *Portrait* and *Huck Finn*, as the primary motivation of the plot—the first element in the sequence that leads most directly to the crisis. In *Portrait*, if Isabel is not rich, the marriage to Osmond does not occur, and in *Huck Finn*, if Huck is not rich, the flight downriver and the friendship with Jim do not occur.

Ralph explains his rationale for making Isabel very rich: "I call people rich when they're able to meet the requirements of their imagination. Isabel has a great deal of imagination." [17] Ironically, Isabel almost immediately reacts to Ralph's gift of power (to meet the requirements of her imagination) by saying, "I'm not sure it's not a greater happiness to be powerless." [18] At the beginning of the novel when Huck abandons his money, his escape from both Pap and "sivilization" expresses a similar sentiment. For the most part, Huck seems to find it a greater happiness to be moneyless and powerless. In a sense, Isabel later imitates Huck's initial attempt at solving his money problem; she gives the problem over to Gilbert Osmond, who claims to know the "correct idea" as to how to use it:

> At bottom her money had been a burden, had been on her mind, which was filled with the desire to transfer the weight of it to some other conscience, to some more prepared receptacle. What would lighten her own conscience more effectually than to make it over to the man with the best taste in the world. [19]

According to Ralph, Isabel possesses her own "natural taste," yet she chooses to obey Osmond's. Taste, as a means of determining value—or direction in Adams's terminology—can be the basis of a spending morality. Whereas Isabel's natural taste is part of her moral character, Osmond's becomes an end in itself. Instead of being expressed in possessions of his own choosing (he actually owns so few), Osmond's taste is the instrument by which he "looks down," as Isabel puts it, on the rest of mankind. Whereas Isabel creates the

16. *The Portrait of a Lady*, ed. Leon Edel (Boston: Houghton Mifflin, 1963), p. 159.
17. Ibid., p. 158.
18. Ibid., p. 190.
19. Ibid., p. 351.

main crisis of her story by failing to exercise her own taste, Huck ultimately resolves his dilemma by discovering, and then exercising, his own taste in determining the value of the "outfit." The problem of taste, then, can be understood as a moral problem in *Portrait*, but *The Rise of Silas Lapham* addresses still more pointedly the question of what the American will do with his money once it has become a possession.

A superficial glance at *Silas Lapham* would seem to distinguish Silas's money from both Isabel's and Huck's, since Silas appears to have earned his wealth over a long period of time. Consider, however, the source of that wealth: "My father found it one day, in a hole made by a tree blowing down." [20] Thus, like Huck's cave loot, Silas's wealth is "earth-money." Moreover, that wealth is not earned in proportion to Silas's sweat. In fact, Silas is paradigmatic of the Gilded Age capitalist: "Their first years there were given to carefully getting on Lapham's part, and careful saving on his wife's. Suddenly the money began to come so abundantly that she need not save; and then they did not know what to do with it." [21] Silas's money, like Huck's and Isabel's, is "more than a body could tell what to do with." As if dramatizing Max Weber's thesis, combining the money-making promoted by the Protestant work ethic with the money-accumulating sanctioned by the Puritan distaste for all but the most frugal consumption, *The Rise of Silas Lapham* is also the rise of the American capitalist. [22] In a sense, Silas's story is "about" the reaching of a critical point in the rise of an American capitalist—the point at which the capitalist makes more money than he knows what to do with. That critical point in the history of the individual capitalist parallels the critical point in the history of the American nation when the frontier closes. Undirected expansion, taking wealth from the "uncovered" ore-beds of the frontier, is no longer possible. At that moment, represented in this mythological narrative by the year 1893—the critical moment in the consciousness of the nation rather than the "legal" or statistically verifiable moment the frontier closes—the capitalist must develop a spending morality, a methodology for determining value, and the nation must develop a methodology for determining economic direction.

Silas gains possession of a large sum of money but is successful in doing only one thing with it: making more money. His morally questionable use of capital when he squeezes his partner out of the paint business is produced by

20. *The Rise of Silas Lapham*, ed. Edwin H. Cady (Boston: Houghton Mifflin, 1957), p. 6.
21. Ibid., p. 21.
22. The situation of the Dryfoos family in Howells's *A Hazard of New Fortunes* (New York: Harper, 1961) is a parallel case, with an even more sudden acquisition of wealth. Partly because of the abrupt ease with which Dryfoos takes his fortune out of the ground—this time by virtue of natural gas—but also because Dryfoos's story is written later than Lapham's, Dryfoos not only worships money-making but also disdains those who cannot earn it out of proportion to their labor: "he began to honor money, especially money that had been won suddenly and in large sums; for money that had been earned painfully, slowly, and in little amounts, he had only pity and contempt" (p. 223). The fact that Dryfoos does not lose his money and that he has less of an individual moral nature than Silas can be attributed, at least in part, to the increased persuasiveness of an economic determinism—in Howells's thought and in the country's thought—as the 1880s became the 1890s.

the same deficiency that characterizes his attempt to buy into Boston society. The Lapham's new house is the focal point of Silas's effort to rise in society, and Silas's attitude toward its construction illustrates his deficiency: "It's just like ordering a picture of a painter. You pay him enough, and he can afford to paint you a first-class picture; and if you don't, he can't. . . . Yes, sir, give an architect money enough, and he'll give you a nice house every time."[23] The problem that the money-making mentality has spending money is not merely a matter of knowing what to buy. It is also having a sense of the worth of a thing in itself, instead of simply what it costs, and having a consciousness of the essentially arbitrary nature of money as a medium of exchange. Silas's equation of "high price" and "first-class" is analogous to the notion of a natural language—wherein there supposedly exists an inherent fitness between the word and the concept it signifies. Silas treats money as a positive term; he believes that it is his money that is exchanged—first-class money for first-class art. He does not perceive that, as the "language" through which signification (value determining) occurs, money is essentially transparent.

That money is transparent is a lesson Huck has ample opportunity to learn as he gets a long look at American culture while floating downriver with Jim. For example, the sum of forty dollars "signifies" several different things during the course of the novel. When the slave-hunters give Huck forty dollars, it is conscience money; when the King sells his chance on the reward for Jim as a runaway slave, it is blood money; and when Tom Sawyer, knowing Jim to be a free man, pays him a wage for "acting" like an imprisoned slave, it is, according to Jim, the fulfillment of a good luck sign that he would be rich.

The fulfillment of Jim's good luck sign represents the resolution of another money dilemma affecting Huck. Jim says that a hairy breast and hairy arms are "a sign dat you's agwyne to be rich" (p. 71). Jim discovers that, in a way, he is rich once he becomes a runaway slave: "I owns mysef, en I's wuth eight hund'd dollars. I wisht I had de money, I wouldn' want no mo'" (p. 73). Jim is worth eight hundred dollars, but he owns that wealth only when he is free— that is, worthless. The contradiction involves an ambiguity, created by the institution of slavery, in the definitions of value and freedom. The contradiction can be resolved only when the free man is no longer a slave—no longer defined as a valuable piece of property. Jim, as a free man, is paid the same forty dollars for which he was sold as a slave. The balance achieved by the manipulation of forty dollars is structurally similar to that achieved by the manipulation of the six thousand. The result of all this money changing hands, and changing "meaning," represents quite an education for Huck, and it is an education that allows Huck, unlike Silas, to make a moral use of his capital, a use that is an expression of his own taste, his own determination of value. Silas does indeed rise above the money-making morality that created his fortune, but the loss of that wealth is a necessary element of his rise. Silas becomes his "free and satisfied" self only after he loses his money. That fact is evident near the end of the novel during Sewell's assessment of

23. *Silas*, p. 55.

Silas: "Sewell was intensely interested in the moral spectacle which Lapham presented under his changed conditions. The Colonel . . . was more the Colonel in those hills than he ever could have been on the back bay."[24] Huck, on the other hand, discovers a way to become his "free and satisified" self by using, not losing, his money; he turns his capital against capitalism; he uses his money to escape from the control "sivilization" would have over his money, and over him.

Huck can do so because he has learned to separate the value of living from the value of "getting a living." Henry David Thoreau perhaps already said it best in "Life Without Principle," commenting on those who would steal their living from the natural resources of the earth (including the resources of the "labor pool"):

> The rush to California, for instance, and the attitude, not merely of merchants, but of philosophers and prophets, so called, in relation to it, reflect the greatest disgrace on mankind. That so many are ready to live by luck, and so get the means of commanding the labor of others less lucky, without contributing any value to society! And that is called enterprise! I know of no more startling development of the immorality of trade, and all the common modes of getting a living. The philosophy and poetry and religion of such a mankind are not worth the dust of a puffball. The hog that gets his living by rooting, stirring up the soil so, would be ashamed of such company. If I could command the wealth of all the worlds by lifting my finger, I would not pay *such* a price for it.[25]

Huck likewise discovers that he is not willing to pay such a price to get a living within a society controlled by the respectable robber's definition of "enterprise," as Thoreau puts it. Huck narrates himself into greater maturity as he encounters aspects of that civilization such as the misanthropic philosophy of Colonel Sherburn, the sentimental poetry of the necrophilic Emmeline Grangerford, and the salvation-for-profit religion of the King's revival meeting.

Huck is able to separate the value of living from getting a living by virtue of his ability and his desire to get along without money even when he has it to spend. When the Duke presses him for ten cents at the beginning of the Phelps episode, Huck admits to the reader, "I had considerable money" (p. 274). He collected a good bit during the course of the novel, and he spends little of it. He demonstrates his frugal nature early in the novel when he gives Jim a counterfeit quarter while holding back the dollar that the judge has just given him. He expresses it also by sneaking under a circus tent, even though he has more than enough money for the price of admission (p. 191). In this way he is, like Thoreau, exploiting the Poor Richard/ Benjamin Franklin economic morality, not in order to get ahead but in order to get *out*. His refined sense of "borrowing" also helps him to get by without spending money. The notion of "borrowing" comes from Pap, who uses it to avoid wasting money that is meant for drinking. However, Huck uses the

24. Ibid., p. 298.
25. In *Reform Papers*, ed. Wendell Glick (Princeton: Princeton University Press, 1973), p. 162.

notion because it enables him to live within, or to move through, an American culture largely created and defined by its money-making—without becoming part of that culture. Thus, Huck's "escape" is a much more sophisticated response than the simple "dropping out" of which he is often accused.

Huck's methodology for determining value, or direction in Adams's terminology, represents an important alternative to the false dilemma created by the respectable robber/money-drunk opposition. He refuses to "buy into" the competitive, expansion-oriented economy of "getting a living," and in so doing he also refuses to accept the proposition that he must either be a respectable robber-capitalist or be a true son of Pap. As indicated earlier, it is significant that the expression of Huck's desire to spend his money on the outfit is followed immediately by the first recognition of Pap's death narrated by Huck. The narrated sequence is important, because it implies that Pap's death is a consequence of Huck's value determination. By expressing a desire to spend his capital, he has rejected the judge's "correct idea" of money; yet that spending does not then become the consumption for its own sake represented by Pap. Huck's alternative is to use his capital to buy out of a capitalistic society. He can do so only because he has a system that determines value independently of the monetary system that defines the Gilded Age, a particular type of independence that is recapitulated, as we all know, in another way. The much-discussed decision to "steal" Jim and to go to hell for it parallels Huck's decision to buy the outfit. Huck knows that Jim is a free man, but he has no philosophy or theology, no language that allows him to say so. Just as he must use capital in order to buy out of capitalism, he must use the only signification system available to him, saying that he is going to steal a slave and go to hell for it, in order to signify that Jim is free. It is that independent spirit, similar to Thoreau's, allowing Huck to live within a society, speaking its linguistic and monetary "vernacular," without being "defined" or controlled by it, that we justly celebrate one hundred years after its creation.

"Interesting, but Tough":
Huckleberry Finn and the
Problem of Tradition

IN Chapter 17 of *Adventures of Huckleberry Finn*, in the course of his admiring description of the Grangerfords' interior decoration, Huck Finn mentions reading *Pilgrim's Progress*. It was a book, he says, "about a man that left his family it didn't say why. I read considerable in it now and then. The statements was interesting, but tough." At first, this offhand characterization seems to be merely one of the novel's many tossed-off gibes at organized religion, religious literature, and conventional piety. And of course it does work this way, as Huck's naiveté permits Mark Twain to satirize the ageless hypocrisies of human nature and the pretensions of genteel culture from behind the mask Huck's voice provides him. But Huck's puzzlement over *Pilgrim's Progress*, I think, marks subtle and pressing problems for him as vernacular narrator and for his creator, Mark Twain, as self-described "jackleg novelist." In fact, Huck's response to Bunyan may serve as an illustration of some of the principal issues of the novel, from the nature of Huck's character and narrative voice to the question of how both the protagonist and the beguiled reader discern meaning in the sequence of events that constitutes experience.

For one thing, Huck's description of the work as the story "of a man that left his family it didn't say why" surely touches upon his own condition as a runaway orphan alternately bullied and deserted by his father. Homeless and often lonely, he wonders why any story would have a man leave a perfectly good family, and not say why. Additionally, Huck's remark that he read in *Pilgrim's Progress* "considerable," and on more than one occasion—the only book he honors by such attention in the novel—raises the delicate issue of the level of his participation in his culture. While for purposes of satire Huck must be ignorant of convention and tradition, there are certain things even an ignorant thirteen- or fourteen-year-old boy from Missouri would know if, like Huck, he learned to read a little; chief among these would be the Bible, at least its most familiar stories, and a sort of rough and ready familiarity with the frontier religious tradition based upon it. In this context, it is not so surprising that Huck should know Bunyan's allegory, for next to the Bible itself, *Pilgrim's Progress* was probably the book most likely to be found in all kinds of American houses in the nineteenth century.

But Huck's principal response to *Pilgrim's Progress* is puzzlement. The book was interesting, but tough, he says, because it failed to supply a satisfactory rationale for its plot. What Huck finds simultaneously compelling and mystifying is the implied layer of allegorical meaning in Bunyan's work. What does this mean? he asks, for he knows intuitively that the literal narrative does not constitute the essence of the story. The symbolic journey of Christian intrigues him, perhaps, because he too is on a journey or even a quest whose significance is obscure, and he is dimly conscious that some larger frame of reference is necessary if he is to make sense of things and if things are to make sense.

Viewed in this light, Huck's critique of Bunyan illustrates what is perhaps the central problem for Huck himself as a character and for Mark Twain as realistic novelist: how is Huck to extract meaning or significance from the apparently random, episodic string of experiences that he moves through? How is Twain to suggest, without violating the credibility of his unsophisticated and literal-minded narrator, the deeper import of events, especially as regards what might be termed the novel's dominant theme, the theme of freedom and the corollary inner conflict Huck faces over helping Jim escape from slavery?

I think Twain achieved a partial answer to these questions through the adumbration of the only sources of mythic themes and images that Huck could know that were also personally resonant to Twain himself: the most familiar and powerful stories and scenes from Scripture—especially the Old Testament—and Christian religious tradition. These are images and stories that even Huck, mostly growing up in his sugar hogshead, would know (though, like his response to Bunyan, he usually finds them "tough": Miss Watson's description of heaven, for example, fails to excite his ardor). These were also images and stories with which Twain's own imagination was suffused—both unconsciously as a product of that same frontier culture, in which Bible stories affected the very shape of experience itself, and consciously as an artist increasingly tormented by religious questions. Consequently, one finds biblical analogues and allusions in at least two different forms in the novel: overt ones deliberately employed by Twain and filtered through Huck's consciousness, usually for comic or satiric effect; and more submerged ones, probably unconscious on Twain's part, that are, like the Bible in the culture, embedded in the very texture of experience itself.

Let me emphasize that I am not suggesting that there is a subtext of religious meaning, or worse, in Melville's phrase, a hideous and intolerable allegory in *Huckleberry Finn*. The current flows in the other direction; the biblical myths and images help to figure forth and amplify the secular themes of the novel, and in fact they are often inverted or displaced in order to undercut the conventional morality associated with the stories themselves.

The problem with these images and allusions in the novel is that they establish patterns and themes that are not, it seems to me, resolved. I doubt that Huck ever does figure out the "why" of *his* leaving home; and the novel itself, by its shifts of imagery and theme in the second half, tends to suggest that the matter remained an agonizing mystery to Twain as well. To consider this problem we will need to look at the circumstances of the novel's composition; but first let me try to sketch where and how I see these patterns and images appearing in the novel and suggest how they seem to amplify its themes.

The first adumbration of the dominant theme articulated in this fashion comes early in the first chapter, when the Widow Douglas, as part of her program for "sivilizing" Huck, gets out her Bible and, as Huck says, "learned me about Moses and the Bulrushers." Huck professes indifference: "and I was in a sweat to find out all about him; but by-and-by she let it out that Moses had been dead a considerable long time; so then I didn't care no more about him; because I don't take no stock in dead people" (p. 18). I say he professes indifference, because we know from his thoughts in many places in the novel that Huck's imagination may even be said to be preoccupied with thoughts of death and dead people. His indifference here amounts to a sort of initial denial of his call, for the biblical story of the boy set adrift by his mother in the great river, whose destiny it was to grow up and lead his people out of bondage, is a clear prefiguration of Huck's central dilemma and mission in the novel, helping Jim to gain freedom.

A few pages later, at the beginning of Chapter 3, comes Huck's only extended description of his religious training:

> Miss Watson she took me in the closet and prayed, but nothing come of it. She told me to pray every day, and whatever I asked for I would get it. But it warn't so. I tried it. Once I got a fish-line, but no hooks. It warn't any good to me without hooks. I tried for the hooks three or four times, but somehow I couldn't make it work. By-and-by, one day, I asked Miss Watson to try for me, but she said I was a fool. She never told me why, and I couldn't make it out no way.
>
> I set down, one time, back in the woods, and had a long think about it. I says to myself, if a body can get anything they pray for, why don't Deacon Winn get back the money he lost on pork? Why can't the widow get back her silver snuff-box that was stole? Why can't Miss Watson fat up? No, says I to myself, there ain't nothing in it. I went and told the widow about it, and she said the thing a body could get by praying for it was "spiritual gifts." . . . Sometimes the widow would take me one side and talk about Providence in a way to make a body's mouth water; but maybe next day Miss Watson would take hold and knock it all down again. I judged I could see that there was two Providences, and a poor chap would stand considerable show with the widow's Providence, but if Miss Watson's got him there warn't no help for him any more. I thought it all out, and reckoned I would belong to the widow's, if he wanted me, though I couldn't make out how he was agoing to be any better off then than what he was before, seeing I was so ignorant and so kind of low-down and ornery. (Pp. [29]–30)

Once again, the passage is a brilliant example of Twain's mastery of the naive narrator for satiric purposes. Huck's ignorance, and his literal-mindedness, lead him to conclude that the widow and Miss Watson must be talking about two entirely different deities, permitting Twain to expose the discrepancies in the beliefs of these two professing Christians without risking blasphemy himself. But there is also a deeper import to the passage. With his sound heart Huck touches instinctively a central tension in the heterogeneous, home-grown Protestantism of the frontier: how to reconcile the just and wrathful God of Calvinism and the Old Testament (Miss Watson's Providence) with the merciful, loving God of the New Testament (the widow's Providence). We see that Huck has thought about such issues as the efficacy of prayer, the nature of divine justice, the relationship of man to a creator, and his own unworthiness. His haphazard religious education has provided him with random scraps, at least, of biblical and primitive Christian religious tradition that give him an inchoate system of patterns and referents by which he can attempt to shape and understand his experience. Likewise, whatever Twain's own bitter personal rejection of orthodox belief in his later years, these religious myths and traditions exerted a powerful influence on his own imagination and still offered, at least at the time he began *Huckleberry Finn*, potentially positive sources of value and meaning by which he could endow the quest of his young protagonist with the dignity and significance that belonged to it. Huck's determination to belong to the widow's Providence is roughly analogous to the veneration for Jesus that Twain preserved despite his attacks on religion.

The invocation of religious and especially biblical myths is concentrated almost exclusively in the first half of the novel, especially in those chapters that describe the growth of Huck and Jim's friendship on Jackson's Island and the beginning of their voyage down the Mississippi. Before turning to these central episodes, however, I should mention another early and seemingly joking allusion that establishes an important motif. When Huck has been kidnapped, taken across the river, imprisoned, and at one point nearly murdered by his own father (an episode that suggests a kind of mordant inversion of the story of Abraham and Isaac), he describes Pap's appearance after he has been on a spree: "He had been drunk over in town, and laid in the gutter all night, and he was a sight to look at. A body would a thought he was Adam, he was just all mud" (p. 49). This figure is a startlingly apt description of Pap Finn's character and cultural significance in the novel as a part of what I might call Twain's countermythology of the frontier. Huck's image suggests the original baseness of man—the uninspired clay from which he was formed, mythically—and simultaneously invokes the failed promise of the frontier as new Eden populated by American Adams: here is the *real* American Adam, Pap, living in the wilderness not in pristine innocence and nourishing contact with nature, but in an almost subhuman ignorance and squalor. The image of man as mud, moreover, is a pervasive one that can be traced in Twain's accelerating disgust with human nature; he returns to it later in the novel, as we shall see, again invoking its negative edenic implications. But he lays it on thicker, so to speak, in *A Connecticut Yankee in King Arthur's Court*, in the conclusion to which Hank Morgan, despairing of mankind itself and abandoning any hope of reforming it, dismisses it as so much "human muck." Later still, Philip Traum in *The Mysterious Stranger* observes that man "begins as dirt, and departs as stench."

But there is a countervailing and at least partially positive invocation of Creation in this portion of the novel, centered around the life of Huck and Jim on Jackson's Island and the early stages of the raft journey. In fact, I would suggest, the imaginative power of this section, surely the mythic heart of the book, with its famous scenes of escape and drift and freedom that dominate the popular imagination as well as academic criticism, derives largely from Twain's invocation of the twin and parallel biblical myths of Creation and Flood; that is to say of Genesis and the story of Noah, the stories of beginning and beginning again, and the promises of creation from nothing and of the preservation of an island of goodness in a wicked world.

It is on Jackson's Island that Huck Finn may be said really to be born or to begin to emerge as a fully realized character. His arrival there constitutes a kind of second beginning for the novel, in fact, for Huck has just shed his former identity by his Tom Sawyeresque faked "murder" at Pap's cabin and is about to begin his new life; as though Twain realized at this point that Huck was more than a comic appendage or foil to Tom Sawyer and that his "autobiography" required a fresh start commensurate with its potential significance. On this uninhabited island Huck meets the runaway slave Jim, fleeing from Miss Watson's plan to sell him down the river. Appropriate to Twain's inversion of Genesis, they are brought together by a snake. Together they explore the island and begin, tentatively, to form a bond not based upon their former, culturally determined identities—white boy with a "conscience" that tells him slavery is morally correct, and black man whom we have earlier seen only as a kind of comic darky. The island is more than a neutral territory where these socially conditioned roles no longer apply; it is a kind of eden to be explored by its original pair. It is early summer, and fruits and berries are beginning to ripen; there are catfish on the lines, and there is a cavern to shelter Huck and Jim from the weather. Jim instructs Huck in the meaning of natural signs, and the birds warn them of storms so they can stay dry. When the water begins to rise over the island, the animals become so tame "that you could paddle right up and put your hand on them if you wanted to" (p. 76). There is at first neither strife nor toil, but only contentment: "Jim," Huck says, "I wouldn't want to be nowhere else but here. Pass me along another hunk of fish and some hot corn-bread" (p. 76).

Twain introduces another serpent into this Eden, however, to play a variation on the mythic themes of temptation and fall. One day Huck discovers a rattlesnake in the cavern and kills it. He decides to play a joke on Jim, so he curls up the dead snake at the foot of Jim's bed to scare him. When Jim comes in, the dead snake's mate is there and bites him. That the second snake, faithful to its dead mate, bites Jim suggests that the snake is merely an agent or instrument and not the cause of the trouble. The snake acts naturally, even nobly, in defending its mate; it is Huck who brings pain and discord into this world, tempted by the prospect of a Tom Sawyer–like trick. (It was Tom, of course, early in the novel, who established the pattern of playing tricks on Jim, hanging his hat on a limb while he was asleep so Jim would think he'd been ridden around the world by witches.) The moral equivalent of original sin in this paradise is the comic version of what the "unpardonable sin" was for Hawthorne; the demeaning joke or gratuitous trick that involves treating another human being as an object to be manipulated and to suffer for the trickster's amusement. The fundamental basis for Twain's attack on the conventional Romantic sensibility in the novel, for which Tom

Sawyer is the chief spokesman, is just this: to enact the conventions or to play the tricks involves denying the humanity and the dignity of the game's object. Like the snakeskin in this episode, this attitude is the source of continuing mischief in the novel; and like the snakeskin, it is not through working its mischief on the characters, for Huck will continue to play jokes on Jim and to have moral relapses (or attacks of conscience, as he considers them), during which he will reconventionalize Jim as a slave. In fact, it is mostly in such brief and fortunate falls as this one, when Huck is forced to confront the real consequences of such attitudes toward Jim, that he may be said to awaken morally.

The Mississippi's annual rise, overflowing the island and making the animals tame, provides Twain the occasion for his most intricate invocation and inversion of a biblical story. During the flood (in a scene that precedes the rattlesnake episode) Huck and Jim see a house floating downriver past the island. They paddle out, rummage through it, and bring back a load of plunder. But they also find in this house a man's naked corpse. Jim warns Huck not to look at his face—"it's too gashly" (p. 77), he says—and covers the dead man with some rags. Later, Huck wants to speculate about the dead man, but Jim deflects his questions.

The floating house, as well as the flood itself, suggests the story of Noah and the ark.[1] But Twain's allusion here is at once more specific, more complex, and more significant. In the biblical account, after the flood subsided Noah drank too much wine, became drunk, and lay uncovered in his tent. One of his sons, Ham, observed this shameful state, and told his other brothers, Shem and Japheth, who backed into the tent where their father lay, in order not to see him, and covered him up. When Noah recovered he blessed Shem and Japheth (the progenitors of the Israelites and the Gentiles, respectively). But he cursed Ham, the ancestor of the African peoples, and prophesied that his descendants would be slaves.

According to Allison Ensor, the story of Noah, along with the story of Creation and the story of the prodigal son, was one of three biblical episodes that had the most persistent fascination for Twain.[2] At various times during his career he planned to write a book about Noah; and in the summer of 1876, when he wrote the first part of *Huckleberry Finn*, one of the unfinished manuscripts he may have brought with him to Quarry Farm, and certainly a project that was on his mind at the time, was a work called "Shem's Diary."[3] But he would have had a further reason to recall the cursing of Ham in the context of his current project, for in the antebellum South of Twain's youth, which is the world of *Huckleberry Finn*, Genesis 9 furnished the principal justification for slavery. It was persistently cited and preached from

1. I am grateful to Tom Quirk for first pointing out to me the suggestive parallels between this section of the novel and the biblical account of Noah; see his "The Legend of Noah and the Voyage of Huckleberry Finn," *MTJ* 21 (1982): 21–23.

2. *Mark Twain and the Bible* (Lexington: Univeristy of Kentucky Press, 1969), pp. 30, 61–71.

3. Walter Blair, *Mark Twain and Huck Finn* (Berkeley: University of California Press, 1960), p. 93.

pulpits; everyone knew that this was the origin of the black race and of slavery as well: Noah said of Ham, "A slave of slaves shall he be to his brothers." What could be clearer than that?

Twain's variation on this familiar story is an almost perfect inversion of the biblical episode that powerfully amplifies the theme of freedom and the reader's growing sense of Jim's humanity in this section of the novel. The dead man lying naked in the floating house, of course, is Huck's father, the drunkard Pap. But it is not his son Huck who covers his nakedness and shame, but Jim, the black man, the descendant of Ham, who protects Huck from the shock of seeing the corpse of his debauched father. Here is one of Twain's most daring essays in creating a "countermythology." Twain turns the story of Ham's curse inside out by having the slave perform the office of covering the body of the naked father, to spare the white child. Both literally and symbolically Jim reverses the sin of Ham; and the reader, I think, completes the reversal by blessing Jim (whether or not he is conscious of the allusion) for his instinctive act of kindness and respect. This episode enhances Jim's stature even further if we recall that Pap Finn, like most of his class on the Southwestern frontier, was an egregious bigot. The reader will remember his famous speech on the "govment" expressing his outrage over the free negro who wore a white shirt and was permitted to vote.

This incident demonstrates the way in which biblical myths may be used to suggest the high seriousness of the quest Jim and Huck are launched upon and simultaneously to criticize what seemed to Twain the cruel and even immoral implications many of these myths, conventionally interpreted, have come to have. In terms of the overall trajectory of the novel, the telescoping of the myths of Creation and Flood that takes place in the Jackson's Island chapters serves primarily to authorize and add impetus to the voyage toward freedom Huck and Jim are about to set forth on. Theirs is a new world in both the Adamic and the Noachian senses. On the one hand, it is edenic in the most persistent American terms, a world of harmony with nature offering a chance to begin life afresh without the traditional weaknesses of socially and historically defined roles. But it is also a fallen and postdiluvian world of merely temporary respite from wickedness and wrath, like Noah's life upon the waters. Their journey offers the hope, at least, of good being preserved out of evil and suggests the moral imperative to flee wickedness; like Noah's, their escape is a moral act, with a similar dignity and sanction. At least until the King and the Duke come aboard, Huck and Jim, like Noah after the flood, operate under a kind of "covenant"; theirs, too, at least for a while, is a purified world. Every reader of the novel, if he remembers little else, remembers Huck's descriptions of the idyllic nature of life on a raft as "mighty free and easy and comfortable"—a peculiarly American confluence of ark and eden, a drifting home in nature.

Numerous other biblical and religious allusions and analogies are sprinkled throughout the first half of the novel and support or amplify the themes of freedom, slavery, and the failed eden of the American frontier. Some of these are direct allusions about which little need be said: the Grangerford parents, for example, are named Saul and Rachel, names that have some relevance to their roles. Others are less obvious but more significant; and generally, the further down the river and into the voyage they occur, the more likely they are to ramify negatively the major themes of the novel. Many of these more significant allusions occur in the series of colloquies or comic "debates" that Huck and Jim stage on the raft.

The first of these takes place before they actually leave the island. Jim tells Huck that to have a hairy chest and hairy arms as he does is a sign that he will be rich some day. In fact, he tells Huck he has already been rich. He once had fourteen dollars but lost it all through a series of bad investments, chief among which were a cow that died and a bank that was to pay him thirty-five dollars at the end of the year for a five-dollar deposit. Jim concludes by telling Huck that, in a sense, he's rich again, for "I owns mysef, en I's wuth eight hund'd dollars" (p. 73). Perhaps the equation of body hair to riches really was a folk belief Twain knew, but in any event Jim's hirsute appearance would remind nineteenth-century readers of the biblical Esau, the hairy man, brother of Jacob. This likelihood is especially strong in the context just described, for like Jim and his investments, Esau is chiefly notable for having been tricked out of his birthright and his father's blessing by his cleverer brother Jacob. Once again, Twain reverses the import of the biblical story, in which Jacob is the hero—the smart one, the favored. Twain, like W. E. B. Dubois in his famous essay on Jacob and Esau, sympathizes with the Esau figure and sees in him the trusting, spontaneous, forgiving character destined to be the victim of the sinister dexterity of the more "civilized" Jacobs of the world.

On their way downriver, Jim and Huck also discuss the wisdom of Solomon. (I should note here that this episode is probably a later interpolation. This and the preceding two chapters dealing with Huck and Jim's adventures on the *Sir Walter Scott* were apparently added by Twain during the final period of composition in 1883 in order to provide Huck with books about royalty for Twain to satirize. So, strictly speaking, this chapter belongs in spirit more to the later sections of the book, although the debate on Solomon's wisdom is germane to the issues that predominate in the first half of the novel.[4]) Once again Twain inverts comically for serious purposes the message of a famous biblical story. Huck alludes to Solomon's wisdom, but Jim will have none of it, citing the story of the child whom Solomon threatened to cut in half. Jim says the dispute was about a whole child, not half a child. Huck says, "But hang it Jim, you've clean missed the point," but Jim is ready for that:

> "Blame de pint! I reck'n I knows what I knows. En mine you, de *real* pint is down furder—it's down deeper. It lays in de way Sollermun was raised. You take a man dat's got on'y one er two chillen; is dat man gwyne to be waseful o' chillen? No, he ain't; he can't 'ford it. *He* know how to value 'em. But you take a man dat's got 'bout five million chillen runnin' roun' de house, en it's diffunt. *He* as soon chop a chile in two as a cat. Dey's plenty mo'. A chile er two, mo' er less, warn't no consekens to Sollerman, dad fetch him!" (P. 112)

4. Ibid., pp. 346–48.

Jim's anger, unusual for him, is well founded, for he knows from experience what it means to be wasteful of children, living as he does in a society where black children, like the legions of Solomon's progeny, were of no particular value except as chattel. Conversely, Jim knows how to value children, for he lavishes on Huck the love that he cannot devote to his own children—who belong to someone else.

Another important allusion, not actually to Scripture but to an event that is so much a part of Christian tradition as to occupy virtually the same status in the popular imagination, occurs when Huck and Jim, floating downriver after escaping from the Shepherdson-Grangerford feud, enjoy their last interlude of unalloyed peace and contentment before the King and the Duke come aboard and the mood of the novel begins to darken. Huck has just given his famous description of a sunrise on the Mississippi, and he then describes nights on the river, including the following bit of cosmological speculation:

> We had the sky, up there, all speckled with stars, and we used to lay on our backs and look up at them, and discuss about whether they was made, or only just happened—Jim allowed they was made, but I allowed they happened; I judged it would have took too long to *make* so many. Jim said the moon could a *laid* them; well, that looked kind of reasonable, so I didn't say nothing against it, because I've seen a frog lay most as many, so of course it could be done. We used to watch the stars that fell, too, and see them streak down. Jim allowed they'd got spoiled and was hove out of the nest. (P. 159)

This discussion not only contrasts Huck's skeptical literal-mindedness with Jim's credulous vitalism but also hints at how Huck's skepticism may actually be more a product of the post-Darwin 1870s and 1880s than of the innocent antebellum frontier: the argument he uses—that it would have taken too much time to make so many—is the very argument that, working its way through biology, geology, and astronomy in the nineteenth century, did the most to undermine belief in Creation. "Jim allowed they was made, but I allowed they happened." In many respects, this sentence encapsulates a central tension of nineteenth-century thought to which we will return.

But the allusion I refer to comes at the end: "We used to watch the stars that fell, too, and see them streak down. Jim allowed they'd got spoiled and was hove out of the nest." This interpretation, I think, irresistibly reminds one of the fallen angels cast out of heaven, and, since the incident is not biblical, the image probably comes to us by way of Milton's *Paradise Lost*, which Twain knew well.[5] Specifically, the allusion is probably either to the general description of the fallen angels "Hurled headlong flaming from the ethereal sky" (1.45), or to the more often quoted description of the fall of Mammon: "from morn / to noon he fell, from noon to dewy eve, / A summer's day; and with the setting sun / Dropped from the zenith like a falling star" (1.742–45).

5. Alan Gribben, in *Mark Twain's Library: A Reconstruction*, 2 vols. (Boston: G. K. Hall, 1980), 1:476, documents frequent references to *Paradise Lost* by Twain as far back as his pilot days on the Mississippi in 1858.

Jim's homely vernacular rendering of this concept is especially pertinent at this point in the novel, for it pertains to the plight of the characters here, their homelessness, and catches up once again the idea of the fall from paradise, the loss of eden. This is in fact the last moment before Jim and Huck reenter the fallen world, the world of con men, cruelty, and demeaning games that makes up the rest of the book. Just around the bend are the King and the Duke, and then Bricksville, where honor demands that Colonel Sherburn shoot the harmless Boggs down in the street, and where loafers pour turpentine on stray dogs and set them afire.

When Huck and Jim arrive at Bricksville, there occurs the final and, I think, climactic invocation of biblical myth in the first half of the novel, culminating the imagery of a failed eden that has been accruing. Huck goes ashore with the King and the Duke, and they reconnoiter: here is a portion of Huck's description of the place, with the passages slightly rearranged for convenience:

> All the streets and lanes was just mud, they warn't nothing else *but* mud—mud as black as tar, and nigh about a foot deep in some places; and two or three inches deep in *all* the places. The hogs loafed and grunted around, everywheres. . . . The houses had little gardens around them, but they didn't seem to raise hardly anything in them but jimpson weeds, and sunflowers, and ash-piles, and old curled-up boots and shoes, and pieces of bottles, and rags, and played-out tin-ware. The fences was made of different kinds of boards, nailed on at different times; and they leaned every which-way. . . . Some of the fences had been whitewashed, some time or another, but the duke said it was in Clumbus's time, like enough. There was generly hogs in the garden, and people driving them out. (Pp. 183, 181)

Like Huck's description of his father as Adam, his account of Bricksville emphasizes the failed promise of the West and the frontier. This new world garden—and the garden is clearly emphasized here—consists, like Pap himself, mostly of mud. And these gardens, with their weeds and trash, offer only more evidence of sterility and cultural exhaustion. Huck's pointed reference to the discovery of America is a reminder of the original promise of the continent, and in the context of these images of decay and decrepitude it provides a savage commentary on the Jeffersonian ideal of small-town western life as consisting of independent freeholders drawing nourishment and virtue from a life close to nature. The description ends with a curiously tableau-like scene being repeatedly enacted—"there was generly hogs in the garden, and people driving them out"—as if life in frontier towns consisted of a perpetually ongoing expulsion from a debased eden.

II

In the second half of the novel, however, there is a radical diminution of the sorts of biblical allusions and underlying mythic patterns so prevalent in the first half. This change in the book's fundamental underlying imagery might be expected, it could be argued, because the themes themselves change in the second half. The satire of institutions and of human nature alike is more pointed, while at the same time the element of burlesque, especially in the last third of the book—the Evasion—threatens to dominate the novel entirely and to push far into the background the quest of Huck and Jim for freedom. Practically the only significant biblical allusion bearing on this original theme occurs when the King and the Duke sell Jim back into slavery for, as Huck bitterly puts it, "forty dirty dollars." This incident would seem to echo the betrayal of Christ by Judas for money (Matthew says it was thirty pieces of silver, though the other evangelists do not specify an amount).

On the whole, however, the rich pattern of allusions established in the first half of the novel fades almost completely away, despite the fact that there are more occasions for religious allusions: the King impersonates a minister, and Silas Phelps is a preacher too, "who never charged nothing for his preaching," Huck says, "and it was worth it, too" (p. 286). But it seems to me that this change does not so much *result from* a difference of theme as presage or even *cause* it, for I would suggest that this shift in underlying motifs signals a profound reorientation of Mark Twain's basic attitudes toward human life and human nature during the seven years that intervened between the inception and completion of *Huckleberry Finn*. The very disjunctiveness or discontinuity of imagery, in fact, may be of more importance than the interrupted pattern itself for our understanding of the novel in its widest genetic, historical, and cultural terms. The disjunction of imagery is finally organic in that it encapsulates both the most important and problematic development in Twain's thought and, in turn, a corresponding change in American culture itself at its deepest levels.

Thanks principally to the work of Walter Blair, the history of the composition of *Huckleberry Finn* is fairly well known, though some uncertainties remain.[6] Twain began the novel in the summer of 1876, clearly intending it as a sequel to *Tom Sawyer* and with the inspiration—momentous, as it turned out, for American literature—to tell the story in Huck's voice. He wrote with great speed and facility, carrying the story forward that summer probably to the end of Chapter 16, the point at which, after drifting past Cairo in the fog, the raft is smashed by a steamboat and Huck and Jim are separated. Here Twain apparently got stuck or lost interest, for he put the manuscript aside. He wrote to William Dean Howells that he liked what he had written only "tolerably well" and thought even to "pigeon-hole or burn the manuscript when it is done."[7]

Over the next six years (and here is where the uncertainty lies) Twain worked only sporadically on the book, perhaps writing as many as six of its forty-three chapters, depicting the feud and the entry of the King and the Duke into the plot. But he did not return to the book with a full head of steam until the summer of 1883 when he wrote the last half of the novel in a

6. *Mark Twain and Huck Finn*, and "When Was *Huckleberry Finn* Written?" *AL* 30 (1958): 1–25; see also Bernard DeVoto, *Mark Twain at Work* (Cambridge: Harvard University Press, 1942), pp. 45–104.

7. *Selected Mark Twain–Howells Letters*, ed. Frederick Anderson et al. (Cambridge: Harvard University Press, 1967), p. 75.

sustained burst of composition between 15 June and the end of August. He was working, he wrote Howells in July, six or seven eight-hour days per week, and averaging about three thousand words per day—a prodigious amount, but not unusual for Twain when the juices were flowing.[8]

Thus, it is hardly surprising that there are deep differences between the first and second halves of *Huckleberry Finn*, for the history of its composition shows that, while it was written over a seven-year period, its evolution was not gradual: most of the first half and all of the second half were actually written in two brief but intense spurts of composition seven summers apart. What happened to Twain and, more importantly, what affected his thinking and his imagination during these years that might account for a profound shift in his deepest level of conceptualizing his story?

Superficially, these years were no more troublesome or frenetic than usual for Twain. He traveled extensively in Europe in 1878 and 1879 and used this experience for *A Tramp Abroad* (1880). In 1881 he began the investments in the Paige typesetter that would eventually bleed him and cause his bankruptcy in 1894. He read European history voluminously and turned it to account in *The Prince and the Pauper* (1882). In that year he also revisited the Mississippi and Hannibal for the first time since the Civil War, and the following year he published *Life on the Mississippi*. Convinced that his publishers were cheating him, he started his own publishing company, under whose imprint he would issue *Adventures of Huckleberry Finn*. He was supervising personally a multitude of projects, both literary and financial, while his imagination was continually spinning new ideas for articles, books, dramas, inventions, investments, travel, living arrangements, and so on. He hobnobbed with the social and literary elite in Hartford, Boston, and New York; moved his large household entourage around frequently; and fumed because he lacked the time or peace to write.

But there was, at the same time, as Emily Dickinson says, internal change, where the meanings are. What this change involved can perhaps most dramatically be suggested by juxtaposing two talks Twain delivered before the Monday Evening Club, a regular gathering of Hartford friends. The first one was given in the winter of 1876, shortly before Twain wrote the first half of *Huckleberry Finn*, and the second in the winter of 1883, shortly before he wrote the second half of the novel. The first sketch, later published in the *Atlantic*, was called "Facts Concerning the Recent Carnival of Crime in Connecticut." In this fantasy, the author is visited by a deformed dwarf, covered with a sort of mossy fungus, who turns out to be his conscience. The author learns that his conscience torments him repeatedly for the same transgressions not to improve him but merely to make him miserable. He also learns that his conscience is shrunken and deformed because of changes in *his* character; he learns that some virtuous people he names have colossal, handsome consciences, and that certain mean snakes of his acquaintance (a publisher, especially) have consciences so shrunken as to be invisible under a microscope. By an intricate twist the author manages to kill his conscience,

8. Ibid., p. 212.

at which point he becomes a free and deleriously happy man, kills everyone who has ever offended him, gleefully swindles a widow and orphans out of their last cow, and so on.

It is tempting to relate both the subject and the mood of exasperation in this sketch to the genesis of *Huckleberry Finn*. One might speculate that by projecting himself through and into the character of Huck, Twain could give expression to that side of his nature that craved release from the restraints of both civilization and conscience. Huck's conscience was not a reminder of sin or guilt such as Twain was tormented by all his life but a spokesman instead for evil, for socially inculcated values and civilization itself. Huck is only troubled by his conscience when he feels bad for not returning Jim to slavery—emotions that we, of course, perceive as arising from his innate goodness. Huck's struggles with his conscience, then, are precisely the opposite of the sort Twain describes in "Carnival of Crime" and perhaps represent a powerful wish fulfillment: Huck's conscience (as Twain himself later described it) is "deformed" too, but unlike the author's deformed conscience it is warped in such a way as to make Huck appear *good*.

It would be tempting to follow this inversion as a kind of "germ" of the novel, but more to the present point is the fact that "Carnival of Crime," while it treats the issue in a detached, comic manner, does not seriously challenge the concept of individual moral responsibility. The fantasy merely dramatizes the violent desire to be free of that responsibility. In fact, the violence of the fantasy argues for the strength of the traditional value structure still in place.

A paper Twain read before the same Monday Evening Club seven years later, just before beginning the last half of *Huckleberry Finn*, is quite a different matter and constitutes, in fact, the core of what Twain later referred to as his "gospel," the deterministic, quasi-philosophic treatise called *What Is Man?* Here he articulated for the first time convictions that had been slowly developing over the years: namely, he denied "that there is any such thing as personal merit; . . . a man is merely a machine automatically functioning without any of his help. . . . I observed," Twain said, "that the human machine gets all its inspirations from the outside and is not capable of originating an idea of any kind in its own head; . . . there is no such thing as free will and no such thing as self-sacrifice."[9]

It would be an oversimplification to claim that these two essays are points in an intellectual system that can be connected by a straight line. Nevertheless, insofar as each work was representative of Twain's state of mind at the time he wrote it, they do suggest if not the trajectory then at least the drift of his thought during these years. When he began *Huckleberry Finn*, his inherited, traditional system of belief was more or less intact, though, like the conscience in the story, it may have been shrinking. He might indulge in a fantasy about killing his conscience, but the forces that underlay that conscience were still very much alive, as dramatized by the fact that he could, at first, project and sustain imaginatively in *Huckleberry Finn* a fictional world

9. Blair, *Mark Twain and Huck Finn*, p. 337.

in which individual moral responsibility, in the character of Huck, was achingly at issue.

By 1883, however, he had become a professed determinist, forthrightly denying individual moral responsibility—not because he had succeeded in killing his conscience but because the system of belief upon which its power was based was dead, replaced by his new gospel arising from positivistic and scientific thought. This system demonstrated to Twain's satisfaction that everything could be accounted for by a chain of material cause and effect, heredity or environment, biological necessity or social conditioning. In Twain's apt but not particularly original figure, man was a machine, totally dependent upon extrinsic forces, incapable of generating anything from within.

I doubt that Twain moved to this extreme materialism merely, as critics have suggested, as a way of escaping the pressures of his Calvinistic conscience. What he was reading during the 1870s and 1880s would suggest that, to the contrary, he was responding energetically to the ascendant ideology of the age. He was reading historians and social thinkers such as Taine, who stressed the influence of heredity and environment in determining the course of history; and the ethical historian W. E. H. Lecky, who presented the sort of simplified, thesis-ridden, narrative history that had the effect of stressing—especially to an untrained amateur like Twain—the inexorable march of events and the concomitant helplessness of the individual. At the same time, he was reading Darwin's *The Descent of Man*, and he grasped vividly, with all their chilling implications for the nineteenth-century mind, Darwin's theories as now *specifically* applied to human nature: that there is no intrinsic difference between man and other animals, and that our existence is the result solely of accidental variations in lower organisms responding to environmental pressures.[10] As Emerson foresaw, the new science, for all its power, contained a time bomb: "I see not," he had said in "Experience," "if one be once caught in this trap of so-called sciences, any escape from the links of the chain of physical necessity. Given such an embryo, such a history must follow." But for Twain, as for the century itself, the fatal first step had been taken, and there was no turning back.

When we look at the second half of *Huckleberry Finn* with this history in mind, I believe we can actually see the seam, the point at which Twain's new habit of mind grafts itself upon the original conception of the work and, as it were, takes command of the fable. This seam lies between Chapters 21 and 22, just halfway through, between the shooting of Boggs by Colonel Sherburn and Sherburn's speech facing down the mob that comes to lynch him. In the first episode, Huck and his party see the drunken Boggs, a stock comic character out of Southwestern fiction, come swooping into town raising hell and generally cussing and threatening everyone in sight. Huck is afraid of him, but the bystanders assure him that Boggs is harmless: "He's the best-naturedest old fool in Arkansaw—never hurt nobody, drunk nor so-

10. Ibid., pp. 135–45, 179; see also Gribben, *Mark Twain's Library*, 1:400–402, 2: 683–84, and Rodney B. Rogers, "Twain, Taine, and Lecky," *MLQ* 34 (1973): 436–47.

ber." But Boggs insults Colonel Sherburn, the town's biggest shopkeeper. Since Sherburn is a gentleman, he shoots the unarmed Boggs down in the street while the drunk's friends are trying to hustle him away. Sherburn is a thoroughly despicable character here, one of the debased "aristocrats" like the Shepherdsons and Grangerfords, whose veneer of gentility and honor masks a murderer's heart. To emphasize the brutality of Sherburn's act, Twain shows Boggs's sixteen-year-old daughter throw herself screaming and crying across the body of her father.

In the next chapter, a mob gathers and goes whooping up to Sherburn's house to lynch him. Sherburn steps out on the porch with a shotgun and coolly faces them down. He delivers a scathing speech that scatters the crowd, a part of which goes as follows: "Do I know you? I know you clear through. I was born and raised in the South, and I've lived in the North; so I know the average all around. The average man's a coward." This denunciation of the average man is striking, but even more startling, I think, is the fact that from Chapter 21 to Chapter 22 Sherburn has been transformed from a thoroughgoing villain to a spokesman for the author's own ideas, for his speech follows closely the sentiments of a passage Mark Twain had written in his own voice earlier that year for *Life on the Mississippi*. When we combine this information with Walter Blair's judgment, based on textual evidence, that Sherburn's speech marks the point where Twain took up the novel again in the summer of 1883, we can begin to understand why the imagery and the theme of the second half of the book are so different from those of the first.[11]

Sherburn's chastisement of the mob is, in a sense, Twain's first public testament of rejection of the damned human race; it registers his new convictions, precipitated by his reading in history and science, that humanity was hopelessly weak, brutal, and incapable of directing itself; that such things as individual merit or responsibility could not even exist if mankind were wholly the product of outside forces. Sherburn's speech sounds as though the author were pointing out to his assembled characters the absurdity and uselessness of their masquerade.

This feeling or conviction, I think, propels the second half of the novel in much the same way the fantasy of freedom propels the first half. The significant difference between the two halves, then, is that the quest for escape and freedom in the first half was conceived and executed under the influence of mythic analogues that made the quest meaningful and important. Human action and individual responsibility attained weight and significance by acquiring mythic dimensions. In the second half of the novel, however, the system of belief that had undergirded these mythic patterns, and from which the corresponding images had arisen, had been succeeded in Twain's imagination by a kind of despondent materialism that could still see suffering and corruption but could not assign to that suffering or struggle any purpose. There Twain's view—that science and technology finally offer only "results" and not answers—is clearly implied, to be registered much more explicitly

11. *Mark Twain and Huck Finn*, p. 441 n.

in his next two important novels, *A Connecticut Yankee* and *Pudd'nhead Wilson*, which focus on the questions of whether there is any escape from the determinism of environment and heredity respectively. Both decide the question in the negative, and in each technology shows itself to be powerless to affect destiny.

To speak in radically foreshortened terms, when Huck and Jim are projected into the world of the second half of the novel they are anachronisms, characters born to a world of mythic resonance and individual moral responsibility only to be thrust into the post-Darwinian world of dissolving belief where meaning itself is in doubt because the traditional authority that guaranteed it has been discredited.

Critics who have confronted the sense of most readers that the Phelps episode, with its extended burlesque of Tom Sawyer's Evasion, is disappointing, have typically charged Twain with a kind of failure of nerve. He is charged, not unreasonably, with an evasion of his own in failing to carry out the potentially tragic implications of his plot, which has Jim and Huck floating farther and farther into slave territory on their quest for freedom. Twain ducks the issue, the argument goes, by having Tom Sawyer reappear, by turning the last part of the book into an expanded parody of Romantic fiction, and by having Jim freed by Miss Watson's implausible deathbed change of heart.

The reading of the novel I have been developing would put a somewhat different slant on the ending. It would suggest not that Twain was unwilling to face the tragic implications of his plot and theme, but rather that tragedy itself was no longer meaningful or even possible. Decisions based on the illusion of full choice turn out to be just that—illusions—hence Huck's famous "All right, then, I'll *go* to hell" (p. 272), usually pointed to as the moral climax of the novel, actually has no consequences, for Huck never has to act upon or live with this decision. In Twain's new deracinated world, the overstuffed burlesque of the ending is as plausible as anything else might be. Why not have Huck, hundreds of miles from home, walk into a strange house and be hailed as Tom Sawyer? Why not have Tom Sawyer show up the very same day? Why not have Miss Watson, who had intended to sell Jim down the river, free him instead?

Twain's considerable facility for spinning out parody or burlesque was perhaps made still more effortless because he apparently no longer believed that the quest of his protagonists could be completed meaningfully. His working notes for this section of the book bespeak horrors that, fortunately, we are spared, but that indicate the essential lack of seriousness with which he now conceived the work. One idea he had for extending the plot, for example, was: "Farmer has bought an elephant at auction. Gives him to Tom Huck & Jim & they go about the country on him & make no end of trouble." [12]

The often-noted structural "flaw" of *Huckleberry Finn*, I would argue, embodies organically the historical disjunction that Twain himself was perhaps never capable of articulating conceptually, but that nevertheless under-

---

12. DeVoto, *Mark Twain at Work*, p. 77.

lies and makes historically plausible the pessimism of his later years. His response to this disjunction allies him, perhaps unexpectedly, with Henry Adams, who, in the *Education*, articulated and symbolized this same disjunction in the "failure" of his own life. Each man was the product of an age of belief, belief that was probably restrictive and frightening but that gave significance to human aspiration and suffering. Each man found himself carried with an artist's sensibility into the world of the twentieth century, with the disjunction itself as the predominant fact of life. Speaking of this ultimate "similarity of vision" in Twain and Adams, Tony Tanner has written:

> It is their inability to disburden themselves of the mental framework which accompanied belief that makes both determinists of one kind or another. God had either fled or been reduced to a thing—. . . . but the feeling of predestination lingered on just beneath the surface of the conscious mind. To this we can trace the persistent image of the voyage in so much nineteenth century American literature, but now what was the destiny to which man had been predestined? The compasses were not functioning, the chart of infallible absolutes was completely useless on these novel seas. . . . It seems that without the one all-solving deity the world collapsed into an amorphous, inexplicable mess before which the only reaction was one of sterile horror. Not that either man wanted the old God back, but they were equally dismayed at America's failure to provide any substitute ideal purpose or explanation.[13]

To make one final comparison, like Herman Melville some thirty years earlier, Twain had become a famous author before he began to be an educated one. Like Melville, his early popular success had introduced him to the world of literary people, books, thought, the life of the mind. Like Melville, he became a voracious but undisciplined reader, responding vigorously to the philosophical questions of the day but lacking the conceptual framework a formal education might have given him; he determined to raise himself above the level of his popular successes but plunged into religious and metaphysical doubts that tormented him all his life. Like the Melville of Hawthorne's description, Twain became a man who could "neither believe, nor be comfortable in his unbelief."

The greatness of *Huckleberry Finn* seems inextricably bound up with its greatest flaw, the discordance of its ending. Structural flaw though that may be, the novel's shift in imagery and theme is a kind of seismographic quiver that records the collision, or rather the rupture, of worlds far below the surface. If the potential of the Bible and religious tradition to help Huck and Twain impose meaning and order on experience was at best a possibility that was interesting, but tough, the new order of things offered even fewer clues to an eighteenth-century sensibility projected into the twentieth century, where the world itself didn't say why.

13. "The Lost America—The Despair of Henry Adams and Mark Twain," *ModA* 5 (1961): 307–8.

23   STANLEY BRODWIN

Mark Twain in the Pulpit: The Theological Comedy of *Huckleberry Finn*

WHILE "speaking from the grave" on 31 July 1906, Mark Twain contemplated the fate of his fellow humorists—Artemus Ward, Josh Billings, and others—and came to the conclusion that they perished because they were "only" humorists. But how did he, Mark Twain, escape this dread fate of the other "sparkling transients"? The answer is:

> Humor must not professedly teach, and it must not professedly preach, but it must do both if it would live forever. By forever, I mean thirty years. . . .
> . . . I have always preached. That is the reason I have lasted thirty years. If the humor came of its own accord and uninvited, I have allowed it a place in my sermon, but I was not writing the sermon for the sake of the humor. I would have written the sermon just the same, whether any humor applied for admission or not.[1]

We may regard this as yet another example of Twain's own ironic truth-bending, his comic way of handling lifelong doubts about whether he was, in fact, a literary buffoon or a truly serious comic artist. Fortunately he was wrong about one thing: his "sermons" have lasted beyond thirty years and give every sign of engaging us well into the future. And no one doubts that *Adventures of Huckleberry Finn* is his *carte d'visite* to "immortality," a novel still challenging us to grasp the spiritual dynamic that integrates its "sermon" and humor.

But whether meant ironically or not, perhaps we should take Twain's comments at face value, for there is certainly evidence that at the heart of his comic imagination there dwelt the impulses of a preacher, a "preacher-manqué," to be sure, because or in spite of a radical predilection to test his own theological and cultural values against the entrenched contradictions he encountered in everyday experience.

Twain had more than an intimation of this "calling" himself. He once wrote to his brother Orion that he might have become a preacher if not for his "calling" to "literature of a low order, i.e., humorous," to exciting "the *laughter* of God's children,"[2] instead. And so in good Puritan-Calvinist tra-

1. Bernard DeVoto, ed., *Mark Twain in Eruption* (New York: Harper & Brothers, 1968), pp. 202–3.
2. Quoted in Jeffrey R. Holland, "Soul-Butter and Hog Wash: Mark Twain and Frontier Religion," in *"Soul-Butter and Hog Wash" and Other Essays on the American West*, ed. Thomas G. Alexander (Provo: Brigham Young University Press, 1978), p. 14. Other good studies on how frontier Presbyterianism shaped Twain's mind are John Q. Hays, "Mark Twain's

dition, he took his "low" calling and turned it to the service of God's world, although he would gradually come to assault that Deity and rage against the consequences of man's fall, exposing the tragic "joke" in the Revealed Word: "Father Adam & the apple—he didn't know it was loaded." [3]

Certainly by the time he began *Huckleberry Finn* in 1876 Twain found himself locked into his tension-ridden role of being a preacher-artist—a "moralist in disguise" [4] he called himself—who was disaffected from his own Protestant dogmas and institutions and whose "texts" daringly attacked the received orthodoxies of his time by creating a "countertheology" embodied in his indigenous Western comic forms. Through his readings in deistic writers like Tom Paine and Voltaire, as well as his familiarity with Darwin and the "Higher Criticism" of the Bible, he was able to free himself from traditional fundamentalism, although emotionally and in his art he remained its captive, hounded by his "Presbyterian Conscience." [5] More significantly, he justified his alienation from the "sham" of religion on a level most deeply related to his native genius: "I cannot see how a man of any large degree of humorous perception can ever be religious—except he purposely shut the eyes of his mind & keep them shut by force," he wrote in 1887–1888. [6] A comic preacher-artist was therefore a contradiction in terms for Twain, unless some way could be found to harmonize the "sermons" of a new Gospel with the humor ready to apply for "admission."

Not surprisingly, as early as the late 1860s and early 1870s, Twain came to the position that not in the "drowsy pulpit" but through "*Narratives of generous deeds*" [7] his "calling" could best be realized. Either as rationalization or simple surrender to psychological necessity, the decision was momentous, signaling Twain's recognition that narrative art was the only strategy that could effectively harness both his preaching and his comic impulses. When he began work on *Huckleberry Finn,* he had already left his fellow literary comedians in his artistic wake, having reshaped his inherited cultural forces

Rebellion Against God: Origins," *Southwestern American Literature* 3 (1973):27–38; Lloyd A. Hunter, "Mark Twain and the Southern Evangelical Mind," *Bulletin of the Missouri Historical Society* 33 (July 1977):246–64; and, finally, Kenneth R. Andrews, *Nook Farm, Mark Twain's Hartford Circle* (Cambridge: Harvard University Press, 1950), chap. 2, "The Varieties of Religious Experience," still the best account of how the liberal Bushnellian atmosphere of Hartford, with especially fine ministers like Joseph Twichell, stimulated Twain's lifelong concern with religious issues.

3. Robert Pack Browning et al., eds., *Mark Twain's Notebooks and Journals, 1883–1891* (Berkeley: University of California Press, 1979), 3:306. Hereafter cited as *MTNJ.*

4. Paul J. Carter, Jr., "Mark Twain: 'Moralist in Disguise,'" *University of Colorado Studies in Language & Literature* 6 (January 1957):65–78, analyzes the consistent way Twain saw himself as a "moralist" and the conflicts it created for him and his audiences.

5. For a discussion of these issues and the significance of the Adamic myth in Twain's imagination, see my "The Humor of the Absurd: Mark Twain's Adamic Diaries," *Criticism* 14 (Winter 1972):49–64; and "The Theology of Mark Twain: Banished Adam & the Bible," *MissQ* 29 (Spring 1976):167–89.

6. *MTNJ,* 3:389. Compare Twain's comment to Orion in 1860: "What a man wants with religion in these breadless times surpasses my comprehension." In *Mark Twain's Letters,* ed. Albert Bigelow Paine (New York: Harper & Brothers, 1917), 1:45.

7. ". . . Remains of George Holland by the Rev. Mr. Sabine" (1871), in *What Is Man? and Other Philosophical Writings,* ed. Paul Baender (Berkeley: University of California Press, 1973), p. 53.

to make them available to his art. The result was a fresh theological and social vision that was to find its most complete expression in Huck's language and comic adventures. It was in fact a *counter*theology, rooted in three central principles that dominated the Christian ethos Twain had absorbed and then transformed: the "myth" of Providence, man's reprobate and lying nature, and the imperative of spiritual conversion and social reform.[8] Always theologically supporting this triad was the primary Adamic myth itself, man's banishment from an edenic condition that thrust him into a world of salvational drama. Indeed, these inverted or "counter" concepts form a "deep-structure" or *episteme* in much of Twain's work, theologically energizing his "low" comic forms and transforming them into a "higher" and sophisticated comic art.

A profound analysis of the way such a transformation can take place is offered by Søren Kierkegaard, whose existential theology placed the dynamics of humor as a mediating and defining bridge between the "ethicist" and religious individual in man's development from the pure "immediacy" of existence toward his total involvement with God. In such an existential dialectic—and here we must necessarily oversimplify Kierkegaard's complex discussion—the humorist apprehends the spiritual nature of his "inwardness" in ethical strivings grounded in guilt, doubt, and despair and absorbs the full reality of the contradictions those strivings reveal. Thus the humorist

> sets the God-idea into conjunction with other things and evokes the contradiction—but he does not maintain a relationship to God in terms of religious passion . . . he transforms himself instead into a jesting and yet profound exchange-center for all those transactions, but he does not himself stand related to God. The religious man does the same, he sets the God-idea into juxtaposition with everything and sees the contradiction, but in his inmost consciousness he is related to God.[9]

The persistent irony for Mark Twain is that he directed his religious "passion" angrily against the contradictions his God-idea or countertheology

---

8. See the many short pieces Twain wrote attacking the "Myth of Providence," in *Mark Twain's Fables of Man*, ed. John S. Tuckey (Berkeley: University of California Press, 1972). The concept of "special providence" especially "nauseates me," Twain wrote in 1886–1887, *MTNJ*, 3 : 246. Also see Robert Lee Cody, "Providence in the Novels of Mark Twain" (Ph.D. diss., University of Florida, 1978), a valuable account of the way Twain used the idea as a structural principle. And in 1885 Twain wrote a short piece, "The Character of Man," which describes the essence of man as a "lie" in every aspect of his being (*What Is Man?*, p. 61). By 1901 Twain's sense of man's sin was so deep that Twichell complained he was "too orthodox on the Doctrine of Total Human Depravity" (quoted in Andrews, *Nook Farm*, pp. 47, 253). I have examined the relationship in Twain's work among the ideas of Providence, lies, and reform, which I call his "countertheology." See my "Mark Twain's Myth of the Daring Jest," in *The Mythologizing of Mark Twain* (Tuscaloosa: University of Alabama Press, 1984).

9. *Kierkegaard's Concluding Unscientific Postscript*, trans. David F. Swenson, ed. Walter Lowrie (Princeton: Princeton University Press, 1941), p. 451. Also see Marie Collins Swabey, *Comic Laughter: A Philosophical Essay* (New Haven: Yale University Press, 1961), p. 91, to whose study I am indebted. See, too, Bruce E. Miller, "*Huckleberry Finn*: the Kierkegaardian Dimension," *Illinois Quarterly* 34 (1971):55–64. While one can accept Miller's contention that Huck is investigating his surroundings and responsibilities in an existential manner, it is difficult to accept his statement that Huck's lighting out is theologically similar to Abraham's pilgrimage to Mt. Moriah. See my argument in "The Humor of the Absurd."

evoked, thus preventing him from resolving them through "a leap of faith." Yet in *Huckleberry Finn* he did find a way of dealing with those cosmic and social contradictions ultimately voiced by Satan in *The Mysterious Stranger* stories. Again, Kierkegaard gives us the key:

> The tragic and the comic are the same, insofar as both are based on contradiction; but the *tragic is the suffering contradiction, the comical, the painless contradiction.* . . .
>
> . . . Satire entails pain, but this pain has a dialectic which gives it a teleology in the direction of a cure. The difference between the tragic and the comic lies in the relationship between the contradiction and the controlling idea. The comic apprehension evokes the contradiction and makes it manifest by having in mind the way out, which is why the contradiction is painless. The tragic apprehension sees the contradiction and despairs of a way out.[10]

As the unconscious ironist of his own story, Huck consistently finds his "way out" of those contradictions he experiences. In his clash with reality, Huck comes to accept the futility of reform or change and to "exchange" the burdens of conscience and human evil for that "painless" or "comfortable" state he seeks. He can be driven to tears over Buck's death or the con men's treatment of Jim; indeed, he will dream of the feud "lots of times" (p. 154). Whatever the circumstance, superficial or dread, the implicit tragedy is exchanged for—*converted to*—a painless condition because his "innocence," naiveté, and active sense of survival find a "way out"; if anything, his spirit of adventure, reinforced by his thoughts of Tom in almost every situation, stays alive, carrying him from crisis to crisis, stoically unscathed. The humor he thus creates becomes *our* release from pain and may be called authentically "Adamic."

An extraordinary aspect of Twain's achievement in *Huckleberry Finn* is the way this kind of humor, intrinsic to Huck's "exchange" psychology, becomes an organic part of a long and complex literary tradition from which Twain could, and did, draw some of the fundamental narrative patterns in the novel. For the "providential tradition" was a longstanding one in Western theology and literature, and its most popular pattern was the spiritual autobiography epitomized in its different literary forms by Bunyan's *The Pilgrim's Progress* (1678) and Defoe's *Robinson Crusoe* (1719). In *Huckleberry Finn* both works are alluded to implicitly and explicitly.[11] In addition,

---

10. *Kierkegaard's Concluding Unscientific Postscript*, pp. 459–63.

11. J. Paul Hunter, *The Reluctant Pilgrim* (Baltimore: Johns Hopkins University Press, 1966), gives a thorough overview of the "providence" tradition and Defoe's reliance upon it. George A. Starr, *Defoe and Spiritual Autobiography* (Princeton: Princeton University Press, 1965), also studies this tradition, stressing Defoe's view that merely "trusting" in Providence was a "lethargy" unless accompanied by insight and responsibility (p. 190). Jacob Viner, *The Role of Providence in the Social Order* (Philadelphia: American Philosophical Society, 1972), offers illuminating insights into the history of this crucial concept and the way it informed Western civilization's views on economic expansion, nationalism, and imperialism. Martin Green, *Dreams of Adventure, Deeds of Empire* (New York: Basic Books, 1979), pp. 245–46, shows how Twain introduced "sordid" elements of the American frontier into Defoe's great mercantile "myth" pattern of adventure. For all details concerning Twain's knowledge and use of Bunyan and Defoe, see Alan Gribben, *Mark Twain's Library: A Reconstruction* (Boston: G. K. Hall, 1980), 1:111–12, 180–82.

Voltaire's *Candide* (1759) may have offered Twain a narrative model satirically deflating eighteenth-century philosophical abuses of a benevolent, optimistic providentialism. Especially in *Robinson Crusoe*, Twain would have found, as did other generations of readers, an exciting fusion of a recognizable, "middle-class" hero's worldly adventures with the revealed moral (and economic) lessons of a divine Providence. The providential narrative, be it allegorical, realistic, or a synthesis of both, usually ended with the protagonist's "conversion" to a true awareness of God's divine theodicy and moral order, an order Twain always challenged and unequivocally denied by the 1880s. That denial was firmly predicated on man's reprobate nature and the often cruelly absurd workings of God's will, which were nevertheless submissively accepted by a "sham" Christian civilization. Above all, mankind's inability to reform, its penchant to invent all kinds of strategies to avoid reforming, laid the grounds for his pessimistic determinism or his view of an amoral, inverted "providential" order. The damned human race was damned precisely because it was subject to a traditional Christian theology that masked these "truths" by nurturing false and unreal hopes of salvation. If, in his last years, he gave Satan the task of thundering this sermon from the pulpit, in *Huckleberry Finn* it was mediated through an unconsciously Adamic innocent whose providential adventures carry him into a fallen American heartland.

Because Huck's "natural" innocence is attuned to a "natural" Providence, he necessarily questions the "two Providences" taught him by Miss Watson and the Widow Douglas—the path of damnation and the path of salvation—concepts that immediately trigger theological and structural tensions.[12] We are in the Mississippi current of providential adventuring, reaching back to Bunyan and Defoe, but with the added dimensions of Twain's Adamic humor and countertheology energizing in complex ways the familiar picaresque framework of a nineteenth-century boys' book. It is remarkable enough that Twain managed so remarkable a fusion, but the critical task is to observe how these new elements mold the book into an American theological comedy, *sui generis*.

All these grand themes and their structural interrelationships begin appropriately enough in Chapter 1. The atmosphere of that Bunyanesque "Delectable Land" that bathes the opening of *Tom Sawyer* is compromised by Huck's fictive separation from Mr. Mark Twain, in whose novel of adventures "stretchers" abounded. Huck's fictional reality, like that of Cervantes's *Don Quixote*, is established as a "truth"-telling narrator whose narrative technique is the "lie" that illuminates by contrast the moral and epistemological confusions inherent in society's theological way of viewing itself. "I never seen anybody but lied, one time or another" (p. [17]),[13] Huck observes, excepting only Aunt Polly and "maybe" Mary; he then goes on to

12. Edgar M. Branch treats the structural significance of this passage in "The Two Providences: Thematic Form in *Huckleberry Finn*," *CE* 11 (1950):188–95.

13. *The Writings of Mark Twain*, ed. Albert Bigelow Paine, 37 vols. (New York: Harper & Brothers, 1923). All references to Twain's works, except those to *Huckleberry Finn*, will be to this edition.

describe the widow's and Miss Watson's salvational roles, the former saving Huck, like Moses, from the "bulrushers," the latter teaching him about the "good place" and the "bad place." But Huck takes no stock in "dead people" and wants to go anywhere Miss Watson is not, though "I never said so, because it would only make trouble, and wouldn't do no good" (p. 18). Huck's wise passivity, which is an integral part of his "sound heart"[14] or God-idea springing from his "natural theology" of superstition, compassion, and instinctual sense of freedom, here avoids an ugly confrontation with what he perceives as a contradiction between teacher and doctrine. The "salvation" he does achieve is ironically managed in other instances by his supreme, Odysseus-like capacity to lie, a capacity that will also enable him to survive his adventures with Tom and Jim. Moreover, the world of superstition and "natural" innocence they share in their differing ways (including admiration for Tom's "style") adds a major counterpointing dimension to the novel's theological structure, a pagan providence of "signs" Jim is especially adept at reading. Thus the book expands theologically its commentary on the central characters' individual versions of freedom and the external or Providential forces acting upon them. In that context, Huck's brooding upon death and his recurring sense of loneliness may be seen as a psychological result not only of his social alienation but also of his theological "lostness" or "abandonment" that emerges in moments of solitude, the Sunday stillnesses in Nature or at the Phelps farm, and when his "orneriness" weighs upon him. With Jim on the raft out on the Mississippi he does feel a joyful freedom—even with Pap he can temporarily feel "comfortable"—but truly alone his alienation appears as a form of religious insecurity Miss Watson's Christianity only intensifies, which explains why the widow's benevolent version of Providence makes his "mouth water." It is no wonder that Twain himself was already formulating tracts and fables out of his Deism and determinism in order to neutralize or explain away that rage of insecurity his loss of faith exacerbated. But in *Huckleberry Finn* the novelist subsumes the "philosopher" by artistically illuminating Huck's struggle to find a "secure" freedom, a way out of his dilemmas far more profound than the need to escape from conventional social restrictions against smoking or swearing. His "inner" freedom, unlike Tom's or Jim's, will be gained by his capacity to reconcile the contradictions encountered during his pilgrim's progress through a fallen world. In that world, "disgusting" (p. 212) as it sometimes becomes for him, he is quite at home.

As I have already suggested, this is a world defined by lies, for Twain one of the most self-evident manifestations of sin. But just as there are "two Providences," there are also two kinds of lies, the lies of innocent deception that can console and ensure survival—the paradox of moral hypocrisy—and the adult world's malevolent motives. Throughout the novel these two kinds of lies are counterpointed, developing a tension between the possibil-

14.   See Henry Nash Smith, *Mark Twain: The Development of a Writer* (Cambridge: Harvard University Press, 1962), pp. 113–37, for a discussion of Twain's description of *Huckleberry Finn* as a clash between a "sound heart" and a "deformed conscience."

ities of prelapsarian life and the realities of a postlapsarian condition. In true theological fashion, the battleground is the Self that must experience and choose between these realities in its compulsion to "reform." The novel's rich texture of moral and comic irony results from the way Huck passively and actively engages these forces and the "adventures" they precipitate. Thus, as soon as Huck returns from his first-night adventure with Tom's "gang," he is taken by the literal-minded Miss Watson (see Matt. 5:6) into the "closet" to pray (p. [29]), initiating his comic meditation on the efficacy of prayer, for he has been taught that there exists a wise Providence to hear and respond. When he is upbraided by Miss Watson for praying for material things ("Once I got a fish-line, but no hooks") instead of "spiritual gifts" and told that he must "help other people" (p. [29]), Huck takes the only way out he knows: "I went out in the woods and turned it over in my mind a long time, but I couldn't see no advantage about it—except for the other people— so at last I reckoned I wouldn't worry about it any more, but just let it go" (p. 30). But as we know, the release from prayer is only temporary, foreshadowing his agony over Jim much later. Miss Watson and the widow do not let up on him, however, and continue to catechize about their respective Providences. Indeed, this whole passage is a paradigm of the Providence-lies-reform theme and narratively prepares us for a genuinely painful adventure to follow. For no sooner does Huck "choose" the widow's mouth-watering salvational Providence, even as he questions how God was "agoing to be any better off than what he was before" (p. 30), then the ominous signs of Pap's presence appear: a drowned body, supposedly Pap, was only a woman dressed up in a man's clothes, and so Huck is "uncomfortable" again. Providence is ironically preparing its coils while Huck reenters Tom's world of make-believe A-rabs and elephants. The chapter now ends as it began, with a satirical thrust at Tom Sawyer's "lie" of the genies and Aladdin's lamp, which Huck converts into all the "marks of a Sunday school" (p. 33). The religious teachings he has questioned are no less fantastic than the *Arabian Nights*. He now knows that neither prayer nor "enchantments" can change reality, and it is upon that truth that all moral struggle and adventure is finally based.

Still, the presence of a dark, ironic Providence lingers on, as months later Pap's sign, a "cross in the left boot-heel made with big nails, to keep off the devil" (p. 35), compels Huck to sell his property to the Judge. And again a troubling episode is countered with the need to read Providence, this time in the form of Jim's pagan "hairball" prophecy that hedges all bets but points to the central spiritual drama of the Self: two angels, one black and one white, will contest for Pap's soul and a "body can't tell, yit, which one gwyne to fetch him at de las'" (p. 37), while Huck will have "considable" trouble and joy.[15] "You wants to keep 'way fum de water as much as you kin," Jim warns in a wonderful false prophecy, "'kase it's down in de bills dat you's

15. Daniel G. Hoffman, *Form and Fable in American Fiction* (New York: Oxford University Press, 1961), pp. 317–42, is still the best study of Jim as pagan-prophet. A biblical perspective of Jim's relationship to Huck is offered by Kenneth S. Lynn, "Huck and Jim," *YR* 47 (1958):421–31.

gwyne to get hung" (p. 38). Of course, here is the beginning of Jim's relationship to Huck as black guru-father, and so we are not surprised when Pap, the "fish-belly white" (p. [39]) and truly "dead" father, shows up in all his devilish glory. Yet Pap's arrival, horrible as it is with his vicious "cracker" racism and hatred of learning, ends with a superb comic demonstration of his conning the new judge's maudlin reform evangelism, dramatizing one of Twain's most cherished convictions about the matter: "He [the new judge] said he reckoned a body could reform the ole man with a shot-gun, maybe, but he didn't know no other way" (p. 44). With that statement, Huck foreshadows also a truth about himself in a different way, when, with "Providence slapping [him] in the face" (p. 270), he goes through his moral anguish over Jim, chooses hell and "never thought no more about reforming" (p. 272)—the perfect "way out."

On a profound symbolic and characterological level, Huck and Pap are indeed father and son. The son is an Adamic innocent who achieves "salvation" by necessarily rejecting the orthodox providences of his society; the father is a powerful image of a truly fallen Adam. Pap, drunk and having slept in the gutter all night, is described by Huck as looking like "Adam, he was just all mud" (p. 49). This metaphor projects Pap as the earthy, flawed, and filthy side of Adam's being, going beyond the traditional implications of the biblical passage that was taken as literal demonstration of God's power in transforming "dust" or "earth" into a "living soul" (Gen. 2:7). For Mark Twain, the term *mud* carried strong personal (the Mississippi is "old muddy") and pejorative connotations. In 1897, lamenting the death of Susy, he wrote to Howells calling himself a "mud image" in contrast to the self that "writes, and has comedy-fancies." [16] And in the "Chronicle of Young Satan," Philip Traum comments, "Man is made of dirt—I *saw* him made. I am not made of dirt." [17] Indeed, the imagery of man entrapped in mud, dirt, and flesh powerfully informs some of the main theological themes in The Mysterious Stranger stories. [18] We may also regard the image of Pap as Adamic mud as a vernacular inversion of the way Victorian piety and iconography imaged Adam as a noble, pure being who only becomes "mud" spiritually, *after* the fall. Huck's vivid, natural perception of "natural" man— his biological father—points to the ultimate theological "twain-ness" in humanity. Huck is a true "unfallen" Adam, while Pap, the fallen natural man, lives with nothing but alcohol and anger and so cannot cope, as does his son, with the world. Hence he degenerates and passes out of the novel's landscape, to be replaced by the Duke and King, "his kind of people" (p. 166), as Huck knows.

Once we recognize that Huck and Pap spring from the same Adamic source, however much they diverge from it, Huck's preference for Pap's existence over that of "sivilization" becomes psychologically and spiritually ex-

16. Henry Nash Smith and William M. Gibson, eds., Mark Twain–Howells Letters (Cambridge: Harvard University Press, 1969), 2:664–65.
17. In Mark Twain's Mysterious Stranger Manuscripts, ed. William M. Gibson (Berkeley: University of California Press, 1969), p. 55.
18. See my "Mark Twain's Masks of Satan: The Final Phase," AL 45 (1973):207–27.

plicable. Both father and son wish to live off the fat of the land, do no work, and yet be content. It is only Pap's violence that drives Huck away from his new eden and providentially to Jim, sold down the river. By creating the lie of his death through his ritual killing, a mythically resonant "way out," Huck will survive, free to bind himself to Jim's own need for the secrecy his skin always threatens to betray. Inevitably, the river looms as the dynamic instrument and metaphor of freedom-in-adventure. But it is also an instrument of nature's Providence, giving, as the sea and island give to Crusoe and Friday, the means of survival and companionship. Thus the river offers first a canoe to Huck and then the raft; the wrecked steamboat with its criminals brings them money and knives; and, finally, the storm separates them, ending in Jim's symbolic interpretation of Huck's dream-trick as "signs" that they would reach the free states and "then be out of trouble" (p. [115]).

Jim's analysis is a brilliant piece of vernacular typology, reading into the river's elements both his and Huck's spiritual adventure. Evoking now the contradiction within himself, Huck brashly presses Jim to interpret the debris on the raft. Jim's answer leaves Huck no way out. But the pain of humiliation from Jim's noble answer is a pain Huck gladly accepts, turning it into a heightened moral experience. Here Twain manipulates the long tradition of Bunyanesque salvational dream-interpretation with its providential signs and symbols, making Jim the minister of nature's texts, and making the "trash" both a symbol of sin and a democratic, spiritual equality. By displacing and inverting the relationships in this scene—and in others—Twain presents a democratic version of the spiritual-adventure autobiography his Protestant culture so assiduously read and took consolation from. Perhaps Twain wished to underline the significance of this transformation by making Huck later tell us that he read "considerable" in *Pilgrim's Progress*, even though the "statements was interesting, but tough" (p. 137). The irony becomes more trenchant when we realize that in the world of *Huckleberry Finn*, Bunyan's Providence only provides the occasions to lie, and the need for the moral reforms that people try to escape, parody, or pervert.

I have called this countertheological pattern the *episteme* or "deep-structure" of the narrative, and it continues into the middle section of the book where the obvious raft/shore tension provides another structural dimension of meaning. Nevertheless, Huck remains an "exchange-center" revealing contradictions and converting what should be tragic despair into comic acceptance or Adamic painlessness. Surely the essential contradiction inherent in the Grangerford-Shepherdson feud is evoked by Huck's reaction to the sermon he hears during a lull in the killing:

> It was pretty ornery preaching—all about brotherly love, and such-like tiresomeness; but everybody said it was a good sermon . . . and had a powerful lot to say about faith, and good works, and free grace, and preforeordestination, and I don't know what all, that it did seem to me to be one of the roughest Sundays I had run across yet. (P. 148)

The surface humor may result from Huck's garbled account of standard "Presbyterian" theology (he is to do the same with Shakespeare), but the scene's deepest thrust exposes a society so morally incorrigible and unaware of its sin that any rage or satirical anger a reader ought to feel at the situation is nullified. We laugh instead while acknowledging the moral farce and slaughter to follow, in which comedy and tragedy form two sides of the providential coin. There is no reform from lies here, but Huck's Adamic stance reconciles us to this through laughter. The accumulation and consistent pattern of such comic effects throughout the novel place its vision beyond the level of social satire and into the realm of religious comedy.

Unquestionably, the scene immediately following Huck and Jim's escape from the feud embodies the novel's most complete Adamic moment. Now "free and easy and comfortable" (p. 156) on the raft, Huck and Jim float into their Eden as if it were a prolonged first day of creation. In Huck's perception all objects are seen and heard with a pristine vividness.[19] He reacts to all the threats that surround him, particularly the snags waiting there destructively. As he begins to see more in the light, he observes a woodyard "piled by them cheats so you can throw a dog through it anywheres; then the nice breeze springs up" (p. 158). Man's evil and the soothing powers of nature are merged into a single pattern of perception. The breeze brings the fresh, sweet smell of flowers but also of "dead fish laying around," an ugly intrusion that in no way mars the ecstatic conclusion of the sunrise: "and next you've got the full day, and everything smiling in the sun, and the songbirds just going it!" (p. 158).

So primitive or prelapsarian is their condition that they even play out an original experience from man's earliest cultural stages: mythmaking.

> It's lovely to live on a raft. We had the sky up there, all speckled with stars, and we used to lay on our backs and look up at them, and discuss about whether they was made, or only just happened—Jim he allowed they was made, but I allowed they happened; I judged it would have took too long to *make* so many. Jim said the moon could a *laid* them; well, that looked kind of reasonable, so I didn't say nothing against it, because I've seen a frog lay most as many, so of course it could be done. We used to watch the stars that fell, too, and see them streak down. Jim allowed they'd got spoiled and was hove out of the nest. (P. 159)

The passage is at once mythopoeic, lyrical, touching, cosmic. It is a description of primitive theology whose subject *is* Creation. Huck, the innocent primitive, is so awed by the multitude of stars that the idea of a Creator seems impossible to him; instead, his capacity for wonder attributes a spontaneous, living force to the heavens. In this moment there is no place for the biblical account of Creation, only for Adamic humor as Huck pragmatically argues the great subject with his black interpreter. Myths of the moon and Huck's experience of the way frogs reproduce merge to form an "edenic" epistemology, a primitive instrument of knowledge capable of searching out the origins of things.

The entire opening of Chapter 19 can therefore be read as Mark Twain's

19. Charles Clerc, "Sunrise on the River: 'The Whole World' of *Huckleberry Finn*," *MFS* 14 (Spring 1968):67–78, gives a thorough analysis of the rhetorical devices Twain uses in this passage.

penetration into the religious dimensions of his characters and the benign non-Christian countertheology that informs their world. Here Twain reaches the height of his cosmic and comic vision of life and mediates it through the humor of tolerance, which may, for a brief moment, harmonize the tension between the good and evil signs in nature, as well as the gulf between boy and man, white and black. By so doing, the mythmaking neutralizes the lurking forces of the two Providences, the two lies and the compulsion to reform waiting to reenter Huck's world. With the King and Duke, those forces come aboard.

We know that these characters entered the composition of the novel probably during a period from late 1880 to early 1883, when Twain was shaping the great episodes about Bricksville, Sherburn's murder of Boggs, the circus, and the Royal Nonesuch.[20] Nevertheless, through the Duke and King, Twain kept his thematic and structural patterns remarkably consistent, expanding and making more thematically explicit the dynamics of Providence-lies-reform. He accomplished this by making the con men function as mock honor-code figures and mock evangelists, who exploit both roles while revealing the spiritual hollowness and vulgarity of those they exploit. In the revival meeting, the King knows that repentance is the catchall stance that can bring money and tears from any audience. Better to act as a reformed pirate than a missionary reforming heathens: "The king said, take it all around, it laid over any day he'd ever put in the missionarying line" (p. 175). And in their use of the honor code, they play out dramatically the theme of royal disinheritance that underscores their personal sense of exile from society as a whole and that structurally counterpoints the "exile" of Huck and Jim. With their theatrical lies, they farcically pervert the gospel message of reform and their own human dignity, while Huck and Jim maneuver patiently to survive and escape from them. Above all, like Huck himself, they too mechanically rely on Providence. Twain will use this fact to introduce a major structural change in the narrative: Providence will take them all off the river at last. For in Chapter 24, they come to two Arkansas villages and cannot decide on their next move. But the King trusts in "Providence to lead him the profitable way—meaning the devil, I reckon" (p. 204), as Huck observes. Wearing black, parsonlike clothes now, and startling Huck by how "clothes could change a body" (p. 204), the King makes a momentous decision that leads him to the young man who tells them about the Wilks girls, their inheritance, and the returning brothers. All "full of tears and flap-doodle," they worm their way in and get the money:

> It ain't no use talkin' [the King says]; bein' brothers to a rich dead man, and representatives of furrin heirs that's got left, is the line for you and me, Bilge. Thish-yer comes of trust'n to Providence. It's the best way, in the long run. I've tried 'em all, and ther' ain't no better way. (P. 214)

But the devil's Providence takes them into their worst corruption as they sell the girls' slaves down the river (thematically reinforcing Jim's fate), a situa-

---

20. See Walter Blair, *Mark Twain and Huck Finn* (Berkeley: University of California Press, 1962), pp. 270–84, for details on the sources of some of these episodes and characters.

tion that thrusts Huck into a new set of moral dilemmas involving his need to lie and struggle to reform. Huck is forced to meditate on his strategy of telling the truth or lies to Mary Jane:

> I says to myself, I reckon a body that ups and tells the truth when he is in a tight place, is taking considerable many resks, though I ain't had no experience, and can't say for certain; but it looks so to me, anyway; and yet here's a case where I'm blest if it don't look to me like the truth is better, and actuly *safer* than a lie. (P. 240)

After exposing the Duke and Dauphin, Huck makes Mary Jane leave the house and advises her to keep up appearances to the frauds. When she objects, he falls back into his natural way of using lies to keep peace:

> "Well, then, it shan't be." It was well enough to tell *her* so—no harm in it. It was only a little thing to do, and no trouble; and it's the little things that smooths people's roads the most, down here below; it would make Mary Jane comfortable, and it wouldn't cost nothing. (Pp. 243–44)

In the world of "down here below"—Huck's own term for a fallen world— the most moral act a man can perform is to help make comfortable a life that is a tissue of falsehood, hypocrisy, and greed. And "comfortable" here means consolation in its fullest spiritual and religious meaning. Huck brings healing, and Mary Jane knows this. She will pray for Huck, whose characteristic response is touchingly ironic—Adamic humor, again, because the convinced "sinner" and innocent skeptic is himself consoled by a spiritual act whose efficacy he has already rejected:

> Pray for me! I reckoned if she knowed me she'd take a job that was more nearer her size. But I bet she done it, just the same—she was just that kind. (P. 245)

The stage is prepared for yet another descent into the comically tortured dialectics of Providence-lies-reform as Huck, outwitting the con men and saving the girls' inheritance, inherits the full pain of his commitment to Jim, sold again for "forty dirty dollars" (p. 269). We are left wondering if Mary Jane's prayers somehow will fill the void for Huck, who, with Providence "slapping" him in the face to reform before "One that's always on the lookout" (p. 270), finds he cannot pray his lie. If Huck's decision to "*go to hell*" (p. 272) is the ultimate ironic triumph of a prelapsarian mentality over a deformed postlapsarian world, it is also, perhaps on its deepest level, a "counter-conversion"[21] whose meaning and humor affirm that the reward of providential adventuring is the painless grail of freedom from reform. "I . . . never thought no more about reforming" (p. 272) may be taken as Huck's deepest conviction and best way out. But this is not only a release from his two doctrinal providences; it is at the same time a freedom to engage in more adventure shaped by a natural Providence that will do with Huck as it wills, a truly "free" and spontaneous force. At the Phelpses' farm, then, Huck goes "right along, not fixing up any particular plan, but just trusting

---

21. See Norris W. Yates, "The 'Counter-Conversion' of *Huckleberry Finn*," *AL* 32 (1960): 1–10, for an excellent study of Huck's famous decision. I would only add that this "counter-conversion" is a microcosm of the structural countertheology in the novel as a whole.

to Providence to put the right words in my mouth when the time come; for I'd noticed that Providence always did put the right words in my mouth, if I left it alone" (p. 278). And when Aunt Sally says, "It's *you*, at last!—*ain't* it?" Huck blurts out: "Yes'm" (p. 279). But "Providence had stood by me this fur, all right" (p. 281), Huck thinks, and is ready to "risk the truth" to Aunt Sally when she providentially hides him in order to surprise the worried Uncle Silas. With no chance to tell the truth Huck finds himself "born again" (p. 282) in the glorious truth/lie that he is Tom Sawyer. The boon of this playful Providence is to prepare one last adventure of disguises, freedom, lies, and reform, soon to be directed by a providential appearance of Tom, the spirit of adventure incarnate.

After hearing of Huck's "grand" and "mysterious" adventures (p. 285), Tom is fired into creating the final providential jape of all: setting an already freed slave free. It may disconcert Huck to know that Tom is a "*nigger stealer*" (p. 285), but this is only one thread in the texture of ironies that form the last section of the novel. The real purpose of the adventure-obsessed mind—of the adult or of the child—is to move from the conventional and safe structures of normal life into the domain of the "unreal," realms of heightened danger where the self's courage and ingenuity can be tested and physical and spiritual excitement can be plucked out of the inertia-locked boredom of everyday life. If the self triumphs it is comedy; if it fails it is pathos or tragedy. Huck's very real admiration for Tom's "style" makes him a willing partner in this quest, despite his normally passive nature, but it is significant that their first effort—saving the King and Duke— fails. Guilt-ridden, Huck learns that "it don't make no difference whether you do right or wrong, a person's conscience ain't got no sense, and just goes for him *anyway*" (p. 292). In spite of his earlier triumph over conscience, guilt has become an "existential" part of him, for he *knows* he "hadn't done nothing" (p. 292). And to that extent he will always welcome a way out, however farcical or cruel it may seem to a reader. Is this not the profoundest level of his attachment to Tom's ways, and of Tom to his? I believe this crucial scene justifies that interpretation and is often overlooked in trying to make sense of these final episodes of Twain's so-called moral lapse.

In this scene Twain makes it abundantly clear what binds Huck and Tom. For Tom, the self that has "adjusted" to a world of respectability, despite his boyish protests and pranks, acknowledges Huck's description of the agony of conscience and the need to "pison" it: "Tom Sawyer he says the same" (p. 292). Tom has followed Huck in this compassionate instance—let us not forget that. But the venture has failed, revealing a savage spectacle of human cruelty; their second venture, softened by Huck making Tom "let on" or subversively pretend to fulfill the absurd rules of *The Count of Monte Cristo*, will end in a comic triumph. From the boys' point of view, the spirit of adventure must now take them into a world of danger, heightening, even to the point of facing real death, their sense of reality; yet it must also give them the satisfaction of defeating and discomforting the adult world that denies them their "forbidden" experiences. They demand the freedom to both fail and succeed. This, then, is the true thrust of Tom's "Evasion" (p. [364]).

In concentrating upon Jim's discomfort, we have forgotten that the real victims of the adventure are the good but bumbling and ineffectual Uncle Silas,[22] Aunt Sally, and the wildly befuddled community of which Sister Hotchkiss is a hilarious example. The Evasion is truly a comic drama of children making one last assault (so Providence provides) to preserve that freedom-in-possibility that must soon accommodate itself to a fallen world with its dogmatically defined providences of Christian "sivilization." Necessarily, there is a price to be paid on both sides, and Mark Twain sees this with astonishing comic clarity. That is why Jim's high moral stature must be temporarily "reduced"; he must play his part in the assault. The novel's comic strategy demands that "innocent" adventures skirt or confront genuine tragedy; thus Jim is *almost* lynched, Tom *almost* killed, the Evasion *almost* a tragedy. Only Twain's consistent vision of comic adventure, freedom-in-possibility, and the need to deny the pain of his heroes' predicament prevents real defeat. The heroes cannot be in any real danger, even Jim, although as a slave he is the most vulnerable to the corrupt contradictions and violence of society. In this way, the Evasion both burlesques and affirms its own providence-adventure form and brings with it the only kind of salvation Huck and Tom can have before finally lighting out of boyhood. Jim's dignity and freedom are clearly asserted, and the boys' book-fed jokes are painless compared to the reality of the townspeoples' first impulse to hang him. The daring comic jest with which the novel ends is justified in light of its entire pattern: Jim is as "free as any cretur that walks this earth!" (p. 360). This is entirely what Twain intended, nor did he wish to explore, in this book, the future travails of a black man freed into a white slave-society. That will be reserved for *Pudd'nhead Wilson*.[23] The first and most important step was, after all, to *be* freed from slavery itself, and Miss Watson's *ex machina* will is a providential gesture to that end, in accordance with the "rules" of the

22. Allison Ensor, "Twain's *Adventures of Huckleberry Finn*, Chapter 37," *Expl* 26 (1967): item 20, and Robert D. Arner, "Acts Seventeen and *Huckleberry Finn*: A Note on Silas Phelps' Sermon," *MTJ* 16:2 (1972):12, both point to Twain's satiric allusion to St. Paul's call for "brotherhood," in order to indict the "good" but slaveholding morality of Uncle Silas. From my perspective, the allusion to St. Paul's courageous "sermon" in Athens also draws an ironic contrast between Paul, the great proselytizer and "anti-feminist," and Silas, the "hen-pecked" preacher, constantly fooled by boys' tricks. Thus, even when Twain creates a "good" preacher, he must still present him as unworldly and ineffectual, at least in the world of *Huckleberry Finn*. The dread irony and contrast is that it is Colonel Sherburn who gives a truly effective "sermon" on moral cowardice.

23. It would be impossible to cite all the studies, pro and con, about the ending of the novel, but Neil Schmitz, "Twain, *Huckleberry Finn* and the Reconstruction," *AmerS* 12 (1971):59–67, gives one of the best defenses of the ending, seeing Jim's plight as a parody of the true state of affairs for blacks whose "freedom" was eroded by postbellum politics. I believe the ending reflects the triumph of adventure over the satanic countertheology of civilization, which, according to its own rules, "frees" Jim while reasserting his dignity. In the context of that perspective, the ending would have been complete if Jim had been reunited with his family. But I do not feel this undermines the "liberating" comic vision in the novel as a whole. But see Thomas Blues, "The Strategy of Compromise in Mark Twain's 'Boy Books,'" *MFS* 14 (Spring 1968): 21–31, for a different approach arguing that Twain's boys "harbor aggressive designs against the community," though they stop short of isolating themselves from it. Finally, David F. Burg, "Another View of *Huckleberry Finn*," *NCF* 29 (1973):299–319, insightfully demonstrates that the ending joins a vision of the "absurd" within a circular structure, while rejecting all "conventional" morality.

book that demand that external help be sometimes given to the entrapped adventurers. But while entrapped in "sivilization" each boy must respond in his fashion to the dangerous conditions it creates. Consequently, Huck must play out his role of "exchange-center" and moral wrestler, and Tom must project heroic adventures even "to the mouth of the river" and bring Jim home as a hero. We may accept Huck's observation on these future plans as Twain's, too: "But I reckoned it was about as well the way it was" (p. [364]). It is a perfect Adamic statement, characteristic of the way the novel's comic vision brings an appropriate response of tolerance and relief to Tom's defining claim that all was done for the "*adventure* of it" (p. 361).

Both Tom and Huck have now announced their special strategies of triumph over the providences, lies, and reformers of "sivilization." In his countertheology Twain has dramatized a radically "new" dynamic of providential adventure, asserting its own autonomy in the lives of his heroes. At the same time the humor has emerged from the tensions created by the gulf between society's Divine Ideals and its hypocritical actions. We have seen how Huck, the comic "exchange-center," coped with that contradiction and its challenge to authentic faith. Yet neither Huck nor his society can entirely escape its cultural forces and personalities and so "leap" into a consciously higher sphere of religious existence. Therefore the categories of "optimism" or "pessimism" really do not apply to *Huckleberry Finn*'s final view of the human condition, not, at least, in their conventional theological meanings. For instead of having clearly defined religious goals that must be gained or at least authentically strived for lest the "sinner" be doomed, as in Bunyan and Defoe, we have the gift of Adamic humor, the *affirmation* of adventure and its calls to "light out," and the defeat, however temporary, of the satanic lies and shams controlling society. It was very much a revolutionary "lay sermon" as Twain described it in 1895,[24] but the lay sermon of a preacher who knows how to artistically shape his own comic countertheology. The salvation that Mark Twain offers in Huck's spiritual autobiography is one that neither Bunyan nor Defoe would have easily comprehended, though surely they would have recognized ruefully the lineaments of moral hypocrisy in the New World carried over from the Old. It remains for us to see that, in its pervasive comic and theological realism, *Huckleberry Finn* stands as a unique Protestant-American epic, challenging the old entrenched assumptions about America's providential mission and its heroes and offering in their place a dynamically subversive comic "theology," destined to live "forever."

24. Blair, *Mark Twain and Huck Finn*, pp. 143–44.

24 JAMES M. COX

A Hard Book to Take

$\mathbf{M}$Y title may seem at first glance all wrong. If any book has been easy to take for the last hundred years, surely it is *Adventures of Huckleberry Finn*. Read by people of all ages, loved throughout the nation, it finally made its way into the academy so that professors of literature—at least a good number of them—have come to take both confidence and pleasure in deeming it a masterpiece of American literature. Yet if Huck's story seems to tell itself upon a current of ease, he says at the end that it was a hard book to write. And it was from the beginning a hard book to take in some quarters. For example, the Public Library Committee of Concord, Massachusetts— home of Emerson, Thoreau, and Hawthorne—banned it. The *Boston Transcript* approvingly reported the committee's judgment that the book was rough, coarse, and inelegant, "the whole book being more suited to the slums than to intelligent, respectable people." The *Springfield Republican* condemned the book on the ground that it was trashy and vicious. Recalling that, eight years earlier, Mark Twain had shown a singular lack of propriety at the Whittier birthday dinner, the *Republican* averred that the book degenerated into "a gross trifling with every fine feeling."

It became so easy to flog those dear old genteel custodians of New England culture for their utter failure of taste, that a generation of academic custodians of literary culture could forget how long it took for Mark Twain to displace the New England worthies in the schools. They could forget, for instance, that Jim's observation about Frenchmen and the French language is not quite so hilarious to Frenchmen (so I have been told) as it is to us; they could forget that the jokes on religion might not be so funny to a devoutly Primitive Baptist; or that the exposures of village cruelty and Southern mores, pursued with the zeal characteristic of so many published interpretations of the novel, might prove a trial to the humor of rural conservative Southerners. These could be forgotten because the enlightened audience of today does not have to worry about any of these groups. The French, who are far away in their own language, will just have to take the little joke (it is really quite a big one), or, if they cannot, somehow mute the joke in translation; the primitively religious do not really count any more than the Southern rural conservatives. They can stay in their communities, for one thing; for another, they can probably find other books to ban since by nature they distrust the literary imagination. Such was the essentially complacent attitude of the academic establishment that put Mark Twain among the major American writers.

I am part of that establishment, and I have helped put to rout the last traces of the genteel remnant in the academy. Even those professors, refined in taste or devoted to the art of real artists (artists like Henry James or Dante), who used to dismay us with their scorn of the ending of *Huckleberry Finn,* have now been worn down or fatigued by our adroit defenses of the ending. And so they are silenced, as they should have been silenced in 1950 when T. S. Eliot, the very embodiment of high art, affirmed that the book—the whole book, ending and all—was incontrovertibly a work of art. But then we who subsequently went on defending the ending should have also rested, at once silent and content in the knowledge of Eliot's magisterial affirmation. But how could we have known that Eliot's judgment, like so many of his decisions, was to be the literary law of the land, making our subsequent interpretations nothing more than glosses on an approved text.

Despite our confident assurance about the book's quality, there has been, in the last fifteen years, another group—steadily increasing in numbers—that finds the book hard to take. I mean of course black Americans. Since they do, our complacency is, or should be, shattered. We used to be able to assure them—when they were little more than token presences in what we are pleased to call the world of higher education—that they could surely see that the book was in no way really prejudiced against Jim or the Negro (as we used to say before Malcolm X sought to set us free). The presence of the word *nigger* throughout the book, we would go on to say, merely reflected the time and place of the novel and was a manifestation of Mark Twain's celebrated realism. To take the term personally or negatively was to fly in the face of the whole intention of the novel. Editions of the novel that took up the matter at all did what they could to defend Mark Twain, or, in one instance that I remember, to declare complaints about Mark Twain's usage irrelevant, since the author's good racial intentions were manifestly visible.

However much we may recognize those good intentions, we nonetheless know, both historically and personally, that racial objection to that word is not irrelevant. If Mark Twain could use the word in the nineteenth century with a certain freedom and could not use all the four-letter words we have lately allowed to pass the censor, we feel a greater inhibition about that word than we can quite believe Mark Twain ever felt and certainly more hesitation about it than about the four-letter words we are using more easily. Let me come closer home. Almost every student of Mark Twain has felt that he exaggerated the matter of social censorship on writers. To be sure, we know that the Gilded Age had overrefined standards of taste and usage. But even Brooks and DeVoto, both of whom lamented the stifling pressures of New England gentility, ultimately concluded that Mark Twain, more than his society, was primarily responsible for the censorship against which he railed.

The fact remains, however, that *Huckleberry Finn,* alone among the masterpieces of nineteenth-century American literature, remains to this day threatened with censorship. School boards in New York and Pennsylvania have recently considered removing it from assigned reading lists; and recently the Mark Twain High School (of all names!) in Fairfax County, Virginia, within a stone's throw of the nation's capital, found itself determined to remove the book from circulation. There were the usual high-minded editorials defending the book and lamenting the bigotry that keeps failing to understand it. Yet for all the familiar defenses and for all my belief in freedom of the press and my love for the book, I know in my heart that, if I were teaching an American literature course in Bedford Stuyvesant or Watts or North Philadelphia, I might well find myself choosing *Tom Sawyer* or *A Connecticut Yankee* rather than *Huckleberry Finn* to represent Mark Twain.

Such a decision would not necessarily be reprehensible. After all, Huck himself often acted precisely along such lines. He had learned from Pap that the best way to get along with scoundrels like the King and the Duke (and Pap, too, for that matter) was to avoid trouble with them. Even to remember the novel is to remember that Pap had something to teach Huck by precept as well as by forceful presence. He taught Huck to "take a chicken when you get a chance, because if you don't want him yourself you can easily find somebody that does, and a good deed ain't ever forgot" (p. 95). Those who find such wisdom immoral would do well to remember that Thoreau thought the wood he stole made the sweetest fire.

To say a word for Pap may seem to many readers of the book—and good readers—nothing short of sacrilege. Yet entertainment of Pap's humanity—which is, after all, immensely entertaining—can provide an avenue for comprehending as well as acknowledging the power and wisdom of the book. On the one hand he is fiercely cruel, and his cruelty runs directly athwart two of the sacred values the book exploits. First of all, his treatment of Huck convicts him of child abuse; but more important, he is a classic exemplification of racial bigotry. Set against the values the book seems so clearly to uphold, these two forms of behavior characterize Pap as a reprobate.

At the same time, Pap is truly a performer. His speech against the government *is* hilarious as long as we can bring ourselves to laugh at it. But the matter of that speech crosses our sense of humane and rational ideals enough to make us displace our humorous response with a harsh moral judgment when we are writing criticism approved for publication in the journals. Even so, the humor is undeniably present right through Pap's performance. For if Pap is a miscreant, he is also helplessly humorous. Listen to his lament:

> "A man can't get his rights in a govment like this. Sometimes I've a mighty notion just to leave the country for good and all. Yes, and I *told* 'em so; I told old Thatcher so to his face. Lots of 'em heard me, and can tell what I said. Says I, for two cents I'd leave the blamed country and never come anear it agin. Them's the very words. I says, look at my hat—if you call it a hat—but the lid raises up and the rest of it goes down till it's below my chin, and then it ain't rightly a hat at all, but more like my head was shoved up through a jint o' stove-pipe. Look at it, says I—such a hat for me to wear—one of the wealthiest men in this town, if I could get my rights." (P. 49)

For all its irony, the passage discloses Pap's incomparable stage presence. In playing, or rather replaying, his public speech before Huck, Pap is in all probability exaggerating, yet the exaggeration is an integral part of his histrionic sense of himself. His unforgettable description of his hat brings him to the edge of a self-consciously humorous grasp of his own image that all but betrays the limitations of illiteracy and cruelty in which his character is conceived. At such a moment the performer is at the brink of eluding the ideational constraint upon his character.

When, in his next breath, Pap launches into his matter of the free Negro professor whose presence in his memory outrages him, we are at the true threshold of the novel. The measure to which the humor—continuing throughout the passage—will be drowned out depends on the indignation the critical audience feels in relation to the matter of the speech. Since that matter is directly racist, it possesses both the volatility and the simplicity to reduce as well as to define its audience. Listen again:

> "Thinks I, what is the country a-coming to? It was 'lection day, and I was just about to go and vote, myself, if I warn't too drunk to get there; but when they told me there was a State in this country where they'd let that nigger vote, I drawed out. I says I'll never vote agin. Them's the very words I said; they all heard me; and the country may rot for all me—I'll never vote agin as long as I live. And to see the cool way of that nigger—why, he wouldn't a give me the road if I hadn't shoved him out o' the way." (P. 50)

In the public and social terms of the novel—let us say in its relation to the national conscience—the irony is sufficiently savage to cut athwart the irrepressible humor that continues to ripple the current of Pap's speech. Though the humor reinforces, it nonetheless qualifies the irony of the performance. Thus when Pap says he was about to vote if he "wrn't too drunk to get there," his acknowledgment of his condition is at once in character yet again brings him to the threshold of a self-consciousness that belies his relentless hostility to blacks. I don't mean at all that Pap himself is any freer from his bigotry by virtue of his humor; I do mean that in his act of performance— and in Mark Twain's management of that performance—his admission (or is it his boast?) of his drunkenness is very much designed to draw a laugh. It is surely so designed by Mark Twain; even Pap, who remains throughout his replay of his speech insistently aware of his own performance, is all but masterfully producing one of his effects. When he subsequently tumbles over the tub of salt pork, barking his shins, and then, rising and cursing, proceeds to give the tub an unfortunate kick with the foot that has two toes "leaking out the front end" of its boot, he bursts forth with an agonized string of curses that he later says "laid over anything he done previous." Consciously casting himself in the role of a master performer, Pap sees himself as an actor in the great tradition of Sowberry Hagan.

I begin with Pap because his presence and identity are characteristic of a central aspect of the novel. The more seriously we take the matter of the book—I mean the matter of race and slavery—the less we are likely to want the humor to rise to the surface of this passage. If we refuse the rise of humor, in the system of emotional exchange that runs through the book the indignation at Pap's brutality and racism has freer play. Acknowledging the humor—which is to say *experiencing* it—involves an instinctive recognition of Pap's humanity. For if Pap is fierce in being, he is a delight in performance. The delight comes first of all from the exposed ironic relationship between his attitudes and his behavior. Equally important, it comes from the economy of pity we enjoy upon seeing him so justly and so visibly in pain. We are, by virtue of the irony, spared the expenditure of sympathizing with him.

The pity we save at Pap's expense we fairly lavish on Jim as the novel proceeds. Seeing the terms of this emotional exchange is to see Pap's vital function and placement in the book. In terms of affect, he is the figure who opens the way for Jim to be a center of sympathy; in terms of theme, his behavior and his departure make it possible for Jim to displace him as Huck's loving father. Even more important, Pap's inimitable performance literally initiates the racial theme just as Pap himself literally drives Huck out of the childhood world of Tom Sawyer and into the arms of the escaped Jim. The two fugitives—the one from Pap, the other from Miss Watson—find in each other the resources that lift their journey into mythic significance. Borne southward on the great river into the very heart of slavery, they nonetheless embody in their relationship what is probably the most powerful expression of our national dream of freedom.

Yet the fact that the direction of this dream of freedom is into the land of slavery should keep us in touch with the profound contradictions of the book. The novel generates a wish for both freedom and brotherhood embodied in a magically simplified image of human relationship between a black man and a redneck boy. But that simplification, as Pap's presence already indicates, is built upon a series of remarkably complex trades and exchanges. Thus, we can see that, although Pap's speech exposes his viciousness, the matter of that speech would or could still offend a particular audience. That very speech is one I could easily imagine *not* reading to a highschool class in Harlem. Yet if I can imagine such self-censorship in the face of external social pressure, I can just as easily imagine a self-indulgent public emphasis on the negative character of Pap in order to expose his bigotry to the lash of criticism—censoring in the process the humor that is so irrepressibly present in the speech. To censor the humor is to deny Pap the humanity he ineffably possesses.

Even more important, failure to recognize his humanity results in a corresponding reduction of Jim's humanity. For if Pap is often reduced to his racism, Jim is just as often simplistically elevated into sainthood. Here again the simplification results from a refusal to see the humor of Jim's performance. For Jim, like all the characters in this novel, is in the business of humorous performance. If Pap's humor threatens to redeem him from simple racism, Jim's humor threatens him with a minstrel identity. It is just this identity that makes modern audiences—whether black or liberal white—uncomfortable. Thus it is not only the word *nigger*, so liberally distributed throughout Huck's narrative, that publicly troubles us. It is the role Jim plays, or is forced to play. Yet diminishing that aspect of Jim's character results in an emphasis on his goodness, generosity, and essential humility. To be sure, Jim manifestly possesses these qualities in abundance, but they come to the fore almost inevitably at the expense of his intelligence. In other words, the more

Jim is made a saint the more he is likely to be the humble victim lacking any semblance of the shrewd humanity Huck so amply possesses.

Yet surely Jim is shrewd, as shrewd as Huck. If we take the incident in Chapter 2, in which Tom lifts the sleeping Jim's hat and hangs it on a tree above his head, we cannot be quite sure, in this world where everyone is involved in tricks, deceit, and confidence games, that Jim is even asleep. If we see in Pap's racism the traces of a humorous consciousness of his own performance, we should be able to detect in Jim's gullible account of being bewitched the apparition of a master of the tall tale. To exclude such a "superstitious" presence is to settle for Huck's complacent feeling of superiority to Jim's gullible belief in superstition. Using this episode as the most genial and disarming initiation into Jim's relation of narrative and relation to the narrative, we can go much further. We know and admire Huck as a liar but are prone never to realize that Jim lies to Huck about Pap's death. He does not elaborate a lie about it; he simply conceals his knowledge from Huck. Though one of his motives for evading Huck's query about the dead man in the floating house may be his tender wish to spare Huck the knowledge of being an orphan, Jim has good reason to suspect that a Huck free of his Pap might leave him high and dry.

The possibility that Huck will abandon or betray Jim is, after all, at the very center of the whole journey—and the two fugitives can never believe in each other sufficiently to annihilate it. That possibility is, after all, nothing less than the likelihood that the social reality from which they both are fugitive will intrude at any time to split asunder their precarious pastoral on the raft. Given this reality, Jim and Huck have confidence in each other at the same time they con each other. There is no better revelation of their relationship than the sequence extending from Huck's apology to Jim after deceiving him about the fog (in Chapter 15) to his wonderful lie to the slave-hunters in the very next chapter.

The fact that two pages after he humbles himself to Jim—that action for which Huck has received so much critical praise—he begins to think about turning Jim in should give us considerable pause. Is Huck's reversal merely a reflection of Mark Twain's carelessness, or is it Huck's own inconsistency of character? Or, more likely, is his rising social conscience integrally related to his sense of guilt at having mistreated Jim about the fog? It is hardly accidental that at the very moment Huck has "matured" in our own eyes by having recognized Jim's humanity he should begin to think about being a good boy in relation to the authority of his own society.

The problem, of course, is that if Huck's determination to be kind to Jim makes him a good boy in our eyes, his wish to be a good boy in his own society puts Jim in great jeopardy. But the paradox runs much deeper. For the fact of the novel is that the passage in which Huck apologizes to Jim literally marks Huck and Jim's passage by Cairo, the Ohio, and freedom. Put another way, the good feeling evoked by Huck's sincere apology literally masks the fact that Jim has irrevocably passed his chance for freedom. As if this were not enough, Huck no sooner ends Chapter 15 asserting that he was glad to have apologized to Jim and "didn't do him no more mean tricks" than he is inwardly planning to turn Jim in. Surely this would be the meanest trick of all. Yet Huck himself betrays no consciousness of his contradiction. Fearing immediately after his apology that they might miss Cairo, Huck proposes to go ashore to discover their exact whereabouts. As he prepares for this excursion, he becomes uncomfortably conscious of Jim's bold anticipation of being free. Troubled by his complicity in Jim's determination to be free, he accuses himself of ingratitude to the respectable people who have tried to help him. His sense of his own wrong is sufficiently acute to repress for the moment the moral enormity of turning Jim over to the authorities. And so, just as our serious approval of Huck's apology to Jim keeps us from seeing that freedom was being lost at precisely that moment, Huck's serious recognition of his own criminal activity is sufficient to keep him from seeing that he is about to do Jim the meanest of mean tricks. Mean tricks are of course in the world of Tom Sawyer and childhood; and Huck, doubtless feeling and even liking his own maturity as much as we feel and applaud it, cannot see this adult effort to be socially responsible as a mean trick. Besides, Jim is talking bolder, and why shouldn't he? Not only does he think freedom is around the bend; he has also just put Huck in his place. As for Huck, if he has humbled himself to Jim, small wonder that from his new perspective Jim suddenly seems proud.

These observations in no way denigrate the nobility of Huck's apology, but they do gauge the emotional exchange in the book. The smoothness, swiftness, and disarming flow of Huck's narration conceal the snags, reefs, and channel crossings that the narrative is constantly negotiating. Moreover, our tentative scrutiny of this particular sequence in the novel prepares us for the wonderful exchange Huck has with the slave-hunters he is about to meet. Even before he can shove off in the canoe with the ostensible mission of finding out just where he and Jim are on the river—and with the secret intention of reforming himself by turning Jim over to society—Jim just may have divined what we might call a honky in the woodpile. Listen to his heartfelt farewell to Huck and to the response it arouses in Huck:

> "Pooty soon I'll be a-shout'n for joy, en I'll say it's all on accounts o' Huck; I's a free man, en I couldn't ever ben free ef it hadn't ben for Huck; Huck done it. Jim won't ever forgit you, Huck; you's de bes' fren' Jim's ever had; en you's de *only* fren' ole Jim's got now."
>
> I was paddling off, all in a sweat to tell on him; but when he says this, it seemed to kind of take the tuck all out of me. I went along slow then, and I warn't right down certain whether I was glad I started or whether I warn't. When I was fifty yards off, Jim says:
>
> "Dah you goes, de ole true Huck; de on'y white genlman dat ever kep' his promise to ole Jim." (P. 124)

In this exchange we have the full force of the idyllic myth: Huck, the good-hearted boy possessing an innocence tied to irony and cunning; and Jim, the long-suffering man who is equally innocent, but whose innocence is expressed in terms of gullibility and humility. At the same time, we have a Huck with bad intentions and a Jim voicing praise sufficiently intense to betray an intelligence that knows betrayal may be at hand. Such an analysis of their exchange does not deny so much as it qualifies their affection for each other. That is why both language and drama are profoundly in harmony. Jim's speech, with an auditory trace of confidence in its performance, is penetrating Huck's vulnerable psyche precisely because the speech is penetrating and the psyche vulnerable.

Huck has no sooner heard Jim's farewell praise than he is confronted by the very society to which he has intended to hand over Jim. It comes in the form of two men hunting not one but five fugitive slaves. With Jim's affectionate voice still sounding in his ears, Huck, unable to tell the two men the truth, helplessly drops into one of his best lies. When he lied to Judith Loftus, he had been caught in the lie (or did he let himself be caught?) and then, in the teeth of her pleasurable self-congratulation at having caught him, he told her a bigger and bolder lie. This time he lies by implication and withdrawal. Asked whether the man on his raft is black, Huck hesitantly replies that he is white. And to the series of questions that follows, Huck says that the man is his father and is sick. When he adds blubberingly that his mam and Mary Ann are also sick and that no one will help them, the men themselves begin to fill in the blanks, concluding that the whole family has smallpox. If Judith Loftus had helped Huck out when, realizing he was not a girl, she supplied him with the details of the identity (an apprentice who had been badly treated) on which he in turn built his second lie to her, the slave-hunters do even better. Keeping their distance to avoid the disease, they are nonetheless so touched by Huck's narrative (which they themselves have fearfully concluded) that they give Huck forty dollars. And Huck takes it. When he returns to the raft so near at hand, Jim is there to praise Huck's performance as much as he had earlier praised his character:

> "I was a-listenin' to all de talk, en I slips into de river en was gwyne to shove for sho' if dey come aboard. Den I was gwyne to swim to de raf' agin when dey was gone. But lawsy, how you did fool 'em, Huck! Dat *wuz* de smartes' dodge! I tell you, chile, I 'speck it save' ole Jim—ole Jim ain't gwyne to forgit you for dat, honey." (P. 128)

They take the money and share it in a moment worthy of the King and the Duke, yet you may be sure that there has been little criticism directed toward pointing up that analogy. As for the two slave-hunters, they have never to my knowledge been given their share of moral credit for their all but spontaneous and certainly heartfelt contribution to Huck's welfare.

Of course they do not know, as we do, that Huck is concealing Jim. Yet they are charged with their intention of hunting runaway slaves at the same time that they are robbed of the moral credit they deserve for sympathizing with what they believe to be Huck's stricken plight. Reflection on the slave-hunters and their fate at our hands, and further reflection on this whole episode, affords an opportunity to ask some genuine moral questions about *Huckleberry Finn*. Having already seen the humor in Pap's racism, the confidence in Jim's gullibility and in his loyalty, the abrupt reversal between the Huck of the apology and the Huck intending to betray Jim to the authorities, and the way in which the emotion of Huck's apology literally displaces

the fact that these two travelers have forever passed by Cairo and freedom—
having seen so much, we are faced with the forty-dollar charity display of
the slave-hunters. We cannot help applauding Huck's dodge as much as Jim
applauds it. Yet even allowing for the fact that the men are slave-hunters and
that their charity has about it a strong element of payoff in order to avoid
the plague they have imagined, they still seem to me a wonderful snag in the
moral current of the narrative. Aren't they really as good as anyone in the
book? Is there anyone else's charity that is really superior to theirs? And
aren't Huck and Jim, by taking their money, just as bad as the King and the
Duke, who are waiting in the wings? Of course these questions go against
our feelings—they go against the master current of the fiction. Yet not to ask
them is to settle for a far tamer stream than the shifting, magnificent Mississippi that absolutely underlies the book.

These questions point us back to a particular kind of moral and emotional
exchange that is always going on in the book. The value we are holding to as
if it were the measure of all others is, of course, Jim. Huck's relation to and
involvement in Jim's freedom lift him out of the childhood world and lift his
lies from what we might call the world of low picaresque into what we want
to see as the realm of higher humanity. The antislavery sentiment affixed to
Jim and his freedom functions as an absolute moral yardstick by which to
measure other values. Thus our sense of Pap's anguish is crowded out by our
indignation at his racism; thus the slave-hunters' sympathy for Huck's fictive
family is set at naught because they *are* slave-hunters; and thus the King and
Duke cease to be amusing once they go beyond fleecing the rural, evangelical, and illiterate white communities strung out along the river and take
up the business of trading off the Wilks slaves. And Huck himself ultimately
loses value when he goes along with Tom's travesty of freeing Jim according
to the rules.

Yet Huck has always done all he could to go along with the more powerful
forces he confronts—and so many of those forces are more powerful than
he, a mere orphan adrift upon the mighty river. His great value lies precisely
in his negative relation to the banks of both right and wrong between which
both his narrative and his life so beautifully and powerfully run. Look at his
own appraisal of the incident involving the slave-hunters:

> They went off, and I got aboard the raft, feeling bad and low, because I
> knowed very well I had done wrong, and I see it warn't no use for me to try to
> learn to do right; a body that don't get *started* right when he's little, ain't got no
> show—when the pinch comes there ain't nothing to back him up and keep him
> to his work, and so he gets beat. Then I thought a minute, and says to myself,
> hold on,—s'pose you'd a done right and give Jim up; would you felt better than
> what you do now? No, says I, I'd feel bad—I'd feel just the same way I do now.
> Well, then, says I, what's the use you learning to do right, when it's troublesome
> to do right and ain't no trouble to do wrong, and the wages is just the same? I
> was stuck. I couldn't answer that. So I reckoned I wouldn't bother no more about
> it, but after this always do whichever come handiest at the time. (Pp. 127–28)

This, it should be emphasized, is his reflection on the action he has all but
helplessly had to take—an action which, *negative* in its nature, leaves him

feeling *bad* and *low*. Out of that depression and regret he would like to think that had he done the opposite he would have felt better, but he knows that he would have felt no better (he does not say he would have felt worse); and so he concludes with the determination to do in the future only what is handiest or easiest. Thus the essential pleasure principle of ease and handiness that he affirms arises out of a helpless action—and the minute we pursue the origins of that action we are led back to Huck's bad intention of betraying Jim, back from that to his apology for having lied to Jim about the fog, and on back to the encompassing narrative fact that the fog itself along with Huck's apology constitute Mark Twain's own dodge for eliminating the possibility of an Ohio ending for his novel. Yet if the episode of the fog, Huck's lie to Jim, and his subsequent apology literally displace their loss of freedom, this narrative sequence just as surely constitutes Huck's much approved "moral growth" that forms the basis for the serious sentiment on which the novel depends.

There, it seems to me, is a fairly clear analysis of the sequence leading to Huck's affirmation of his pleasure principle. His pleasure principle, of course, involves a bold program, so bold that he himself cannot keep it up, and no reader of the novel should have to be told where he fails. The failure is, as a matter of fact, at the heart of his greatest success—the moment when he determines to set Jim free. That moment is a remarkable variation on both the action and reflection we have just examined. This time, however, Huck is alone, the King and the Duke having "stolen" and sold Jim for "forty dirty dollars," to use Huck's description of the transaction when he learns of it. Realizing Jim's plight, Huck thinks at first of writing Miss Watson, on the premise that Jim will be treated better upriver than where he now is. He decides on second thought not to write because he fears that Miss Watson might vengefully sell Jim back downriver. But then the greater fear of what people will think of *him* for abetting a fugitive slave gets the better of him— and out of that fear emerges his conscience to upbraid and shame him for his wickedness until he finally decides to write Miss Watson of Jim's whereabouts. In the midst of the flush of self-approval that follows hard upon the completion of his letter, the image of Jim looms in Huck's mind as a rebuke to his first act of writing. Benignly presiding over and pervading Huck's highly compressed mental rehearsal of the journey, Jim stands as the figure against whom Huck, remembering incident after incident of their journey, cannot harden his heart:

> and at last I struck the time I saved him by telling the men we had small-pox aboard, and he was so grateful, and said I was the best friend old Jim ever had in the world, and the *only* one he's got now; and then I happened to look around, and see that paper.
>
> It was a close place. I took it up, and held it in my hand. I was a trembling, because I'd got to decide, forever, betwixt two things, and I knowed it. I studied a minute, sort of holding my breath, and then says to myself:
>
> "All right, then, I'll *go* to hell"—and tore it up. (Pp. 271–72)

No attentive reader of the novel can ever wish that Huck had concluded otherwise. Yet his choice, if we take it seriously—and if anything in the novel is to be taken seriously, surely this decision is—seems to run directly athwart his prior determination to do whatever came easiest and handiest. The more seriously the decision is taken—the more it is seen as Huck's "crisis of conscience"—the more disappointing the ending of the novel will be. For instead of living solemnly by his decision, Huck merely submits to Tom Sawyer's extravaganza of freeing Jim. Moreover, Tom's farce is predicated on his concealed knowledge that Jim is already free—and freed by Miss Watson, of all people! She, the moralist of the old order, who has been advertised in the fiction as the person who would sell Jim down the river, turns out to make the will that legally sets him free. How could Mark Twain play such a mean trick? The least he could have done was to plot his novel better and make Jim the property of the Widow Douglas.

Of course he had given us this authorial warning through a G. G., Chief of Ordnance (could those initials stand for General Grant?):

> Persons attempting to find a motive in this narrative will be prosecuted; persons attempting to find a moral in it will be banished; persons attempting to find a plot in it will be shot.

Given such a series of threats, we had perhaps better not even wish for a plot, let alone seek one. Here again, it is worth noting that Mark Twain is not denying the presence of motive, moral, or plot but asserting the danger of seeking for them. We do not wish to take this warning seriously, yet all the criticism written about this narrative, including this essay, is testimony to the book's resistance to motive, moral, and plot.

What, after all, is the almost universal disturbance about the abortive ending but a complaint about Mark Twain's rather high-handed (or was it his casual, or worse, his unwitting?) dismissal of whatever motive, moral, or plot his narrative had generated? And the ending does indeed seem to abort the motive (Huck and Jim's wish for freedom), the moral (the triumph of the natural good intentions of a sound heart over a deformed conscience), and the plot (a young picaro's account of his discovery of a slave's humanity and his subsequent attempt to steal the slave out of slavery). In those last ten chapters Huck and Jim no longer visibly wish for freedom but become passive slaves to Tom Sawyer's "plot"; Huck's sound heart is so still that he seems as heartless as Tom Sawyer; and the act of stealing a slave becomes Tom's charade of enslaving a free man.

No wonder such an ending has driven critics of sound mind to distraction. If it has never really bothered children, there is not all that much evidence that so many of them actually read it. It bothered Leo Marx enough to make him mount an attack on Lionel Trilling and T. S. Eliot, who he felt had not been bothered enough by it. And it has more recently motivated John Seelye to rewrite the book under the title of *The True Adventures of Huckleberry Finn*. Putting in all the four-letter words that Mark Twain left out, Seelye, obeying liberal and even radical intentions, has Jim killed so that Huck, speaking in the dark, can conclude the narrative with these words: "I didn't care whether the goddam sun ever come up again."

The happy effect of Seelye's tour de force, giving us a dead rather than a free Jim, should enable us to realize that such a substitute ending, though it may satisfy those who long for something more serious than Tom's farce and something more real than his fantasy, is little better than a conventional happy ending would have been—an ending that would have had Huck, not Tom, free Jim—and not a *free* Jim either, and certainly not according to the rules. To have accomplished that, Mark Twain would have needed to put the fog and apology far enough upstream (since no one would want them removed) to leave Huck time and space to have his crisis of conscience above Cairo. Or, if he had them pass it in order to have his great Arkansas scenes, he would have needed to have them use that forty dollars they got from the slave-hunters to buy passage on a steamboat (as Jim suggests at one point) and come to freedom in style. But we couldn't stand that ending either, because then the slave-hunters would have provided Huck and Jim's passage to freedom. The more anyone thinks about such substitutions, the more Mark Twain's mean trick of an ending seems as good as we are likely to get. He had Tom give Jim forty dollars for being such a good prisoner, and Tom even hoped to take Jim back on a steamboat and have a circuslike celebration in St. Petersburg.

Mean trick though Mark Twain's ending may be, it is probably the best ending we shall ever have. By making us wish for something else, it remains its own discordant reality principle. If we want Huck to have freed Jim, we just want Huck to be a charitable good little abolitionist. Mark Twain might just as well have sent him across the yard in Hartford to Harriet Beecher Stowe's house to ask for Eva, the good little Christian. If, however, we continue to look at the novel in terms of emotional exchange, we can see that Mark Twain determined to save both Huck and Jim at the expense of Tom Sawyer. In the world of literary interpretation, poor old Tom never has got over that decision, and he never will. In the light of those interpretations, we have to see that Mark Twain so loved Huck and Jim that he sacrificed Tom Sawyer for them.

To review Mark Twain's mean trick and his sacrifice of Tom is to be taken back once more to Huck's mean trick and his apology. Remembering just how that remarkable sequence displaced the actual passage by Cairo and the irrevocable loss of freedom ought to instruct us about the implicit vision behind the mean trick of the ending. Surely this second trick discloses that, far from being free, humanity is in slavery. The travesty of Jim's "freedom" in the closing narrative movement reveals in a way that no other ending could that he is not free and will not be. Why else and how else could we, after one hundred years of the book's life, keep being drawn into the splendid lie of a young boy deciding to steal a slave out of slavery? Let me offer three tentative reasons for our being sold by as well as sold on the book. First, deep down we know and know socially every day that neither we nor Jim is free despite the fictions of history and the Thirteenth Amendment; second, we do not even want Jim to be free, in order that we can continue to enjoy the perennial self-approval of freeing him; and third, we tell ourselves he is free because we, like all the characters in the book, want to be lied to. If that last is what the King and Duke know so well, it is also what Huck knows. The lie is, in a world of lies, what comes easiest and handiest to mind and mouth. Knowing so much, Huck, like the King and the Duke, can easily enlist the help of his interlocutors. As he says of Aunt Sally and Uncle Silas when he lies to them about having been on a steamboat that blew its cylinder head, "If I'd a called it a bolt-head it would a done just as well" (p. 283).

The truth we most deeply need to believe in a free country is that we are free—and freedom in this country, first defined as freedom from tyranny, came to be defined as freedom from slavery. Freeing the slaves—emancipation—was the great international and political movement in the West in the nineteenth century. Predicated on the twin humanitarian emotions of indignation at the cruelty to the downtrodden of the earth and sympathy for their plight, emancipation volatilized the American dream of freedom into the war that freed the slaves. Having lived on the great Mississippi that had run directly between freedom and slavery and having come across that river to take up residence next door to Harriet Beecher Stowe—the very embodiment of Christian indignation and sympathy—Mark Twain knew that the current of that emotion was as powerful and deceptive in history as the current of the river. But beyond that he knew that official religions, national claims to truth, moral interpretations of history, the Christian conscience, and even God himself were lies. If he himself had a great sympathetic heart, he had also seen every form of fraud and was himself, as he well knew, hardly exempt from greed and mendacity.

Nietzsche, it is well to remember, during the very years in which Mark Twain was writing *Life on the Mississippi*, *Huckleberry Finn*, and *A Connecticut Yankee*, was projecting a whole long series of notes, aphorisms, and speculations for a book to be called *The Will to Power*. He saw and felt, with perhaps more clarity and intensity than Mark Twain could see, the lie of the nineteenth century. Indeed his book in every respect constitutes fine parallel reading with *Huckleberry Finn*. One quote from it will suffice to show how Nietzsche defined the lie:

> The holy lie therefore invented (1) a *God* who punishes and rewards, who strictly observes the law-book of the priests and is strict about sending them into the world as his mouthpieces and plenipotentiaries; (2) an *afterlife* in which the great punishment machine is first thought to become effective—to this end the *immortality of the soul*; (3) *conscience* in man as the consciousness that good and evil are permanent—that God himself speaks through it when it advises conformity with priestly precepts; (4) *morality* as a denial of all natural processes, as reduction of all events to a morally conditioned event, moral effects (i.e., the idea of punishment and reward) as effects permeating all things, as the sole power, as the creator of all transformation; (5) *truth* as given, as revealed, as identical with the teaching of the priests: as the condition for all salvation and happiness in this life and the next.[1]

Nietzsche concluded that the origin of this holy lie was nothing more or less than the *will to power*. That will was at once the motive and the end of the

1. Friedrich Nietzsche, *The Will to Power*, trans. Walter Kaufmann and R. J. Hollingdale (New York: Random House, 1967), pp. 90–91. For the quotes that immediately follow concerning the Great Man, see p. 505.

institutions of knowledge, morality, imagination, and society, which is to say that it was the motive of schools, churches, literature, and nations. He longed for a great human being who lacked "the virtues that accompany respect and 'respectability' and altogether everything that is part of the 'virtue of the herd,'" who "when not speaking to himself wears a mask," who "rather lies than tells the truth," and whose strength of will is "the freedom from any kind of conviction."

Surely anyone familiar with Mark Twain's overt attitudes and expressed observations knows how much he shared Nietzsche's premises. Indeed, Huck Finn is in an uncanny way Mark Twain's expression or version of Nietzsche's great human being. For Mark Twain recognized that the holy American nation, having fought out the battle of good and evil along the lines and under the terms of freedom against slavery, was itself moving toward the goal of imperial power. And if we survey our progress in the one hundred years since the publication of *Huckleberry Finn*, we see how much we are at the threshold of George Orwell's *1984*, in which the Ministry of Truth projected the following slogans:

WAR IS PEACE

FREEDOM IS SLAVERY

IGNORANCE IS STRENGTH

In Orwell's world, Winston Smith, under the vigilant electronic eye of Big Brother, is commissioned to rewrite history each day, first by removing every aspect of it that fails to conform to the originating policy changes of the Ministry of Truth, and second by translating the narrative into Newspeak— a language designed to purge ambiguity, to eliminate irregular verbs, and to use nouns, verbs, adjectives, and adverbs interchangeably so as to annihilate as much as possible the distinctions between act and thing, and between individual and class. In addition, Newspeak built up a vocabulary of compound words with the design of making the political component the absolute dominant power of language. Here good and evil, as defined by the state, could instantaneously be communicated into conceptual linguistic designations such as *goodthink* and *crimethink*, *crimesex*, and *goodsex*, all for the purpose of regulating the lives of the citizens of Oceania.

Having lived through 1984, we may feel sufficiently unthreatened by Orwell's book to contend that history is not corroborating his dystopic vision. Yet each day the paranoid camera eye is projected through an electronic image of a world where an incredible array of missile clusters, called densepacks, are being projected into a projectile called the Peacemaker; where the way to arms reduction lies in the production of more arms; and where the institution for waging absolute destructive war is called the Department of Defense. And all this defense is being stockpiled to keep our national freedom secure from the slavery of rival political ideologies.

The discordant reality principle of Mark Twain's ending in its very act of travesty exposes an implicit vision profoundly related to Nietzsche's holy lie and Orwell's Big Lie. Mark Twain, who had lived across the division of his own nation, could see the holy lie of religion as well as the big national lie of freedom. Yet however much we might see Mark Twain's relation to Nietzsche and Orwell, we unfailingly know that neither the narrative nor the narrator of *Huckleberry Finn* can quite be subordinated to that relationship. By way of pointing up the difference that qualifies the relationship, we can take another passage of the book which, appearing only five pages after Huck's much heralded crisis of conscience, records an exchange between Huck and Aunt Sally just after he lies to her about being on a steamboat that blew its cylinder head. Showing immediate concern, she asks,

"Good gracious! anybody hurt?"
"No'm. Killed a nigger."
"Well, it's lucky; because sometimes people do get hurt." (P. 280)

That brief exchange, surely one of the most universally approved passages in the book, is usually quoted to illustrate the instinctive heartlessness of a slaveholding society. Yet the exchange raises all the moral questions of earlier passages we have examined. How, after all, *are* we to take Huck in the exchange? In light of his long experience with Jim and his recent declaration of love for him, is Huck consciously going along with the value system he knows Aunt Sally to believe in? Is he deliberately or merely instinctively withholding that part of himself that is dedicated to freeing Jim? Or is he impervious to an awareness beyond his individual experience with Jim that "niggers" count as people? Or has he literally forgotten his relation to Jim in this new tight place in which he finds himself? If he continues to refer to Jim as a nigger—which he does right through to the end—can he really think that Jim counts as a person? All these questions point to vital aspects of Huck's character that assume negative relations to a positive and principled desire for Jim's freedom, leaving only our wish that Huck remember his knowledge of and experience with Jim—for if Huck remembers he does not show it. As for Aunt Sally, her earnest remark that people sometimes do get hurt all but convicts her of the cruelty from which we might wish to exempt Huck. Yet the fact remains that both she and Huck are unquestionably kindhearted characters, and *both are momentarily sacrificed in order to produce the vividly savage satire upon the society in which both helplessly exist.* Both, in other words, are made by Mark Twain to perform the little drama intended to expose the cruelty of a benighted society.

To subject this passage to the scrutiny that we have directed upon other memorable and much-approved passages is to come full circle back to the fact that this is a hard book to take. For we see once more that directing satiric scorn harshly upon the slaveholding society robs Aunt Sally of her good intentions and even throws Huck's good heart into question. Moreover, the satiric irony of the passage, no matter how manifest, cannot really make up for the *matter* of the passage—the fatal word—to a black audience. To the audience content to feel a pleasurable thrill at seeing the slaveholding society of the old South or the segregated society of the intermediate South flogged once more, we should be able to say, in the presence of the new South, that they are taking pleasure in flogging a dead horse. Rather than continuing to do that, such an audience ought to be glad that a new black audience is rising in force to object to the book. Such objection is assurance that the book is alive in a living, shifting society and cannot be complacently approved by the new academic tradition that has replaced the old genteel tradition.

Is there a way out of these mean tricks that begin to bare themselves wherever the book is indulgently approved? Just possibly. If we go on to read the lines directly and happily following that famous passage, we find Aunt Sally going on to say,

> "Two years ago last Christmas, your Uncle Silas was coming up from Newrleans on the old *Lally Rook*, and she blowed out a cylinder-head and crippled a man. And I think he died afterwards. He was a Babtist. Your Uncle Silas knowed a family in Baton Rouge that knowed his people very well. Yes, I remember now, he *did* die. Mortification set in, and they had to amputate him. But it didn't save him. Yes, it was mortification—that was it. He turned blue all over, and died in the hope of a glorious resurrection. They say he was a sight to look at." (P. 280)

There again is the beautiful principle of emotional exchange at work. If we are indulgently indignant at the cruelty of the slave society, we do not even want to remember the poor Baptist. Certainly we are not meant to sympathize with his fate. But if we care about the humor of the book we cannot do without him. Aunt Sally in this instance is made a little more stupid than she really is, but her sentimentality and kind-heartedness are somehow retained in Mark Twain's determination to move from the savage irony of satire into the dissolution of helpless humor. There is no sign that Huck laughs at this turn of events. He is as silent on the subject as he is about his knowledge of Jim, but the humor of his narrative is undeniably there. If we do not helplessly laugh it is only because we have been unduly arrested by our pleasure in the satiric cruelty that initiates the exchange.

Huck's apparent lack of memory about Jim and his deadpan about the humor are surely the great redemptive facts about this book. Like Nietzsche's great human being, Huck retains a true freedom from all conviction. He truly does belong on the current of the Great Mississippi running between the banks of good and evil, between freedom and slavery, and still running in its lower reaches, between banks where slavery is on both its sides, toward an open sea. We have to recognize, or surely would want to, that even when he chooses to go to hell, he is even then somehow, like the running river, taking the path of least resistance. It is surely easier and handier for him to betray Miss Watson than to betray Jim. His lies are, in their final analysis, better than the truth that our own socially and morally approving conscience would confer upon him. If the people in the black audience find the fatal word and the stereotypical minstrel characterization of Jim hard to take, they are only telling us that we ought to find its manifest and indulgent good intentions as well as its implicit nihilism—a nihilism utterly but oh so humorously explicit in its final sentences—harder to take than we do.

It would not be so bad if the book were banned in the public schools. Then we might read it anew and find another passage as central as the much-quoted passages I have cited. When Huck first embarks upon the river after his escape from Pap and before he meets Jim, he writes (for he is a *writer*, we must remember):

> I didn't lose no time. The next minute I was a-spinning down stream soft but quick in the shade of the bank. I made two mile and a half, and then struck out a quarter of a mile or more towards the middle of the river, because pretty soon I would be passing the ferry landing and people might see me and hail me. I got out amongst the drift-wood and then laid down in the bottom of the canoe and let her float. I laid there and had a good rest and a smoke out of my pipe, look-ing away into the sky, not a cloud in it. The sky looks ever so deep when you lay down on your back in the moonshine; I never knowed it before. And how far a body can hear on the water such nights! I heard people talking at the ferry land-ing. I heard what they said, too, every word of it. One man said it was getting towards the long days and the short nights, now. 'Tother one said *this* warn't one of the short ones, he reckoned—and then they laughed, and he said it over again and they laughed again; then they waked up another fellow and told him, and laughed, but he didn't laugh; he ripped out something brisk and said let him alone. The first fellow said he 'lowed to tell it to his old woman—she would think it was pretty good; but he said that warn't nothing to some things he had said in his time. I heard one man say it was nearly three o'clock, and he hoped daylight wouldn't wait more than about a week longer. After that, the talk got further and further away, and I couldn't make out the words any more, but I could hear the mumble; and now and then a laugh, too, but it seemed a long ways off. (Pp. 58–59)

How much is beautifully there. The fugitive boy in the stolen canoe running away upon the running river with no time to lose,.yet time enough in the idle moment to see the depth of the heavens above him, and ears acute enough to hear the conversation far across the water. And then the wonderful conver-sation itself with the stupid jokes—showing that for every two people who share a joke there is likely to be a third who finds nothing funny, and show-ing too humanity's inveterate need to repeat itself in an act of performance. And the stupidity and the corny jokes made incredibly humorous as Huck's written rehearsal redeems those dear old yokels. And finally the voices fad-ing, leaving the mumble and the laughter trailing in the wake of the passage. With no time to lose, how much is gained!

On a great muddy river where, unlike the blue stillness of Walden Pond, the water's action makes reflection impossible just as its color hides its depth, the instinct of both Huck's deviant language and deviant character is equal to the mulatto solution of the current. That is why Huck's being and lan-guage are magically and mysteriously identical with the current, and also why the humor he both evokes and records keeps him free from the prin-ciple of freedom, the principle that in the economy of moral exchange al-ways threatens to create two rednecks for every slave it frees. Mark Twain knew as well as we know how utterly necessary that principle is for Ameri-can society. It was the principle we believe we believed in enough to fight the one war when God was truly on our side. Yet the war was bloody and di-visive, involving catastrophic loss of life. The humor of *Huckleberry Finn* literally displaces that loss with a gain of helpless and overt pleasure. Such pleasure, a manifest and true expression of the pleasure principle at the heart of all life, serves to disarm the pleasure of principle that is the armor of adult society. The point is that it disarms it but does not overtly attack it. No adult society can do without the pleasure of principle, which, after all, is at once the purpose and conscience of civilization. Mark Twain believed in it enough to sacrifice Tom Sawyer to it—and we cannot forget that Tom was the character through whom he had discovered Huck Finn. Yet he would not sacrifice Huck to it. Instead he let Huck reject civilization and the adult conscience in the very last pages of his book—an ending that is, as Eliot so rightly realized, as perfect as any in literature.

Holding to the beauty of this humor, yet remembering always that humor involves an exchange that threatens somebody, we should be able not only to stand but to understand civilization's impulse to ban the book. The banning would express society's discomfort with the book just as Huck's rejection of civilization is an expression of his discomfort with adult society. Even if the book were banned in all the schools, we would only be reminded that its very language was proof from the beginning that it never was for the schools. When the book was banned in Concord, Mark Twain applauded the action on the grounds that it would sell thirty-five thousand copies. As both inventor and publisher of *Huckleberry Finn*, he lived in a world where abrupt exchanges were conducted in as well as between the realm of the moral indignation and the arena of the marketplace. Huck observes at the outset of the novel that he doesn't like the widow's food because everything is cooked by itself. He likes things cooked together, as if in a barrel of odds and ends, where "things get mixed up, and the juice kind of swaps around, and the things go better" (p. 18). Later, observing the early morning sun shining through the forest leaves on Jackson's Island, he notes the freckled places in the gloom, which "swapped about a little, showing there was a little breeze up there." Lost in the fog on the river and calling out to Jim, he cannot place Jim's answering whoops because he "never knowed a sound dodge around so, and swap places so quick and so much." Finally at Aunt Sally's, when he discovers that he is supposed to be Tom Sawyer and almost slumps through the floor in relief, he regrets that "there warn't no time to swap knives" as Uncle Silas forcibly hustles him into his new identity with a barrage of questions that he happily *can* answer. Swapping, it turns out in this humorous and devious world of moral relativity, leads to possibilities of taste, beauty, anxiety, and pleasure.

Having experienced the manipulative, shifty, shrewd, and humorous exchanges constantly taking place both on and beside the moving Mississippi, we should be able to contemplate with a degree of equanimity the possibility of widespread removal of *Huckleberry Finn* from school and library shelves. In the face of such censorship, we would still be left with the happy choice of pursuing the pleasure of principle with a serious—even outraged—public defense of the book against those who found it hard to take, or indulging the pleasure principle by reading the book in private where we could blessedly take it easy.

Selected Bibliography of Criticism 1968–1983

Bibliographical Works

The following section is primarily intended to aid those unfamiliar with *Huck Finn* scholarship. The absolute novice might want to start with the Norton Critical Edition of *Adventures of Huckleberry Finn*, listed below under Sculley Bradley, which offers an annotated text, sources, essays in criticism, and a short bibliography all inside one cover. In fact, if one simply wants to get a "feel" for what has been written on *Huck Finn*, one could find plenty of reading in any of the several collections of criticism listed below.

Those interested in undertaking more serious research on *Huckleberry Finn*, on other works by Mark Twain, or on the life of Samuel Clemens, would do well to consult first Thomas Tenney's *Reference Guide* and his annual supplements to that guide appearing in *American Literary Realism*. Tenney's items are well annotated, and his list is by far the most comprehensive. Tenney has also taken over the *Mark Twain Journal*; thus, the journal will no doubt become increasingly the showplace for much of the best in Mark Twain criticism. Of course, the annual MLA bibliography, particularly with the recent advancements promised by the new computerized format's subject and keyword indexing, is also a logical place to start, as is the annual bibliographical essay in *American Literary Scholarship* by Louis J. Budd, John C. Gerber, and Hamlin Hill. The annual annotated checklist in *Mississippi Quarterly* and the lists of recent criticism in *American Literature* and *Western American Literature* should also be consulted. Finally, even though it is not a bibliography of criticism, I have listed Alan Gribben's *Mark Twain's Library* below, because it too should be a starting point for serious research.

For those who are already familiar with the research process but who are either turning to *Huck Finn* criticism for the first time or wanting to keep current, the selected bibliography of criticism following the list of bibliographical works can be treated as an update of Maurice Beebe and John Feaster's checklist in *Modern Fiction Studies* (1968). The list does not pretend to be exhaustive, excluding, as it does, most foreign criticism, but it is comprehensive.

Anderson, Frederick, ed. *Mark Twain: The Critical Heritage*. London: Routledge & Kegan Paul; New York: Barnes & Noble, 1971. Pp. 121–35.

Beebe, Maurice, and John Feaster. *MFS* 14 (1968):93–139.

Bowen, James, and Richard VanDerBeets, eds. *"Adventures of Huckleberry Finn" with Abstracts of Twenty Years of Criticism*. Glenview, Ill.: Scott, Foresman & Co., 1970.

Bradley, Sculley et al., eds. *"Adventures of Huckleberry Finn": An Annotated Text, Backgrounds and Sources, Essays in Criticism*. 2d ed. A Norton Critical Edition. New York: Norton, 1977.

Branch, Edgar M. "Mark Twain Scholarship: Two Decades." In *"Adventures of Huckleberry Finn" with Abstracts of Twenty Years of Criticism*, pp. 344–49. Glenview, Ill.: Scott, Foresman & Co., 1970.

Budd, Louis J., ed. *Critical Essays on Mark Twain, 1867–1910.* Boston: G. K. Hall, 1982.

Clark, Harry H. "Mark Twain." In *Eight American Authors.* Edited by James Woodress, pp. 273–320. New York: Norton & Co., 1971. Original essay completed following Clark's death by J. C. Mathews (MLA, 1956) with additions by Howard Baetzhold in 1971.

Gerber, John C., ed. *Studies in "Huckleberry Finn."* Columbus, Ohio: Charles E. Merrill Publishing Co., 1971.

Gribben, Alan. *Mark Twain's Library: A Reconstruction.* 2 vols. Boston: G. K. Hall, 1980.

———. "Removing Mark Twain's Mask: A Decade of Criticism and Scholarship." *ESQ* 26 (1980):100–103, 149–71.

Hill, Hamlin. "Who Killed Mark Twain?" *ALR* 7 (1974):119–24.

Kesterson, David, ed. *Critics on Mark Twain: Readings in Literary Criticism.* Coral Gables, Fla.: University of Miami Press, 1973.

Leary, Lewis, and John Auchard. *Articles on American Literature, 1950–1967.* Durham, N.C.: Duke University Press, 1970. Pp. 56–77.

———. *Articles on American Literature, 1968–1975.* Durham, N.C.: Duke University Press, 1978. Pp. 72–86.

Schmitter, Dean Morgan, ed. *Mark Twain: A Collection of Criticism.* New York: McGraw-Hill, 1974.

Tenney, Thomas A. *Mark Twain: A Reference Guide.* Boston: G. K. Hall, 1977. Updated by annual supplements in *ALR.*

Articles in Periodicals

Agarwal, B. B. "Educational Ideas in *Huckleberry Finn.*" *MTJ* 21:4(1983): 2–4.

Anderson, David. "Basque Wine, Arkansas Chawin' Tobacco: Landscape and Ritual in Ernest Hemingway and Mark Twain." *MTJ* 16:1(1971): 3–7.

———. "Three Generations of Missouri Fiction." *MMisc* 9(1981):7–20.

Andrews, William L. "Mark Twain and James W. C. Pennington: Huckleberry Finn's Smallpox Lie." *SAF* 9(1981):103–12.

Arikawa, Shoji. "Huckleberry Finn in Japan." *EngR* 21:3(1971):20–26.

Arner, Robert D. "Acts Seventeen and *Huckleberry Finn*: A Note on Silas Phelps' Sermon." *MTJ* 16:2(1972):12.

Ashely, L. F. "Huck, Tom and Television." *English Quarterly* 4(1971):57–65.

Aspiz, Harold. "Mark Twain and 'Doctor' Newton." *AL* 44(1972):130–36.

Atherton, James S. "To Give Down the Banks and Hark from the Tomb!" *JJQ* 4 (1967):75–83.

Baldwin, David. "Humor in Mark Twain's 'Buck Fanshaw's Funeral.'" *MTJ* 20: 4(1981):16–18.

Banta, Martha. "Rebirth or Revenge: The Endings of *Huckleberry Finn* and *The American.*" *MFS* 15(1969):191–207.

Barchilon, Jose, and J. S. Kovel. "*Huckleberry Finn*: A Psychoanalytic Study." *JAPA* 14(1966):775–814.

Barnett, Louise K. "Huck Finn: Picaro as Linguistic Outsider." *CollL* 6(1979): 221–31.

Barsness, John A. "Platform Manner in the Novel: A View from the Pit." *MASJ* 10(1969):49–59.

Beaver, Harold. "Run, Nigger, Run: *Adventures of Huckleberry Finn* as a Fugitive Slave Narrative." *JAmS* 8(1974):339–61.

Bell, Millicent. "*Huckleberry Finn*: Journey without End." *VQR* 58(1982):253–67.

Bellman, Samuel I. "Peripheral(?) Characters in *Huckleberry Finn* and *Catcher in the Rye*." *MTJ* 19:1(1977–78):4–6.

Belson, Joel Jay. "The Argument of the Final Chapters of *Huckleberry Finn*." *MTJ* 21:3(1983):11–12.

———. "The Nature and Consequences of the Loneliness of Huckleberry Finn." *ArQ* 26(1970):243–48.

Bendixen, Alfred. "Huck Finn and *Pilgrim's Progress*." *MTJ* 18:3(1976):21.

Benoit, Raymond. "Again with Fair Creation: Holy Places in American Literature." *Prospects* 5(1980):315–30.

Benson, Jackson J. "John Steinbeck's *Cannery Row*: A Reconsideration." *WAL* 12 (1977):11–40.

Berger, Arthur Asa. "Huck Finn as an Existential Hero: Making Sense of Absurdity." *MTJ* 18:2(1976):12–17.

Berkove, Lawrence I. "The Free Man of Color in *The Grandissimes* and Works by Harris and Mark Twain." *SoQ* 18:4(1980):60–73.

———. "The 'Poor Players' of *Huckleberry Finn*." *Papers of the Michigan Academy of Science, Arts, and Letters* 52(1982):291–310.

Bier, Jesse. "A Note on Twain and Hemingway." *MQ* 21(1980):261–65.

———. "Bless you, Chile': Fiedler and 'Huck Honey' a Generation Later." *MissQ* 34(1981):456–62.

Billinsley, Dale B. "'Standard Authors' in *Huckleberry Finn*." *JNT* 9(1979):126–31.

Birchfield, James. "Jim's Coat of Arms." *MTJ* 14:4(1969):15–16.

Black, Linda. "Louisa May Alcott's *Huckleberry Finn*." *MTJ* 21:2(1982):15–17.

Blair, Walter. "Was Huckleberry Finn Written?" *MTJ* 19:4(1979):1–3.

Boland, Sally. "The Seven Dialects in *Huckleberry Finn*." *NDQ* 36:3(1968):30–40.

Branch, Edgar M. "Mark Twain: Newspaper Reading and the Writer's Creativity." *NCF* 37(1983):576–603.

Branch, Watson. "Hard-Hearted Huck: 'No Time to be Sentimentering.'" *SAF* 6 (1978):212–18.

Brazil, John R. "Perception and Structure in Mark Twain's Art and Mind: *Life on the Mississippi*." *MissQ* 34 (1981):91–112.

Briden, Earl F. "Huck's Great Escape: Magic and Ritual." *MTJ* 21:3(1983):17–18.

———. "Huck's Island Adventure and the Selkirk Legend." *MTJ* 18:3(1976):12–14.

Brogunier, Joseph. "An Incident in *The Great Gatsby* and *Huckleberry Finn*." *MTJ* 16:1(1967):1–3.

Brown, Spencer. "*Huckleberry Finn* for Our Time: A Re-Reading of the Concluding Chapters." *MQR* 11(1967):41–46.

Bryant, Katie. "The Slavery of Dialect Exemplified in Mark Twain's Works." *MTJ* 19:3(1979):5–8.

Bugliari, James. "The Picaresque as a Flaw in Mark Twain's Novels." *MTJ* 15:4 (1971):10–12.

Burg, David F. "Another View of *Huckleberry Finn*." *NCF* 29(1974):299–319.

Burns, Graham. "Time and Pastoral: *The Adventures of Huckleberry Finn*." *CR* 15(1972):52–63.

Burns, Rex. "The Artful Photograph: Mark Twain's Eye." *ALR* 15(1982):62–73.

Burns, Stuart L. "St. Petersburg Re-Visited: Helen Eustis and Mark Twain." *WAL* 5(1970):99–112.

Byers, John R., Jr. "Mark Twain's Mary Jane Wilks: Shamed or Shammed?" *MTJ* 17:1(1973):13–14.

———. "Miss Emmeline Grangerford's Hymn Book." *AL* 43(1971):259–63.

———. "The Pokeville Preacher's Invitation in *Huckleberry Finn*." *MTJ* 18:4 (1977):15–16.

Carkeet, David. "The Dialects in *Huckleberry Finn*." *AL* 51(1979):315–32.

––––––. "The Source for the Arkansas Gossips in *Huckleberry Finn*." *ALR* 14 (1981):90–92.

Casey, Daniel J. "Universality in *Huckleberry Finn*: A Comparison of Twain and Kivi." *MTJ* 14:1(1967):13–18.

Cecil, Moffitt L. "The Historical Ending of *Adventures of Huckleberry Finn*: How Nigger Jim Was Set Free." *ALR* 13(1980):280–83.

Christopher, J. R. "On the *Adventures of Huckleberry Finn* as a Comic Myth." *CimR* 18(1972):18–27.

Clark, Marden J. "No Time to be Sentimentering." *MTJ* 21:3(1983):21–23.

Cloutier, Arthur C. "'Dear Mr. Seelye . . . Yours Truly, Tom Sawyer.'" *CE* 34(1973): 849–53.

Coard, Robert J. "Huck Finn and Mr. Mark Twain Rhyme." *MQ* 10(1969):317–29.

––––––. "Huck Finn and Two Sixteenth Century Lads." *MQ* 23(1982):437–46.

Cohen, Edward H. "The Return to St. Petersburg." *IEY* 23(1973):50–55.

Collins, Billy G. "Huckleberry Finn: A Mississippi Moses." *JNT* 5(1975):86–104.

Colwell, James L. "Huckleberries and Humans: On the Naming of Huckleberry Finn." *PMLA* 86(1971):70–76.

Coplin, Keith. "John and Sam Clemens: A Father's Influence." *MTJ* 15:1(1970):1–6.

Cox, James M. "Humor and America: The Southwestern Bear Hunt, Mrs. Stowe and Mark Twain." *SR* 83(1975):573–601.

––––––. "Toward Vernacular Humor." *VQR* 46(1970):311–30.

Cox, John F. "On the Naming of Huckleberry Finn." *PMLA* 86(1970):60–62.

Cross, Randy K. "*Huckleberry Finn*: The Sacred and the Profane." *MTJ* 21:3 (1983):27–28.

Cuddy, Lois A. "Eliot and *Huck Finn*: River and Sea in 'The Dry Salvages.'" *TSER* 3:1–2(1976):3–12.

Cude, Wilfred. "'False as Harlots' Oaths': Dunny Ramsay Looks at Huck Finn." *SCL* 2(1977):164–87.

David, Beverly R. "Mark Twain and the Legends for *Huckleberry Finn*." *ALR* 15 (1982):155–65.

––––––. "The Pictorial *Huckleberry Finn*: Mark Twain and His Illustrator, E. W. Kemble." *AQ* 26(1974):331–51.

Davidson, Loren K. "The Darnell-Watson Feud." *Duquesne Review* 13(1968): 76–95.

Delaney, Paul. "You Can't Go Back to the Raft Ag'in Huck Honey!: Mark Twain's Western Sequel to *Huckleberry Finn*." *WAL* 11(1976):215–29.

Desai, S. K. "Time in *Huckleberry Finn*." In *Indian Studies in American Fiction*, edited by M. K. Naik, S. K. Desai, and S. Mokashi-Punekar, pp. 68–76. Dharwar: Karnatak University; Delhi: Macmillan India, 1974.

Desmond, John F. "*Huckleberry Finn* and the Failure of Anamnesis." *MTJ* 21:4 (1983):8–10.

Donaldson, Scott. "Pap Finn's Boy." *SAB* 36:3(1971):32–37.

Duncan, Jeffrey L. "The Empirical and the Ideal in Mark Twain." *PMLA* 95(1980): 201–12.

Elsbree, Langdon. "Huck Finn on the Nile." *SAQ* 69(1970):504–10.

Ensor, Allison. "The Location of the Phelps Farm in *Huckleberry Finn*." *SAB* 34 (1969):7.

––––––. "The 'Opposition Line' to the King and the Duke in *Huckleberry Finn*." *MTJ* 14:3(1968):6–7.

Fetterly, Judith. "Disenchantment: Tom Sawyer in *Huckleberry Finn*." *PMLA* 87 (1972):69–74.

Fiedler, Leslie. "Literature and Lucre: A Meditation." *Genre* 13(1980):1−10.

Fischer, Victor. "Huck Finn Reviewed: The Reception of *Huckleberry Finn* in the United States, 1885−1897." *ALR* 16(1983):1−57.

Fite, Montgomery. "Mark Twain's Naming of Huckleberry Finn." *AN&Q* 13 (1975):140−41.

Frazer, Timothy C. "A Note on Mark Twain's Use of Dialect in Earlier Writings." *MTJ* 20:2(1980):8−9.

Galligan, Edward L. "True Comedians and False: Don Quixote and *Huckleberry Finn*." *SR* 86(1977):66−83.

Gardner, Joseph H. "Gaffer Hexam and Huck Finn." *MP* 66(1968):155−56.

Gaston, Georg Meri-Akri. "The Function of Tom Sawyer in *Huckleberry Finn*." *MissQ* 27(1973):33−39.

Georgoudaki, Catherine. "Women's Original Compositions in *The Adventures of Tom Sawyer, Life on the Mississippi*, and *Adventures of Huckleberry Finn*." *ArAA* 4(1979):71−78.

Gerber, John C. "Practical Editions: Mark Twain's *The Adventures of Tom Sawyer* and *Adventures of Huckleberry Finn*." *Proof* 2(1972):285−92.

Goldstein, Wallace L. "Mark Twain's Use of Diction in *The Adventures of Huckleberry Finn*." *EngR* 31(1980):11−13.

Gollin, Richard and Rita. "*Huckleberry Finn* and the Time of the Evasion." *MLS* 9(1979):5−15.

Goodyear, Russell H. "Huck Finn's Anachronistic Double Eagles." *AN&Q* 10 (1971):39.

Goudie, Andrea. "'What Fools These Mortals Be!' A Puckish Interpretation of Mark Twain's Narrative Stance." *KanQ* 5:4(1973):19−31.

Graves, Wallace. "Mark Twain's 'Burning Shame.'" *NCF* 23(1968):93−98.

Gregory, Stanford, Jr., and Jerry M. Lewis. "Huck Finn and the Game Model Gloss." *Qualitative Sociology* 3(1980):136−51.

Grenander, M. E. "*Benito Cereno* and Legal Oppression: A Szaszian Interpretation." *Libertarian Studies* 2(1978):337−42.

Griska, Joseph M., Jr. "Two New Joel Chandler Harris Reviews of Mark Twain." *AL* 48(1977):584−89.

Gupta, Rameshwar. "The Central Theme in *The Adventures of Huckleberry Finn*." In *Indian Studies in American Fiction*, edited by M. K. Naik, S. K. Desai, and S. Mokashi-Punekar, pp. 55−67. Dharwar: Karnatak University; Delhi: Macmillan India, 1974.

Hakar, John. "*Huckleberry Finn*: A Copy Inscribed in 1903." *ABC* 20:1(1970):7−9.

Hanson, R. Galen. "Tom Sawyer's Gang as Social Ritual: Implications for Modern Social Organization." *MTJ* 21:3(1983):33−34.

Harkey, Joseph H. "Mark Twain's Knights and Squires." *MTJ* 20:3(1980):6−13.

———. "When Huck Finn Smouched that Spoon." *MTJ* 15:2(1970):14.

Harris, John. "Principles, Sympathy and Doing What's Right." *Philosophy* 52 (1977):96−99.

Harris, Susan K. "'This Peace, This Deep Contentment': Images of Temporal Freedom in the Writings of Mark Twain." *ELWIU* 7(1980):201−12.

Harwood, C. Edwin. "Twain's Huckleberry Finn, Chapter XIV." *Expl* 28(1969):item 36.

Haslan, Gerald W. "*Huckleberry Finn*: Why Read the Phelps Farm Episode?" *RS* 35(1967):189−97.

Haupt, Garry. "The Tragi-Comedy of the Unreal in Ralph Ellison's *Invisible Man* and Mark Twain's *Adventures of Huckleberry Finn*." *Interpretations* 4(1972):1−12.

Hearn, Michael Patrick. "Mark Twain, E. W. Kemble, and *Huckleberry Finn*." *ABC* 2(1981):14–19.

Hoffman, Michael J. "Huck's Ironic Circle." *GaR* 23(1969):307–22.

Holland, Laurence B. "A 'Raft of Trouble': Word and Deed in *Huckleberry Finn*." *Glyph* 5(1979):69–87.

———. "Authority, Power, and Form: Some American Texts." *YES* 8(1978):1–14.

Hook, Andrew. "Huckleberry Finn and Scotland." *EngR* 21:2(1970):8–14.

Howell, Elmo. "Mark Twain and the Phelps Farm Episode: Another Look at *Huckleberry Finn*." *Interpretations* 5(1973):1–8.

Hoy, James F. "The Grangerford-Shepherdson Feud in *Huckleberry Finn*." *MTJ* 18:1(1975):19–20.

James, Stuart B. "The Politics of Personal Salvation: The American Literary Record." *DQ* 4(1969):19–45.

Karnath, David. "Mark Twain's Implicit Theory of the Comic." *Mosaic* 9(1976): 207–18.

Keetch, Brent. "Mark Twain's Literary Sport." *MTJ* 18:2(1976)7–10.

Kellner, Robert Scott. "Mark Twain and the Mental Cripple: The Challenge of Myth." *MTJ* 21:4(1983):18–20.

Khouri, Nadia. "From Eden to the Dark Ages: Images of History in the Work of Mark Twain." *CRevAS* 11(1980):151–74.

King, Bruce. "*Huckleberry Finn*." *ArielE* 2:4(1971):69–77.

Kinghorn, Norton D. "E. W. Kemble's Misplaced Modifier: A Note on the Illustrations for *Huckleberry Finn*." *MTJ* 16:4(1973):9–11.

Kirkham, E. Bruce. "Huck and Hamlet: An Examination of Twain's Use of Shakespeare." *MTJ* 14:4(1969):17–19.

Kolb, Harold H., Jr. "Mark Twain, Huck Finn, and Jacob Blivens: Gilt-Edged, Tree Calf Morality in the *Adventures of Huckleberry Finn*." *VQR* 55(1979):653–69.

Krauss, Jennifer. "Playing Double in *Adventures of Huckleberrry Finn*." *MTJ* 21:4(1983):22–24.

Krauth, Leland. "Mark Twain: The Victorian of Southwestern Humor." *AL* 54 (1982):368–84.

Kravec, Maureen T. "Huckleberry Finn's Aristocratic Ancestry." *MTJ* 18:2(1976): 19–20.

Laidlaw, R. P. "More Huck Finn in *Finnegans Wake*." *WN* 5(1968):71–73.

Leary, Lewis. "Troubles with Mark Twain: Some Considerations on Consistency." *SAF* 2(1973):89–103.

Lee, Mary K. "The Overt, Unreliable, Naive Narrator in the Tall Tale and *Huckleberry Finn*." *MTJ* 21:3(1983):39.

Levy, Alfred J. "The Dramatic Integrity of Huck Finn." *BSUF* 20:2(1979):28–37.

Lewis, Stuart. "Twain's Huckleberry Finn, Chapter XIV." *Expl* 30(1972): item 61.

Light, James F. "Paradox, Form, and Despair in *Huckleberry Finn*." *MTJ* 21:4 (1983):24–25.

Light, Martin. "Sweeping out Chivalric Silliness: The Example of Huck Finn and *The Sun Also Rises*." *MTJ* 17:3(1974):18–20.

Lowrey, Captain Robert E. "The Grangerford-Shepherdson Episode: Another of Mark Twain's Indictments of the Damned Human Race." *MTJ* 15:1(1970):19–20.

Loyd, James B. "The Nature of Twain's Attack on Sentimentality: *The Adventures of Huckleberry Finn*." *UMSE* 13(1972):59–63.

Lynn, Kenneth S. "Welcome Back from the Raft, Huck Honey!" *ASch* 46(1977): 338–47.

McCullough, Joseph B. "Uses of the Bible in *Huckleberry Finn*." *MTJ* 19:3 (1978):2–3.

McKay, Janet H. "Going to Hell: Huck Finn's Great Debate." *Interpretations* 13 (1981):24–30.

———. "'Tears and Flapdoodle': Point of View and Style in the *Adventures of Huckleberry Finn*." *Style* 10(1976):41–50.

McMahan, Elizabeth E. "The Money Motif: Economic Implications in *Huckleberry Finn*." *MTJ* 15:4(1971):5–10.

McNamara, Eugene. "*Adventures of Huckleberry Finn*: Chapter One as Microcosm." *MTJ* 18:4(1977):17–18.

Manierre, William R. "Contemporary Relevance of *Huckleberry Finn*." *AAus* 3 (1974):77–94.

———. "On Keeping the Raftsmen's Passage in *Huckleberry Finn*. *ELN* 6(1968): 118–22.

Marks, Barry A. "The Huck Finn Swindle." *WAL* 14(1979):115–32.

———. "The Making of a Humorist: The Narrative Strategy of *Huckleberry Finn*." *JNT* 12(1982):139–45.

Marshall, Gregory. "Blood Ties as Structural Motif in *Huckleberry Finn*." *MTJ* 21:3(1983):44–46.

Martin, Jay. "The Broken Speech: Mark Twain and Henry Miller." In *Proceedings of a Symposium on American Literature*, edited by Marta Sienicka, pp. 213–24. Poznań: Universitet w Poznaniu, 1981.

May, Charles E. "Literary Masters and Masturbators: Sexuality, Fantasy, and Reality in *Huckleberry Finn*." *L&P* 28(1978):85–92.

Mayberry, George. "Huckleberry Finn Enriched." *Nation* 207(26 August 1968): 154–57.

Michelson, Bruce. "Huck and the Games of the World." *ALR* 13(1980):108–21.

Miller, Bruce E. "*Huckleberry Finn*: The Kierkegaardian Dimension." *Illinois Quarterly* 34(1971):55–64.

Miller, Lee. "Huckleberries and Humans." *PMLA* 87(1972):314.

Miller, Michael G. "Geography and Structure in *Huckleberry Finn*." *SNNTS* 12 (1980):192–209.

Millichap, Joseph R. "Calvinistic Attitudes and Pauline Imagery in *The Adventures of Huckleberry Finn*." *MTJ* 16:1(1971):8–10.

Mills, Nicolaus C. "Prison and Society in Nineteenth-Century American Fiction." *WAL* 24(1970):325–31.

———. "Social and Moral Vision in *Great Expectations* and *Huckleberry Finn*." *JAmS* 4(1970):61–72.

Monteiro, George. "Innocence and Experience: The Adolescent Child in the Works of Mark Twain, Henry James, and Ernest Hemingway." *EAA* 1(1977):39–57.

Morsberger, Robert E. "Pap Finn and the Bishop's Candlesticks: Victor Hugo in Hannibal." *CEA* 31:2(1969):17.

Mulqueen, James E. "Huck Finn, Imagist Poet." *CEA* 37:3(1975):14–15.

Nagel, James. "Huck Finn and *The Bear*: The Wilderness and Moral Freedom." *ESA* 12(1969):59–63.

Oehlschlaeger, Fritz. "Huck Finn and the Meaning of Shame." *MTJ* 20:4(1981): 13–14.

Opdahl, Keith M. "'You'll Be Sorry When I'm Dead': Child-Adult Relations in *Huck Finn*." *MFS* 25(1979):613–24.

Oriard, Michael. "From *Tom Sawyer* to *Huckleberry Finn*: Toward Godly Play." *SAF* 8(1980):183–202.

Ostrom, Alan. "Huck Finn and the Modern Ethos." *CentR* 16(1972):162–79.

Passon, Richard H. "Twain and Eighteenth-Century Satire: The Ingenu Narrator in *Huckleberry Finn*." *MTJ* 21:4(1983):33–36.

Patterson, Robert G. "Death on the Mississippi: Mark Twain's *Huckleberry Finn*." *Psychological Perspectives* 7(1976):9–22.

Pauly, Thomas. "Directed Readings: The Contents Tables in *Huckleberry Finn*." *Proof* 3(1973):63–68.

Pearce, Roy Harvey. "Huck Finn in His History." *EA* 24(1971):283–91.

Pease, Ralph. "Huckleberry Finn Talks about What Mr. Twain Did to His Story." *MTJ* 21:3(1983):48–49.

Peck, Richard E. "A Mark Twain 'Literary Offence.'" *MTJ* 14:3(1968):7–9.

Pettit, Arthur Gordon. "Mark Twain, the Blood-Feud, and the South." *SLJ* 4:1 (1971):20–32.

———. "Mark Twain, Unreconstructed Southerner, and His View of the Negro, 1835–1860." *Rocky Mountain Social Science Journal* 7(1970):17–27.

Piacentio, Edward J. "The Significance of Pap's Drunken Diatribe Against the Government in *Huckleberry Finn*." *MTJ* 19:4(1979):19–21.

———. "The Ubiquitous Tom Sawyer: Another view of the Conclusion of *Huckleberry Finn*." *CimR* 37(1976):34–43.

Pinsker, Sanford. "Huckleberry Finn, Modernist Poet." *MQ* 24(1983):261–73.

Quirk, Tom. "The Legend of Noah and the Voyage of Huckleberry Finn." *MTJ* 21:3(1983):21–23.

Rachal, John. "Scotty Briggs and the Minister: An Idea from Hooper's Simon Suggs?" *MTJ* 17:2(1974):10–11.

Rao, B. Ramachandra. "Structural Devices in *The Adventures of Huckleberry Finn*." *BP* 14(1970):23–29.

Rearden, John D. "'Shakespearean Revival!!!': Satire of American Elizabethans." *MTJ* 21:3(1983):36–38.

Ridge, Stanley G. M. "'Sivilization' and Huck Finn." *Crux* 13:2(1979):53–56.

Roberts, Bette B. "Huck Finn and Ed Gentry: The River Revisited." *IEY* 30(1980):14.

Robinson, Forrest G. "The Silences in *Huckleberry Finn*." *NCF* 37(1982):50–74.

Rodnon, Stewart. "The Adventures of Huckleberry Finn and *Invisible Man*: Thematic and Structural Comparisons." *NALF* 4(1970):45–51.

Rubin, Louis D., Jr. "Southern Local Color and the Black Man." *SoR* 6(1970):1011–30.

Rulon, Curt M. "Geographical Delimitation of the Dialect Areas in *The Adventures of Huckleberry Finn*." *MTJ* 14:1(1969):9–12.

Sapper, Neil G. "'I Been There Before': Huck Finn as Tocquevillian Individual." *MissQ* 24(1970):35–45.

Sawey, Orlan. "The Consistency of the Character of Nigger Jim in *Huckleberry Finn*." *TAIUS* 4(1971):35–41.

Scafella, Frank. "Models of the Soul: Authorship as Moral Action in Four American Novels." *Journal of the American Academy of Religion* 44(1976):459–75.

Schact, Paul. "The Lonesomeness of Huckleberry Finn." *AL* 53(1981):189–201.

Schafer, Jurgen. "Huckleberry, U.S." *ES* 54(1972):334–35.

Schieck, William J. "The Spunk of a Rabbit: An Allusion in *Huckleberry Finn*." *MTJ* 15:4(1971):14–16.

Schmitz, Neil. "On American Humor." *PR* 47(1980):559–77.

———. "The Paradox of Liberation in *Huckleberry Finn*." *TSLL* 13(1971):125–36.

———. "Twain, *Huckleberry Finn*, and the Reconstruction." *AmerS* 12(1971):59–67.

Schonhorn, Manuel. "Mark Twain's Jim: Solomon on the Mississippi." *MTJ* 14:3 (1968):9–11.

Schultz, Lucille M. "Parlor Talk in Mark Twain: The Grangerford Parlor and the House Beautiful." *MTJ* 19:4(1979):14–19.

Seib, Kenneth. "Moses and the Bulrushers: A Note on Huckleberry Finn." *MTJ* 18:4(1977):13–14.

Shaw, Patrick W. "Huck's Children: The Contemporary American Picaro." *MTJ* 21:4(1983):42–43.

Shear, Walter. "Games People Play in *Huckleberry Finn*." *MQ* 20 (1979):378–93.

Simonson, Harold P. "*Huckleberry Finn* as Tragedy." *YR* 59(1970):532–48.

Singer, Glen W. "Huck, Ad, Jim, and Bugs: A Reconsideration—*Huckleberry Finn* and Hemingway's 'The Battler.'" *Notes on a Modern American Literature* 3(1978):item 9.

Skerry, Philip J. "*The Adventures of Huckleberry Finn* and *Intruder in the Dust*: Two Conflicting Myths of the American Experience." *BSUF* 13:1(1972):4–13.

Snyder, John. "James' Girl Huck: *What Maisie Knew*." *ALR* 11(1978):109–23.

Solomon, Andrew. "Jim and Huck: Magnificent Misfits. *MTJ* 16:3(1972):17–24.

Solomon, Jack. "Huckleberry Finn and the Tradition of the *Odyssey*." *SAB* 33 (1968):11–13.

Sommers, Jeffrey. "'I Never Knowed How Clothes Could Change a Body Before': The Dual Function of Clothing in *Huckleberry Finn*." *MTJ* 20:4(1981):19–21.

Stein, Allen F. "Return to Phelps Farm: Huckleberry Finn and the Old Southwestern Framing Device." *MissQ* 24(1971):111–16.

Sten, Christopher. "'When the Candle Went Out': The Nighttime World of Huck Finn." *SAF* 9(1981):47–64.

Stephens, Gary. "Haunted Americans: The Endurance of American Realism." *PR* 44(1977):73–84.

Strickland, Carol C. "Emmeline Grangerford, Mark Twain's Folk Artist." *BNYPL* 79(1976):225–33.

———. "Of Love and Loneliness, Society and Self in *Huckleberry Finn*." *MTJ* 21:4(1983):50–52.

Sullivan, Jeremiah J. "Conflict in the Modern American Novel." *BSUF* 15(1974): 28–36.

Sykes, Robert H. "A Source for Mark Twain's Feud." *West Virginia History* 28 (1968):191–98.

Talbott, Linda H. "*Huck Finn*: Mark Twain at Midstream." *Nassau Review* 1(1969): 44–60.

Tate, Allen. "Faulkner's *Sanctuary* and the Southern Myth." *VQR* 44(1968):418–27.

Thomas, Brook. "Language and Identity in the *Adventures of Huckleberry Finn*." *MTJ* 20:3(1980):17–21.

Towers, Tom. "Love and Power in *Huckleberry Finn*." *TSE* 23(1978):17–37.

Trachtenberg, Alan. "The Form of Freedom in *Adventures of Huckleberry Finn*." *SoR* n.s. 6(1970):954–71.

Von Frank, Albert. "Huck Finn and the Flight from Maturity." *SAF* 7(1979):1–15.

Wagenknecht, Edward. "Huckleberry Finn as the Devil's Disciple." *Boston University Studies* 18(1970):20–24.

Wagner, Jeanie M. "*Huckleberry Finn* and the History Game." *MTJ* 20:1(1979): 5–10.

Wall, Cary. "The Boomerang of Slavery: The Child, the Aristocrat, and Hidden White Identity in *Huckleberry Finn*." *Social Studies* 21(1982):208–21.

Walters, Thomas N. "Twain's Finn and Alger's Gilman: Picaresque Counter-Directions." *Markham Review* 3(1972):53–58.

Warren, Robert Penn. "Mark Twain." *SoR* 8(1972):473.

Weaver, Thomas, and Merline A. Williams. "Mark Twain's Jim: Identity as an Index to Cultural Attitudes." *ALR* 13(1980):19–29.

Weeks, Robert P. "The Captain, the Prophet, and the King: A Possible Source for Twain's Dauphin." *MTJ* 18:1(1975):9–12.

Wells, Anna Mary. "Huck Finn, Tom Sawyer, and Samuel Clemens." *PMLA* 87 (1972):1130–31.

Wells, David. "More on the Geography of *Huckleberry Finn.*" *SAB* 38:4(1973): 82–86.

Wexman, Virginia. "The Role of Structure in *Tom Sawyer* and *Huckleberry Finn.*" *ALR* 6(1973):1–11.

Wiener, Gary A. "From Huck to Holden to Bromden: The Nonconformist in *One Flew over the Cuckoo's Nest.*" *Studies in the Humanities* 7(1979):21–26.

Wilcox, Earl. "Jake and Bob and Huck and Tom: Hemingway's Use of *Huck Finn.*" *Fitzgerald/Hemingway Annual, 1971*, edited by Matthew J. Bruccoli and C. E. Frazer Clark, pp. 322–24. Washington: NCR Microcard Editions, 1971.

Williams, Philip. "*Huckleberry Finn* and the Dialectic of History." *ESELL* 51(1967): 59–98.

Wilson, James D. "*Adventures of Huckleberry Finn*: From Abstraction to Humanity." *SoR* 10(1974):80–93.

Yu, Beongcheon. "The Ending of *The Adventures of Huckleberry Finn.*" In *Indian Studies in American Fiction*, edited by M. K. Naik, S. K. Desai, and S. Mokashi-Punekar, pp. 68–76. Dharwar: Karnatak University; Delhi: Macmillan India, 1974.

Zambano, Ana Laura. "Huckleberry Finn: A Study in Moral Growth." *MSpr* 70 (1976):115–18.

Zimmer, Giles. "Grangerford and Cory: Similar Creations." *MTJ* 21:3(1983): 59–60.

Books

Allen, Walter. *The Urgent West: The American Dream and Modern Man.* New York: E. P. Dutton & Co., 1969. Pp. 168–79.

Baetzhold, Howard G. *Mark Twain and John Bull: The British Connection.* Bloomington: Indiana University Press, 1970.

Banta, Martha. *Failure and Success in American Fiction: A Literary Debate.* Princeton: Princeton University Press, 1978. Pp. 345–57.

Bier, Jesse. *The Rise and Fall of American Humor.* New York: Holt, Rinehart & Winston, 1968. Pp. 117–61.

Blackburn, Alexander. "Confidence Men in *Huckleberry Finn.*" In his *The Myth of the Picaro: Continuity and Transformation of the Picaresque Novel 1554–1954*, pp. 178–87. Chapel Hill: University of North Carolina Press, 1979.

Blair, Walter. "Mark Twain and the Mind's Ear." In *The American Self: Myth, Ideology, and Popular Culture*, edited by Sam B. Girgus, pp. 231–39. Albuquerque: University of New Mexico Press, 1981.

Blair, Walter, and Hamlin Hill. *America's Humor: From Poor Richard to Doonesbury.* Oxford: Oxford University Press, 1978.

Blair, Walter, ed. *Mark Twain's Hannibal, Huck and Tom.* Berkeley: University of California Press, 1969.

Bluefarb, Sam. "*Huckleberry Finn*: Escape from Conscience and the Discovery of the Heart." In his *The Escape Motif in the American Novel: Mark Twain to Richard Wright*, pp. 12–24. Columbus: Ohio State University Press, 1972.

Blues, Thomas. *Mark Twain and the Community.* Lexington: University of Kentucky Press, 1970.

Budd, Louis. "Introduction." *Adventures of Huckleberry Finn*. Facsimile of the Manuscript. 2 vols. Detroit: Gale Research Co., 1983. Pp. ix–xx.

———. *Our Mark Twain: The Making of His Public Personality*. Philadelphia: University of Pennsylvania Press, 1983.

Cady, Edwin H. "Huckleberry Finn by Common Day." In his *The Light of Common Day: Realism in American Fiction*, pp. 88–119. Bloomington: Indiana University Press, 1971.

Carrington, George C., Jr. *The Dramatic Unity of "Huckleberry Finn."* Columbus: Ohio State University Press, 1976.

Egan, Michael. *Mark Twain's "Huckleberry Finn": Race, Class and Society*. London: Published for Sussex University Press by Chatto & Windus, 1977.

Ensor, Allison. *Mark Twain and the Bible*. Lexington: University of Kentucky Press, 1969.

Gale, Robert L. *Plots and Characters in the Works of Mark Twain*. 2 vols. With foreword by Frederick Anderson. Hamden, Conn.: Archon Books, 1973.

Geismar, Maxwell. *Mark Twain: An American Prophet*. Boston: Houghton Mifflin Co., 1970.

Gibson, William M. *The Art of Mark Twain*. New York: Oxford University Press, 1976.

Gottfried, Leon. "The Odyssean Form: An Exploratory Essay." In *Essays on European Literature in Honor of Liselotte Dieckmann*, edited by Uwe Hohendahl et al., pp. 19–43. St. Louis: Washington University Press, 1972.

Gunn, Giles. *The Interpretation of Otherness: Literature, Religion, and the American Imagination*. New York: Oxford University Press, 1979.

Habegger, Alfred. *Gender, Fantasy and Realism in American Literature*. New York: Columbia University Press, 1982.

Harris, Susan K. *Mark Twain's Escape from Time: A Study of Patterns and Images*. Columbia: University of Missouri Press, 1982.

Hearn, Michael Patrick, ed. *The Annotated Huckleberry Finn*. New York: Clarkson N. Potter, 1982.

Hill, Hamlin. *Mark Twain: God's Fool*. New York: Harper & Row, 1973.

———. "Samuel Langhorne Clemens (Mark Twain)." In Donald Pizer and Earl N. Harbert, eds., *American Realists and Naturalists (Dictionary of Literary Biography, Volume Twelve)*, pp. 71–94. Detroit: Gale Research Co., 1982.

Holland, Jeffrey R. "Soul-Butter and Hog Wash: Mark Twain and Frontier Religion." In *"Soul Butter and Hog Wash" and Other Essays on the American West*, edited by Thomas G. Alexander, pp. 5–32. Provo, Utah: Brigham Young University Press, 1978.

Jefferson, Douglas W. "Mark Twain: *Adventures of Huckleberry Finn*." In *Der amerikanische Roman: Von den Anfangen bis zur Gegenwart*, edited by Hans-Joachim Lang, pp. 142–67. Düsseldorf: August Bagel, 1972.

Johnson, James L. *"Adventures of Huckleberry Finn."* In his *Mark Twain and the Limits of Power: Emerson's God in Ruins*, pp. 70–119. Knoxville: University of Tennessee Press, 1982.

Kaplan, Harold. *"Huckleberry Finn*: What It Means to Be Civilized." In his *Democratic Humanism and American Literature*, pp. 225–52. Chicago: University of Chicago Press, 1972.

Linberg, Gary. *The Confidence Man in American Literature*. New York: Oxford University Press, 1982.

Loos, William H. "Afterword: A Note on the Manuscript; or, Huck Finn in Buffalo." *Adventures of Huckleberry Finn*. Facsimile of the Manuscript. 2 vols. Detroit: Gale Research Co., 1983. Pp. 723–25.

Lynn, Kenneth S. *Visions of America*. Westport, Conn.: Greenwood Press, 1973. Pp. 49–59.

McKay, Janet H. "*Adventures of Huckleberry Finn*: Sophisticated Naivete." In her *Narration and Discourse in Realistic American Fiction*, pp. 138–88. Philadelphia: University of Pennsylvania Press, 1982.

Martin, Terence. "The Negative Character in American Fiction." In *Toward a New American Literary History: Essays in Honor of Arlin Turner*, edited by Louis Budd et al., pp. 230–43. Durham, N.C.: Duke University Press, 1980.

Matthews, Greg. *The Further Adventures of Huckleberry Finn*. New York: Crown Publishers, 1983.

Miller, J. Hillis. "Three Problems of Fictional Form: First-Person Narration in *David Copperfield* and *Huckleberry Finn*." In *Experience in the Novel*, edited by Roy Harvey Pearce, pp. 21–48. New York: Columbia University Press, 1968.

Norton, Charles A. *Writing Tom Sawyer: The Adventures of a Classic*. Jefferson, N.C.: McFarland & Co., 1983.

Parker, Hershel. "Aesthetic Implications of Authorial Excisions: Examples from Nathaniel Hawthorne, Mark Twain, and Stephen Crane." In *Editing Nineteenth-Century Fiction*, edited by Jane Millgate, pp. 99–119. Toronto: Toronto University Press, 1977.

Past, Ray. "Huck's Luck." In *Homage to Faye Laverne Bumpass*, edited by Roberto Bravo-Villarrod et al., pp. 61–67. Lubbock: Texas Tech University Press, 1981.

Pettit, Arthur Gordon. *Mark Twain and the South*. Lexington: University of Kentucky Press, 1974.

Pinsker, Sanford. "The Urban Tall Tale: Frontier Humor in a Contemporary Key." In *Comic Relief: Humor in Contemporary Culture*, edited by Sarah Cohen, pp. 249–62. Urbana: University of Illinois Press, 1978.

Rose, Alan Henry. "A Prisoner of Style: The Uses of Art in *Huckleberry Finn* and *Pudd'nhead Wilson*." In his *Demonic Vision: Racial Fantasy and Southern Fiction*, pp. 86–96. Hamden, Conn.: Archon Books, 1976.

Rubin, Louis D., Jr. "Mark Twain's South: Tom and Huck." In *The American South: A Portrait of a Culture*, edited by Louis D. Rubin, Jr., pp. 190–205. Baton Rouge: Louisiana State University Press, 1980.

Seelye, John. *Mark Twain in the Movies: A Meditation with Pictures*. New York: Viking, 1977.

———. *The True Adventures of Huckleberry Finn*. Evanston, Ill.: Northwestern University Press, 1970.

Simpson, Claude M., Jr. "Huck Finn after *Huck Finn*." In *American Humor: Essays Presented to John C. Gerber*, edited by O. M. Brack, Jr., Scottsdale, Ariz.:Arete, 1977.

Simpson, Lewis P. "The Southern Literary Vocation." In *Toward a New American Literary History*, edited by Louis Budd et al., pp. 19–35. Durham, N.C.: Duke University Press, 1980.

Sloane, David E. *Mark Twain as a Literary Comedian*. Baton Rouge: Louisiana State University Press, 1979.

Smith, Henry Nash. "Guilt and Innocence in Mark Twain's Later Fiction." In his *Democracy and the Novel: Popular Resistance to Classic American Writers*, pp. 104–27. New York: Oxford University Press, 1978.

Spengemann, William. "Mark Twain." In his *The Adventurous Muse: The Poetics of American Fiction, 1789–1900*, pp. 213–40. New Haven: Yale University Press, 1977.

Wadlington, Warwick. "But I Never Said Nothing: *The Adventures of Huckleberry Finn*." In his *The Confidence Game*, pp. 241–84. Princeton: Princeton University Press, 1975.

Young, Philip. "*Huckleberry Finn*: The Little Lower Layer." In his *Three Bags Full: Essays in American Fiction*, pp. 136–53. New York: Harcourt Brace Jovanovich, 1972.

The Contributors

Millicent Bell is Professor of English at Boston University. She is the author of many articles and reviews on American and English literature, editor of *Hawthorne's Complete Novels* for the Library of America, and author of *Hawthorne's View of the Artist, Edith Wharton and Henry James,* and *Marquand: An American Life.* She is currently at work on a literary biography of Henry James and a study of form in the nineteenth-century American novel, which will include the revisionary views of *Huckleberry Finn* presented in the present volume.

Stanley Brodwin is Professor of English at Hofstra University. He has published a number of articles exploring the theological dimensions of Mark Twain's works, as well as studies on Emerson, Melville, Hawthorne, Franklin, Whitman, and Bryant in such journals as *PMLA, Prospects, Journal of the History of Ideas,* and the *Nathaniel Hawthorne Journal.* He has also contributed a study of James Boswell to the *Philological Quarterly* and one on Thomas Mann to *Modern Fiction Studies.* In 1978 he was an NEH-sponsored fellow at the Jewish Theological Seminary in New York. He is currently preparing a book on Mark Twain's theological imagination.

Louis J. Budd is James B. Duke Professor and former chairman (1973–1979) of the Department of English at Duke University; he is also Managing Editor of *American Literature.* His publications deal mostly with Mark Twain, such as *Mark Twain: Social Philosopher* (1962) and *Our Mark Twain: The Making of His Public Personality* (1983). He is currently preparing a volume of Mark Twain's shorter writings for the Library of America.

George C. Carrington, Jr., is Professor of English at Northern Illinois University and has written *The Immense Complex Drama: The World and Art of the Howells Novel,* and articles on Howells's fictional sketches. He is also the author of *The Dramatic Unity of "Huckleberry Finn."* At present Carrington is interested in the farcical vision in American fiction.

James M. Cox is Professor of English at Dartmouth College and has written extensively on American literature. Besides his book *Mark Twain: The Fate of Humor* (1966), his published research includes essays on Poe, Hawthorne, Jefferson, Frost, Twain, and Henry Adams.

J. Donald Crowley, co-editor, is Professor of English at the University of Missouri–Columbia. He has published essays on Hawthorne, Frost, and Jane Austen and has edited *Hawthorne: The Critical Heritage* (1971), *The Strange Surprising Adventures of Robinson Crusoe* (1972), three volumes of Hawthorne's tales and sketches for the Centenary Edition (1974), and *The Wings of the Dove* (1978).

Victor Doyno is Associate Professor of English at the State University of New York at Buffalo. His publications include essays on Fitzgerald, Twain, and William Blake. His essay on Twain's revisions of the *Huck Finn* manuscript draws on a larger study of the subject currently in preparation.

Allison R. Ensor is Professor of English at the University of Tennessee, Knoxville. He is the author of *Mark Twain and the Bible* (1969) and editor of the Norton Critical Edition of *A Connecticut Yankee in King Arthur's Court* (1982). His articles on Mark Twain have appeared in such journals as *American Literature, American Literary Realism, South Atlantic Quarterly,* and the *Mark Twain Journal.*

John C. Gerber is M. F. Carpenter Professor Emeritus of English at the University of Iowa and Professor Emeritus of English at the State University of New York at Albany. He was chairman of the editorial board of the Iowa-California Edition of the Works of Mark Twain, 1962–1982, and was historical editor of the Tom Sawyer volume in that series. He has written over ten critical and bibliographical articles about Mark Twain and his works, edited *Studies in "Huckleberry Finn"* (1971), and lectured widely on the author not only in the United States but also in Egypt, France, Korea, and the People's Republic of China.

Stephen Gilman was a student of Américo Castro. At present he teaches Spanish literature at Harvard University. He has published books on *La Celestina,* Galdós, and Cervantes. Because of his interest in *Don Quixote,* he has written several essays on its contribution to the modern novel in other languages. Currently he is concerned with Henry Fielding as a reader of the Spanish masterpiece.

Jan B. Gordon teaches in the English Department at the Tokyo University of Foreign Studies, Japan. He is currently at work on a book on the semiotics of gossip and its modes of repression in nineteenth-century fiction, chapters of which have recently appeared in *Dickens Studies Annual, ELH,* and the *Journal of European Studies.* Together with Masao Shimura, he is also completing a translation of a novella by Kawabata entitled *The Dandelions.*

Alan Gribben is Associate Professor of English at the University of Texas at Austin and previously served on the editorial staff of the Mark Twain Papers at Berkeley. He is author of *Mark Twain's Library: A Reconstruction* (1980), and numerous articles about Twain's reputation and literary works. Recently his essay about Twain's fascination with the occult appeared in *The Haunted Dusk: American Supernatural Fiction, 1820–1920,* and his "Autobiography and Property: Mark Twain and His Legend" was included in *The Mythologizing of Mark Twain.* Professor Gribben is now completing a study of dominant themes in Mark Twain's writing.

Hamlin Hill is Professor of English and American Studies at the University of New Mexico; in 1984–1985 he is Resident Scholar in American Studies for the United States Information Agency. He is the author of *Mark Twain and Elisha Bliss* (1964), *Mark Twain: God's Fool* (1973), and (with Walter Blair) *America's Humor from Poor Richard to Doonesbury* (1978). He is the editor of *Mark Twain's Letters to His Publishers* (1967) and wrote the "Mark Twain" chapter for *American Literary Scholarship* from 1969 through 1975.

William E. Lenz is Assistant Professor of English and Director of the Writing Program at Chatham College. His study of American fiction, *Fast Talk and Flush Times: The Confidence Man as a Literary Convention,* will be published by the University of Missouri Press in 1985. He is currently exploring the influence of nineteenth-century Antarctic expeditions on the American literary imagination.

Jay Martin is Bing Professor of English at the University of Southern California; lecturer in the Department of Psychiatry and Human Behavior at the University of California–Irvine Medical School, and a psychoanalyst in private practice. He is the author of ten books on American literature. His essay was written under a grant from the National Endowment for the Humanities and revised in the facilities of the Rockefeller Foundation Study and Conference Center in Bellagio, Italy.

Fritz Oehlschlaeger is Associate Professor of English at Virginia Polytechnic Institute and State University. Previously he has co-edited *Toward the Making of Thoreau's Modern Reputation* and published work on various subjects in American literature in such journals as *American Literature, American Literary Realism, Essays in Literature, Colby Library Quarterly,* and *Midwest Quarterly.* At present he is working on the Transcendentalist F. B. Sanborn, on Willa Cather, and on a collection of frontier humor from the *St. Louis Reveille.*

Roy Harvey Pearce is Professor of American Literature at the University of California, San Diego. His principal books are *The Savages of America* (1953, revised edition, 1965), *The Continuity of American Poetry* (1961), and *Historicism Once More* (1969). He is a general editor of the Centenary Edition of the *Works of Nathaniel Hawthorne* (1962–). Recently he has edited, for the Library of America, the *Tales and Sketches* of Nathaniel Hawthorne (1982) and has co-edited *Progress and Its Discontents* (1982). He was awarded, in December 1984, the Hubbell Medal of the American Literature Section of the Modern Language Association of America.

Tom Quirk is Associate Professor of English at the University of Missouri–Columbia. He is the author of *Melville's Confidence-Man: From Knave to Knight* (1982) and has written on a number of American literary figures, including Nathaniel Hawthorne, Mark Twain, Herman Melville, Jean Toomer, Joyce Carol Oates, and F. Scott Fitzgerald. He is currently engaged in writing a book on philosophical vitalism in American life and letters, a chapter of which will be published in *Prospects* in 1985.

Robert Regan is Professor of English at the University of Pennslyvania and began studying Mark Twain under Henry Nash Smith at Berkeley. After the Ph.D., he taught at the University of Virginia and, as Fulbright Lecturer, at the University of Montpellier before joining the Penn faculty. More recently he was Visiting Professor at King's College, London. His publications include *Unpromising Heroes: Mark Twain and his Characters* and *Poe: A Collection of Critical Essays.* He hopes soon to complete an edition of Mark Twain's shorter travel writing.

Robert Sattelmeyer, co-editor, is Associate Professor of English and Director of Graduate Studies in the Department of English at the University of Missouri–Columbia. He is the co-editor of three volumes of Thoreau's *Journal* in the Princeton Edition of *The Writings of Henry D. Thoreau* and a member of the Edition's Editorial Board. He is also the author of a number of articles on American writers, including Lewis and Clark, Hawthorne, Thoreau, Melville, and Hemingway.

David Sewell is Assistant Professor of English at the University of Rochester and has published on Herman Melville. His essay in this volume forms part of a study on varieties of language in Mark Twain's writing.

Robert Shulman is Associate Professor at the University of Washington. He has written on Melville and on most of our major nineteenth-century authors. His recent work includes "Community, Perception, and the Development of Stephen Crane" (*American Literature*), "The Artist in the Slammer: Hawthorne, Melville, Poe and the Prison of Their Times" (*Studies in English Literature*), and "*Song of Myself*: Whitman's Individualism and Market Society in America" (*Lamar Journal of the Humanities*). His essay on *Huckleberry Finn* is part of a recently completed book, *Social Criticism and Nineteenth-Century American Fiction*.

Eric Solomon, Professor of English at San Francisco State University, is the author of *Stephen Crane in England* (1964) and *Stephen Crane: From Parody to Realism* (1966). His other work includes essays on *Jane Eyre, Wuthering Heights, Adventures of Huckleberry Finn*, and Civil War fiction. He is currently completing two books: *Jews, Baseball, and the American Novel* and *Robert Benchley's "New Yorker" Writing*.

Jeffrey Steinbrink is Associate Professor of English at Franklin and Marshall College, where most of his teaching is in nineteenth-century American literature. He has published essays on a number of American writers, including Cooper, Emerson, Hawthorne, Thoreau, Whitman, Dickinson, and Ellison. For the past three years he has been working almost exclusively on Mark Twain and is currently focusing on Twain's life and work in three environments—Buffalo, Elmira, and Hartford—between 1867 and 1874.

Paul Taylor is currently a Ph.D. candidate in the Department of English and a law student at the University of Missouri–Columbia. He has written previously on Henry James and is currently working on a study of Henry Adams.

Nancy Walker is currently serving as Executive Assistant to the President of Stephens College, where she has taught American literature since she received her Ph.D. from Kent State University in 1971. She has published a number of articles on writers such as Dickinson, Woolf, Drabble, O'Hara, and John Irving and has recently co-edited an anthology of American women's humorous writing from 1840 to the present. Walker is the guest co-editor of a special humor issue of *Open Places* and is currently working on a study of women's letters as a literary genre.

Index

WITHDRAWN